PERSONNEL ADMINISTRATION

A Point of View and a Method

Personnel Administration

A Point of View and a Method

By Paul Pigors

and Charles A. Myers

Associate Professors of Industrial Relations
Industrial Relations Section
Department of Economics and Social Science
Massachusetts Institute of Technology

FIRST EDITION
THIRD IMPRESSION

McGRAW-HILL BOOK COMPANY, INC.

NEW YORK AND LONDON

1947

PERSONNEL ADMINISTRATION

Preface

This book is addressed primarily to students, to persons just entering personnel positions in industry, and to personnel administrators who wish to reevaluate their own techniques and principles. In classes at the Massachusetts Institute of Technology, however, the authors have found that this subject is also of interest to those who are preparing themselves for engineering and executive positions. And comments later received from graduates testify to the value of the personnel approach in understanding and handling the human problems that confront supervisors and technical men. This is in line with the conviction that the personnel point of view is most useful when it permeates the entire management structure.

Each chapter briefly presents the elements of one topic, hitting only the high spots. Instead of attempting a detailed discussion of any one area, the authors have preferred to sketch in the whole field by giving a general approach to the understanding and treatment of personnel problems. They believe that this point of view has validity in a wide range of industrial and nonindustrial situations, both for large and for small organizations.

After a general discussion of the nature of personnel administration in Sec. A, the point of view is developed in three different ways. First, in Sec. B, a method of understanding is presented. No claim is made that it is superior to all others in every situation. But experience has shown that it meets the pragmatic test. In other words, it works. Second, using this method for asking questions, how a personnel administrator may assess individual and organizational stability in his company is shown in Sec. C. Third, in view of these findings, he can help to formulate, complete, or evaluate a personnel policy system. Such a system is essential for building and maintaining effective work teams. The whys and hows of this important aspect of personnel work are discussed at some length in Secs. D through F. All the text material comprises Part I of the book.

Part II gives case material to illustrate the subject matter of the chapters. Most of these cases have been taken from unionized firms and are therefore representative of typical industrial situations in America today. Each case is primarily related to one chapter. But, since the situations described are real, though the names of individuals and companies are disguised, all the cases illustrate more than one point. As they stand, they offer better practice in situational analysis and in understanding personnel problems than if they were artificially pruned of all their side branches.

Chapters and cases together form a more comprehensive approach than either could alone. But, even so, the subject is by no means exhaustively covered. No single book of readable length could adequately present all the details of the whole picture, but the text is supplemented with selected references to personnel literature. This bibliography is intended for use especially by advanced students.

The authors' debts to personnel administrators, top-management officials, first-line supervisors, other line and staff representatives, union leaders, other teachers, and alert students are too numerous to itemize here. Much of what is said is based on the best practice in the personnel profession. Much has also been learned from books and tested by experience. The greatest intellectual debt, as will be apparent, is to Dr. Elton Mayo and his colleagues, particularly Prof. F. J. Roethlisberger, at the Harvard Graduate School of Business Administration. Other useful knowledge has been gained from study of actual problems confronting supervisors and union officials, especially in situations where the authors served as consultants. Certain conclusions have been hammered out on the anvil of class discussion to meet the searching questions of students.

Special gratitude is due Profs. Douglass V. Brown and Douglas McGregor, who have not only criticized every chapter of the text but in daily work association have taught the authors much about the personnel point of view. E. Robert Livernash, formerly of M. I. T. and chairman of the Regional War Labor Board, has also made many constructive suggestions. The authors are also grateful for the criticisms and suggestions of several readers to whom the publishers sent parts of the manuscript for review.

Thanks are extended to Faith Pigors and Beatrice A. Rogers for valuable editorial assistance.

The authors are also grateful to Barbara Klingenhagen for helping with the bibliography and to Dorothy Spence, who typed all the manuscript, not once but many times.

CAMBRIDGE, MASS.   PAUL PIGORS
    October, 1947.   CHARLES A. MYERS

Contents

vii

Part II

CONTENTS ix

Part I

A. The Nature of Personnel Administration

B. Handling Personnel Problems

C. Diagnosing Organizational Stability

D. Building and Maintaining Work Teams

E. Wages and Hours

F. Employee Services and Programs

A.   THE NATURE OF PERSONNEL ADMINISTRATION

Chapter 1

What Is Personnel Administration?

> Management is the development of people and not the direction of things. . . . Management is personnel administration.
>
> LAWRENCE A. APPLEY[1]

During the past thirty years, there has been increasing emphasis on the personnel function in management. The labor shortages of the First World War, the growing attention by management to the welfare of employees, and, most of all, the "scientific management" movement inaugurated by Frederick Taylor, an engineer, led to what we know today as personnel administration. In subsequent years, other developments left their imprint on the growth of personnel administration. The spread of unionism; the great depression; increasing government intervention in employee-employer relationships; personnel research using the social sciences of psychology, sociology, anthropology, and economics; and the labor problems of the Second World War have helped personnel administration to grow.

We are now on the threshold of a new profession that promises much. There is no greater challenge than the opportunity to bring out the best in free people working in an organization so that they will genuinely enjoy their work and thus enable the organization to accomplish its purpose.

THE NATURE OF MANAGEMENT

In the public mind, however, there is much confusion about the nature of personnel administration. During the Second World War, many businessmen decided for the first time that they needed a personnel director, and job opportunities in the field increased so greatly that many inadequately prepared persons were thrust into positions where they were

[1] "Management The Simple Way," *Personnel*, Vol. 19, No. 4, pp. 595–603, 1943.

expected "to handle personnel problems." These businessmen, and frequently also the personnel people they hired, viewed personnel administration as a separate part of the management function. They thought that it must be separate because it deals with human beings, while production management is concerned with materials and equipment, financial management with costs and income, and sales management with selling.

To clear up this confusion, we must ask: What is management? Is it the organization of production through the design of the product or service, the layout of machinery and equipment, the balancing of processes, the routing of materials and orders, the attainment of technical efficiency? Is it skill in purchasing, marketing, or selling? Is it careful handling of income and outgo?

The practice of management includes all these subjects, and many books and articles have been written about them. A common thread is lacking, however, in such partial concepts of management. Machines and equipment do not function without people to operate them and keep them in repair. Materials are not always automatically conveyed. The efficient operation of a factory or any other organization is not solely a *technical* problem requiring only the skill of the engineer. Purchasing and accounting also involve relations with people, both inside and outside the organization. And in sales we see clearly that results are proportionate to the extent that an effective force of salespeople is developed to sell goods or services to other people—the customers.

MANAGEMENT AND PERSONNEL ADMINISTRATION

Good management, therefore, has always meant getting the cooperation of other human beings. Reduced to its essence, *good management means getting effective results with people*. Think of any enterprise that is generally regarded as successful, or of any manager who stands head and shoulders above his fellows, and ask the reason for success. The answer will usually be found in the effective work team that has been developed by managerial skill in working with people. The successful administrator gets people to work *with* him, not primarily because he has power over them and can order them about, but because he is the kind of leader for whom they want to do their best.

A successful enterprise, of course, also requires technical competence.[1] Manpower is only one of the resources that the executive must marshal in

[1] By "technical competence" we mean primarily the other aspects of management such as production planning, machine design, product design, marketing, and financial planning. These special technical skills of management are outside the scope of personnel administration, although the personnel administrator's effectiveness with other managers is increased if he is at least familiar with these special fields.

order to accomplish the objective for which the organization was created. He must have adequate materials, efficient methods, and good machinery and equipment, and he must know how to combine them effectively. But he does this *with the collaboration of other people in his organization*, and all the technical competence in the world will not suffice if his subordinates are working *against* him, or grudgingly *for* him, rather than enthusiastically *with* him. This problem of winning wholehearted cooperation is the central, ever-present problem of management.

The simple truth—that "management is the development of people and not the direction of things"—leads clearly to an important conclusion well stated by Lawrence A. Appley: ". . . management and personnel administration are one and the same. They should never be separated. *Management is personnel administration.*"[1]

Some who read this striking statement by Mr. Appley will feel that his definition of management is too narrow—that too much is being claimed for personnel administration. But consider virtually anything a manager does. Is it accomplished successfully without the willing assistance and cooperation of other people?

The skillful manager—the executive or supervisor who consciously or unconsciously follows the principles of good personnel administration—gets effective results with people by bringing out the best efforts in each through real leadership, not "drivership." He sets up a number of smaller standards or objectives that must be reached if the major objective of the organization is to be accomplished. He gives clear instructions and effective training so that people will know and be able to do what is expected of them. And he checks their performance from time to time to tell them how well they are meeting standards. He is constantly trying to get better performance, not by "using the whip," but by stimulating and encouraging in his subordinates the will to work.

Personnel Administration Defined

The essence of what we mean by personnel administration is contained in the following definition, the considered opinion of Thomas G. Spates, a leader in the profession:

Personnel administration is a code of the ways of organizing and treating individuals at work so that they will each get the greatest possible realization of their

[1] "Management the Simple Way," *Personnel*, Vol. 19, No. 4, pp. 595–603, 1943. At that time, Mr. Appley was vice-president of the Vick Chemical Company and on leave as executive director of the War Manpower Commission. In 1946, he became vice-president for personnel and public relations of Montgomery Ward and Company, Inc.

intrinsic abilities, thus attaining maximum efficiency for themselves and their group, and thereby giving to the enterprise of which they are a part its determining competitive advantage and its optimum results.[1]

Let us consider the parts of this definition. First of all, personnel administration is based on a code from which are derived its point of view and a set of techniques of handling people at work. Its professional standards have been tested by experience. It is a skill that, though expressed long ago in the golden rule, has been consciously studied and professionally applied only within recent years. Far more time and effort have been spent in developing machines and things than in trying to understand and develop people. The word "code" suggests that, even in a young and emerging profession, there are some guiding principles. These we shall discuss throughout the book and summarize in our final chapter.

Another important emphasis in the definition is on personal development. Good personnel administration helps individuals to utilize their capacities to the full and to attain not only maximum individual satisfaction from their work but also *satisfaction as part of a work group*. Though he is merged in the group, the individual is not necessarily submerged in it. He need not lose his identity because he becomes part of a team. His degree of success as a team member largely reflects the successful application of the personnel point of view and the personnel program.

Also important in the definition quoted is the assumption that, if people are skillfully handled both as individuals and as group members, they will respond by giving their best work to the organization of which they are a part. This is another way of saying that democracy is stronger and more effective than authoritarianism and that, in business as well as in government, where men and women are free they will be happier and work more effectively than if they are regimented. One of the greatest rewards of personnel administration is in the realization and demonstration of this truth.

PERSONNEL ADMINISTRATION AND COSTS

To the hard-boiled school of management, this definition and point of view of personnel administration may seem soft and sentimental. They may assert that they will have none of it. Let such critics consider again the basic question of how any organization achieves its long-run purpose. Does it succeed without the cooperation of all employees? Can this cooperation be secured by fear and threats, by picnics and Christmas baskets, by high

---

[1] *An Objective Scrutiny of Personnel Administration*, p. 9, Personnel Series No. 75, American Management Association, New York, 1944. Mr. Spates is vice-president of the General Foods Corporation.

wages and nothing else? Or is it primarily the result of a relationship between management and employees that is the realization of the
personnel-administration concept? A closer examination of a specific
case would probably reveal that a successful "hard-boiled" manager
had, in fact, adopted the kind of personnel approach that we are
discussing.

Good personnel administration is not simply making employees happy
in their work. The personnel administrator must be "cost-conscious" in
advising management on the formulation of personnel policies and the
adoption of a personnel program. He may be expected to justify a proposed
expenditure and to estimate the probable savings, tangible or intangible,
that are likely to result. To be effective, he must talk the cost language of
top management. On numerous occasions, however, he will be unable to
demonstrate immediate monetary savings to be derived from a proposed
program. Then he must be a proponent of the point of view that developing a congenial work team of individuals is of long-run value to an
efficient enterprise.

Personnel Administration: Basic

If management means getting effective results with people, then personnel administration is a basic management function. It permeates all *levels*
of management, since the chief executive can be effective only to the extent
that he achieves results with the assistance of his vice-presidents and general
managers, who, in turn, depend upon the cooperation and skill of the
superintendents, foremen, and supervisors under them. And first-line
supervisors must build an effective work team of people whose performance
will meet or exceed expected standards.

Personnel administration also permeates all *types* of management, such
as production management, financial management, and sales management.
Unless these managers are themselves to perform all the functions for
which they are responsible, they have to secure the cooperation of other
people whom they have employed to assist them.

In short, every member of the management group, from the top down,
must be a "personnel administrator" in the vital sense that he seeks to get
effective long-run results through the efforts of the people who look to him
for direction and leadership. The responsibility for personnel administration, therefore, is clearly not something that can be assigned to a minor
functionary in the organization—a glorified office boy and backslapper
who will "handle personnel problems" and keep the employees happy,
"managing the men" while other more important executives manage
machines, materials, and money.

The Need for a Personnel Administrator

This does not mean, however, that an organization can dispense with an officially designated personnel administrator. Too often, personnel programs are regarded as something superficial, like the frosting on a cake. Too often, they are postponed or assigned to a minor official so that top executives can devote their entire attention to the "important" problems of production or sales.

In every organization, there should be someone who is primarily concerned with helping to develop in operating officials the point of view and skills of personnel administration. As we shall see in the next chapter, the personnel administrator can be friend and aide to the harassed executive or supervisor—an aide who does not usurp the executive's responsibilities for getting effective results with people, but one who helps him to perform them better. Is there any organization that does not need this kind of assistance?

Another important contribution of the personnel administrator, which we shall consider in greater detail in the next chapter, is helping top management to formulate clear personnel policies on such matters as hiring, transfer, promotion, layoff, discharge, etc. Furthermore, the presence of a personnel specialist in top-management councils is assurance that, in any important company plans, the effect on personnel will be given full consideration.

For example, if a proposal to purchase and install new machinery is being discussed, the personnel administrator may be expected to make recommendations on the timing and rate of installation, discussions with employees in advance, setting new wage rates, and getting employee acceptance of the new output standards. If the stability and morale of the organization are poor, he may even contend that it is unwise to make a change at the present time.

In many small firms, it is thought that personnel matters can be handled as a side line by the superintendent or by the employment manager. This is a serious misconception. We agree in general with the conclusion reached by a conference of the American Management Association that "no plant is too small to have someone whose primary job it is to specialize in personnel administration and the study and elimination of causes of misunderstanding and resentment on the part of employees and supervisors."[1] In a very small firm, where there may be only one management official, he will

---

[1] SPATES, THOMAS G., The Shifting Scene in Industrial Relations, in *The Status of Industrial Relations*, p. 5, Personnel Series No. 32, American Management Association, New York, 1938.

find it advantageous to check every policy and problem from the personnel point of view.

A sound personnel program and the wholehearted acceptance of the personnel point of view are not achieved overnight in companies or organizations that have previously been without them. Faced with increasing personnel difficulties, some employers have hired a personnel manager to "solve" these problems. This expectation is a delusion, which, if not dispelled at the outset, will confront the new personnel man with an impossible task and embitter the chief executive later. One newly appointed personnel officer accepted a position with a large firm only on the understanding that he would not be expected to accomplish much in the first few years. His modest prediction is undoubtedly on the pessimistic side, but it is a healthy sort of pessimism.

There are no panaceas or miracle cures in personnel administration. Consultants or management-engineering concerns that promise to solve a firm's personnel problems in a few weeks or months are offering a doubtful service that may do great harm. The conversion to a sound personnel program is a lengthy one, requiring as it does new insight on the part of all members of management, from the top executive down to first-line supervisors. It is better to proceed slowly, introducing one change at a time, than to attempt to do all at once everything that needs to be done. Furthermore, a certain program that has worked well in some firms and organizations may not work well in others. The personnel program, although based on the experience of others, must be adapted to the needs and desires of the people who constitute the organization in which it is used.

In achieving success in a program of personnel administration, top-management support is absolutely essential. Many personnel specialists have learned this the hard way. The best paper programs will not succeed without a recognition by operating officials of the importance of the personnel point of view and personnel-administration methods in getting effective results through people. This means a willingness on their part to give weight to the personnel point of view in determining and administering the policies of the organization.

Although top-management support is essential, the personnel point of view and program must be "sold" to the operating officials down the line, not forced upon them. At the outset, the new personnel administrator often encounters resistance to his recommendations for change because his suggestions are regarded as criticisms. This initial opposition by some members of the management group is not easily overcome. But patience, understanding, persuasion, and trying to be of service in other ways are more likely to win the opposition over to the personnel administrator's point of view than is open conflict.

WIDER APPLICATIONS AND TERMS

Personnel administration, as we conceive it, is not restricted to factories and wage earners. It is also important in offices, sales departments, laboratories, and in the ranks of management itself, where top officials must win the cooperation of their subordinates. Nor is good personnel administration something needed by private industry alone. Nonprofit institutions, government, and the armed services have added personnel officers to their staffs, in the belief, as expressed by the Army Air Forces, that "every officer in command of men" must utilize "personnel practices and procedures designed to make them effective in their jobs to the maximum extent."[1]

Two other terms have been used frequently in discussions of personnel problems and techniques: "labor relations" and "industrial relations." Sometimes these are used interchangeably with "personnel administration," but it is useful to distinguish between them.

The term "labor relations" refers primarily to the relations between management and organized labor. The subject matter of labor relations includes the negotiation of contracts with unions and day-to-day relationships with union stewards and business agents in the handling of differences arising under the contract, arbitration, and governmental regulation of the terms and conditions of employment.

Some companies have a "labor-relations director" whose primary job is to advise and assist top management, superintendents, and foremen or department heads in their dealings with union representatives. This official may or may not report to the personnel administrator, although in our judgment this function should be subordinate to personnel administration in the broad sense. In a unionized company where there is no labor-relations director, the personnel administrator should therefore include these duties among his own.

The personnel administrator, whose primary objective is in assisting these same company officials to get more effective results with people, cannot neglect the possibility of developing constructive relationships through unions. On the contrary, in unionized firms, he is seriously concerned with helping to make this possibility a reality. More will be said on this point

[1] *Personnel Management Manual*, p. 1, Headquarters, Army Air Forces, Washington, D. C., February, 1945.

in Chap. 3 and in many of the case illustrations in this book. But contract negotiations and dealings with representatives of organized labor are not the primary functions of personnel administration. They are a responsibility of the operating managers of the business, who may receive advice and assistance from a specialist in labor relations or from the personnel administrator.

An industrial-relations director or vice-president in charge of industrial relations is usually an officer who serves as a specialist in both labor relations and personnel administration in a large industrial concern. He may assist (or even represent) top management in negotiations with unions, and he may also be responsible for carrying out the personnel service functions in the entire organization.

But in this country "industrial" means "private industry," and the scope of personnel administration is much broader. Good personnel administration is needed wherever managers have the problem of getting the cooperation of people. Therefore, we shall use the term "personnel administration" to describe the function that, in many firms, is called "industrial relations."

Summary

Personnel administration is a method of developing the potentialities of employees so that they will get maximum satisfaction out of their work and give their best efforts to the organization. It is a point of view and a set of techniques. Personnel administration is not a separate part of management, to be considered apart from the problems of product design, production, accounting, or sales. Rather it is a basic management function, permeating all levels and types of management. Good management gets effective results with the cooperation of other people, and this is personnel administration.

This emerging profession has developed out of a belated recognition that, in our rapid technological progress, we have failed to devote enough attention to the human factor on which the success of any organization depends. In progressive enterprises, the personnel function has achieved the consideration that it deserves. Personnel policies have "moved into the front office," and personnel administrators have achieved higher standing than they formerly enjoyed in many companies.

This suggests the proper place of personnel administration, but we must explore the subject further. Where does the personnel administrator fit into the company organization, and what are his responsibilities? In other words, what are the primary functions of the personnel administrator? What methods of approach and what techniques does he use? These questions are broadly answered in the next chapter.

Chapter 2

The Place and Functions of the Personnel Administrator

> Unless there is a sound organization structure, a major
> personnel officer reporting to the president, and a con-
> tinuous coordination of the personnel department with the
> line organization, the personnel program of the company
> does not reach its highest degree of effectiveness.
>
> HAROLD B. BERGEN[1]

The establishment of a personnel department is no guarantee that personnel difficulties will end. On the contrary, they may increase if the chief
executive, lower operating management, and the personnel administrator
are confused as to the proper place of personnel administration in the
company organization.

The newly designated personnel administrator cannot by himself
"solve" personnel problems. He is no miracle worker. Rather, he is an
adviser to operating management on personnel problems and an exponent
of a point of view and methods designed to help in getting effective results
through people. He cannot establish policies and make decisions himself
without usurping the authority and responsibilities of operating management. Yet these fairly obvious truths are frequently ignored in practice.

SOME COMMON MISCONCEPTIONS

Some of the common misconceptions concerning the proper place of
the personnel administrator are illustrated by the following examples.
The president of one small firm, feeling that he ought to have a personnel
specialist, decided to hire one. He was willing to give this official full
responsibility in handling personnel problems, because he wanted to be

[1] "Fundamentals Of a Personnel and Industrial Relations Program," *Personnel*, Vol.
13, No. 2, pp. 46–54, 1936.

relieved of the necessity of dealing with them himself so that he could devote all his time to other matters. Consequently, the new personnel administrator began with an impossible job. His role in the organization had not been properly defined. He was expected to "get results," yet he found himself at swords points with the superintendent and department heads who misunderstood his position and felt that he was interfering with their rightful functions.

A similar case is that of the new personnel administrator who lacked proper perspective for his own job and tried to make decisions on personnel matters that were properly the responsibility of the superintendents and foremen. He took over more and more power, partly because he thought it increased his own prestige and partly because he believed it would be an easier and more effective way to handle personnel problems. He relieved the foremen of the responsibility for discipline, rate changes, promotions, and other matters on which properly he should only advise operating management. When some of the foremen vigorously objected that they were no longer permitted to run their own departments, he was puzzled and hurt by their lack of appreciation of what he was trying to do.

A final illustration is the superintendent who urged that either a labor-relations or a personnel administrator be employed to handle problems with a newly organized union. Dealings with the union business agents were taking too much of his time, and he felt that these matters should be assigned to a specialist. The new man was hired and given free rein to settle grievances "so long as you don't interfere with production." The plant manager and the superintendent rejoiced in this move, with the comment that "now we will have more time to run the plant." They were disappointed to find that most grievance cases still came to them for final settlement.

LINE AND STAFF RELATIONSHIPS

These examples illustrate the basic confusion over "line" and "staff" functions in sound company organization. *Line*, or operating, officers are those who have direct responsibility for receiving orders from their superiors and for carrying them out by giving instructions to and getting the cooperation of their own subordinates.

This is often known as the "military" form of organization, and it involves delegation of authority from the top downward with the subordinates held responsible for results by their superiors. It is authoritarian in nature (though not necessarily in methods), because authority spreads outward and down from the top to the bottom, as in a pyramid. The president is the chief executive, deriving his authority from the board of directors and stockholders, and under him at successive levels are the operating vice-president or general manager, the superintendents, department heads, and foremen or other first-line supervisors.

Staff officers, on the other hand, are those who provide specialized services to the line officials and advise and assist them in the performance of their duties. An example of this is the company attorney, who provides legal assistance and advice to company management. The cost accountant has, or should have, a similar relationship. He keeps control records that enable him to advise the chief executive on prices to be charged for products or services, but he does not set the prices himself. Further, he tells department heads and foremen when their costs exceed "standards" but it is not his responsibility to correct them. Sometimes this function is called a "control" function, but the control should be exercised *through* the line and not *on* the line.

Other examples of proper staff functions are purchasing, engineering, research and development, and traffic. The chiefs of these departments are all responsible, of course, for giving orders to their own subordinates; *i.e.*, they have line authority over their own departments. But they should advise, counsel, assist, and service the central operating management of the organization. They should not exercise direct authority over operating officials, such as the manufacturing superintendent.

The position of such officials as the sales manager or advertising director, however, is less clear. In some companies, these officials have line responsibilities for functions that supplement manufacturing operations, and they can scarcely be considered "staff" officials. Thus they are line or operating officials performing a function of equal importance with manufacturing.[1]

PLACE OF THE PERSONNEL ADMINISTRATOR

What is the role of the personnel administrator in a sound company organization? He is clearly a staff official, and he should report directly to the chief executive of the organization. He should not issue orders in his own name to members of the line organization or to employees, even when personnel matters are involved. Instead, he should advise the president and other top executives on good personnel policies and on

[1] For further discussion of line and staff, see PAUL E. HOLDEN, LOUNSBURY S. FISH, and HUBERT L. SMITH, *Top-management Organization and Control*, Secs. 2 and 3, Stanford University Press, Stanford University, Calif., 1941. A different approach to organization, in terms of "doing," "planning," and "seeing" functions, is presented by ALVIN BROWN, *Organization: A Formulation of Principle*, Chaps. 8 and 9 especially, Hibbard Printing Company, New York, 1945.

their consistent, uniform application throughout the organization. He may initiate the formulation of personnel policies, but he should not have the final authority to establish them.

The responsibility for making policy decisions should rest with the chief executive, and the responsibility for carrying them out belongs to his subordinates in the line organization. The personnel director may also advise and assist the lower line officials in administering personnel policies and in handling personnel problems. But he should not give orders to the line management. He issues orders only to his own subordinates, who are members of a staff department with numerous service functions to perform for the whole organization.

When he differs from line officers and supervisors about personnel methods, or with their interpretation or application of company personnel policies, he should not exercise direct authority over them. If he cannot persuade or convince the line official of the wisdom of his approach or of his interpretation of established policies, then he should report the disagreement to the man's superior or to the chief executive. He may thus perform a control or "check-up" function for the president, who, it is assumed, desires consistent observance of company policies and good personnel practices.

But, if he is to win the confidence and cooperation of lower line management, the personnel administrator must exercise this control function sparingly. Persuasion is his tool, and his personality must be the kind that makes other officials want to work with him instead of against him. If he has any "authority," it is the authority of established personnel policies and procedures that he has helped to formulate, rather than the authority of his position.

Sound Organizational Relationships

The proper relationships that should exist between the personnel administrator and line management are more clearly seen in a formal organization chart. Figure 1 shows a sound company organization, with the personnel administrator on equal footing with other staff officials and reporting directly to the president. The relationship of delegated authority from president down to foremen is shown by heavy solid lines. The president also gives orders to his staff officers. Therefore, a line relationship is also indicated between them, as well as between the personnel administrator and his own subordinates. The staff officials are primarily advisors and service agents, not only to the chief executive, but also to each other and to the lower levels of line management.

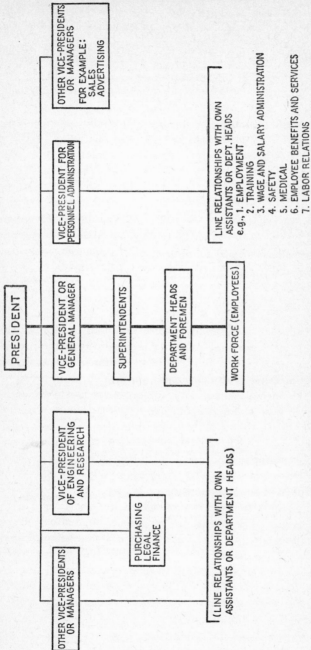

Fig. 1. — An organization chart showing line and staff relationships and the place of the personnel administrator.

An excellent summary statement of the relationships between the personnel department and line organization is the following:

The activities of the personnel department are directed toward making line control of the human element stronger and more effective—not toward usurping that control. . . . In short, the personnel staff *recommends*, *cooperates*, and *counsels*, while line management actually *adopts* and *applies* the policies, techniques, and procedures in its operations.

It has been repeatedly affirmed that, no matter how capable the members of the personnel staff may be, no matter how excellent the plan on which their activities are based, the personnel program cannot be successful unless the line organization is "doing a good personnel job at the workbench." Therein lies the major clue to the proper relationship between the line and staff organizations in the matter of personnel policy and practice.[1]

Thus the success of the personnel administrator in any organization is measured by the extent to which he has helped every line or operating manager to become a good administrator of personnel. Like these other managers, he also gets his results through other people.

SUPPORT FROM THE TOP

No staff officer can be really effective without full support from top management. He needs the confidence and backing of the president, not only in policy formulation but also in the administration of policies by the line organization. The personnel administrator is no exception. Unless he has the encouragement and support of the chief executive, he can accomplish very little, for line officials will soon realize that their chief is not really behind the personnel program.

Support from the top for the personnel program involves not only backing from the chief executive in the "home office" but also cooperation from branch managers or plant superintendents who may be the local chief executives. The branch plant of a large food-processing concern, for example, was instructed by the Chicago office to add a personnel director to its staff. The local manager thought this was all "poppycock," but he had to carry out the order. He hired a personnel director and gave him a desk in a corner of the accounting department. For use as a wastebasket, the personnel man was given a 5-gallon oil drum with the top cut off. His location and equipment truly symbolized his status, for he had no influence, was never consulted by the branch manager, and accomplished practically nothing.

---

[1] *How to Establish and Maintain a Personnel Department*, pp. 12–13. Research Report, No. 4, American Management Association, New York, 1944.

The role of the personnel administrator attached to a branch plant is a particularly difficult one. He is responsible to the branch-plant manager and subordinate in a functional or staff sense to the chief personnel administrator in the home office. He must try to develop in the branch the personnel program and policies that have been established for the whole company. Yet, in seeking to gain acceptance of these, he will not have the support of the branch manager unless the latter is as impressed with the importance of good personnel administration as is the chief executive of the company in the home office. As a staff officer, the branch personnel man cannot give orders to the branch plant manager. If he cannot sell his point of view, he can only report his difficulties to his own superior, the chief personnel officer, who will then endeavor to get from the president of the company better support down the line for the personnel program.

Broad Functions of the Personnel Administrator

Our discussion up to this point enables us to outline the role of the personnel administrator, in terms of his broad functions and his relation to the line organization. His principal functions can be summarized as follows:

1. To advise and assist the line organization in the personnel approach; in other words, to be an effective exponent of the personnel point of view in formulating and administering policies and in the problems handled by the line officials, from the top down.

2. To diagnose the stability or morale of the organization as an effective work team, by means of various indexes of teamwork such as productive efficiency, absenteeism, accidents, labor turnover and internal mobility, and complaints and grievances; and to keep the line management informed of actual or potential difficulties that need their joint attention.

3. To provide personnel procedures and services, such as recruitment, hiring, selection, training, wage and salary administration, safety education, etc., as an aid to the line officers in getting more effective results through the people under them.

4. To secure coordination and control of these activities through top management, which has the final responsibility for seeing that they are uniformly and consistently administered.

Points 1 and 4 summarize much of what has already been said in this chapter and in Chap. 1. The approach of the personnel administrator is further discussed in the three chapters in Sec. B on Handling Personnel

Problems. Point 2 is elaborated in the three chapters of Sec. C on Diagnosing Organizational Stability. Personnel procedures and services (point 3) are the subject matter of the remaining chapters of the book, which are grouped in the sections headed Building and Maintaining Work Teams, Wages and Hours, and Employee Services and Programs. In these chapters, more emphasis is placed on the kinds of policies that need to be developed and the kinds of problems that are likely to arise in their formulation and application than on the details of the particular policies or procedures.

Personnel Procedures and Services

At this point, an outline of the most important areas for policies, procedures, and services found in a well-rounded personnel program will give us a bird's-eye view of the kinds of problems that confront the personnel department. These are subjects on which the personnel administrator advises top management in policy formulation and assists lower line management in carrying out policies. In these areas also, the personnel department provides certain services for the whole organization.

1. *Recruitment, Selection, and Placement* (Chap. 10).—Centralized hiring procedures; subsidiary policy requirements; requisitioning workers; recruitment and sources of labor supply; selection through the employment interview, the application blank, the physical examination, and employment tests; placement on the right job.

2. *Selection and Training of Supervisors* (Chap. 11).—The supervisor's functions and responsibilities; methods of selecting supervisors; training for future supervisors; specific training for present supervisors.

3. *Employee Induction and Training* (Chap. 12).—Responsibility for induction and training; induction as a part of training; types of employee training; developing a training program; training techniques; training as a continuing function.

4. *Employee Rating and Promotion* (Chap. 13).—What a good rating plan does; developing and administering a rating plan; promotion and upgrading; seniority and ability in promotions; other policy elements in promotions; handling promotions; disputes over promotions.

5. *Transfer, Downgrading, and Layoff* (Chap. 14).—Types of transfers; transfer policy; skill in handling transfers; downgrading vs. layoff; use of rating in downgrading and layoffs; formulating a layoff policy; other aspects of layoff policy; employment stabilization.

6. *Discipline and Discharge* (Chap. 15).—Foundations of constructive discipline; formulating plant rules; types of disciplinary action; informing employees of disciplinary policy; "talking it over;" a situational approach

THE PERSONNEL ADMINISTRATOR 21

to discipline; taking disciplinary action; discharge as a last resort; elements of a discharge policy.

7. *Wage Policies and Wage Administration* (Chap. 16).—Relation of wages to the personnel program; the general level of wages; making wage surveys; other factors affecting wage levels; internal wage and salary relationships; job description and analysis; elements of job evaluation; advantages of job evaluation; limitations and problems in job evaluation; advancing individuals within rate ranges; rates on women's jobs; responsibility for wage and salary administration.

8. *Methods of Wage Payment; Output Standards* (Chap. 17).—The personnel administrator's role; basic methods of wage payment; employee attitudes on wage incentives; requirements of a good wage-incentive system; group and plant-wide incentives; getting employee acceptance of new output standards; sharing the gains; the place of profit sharing; annual wage and guaranteed employment plans.

9. *Hours of Work and Shifts* (Chap. 18).—Optimum hours of work; trends in working hours; payment for overtime work; responsibility for scheduling hours; shift operations; characteristics of different shifts; meeting shift problems; rest and meal periods; paid vacations and holidays.

10. *Services for Employees* (Chap. 19).—The scope of employee services; how should services be offered; services in a large company; limitations necessary for mutual protection; special services; questions to be asked in considering a program.

11. *Employee Health and Safety* (Chap. 20).—Policies for health and safety; planning for health; organization for health; organization for safety; the safety director's qualifications; his place and functions; accident analysis; safety committees; relation to other personnel activities.

12. *Employee Participation in Production Problems* (Chap. 21).—Employee interest in production problems; suggestion systems and their requirements; acting upon suggestions; joint suggestion committees; limitations of a suggestion system; meetings with supervisors on improving efficiency; joint labor-management committees; union-management cooperation on production problems; and conditions necessary for its success.

The Need for Personnel Policies

In a well-run organization of moderate or large size, formal statements of company policies on each of the 12 areas outlined above are needed. The personnel administrator should participate in the formulation of these policies, since in these matters he may be expected to possess a special competence. He prepares tentative policy drafts for top-management consideration, and, through study of the personnel needs of the organization, he plans for a well-rounded personnel-policy system. But, to repeat, it is not his function to make final decisions on personnel policies.

What is a policy? Briefly, it is a statement of intention that commits management to a general course of action in order to accomplish a specific purpose. For example, when a firm announces that "work requirements and employee performance shall periodically be reviewed for the purpose of establishing and keeping up to date a system of grading jobs and rating men," it is making a commitment for action with a definite objective in mind.

The application of a policy involves many details, but at the outset it is necessarily stated in broad terms. A policy should not be so categorical as a rule, since it is intended as a guide for management representatives who are expected to use some judgment in applying it. Finally, a policy must bear a consistent relationship to other policies and company practices that, taken as a whole, enable supervisors and employees to understand, anticipate, and cooperate with the central purposes of top management. The most important feature of a policy, however, is that it commits management to a particular course of action.

Personnel policies are necessary in an organization because management cannot deal with each employee *solely* as an individual. An obvious example of this is the fact that no firm can permit its employees to come to work or leave work at their convenience. Coordination of operations in order to produce an article or perform a service demands that employees come to work on a definite schedule. Special hours may be provided for part-time workers, as in the 4-hour "victory shifts" during the war, but this is done primarily to tap an otherwise unavailable portion of the labor supply and not to accommodate some particular individual.

To be sure, good personnel administration recognizes every employee as an individual with interests, rights, and duties other than those associated with his position and function in the organization. Before he was employed, he was a person who had problems and hopes and fears. He is no less a person when he enters the organization.

But, in going to work for an organization, the individual also becomes a member of smaller groups to which certain policies apply. He may be a union member, some of whose rights and duties are covered by a labor agreement. In addition, he is either a probationer or a regular employee; a learner, an apprentice, or a classified job holder; an unskilled, semiskilled, or skilled worker, or a technical or professional employee; a shop or office worker; a salaried or an hourly rated employee, a production or a nonproduction worker, a young or short-service employee, married or unmarried, or a member of many other subgroups or classifications. Policies that commit the organization to certain lines of actions with respect to these subgroups are the keystone of a constructive program of personnel administration.

FORMULATING AND ANNOUNCING PERSONNEL POLICIES

The personnel administrator helps to formulate policies and procedures, therefore, that consider the individual as (1) an employee of the organization and (2) a member of specific groups within the organization. Consequently, instead of concerning himself exclusively with the problem of how a certain employee can be given a satisfactory start in his new job, the personnel administrator gets top-management approval of a good induction program that can be applied to all new employees. In management councils, he takes a stand for similar policies and procedures concerning such matters as transfer, promotion, layoff, wage levels, and changes.[1] When these are incorporated in a written union agreement, there is still the need to help formulate interpretations to management representatives in the application of these policies and to develop other policies that are consistent with but not covered by the general framework of the agreement.

An important contribution of the personnel administrator to the formulation of personnel policies is his experience with similar situations earlier in the same organization, or in other organizations, and his familiarity with the literature on personnel policies.[2]

Once formulated, how should personnel policies be made known to all employees? They should certainly be stated in writing, and probably the most effective method of informing employees is through an employee handbook. If it is clearly written, the handbook has the great advantage of telling employees, particularly new ones, the things most of them want to know: what opportunities and benefits does the organization offer its

---

[1] Chapter 4 gives a more extensive discussion of policy thinking.

[2] This material is reported in such professional journals as *Personnel* (American Management Association), *Advanced Management* (Society for the Advancement of Management), *Personnel Journal* (Personnel Research Foundation), *Personnel Digest* (National Association of Personnel Directors), *Conference Board Management Record* (National Industrial Conference Board, Inc.), *Executives Service Bulletin* (Policyholders Service Bureau, Metropolitan Life Insurance Company), *Personnel Administration* (Society for Personnel Administration), *Supervision* (National Association of Foremen), and *Factory Management and Maintenance* (McGraw-Hill Book Company, Inc.), as well as in special books and monographs (such as the NICB's Studies in Personnel Policy or the AMA's Personnel Series), and in papers presented at annual meetings of the professional societies. The journals in the social sciences, particularly those in applied psychology, social anthropology, and economics, should not be overlooked by the personnel administrator interested in the experience of others.

employees, and what policies will affect their continued employment and advancement? Even if a firm has a printed contract with a union, the employee handbook is still a useful supplement.

In addition to the handbook, some firms also prepare a special printed statement of personnel policies for distribution to employees.[1] Changes in personnel policies are generally announced in employee magazines, on bulletin boards, and verbally by supervisors. The supervisors are kept informed of established personnel policies and revisions in them by means of periodic supervisory conferences and loose-leaf policy manuals, which can be kept up to date. This is an important aspect of the training of supervisors, which is discussed in a later chapter. But it is well to supplement this material for supervisors with printed information on company policies for all employees.[2]

Without clear information on personnel policies, employees are likely to be confused, do not know what is expected of them, and are apt to believe that favoritism and "pull" are the major factors in hiring, promotion, wage and salary changes, layoff, discipline, and discharge. Needless to say, however, written policy statements are worthless if management does not intend to carry them out honestly and consistently. Nothing should be put in writing to which employees, knowing that management's professed policies do not square with its practices, could answer, "bunk."

Summary

The place of the personnel administrator in the company organization should be clearly defined at the outset. He is a staff man, without line authority except over his own assistants, and he should report directly to the chief executive of the organization. Unless he has top-management support, he can accomplish little.

The personnel administrator is the exponent of the personnel point of view in policy formulation and administration, as well as in handling special personnel problems. He is expected to keep his finger on the pulse of the organization—to diagnose its stability and morale—and to help develop sound personnel procedures and services designed to maintain high morale and correct poor conditions.

[1] An example is *Employee Relations in General Foods*, 2d ed., General Foods Corporation, New York, May 19, 1941.

[2] For a stimulating discussion of this subject see, "Written Statement of Personnel Policy," *Studies in Personnel Policy*, No. 79, National Industrial Conference Board, Inc., 1947.

Personnel policies are needed in any organization, because each employee cannot be treated solely as an individual. The personnel administrator can make an important contribution in helping to formulate these policies and in reducing them to writing.

In unionized firms, many of the matters covered by personnel policies involve discussions with union officials. The resultant agreement is embodied in a labor contract between the parties, and the personnel administrator or the industrial-relations director may again play an advisory role to top management when this contract is being drawn up. Furthermore, in the day-to-day administration and application of the terms of the contract, differences in interpretation frequently arise. These involve relationships with union representatives, and the personnel administrator, as adviser to line management, has an opportunity to help determine these relationships. The possible alternatives are the subject of the next chapter.

Chapter 3

Personnel Administration and Unions

> Where we are dealing with organized labor, we are going
> to get about the type of leadership that we are ourselves.
>
> Cyrus S. Ching[1]

The economic and political power of organized labor has grown tremendously since 1933, leaving its imprint upon personnel work. This development has broadened the staff responsibilities of the personnel administrator, and it has brought a reconsideration of the content of many personnel policies, as well as their method of formulation.

The development of personnel administration has, in some respects, paralleled that of organized labor. During the First World War, labor shortages brought a recognition of the importance of sound hiring and employment practices, and through this personnel work got its start. Unionism also grew in strength, reaching a peak membership of 5,000,000 in 1920. Here the parallel breaks down, however, for union membership fell off drastically during the twenties, while personnel programs continued to be more widely adopted. In fact, in many firms they became a device to weaken or avoid unionism. There were welfare schemes that smacked of paternalism, and many companies sponsored employee representation plans. At the same time, government and the courts were lukewarm, if not openly hostile, toward unions. This did not change until about 1932.

The depression of the thirties and the resurgence of unionism brought renewed vitality and a new point of view to personnel work. Widespread unemployment emphasized the social responsibilities of management, and collective bargaining through unions involved new obligations. This was the period when personnel policies finally "moved into the front office."

[1] "Problems in Collective Bargaining," *Journal of Business of the University of Chicago*, Part 2, p. 40, January, 1938.

Why Workers Join Unions

Today it is shortsighted to discuss personnel administration without considering unionism. Wartime union strength of 14,000,000 workers—nearly one-third of the civilian labor force—may drop off somewhat in the postwar years, but managements that count upon a repetition of the drastic decline in union strength that occurred during the twenties are overlooking essential differences. Not only is union membership relatively stronger than it was in 1920, but the right of workers to organize and bargain collectively is now firmly established and protected in our public policy, especially in the National Labor Relations (Wagner) Act of 1935, which forms an important part of the new labor-management relations (Taft-Hartley) act of 1947.

Given governmental protection, unionism derives its strength from its representation of the basic attitude and aspirations of wage earners in an industrial civilization, which are not greatly different from the hopes and objectives of other persons. Extensive interviews with workers by the Division of Labor Studies of the Institute of Human Relations, Yale University, revealed the following as goals that every worker seeks:[1]

1. The society and respect of other people.
2. The degree of creature comforts and economic security possessed by the most favored of his customary associates.
3. Independence in and control over his own affairs.
4. Understanding of the forces and factors at work in his world.
5. Integrity—the desire to be treated as a human being.

According to the Yale study, workers voluntarily join a specific union if membership in that union will help them realize these goals. For example, as "a good union man," a worker feels part of a group and has the respect of his fellows. If he becomes a union officer or steward, he may even be a "fellow your buddies look to" in the group. The economic motive for joining unions is also a strong one; and the fact that a union in the plant or in a near-by firm has used its bargaining power to win increased wages, shorter hours, and a greater degree of economic security for its members attracts nonunion workers to "join up."

But perhaps too much emphasis has been put on the economic reasons for union membership. One of the strongest drives toward unionism today is the desire of workers to participate, as members of a group, in decisions that affect them. They want a larger measure of control over their own affairs, and a union helps to give them this by placing certain restrictions

[1] Bakke, E. Wight, "Why Workers Join Unions," *Personnel*, Vol. 22, No. 1, pp. 37–46, 1945. See also Golden, Clinton, and H. J. Ruttenberg, Motives for Union Membership, in *The Dynamics of Industrial Democracy*, Chap. 1, Harper & Brothers, New York, 1940.

on management's previously unchallenged authority. The union must now be consulted and in some cases even agree to changes before they are made. Still another method of increasing workers' "control over their own affairs" is through political action by unions in local, state, and national elections and in legislative activity.

Union educational activities may help the worker to gain a better understanding of the forces and factors at work in his world, though only from the union point of view. Moreover, the worker's desire to be treated as a human being may be realized through membership in a given union if this affords him a new self-respect. Furthermore, as a union member, or union officer, he may get a new kind of respect from his foreman, or at least feel that the union will back him up in some long-nursed griev-ance. He now has an avenue of communication right to the top, if necessary.

For these reasons, the American factory worker today is strongly pro-union.[1] Failures by some employers to provide decent wages and working conditions and to treat their workers humanely have, of course, hastened the growth of unions in some firms and industries. But many managements have learned that high wages and other economic benefits, which they thought their employees wanted, do not prevent unionization. Strong pressures for group relationships and for an increasing measure of control over the things that affect them have led workers to join unions even in "good" firms. This has been most evident in indus-tries that had already been largely organized by strong international unions.

Employers who have tried to do everything *for* their employees are often bewildered, hurt, and angered when these employees want to do something for *themselves* through membership in an outside union. In our experience, such employers make a mistake in regarding unionization as an insult or as an evidence of failure on their part. This attitude can only result in heart-aches and bitterness that will delay the necessary readjustments to the new situation. The real challenge is for these managements to deal construc-tively with this new organization which their employees have chosen to represent them.

[1] A recent opinion survey of a sample of 17,000,000 wage earners in manufacturing showed that (1) "The factory worker is strongly prounion. In 7 cases out of 10 he is a union man," (2) "He believes firmly that the worker's best chance of making a good living lies in joining a union." Even 39 per cent of the nonunion workers advocated joining a union, although 37 per cent of the total interviewed said that workers were forced to join unions through some form of the "union shop." "What the Factory Worker Really Thinks about Post-war Jobs and Labor Unions," *Factory Management and Maintenance*, Vol. 102, No. 10, pp. 81–92, 1944. The survey was made by the Opinion Research Corporation of Princeton, N. J.

The Difference Made by Unionism

When a firm is first unionized, what are the effects? A basic social change occurs in the structure of employer-employee relationships. A wedge seems to have been driven between the company and its employees. Many of these employees now profess an allegiance to an outside organization that, if it is affiliated with a national union, has broader interests and problems than those confronting the individual employer. In the initial stages of union relations, therefore, conflict is more probable than cooperation, especially if recognition of the union has followed a bitter period of name calling, electioneering, or possibly a strike.

With the entry of a union, furthermore, top management can no longer make unilaterial decisions about employee relationships. Company policies on wages, transfer, layoff, and discharge, to mention only a few, must now be discussed with union representatives and formally incorporated in a written agreement. Decisions on the administration of these policies may still rest with management, but they are frequently subject to questioning and criticism by union representatives under a formal grievance procedure. As one keen student of labor-management relations has observed, "A union is an employer-controlling device. It seeks to control the discretion of employers . . . at every point where their action affects the welfare of the men."[1] This relates to the question of management's "prerogatives," which have been the subject of much discussion and conflict in labor-management relations. Faced with an effective challenge to its decision-making authority, top management naturally finds it difficult wholeheartedly to accept the new organization without fear of the future.

Difficult as this adjustment is for top management, it is frequently even more difficult for lower line officials. Superintendents and foremen now find their authority challenged. There is another person, the "shop steward," who, though subordinate to the foreman in the company organization, has a position in the union that is on the same level as the foreman's position in the company. This is illustrated in Fig. 2, which shows a typical complaint and grievance procedure.[2]

The steward holds his position through appointment by union officers or election by union members in his department. In carrying out his duties,

[1] BAKKE, E. WIGHT, Labor and Management Look Ahead, in *Reconciling Labor and Management Philosophies*, p. 13, Personnel Series No. 98, American Management Association, New York, 1946. This paper, based on interviews with about 60 management leaders and 60 union leaders during the fall of 1945, is pertinent to much of the point of view expressed in this chapter, and it is especially enlightening on the issue of management prerogatives (pp. 13–15).

[2] A fuller discussion of complaints and grievances and of the appropriate procedures is presented later in Chap. 10; at this point, we are concerned only with the relative organizational positions of the foreman and steward in a unionized firm.

he is responsible to them, not to the foreman. Workers come to him with complaints and grievances. Acting as the workers' representative, he takes these matters up with the foreman. New stewards, especially in newly unionized firms, are likely to feel that they "are now running the department," and friction with the foreman often develops. This is a very difficult

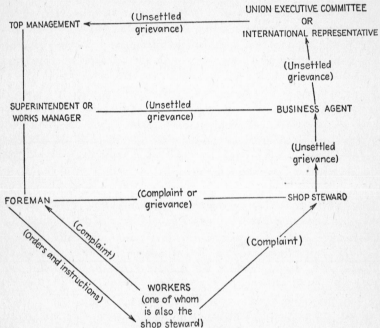

FIG. 2. — Place of the foreman and shop steward in the complaint and grievance procedure.

period of readjustment for the foreman, who may be especially disturbed unless he understands clearly top management's attitude and policy toward the union.[1]

POSSIBLE ALTERNATIVES FOR MANAGEMENT

When a union first secures bargaining rights, management's position toward this new organization can be the result of a choice among several attitudes and policies. What are these possible choices?

First, management may decide to fight the union indirectly. If this decision is put into effect, it must be done in subtle ways, since outright

[1] For a more extended discussion of newly unionized situations, see BENJAMIN M. SELEKMAN, *Labor Relations and Human Relations*, McGraw-Hill Book Company, Inc., New York, 1947, especially Ch. II, "When the Union Enters." Practical suggestions for foremen in adjusting themselves to and dealing with union stewards are found in GLENN GARDINER, *When Foreman and Steward Bargain*, McGraw-Hill Book Company, Inc., New York, 1945.

opposition to union membership and refusal to bargain collectively are unlawful under the National Labor Relations (Wagner) Act of 1935. Management may indulge in subtle forms of discrimination and efforts to discredit the union. But such activities usually bring retaliation in kind from union leaders. Peaceful relations and responsible unions are not developed by this approach. Instead, labor relations are characterized by bitter accusations on each side, evidences of bad faith, and underhanded tactics.

Second, management may deal with the union "at arm's length," making no real effort to establish a cooperative relationship and hoping for disappearance of the union sometime in the future. This is a fairly common attitude on the part of those managements which accept unionism grudgingly and wish to have as little to do with it as possible. The frigid reception and lack of understanding tend to become reciprocal—the union knows that it is the unwanted stepchild and behaves as such. Although labor relations are less primitive than in the first type of relationship, they are still characterized by mutual suspicion and distrust.

Third, management may accept unions as a permanent and positive force in our present-day industrial civilization and attempt to work out constructive cooperative relationships with them. This alternative involves the recognition by management that it has an opportunity to help unions become responsible by taking the initiative in seeking to establish friendly relations based on fair dealing and understanding of each other's problems. Increasingly, this third policy is being adopted by American management, though it requires a great deal of time and patience.

Cyrus S. Ching, vice-president of the United States Rubber Company and an outstanding management spokesman in industrial relations, expressed this point of view in a widely quoted address in 1937:

> In our company . . . we are going to get about the type of labor leadership that we develop by our own actions. If, in dealing with labor organizations, we are ethical, are entitled to the confidence of people, use fair tactics and use friendly attitudes, we will get that in return; if we are going to be militant, use underhanded tactics, and fight all the time, that is the type of organized labor leader we will get. So I think we all must realize that, where we are dealing with organized labor, we are going to get about the type of leadership that we are ourselves.[1]

[1] "Problems in Collective Bargaining," *Journal of Business of the University of Chicago*, January, 1938, Part 2, p. 40. Eight years later, after continued experience with unions in his own company and as industry member of the National War Labor Board, Mr. Ching had not changed his views: "I feel very, very strongly that industry has the responsibility of selling itself to organized labor on the basis of its integrity and businesslike methods. . . . Industry has a responsibility for the type of labor leadership we have . . . and shall have in the future." "As Management Sees Our Postwar Labor Problems," *The Controller*, Vol. 13, No. 2, pp. 58ff., 1945.

In August, 1947, Mr. Ching became director of the new Federal Mediation and Conciliation Service.

THE BASIS FOR UNDERSTANDING

This statement is of course a generalization, and many employers dealing with unions can cite cases in which union officers, business agents, and stewards failed to respond favorably to tactful and honest treatment. But too many employers have never made a genuine attempt to take the initiative in friendly dealings. They wait, often in vain, for union leaders to "become responsible." Granting that there are exceptions, it is nevertheless borne out in many collective-bargaining experiences that, when management is frank and decent and friendly, union leaders will gradually come to act in the same way. When management goes halfway or even more, union leaders will, in most cases, come to meet them, and mutual understanding is then possible.

If an employer chooses this third policy, which is the only road to peaceful and constructive relationships in a unionized society, his effort to achieve understanding with union leaders must be genuine. He must put all his cards on the table. If the facts necessary to understanding are withheld, collective bargaining can never become more than horse trading, and union demands will continue to be unreasonable. In the words of Alexander Heron, "We have seen examples of facts twisted to suit a program of agitation, facts half told in order to create conflict between employer and employee. The more we have barred the sources of information to union representatives, the more dramatic and unfavorable has been their use of the fragments they did obtain; and the more persistent and circuitous have been their methods of obtaining what they could use. Frankness toward the so-called labor politician helps him to become a labor statesman."[1]

When an employer has committed himself to this third policy, he may discover that relationships with a responsible union can mold the organization into a better work team, rather than making it a house divided against itself. Certainly many firms learned during the war that union leaders can provide an effective channel of communication between top management and the work force and that this can help workers feel that they have an integral part in the enterprise, rather than being *apart* from it. Successful experiences in union-management cooperation on production problems

[1] *Sharing Information with Employees*, p. 177, Stanford University Press, Stanford University, Calif., 1942. Mr. Heron was then director of industrial relations, Crown-Zellerbach Paper Company.

The reader interested in concrete collective-bargaining case studies that bear out the position we have taken should consult H. A. MILLIS, editor, *How Collective Bargaining Works*, The Twentieth Century Fund, New York, 1942. See also WILLIAMSON, S. T. and HERBERT HARRIS, *Trends in Collective Bargaining*, The Twentieth Century Fund, New York, 1945.

and with labor-management committees during the war, which we shall discuss in a later chapter, supply ample evidence on this point.

The development of friendly, cooperative relationships with management, however, may involve risks for union leaders. In a democratic union, where the real power rests with the membership, the leader must always consider the *political* effects of his actions. He cannot be too far in front, for there is danger that he might be denounced and unseated as a "management boy." He must try to educate the membership to the realities of the labor-management relationship as he sees them from his "inside" position. His job is easier if management does nothing to weaken his standing but instead provides him with accurate information and settles grievances or contract demands in good faith.

Management should realize that the structure of a democratic union is almost exactly the reverse of a company's organizational structure. The power of decision making is at the bottom of the structure, in the rank-and-file membership, rather than at the top, as in the board of directors or chief executive of a business enterprise. It requires sympathetic understanding to appreciate that the average union leader in a democratic union is expected to be responsive to the wishes of his membership and also to be responsible in his dealings with management. In unions that lack democratic procedures, this problem is not so serious. But managements often criticize unions for being undemocratic; and, if they hope for democracy in the unions they deal with, they must try to understand the problems facing union leaders.[1]

The Personnel Administrator and Unions

How does all this affect the personnel administrator? As a staff officer, he is not responsible for making policies, nor can he directly commit management to one of the three policies for the organization of which he is a part. But, in his role as advisor to top management, he can *influence* attitudes and policy making. He can also help to determine the way in which policies are administered by lower management, because he is an adviser and aide to all members of the line organization in matters affecting personnel. And unquestionably his attitude toward unionism in general and toward the union officials in the company should be a strong influence in management thinking and action all the way up and down the line.

In our judgment, the personnel administrator will debase professional standards if he regards the personnel program as an instrument for keeping

[1] *Cf.* SELEKMAN, BENJAMIN M., *op. cit.*, especially Ch. VIII, "Wanted: Mature Labor Leaders."

out or getting rid of a union. As one member of the profession has said, "To the eternal good of all concerned, the personnel man has evolved from one who tried to keep *from* working with the unions to one whose job is working *with* the unions."[1] Sound personnel procedures and practices are needed whether or not there is a union. But any attempt to use them to weaken and undermine a union will only bring to the front the worst elements in the union.

In distinguishing earlier between "personnel administration" and "industrial relations" or "labor relations," we said that dealings with organized labor are not the primary concern of the personnel administrator. In unionized concerns that have no separate labor-relations or industrial-relations director, however, the personnel administrator is likely to be drawn into these problems. If he is clear about his proper staff role, he will avoid being put in the position where he has to make decisions in the name of management on complaints or grievances or on contract demands. Even in the grievance procedure, he remains an adviser, and line management at various levels has the responsibility for decision making.

In his capacity as adviser, however, the personnel administrator should know something about the experience of other managements in dealing with organized labor, especially in terms of the three possible policies discussed earlier. If he recommends the third, as we believe he should, he can also assist top management in getting this policy understood and carried out down the line, especially at the supervisory level. New supervisors and most supervisors in newly unionized firms need suggestions on building constructive relationships with shop stewards, and here the personnel administrator has an opportunity to bring to their attention the accumulated experience of others in meeting similar problems. In the words of the industrial-relations director of a large manufacturing firm that has dealt with unions for 50 years:

Our attitude and procedure in dealing with the union representative who is inconsiderate and overaggressive, who exaggerates, who talks without thinking, who doesn't have the facts, etc., will often determine how long this type of man will stay at the top. If we are rough, scheming, or clever in dealing with him, we become a sounding board for him, and this will prevent good relations for a long time to come. Such a situation is beneficial neither to the employees nor to the company but will often cost both sides a great deal.[2]

[1] BURK, SAMUEL L. H. (director of industrial relations for Pittsburgh Plate Glass Company, and wartime director of industrial relations for Triumph Explosives, Inc.), The Personnel Profession—Its Present and Future Status, in *Personnel Organization and Professional Development*, p. 42, Personnel Series No. 74, American Management Association, New York, 1943.

[2] WARREN, RAY, *Working with Unions to Prevent Grievances*, pp. 13–14, Personnel Series No. 57, American Management Association, New York, 1942. See also GARDINER, GLENN, *op. cit.*

In handling personnel problems, furthermore, the supervisor needs a point of view and certain skills that the experienced personnel administrator can help him acquire. Inadequate consideration of all the facts, jumping to conclusions, and hasty action are always injurious to employee morale; but, when a union is present, their consequences may be particularly serious and time-consuming, especially for other company officials. The supervisor must therefore, develop a skill in case analysis, and as an aid to understanding he must view each situation from the standpoint of its policy implications and the persons involved in it. He also needs to know how to be a good listener when an employee has something on his mind; in other words, how to interview. These are the skills of the personnel administrator, whose success is in part measured by the extent to which members of the line organization themselves acquire and use these skills.

Summary

Unionism springs from the basic aspirations of wage earners who, in specific situations, become convinced that they can get more satisfaction by membership in a union than by "going it alone." This feeling is so widespread that even "good" firms are unionized. Instead of regarding this as an insult or as an evidence of their failure, managements should take the initiative in developing constructive relationships.

The personnel administrator has the opportunity (1) to influence top-management policies toward unions, (2) to assist in the understanding and administration of these policies by lower line management, and (3) to help supervisors handle the kinds of problems that arise in newly unionized firms.

As an aid to understanding personnel and labor-relations problems, the supervisor needs to develop a skill in situational thinking—in viewing each situation from the standpoint of its policy implications and of the persons involved in it. He also needs skill in case analysis and in basic interviewing technique. These are some of the skills of the personnel administrator which are discussed in the following three chapters.

B. HANDLING PERSONNEL PROBLEMS

Chapter 4

Situational Thinking

In coping with complex and fluid situations we need thinking which is relational and which searches for cross bearings between areas; this is thinking in a context. By its use it is possible to reach an understanding of historical and social materials and of human relations, although not with the same degree of precision as in the case of simpler materials and of recurring events.

General Education in a Free Society,
REPORT OF THE HARVARD COMMITTEE[1]

In orienting ourselves to any human situation, we may begin either with a general view of the whole or with an intensive study of the parts. Whichever way we start, each method is needed, sooner or later, to supplement the other. We can neither thoroughly comprehend the whole without understanding the parts nor grasp the entire meaning of each part without knowing the significance of the whole. And, in trying to understand people, we need to think about relationships among individuals, and between individuals and the "wholes" to which they belong.

Moreover, it is helpful to know not only what relationships obtain but also of what relationships each person is currently aware. A foreman's future is partly determined by his position in the network of organizational relationships. But his actions at any given moment may fail to reflect certain important relations that are not present in his mind. This simple fact gives us a clue to significant differences in his behavior, *e.g.,* in his manner to a subordinate according to whether or not his superior happens to be present.

An understanding of significant relationships is possible only when we have a good grasp of the total situation. We are fortunate, therefore, when previous experience enables us to begin our intensive study of details with some understanding of the general pattern, *i.e.,* the general type of situ-

[1] Harvard University Press, Cambridge, Massachusetts, 1945, p. 66.

ation. Then we can say, "*This* is a layoff" or "*That* is the type of problem common to a rapidly expanding organization."

If, however, we have to start from scratch in an unfamiliar situation, we should begin by observing as many facts as we can. By this detailed observation, we hope to discover the basic elements. We can then explore their interrelationships and in this way evolve a picture of the larger pattern. When we begin by observing the parts, we need a method for differentiating between the relevant and the irrelevant. Otherwise we become confused by the mass of detail. What we want is a method for posing fruitful questions. If we evolve a comprehensive system, of course we shall find that not every question is useful in every situation. But, if we have them all to fall back on, we stand a better chance of finding significant leads. What kinds of question can usefully be asked when we seek understanding of human problems in industry?

BASIC VARIABLES

Experience in personnel administration indicates that the basic elements into which we need insight are (1) technical features, (2) the human element, (3) principles and policies, and (4) the time factor.

Technical Features.—Modern management and engineering have brought the techniques of organization and productive enterprise to a high level of efficiency.[1] In fact, progress in this direction has far outrun our capacity for dealing efficiently with people. More than that, the inclination to concentrate on mechanical systems and on the logic of efficiency has often led management to subordinate the individual to technical requirements. In what has been called the "machine age," human beings have too often been looked upon as mere functional entities and adjuncts to machines. The development of personnel work in itself was an inevitable reaction to this overemphasis on the technical element.

The Human Element.—The individual in industry should be studied in two ways. First, the personnel administrator should think about the individual's needs and behavior as determined by his current situation and according to whether the person is a male or female worker, a probationer or regular employee, a skilled or unskilled operator, or a unionized or nonunionized worker. Second, if there are special problems, the personnel administrator needs to ask: Why is this person making or confronting diffi-

---

[1] We include no discussion of ways to study and control the technical factor. Scientific literature on such subjects as production planning and control, time and motion study, and quality and cost control is abundantly available and should be familiar to the personnel administrator.

culties? What is unique about his personal situation or temperament? Has this any bearing on the problem at hand? What demand is the work situation making on him that he is unable to meet? Conversely, what demands is he making on his work situation that are not being satisfied? This approach may be called *person-centered thinking*.

Emphasis on the human element meant a step forward in the sense that management no longer defended the proposition that industrial progress can be achieved by a solution of purely technical problems. But over-emphasis on the person-centered approach is just as misleading as the tendency from which it was a reaction. In fact, the study of human problems in industry cannot intelligibly be divorced from the technical setting in which they arise. A more comprehensive view attempts to balance and relate technical and human factors within an inclusive system.

Principles and Policies.—The personnel administrator finds it useful to relate his observation of people and of the mechanical element by means of his understanding of the general principles[1] that apply to human situations. This approach may be called *policy-centered thinking*. Modern management thinks about such principles when formulating and administering policies for large-scale situations. These policies relate general principles to specific situations in such a way as to form a guide to action at all organizational levels. But policy thinking is useful not only as a means of achieving uniformity throughout a large organization. It is also needed in a situation where only two people are concerned. Whatever the scale of relationships, clear and consistent policies enable us to act in a way that reconciles the different requirements made by the mechanical system and by the participating individuals. These policies form the basis for reasonable and consistent behavior.

When the personnel administrator has the opportunity to make recommendations in advance of executive action, he asks: Which policies are applicable to this type of situation, in this company, at this time, and for these individuals? If, on the other hand, he is called in after problems have developed, policy thinking may again provide the clue. Are the necessary policies being applied at all? Are they well administered and clearly inter-

[1] Consideration of principles that underlie policies constitutes an important area of study. But, since there is at present no clear-cut agreement as to what these principles should be, inclusion of our opinion on this subject would serve no useful purpose at this time. For this reason (except for a brief introduction to Secs. D through F), we have confined ourselves to a consideration of policies that apply principles to specific situations. Within recent years, there has been considerable advance in policy thinking, but an essential step for further progress in personnel administration is a clarification of fundamental principles of human behavior in organizations.

preted? Are some policies being applied but proving inadequate because other parts of a complete policy system are lacking?

The Time Factor.—In seeking understanding of human and technical elements, as well as of the principles that integrate both, the observer finds that he must also consider various aspects of the time element. How *far back* must we look in order to understand the meaning of what is happening now? What future events are we *moving toward*? What is the *sequence* of key facts? What *developmental* stage has been reached by this person or in this relationship? And how fast is the *pace*? Are events moving at such a rate that it is too late for the the slow influence of group thinking to take effect? Such questions as these may lead toward understanding of the ways in which time, as process, affects human experience.

METHOD OF STUDY

Obviously a wide range of questions concerning the various elements in industrial situations cannot be asked all at once. In learning to find our way about in any system of relationships, we have to study each element separately. As we do this, we find that the edges of each subsituation are blurred. For instance, when we focus attention on human problems, we soon find that we can accurately understand what these are only as we come to appreciate the technical and organizational aspects of the situation in which they have arisen. And we also need to trace the influence of the time factor in their development if we are to grasp their meaning. This somewhat inconvenient blurring of the various elements may serve to remind us that all of them are, in actuality, inseparable. Nevertheless, a preliminary separation is worth while as a practical method of study, because it enables us to observe more facts than we otherwise could.

Granted, then, that the basic variables are to be studied one by one, with which should a personnel administrator begin? This question has two answers according to whether it is posed as a practical assignment or as a logical problem.

The practical answer to the question of where to begin is found in the situation and in its stage of development. For this reason, it is essential that a personnel worker be flexible and able to think on his feet. For instance, when asked to help with a human problem, the personnel administrator may meet the most acute need by beginning with the person-centered approach, probably in an interview.

However, even then the personnel administrator fits purely personal facts into the framework of policy requirements. This type of policy-centered thinking should be going on in his mind first, last, and all the time.

The logical answer, therefore, to the sequence of his approach to under-standing is that policies come first.

PUTTING POLICY REQUIREMENTS FIRST

When using policy-centered thinking as a problem-solving technique, the personnel administrator begins by thinking about policy requirements. For example, if he is asked to look into the friction between two department heads, he may well begin by inquiring whether there is a suitable organ-ization policy. Perhaps he finds that the two officials' duties and scope of authority were never clearly defined and that the consequent overlapping and inefficiency are sources of chronic irritation to both men. In fact, any two people placed in a similar situation would be likely to find themselves in the same kind of difficulty. If this is the case, the personnel administra-tor's first recommendation would be that management clarify this feature of their common work life by establishing an appropriate organization policy, indicating lines of authority as well as the duties and responsibilities of all concerned.

Perhaps, however, the personnel administrator finds that needed policies have been aptly formulated but are being misapplied. In that case, he shifts his policy-centered thinking from the immediate difficulty to the future. For instance, to prevent the recurrence of similar difficulties in this or another situation, it may be necessary to maintain more effective com-munication down the line in regard to policies and to establish more adequate follow-up of policy activity.

Finally, the personnel administrator may find that some needed policy is not being applied at all. This may be either because the management official who is responsible for action does not know that the company has a suitable policy or because there is none. In the first case, the failure is probably again one of communication down the line, although it may be lack of ability or of training to think in terms of policy. Then there is need for better training of the management representative at fault here and probably also of others in the company.

On the other hand, if policy needs are not being met because (1) exist-ing policies no longer fit the evolving situation or (2) policies are inade-quate to cover all the necessary features or (3) they are not genuine policies at all, then constructive policy thinking must be done at higher levels, ultimately by top management itself.

In such ways, policy thinking helps us to get a perspective on human problems. But, while sorting out the policy implications of a given situ-ation, the personnel administrator does not withhold attention from the other component elements. These different modes of thinking are complementary. For instance, his policy thinking is enriched if he can achieve a sound understanding of technical and human factors in the evolving situation. Thus his first practical step in a problem situation may be to hold an interview.

UNDERSTANDING PEOPLE

Suppose, for instance, he is asked to find out what is the matter with Bill. This otherwise valuable employee has occasional outbreaks of violence during which he indulges in such behavior as taking out his temper on the machine. The supervisor has reasoned with him and threatened to no avail. What can be done?

A personnel administrator knows that there is some reason for this explosive behavior on Bill's part. The question is, what? In order to reach the heart of this unique situation, we may need to start from the periphery, where we understand what is true of Bill because it is true of everyone. For each of us, the idea of what we need and want in life is reflected in our behavior. Our regular way of life is predominantly either a planned method for achieving this goal or a more or less haphazard set of reactions, largely conditioned by the behavior of those with whom we have associated. However our way of life has been developed, each of us tends to be upset when it is interfered with. To be upset or to feel insecure normally leads to some effort to reestablish one's balance and to protect what is being threatened. Different people do this in different ways. Those whose way of life is planned may be able to think out constructive alternative methods. But most people react from feeling rather than from thought. When they are frustrated, they are apt to take out their feelings of resentment in some nonlogical way. Often this creates problems for others. In modern American industry, rigid rules to prohibit fighting and quarreling prevent Bill from working off his annoyance directly on other people. So he takes out his temper on his work or on the machine. This, in turn, brings him in conflict with the supervisor whose duty it is to get out quality work and maintain the equipment in good order. Warnings, reprimands, and penalties merely aggravate Bill's uncooperative attitude.

How can this whole vicious cycle be broken? If Bill is fired, his problems are merely taken somewhere else, and management has found no solution for the same behavior when it crops up in other cases. Furthermore, management has done nothing constructive. The intelligent way to help Bill and others like him is to find out what this undesirable behavior means in terms of Bill's own way of life.

THE PERSON-CENTERED APPROACH

Looked at only in the setting of the shop situation, Bill's behavior may be entirely unreasonable. "Nobody was bothering him. The material was up to specifications, and he had all the necessary tools. He must be crazy." This is the way a supervisor who is untrained in situational thinking naturally sees and judges Bill.

But, realizing that there is some reason for every kind of behavior, we know that, if it is not to be found in the work situation, it must lie in some other area of Bill's life. He may be grappling unsuccessfully with a problem that is not related to his work at all but is central at this time to his life as a whole. In that case, his outbreaks of temper may be an expression of his sense of defeat. Perhaps they are an ill-advised but natural effort to restore his self-respect by proving to himself that he can exercise power over something. Working on the assumption that Bill's logically unreasonable behavior may be based on some emotional reasoning, how can we go about tracking down the origin of his resentment?

Fortunately, each of us is not only in a unique life situation but also in a situation that is in some respects typical of everyone. Therefore, we all have much, though not everything, in common. In seeking insight into what may be creating difficulties for someone else, we can therefore take a short cut by generalizing from our experience with ourselves and other people.

In general, the major forces and areas of human life are the same for us all. A detailed discussion of these forces would be out of place in this text. But, for our present purpose, they may be summarized in tabular form, according to the areas in which they operate. (See page 45.)

Only a psychiatrist or social worker could spend the time and would have the skill needed to probe thoroughly into all these factors. But whoever undertakes to help another person should know that difficulties may arise in any of these areas, and he should be ready to consider them. Even a busy supervisor, when previously coached in the personnel point of view, can make use of the chart below to broaden his understanding of subordinates.

For instance, before interviewing Bill, the supervisor should ask himself, "What do I already know about him that may give me a lead? Is he a family man? Has he ever mentioned any worries at home? Has he friends and hobbies? Is his work suited to his abilities and ambitions? What is his informal status in the work group, his formal standing in the company? Is he a newcomer in the community, with irritating problems of housing and transportation? Does he belong to a minority group in race or religion?" If the answer to any of these questions suggests that Bill is trying to cope with some problem too big for him, the supervisor may in a preliminary interview want to urge Bill to take advantage of some feature in the company's service program, even if only in the form of further interviewing by an expert.[1] Or perhaps all that is needed is an

WHAT TO LOOK FOR AND WHERE TO LOOK[1]

Forces	Area		
	Within the individual	Within the company	In the community
Physical	Physical, *i.e.*, organic changes Health	Physical conditions of work Physical demands made by the job	Neighborhood Housing Transportation Living standards
Mental	Mental, *i.e.*, psychological changes Preoccupations Emotional maturity Morale	Intellectual and emotional demands Facilities for training Stimulating contacts	Intellectual and emotional environment Schools Religion Recreation
Social interaction with others	Attitudes His idea of himself Degree of participation and responsibility Sense of membership	Social conditions and opportunities Office or shop Nature of work group Nature of work shift Single-machine job or line assembly Job status Type of organization; formal or informal Hourly rated or salaried	Activities Group status: dominant or minority group Class distinctions Position in family structure

[1] This table is adapted from F. J. ROETHLISBERGER and W. J. DICKSON, *Management and the Worker*, p. 327, Harvard University Press, Cambridge, Mass., 1939.

informal interview by the supervisor himself, to show a friendly interest in Bill as a person and give him a chance to "get his gripe off his chest."

EACH PERSON'S SITUATION IS UNIQUE

Whether help is offered by an expert or by an amateur, it is essential to start from where the person in difficulty is. Not only do we need to

[1] For discussion of appropriate ways to help employees, see Chap. 19.

understand what his difficulty *is*, but also what he *thinks it is*, and why he has chosen this specific means of meeting it. To do this, we need to get his view of the situation; to see, from his angle, where he stands. Normally, in his own eyes, each person stands in the center of the picture. He sees his own needs as being predominantly important and appreciates the strength of his own feelings. This view, though not the whole truth about any situation, is one feature to be dealt with. Therefore, we need to recognize it. Only when we do are we likely to be able to help him enlarge his view and comprehend the needs and feelings of other people, the technical requirements of the company, and the principles by which all the basic needs and differences can be integrated.

Fortunately, only a small minority of cases in any normal industrial situation call for the time-consuming person-centered approach. If, for instance, the company is involved in a layoff, this may come to some workers as a welcome opportunity for an extra vacation. To the majority, unless the layoff is prolonged, it will probably not be a matter of vital importance. But for a few employees it may present problems that they cannot solve alone. To one it may be the last straw in a financial crisis. Another may find it an insupportable insult to his pride. By the person-centered approach we attempt to see what demands this situation is making on each person and what tensions are set up when the situation clashes with the demands that he makes of life in general and of work in particular. In order to form a comprehensive picture from these two sets of conflicting demands, we have to achieve some understanding of the individual pattern created by the person's heredity, temperament, experience, and outlook. This pattern is in some respects unique. And it is constantly changing.[1]

Combined Understanding

A sound means for building situational understanding of individuals is to pool the insight achieved by people in different positions. No one can quite put himself in Bill's place. But different people can see different bits of Bill's experience, because each has shared one part. The supervisor knows something about Bill's situation, because they both are daily in the same place and he knows Bill's work. If the supervisor has previously been a member of the rank and file, he has had some experience of what that means, too. A union official has a different angle on Bill's situation.

[1] The fluidity of all human experience is one of the blurred edges referred to above. It is accounted for by the fact that time, as process, is an element in all human experience.

And a fellow employee on the same job, especially if he is a member of Bill's work unit, has further special opportunities for understanding. It may be worth while for the personnel administrator to talk also with the company doctor and even with some member of Bill's family, in order to find the missing piece without which the picture puzzle of Bill's life situation cannot be put together.

It usually takes time to understand all these interrelationships. But, if company policies permit and if cooperation is adequate between line and staff officials and between officers of the company and of the union, such exploration can help to reestablish a potentially valuable employee. When understanding of Bill's unique situation is related to understanding of company policies and technical requirements, there is a good chance for someone in the company to evolve a practical method of helping Bill to help himself.

And often a gain in understanding by a company official of some unique situation can lead to further gains in understanding by other people of technical requirements or of policy implications. For it is not only misunderstandings that have snowballing tendencies. Insight, too, can grow and spread. When we come to understand a subjective difficulty, we may at the same time learn how to help others think objectively. When we achieve enough insight *into* an individual situation, we stand a better chance of helping the person to look *outward* instead of being excessively preoccupied with his own difficulties.

Once understanding has been set in motion, it may work both ways and spread in all directions. While using the person-centered approach, the interviewer has presumably gained new insight into a unique problem. He is then in a better position to help build understanding by the employee's immediate supervisor, by interested union officials, and by the employee himself. All these people probably need a clearer picture of the company's technical situation at the time and of top management's policies. A group conference or private interview initiated to discuss a unique problem can often be broadened to include an explanation of technical demands that the company has to meet (such as those produced by the current economic situation, by the supply or condition of raw materials) and of methods that are used to meet them, such as production scheduling and temporary layoff. Usually there is also a need for reinterpreting the personnel policies by which both technical and human needs are balanced. This approach, in which generally valid principles of behavior are formulated as guides to action in specific types of situation, has already been referred to as policy-centered thinking.

Policy-centered Thinking

When we said that, in normal industrial situations, the cases of serious individual difficulties should be relatively few, we were assuming that personnel policies are wisely formulated, efficiently administered, and well interpreted. If this is not the case, problems multiply, both for individual workers and for the company in its labor relations. Unique problems cannot all be met in advance by policy thinking. But they can be kept to a minimum when by this means management provides for fair and uniform action at all levels and in all areas of the organization, especially when these policies are made known in advance to all concerned.

As we said in Chap. 2, decision making on policies is the responsibility of top management. As such, it should be carried out in advance of executive action. But policy thinking should not be confined to the executive level. It is essential that the supervisors who administer policies should understand and share their aims. This fact seems obvious in theory, but in practice supervisors often fail to understand how personnel policies relate to the problems that confront them.[1] Sometimes, indeed, supervisors are just as much in the dark as workers about the purposes that underlie top-management policies. They need help from someone who, like the personnel administrator, is versed in understanding both a variety of unique human situations and the whole set of principles that together form the basis of management's policy system. When these can be clarified for supervisors, the unifying influence of top-management purpose can become effective at the work level.

Helping Supervisors to Interpret Policy Aims

In his capacity as liaison official, the personnel administrator can do much to help first-line supervisors interpret and administer policies. He knows that foremen are constantly confronted by appeals for special action in "exceptional" cases. When dealing with these, supervisors necessarily receive some practical training in the person-centered approach. In his daily contacts with workers, a foreman is kept aware of

[1] For instance, in October, 1945, one of the authors talked to 95 supervisors from 35 representative companies in a small New England city. When he asked the question, "How many of you fellows have been informed by top management what the company's personnel policies are?" only three men signified that these had been explained to them. Others were silent or stated that, as far as they knew, there were no personnel policies in their company. Subsequent discussion with smaller groups verified the fact that most supervisors have little or no training along policy lines. Experience with similar groups shows that such ineffectual policy thinking is not unusual.

the many claims for special treatment that seem fair enough to the individual making the request. But often he is given little or no training in the kind of thinking by which individual claims alone can be met within the broader pattern of principles that are fair to all. And, unless a supervisor understands and can interpret to workers the *intent* of each policy, employees cannot reasonably be blamed for making their own interpretation of company *events*.

For example, in one firm the policy on sickness and absence was such that a worker with an infected tooth was excused one afternoon in order to go to the dentist. No explanation was made to workers as to the purpose and general application of the policy involved. The next week, an employee in the same section applied for time off to get her hair set. She was indignant when the supervisor refused. "Mary got time off last week—why can't I get off today?" With no understanding of policy requirements and purposes, how could this worker be expected to see that "time off" was not the common denominator in these two situations?

HELPING TOP MANAGEMENT IN POLICY FORMULATION

Sometimes, interpretation of policy thinking is all that the personnel administrator needs to do for line management and for workers in this field. But often he is also called upon to help in formulating policies when previously only expediency and individual judgment have guided action.

The Logical Phase.—When making recommendations to top management for new policies, the personnel administrator thinks first about the situation in general terms. He asks himself, "What principles need to be applied so that the proposed arrangements shall be fair to all concerned?" In reaching such a judgment, he thinks about the common denominator in the experience of everyone concerned and makes a composite picture from all the individual cases within his experience. He takes into account not only the features that are common to these but also the unique variations. Thus he can determine in what respects the policy should leave room for discretion. Having tentatively formulated a policy that covers all these situational features and that also conforms to the requirements of a genuine policy (see Chap. 2, page 22), he can then move on to the next stage of policy making.

The Comparative Phase.—Nowadays, no one has to "go it alone" after he has formulated a tentative policy. For one thing, the policy can be tested by comparison with the large body of written material that represents the accumulated experience of the personnel profession and of personnel-minded executives.

Second, every well-organized company has personnel policies and established procedures in some areas of activity with which the proposed policy can be compared. The new policy will be more effective and easier to explain and apply if it is evidently in line with other procedures that have already won acceptance in the company as a whole. Time and trouble are well spent in wording and interpreting policies in order to show that they are consistent with previous practice.

Third, enlightened executives will want assurance that any new or altered policy points toward action that will compare favorably with current practice in the community or in the industry at large.

Fourth, in a unionized company, the proposed policy will need to be checked against relevant clauses in the union contract in order to prevent actual or apparent violation of a previous agreement.

If the tentative policy compares well with such ideas, practices, and agreements, it is ready to be submitted for top management's approval.

In such ways, a personnel administrator can use policy thinking as a preliminary to the person-centered approach in helping top management and supervisors to understand and treat human problems. Both these approaches also depend for success on an appreciation of the third element, common to all human situations—time itself.

THINKING ABOUT TIME AS PROCESS

The time factor makes itself felt in human experience in five different, though related, ways. All these need to be taken into account by anyone who tries to understand and help people.

The *continuity* of events and experience means that each moment contains within it elements both of the past and of the future. The present cannot be fully understood when examined in isolation. What was said and done before partly determines what is being said and done now. Thus the past should enter into what is being planned now, because it limits what can effectively be said and done hereafter. The future, too, exists in each bit of the present. It is in the minds of people in the form of hopes and fears and so determines their behavior. Moreover, the future is constantly merging with the present in actuality.

This *fluidity* of events and experience is another temporal feature that needs to be remembered. Any situation that we are studying is constantly changing. Nothing human remains static. For this reason, it is unrealistic to make "final" judgments about people. New evidence may at any moment offer new insight to those who are on the alert for it. We need to have working hypotheses, but we need also to keep a weather eye open for new elements in the evolving situation. In policy thinking we need to remember that we cannot sit back and say, "Well, thank goodness, we've got that settled once and for all." Rigid policies are dead policies. This kind of thinking may become positively disruptive in personnel relations if it operates like the "dead hand" that rules situations when the thinker is no longer alive to take account of new elements in the situation.

Yet, within this pattern of ceaseless change, there is a *sequence* of events that we need to know if we are to see significant relationships. What preceded and what followed that act or word? The meaning of each bit of the present is partly determined by its place in relation to other events. Did he smoke before or after he was told that this was contrary to the safety rules? If before, it was merely careless. If after, it may have been willful disobedience. We cannot know how best to evaluate behavior unless we can place it in its temporal setting as well as understand the person whose act it was.

Setting Up A Time Frame.—The fluidity and continuity of events mean that we can never wrap up experience in neat parcels and put it away for future reference. But, in view of the importance of establishing the sequence of events, we need some device for temporarily setting apart certain segments of time for intensive study. When a personnel administrator is called upon to recommend a solution to some problem situation, he may therefore resort to the practical expedient that we call setting up a time frame for understanding. In doing so, he makes a compromise between the impossible feat of examining the limitless past and future that are inseparably connected with the problem episode and the unrealistic procedure of examining only the episode itself. He learns to select for study a span of time long enough to form a comprehensible unity within which significant words and acts make sense.

Setting up a time frame helps us to see subsituations within a larger context, just as we appreciate the meaning of separate scenes when we see a whole play. In order to understand a scene in the middle, we have to know what has happened before and the characteristics of the principal actors, whether they were on the stage or behind the scenes when we came in. And we are helped to see the meaning of their behavior because we can guess both what lies ahead and what they are expecting. Similarly, in real life, we learn what kind of behavior is "in character" for the people whom we are trying to help when we know what they have done over a period of time. Then, if we want to make constructive suggestions for action, we are in a better position to know what kind of solution would be acceptable to these people.

In all these ways, an appreciation of the time factor enables us to be more realistic in understanding and helping people. When we study industrial situations as also including technical features, and if we can equate both human and technical factors by means of appropriate principles, we stand a good chance of evolving a workable solution for any ordinary problem.

Two Other Temporal Features.—Another temporal feature that we need to study, in regard to both individuals and their interrelationships, is their *developmental stage.* Was the offender a boy and a new worker on probation, or was he a regular employee and a mature man? Does this layoff concern a girl in her teens or a man with twenty years of service? A worker's "age," both chronologically and in terms of his relation to the company, is a factor that helps us to appreciate what his own responsibilities and expectations are likely to be and what responsibilities the company has toward him. A wise personnel administrator will not offer advice in a situation unless he knows the facts about the stage of development that has been reached.

Lastly, we need to think about the *pace* of people and events. This is related to their stage of development. In a union-management dispute, for example, are we at the climax, where the tempo is too rapid for policy thinking by the group? If so, there is no use in attempting to introduce it now. Or, in regard to a worker who is to be discharged because he "dawdles," what is his natural pace? If he is in other respects a satisfactory employee, can he not be put at some job where the pace is slower? Or can he be helped to work faster after he clearly sees the situational demands for more speed? Or is his "dawdling" merely a sign that he is getting old? If we anticipate and accept a slower pace, transfers may save older workers from accidents and put them where steadiness of performance is of more value to the company than speed.

SUMMARY

By each of these modes of thinking, we seek an understanding of significant relationships, and in each we get perspective by examining situations from a different point of view.

Policy formulation is a study of essential relationships. Its success depends on ability to relate human and technical demands on the basis of sound and acceptable principles. By putting policy requirements first, it is possible to integrate different kinds of demand and to evolve general directives that secure fairness to all. Top management usually needs help in this type of thinking. Executives in a large organization cannot keep track of current developments unless these are brought to their attention. When new features in an evolving situation are related to policy requirements, they may call for reformulation of existing policies. A personnel administrator can also help first-line supervisors and members of intermediary management to see the relationship between top management's central purposes and the myriad everyday problems that arise in the shop.

Person-centered thinking, on the other hand, helps us to focus attention on unique factors. Using a system such as "what to look for and where to look," we may delimit the field where we are called upon to understand special variations of the general pattern. And this final feat of imagination is more likely to succeed when insight is pooled by different people each of whom shares some part of the unique experience.

Third, when we think about time as process, we get a different perspective on evolving situations.

Taken together with technical features, all these different kinds of relationship make up as complete a picture of reality as we can grasp. In the next chapter, we shall discuss the ways in which a personnel administrator uses this method of understanding to work on actual cases.

Chapter 5

Getting Down to Cases

> The statements of participants . . . are often interpretive of events much more than descriptions of events. They are notoriously unreliable, and can safely be used, like the patient's statements of symptoms, only by one skilled in interpreting such statements and possessed of a thorough knowledge and experience.
>
> CHESTER I. BARNARD[1]

The personnel administrator can be of service to line management and to workers by relating and interpreting the various subjective statements made by participants about events. In doing this, his aim is to get the whole story, of which each statement is a part. He knows that he can never be sure of seeing and interpreting the whole truth; but at least he never rejects any bit of truth that he does see, no matter how severely he may be tempted to do so.

At times, when confronted by an inconvenient or apparently incomprehensible fact, he feels like a person who finds one piece of a picture puzzle that will not fit. Perhaps he would like to throw it away. But he knows that it must fit because it is part of the whole picture that he has set himself to put together. He is likely to succeed if he keeps on trying, and he can do so most easily if he has an orderly method. Wherever he begins, he always works outward as far as he can from the bits he begins with until he can finally combine all the parts into one whole.

No piece in the puzzle can be considered unimportant, however small it is in itself, because all must be fitted together in order to finish the picture. Similarly, when difficulties arise in personnel relationships, no persistent complaint should be overlooked, however trivial it seems, because it may supply the key to larger issues.

[1] "Riot of the Unemployed at Trenton, N. J., 1935. A Lecture at Harvard University, 1938–1941, Presenting a Case in Concrete Sociology." Privately Printed.

Complaints should be settled by the foreman directly with the worker or by cooperation between the foreman and the shop steward. But, in some instances, misunderstandings cannot be straightened out between the parties themselves. In such cases, the personnel administrator is called upon to advise line officials or to lead discussions between union and management officials.

Many grievances seem relatively trivial, of vital importance only to the people who are immediately involved. Others clearly have policy implications because their solutions affect the plant as a whole or point toward needed changes in formal agreements. But, whether these difficulties are large or small, success in meeting them is essential to satisfactory personnel relations.

As an adviser, the personnel administrator can be of genuine help to line executives in solving personnel problems. In the first place, as a staff official, he is outside the problem situation. Second, unlike the line executive, who is constantly required to meet technical as well as human requirements, the personnel administrator is free to concentrate for considerable periods on human needs. Third, as a specialist in human relations, he may be presumed to have both competence and training in this field. More specifically, as an investigator of human problems, he is expected to know how to get down to cases, how to differentiate between opinions and facts, how to achieve the realistic understanding that must precede a satisfactory solution, and how to make an orderly, impartial presentation of the whole story. In what ways does he work on a case in order to get, to evaluate, and to relate the facts?

GETTING INSIDE THE SITUATION

One objective in case analysis is to understand the situation, insofar as it is possible, like an insider. In trying to do this, the observer should be wholly receptive as a neutral but understanding person. He comes to the situation with an open mind and absorbs the impressions that give him local color and a feeling for unique contexts. Although it seems that at this stage the observer is doing nothing, an intense mental effort is required to assimilate the new material *while withholding judgment*. Getting to understand essential relationships is like mapping the salient features of a new terrain. Only in this way can one acquire the easy familiarity with details that makes one at home in a new world of experience.

If the preliminary survey has been thorough, certain features emerge as problems for further study. These often strike a newcomer with peculiar force because he has a fresh view of the situation as a whole. A person who is habituated to a given scene easily overlooks significant details.

Getting the Whole Story

Another means of getting insight is listening to expressions of dissatisfaction by those who are involved in the situation. Such statements need not be accepted at their face value. Nevertheless, it is essential to know what they are, because the complainant's attitude, reasonable or otherwise, is one of the factors to be dealt with.

Because feelings color facts, the process of getting the story must be broken down into at least three stages. First, the person trained in the personnel approach gets the complainant's angle on the problem. He tries to visualize this subsituation from the inside, although without letting his own feelings become engaged. This, of course, is done by the person-centered approach. Next, he tries to get a more inclusive view of the same problem by looking at it through the eyes of other participants in the environment. This entails getting "the other fellow's story." Lastly, the interviewer tries to get a still wider perspective and to see the picture as it "really is." This involves relating all the partial views to each other in the specific setting of company policies and procedures.

1. *The Complainant's Story.*—Since the complainant is emotionally involved, he probably has a one-sided picture of the problem. Anyone who is upset selects facts, consciously or unconsciously, to express his feelings, to support his interpretation, or to advocate his solution. Even if the aggrieved person thinks he has a perfectly unprejudiced view, he inevitably sees things in the perspective of his national, social, and occupational background. Further slanting derives from his temperament, industrial status, and current preoccupations.

Because the personnel administrator is aware of this inevitable bias, he is on the lookout for significant omissions and for subjective judgments offered as facts. He knows that what is being communicated is the unique pattern of one person's experience, which is obviously not the same as the objective pattern of the whole situation. The personnel administrator's avowed intention of getting other pictures of the same situation in no way implies distrust of the complainant's honesty. In fact, even a passionate advocate will usually be quick to accept the need for checking one account against another. He is confident that the facts are in line with his contentions.

2. *Other Angles.*—The complainant's story usually involves at least one other person, even if only by implication. Thus there is always another inside view of the same situation, probably equally biased and highly colored. Indeed, it may be that a second party looks upon himself not as the defendant but rather as the chief complainant. And very likely his

story is as compelling as the first. Yet the facts in the case are so differently interpreted and aligned that they march to quite another conclusion. An inexperienced listener may be completely bewildered by the apparent incompatibility of two such accounts and may easily conclude that it is impossible to separate fact from fiction. If he has allowed his feelings to be swayed, first by one party and then by the other, he will probably be disturbed to find that he is equally convinced by both in turn and unable to decide which is right.

3. *Integrating the Partial Stories.*—The trained personnel administrator avoids both kinds of difficulty by not accepting any statement as factual until he has had an opportunity to verify it and by keeping his feelings under careful control. His major contribution is to impersonalize the situation. Throughout the listening stage, he sifts and weighs the material presented. He prunes the various stories of irrelevant details that obscure essential outlines. He looks for areas of logical agreement and relevant differences. For example, although two contending parties may disagree as to certain facts or as to their interpretation, they can usually agree about what needs to be discussed. The union contends that worker A, like worker B, is able to do the work required. Management agrees that worker A meets minimum requirements but contends that worker B is more efficient. Basically, talk centers on *minimum requirements*, although management stresses the concept of qualitative difference. According to contractual agreements or informal understandings, this factor may or may not be relevant to the situation. These data the personnel administrator fits into his understanding of the total situation as gained through his knowledge of the work environment, the company organization, contractual agreements, customary procedures, and key figures.

CLEARING UP MISUNDERSTANDINGS

Situational thinking is often useful in clearing up misunderstandings. It helps us to be alternately insiders (with our feelings) and outsiders (with our judgment). In this way, we may be able both to appreciate subjective values and also acceptably to present the objective truths and principles that form the basis for action in accordance with policy requirements. A case in which these techniques were successfully used may briefly be described in order to illustrate how the method works.

THE STORY OF GIUSEPPE LICCARDI

In a company that had rapidly expanded from two men in a basement laboratory to a thousand employees in a modern plant, deep dissatisfaction was felt by Giuseppe Liccardi, who had originally been the only employee.

By using the person-centered approach, the following "facts" were elicited from Giuseppe by the personnel administrator. During the grueling days and nights of initial research, the inventor of a revolutionary manu-facturing process had exuberantly assured his coworker Giuseppe (a tem-peramental individual) that "when this business grows up, you'll rise with it." Giuseppe, who was generously contributing time and energy, even working without pay when money was short, took this to mean that he would always maintain his close working relations with the chief and, moving upward with him, would eventually become vice-president of a large company. His stereotype of such a position was a picture of himself smoking fragrant Havanas with his feet on a splendid desk. While loyal subordinates carried on the work, he would thus be repaid for all his initial struggles and hardships.

When subsequently he got no farther than being a section head who had little or no contact with the president, he felt aggrieved at such a "breach of faith." At first, he sentimentalized the situation: "In his heart, the chief feels the same as ever toward me." (This impression was deepened on such occasions as annual banquets and employee picnics, when the successful inventor-president would reminisce about the early struggles and speak in glowing terms of his first employee-associate.) "It's too bad he's so busy with all these big shots from New York and Washington. He's lost touch with the real life of the business. Of course, the board of directors and the bankers put pressure on him to get key positions for their friends. If he could only shake off these outside influences and come back to the shop, he would surely remember his real friends. Then everything would work out all right."

But, as year after year went by, without bringing to Giuseppe any further promotion, he felt increasingly bitter. He made no secret of his dissatisfaction and became a demoralizing influence among employees.

His never-ending complaints led the president to develop a grievance of his own. This the personnel administrator pieced together, as follows: As a reward for his early zeal, Giuseppe had been made a section head, although his abilities were not quite commensurate with this job. Yet, here he was "squawking his head off because he wasn't a vice-president. There's gratitude for you."

After the personnel administrator had a clear picture of both sides of the story, he knew how to start showing each person's side to the other. When the president had listened to a rational account of Giuseppe's griev-ance, he was able to appreciate his employee's feelings. After that, he no longer regarded Giuseppe merely as an ungrateful troublemaker and became interested in helping him to see the developing situation in its proper perspective. Giuseppe likewise felt differently after he understood that the president was obligated to act not only as his friend but primarily as chief executive of a growing business.

CLARIFYING ISSUES BY POLICY THINKING

Useful as the person-centered approach proved to be, this pair of misunderstandings could never have been cleared up without policy thinking. The issue was clarified by the personnel administrator, who, thinking along policy lines, saw the situation as a typical transition problem with a special need for communication.

In an expanding business, the owner-manager inevitably finds it increasingly difficult to keep in touch with the members of his original force whose abilities are not commensurate with his. They get left behind, and executive positions are given to qualified newcomers. Unless appropriate explanations are made about the new relationships in the developing situation, disappointed employees have a justifiable cause for dissatisfaction. Often, however, the necessary explanations are indefinitely deferred because the subject seems too delicate to talk about.

Of the two policies called for by such a situation—on organization and on communication—only the former had been applied. The president was certainly justified in not promoting to vice-president a man unqualified for this executive position. But he was ill-advised in not communicating his decision and the reasons for it before Giuseppe's natural disappointment had developed into a full-fledged grievance. Giuseppe had the right of every employee to know where and how he stood with higher management and what were his chances of promotion.

The study of Giuseppe's "personal" problem high-lighted the need for a more adequate communication policy, and the person-centered approach was essential to gain understanding of his situation. But fresh insight into policy implications would not have been achieved if Giuseppe's case had been studied only by the person-centered approach and treated solely as an individual complaint. And, if Giuseppe's problem had been discussed with him only as a personal issue, he would not have been helped to see his situation in terms of policy requirements. But, when Giuseppe was able to see the whole picture, he could more easily concentrate on his real opportunity to make the most of his abilities.

WHAT IS THE ISSUE?[1]

In probing into any kind of disagreement or difference of opinion, we need to center attention on significant differences among the various

---

[1] Of course, it often happens that there are many issues; but even so, they should be formulated one at a time.

pictures that are brought to light. There may be disagreement as to what the facts were. Or there may be differences of opinion as to what the parties want to have happen. The personnel administrator cannot decide how to go about his investigation until he knows whether his technique is to be one of fact finding or whether he must attempt the more delicate task of integrating different objectives on the ground of mutual interests and policy aims.

Sometimes, as in arbitration, the case is presented to the analyst with an issue already formulated by the parties to the dispute. But even here the issue must be carefully inspected to determine whether, as formulated, it represents merely legalistic verbiage or whether it reaches down to the level of actual differences. A too narrowly defined issue will tie the arbitrator's hands and prevent his being of much service in the situation. Likewise, in the less formal approach of everyday personnel work or research, an ineptly phrased issue may blur or distort relevant facts or throw the investigator off the track.

Investigation

When the issue has been carefully formulated, the next step is a thorough investigation. If the issue concerns past events, the investigator works toward a solution by making a finding of fact on the basis of available evidence. This is not always so simple as it would seem, since it may involve interpretation of behavior. For instance, in a case involving maintenance of membership, is Mr. Peterson still a union member, or did he resign as he claims? The decision hinges on the significance of Mr. Peterson's oral statement to the union treasurer that he was "fed up with the union" and no longer wanted to belong. He followed up this assertion by failing to pay dues or attend meetings and maintained that his statement and subsequent inaction constituted his resignation. Investigation disclosed, however, that, according to union bylaws, formal application for membership and notice of resignation had to be submitted in writing to the secretary, whose duty it was to keep the membership file up to date. Mr. Peterson was familiar with these requirements and had at one time notified the secretary by mail of the fact that he had moved to another street. His outburst to the treasurer, made as it was in a barroom, had been discounted as a sign of bad temper. He had been classified as a delinquent dues payer but was still kept on the membership list.

In any fact-finding investigation, the personnel administrator must see that all relevant facts and understandings are brought to light. If the situation is fairly simple, the findings may be such that it is possible to make a prompt decision as to what the facts are and in what direction they point.

Frequently, however, in the course of the investigation, new data are brought to light that call for a reformulation of the issue. It may be found that the point of difference as originally stated refers only to a surface phenomenon and that the real issue lies deeper. Thus what began as an inquiry into facts may be continued as a search for common understandings and mutually acceptable principles.

For example, in a management-labor dispute that was brought to arbitration, the following issue was formulated by the parties: [1] "Was Bill Thompson discharged in good faith by the company on June 6, 1945?"

Management asserted that Thompson had been discharged because he had disobeyed an order. The collective-bargaining contract expressly stated that "Employees may be discharged for cause at any time provided such discharge is made in good faith." Management maintained that the phrase "in good faith" meant "without pretense and for the cause alleged" and insisted that the arbitration be confined to an interpretation of this narrow issue.

The union contended that the order had been unreasonable and that, under the circumstances, Thompson had acted within his rights in disobeying.

Even this superficial introduction suggested that the key question was primarily not a matter of fact but rather one of understandings and policies. The use of a phrase such as "in good faith," although it is somewhat of a stereotype in union circles, suggests distrust of management by the union at the time when the contract was drawn. There was evidence that this feeling still existed. The union accused management of deliberately provoking the incident that culminated in Thompson's discharge and thus of acting in bad faith. The facts behind this accusation gradually emerged.

For one thing, Bill Thompson was a long-service employee (22 years and 10 months), an efficient worker whose services the company was admittedly reluctant to lose. Why, then, should management suddenly resort to such extreme disciplinary action without making an attempt to reason with him? It became clear that Thompson was the victim in a clash of wills. There had been disagreement between management and the union as to job classifications (especially longshore work) and rates of pay.

The first test question became, "Should Thompson, who is classified and paid as an ironworker in the mechanical department, be paid at the higher rate of a longshoreman when doing longshore work?" Management

[1] The company was a large processing enterprise that did its own stevedoring, unloading bulk cargoes of raw material. The union was an industrial unit that represented all the hourly rated workers of the company.

would not agree to do this. The union then insisted that Thompson should not be permitted to undercut the longshore rate by performing this type of work. Management acceded to this demand, and an "understanding" was reached that Thompson be relieved of *all longshore work*.

Unfortunately, no definition of longshore work was offered by either party, and each side had a different understanding on this key point. Thompson was told by a member of the union committee that he was "all done with the job *on the ship and on the dock*." Management's understanding at this time was that Thompson should be relieved only of work *on the ship*. This difference in understandings inevitably led to further difficulty between management and the union, with Thompson still taking the brunt of it. For instance, when Thompson had been ordered to transport ship's tackle from the dock to the blacksmith shop, he did so under protest, and he was warned by the union to refrain from engaging further in longshore work. He was reminded of their interpretation of management's agreement.

At a subsequent meeting between management and the union (held 1 hour before Thompson's discharge), management clarified its position, bringing it into line with the generally accepted definition of longshore work.[1] The union accepted this clarification, which would involve a broadening of Thompson's area of activity. But, before they had an opportunity to inform him of their new understanding with management, he had been given a test order and discharged.

Evaluation of all the testimony indicated that management had not acted in good faith, since Thompson's supervisor had discharged him without bringing him up to date in regard to his precise duties. Thompson was living up to his understanding of the agreement between management and union officials. When management and union instructions came into conflict, he naturally preferred to avoid getting into further trouble with his own organization.

Since this was a case for arbitration, the analyst's official responsibilities ended with the award and precluded further attempts to reach a settlement of more basic issues. If the arbitrator had been acting as a personnel administrator, he would have been duty-bound to continue his explorations until he was satisfied either that he understood all the issues at stake or that he could not, in the time allowed, get any further. In this case, for instance, he would have continued the phase of investigation until he clearly saw to

---

[1] The recognized categories of longshore workers are "hold" men, "deck" men, and "dock" men, the latter working only *on the apron* of the pier, loading and unloading the ship. This division of the dock meant that management was entitled to order a mechanical worker to transport materials to and from the pier, on the shore side of the apron.

what extent, and in which of the following areas, errors had been made by both parties to the dispute:

1. In the area of job description, both management and the union started with mistaken conceptions as to what properly constitutes longshore work. Management took steps to correct its error before the union did.

2. In the area of procedure, both sides were lacking in skill, especially in conference method.

3. In the area of management-union cooperation, both parties were at fault. Everyone is bound to lose when a test case is fought out over the person of an employee instead of being fully clarified in conference.

As the case analyst concludes the phase of investigation, he marshals his evidence differently according to whether he will only be required to make a report of his findings or whether he is also expected to outline a program for action.

PLANNING THE SOLUTION

If he is asked to determine what needs to be done, the personnel administrator looks primarily to the future. He seeks a solution that is compatible with constructive relationships and policies. He never aligns himself with either party against the other in a destructive attempt to settle old scores. He is interested in the past only insofar as it helps him to understand the present and to build for the future. In planning a program to resolve current disputes, he tries to evolve one that will forward the basic interests of both parties and actively promote better understanding. This does not mean that he looks for a compromise in which there is an inevitable loss to both sides. Instead, he attempts to find a way out of the current dispute by widening the existing areas of agreement and preserving what is essential to each.

With this forward-looking objective in mind, the personnel administrator asks not only "What should be done?" and "Who should do it?" but also "When should it be done?"

TIMING FOR ACTION

In recommending action, the personnel administrator needs to think about timing. The stage and pace of events limit what can usefully be said and done. Experienced executives act on this insight, although they cannot always put into words the reasons for their intuitive behavior. A simple solution to a problem that might have been acceptable at the beginning of a misunderstanding is unacceptable after a long delay or when differences of opinion have hardened into opposing convictions. An explanation given in time may avert dissatisfaction and win acceptance. If offered belatedly, when misunderstandings have already developed, the explanation may become an additional source of irritation.

In a double sense, we need to take our cue from a developing human situation. Both what needs to be done and when it can best be set in motion are indicated by the pace of contemporary events and the tempo of the people who need our help. Is the situation rapidly moving toward a crisis that calls for immediate interference, or is there time for the slow forces of education to take effect? Is this person quick to take a hint, or does his mind react slowly in assimilating new facts? Can he accelerate his pace to cover more ground, or can he be successful only in a job whose area is more limited than that over which his present duties extend? Only when we can answer such questions as these can we feel some confidence that the new element introduced by our solution will gear in with other moving parts and not have the effect of a monkeywrench thrown into the works.

When the personnel administrator has made preliminary decisions on such points, he is ready to take the last step before making a recommendation to management.

Pretesting the Solution

In most situations, there are a number of possible solutions. Two vital questions to ask about each are: How will the proposed solution work out in this situation? Will it be likely to meet more of the basic needs than another? A sound solution is one that conforms to generally valid principles but is tailored to fit the specific situation. No solution should be selected merely because it has worked successfully before or because it seems expedient, though impolitic, at the moment. It should be designed to meet long-run as well as short-run requirements. It should not only solve current issues but also be consistent with the system of policies applied in the organization as a whole and well suited to the personnel who are to put it into effect. If the only sound solution is inconsistent with established policies and procedures, the personnel adminstrator should recommend that policies and procedures be revised to conform to the proposed remedy.

When the tentative solution has been examined in the light of its probable consequences and of its consistency with governing principles of the organization, it can be presented to management as a recommendation. If top management approves the recommendation, there is still another step to be taken before a final decision is made. The tentative solution should be discussed with union leaders and with key workers whenever it is likely to involve changes that are important to workers. The significance of such discussions is threefold. Management has an opportunity to show that it values the opinion of workers and to give them notice of changes to come. And workers have a chance to participate in policy thinking. This is a valuable exercise in itself and also increases the likelihood of acceptance at the work level of underlying principles. In these discussions, the personnel administrator can often be of considerable service as an interpreter. His active participation normally stops here. But, if he loses track of the case at this point, his own technique as a student of human relations is faulty.

FOLLOW-UP AND EVALUATION

Whenever possible, the personnel administrator follows the case in its subsequent developments in order to test his judgment and to deepen his insight. Only when he compares the actual results with what he judged to be the probable consequences and when he observes how often the solution of one problem contributes to the formation of another does he take full advantage of the continuing opportunity for learning that is offered by case study. When he has followed up immediate developments and evaluated his own technique throughout the various stages, the case has become an integral part of his clinical experience.

Ideally, the personnel administrator should carefully write up each case while the facts are fresh and while he can still fill in any gaps in his own observation. Often it is not until he attempts to make an orderly account of all relevant facts that the case analyst sees that there are any gaps in his observation. This is one value to be gained from writing up a case. Second, the process of writing helps us to take a more impersonal view of what has been said and done. This helps us to evaluate our own contribution. Moreover, when case data have been recorded, they are permanently available for future reference, and the accumulated body of cases is a fertile source of living knowledge. If this cumulative record is well organized, it can readily be referred to when deeper insight or improved techniques suggest new answers to old questions.

SUMMARY

In getting down to cases, the personnel administrator begins by clarifying his understanding of separate views, or parts of the whole picture. By integrating the various parts, he then achieves an inclusive view of the issue. Finally, in planning and pretesting a solution, he includes in his picture of the situation the larger needs and policies of the company as a whole. Thus his scale of view comprehends the subsituation of individuals, the inclusive company situation, and the principles that usefully serve as a means for integrating differences. The time element is taken into account during the stages of preliminary survey and of subsequent investigation, as well as in planning how and when to introduce a new element, in the form of a proposed solution.

During almost every phase, interviewing plays a part. By this means, the personnel administrator tries to understand what others think and feel, as well as to learn the relevant technical facts and the various features of the time element as these affect the situation. By this same technique, he communicates or interprets policies that have a bearing on personnel problems. Interviewing is such a valuable technique for acquiring and spreading understanding, as well as for building satisfying personnel relationships, that we have devoted to it the entire next chapter. Interviewing is also important in diagnosing organizational stability, as we shall see in the section following the next chapter.

Chapter 6

Interviewing

When I am confronted with a complex situation involving the interactions of people, what people say is necessarily an important part of the data from which I have to make a diagnosis. Therefore, my first object is to get people to talk freely and frankly about matters which are important to them. . . . In the interview I use a number of simple rules or ideas. I listen. I do not interrupt. I refrain from making moral judgments about the opinions expressed. I do not express my own opinions, beliefs, or sentiments. I avoid argument at all costs. I do this by seeing to it that the speaker's sentiments do not react on my own.

F. J. ROETHLISBERGER[1]

In personnel administration, there are many different types of interview, such as employment, induction, follow-up, and exit. As part of standardized employment procedure, these kinds of interview will be discussed briefly in Chaps. 10 and 12. In the first three, the interviewer roughly knows before he begins what facts will form the subject of the talk. Thus, in a brief interview, largely directed by himself, he can rely on getting the necessary information chiefly from answers to direct questions.

But there is another kind of interview in which the objective is to find out what employees think and feel. The exit interview often falls in this category and sometimes the follow-up interview also. More important, however, are interviews in problem situations that confront supervisors and personnel administrators. In such situations, the interviewer makes a mistake if he conducts a formal interview or attempts to control the subject. He can best find out what he needs to know by letting the interviewee say whatever he wants to say.

Both directed and undirected interviews have in common the fact that they are an experiment in human relations, during the course of which

[1] *Management and Morale*, Harvard University Press, Cambridge, Mass., 1942, pp. 92–93.

greater understanding is sought between two people. Because this aspect of interviewing is commonly overlooked, we make it the central theme of our chapter.

Interviewing is more than a technique. It is an art in which subsidiary skills are used with varying success by persons with different degrees of natural aptitude. Every interview ought to be a satisfying experience. Whatever its specific objective, the general purpose is always to promote mutual understanding and confidence. If this inclusive purpose is kept in

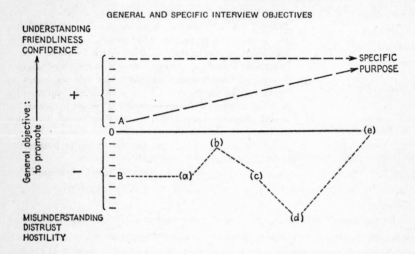

mind, the interview can usually be made a satisfying, or at least an acceptable experience, and the general rules for successful interviewing follow naturally.

THE INTERVIEW AS A DEVELOPING SITUATION

Ideally, understanding and confidence should grow during every interview, however little it succeeds in achieving the specific purpose for which it was held. No interview need be a total failure in regard to its general objective. The interviewer can always get some kind of insight, whether or not it is just what he was hoping for. And the interviewee should always have the benefit of being recognized as a person sufficiently interesting to be worth listening to. He, too, can get new light if he wants it, both on himself and on his situation, as well as about management's technical situation and general purposes.

The range of opportunity offered in the course of an interview may be diagramed as shown above.

Lines A and B indicate states of mind of two different workers during interviewing and represent degrees of success achieved during the interview in both general objective and specific purpose.

Line A starts at the neutral plane where strangers meet and progresses smoothly upward and forward to reach both aims. This is practically an ideal interview, a rare event.

Line B represents an actual interview with a person who was hostile to the interviewer at the start. After preliminaries, the interview progressed toward greater understanding b but then lapsed into increased misunderstanding and distrust—c and d—probably because of something the interviewer said. The interview might have ended on this negative note, but by luck or good technique the interviewer in this case was able to reach the neutral plane e.

An Example of a Poor Interview

The following interview was held by a personnel consultant who was employed to help build a work team and raise morale in the frosting department of a small bakery that lacked a personnel department. By individual interviewing, he was preparing the way for a group conference in which, through participation to remedy unsatisfactory conditions, the girls in the frosting department could learn more about how to think and act as a team.

Mary Ryan was an aggressive worker who, before the interview, had branded the consultant, Mr. Anderson, as "just another of those five-day experts hired by the company to make us all work harder." Starting with this handicap, Mr. Anderson proceeded to make matters worse during the interview by breaking most of the rules for sound procedure.

The interview was held in a little room above the frosting department. Advance notice to Mary Ryan had been given without explanation by the forelady, whom she heartily disliked.

1   Mary (*somewhat defiantly*): Well, here I am. They told me you wanted to talk with me.

Mr. A.: Thank you for coming, Miss Ryan. Won't you sit down? I should like to talk to you if you can give me a few moments. My name is

5   Anderson. I'm interested in trying to find out how people get along in a small plant like this; whether they like the work and feel they are treated right. Of course, you don't have to talk to me if you'd rather not.

Mary: Oh, I'm not afraid. I just don't see any point in it.

10   Mr. A.: Don't you believe in people getting together and talking things over?

MARY: Sure. Only we don't know you. You come in from the outside and we don't know what you're really after. You say you aren't working for Morgan Brothers Bakery as a . . . a . . . what d'you call it! . . . effi-
15 ciency expert, but how do we know?

MR. A.: I'm glad you're frank about it. You're not afraid to talk, but you're suspicious of me. Is that it?

MARY: Yes.

MR. A.: Well, I don't blame you for that. After all, you don't know me.
20 But that's one reason for my wanting to talk to you. I want to explain who I am, why I'm here, and what I'm trying to do. I had hoped to convince you that I'm here to help you girls, but if you won't take my word for it, of course I can't make you.

MARY: Why should we believe you? We never met you before. The fore-
25 lady said you're all right. But we don't know you. Besides I can't understand what you want to do.

MR. A.: That's why I asked you to come and talk to me. I thought this would be a good chance to explain. I should be glad to tell you any-thing you would like to know.

30 MARY: Well, just what are you trying to do here?

(a) MR. A.: I should like to talk to you girls and find out what you do, how you like your work, and whether you have any suggestions as to how your department could be improved. I'm interested in anything you have to say about your job.

35 MARY: Oh, I see. . . . Well, we're all very happy. At least I am.

MR. A.: I'm glad to hear that. What do you do?

MARY: I'm a froster.

MR. A.: Do you work at that all the time?

MARY: No, as a matter of fact that's one thing that isn't quite right.
40 You see, it takes a long time for a froster to learn her job. For that reason she should get some consideration. But you don't find that here. It doesn't make any difference whether you're just a shipper or a fros-ter or only a beginner; they treat you all alike. I think beginners should do some of the dirty jobs. But if the forelady isn't in the right
45 mood, she'll set the green girls to work frosting cakes and make us pick up and clean, or work on stales.

MR. A.: What does "work on stales" mean?

MARY: Oh, stales are the returns from the shops. Most of it is thrown away or sent to the pigs or something. But if the cakes are still in good con-
50 dition, they're shipped to the stales stores, where they are sold very cheap.

MR. A.: I see.

MARY: Anyway, I don't think good frosters should be called on to do that kind of work.

55 MR. A.: How many good frosters are there?

MARY: Really good frosters?

Mr. A.: Yes, girls who are expert on the job.

Mary: Well, there are two girls who are really good.

(b) Mr. A.: That's interesting. I have a good idea who they are.

60 Mary: Who?

Mr. A.: The Kearney sisters, isn't that so?

Mary: Yes, all the girls know those two are the best frosters.

Mr. A.: How about the others?

Mary: Oh, there are three or four who are not so bad. But I suppose
65 there's not much difference, really. Some of the shippers can slap it on
pretty good.

Mr. A.: Would it be better if some of the good frosters had nothing to do
but that?

Mary: Yes, it would. But I'm satisfied anyway. I've no complaints to
70 make.

Mr. A.: I'm not looking for complaints. All I'm interested in is to find out
how things could be arranged differently so as to make the work more
satisfactory. Wouldn't it be foolish if we could improve working conditions and didn't do it?

75 Mary: Maybe. But even if I'm not entirely happy, I'm satisfied.

Mr. A.: I'm sorry to hear that you're not entirely happy. Has it to do with
things at the plant?

Mary: Oh, no. Not at all. Things are all right here.

(c) Mr. A.: Has it to do with things outside?

80 Mary: Maybe it has. Maybe it hasn't. But I wouldn't tell you. Why do
you want to know, anyway? I don't see what it has to do with you.

Mr. A.: Oh, I know it isn't any of my business, and I don't want to butt
into your private affairs. I just thought it might help you to talk about
it.

85 Mary: No there's nothing you can do.

Mr. A.: I'm sorry.

Mary: Is there any more you want to know? I think Mildred will start
looking for me.

Mr. A.: Don't worry. She knows you're talking to me and has agreed to
90 let you stay away from work and talk to me as long as you like.

Mary: Well, I think I ought to get back to work.

(d) Mr. A.: Then don't let me detain you. Thank you for coming and giving
me as much help as you did.

Mary: I don't see where I've helped you any.

95 Mr. A.: You've helped a lot, and I'm much obliged.

(e) Mary (turning at the door): Well, maybe you're all right. But do you know
what? I think you would do better to have a meeting. Why don't you
tell the girls we can have a meeting? Then they won't be so afraid to
talk.

100 Mr. A.: Thanks for the tip. I think that's a good idea, and I'll see whether
a meeting can be arranged.

MARY: O.K.! Well, 'by now.

103   MR. A.: Good-by.

ANALYSIS OF THIS INTERVIEW

As we briefy analyze this interview, it is evident that Anderson had two strikes against him before he started and practically put himself out by his unfortunate beginning and by his persistent attempt to elicit from Mary facts that she was unwilling to discuss. At *a* (lines 31 to 34), when he switched to a line of questioning about the work situation, Mary began to open up and was giving him both valuable information and some degree of confidence until he put her off by his remark at *b* (line 59).

From then on, Mary ceased to cooperate. If he had been more discerning and experienced in interviewing, Mr. Anderson would have realized at this point that he must postpone pursuit of his specific purpose until he had reestablished a satisfactory relationship. Once the barometer indicating an interviewee's confidence has dropped below the "fair-weather" level, the more an interviewer pursues his current course, the worse the situation becomes. An aggressive worker becomes antagonistic; a timid employee gets more nervous.

In this interview with Mary Ryan, Mr. Anderson seems to have been unaware of what was happening. At *c* (line 79), for instance, he proceeded to make matters worse by trying to get Mary to discuss her private affairs. At *d* (lines 92 to 93), he finally cut his losses and admitted his failure. But his unwavering good nature and courtesy throughout the interview seem to have appealed to Mary, who at *e* (line 96) suddenly repaid him with the suggestion that he was hoping she would make. His success may, of course, be attributed merely to luck, an element that, for better or worse, cannot entirely be eliminated even by the most careful planning.

Sometimes luck may be against an interviewer and prevent his making any progress. But, when circumstances are sufficiently favorable to allow him to do his best, how does he go about it?

PREPARING FOR THE INTERVIEW

Interviewing procedures and techniques vary to some extent according to the special type of interview to be held. But, except for those specifically directed at collecting objective facts (such as the employment interview), most interviews held by the personnel administrator attempt to increase understanding of some difficulty experienced or created by the worker. In any such interview, the following steps need to be taken:

1. *Getting Background Information.*—All pertinent information that can be gathered beforehand should be assembled and, if necessary, written. This preparation saves time and mental effort during the coming talk and enables the interviewer to sketch in advance at least a general picture of the interviewee and his difficulty. The details can be filled in later.

2. *Preparing a Schedule or Plan for the Interview.*—The specific character of the outline depends on whether the interview is to be formal or informal and will require chiefly listening or a good deal of directed questioning from the interviewer. These details depend on whether the information to be gathered is needed (1) for action by someone else at a later time, as for policy action by a management committee,[1] or (2) for adjustment by the interviewee in a current difficulty.

Sometimes it is helpful to have a detailed schedule of questions prepared for reference just before the interview,[2] or perhaps all that is needed is an informal plan that can be developed in a few minutes. In either case, the plan envisages what needs to be learned and how the information may best be sought from this specific person in view of what is already known about him. One advantage of making a plan in advance is that the interviewer then has time to think of all the important items on which he lacks information. A second advantage is that, having jotted down the key points, he is less likely to forget to take them up if the interview is interrupted before the whole situation has been explored. Third, having done as much thinking as possible in advance, the interviewer is free to concentrate more attention on listening and observing during the interview itself.

3. *Notifying the Interviewee.*—The person who is to be interviewed should be given advance notice in such a way as to reassure rather than alarm him. In preparing *himself* for the coming talk, an interviewer may easily forget that, from the time when the other person knows there is to be an interview, he is doing something, too. He may be becoming frightened or antagonistic or preparing himself to be noncommittal, fearing that whatever he says will be used against him. Some workers have had such unfortunate experiences with management or are so preoccupied with feelings of guilt or resentment that they inevitably come to an interview in an uncooperative frame of mind. But, too often, unintelligent or discourteous notification brings about this result unnecessarily.

[1] *Cf.* PIGORS, PAUL, and ALFRED D. SHEFFIELD, Interviewing the Employee for Decision-making on Policy (Replacement Transfers of Time-study Men), *Case Studies in Industrial Relations*, Addison-Wesley Press, Inc., Cambridge, Mass., 1944.

[2] See The Case of the Bakers' Helpers, pp. 332–340.

The Setting for the Interview

Success in conducting an interview depends in part on the proper setting. Four requirements may be listed:

1. *Privacy and Comfort.*—Privacy and comfort are generally recognized as aids to free talk. When practicable, interviews are best held in a private room. But privacy and comfort are primarily states of mind. A reasonable degree of privacy can often be attained in a corner of the lunchroom, at a deserted workbench, or in any other place where people are not within earshot. Such semiprivacy may be enough to suit the purpose of the interview, unless it is likely to be of a highly emotional or delicate nature.

2. *Establishing and Maintaining Confidential Relations.*—Even more important than spatial privacy is the feeling of security that comes to a worker when he trusts the interviewer not to abuse his confidence by repeating what has been said in private. Workers who have experienced or, in some cases, even heard about an abuse of confidence are naturally reluctant to talk. Even if this reluctance is not expressed in words, it often underlies the grudging and monosyllabic response that balks an inexperienced interviewer.

If the worker is making a complaint, he naturally wonders how the interviewer's avowed purpose can be *both* to keep confidential what is said in private and to use it as evidence to get action. The apparent incompatibility of these aims can easily be explained. In most cases, the interviewee is only one of many who are experiencing the same or similar difficulties. In reporting these, the interviewer omits names and other identifying features. But when the complaint, *e.g.*, against a fellow worker or supervisor, is purely individual and not part of a situation that involves others, the only way to protect confidence is to leave the decision in the hands of the person being interviewed. He may decide that, in view of the risk, he wants no direct action on his complaint and prefers some indirect remedy such as a transfer out of the group. If, on the other hand, he insists that an accusation be made, he must stand ready to serve as chief witness, however disagreeable this may prove. The interviewer can put the choice clearly before the worker, who thus has an opportunity to make up his mind, knowing that his remarks will go no further until he gives the word.

3. *An Atmosphere of Leisure.*—Another aid to free talk is a feeling of leisure. People cannot be expected to embark on a difficult subject if they feel that they are being hurried through a question and answer period that is expected to take only a few minutes. Under ideal conditions, a successful interview can sometimes be conducted in 10 or 15 minutes. But, even then,

a skillful interviewer will manage to convey the impression that he has plenty of time. Leisure, too, is a state of mind rather than a matter of minutes. When the subject on hand is complex or difficult, an interview may need to be prolonged for 1 or 2 hours, or even continued in another session. However long it takes, the interviewer defeats his central purpose if he shows impatience or in any way indicates that he would rather be doing something else.

For the same reason, interruptions from outside are unfortunate. When an interviewee has thrown caution to the winds and is well launched on a difficult subject, even a telephone call for the interviewer may spoil everything. Given time to think, the worker's impulse to talk may easily be submerged by a return of caution. But, even if the interruption has no such obvious effect, it is undesirable because it emphasizes the fact, only too obvious in daily work life, that the ordinary employee is considered too unimportant to be put first. Ideally, during the interview, he is and should be made to feel as important as that.

4. *The Informal Opening.*—Before actually "getting down to brass tacks," courtesy suggests a brief prelude of general conversation to put the worker at his ease. This is more a part of the setting, contributing to a congenial atmosphere, than it is a technique of interviewing. As a purely social gesture, it comes naturally to anyone who has the knack of handling people and needs no special discussion here.

Conducting the Interview

The following interview techniques are valuable in different degrees according to specific circumstances:

1. *Listening with Intelligence and Sympathy.*—Listening can be valuable to both parties. Whatever other benefit a disturbed worker derives from the interview, he cannot fail to experience a therapeutic value if he is allowed to get his problem "off his chest" to a sympathetic and intelligent listener.[1] The interviewer's attentive silence may be his best contribution. Because the interviewee is offered a hearing, he often makes a special effort to formulate his thoughts. As these are crystallized in words, they may lead to new insight for him either as to his own weaknesses or as to what other

[1] This is the principal reason for instituting a counseling program. *Cf.* ROETHLISBERGER, F. J. and W. J. DICKSON, *Management and the Worker*, Harvard University Press, Cambridge, Mass., 1939, Chapter XXVI, especially pp. 593–604; HIMLER, LEONARD E., The Counseling Interview, *Addresses on Industrial Relations*, pp. 63–74, Bureau of Industrial Relations, University of Michigan, Ann Arbor, 1945, and HOSLETT, SCHUYLER D., "Listening to the Troubled or Dissatisfied Employee," *Personnel*, Vol. 22, pp. 52–57, July, 1945.

people have actually done. Usually a person can answer his own questions better than anyone else, once he has got them clearly stated.[1]

The benefits that accrue to an attentive listener would seem too obvious to mention if it were not that many interviews fail because listening is not carried far enough. Interviewers sometimes become confused as to what they should be listening for. In the interview with Mary Ryan, for instance, Mr. Anderson thought that he did not need to listen when Mary was going to tell him about the skilled frosters. Certainly he did not need to be told who they were. But, by breaking into her account and undertaking to give her the information that she was about to offer him, he committed two tactical errors. When he repeated something he had learned in previous interviews, he may have reminded Mary about the program that she had been trying to disrupt. He also reversed the relationship in which she was acting as his teacher. Her next remarks say in effect, "If you think you're so smart, why come to me for information?"

The unfortunate result in that situation points up the fact that an interviewer needs to listen both because he thus builds the speaker's confidence and because he never knows when a seemingly trivial bit of information may either prove important in itself or lead to something significant that he does not know anything about. Because he does not fully understand the situation, he should be prepared to listen to a number of things that seem off the point. At least they give him a line as to what is important to the speaker.

As a means of helping people to talk, listening may be supplemented by direct questioning. Both techniques are useful when people need help to say (1) what they cannot say unaided (presumably for lack of skill with words) or (2) what they would like to say if they dared.

2. *Defining the Problem.*—Ideally, the interviewee defines the problem for himself with the aid of sympathetic listening and brief directed questioning. When interviewing a worker about some difficulty that he is experiencing, an essential step is to get the problem clearly stated. Questioning is helpful when vague phrases or unsupported statements leave

---

[1] What happens is well described by Dr. Richard C. Cabot, who was by nature a social worker and who for many years used listening both as a diagnostic device and as an effective remedy for troubled persons. "It has been our experience again and again to listen while a patient described his problems, to be stumped by them and appalled at our own failure, and prudently to keep silence and make no answer till that very silence drew the patient on to say more than he started to say. Soon he begins answering himself better than we could have answered him." CABOT, RICHARD C., and RUSSELL L. DICKS, *The Art of Ministering to the Sick*, p. 193, The Macmillan Company, New York, 1936. The excellent chapter on Listening should be read in its entirety.

the interviewer unnecessarily in the dark. Suppose the accusation is, for instance, that "Tom is a stinker and I can't stand working with him any more." Before he can offer a helpful suggestion, the interviewer needs to know what Tom has said or done that "stinks." A considerable amount of listening and questioning may be necessary before this point becomes clear, since strong emotions and clarity of speech seldom go hand in hand.

When the interviewer feels that he "has got the worker's drift," he may terminate this stage of the interview with a summarizing question that asks, "Is this what you mean?" Such questions need to be carefully phrased, since, if they are shaped to indicate a moral judgment or to intrude a bit of advice, they may easily undo all the good that has been accomplished by listening and questioning.

3. *Keeping Alert and Flexible.*—As the interviewer feels his way around in the trouble situation by listening and questioning, he is presumably getting light on how to proceed. This attitude of watchful waiting, to move forward step by step with the interviewee toward better understanding, seems perhaps inconsistent with the statement that the interviewer should be conducting the interview according to a plan. This inconsistency, however, is only apparent. The plan gives something to start from and something to fall back on unless new evidence indicates that another approach might be more successful. But an alert observer may see in the course of an interview that the road undertaken is a dead end, whereas another path that had seemed too unimportant to follow or was not even visible till he got there is really the way to his objective. Alertness and flexibility enable an interviewer to take advantage of the lucky breaks and to counteract the ill effects of any misstep. In interviewing, no amount of advance planning can replace the capacity to think on one's feet.

4. *Using Imagination to Evoke Meaning.*—Even at its best, verbal communication is so clumsy that it cannot give us all we need for understanding. Imagination can fill in the gaps from what is implied but not said. By imagination, one can evoke obscure meanings, interpret significant statements and omissions, and fill out a background that is described only fragmentarily. In such ways, an alert interviewer can get at least part way inside the unique context that is the other person's private world. A competent interviewer also learns much from gestures, expressions, manner and inflection, pauses, and way of responding.

5. *Taking Notes.*—Many interviewers are afraid to use the obvious device of taking notes, believing that it necessarily bothers an interviewee. They might also be concerned because the time and attention given to writing limit what can be spent on observation. This second difficulty is

met by keeping notes in the form of a telegraphic memorandum of significant details and suggestive items. The major difficulty, that note taking may prevent the development of an informal relationship, can be met by good timing.

Notes should never be begun until after a satisfactory relationship has been established. At that point, note taking may produce a favorable effect. When a worker trusts an interviewer, he is likely to be pleased that his remarks are considered sufficiently important to be written down. Thus note taking can immediately and directly contribute to the interviewer's purpose of showing the worker that management is concerned to know how he thinks and feels about a given situation. Sometimes workers enter into the spirit of note taking and jog the interviewer's elbow, as it were, by some such remark as, "Now be sure to get this down. It's important." Whether or not this happens, however, the notes themselves are a significant part of the record by which to evaluate the interview experience.

6. *Concluding the Interview.*—According to the degree of insight attained by the interviewee, he may or may not be able to state his problem clearly by the end of the interview and to visualize a possible solution. If he cannot do this for himself, the interviewer may be able to help him either by a summarizing question or by a crystallizing statement. The interviewer may say, "As I see it, your problem boils down to this." He then briefly summarizes the worker's dilemma or the causes of his tension or the reason for the dissatisfaction that he is feeling or producing for others. In talking over such a problem, the interviewer should be careful, of course, that he does not let his desire to help urge him into (1) promising more than he can perform or should undertake for the company or (2) trying to decide what the worker wants to do.

As the interview ends, the worker often spontaneously evaluates the interview experience by some such remark as, "Well, thanks a lot. I certainly feel better for getting all this off my chest. I never thought the company was interested in the way we feel about things. I surely appreciate your giving me all this time." The interviewer also will want to express his appreciation that the worker has come to the interview and given valuable information. If the interview has been unsuccessful, this may seem an unnecessary or even hypocritical gesture. But it is not, and it may open up a new lead. In any case, it serves to show that the interviewer's good nature is still intact, and it is honest in that even an unsuccessful interview can be informative to the interviewer. He can at least learn from it what not to do again.

EVALUATING NOTES AND TECHNIQUES

When the interview itself is concluded, however, the interviewer's job is still unfinished. He needs to review his notes and consider what he has accomplished. This kind of evaluation requires time and thought, but it is essential if full advantage is to be taken of the interview experience. Each interview is an opportunity to get new ideas about human nature (in oneself and others), about company policies and practices, about current situations and problems, and about what is needed to make talk between two people a worth-while experience for them both. Unless such ideas are fully developed while they are still fresh in one's mind, preferably by writing out a summary of each interview and the situation thus explored, they are apt to disappear.

Writing up his notes so that they form an intelligible statement does for the interviewer something similar to what talking does for the interviewee. It helps to clarify ideas and thus to show what is there. To the personnel administrator, this has several kinds of value. For one thing, the completed interview notes form an important part of a case record. They are valuable for all kinds of special reference—*e.g.*, to review before another interview with the same person.

Furthermore, the record in itself, and even more the cumulative evidence of a number of interview records, reveals significant points about interview method. Everyone can improve his interview techniques if he is clear as to just where and why he is weak. The record provides clues. Failure in one case may be attributed to bad luck. Failure in many cases should be traced to flaws in technique.

Often, study of such interview material reveals that the interviewer has more food for thought than he realized at the time. As he looks over his notes, comparing them with facts gathered before and with any other information he can later get about the person, he may find that something jotted down almost at random, or merely because it seemed important to the interviewee, suddenly stands out in its full significance. Sometimes this growth in understanding does not come until long after the interview, perhaps when another case presents a similar situation for study. If even the meager facts were recorded at the time, evaluation can complete them whenever insight becomes adequate.

SUMMARY

Evaluation brings the process of interviewing full circle by measuring the result against the objective. Was the interview an experience during which both parties gained in mutual understanding and confidence? If not, why not? How can the interviewer do better next time? Did he fail in his specific purpose through inadequate preparation for the interview? Did he permit his own eagerness to get facts, or the interviewee's unco-operativeness, to interfere with the general objective? Was the setting in any way less favorable than he could have made it? In looking back, what evidence is there that the interviewee was bothered by anything that occurred during the course of talk? Were the interviewer's techniques of listening, of questioning, and of summarizing good enough for the purposes of this interview? If so, in what ways could they have been improved, in order to achieve success under more difficult conditions? Was he alert to take advantage of new leads?

If an interviewer checks his results by such questions, he cannot fail to see where he can progressively improve his interviewing skills. In this way, hindsight can lead to greater foresight, and both can contribute to insight.

As a means of achieving insight, interviewing is an essential device for diagnosing organizational stability, a subject that will be discussed in the three chapters comprising the next section.

C. DIAGNOSING ORGANIZATIONAL STABILITY

INTRODUCTION TO DIAGNOSING
ORGANIZATIONAL STABILITY

In making and selling a product or service for profit, management depends not only on effective utilization of technical knowledge but also on getting efficient individuals to work together as a team. This makes for organizational stability, without which any organization is at loose ends and eventually fails in achieving its objective.

A competent personnel administrator can aid line management to preserve and develop organizational stability by studying the outward signs that indicate the level of employee morale and team spirit. This he does by a method similar to that used by a doctor when he helps to prevent the development of a serious illness by detecting and evaluating slight symptoms.

In a small organization, the successful executive senses almost intuitively when morale is low. Output may have dropped, foremen report that tardiness and absenteeism are increasing, long-service workers are quitting, and accidents may be on the increase. This information reaches the front office quickly, without benefit of elaborate statistical analyses and investigations.

As organizations grow in size, however, the chief executive cannot rely upon sporadic information from the numerous line officials or on a "walk through the shop to see how the boys feel." Just as he calls for continuing data on inventories, goods in process, finished products shipped, etc., so the alert management official wants to be constantly informed about the stability and morale of his organization.

The personnel administrator has an important responsibility to interpret for top management and line officials the significance of the various indexes of organizational stability. Most operating officials closely watch the data on productive efficiency, and these are very important for the personnel administrator also. But other indexes of organizational stability that frequently do not receive enough attention from line management are

1. Tardiness and absence from work.
2. The nature and frequency of accidents.
3. Labor turnover.
4. Internal mobility as shown by transfers and promotions.
5. The prevalence and character of employee complaints and grievances.

In the following three chapters, we shall discuss the meaning of these data from the personnel point of view.

Chapter 7

Some Indexes of
Employee Morale

Our modern large corporations . . . need to introduce in
their organizations a skill in human relations comparable
to the skill which they introduce when they hire an engineer.
And as a very large part of this skill, there is required on
the part of the group charged with this responsibility a
"sense of the whole," a concept of the interrelatedness of
the phenomena with which they are trying to deal.

F. J. ROETHLISBERGER[1]

The personnel administrator's special contribution derives in part
from his study of conditions that are unobserved or unreported by line
officials. But often he can also be useful by applying the personnel point
of view to the same conditions that are studied by line management, from
its "purely practical" angle.

Whatever the field of observation, the personnel administrator's
method has certain typical characteristics. As a specialist in human relations, he examines statistics, for instance, not as bald factual records but
rather as clues to the circumstances or attitudes that determined them.
Thus he is concerned not so much with what statistics *directly show* as with
what *shows through* them. He asks himself, "Why are these things happening? What is behind them? Are they the long-run effects of some
activity that was formerly accepted as 'good enough'? Do they point to a
need for preventive action?"

When he finds that something is wrong, he does not indulge in moral-
istic judgments. His attitude is not "*who* is to blame" but rather "*what*
is to blame?" In searching for this kind of insight, he is more interested
in possible significance for the future and in present observable effects of
past failures and tensions than in the actual size of a current figure. And

[1] *Management and Morale*, Harvard University Press, Cambridge, Mass., 1942, p. 115.

he finds that he can often make more headway by analyzing figures for subgroups and for individuals than by merely examining over-all totals.

This point of view can usefully be applied to such statistics as those on productive efficiency. These may show not only how successful an organization is in business terms but also how well it is succeeding in terms of employee morale.

DATA ON PRODUCTIVE EFFICIENCY

Usually operating officials keep a close watch on such productive-efficiency data as the following:

1. Output per man-hour.
2. Actual hours compared with standard hours.
3. Piecework earnings or points.
4. Labor costs.
5. Overhead costs and other cost items.
6. Quality records.

But often these are not recognized as indexes of individual morale and team spirit. Sometimes even the personnel administrator misses the significant clues to be found here, because he thinks that such purely business statistics are not in line with his major interests. For this reason, he may neglect to study the data on productive efficiency. But such an attitude is ill-advised, because, in failing to show an interest in these figures, the personnel administrator is missing an opportunity to meet representatives of operating management on their own ground and to talk their language.

Furthermore, the implications of data on productive efficiency are of special interest to the personnel administrator, whether the figures are high or low. Management may be satisfied by a favorable showing and think no more about it. But the personnel administrator wants to know what human facts determined these figures. A high rate of productive efficiency is not necessarily indicative of satisfactory personnel relations, because considerable efficiency can be achieved for a short period by rigid authority. However, since authoritarianism does not enlist voluntary cooperation[1] or satisfy the highest type of employee, the personnel administrator should point out that efficiency obtained by such methods is unlikely to endure.

On the other hand, if productive efficiency is low, he should not jump to the conclusion that the trouble necessarily lies in the field of personnel

---

[1] A possible exception occurs in the case of members who occupy important positions in the governing hierarchy and whose personal fortunes entirely depend on complete identification with the authoritarian system.

relations. The explanation may be found entirely in the technical area. But, quite frequently, a low rate of productive efficiency does indicate personal maladjustment, unsatisfactory group relationships, or fears that express themselves in deliberate restriction of output. Study of subgroups in large industrial undertakings shows that, in most cases, productive efficiency closely parallels work satisfaction and that both depend on the success of group leaders and minor supervisors in developing effective work teams.[1]

But, taken alone, the rate of productive efficiency is obviously not a sufficient index of employee morale and group stability. The personnel administrator needs to study other indexes and report on them to operating management. One of the most important of these is the attendance record, which shows tardiness and absence.

TARDINESS AND ABSENCE

Although rare instances of tardiness are perceptibly disturbing to group efficiency, they are not of special interest to the personnel administrator, since they probably reflect external circumstances rather than undesirable attitudes. But a record that shows that tardiness is typical of some employee suggests the need for further study. Both lack of integration in the work group and lack of loyalty to the company are exemplified by the tardy members who frequently form a steady nucleus among those who rush the time clock at the end of their working day. Anyone may occasionally want to leave work in a hurry, but those who always stand in line or jostle each other to get away as soon as the clock has jumped to the appointed minute are giving unmistakable evidence of low morale.

When chronic tardiness indicates that something is wrong, interviewing may enable a supervisor or a personnel administrator to uncover the root of the difficulty. It may be that management is partly at fault in such ways as not making work seem important, in appearing to belittle the individual contribution of an unskilled operator, in not providing supervision of a high quality, in failing to promote teamwork of a caliber such that minor discipline is handled within the group, or in having selected employees who are not capable of self-discipline.

The potential value of self-discipline and regulation within each small group is equally clear in regard to absence, which may be a more pro-

---

[1] For a detailed example to substantiate this statement, see the case for Chap. 8, Work Group No. 7 (the effect on work teams of labor turnover and internal mobility). The Western Electric studies are also conclusive evidence on this point. See ROETHLISBERGER, F. J., and W. J. DICKSON, *Management and the Worker*, Harvard University Press, Cambridge, Mass., 1939.

nounced symptom of the same undesirable attitude that produces tardiness.

Various kinds of absence affect group efficiency and stability in different ways and may be significant indications of individual attitudes toward the work team. Occasional and excused absences, arranged in advance with the supervisor's permission, make a minimum disturbance of group activity and may be justified by unusual demands outside the plant, such as illness at home.

Absence that cannot be prearranged may be caused by an emergency and therefore becomes an excused absence if the person promptly notifies his supervisor. Such notification indicates a responsible attitude on the part of the "absentee."[1]

An absence of which the supervisor is not immediately informed is more disruptive of group efficiency, because planning becomes more difficult. In this case, it is impossible to know at the beginning of the workday whether the missing person is to be regarded as late or absent. However, the fact that no notification has been sent does not necessarily indicate a willful disregard of company rules. Sometimes the absence is unavoidable, and for some valid reason notice did not reach the supervisor.[2]

Chronic unexcused absence is most disturbing to group efficiency and morale. It makes an individual unacceptable on a work team, no matter how much he has to offer when he does come to work. More than any other form of absence, such genuine absenteeism indicates both lack of teamwork and poor personnel administration in the organization.

A COMPARATIVE STUDY OF ABSENCES

The close relation between the rate of absence and the administrative factors that make for good teamwork is clearly shown by a study of absences made in the casting shops of three comparable companies in the same community during the months of January, 1942, through May, 1943.[3]

---

[1] The terms "absentee" and "absenteeism" have acquired a moral connotation. For this reason, they should be used with care. Indiscriminate blasts by management against all absences are detrimental to employee morale, because they lump together people whose attitudes and circumstances may be significantly different.

[2] Among such reasons are ignorance of company rules, fear of a supervisor, lack of a home telephone, or forgetfulness on the part of someone who was entrusted with a message. For a case in point, see Chap. 15 on Discipline and Discharge, p. 205.

[3] Fox, JOHN B., and JEROME F. SCOTT, *Absenteeism: Management's Problem*, Harvard Graduate School of Business Administration, Business Research Studies No. 29, Vol. 30, No. 4, 1943. All three concerns were well-established companies making the same product, sharing the same labor market, and with the same environment as to housing, shopping, and transportation.

TABLE SHOWING ADMINISTRATIVE DIFFERENCES IN TWO COMPANIES

Administrative factors	Casting shop of Company *A*	Casting shop of Company *C*
Induction and training of new employees	A new employee was assigned to a caster who needed an assistant. There was no pay adjustment for the trainer	The company had a well-planned induction procedure. The new employee was assigned to a special instructor and given a regular assignment only when he had learned the job
Payment system	Individual piecework or group piecework with caster and helper as payment unit. No financial incentive for intershift cooperation	Group piecework, all the men on all three shifts being considered as a single unit. "It was to the financial interest of the men on one shift to charge a furnace even though that furnace was not going to be poured until the following shift came on"
Shift schedule	Monthly shift rotation. Each foreman stays with his own shift	Monthly shift rotation. Foreman rotating on a special schedule that eventually brings each foreman in contact with every worker on each shift
Hours of work	56 hours a week. If production required an increase in hours, the foreman would ask his men on Thursday if they were willing to work on the following Sunday. Sunday operations were scheduled in terms of the answers received	48 hours in a 6-day work week, Sunday being scheduled just like any other day. Each worker had 1 day off in 7. Workers on the same shift could arrange to swap days off
Record of absences	Foremen kept no record of absences	Foremen kept careful absence records, retaining them in the shop for ready reference
Talking with absentees	Channels of communication easily blocked. Foremen too busy with technical duties. Labor-management committee appointed deputies to talk with absentees but had difficulty in recruiting suitable candidates. Deputies did not like to act as monitors	Foremen instructed to talk patiently with employees, find out reasons for absence, report them up the line. Given supervisory assistance on technical duties to free them for their leadership responsibilities
Disciplinary action	Extreme leniency with regard to unauthorized absences	Strict discipline. Absence from work on Sunday, no matter what the reason, carried with it a penalty of disciplinary suspension on Monday. Furthermore, when an employee who had frequently been absent failed to improve his attendance after due warning, he was reported to the local draft board or discharged

Company A's rate of absence[1] among all workers during this period was slightly above 2 per cent at the beginning and by September had gradually increased to 3 per cent. Then over a period of 5 months there was a steep rise to nearly 11 per cent, after which it dropped in the next 2-month period to 4 per cent.

Company B's rate of absence rose steadily from 2 per cent to 5½ per cent.

Company C, on the other hand, *had an absence rate well below 2 per cent during the entire period.*

As an explanation of these marked differences between Company *A* and Company *C*, the differences in administrative factors are summarized below.

Company *C*, in brief, solved its attendance problem principally by careful training of its supervisors and by relying on the self-discipline of responsible employees and such self-regulation as inevitably develops in an effective work team.

In Company *A*, group discipline was regarded by workers as a form of police work for which management should be responsible. Because of difficulties in securing and holding labor, management was inclined to be lax in exercising this responsibility.

In Company *C*, however, management strictly enforced rules making for good discipline. Over and above this, workers in Company *C* voluntarily participated with management in achieving this important company objective.

When we study an absence record in such a comprehensive manner, we learn something about the current level of employee morale. We also get insight into conditions that affect morale and into the means by which it may be raised. A similar analysis of accidents leads to a gain in understanding on the same three points.

What Can We Learn from Accident Records?

In looking at accidents as an index of the needs and attitudes of people, the two most fruitful methods seem to be comparative analysis and study

[1] In order to minimize *frequency of absences*, any series of consecutive days absent by one man was counted as one absence in the study. However, the formula recommended by the U. S. Bureau of Labor Statistics for computing the absence rate is

$$\frac{\text{Man-days lost}}{\text{Man-days worked plus man-days lost}} \text{ per month}$$

Controlling Absenteeism, Special Bulletin No. 12, p. 13, U. S. Department of Labor, Division of Labor Standards, Washington, D. C., 1943. "Man-days lost," of course, refers to losses due to absences on days when the employee was *scheduled* to work. This excludes vacations, holidays, official leaves of absence, etc. In some firms, separate indexes are computed for "absences for all causes" and "unexcused absences." Rates are also computed, for comparative purposes, by departments, shifts, sex, age, etc.

of the circumstances surrounding special and typical kinds of accident.

A comparative study of accident records throughout the country, such as can be made from the figures published annually by the U.S. Department of Labor, reveals the interesting fact that the lowest percentages of accidents are usually to be found in very small and very large companies. The medium-sized plants have, on the average, a less good record. What does this show? It seems to support the belief, also confirmed by experience, that both engineering and team spirit can play an important part in keeping down accident rates.

In very large companies, engineering for accident prevention has reached a high level of efficiency.[1] In smaller companies, engineering that builds safety into the plant and reduces hazards that cannot entirely be eliminated is necessarily limited because it is so expensive. In very small companies, engineering is even more restricted. In fact, safety engineers are sometimes shocked at the mechanical risks that exist in these plants. Yet, on the whole, workers seem to be relatively safe even under such conditions when the total number of employees is small enough so that everybody knows everyone else and when the owner-manager takes a personal interest in safety. Obviously, the human causes of accidents are here sufficiently reduced to outweigh mechanical hazards. A spirit of teamwork, which manifests itself in safety-mindedness for others, is a significant factor in accident reduction. Moreover, in a very small work force, the skill and intelligence required of all employees means that each member is likely to have the qualifications that make for personal safety. In a medium-sized plant, the caliber of employees is unlikely to be at such a consistently high level, and the sense of belonging to a single company-wide work team is difficult if not impossible to achieve. Thus these companies fall between two stools, as it were. They lack both the most expert engineering and also the conditions of individual skill and group association that make for safety.

An illustration of the type of accident that indicates both inadequate engineering inspection by management and unsafe practice by an employee who was not safety-minded for others is given in the following incident. In a shipyard, "a painter had built himself a temporary scaffold and on finishing his work had departed, leaving it in place. Later when several chippers used the scaffold, under the impression that it had been erected by stage builders for their use, it collapsed and dropped the workers and their equipment to the way."[2] If modern management had developed

---

[1] See Chap. 20 for details.

[2] McElroy, Frank S., and Arthur L. Svenson, "Basic Accident Factors in Shipyards," *Monthly Labor Review*, Vol. 59, pp. 13–23, 1944.

effective procedures of control, as is usually the case in large corporations nowadays, safety inspection would probably have prevented this accident. In a very small concern, the typical safety-mindedness of each worker for all others might be expected to rule out such accidents by eliminating the human cause.

COMPUTING ACCIDENT RATES

This type of comparative analysis should be of interest to every chief executive, yet it seems that many managements do not even know whether their record for safety is comparatively good or bad. Since accidents constitute a major problem in industrial efficiency and for employee morale, and since accident analysis demonstrates that most accidents are avoidable,[1] it is inexcusable for management not even to know the facts in regard to its own accident record. Of course, every executive likes to think that his company record is good. But experience shows that, in many cases, the wish is father to the thought. It is the duty of the safety director (or, if there is none, of the personnel administrator) to find out and report to line management how well the company's injury-accident record compares with that of other companies in the same industry. This can be done by applying the standard formulas[2] to determine the frequency and severity rate. It is also useful to find out what the general liability rate of the industry is as a whole, in comparison with other industries. Both management and workers are naturally interested to know whether accidents in the company are partly attributable to risks inherent in the type of work. Even when this is known to be the case, however, it may be used as a challenge to build a safety program that shall set a record for

---

[1] For example, a causal analysis of over 1,360 longshore injuries reveals that most of the unsafe conditions were not an inescapable occupational hazard but rather were created by the way in which the casual laborers performed their work. The authors conclude: "By and large these unsafe acts represent violations of the most elementary rules of safety; in short, they are the type of unsafe acts which are committed by persons entirely untrained in safety and condoned only by supervisors who are unconcerned with safety. It seems evident that most of the injuries to longshoremen could be avoided if the workers were thoroughly instructed in safety and were given safety-minded supervision." McElroy, Frank S., and George R. McCormack, "Injuries and Accident Causes in the Longshore Industry, 1942," *Monthly Labor Review*, Vol. 59, pp. 1–7, 1944.

[2] The American Standards Association provides the following formulas:

$$\text{Frequency rate} = \frac{\text{number of injuries} \times 1{,}000{,}000}{\text{number of man-hours of exposure}}$$

$$\text{Severity rate} = \frac{\text{total time charges in days} \times 1{,}000}{\text{number of man-hours of exposure}}$$

The man-hours of exposure are the total of man-hours actually worked by all employees. Time charges for permanent disabilities are based on a standard scale of allowances. For greater detail, see *Accident-record Manual for Industrial Plants*, Bulletin No. 772, U.S. Department of Labor, Division of Industrial Hazards, Washington, D. C., 1944.

the industry. That this can be done is proved in statistics published by the U.S. Department of Labor, which show that some companies in each of the most hazardous industries have achieved very low frequency rates.

The comparison of safety records between different departments in one company may throw light on many features of work life and on the level of teamwork. In order to be fair, such comparisons must of course take into account differences in the rate of accident liability attaching to various kinds of work. When such differences are allowed for, the handicap of a given department is eliminated by using the adjusted frequency rate.

In the study of accident records, the frequency rate[1] is a more significant index than the severity rate, because the result of an accident is often a matter of luck. Management's aim should be to eliminate all avoidable accidents and not simply to reduce the cost of injuries. The existence of such a purpose and the extent to which it is incorporated in safety procedures may be studied by analysis of special and typical kinds of accident.

SPECIAL AND TYPICAL ACCIDENTS

Analysis of the circumstances surrounding individual accidents clearly shows that both mechanical and human factors (physical, mental, and emotional) play a part in causing accidents. Responsibility for safety is divided between management and workers, since neither one can do the job alone. But mechanical risks and the quality of supervision are the special responsibilities of management, and even the health and morale of employees are influenced by management activity. Inadequacies in either the mechanical or the human environment of workers have a depressing effect on employee morale and reduce the possibility of achieving effective teamwork. Therefore, whether or not accidents result in serious injuries, management is concerned to learn all it can about its own efficiency in these areas.

Accident analysis may reveal that safety policies that should be formulated by top management do not exist in the company at all or are being neglected or misapplied in supervisory procedures. Two examples indicate the need for this line of inquiry.

A case in point was that of an elderly factory worker who had previously been employed in a grocery store. He had this to say at the end of his first week's work: "I was scared; I thought I wouldn't make it. The foreman showed me how to do the job. I guess I spoiled half of the pieces the

---

[1] This figure would be still more significant if consistently applied on the basis of a careful definition of accidents (see Chap. 20 for discussion of this point). At present, the figures merely show the frequency of disabling injuries.

first week. The foreman bawled me out every day. I was about ready to quit on Friday when I dropped a casting on my foot, and they sent me over to the hospital, and the foreman gave me a bad record for being careless."

No doubt this man was a problem to the foreman. On the other hand, when the personnel director inquired why he was "scared," why he had not made a better production record on a comparatively simple operation, and whether his instruction had been adequate, the worker replied,

"No, I guess he showed me how to do the job all right, but I'd never worked in a shop before. I'd just lost my job that I had been on for fifteen years. I wanted to make good, but I was scared of the noise of the machine shop, I guess. I just couldn't get used to it. And there was a conveyor going over my head carrying some big castings which weighed about fifty pounds apiece. I guess they wouldn't have dropped on me, but I was always looking up at 'em. I guess that's what happened when I dropped the casting on my foot."[1]

Person-centered analysis of this accident suggested that more careful introduction to his work would probably have helped the employee better to adjust to his new situation. This would have aided management by stepping up production and saved both management and the worker from the loss occasioned by an avoidable accident. When analysis uncovers such a situation, it can be used to indicate the need for improvement either in policy thinking or in the practical procedures that should constantly interpret for employees top management's concern for their welfare.

ACCIDENTS AND HEALTH

Study of accident causes also indicates the correlation between health and safety. Other things being equal, employees are less likely to have accidents when they feel well than when they are tired or sick. Moreover, if management fails in any respect to evince an interest in the health of workers, the resentment aroused by such apparent callousness may become a contributory cause of accidents.

In one plant, during the Second World War (where incidentally the accident rate was unnecessarily high), efficiency of the production process required that the humidity be kept as low as possible. To contribute to this end, radiators were promptly installed in a workroom that was located in a recently converted storage warehouse. As autumn drew on, there was an uncomfortable and increasing contrast of temperature be-

---

[1] ARMSTRONG, T. O., The New Employee, in *Industrial Safety*, Chap. 25, p. 281, Roland P. Blake, editor, Prentice-Hall, Inc., New York, 1944.

tween the workroom and the adjoining rest room, where the female operators ate lunch. Since the work was quite strenuous, the chill of the un-
heated rest room was felt all the more keenly during the time when employees were inactive. For this reason, many chose to lunch in the dirty
workroom itself and did not even bother to wash their hands before eating.
It was "understood" that management intended to heat the rest room as
soon as possible. But the vague statements to this effect were insufficient
to appease the women's resentment.[1] As one of them remarked, "This
just goes to show that they'll do anything to make money for themselves.
And you notice they could get radiators all right for the shop. Why should
we believe the phony story they can't get any for the rest room?"

Such examples serve to highlight the need for careful and constant
follow-up of employees. When accidents reveal unsafe practices or unsatisfactory conditions, they are useful indexes of what needs to be done.
The environmental conditions described in the second example are typical
of many situations in which management cannot immediately correct
unsatisfactory conditions. When this is the case, it is all the more important
that supervision be of superior quality. Often employees can accept im-
perfect conditions when the reasons are clearly explained by a supervisor
who convincingly interprets management's regret and good intentions.

ACCIDENTS AND SUPERVISION

When the company has an accident-reporting system that attempts to
determine causes by the use of the standard accident-classification code,
the foreman's report is a significant index in several respects. In order to
follow up the clues given, a series of questions may be asked. For instance,
if one supervisor consistently reports that accidents in his section are the
fault of employees, what does this show? Why should he have an unusually large proportion of incompetent or careless employees? If this is
actually the case, why did he, at the end of the probationary period, accept them as regular employees? Has he done all that he could have done
by further instruction and by clear and thorough order-giving to correct
their careless habits?

[1] The fact that these employees were women probably meant that they were sensitive both physically and emotionally. Accident analysis during the war indicated the
need for special measures to protect the health, safety, and emotional stability of the
many women in industry. This need was especially acute in the case of those who were
not inured to work or to the somewhat uncavalier methods of the average foreman.
Study of avoidable accidents and risks indicated the need for such measures as improvement in working conditions, greater development of first-aid procedures, and better
training for supervisors.

The stupidity of assigning carelessness as a cause of accidents is strongly emphasized by W. Dean Keefer when he says, "Carelessness is not a cause of accidents. Instead it is an alibi for industrial executives, foremen, and others who unthinkingly are placing the blame for accidents on the workers who are injured. It serves as a boomerang, too, for its use condemns the person who uses it; it is an unthinking admission on his part that he is making little or no intelligent effort to control the actions of the workers."[1]

Apparent carelessness may be the result of chronic accident-proneness (due to poor hand-eye coordination) or of temporary ill health of body or mind. If the supervisor is on his toes, he knows what lies behind "carelessness" and does what he can to correct fundamental accident causes.

Yet foremen, if unaided by experts, can hardly be expected, among all the urgent demands that are pressed on them, to think profoundly about accidents as indexes. It is the responsibility of the safety director or personnel administrator to keep supervisors informed of all that can be learned from accident analysis. In this way, staff and line can work together to supplement each other's understanding and efficiency. When this happens, the result is a gain for both management and workers. Accidents can never be altogether eliminated, because human beings will never become entirely stable and perfectly efficient. But, when the accidents that do happen are used as educational material for employees (both management and workers) at all levels, there can be a progressive gain in morale and teamwork. Unless accidents are so used, they not only indicate lapses in morale and teamwork but also are apt to set up a vicious cycle in which the feelings of workers suffer further depression that cumulatively reduces their efficiency of action.

SUMMARY

Such a study of accidents is a practical application of situational thinking. In this way, a personnel administrator seeks understanding by relating people, technical factors, policies, and the time factor. Safety records can be improved when individual idiosyncracies (*e.g.*, accident-proneness) are seen in relation to technical features of the work situation such as job methods and mechanical hazards. Similarly, we need to consider in relation to each other current data on the level of teamwork; the quality of supervision; and the health, strength, and age of individual workers. Moreover, by comparing the company's record with that of the industry as a whole, we know whether the record is relatively good or bad.

[1] KEEFER, W. DEAN, Circumstances Surrounding Accidents, in *Industrial Safety*, Chap. 5, p. 47, Roland P. Blake, editor, Prentice-Hall, Inc., New York, 1944.

And comparison of past and present statistics shows whether the condition is getting better or worse.

Statistics on tardiness and absence need to be examined in the same way if we are to see what they mean in terms of policy requirements. Here again the quality of teamwork and of first-line supervision are to be considered in relation to company policies. Furthermore, the pace and hours of work and the age of workers need to be thought about in connection with the attendance record. When we judge this, in individual cases, we should also consider the developmental stage reached by a worker, and we must know the sequence of events in an evolving situation during which an unsatisfactory record was developed.

Even in studying such data as the figures on productive efficiency, a personnel administrator needs to relate technical and human factors and to study the general principles that are being or should be applied. Is productive efficiency high? If so, does it reflect high morale? If efficiency is low, does the fault lie in technical features of the work situation, in the mechanical inefficiency of individuals, in supervision, or in the current state of labor relations, in the absence or inadequacy of company policies?

In such ways, a personnel administrator examines the record. He asks himself, What are the facts? What do they mean—for workers and for management? In view of this, what needs to be done? This kind of study is an essential preliminary to the improvement of a personnel program. It should also be extended to other indexes of organizational stability such as labor turnover and internal mobility, which we shall discuss in the next chapter.

Chapter 8

Labor Turnover
and Internal Mobility

> Far more important than as a *cause* of demoralization
> among workers is the turnover as a *symptom* of demoralization
> which exists for other reasons.
>
> SUMNER H. SLICHTER[1]

Personnel mobility is of two kinds—movement *into and out of* the company and shifting of employees *within* the organization. The former is "labor turnover;" the latter is a similar manifestation on a smaller scale. To some extent, every suborganization in a company is a self-contained unit. Thus, employee movement among sections, departments, divisions, or even plants presents for management the same kind of opportunities and dangers that are involved in labor turnover proper.

Within due limits, and when skillfully handled, both labor turnover and internal mobility can benefit the entire company as well as the individuals who make the adjustments. Beyond these limits, or when handled without the necessary skills in policies and procedures, personnel mobility is destructive of individual and organizational stability alike.

STABILIZING EFFECTS

Labor turnover promotes company stability insofar as such circulation of employees brings new blood into the organization. The company remains a "going concern" in regard to personnel as long as employees who leave for reasons of age or health are replaced by younger or stronger employees. Moreover, efficiency and morale are raised when necessary management replacements can be supplied by promotions from within the organization rather than from outside the company.

---

[1] *The Turnover of Factory Labor*, D. Appleton-Century Company, Inc., New York, 1921, p. 158.

Similarly, internal mobility may build teamwork when remedial transfers make possible a better adjustment between teammates and when upgrading or promotion meets a worker's needs and thus resolves inner conflicts. An ambitious employee needs to know that promotion will parallel his increased ability and worth to the company. If his job is far below his capacity, he is inevitably wasting ability[1] and is subjected to tensions. Similarly, if he feels that he is in a "blind-alley" job, he is certain to be dissatisfied. The disturbing effect of such strains on his equilibrium may, through him, prove injurious to group morale.

Conversely, an employee who has been placed in a position that is far beyond his abilities is inevitably inefficient and subject to overstrain and may indulge in "griping." Or, where companies operate on shifts, the time of day or pace of the shift may prove ill-suited to certain individuals. The conflicts thus generated are so detrimental to group stability that the readjustments necessitated by transfer are more than worth the temporary inconvenience to all concerned.

Individual needs can also be met by internal mobility in the form of production transfers to avoid layoffs, remedial transfers to solve personal or technical difficulties arising from improper placement or marked changes in individuals, and sometimes even by transfers for such a purely social reason as an employee's desire to join a more congenial work group or, for some personal reason, to swap assignments with another employee. In such ways, labor turnover and internal mobility may promote individual, group, and company interests by increasing work satisfaction, loyalty, and efficiency.

UNSTABILIZING EFFECTS

But, obviously, personnel mobility is not all gain. When a separation occurs for any reason, the organization and the work groups that comprise it must adjust to the loss. Changes in work routine are inevitable, and a group may be shorthanded for a time. If the displaced worker is a valued teammate and is laid off or discharged without adequate explanation, his fellow employees become disturbed. Speculation leads to rumors. Gossip and worry reduce work efficiency. A sense of insecurity and resent-

---

[1] In employment policies that provide both for recognition of ability by promotion within the company, and sometimes even for releasing an employee whose worth cannot be suitably matched by a position in the organization, personnel-minded executives recognize their obligation to develop employees. During the critical period of production for the Second World War, the War Manpower Commission attempted to prevent the waste involved in underuse of an employee by providing for a release when a larger position was open to him.

ment may spread among members until it leads to voluntary quits that further upset the group.

When a new member is introduced into a work group, human adjustments must be made by all concerned. Some adjustments are necessary even when a new member is a transferee. If he is a newcomer to the company, and perhaps also unaccustomed to industrial life, much has to be done before he is assimilated into the work team. The old-timers are inclined to ask each other, "Who's the new guy? He looks kinda dumb." And the "new guy," confronted by a work group that seems to him a clique, may feel at the end of the first day, "Gosh, I'm not going to be able to stand working here." The mutual adjustments by which the group adapts to a new member and the probationer makes a place for himself are often difficult. The strain involved may manifest itself in "scraps," accidents, or quarrels; and, unless the adjustment process can be satisfactorily completed, the whole replacement cycle must be repeated.

Emphasis on such intangibles should help the personnel administrator to convince management that personnel mobility should be handled with care and that everything possible should be done to keep it down to the point where individual and group needs are in balance.

Costs of Labor Turnover

Since personnel mobility requires adjustments by all concerned, it obviously involves some cost that, unless outweighed by a gain, constitutes a loss. In most companies, avoidable separations and unnecessary or unwise transfers produce unjustifiable costs not only in human values but also in money. Yet line officials are often unaware of the extent and nature of the damage done even by such an obvious manifestation of poor management as excessively high turnover rates.

If labor is considered merely as a commodity, a constant need for replacements may seem nothing to worry about in a period of labor surplus. But officials who hold this view are quickly jolted out of their complacency when a tight labor market makes replacements difficult to find. Even in "good times," they might be shocked if they realized all the financial waste involved. In order to reduce the cost of labor turnover to a minimum, it is essential that line officials from the top down be kept supplied with relevant information.

What are some of these costs?

1. Costs of hiring and training each new employee. (If a skilled employee leaves the company soon after his training is completed, obviously this constitutes a considerable loss for the company.)

    a. Employment-department costs—time and facilities used to interview the applicant, prepare necessary records, give physical examinations, etc.

    b. Training costs—time of supervisor, trainer, or other employee who explains work to the new man.

    c. Pay to the learner over and above what he produces, especially if he is on piecework and there is a guaranteed minimum that he does not earn at the beginning.

    d. Breakage, scrap, and wastage of materials in the learning period.

    e. Possible costs in accidents to self or others while skill is being acquired.

2. Cost of overtime work required from regular workers in order to maintain production until the new man can do his share.

3. Loss of production in interval between separation of former employee and the time when his replacement is fully broken in.

    a. Maximum loss while the group is without a replacement.

    b. Loss in group efficiency while regular workers are readjusting to a new member.

4. Expense in productive equipment not being fully utilized during training period.

By pointing out such losses,[1] the personnel administrator has an opportunity to show that he can be cost-minded and that he is not concerned with sentiments alone. In the "cost language" of shopmen, he can make clear the wastes involved and thus enlist the interest of production officials in a program to reduce excessive labor turnover.

However, the costs can be estimated only when we know how much labor turnover there is at any given time and of what kind. Obviously the most unjustifiable extravagance is the waste involved in "avoidable" separations. In order to determine whether or not this item is concealed among turnover figures, the personnel administrator must analyze the current rate of labor turnover and distinguish between avoidable and unavoidable separations.

DIFFERENT TYPES OF LABOR TURNOVER

Here, as with other statistical data that are used to further human understanding, the figures are less useful in the form of over-all totals

---

[1] Some effort has been made to estimate the amount of these costs. For example, an itemized account of expenses involved in the turnover of an hourly rated employee in a boiler-manufacturing company totals $95.47. WALTERS, J. E., *Personnel Relations*, p. 251, The Ronald Press Company, New York, 1945. Walters states further that turnover costs vary from $8.50 for unskilled laborers to $250 for skilled workers. For other estimates, see SUMNER H. SLICHTER, *The Turnover of Factory Labor*, pp. 130–140, D. Appleton-Century Company, Inc., 1919.

than when they are analyzed in more detail. Turnover can be computed for each type of movement in and out of the company. What are these types?

1. *Accessions.*—Hiring new workers or rehiring former employees.
2. *Separations.*—Termination of employment, usually subdivided as follows:
   a. *Quit.*—A separation initiated by the worker. Workers who are absent without authorization for 7 consecutive days are usually listed among the "quits."
   b. *Layoff.*—A termination of employment (expected to last more than 7 days) initiated by the employer because the job is being eliminated or because there is a reduction of operators. Such separation is presumably without prejudice to the employee. (Suspension of operations during inventory periods and suspension of an employee as a form of punishment should both be differentiated from layoff, although in shop language such distinctions are frequently not made.)
   c. *Discharge.*—A termination initiated by the employer because he is dissatisfied with the employee's performance or conduct, and therefore with prejudice to the worker's record.

COMPUTATION OF RATES

Labor turnover is commonly expressed in two rates—one for separations and the other for accessions. The Bureau of Labor Statistics, U. S. Department of Labor, uses the following method to compute the separation rate:

1. Find the average number of employees by adding together the number on the pay roll on the first and last days of the month. Then divide this total by two.
2. Divide the total number of separations during the month by the average employment figure.
3. Multiply this number by 100 to get the rate per 100 employees for the month.

Expressed as a formula, this method is

$$\text{Separation rate (or percentage)} = \frac{\text{Total separations per month}}{\text{average number on pay roll for the month}} \times 100$$

Monthly figures may be converted to an annual rate by multiplying the actual monthly rate by a factor equal to 365 divided by the number of days in the given month. Unless this is done, monthly figures are not strictly comparable with annual figures, since months vary in length.

The rate for accessions, quits, layoffs, and discharges can be computed by the same basic formula. When the separation rate is subtracted from the accession rate, the result is positive or negative according to whether the company's force is expanding or contracting.

COMPARATIVE MEASUREMENT OF TURNOVER

Absolute figures for turnover rates are of little significance, however, unless they are compared with a standard and unless they are used as a point of departure for seeking an explanation of employee dissatisfactions. Whether turnover rates are rising, falling, or standing still in the country or in the industry as a whole, it is important to know how the firm's turnover rates compare with others. These comparative figures appear each month in the *Monthly Labor Review* published by the Bureau of Labor Statistics of the U.S. Department of Labor.[1] A useful chart can be prepared and kept up to date, showing company turnover rates compared with similar rates for the industry and for all manufacturing. The trend of a company's turnover rates over a period of time also shows roughly what is happening to the size of its work force.

ANALYZING TURNOVER DATA

But, even if the company figures compare favorably with others, the personnel administrator should not be satisfied unless he is sure that the rate of voluntary separations is as low as possible and until he knows all that these figures can teach him about how effectively the company is handling its personnel. In following these leads, three sets of questions need to be answered.

1. *Why Are Employees Voluntarily Leaving the Company?*—Is it because employees think they can find a "better job somewhere else"? Are they dissatisfied with working conditions, with supervisors or with fellow employees, with shift assignments, or because they feel they are "getting nowhere"? Or are employees leaving the company for "unavoidable" reasons, such as illness, "needed at home," reopening of school, marriage, pregnancy, etc.?

Frequently, of course, management does not know why an employee leaves the company, if he goes of his own accord. But there are various ways in which the information may be sought. Some reason is usually stated to the foreman or supervisor if the employee gives notice that he is

[1] Data are secured from approximately 5,800 representative firms in 135 different industries. Turnover rates are published for 36 of these industries and for 30 different states. Similar figures are also prepared and published by the National Industrial Conference Board, Inc.

going to leave. But often the reason alleged is not the real one. During the Second World War, for instance, when releases were necessary before changing employment, "ill health" or "needed at home" were frequently stated as reasons for leaving because they were comparatively difficult to "disprove." In many cases, these same employees actually left to take other employment that promised more pay or better conditions.

The exit interview, held when an employee calls for his final pay check, may bring out the real cause for leaving, although, even to a sympathetic listener, the worker may not be able to talk freely if he is still suffering from internal conflict or fears that an argument may ensue. Thus the chief gain of an exit interview may be that it is a friendly gesture from management. A better means of getting the necessary information may be an interview with employees some time after they have left.[1]

Aside from information provided by the worker who is leaving, light may be shed on possible reasons for voluntary separation by investigating a second question.

2. *Where Are Voluntary Separations Occurring?*—What departments or sections are workers voluntarily leaving? What kind of work was being performed, in what conditions, and under whose supervision? The answers to this set of questions are especially significant if there is a disproportionate turnover in some place where it cannot readily be accounted for by the nature of operations or of working conditions. In such a case, the fault may be in the composition and functioning of work teams or in the quality of supervision. For example, in one company, comparisons of turnover in three departments led to further investigations that definitely pointed to the incompetence of a supervisor.

Further insight into reasons for leaving, as well as a more accurate estimate of the expense involved, may be obtained by asking a third question.

3. *What Kind of Employee Is Leaving Voluntarily?*—The age, sex, marital status, nationality, length of service, and skill of the worker who leaves the company of his own volition are items worthy of study. If voluntary separations are chiefly among very young workers of both sexes, on the part of girls who are getting married, in the age group above fifty, or among unskilled workers with less than 6 months of service, there is less cause for concern than when long-service, highly skilled employees between thirty and forty years of age are quitting the company. However, the personnel administrator cannot afford to be satisfied when any employees are leaving without regret. Every worker would feel some re-

---

[1] PALMER, DWIGHT, E. R. PURPUS, and LEBARON O. STOCKFORD, "Why Workers Quit," *Personnel Journal*, Vol. 23, No. 3, pp. 111–119, 1944.

luctance to leave the company if his work and his associations there had been satisfying.

A good deal of unjustifiable smugness is expressed by personnel workers when separations in their company are chiefly among "common labor," for example. It might be more constructive to ask: Could we reduce the number of such separations by improving working conditions or by supplying more and better opportunities for participation and advancement? Similarly, it need not be accepted as true that all young people are flighty. What is being done in the company to make young people feel that their youth is considered an asset to the organization, that their ideas are potentially valuable, and that the abilities they expect to develop will be suitably rewarded? What educational opportunities are being offered in the company that help to stimulate and to apply their desire for self-development?

REDUCTION OF TURNOVER

Answers to the three broad lines of inquiry[1] help the personnel administrator and the line officers he advises to ask the final question: Is there any condition in the organization that could be improved, either by management or by the collaboration of management and workers, in order to reduce excessive labor turnover? Since the answer to this usually is "yes," it is clear that separations furnish the personnel administrator and line executives with a perpetual opportunity for evaluating the effectiveness of their dealings with personnel.

Even when management knows the costs and many of the reasons for high turnover, no single remedy can be used as a cure-all for this symptom of organizational ill health. But, over a period of time, it can be reduced by working to prevent its causes. Consistent application of the personnel point of view throughout the organization provides for employees the genuine satisfactions of membership in effective work teams and in a respected organization.

An example of the way in which careful study of turnover statistics can lead to corrective action is the experience of a large manufacturing firm during the Second World War. When there was plenty of labor, in the period before 1941, this firm kept only a rough record of quits. As late as 1943, this record was not being seen regularly by line executives.

Then, early in 1944, the personnel department began to prepare more detailed turnover reports, showing the reasons for separation and the turnover rates for each of the 26 departments in the company. These

---

[1] 1. Why are employees voluntarily leaving the company?
2. Where are voluntary separations occurring?
3. What kind of employee is leaving voluntarily?

reports were presented each month to the president and vice-president so that departmental rates above the company average could be subjected to further study. More detailed explanations were secured, and necessary improvements were made in supervision, working conditions, and the wage structure.

An exit-interview program was inaugurated to reduce the reported number of "unknown" reasons for leaving. This was also useful in reducing the number of employees who actually quit. Finally, discovery of excessive turnover among new employees in 1944 led to improvements in hiring practices and to the development of a formal induction program. The total separation rate for the company was equal to that reported for the industry at 9 per cent in September, 1942. By the end of the war, in August, 1945, it was only 3 per cent, as compared with 8 per cent for the industry as a whole. The induction program was an important factor in the reduction of the separation rate for employees of 6 weeks' service or less from 29 per cent in March, 1944, to 18 per cent at the end of the war.

Analyzing Internal Mobility

When internal mobility is studied in the same way, similar improvements in the handling of personnel may be achieved. Why do people ask to be transferred from certain jobs and departments? Excessive transfer is a disruptive and costly influence similar to excessive separation. In some ways, the situation is worse, since, whether or not the request for transfer is granted, the employee who was or remains dissatisfied is still a member of the work force and consequently may undermine group morale with his complaints and recriminations. Before concluding that these are unreasonable, management needs to know, for instance, whether there are "blind-alley" or "dead-end" jobs held by employees who are not pensioners. Or are the jobs that employees try to leave simply the lower rungs on established ladders of promotion? If so, is this known to all employees?

Again, are certain departments serving as training groups for personnel and as feeders of promotional material to be used by other departments? If so, why? The reasons for this may be twofold. The work in these departments may be of such a nature that it affords an excellent opportunity for introducing unskilled and semiskilled workers to the company. Or these departments may have limited opportunities for advancing employees who show special promise. In any event, management should be fully acquainted with these conditions in order to give supervisors full credit for the extra work involved in constantly breaking in new employees and developing good men. Conversely, the fact that one department head always asks for promotional material from outside his own department may indicate to management that he is not doing a good job in bringing along his own men.

In these ways, analysis of internal mobility can throw light on local conditions and lead to new insight on what needs to be improved, if it is not to cause dissatisfaction or even excessive labor turnover.

Summary

Labor turnover can promote organizational stability by bringing in new blood. And internal mobility may help individuals and may improve teamwork by raising morale. But both require adjustments in and between people. In labor turnover, particularly, these adjustments represent a cost, both in money and in human values. In order to determine whether this cost is offset by the gains that result, management needs to know what the expense amounts to, why employees are leaving, where voluntary separations are occurring, and who is quitting the firm.

Study of labor turnover by asking such questions gives the personnel administrator clues as to what needs to be done in order to reduce grounds for dissatisfaction. Other leads may be obtained by analyzing internal mobility in the same way. But neither voluntary separations nor requests for transfer should be taken as a reliable index of the amount of instability that exists in the company in the form of employee dissatisfaction. For, when other jobs in the community are scarce, employees are more likely to nurse dissatisfactions on the job than to quit the company. And, even when jobs are plentiful, any one of a number of personal reasons may cause an employee to feel that, whatever his dissatisfaction, he must stay where he is. For this reason, the personnel administrator needs to extend his field of study so as to include other indexes of poor morale, whether such unrest is expressed in acts, in words, or only in behavior patterns so subtle that they commonly escape the notice of management altogether.

Chapter 9

Complaints and Grievances

The true significance of the grievance emerges only when
we recognize the expression of dissatisfaction as a symptom
of friction, of malfunctioning somewhere in this living
structure of shop relationships.

BENJAMIN M. SELEKMAN[1]

The dissatisfactions felt by employees about the company, if they were
all made known to management, would probably be the most significant
single index of stability. As it is, in nonunion companies, many employees
lack the courage to express their dissatisfactions, or "grievances," in the
form of official complaints. Thus, no matter how efficient the company
procedure for handling complaints, management cannot even attempt to
deal with everything that troubles employees. And it cannot be assumed
that what is unknown to management is necessarily unimportant.

A major function of the personnel administrator is to interpret
the workers to management and to aid line supervisors in the exercise of their leadership responsibilities. Employee dissatisfactions are
opportunities for understanding to which the personnel administrator
should be alert.

When a union fulfills the useful function of opening a new channel for
complaints, management has reason to be grateful for this opportunity to
gain understanding and improve conditions. Sometimes, of course, a
militant union treats a relatively trivial dissatisfaction as though it were
a full-fledged grievance. This attitude exasperates feelings instead of
clarifying ideas. However, it is likely to occur only when minor dissatisfactions have piled up because management has failed to maintain free
communication up the line from the bench in the shop to the desk in the
president's office.

[1] *Labor Relations and Human Relations,* McGraw-Hill Book Company, Inc., New
York, 1947, p. 110.

In all discussions of complaints, whether with union officials or directly with workers themselves, it is important to distinguish among the various forms and stages of employee dissatisfaction. For this reason, we use the three words "dissatisfaction," "complaint," and "grievance," rather than using only the term "grievance," as is often done in casual shop language.

What do we mean by these three terms?

DEFINITIONS

An employee *dissatisfaction* may be defined as anything that disturbs an employee, whether or not he expresses his unrest in words. For instance, a worker on incentive may be dissatisfied at the amount of time he has to spend in looking for the small tools he needs.

A *complaint* is a spoken or written dissatisfaction, brought to the attention of a management or union representative. It may or may not specifically assign a cause for dissatisfaction, thus undertaking to locate the responsibility. The worker *complains* to his foreman or shop steward about the shortage of small tools, "Four times this morning I've had to chase around looking for pliers." He may make his complaint more specific by adding, "I think management ought to give each of us all the tools we have to use." Or the complaint may be specifically against a fellow worker, "We didn't have this kind of trouble before Joe came."

A *grievance* is a complaint that has been ignored, overridden, or in the employee's opinion otherwise dismissed without due consideration. From the aggrieved worker's point of view, therefore, a grievance always carries a sense of injustice dealt him by management or sometimes by union officials; it is a wrong that has been done him. After a complaint has been formally or informally brought to the attention of the proper management representative and no action has been taken or satisfactory explanation given, it becomes a grievance against management.

WHAT DO COMPLAINTS INDICATE?

In studying complaints as an index, the personnel administrator considers them as leads to further investigation rather than as nuisances to be disposed of. Such an exploratory approach attempts to go beyond the wording of complaints and to reach the underlying meaning. If management is to act constructively on employee complaints, *i.e.*, to use them as suggestions for improving company practices and procedures, they must be duly verified and evaluated. But this process is not always as simple as it sounds, because not all kinds of complaint are subject to objective verification. It is important to ask, therefore, with what kind of complaint we are dealing.

Three Kinds of Complaint.—In a significant study of employee complaints,[1] three types are differentiated according to content.

The first type of complaint referred to tangible objects in terms that could be defined by any competent worker or engineer and that could be tested by physical procedures. "The machine is out of order," "This tool is too dull," "The stock we're getting now isn't up to standard," "Our cement is too thin and won't make the rubber stick." Relatively few complaints were of this type.

A second kind of complaint was based partly on sensory experience but depended primarily on the attendant subjective reactions. "The work is messy," "It's too hot in here," "This job is too hard." Such statements include terms whose meanings are biologically or socially determined. Hence they cannot be understood unless one knows the complainant's background. Except in extreme cases, they are not entirely verifiable by any objective procedure, scientific or otherwise. Handling wet green hides is a job that would readily be admitted by any reasonable person to be messy. On the other hand, a temperature of 65 degrees Fahrenheit may seem warm to one person and chilly to another.

A third category of complaints involved the hopes and fears of employees. Such complaints cannot be objectively verified unless reworded in such a way that the terms used to state judgments can be agreed upon by all concerned. "The supervisor is a bully," "The pay rates are too low," "Seniority doesn't count as much as it should," "Ability is not properly recognized here." It was this category of complaint that proved most revealing to the investigators, because it showed the importance of determining not only what the employees felt but also why they felt as they did. A necessary step toward remedying the conditions that were occasioning such complaints lay not in verifying the facts (the "manifest content") but in determining the personal reference (the "latent content"). For instance, questioning of the worker who complained that his supervisor was a bully elicited the surprising statement that "he doesn't say 'good morning' to the help." Further talk revealed that the worker's dissatisfaction was rooted in his attitude toward *anyone* in authority rather than in the behavior of the supervisor of whom he complained.

This last type of complaint is most difficult to evaluate, as well as to deal with, because of its intermingling of fact and sentiment. Unfortunately, it is also the most frequent.

[1] ROETHLISBERGER, F. J., and W. J. DICKSON, *Management and the Worker*, pp. 255–269, Harvard University Press, Cambridge, Mass., 1940.

Skill in interviewing and in situational thinking is needed to get at the meaning of "disguised complaints" and to find out what, if any, ground for dissatisfaction exists.[1]

COMPLAINTS ALSO TELL US ABOUT MANAGEMENT

By classifying and sifting complaints in this way, we not only learn what employees are feeling but also get a clue to the way in which first-line supervisors are handling personnel. Additional light is thrown on this point if we study the source and scale of expressed dissatisfactions.

Where Are Complaints Coming From?—Are complaints coming from all over the plant? If so, the fault must lie in some major policy. If, however, complaints cluster in one or a few areas, it is more probable that special conditions of work or of supervision need attention. Lastly, if complaints perpetually stem from a few workers, it may be that these people are misplaced or are suffering from some unnecessary tension or are simply maladjusted individuals.

The Number and Rate of Complaints.—The number of complaints coming from any one part of the company may tell us something. The question is, what? If the quantity is unusually large in any one department, section, or group, it is commonly assumed by management that this is a very bad sign; whereas, if there is little or no expressed dissatisfaction in another part of the company, it is often taken for granted that everything is practically perfect there. Such unjustifiable conclusions are frequently used by executives as the basis for comparisons that are certainly odious to supervisors.

When superficial judgments lead executives to point out to one supervisor that another foreman is more efficient because his employees have fewer complaints, material is provided for dissatisfaction and misunderstanding among supervisors. It is easy for an executive to express such a snap judgment, "Why aren't you all like Tom McCann? His men are perfectly happy." If it were equally easy for McCann's fellow supervisors to say what they feel, they might retort, "That's what you think." Actually, the fact may be (and, if so, other supervisors probably know it) that the absence of expressed dissatisfactions is the result of "strong-arm methods" by which a supervisor refuses to recognize complaints. Another supervisor may be receiving and reporting a large number of complaints because he is the kind of person to whom employees can talk and who is not afraid to report the complaints up the line if they imply the need for policy thinking that is outside his authority.

[1] For an example of a disguised complaint, see the case for Chap. 16, A Wage Complaint of the Polishers. Other interesting material is given by BENJAMIN M. SELEKMAN, *op. cit.*, especially Ch. V, "Handling Shop Grievances."

No one can tell *what* is indicated by the quantity of complaints unless he understands the specific situation well enough to know *why* they are being expressed and *at what rate*. The rate is significant, since a large number within a short interval may indicate a releasing of the floodgates, which is a healthy sign. Wherever there are people, there will be dissatisfactions. This human fact must form the starting point for judgment of complaints as an index. If for any reason dissatisfactions have been suppressed, they will come out fast when they are released. If not released in words, they will certainly be expressed sooner or later in undesirable actions, in requests for transfer, or even in quits. When top management accepts this fact, it will be easier to train supervisors to the point of view that employee complaints are not merely time-consuming nuisances but are opportunities for increased understanding.

Thus a small number of complaints is an insufficient index that employee morale is high. This tentative judgment must be confirmed by taking cross bearings on other indexes in the same group. What is shown by the record for accidents, tardiness, absence, and separations? If all these records are good, can our finding be further confirmed by such positive signs as high productive efficiency and evidences of voluntary participation?

Of course, it may be that a large number of complaints does indicate a low degree of employee morale, a poor quality of supervision, or the absence or malfunctioning of a policy, especially when the complaints are spread over a long interval of time. In that case, the large quantity is not indicative of a sudden improvement in the conditions of communication and therefore probably does point to the need for either policy-centered or person-centered thinking, or for both.

The Nature of the Complaint and Grievance Procedure [1]

Further understanding of whether or not management policy is being implemented to promote organizational stability can be obtained by studying the procedure for handling complaints and grievances. The

[1] It is common practice to use the term "grievance" procedure. But use of this word alone is both unconstructive and inaccurate, because it implies that all the dissatisfactions dealt with in this procedure have been improperly handled by management. It would be more constructive to use the term "complaint" procedure, since this would imply the expectation that management will deal fairly with officially expressed dissatisfactions.

Actually, the procedure changes in character as it moves through different levels. The foreman does, or should, handle complaints. At upper levels, and in arbitration, the dissatisfactions have become grievances.

In order to avoid constant use of the cumbersome though logical phrase "complaint and grievance" procedure, we have, where possible, used whichever word applied to the level of action to which we are referring at the time.

establishment and functioning of this procedure are responsibilities of top management and of the union.

The technical requirements can be briefly outlined:

1. The dissatisfied employee should have an opportunity to express his complaint to the supervisor, without fear of retaliation. Where a union is the exclusive bargaining agent of the employee, the shop steward should be present in all cases involving contractual relations.

2. If the complaint is not settled at the first step, it becomes a grievance and should be reduced to writing. It can then be considered by the next higher line-management representative (department head or superintendent) and, in unionized firms, by the business agent or shop committee. There may be successive intermediate steps after this, depending upon the hierarchy of the management and union organization. (Refer to the chart of a typical grievance procedure in Chap. 3, Page 28.)

3. As a final step *within* the organization, an unsettled grievance reaches the top level of management, the chief executive, and, in unionized firms, the international representative of the union, or the union executive board.

4. In an increasing number of grievance procedures, a final step is appeal to an impartial arbitrator or umpire, whose decision the parties agree in advance to accept. Arbitration here is usually limited to grievances involving disputes over the interpretation or application of terms of the labor agreement and not to grievances that might involve a *change* in the agreement.

But, clearly, the technical structure is not enough to distinguish a good grievance procedure from a poor one. Other criteria are needed. For instance:

1. *Is it definite?*—The definiteness of a complaint and grievance procedure is clearly a matter of policy. A satisfactory reply from management cannot be expected when its policy is characterized by anything as vague as the well-meaning attitude often referred to as "the open-door policy." Employees have a right to know just how their complaints are going to be handled. And only by setting up definite procedures can management reasonably expect employees to cooperate by reporting their dissatisfactions at appropriate times, in suitable ways, and to the proper management representative.

2. *Is it simple?*—The complaint and grievance procedure should be easy to explain to all new employees before they begin working for the company, so that every employee can understand what the procedure is. Since it is intended to facilitate communication and collaboration between workers and management, such a procedure should obviously be not only definite and fair but also clear to all. Simplicity of procedure contributes to clarity and also enables management to fulfill a third essential requirement.

3. *Does it function promptly?*—Prompt action is certainly in management's interest, since any delay is costly in the growth and spread of employee dissatisfaction. During the period while a worker is waiting to see what, if anything, management will do to satisfy him, his dissatisfaction is apt to loom very large in his mind. To management, this may seem unreasonable, since, in proportion to the scale of operations in a large enterprise, employee complaints often seem so small as to be practically invisible. When industrial operations involve millions of dollars, an accidental pay shortage of 21 cents may seem to management so trivial that nobody could possibly get excited about it. But experience shows that this is not the case. Added to other causes of dissatisfaction, even such a trifling matter often contributes to the impression that management does not care how workers feel and that this is simply another instance in which a worker has been "gypped." Thus it is more realistic to recognize the psychological fact that anything that annoys a person is important to him. He will brood over it and magnify its significance. And the longer he broods, the more important it will seem to him, until finally this preoccupation may obscure all his more favorable impressions of management.

But such a growth of dissatisfaction within one individual is not the only harmful effect of delay in handling complaints. Dissatisfactions are freely communicated among workers during lunch and rest periods, in the washroom, and even during work time. In this way, complaints are spread among individuals and groups. They lose nothing in the telling, finding fertile soil in the latent antagonisms that are normally felt by workers toward higher management.[1] Furthermore, any unnecessary delay (from the worker's viewpoint, any delay that he does not understand or sympathize with) in itself constitutes a grievance. In union parlance, it is termed "stalling" and is a frequent and bitter complaint against management.

When the personnel administrator has checked a complaint and grievance procedure to see that it embodies all the general features mentioned above and is workable as to its technical details, he is satisfied that top management has done its share. It then remains to be seen how much ability is being demonstrated by the management officials who administer the procedure. Since the machinery to be used and the union agreement (if any) to be referred to are the same throughout the company, the treatment of each case may show significant differences in individual skill between those who deal with complaints or grievances. However, this test must be used with caution, since the attitudes and skills of union officials are also integral factors in the complaint situation. Nevertheless,

[1] *Cf.* Pigors, Paul, and Faith Pigors, "The Legend of the Big Bad Boss (The Attitude of Workers toward Authority)," *Personnel*, Vol. 22, No. 2, pp. 94–101, 1945.

when due account is taken of specific situational factors, something about management ability in handling personnel is to be learned by observing how many steps of the procedure have to be used in settling employee complaints.

Level of Settlement as an Index

If the majority of complaints in a given department are being handled informally between first-line supervision and the worker who feels dissatisfied, or in cooperation with the shop steward who represents him, the complaint procedure is functioning with maximal efficiency. Management is to be congratulated both on the caliber of its first-line supervision [1] and on the nature of its labor relations.

If, however, most of the complaints are being referred to the shop committee as grievances for official settlement with the department head or superintendent at a management-shop committee meeting, some delay is inevitable. Thus the ill effects of the original dissatisfaction have time to grow and spread. Moreover, when a complaint has to be handled on the level of formal discussion, the opportunities are lost for spontaneous minor adjustments between people who work together and for the growth of mutual understanding that might have taken place during an informal settlement in the shop. In formal discussions, the complaint is usually settled with reference to the union contract—that "formal law of the shop." But, necessary and useful though it is, this contract may not always prove adequate to settle underlying dissatisfactions.

When grievances must be taken higher still for settlement, to the level of top management and officials of the international union, the situation becomes increasingly difficult. The original dissatisfaction has now become a genuine issue that divides management and the union unless and until formal agreement can be reached. By this time, it may also come to be regarded as an isolated incident and is therefore far harder to understand than when it was seen in its shop context through the eyes of insiders.

Finally, a maximum expenditure of time and a considerable loss of employee good will are involved if the grievance cannot be settled at all between management and union representatives but must be made the subject of an official arbitration hearing. [2] When this is necessary, such a

---

[1] The personnel administrator's success as a teacher of his own skills, and the freedom he is given by top management to act as a teacher of these to line officials, may both be reflected in the human efficiency of supervisors. All the skills discussed in Chaps. 4, 5, and 6 are needed in handling complaints.

[2] We do not for a moment wish to underestimate the value of voluntary arbitration as a peaceful method of settling labor disputes. However, no personnel man could deny that it would be far better if dissatisfactions never reached such a point that they required a ruling by an outside party. On the other hand, arbitration is useful not only in settling specific issues but even more because its method may be used as a model. All concerned may learn this method of impersonalizing issues and apply it in the shop.

long interval is inevitably consumed between the first expression of the dissatisfaction and the time the arbitrator's decision finally reaches the worker that personnel relations are inevitably subjected to strain. However, the opportunity for arbitration serves as an assurance that the grievance will finally be resolved.

An appeal to outside arbitration may result from a genuine incompatibility of the parties' interpretations of a clause in the labor agreement. In this case, the arbitrator acts as an interpreter of the agreement. However, continual failure of the parties to agree on the issue is a reflection on the personnel administrator.

Most complaints should be handled almost as soon as they are expressed and at the level of first-line supervision. Any dissatisfactions that become grievances that cannot be handled between workers and management even at top levels indicate that collaboration in this case has broken down.[1] In order to facilitate settlement at the level of first-line supervision, top management and the personnel administrator clearly have the responsibility for formulating policies and interpreting them all the way down the line.

Criteria of Success in Handling Complaints and Grievances

When we say that a management representative has "succeeded" in handling a complaint or grievance, precisely what do we mean? Success in any endeavor is properly rated only in terms of what the person is or should be trying to do. In handling employee complaints and grievances, what is the objective? Sometimes it is considered to be the very limited one of hushing up a person who is "squawking;" of suppressing a "gripe." But, as a branch of personnel work, the major aim in every case must be to advance mutual understanding.

Whenever possible, this gain in understanding should also be extended to other employees who, although not necessarily involved in the occasion of the complaint or grievance, are concerned with the underlying prin-

[1] The breakdown may be as much a fault of the union as of management. In a large machine-tool company, for example, union members revolted against their leaders on the ground that they were becoming too management-minded. A new group was voted into office on the slogan, "We won't compromise with management. We'll take every case to arbitration and win for the union." The result of such shortsighted policy was disastrous. Not only did the grievance machinery become clogged with cases pending arbitration (98 cases on the docket), but, with so many disputes to handle, union officers had little time to make an orderly and convincing presentation of the cases. As a result, in almost every decision the arbitrator had to rule against the union. After 3 months of such unsatisfactory experience, the members lost confidence in their new leaders also.

ciples. With this aim in view, the personnel administrator can never be content with the kind of treatment of a complaint that merely keeps people quiet or represents a compromise on a specific issue.

Union officials likewise give evidence of their interest in the policy aspect of handling grievances. Some unions, for instance, differentiate in their "grievance" files between run-of-the-mill complaints and "policy cases." The latter have plant-wide or industry-wide implications and are referred to in planning for contract negotiations.

As an opportunity to gain and to spread understanding, a personnel administrator may apply four test questions by which to judge success in handling a complaint or grievance:

1. Was the case handled so as to bring out its full significance to the parties directly involved?
2. Was the incident closed with a sense of satisfactory adjustments in regard to the specific complaint?
3. Did the solution also provide for an advance of understanding by everyone directly involved, and perhaps also for a spread of understanding among people not immediately concerned?[1]
4. Did the solution increase production?

THE ROLE OF THE PERSONNEL ADMINISTRATOR

The personnel administrator, of course, should not step out of his role by making decisions in the name of line management on complaints or grievances. His function is to develop better understanding all round in regard to causes of dissatisfactions, presentation of complaints, and treatment of grievances, if any. When he is successful in this function, current dissatisfactions can lead to future improvement.

Unfortunately, however, an overenthusiastic personnel administrator sometimes misconceives his proper role and comes to think of himself as a policeman whose function it is to bring foremen into line and *tell* them how to analyze and handle complaints. The confusion that is apt to result from such a misconception is illustrated by the experience of an electrical-goods manufacturing firm. In this company, it had become accepted practice to hold a formal "hearing" in the industrial relations office whenever the foreman and the shop steward could not by themselves settle a complaint.

[1] This objective is not, of course, always attainable. Achievement of this aim can be facilitated by the circulation of decisions or interpretations involving cases that were settled on the higher levels of the grievance procedure. General Motors Corporation, for example, sends out umpire decisions to all members of management who, in supervisory and management conferences, use this material as the basis for discussion and for the development of policy thinking.

A foreman who was called into the industrial relations office to give "his side of the story" usually considered himself being "called on the carpet" and was therefore "on the defensive." Whereas before, in his own office, he was able to act as a sympathetic listener and "friend," he now found himself in the position of a defendant. The worker and his shop representative were the accusers. The union officials gave their moral support and in a certain sense acted as "legal aids." The supervisor of industrial relations acted as "trial examiner." The atmosphere of the meeting was legalistic, and both sides were more intent on "proving their case" than on trying to understand the underlying causes of employee dissatisfaction. Under these more formal conditions, foremen sometimes became embarrassed and undecided. They gave reasons and arguments different from what had been used in the shop, thereby confusing the issue. On such occasions, the supervisor of industrial relations was placed in the painful position of having to ask the foreman to clarify his statements or even of having to correct him in the presence of workers, shop steward, and other union officials. This tended to place the foreman before the worker as one commanding less confidence than did the shop steward. Foremen naturally resented this, expressing their discouragement as follows: "We are nothing any more. If we don't get licked by the shop steward, we get hauled to the office and get licked there. What's the use? We might just as well sit down and say 'Sure!' to everything they say."[1]

SUMMARY

The personnel administrator's purpose in analyzing complaints and grievances is to improve understanding in order to raise employee morale and increase production. In trying to achieve this, he needs to use situational thinking. He applies both logic and observation to differentiate among dissatisfactions, complaints, and grievances and to distinguish among different types of complaint. By using his imagination and the skills of interviewing, he may be able to evaluate the latent content of a disguised complaint. He can then perhaps bring to light a hidden dissatisfaction and thus clear the way either for improvement of material conditions or for better communication.

Policy thinking applied to employee complaints suggests a study of top-management purposes and administrative practices. Is the official procedure definite, simple, and prompt? Do first-line supervisors succeed in using it to settle complaints in the shop? The person-centered approach may be necessary if a personnel administrator is to understand why some foremen are failing to settle complaints before they harden into grievances.

In evaluating the importance for personnel relations of current complaints and grievances, the level of settlement is a useful index. Among

[1] PIGORS, PAUL, and ALFRED D. SHEFFIELD, *Coordinating Structures and Procedures for Handling Dissatisfactions, Case Studies in Industrial Relations*, pp. 10–11, Addison-Wesley Press, Inc., Cambridge, Mass., 1944.

other things, it determines the length of time during which an individual dissatisfaction can grow and spread.

Other aspects of the time factor that repay study in connection with employee dissatisfactions are the rate at which complaints are coming in and the stage of union-management relations. Is the union so securely established that it can afford to screen out unwarranted and trifling employee complaints? Or is the ruling faction so insecure that it must press unreasonable complaints for fear of incurring the criticism of the rival faction?

Finally, the personnel administrator should ask, "When management does handle complaints and grievances, has understanding grown and spread as much as possible?"

Such a study of employee complaints and grievances as well as of management skills should be helpful in removing legitimate causes for dissatisfaction. And, by keeping track of these and other indexes of organizational stability, the personnel administrator should be able to inform line officials as to the current state of employee morale.

Supplying this information, however, is only part of his job. If he finds that morale is low in some area, what can he recommend that management do to raise it? If morale is high, can he suggest anything to prevent difficulties from arising and to keep conditions such that work in the company is a satisfying experience? And, if team spirit is markedly higher in one section of the company than in others, what can be learned from this that can be constructively applied to raise the level elsewhere?

This constructive and preventive approach applies the method of policy thinking to all management dealings with personnel. After diagnosing the current state of organizational stability and morale, the personnel administrator checks over existing policies and procedures by which the work force is being built, to see whether or not they are promoting a high order of teamwork.

D. BUILDING AND MAINTAINING WORK TEAMS

INTRODUCTION TO BUILDING AND MAINTAINING
WORK TEAMS: A PERSONNEL POLICY SYSTEM

Thus far we have discussed three aspects of the personnel point of view. Section A presented the broad function of the personnel administrator. Section B described a general method of understanding. Section C called attention to methods of diagnosing individual and organizational stability. In these ways, we have seen the personnel administrator thinking and observing. Interviewing was the nearest approach to action. In the following chapters, we shall see how the personnel administrator applies situational thinking to promote stability by procedures that build and maintain work teams.

Management decisions for personnel activities should be integrated into a single policy system. When this is done, all areas of activity have certain features in common. For instance:

1. Every area has its own policies. In each, the most general directives are determined by the chief executive, while more specific principles of action are developed (subject to top-management approval) by the management representatives responsible for that area.

2. All policies and procedures for every area are consistent with the policies and practices in every other area.

If the whole policy system is built around the personnel point of view, it further embodies such general principles of human nature as

1. Every employee is a person and shall be treated as such within the limits of policy requirements. As a person, he has certain rights, such as

   a. To use and to develop those capacities which are relevant to organizational purpose.

   b. To hear and to be heard about what vitally concerns him.

   c. To receive due recognition and reward for services rendered, and appropriate assistance in meeting those needs and responsibilities that are central to his life as a whole.

2. Every individual can be more of a person when he voluntarily participates in an organization whose requirements he recognizes as more important than his purely personal wishes. As a member of the company community, he has certain duties, such as

   a. To meet quality and quantity standards of job performance.

   b. To maintain a responsible attitude toward the company and toward his fellow employees.

c. To participate in company progress by making constructive suggestions and, when necessary, official complaints.

d. To abide by mutual agreements, policies, and rules as long as these are in force.

When these rights and duties characterize the activity toward and by all employees, joint responsibility and mutual service make the company a well-ordered community.

UNITY OF THE EMPLOYMENT PROCESS

In order to keep personnel activity at this level, it is essential that everyone in the employment relationship should recognize the unity of the whole employment process. Each phase in this process should be consistently shaped toward the aim of developing individual and organizational stability from the first employment contact, through all intermediary stages, up to and including the final separation. And all allied procedures should be planned to contribute to the same goal.

Recruitment (attracting a suitable number of desirable and qualified individuals) is the first step in promoting effective collaboration in small work teams, by people who also feel a genuine sense of membership in the company as a whole. The discriminating judgments made in *selection* (eliminating the unsuitable and choosing those who seem technically and humanly qualified) are subsequently confirmed, or in a few cases invalidated, by the evidence given in the first work assignment. This stage of *placement* is both a decision and an experiment in which management and workers begin to find out how they can collaborate.

Induction (introducing the new worker to the nontechnical features of his work life) and *training* (his technical preparation) precede and follow placement as essential steps in helping the newcomer to make the necessary adjustments. *Follow-up* is a continuing procedure through which the judgment made in selection is kept up to date by being confirmed, amplified, or corrected in current work situations, and in which the worker receives the benefit of being recognized as a person. The wise use of *employee rating* leads to the development of many workers through *transfer*, *upgrading*, and *promotion* by avenues of transfer and ladders of promotion that are logically constructed by *job analysis* and made known to all employees. Employee rating and job analysis also play a part in the uncongenial task of *downgrading*. Being known to all in advance, this method of ensuring fairness forms a ground on which union leaders, workers, and management representatives can meet even in the difficult procedures of *layoff* and *discharge*. *Discipline* is consciously related to effective teamwork both as cause and as effect.

A sound *wage policy* and a consistent *wage structure* promote the individual employee's sense of security and also contribute to organizational stability by recognizing the relative values of different kinds of work. Appropriate *methods of wage payment* provide financial incentives to greater production and acceptance of new output standards. Reasonable *working hours* strike a balance between technical demands and human needs.

A program of *employee services* expresses management's recognition of needs and responsibilities other than those directly connected with job requirements. Concern for *employee health and safety* is implemented in ways that further strengthen the sense of mutual responsibility between management and workers. Finally, *voluntary participation* is sought from all company members, as working partners of top management, in meeting problems of production and of group living.

All the procedures to be described in the following sections can be applied through situational thinking, in which management balances policy requirements and individual needs. When such a policy system is thoroughly understood and consistently applied by all management representatives, workers can feel the core of purpose that unifies all levels and types of management. Such unity within the directing group makes it easier for workers to anticipate and cooperate with management in all phases of company activity.

This continuing activity is set in motion for each individual at the beginning of the employment relationship. If the personnel point of view is accepted, its application must begin at this point. How shall it be put into effect?

Chapter 10

Recruitment, Selection, and Placement

> The act of hiring a man carries with it the presumption that he will stay with the firm. Sooner or later his ability to perform his work and to get along in the group in which he works will become matters of first importance. This suggests critical examination of current methods of selecting workers, with a view to developing the best job of placement of which industry is capable.
>
> GUY W. WADSWORTH, JR.[1]

What is the purpose of the three principal hiring procedures, recruitment, selection, and placement? From the personnel point of view, management is trying to do far more than merely to fill current vacancies. If this were all that needed to be done, the simplest formula would be vacancy—requisition—fill. But such an oversimplified hiring process would not promote the larger aim of building morale by achieving a balance between personnel mobility and organizational equilibrium. In order to advance this purpose, certain policy decisions have validity for all companies, despite specific differences in their product or service.

CENTRALIZED HIRING PROCEDURES

In the first place, if the policies of top management are to be consistently and efficiently implemented in plant-wide hiring, all employment activity must center in one place. Decentralized employment procedures, such as those which continue to be practiced in certain organizations and industries (*e.g.*, east coast longshore work), furnish ample evidence of the inefficiency and inconsistency resulting from a failure to coordinate related activities. Only when all requisitions go through one center and all

[1] "Tools of the Personnel Trade," *Mechanical Engineering*, ASME, January, 1940, p. 13.

employment records are kept up to date in the same place is there a maximum possibility for efficiency and for the type of follow-up that progressively improves employment methods by checking on the success of previous hiring.

If the policy of centralized hiring is adequately explained by top management, line officials need not feel that, in accepting the services of staff experts, they suffer any loss in prestige or responsibility. It can easily be shown that the work of the employment department (usually a subordinate unit of the personnel division) is a supplement to the judgment of line officials and not a substitute. Modern hiring procedures include a type of interviewing that requires familiarity with up-to-date psychological knowledge and various kinds of test that need to be administered and diagnosed by experts. This work gears in at various points with the knowledge and training of line officials.

Centralized hiring procedures, properly conceived, are a complement to and not an invasion of the line supervisor's responsibilities. He should still retain the right to accept or reject the applicant sent to his department by the employment manager. But, since he ordinarily has neither the time nor the skill to perform the recruitment and selection process himself, he can benefit by the assistance of a central staff agency.

The personnel administrator has an opportunity to advise top management in planning the recruitment procedures that are part of the centralized hiring that is administered by the employment department. He should therefore develop specific policies of his own. These, of course, are subject to the approval of top management. What are some of them?

SUBSIDIARY POLICY REQUIREMENTS

Since the maintenance of individual and organizational stability is a major aim of management, it should be considered even in the first phase of employment procedure by keeping a balance between the number of people recruited and management's current expectations as to hiring needs in the near future. Management should know at all times how much and what kind of ability is required. Only on the basis of such knowledge can recruitment needs be accurately estimated, taking into account the rate of company expansion or contraction, organizational structure, and current data on labor turnover.[1]

[1] During the Second World War, many firms made a complete inventory of their current man power and future requirements for the first time when they were required to prepare "Manning Tables" for the War Manpower Commission. For each job in the plant, the following information was compiled: (1) minimum training in hours, (2) present number employed, divided by "white" and "other" and subdivided by male and female, (3) the percentage of total departmental and plant employment

Second, promises made during recruitment should not oversell either the company or any job in the plant. If they do, employees will inevitably become dissatisfied when experience shows them the difference between recruitment talk and employment facts. And, in whatever form their dissatisfaction is expressed, it militates against organizational stability. Thus any method of high-pressure recruiting salesmanship defeats the long-run aim of the whole hiring process.

Third, recruitment procedures should be well adapted to relevant differences in the kind of employees to be hired. Every industrial firm needs a comparatively large number of workers, both men and women, to perform unskilled and semiskilled operations in the factory and office, and also workers skilled in various crafts. Members of this group must usually be able to develop versatility, because, in addition to their regular assigned duties, they may be needed as substitutes for other workers, as teachers of new employees, or as understudies for minor supervisory positions (acting as jobsetters, group leaders, etc.). Employees who are differentiated according to these three degrees of skill are commonly classified in one main category as hourly rated workers. A second main category of employees is composed of the comparatively small number of candidates hired primarily for what they will become. This group is needed to assure a supply of management replacements and to form a pool of potential technicians.

Although these two groups are hired for different purposes, there is nothing to prevent able workers from advancing by upgrading and promotion into a higher group. Such advancement is possible both because initial judgments are necessarily tentative and because workers develop experience and ability on the job. Thus no employee who is hired for routine work is barred from advancing to whatever level is warranted by his ability. Conversely, candidates for salaried positions are given special opportunities but not the promise of advancement until they have demonstrated the requisite ability.

---

represented by each job, (4) whether the job could be filled by handicapped workers, (5) whether the job could be reengineered or broken down to utilize a different type of labor, and (6) additional future labor needs on each job, listed according to whether they could be met by upgrading and transfers within the plant or by recruiting from the outside. Successive monthly requirements and maximum needs to meet anticipated production schedules were also indicated, together with the minimum experience required for each job. This information not only gave employers an indication of their future labor requirements on each job but also revealed the necessity for training and upgrading and for better utilization of women, older workers, and handicapped persons. For further details, see "The Manning Table Plan for Manpower Inventory," *Factory Management and Maintenance*, Vol. 100, pp. 74–82, 1942.

Hiring procedures for future technicians and management replacements differ so much in each case that we shall not discuss them here.[1] At least two policy requirements, however, are generally valid. Since this type of employee is essential to have and difficult to find, some firms recruit on the principle that it is impossible to have too much of a good thing. But this proves quite untrue of top-caliber employees. They become restless if kept too long in subordinate positions where their major capacities remain unused and therefore partly undeveloped. Management's aim to promote individual stability can be fulfilled only when recruitment of this group is limited to the number that can be promoted within a reasonable length of time.

A further policy limitation to outside recruitment is imposed by the desirability of leaving room for advancement from the ranks of employees of exceptional ability. This policy has a healthy effect on employee morale and, when it can be put into practice, promotes organizational stability.

In hiring routine workers, procedures vary markedly according to whether these individuals are expected to take skilled, semiskilled, or unskilled jobs, and there should be further slight variations in approach to recognize individual differences. But recruitment, selection, and placement of this group should follow one general pattern.

REQUISITIONING WORKERS

The supervisor's hiring activity begins with the requisition. This should be made on the basis of accurate job specifications to be drawn up by the first-line supervisor in cooperation with a specially trained job analyst (usually from the employment department).[2] Two points of importance in regard to the requisition are that it be clear-cut as to the exact demands of the job (the technical job content being still the same as that stated in the job description) and that it be definite and realistic as to what the foreman wants. Some supervisors submit requisitions that call for supermen. This is apparently done on the theory that, allowing a due margin for errors by "those guys in the employment department," such requisitions will produce candidates somewhere above the level of a moron.

Effective collaboration between supervisors and the employment department is important at this point as at others, for all concerned. If supervisors are cooperative and personnel workers have in the past

---

[1] For an excellent discussion of policies and procedures concerning the recruitment of potential managerial and professional personnel, see CULLEN, G. L., "Recruitment and In-plant Training of College Graduates," *Personnel*, May, 1947, pp. 388–404.

[2] For a discussion of job description and analysis, see Chap. 16.

proved efficient and not officious, good teamwork between line and staff should not be difficult to obtain, and each official can make a special contribution to an employment process that shall attract and develop qualified employees.[1]

RECRUITMENT

Chronologically, of course, recruitment may come before requisition in filling any given vacancy, because the employment department is recruiting all the time. Thus it is to be expected that, except in periods of extreme labor shortage, an appropriate number of promising candidates to fill future vacancies will always be on file in the employment department. This list is gathered from a variety of sources and includes qualified former employees who have been laid off or who for some reason have voluntarily left the company. The employment manager keeps in touch with former employees so that he may inform them when suitable openings occur. As former company members in good standing, they will naturally be given preference over strangers.

Contact with potential candidates not previously employed by the company is established by what amounts to advertising in one form or another. The best means of advertising, because it is both the most effective and the cheapest, is not done by the employment manager at all but is carried on by present or former employees who tell their friends that the firm is a desirable place to work.

The employment manager may usefully make the same point, though obviously with less force. In written advertisements and by personal contacts (formal or informal), he reaches the leaders of a variety of local groups such as schools, churches, trade unions, private employment agencies, clubs, the prison association, etc. These leaders are usually interested in knowing that a reputable company in the community is looking for prospective candidates to fill permanent positions. Obviously, no written or spoken words to this effect will carry weight in the long run except as supported by the testimony of satisfied employees.

In addition to these private groups, the employment manager should also keep in touch with the local office of the public employment service. As a central clearing house for the local labor-market area, the public employment service knows more about the supply of various types of labor, relative to the demand, than does the average employer. It is in a

---

[1] For an amusing description of the minor headaches to which the employment manager is sometimes subjected in his relations with supervisors and department heads, see E. J. CROSBY, "Subterfuges I Have Known," *Personnel*, Vol. 18, No. 6, pp. 355–359, 1942.

position to assist him in recruiting applicants for jobs according to his own specifications. Also, through its interarea clearance system, the public employment service can tap a wider labor market than can ordinarily be reached by a single employer. Known during the war as the U.S. Employment Service, this agency made a valuable contribution to the war effort. Its continued value in peacetime will be determined in large part by the use that employers make of it as an aid in recruitment and selection.

Recruitment procedures may be improved if the personnel administrator carefully studies the correlation between sources of labor, methods of recruitment, and subsequent job performance. He should be able to answer the question, "From what sources and by what methods have we secured our most satisfactory workers?" But, however efficient recruitment becomes, not all the candidates will prove acceptable as regular workers. The next phase, selection, is a more careful screening of potential candidates from the lists made up by recruitment.

SELECTION

In selection, instead of ending with the name of a potential candidate in a file, we are moving toward actual placement on a job. If this is to be successful, management needs to learn and to weigh a number of factors about the potential employee. How shall it be judged whether his employment in this company, under present conditions, in a current opening will actually work out to the advantage both of the company and of the candidate?

In seeking information on all relevant factors, the employment manager may make use of the following techniques[1] though not necessarily in the order given here:

1. *Preliminary Interview.*—The first interview may be conducted by an assistant in the employment department and is management's opportunity for a preliminary decision as to the applicant's suitability. It may be obvious at once that a given individual is not suited to the kind of job for which there are current or expected openings, since he does not meet certain requirements as to size, physical strength, or age. Or it may be apparent that the person will not fit in well with the company's present personnel. Such a decision need not lay management open to an accusa-

---

[1] The reception of applicants is not discussed here, since it is not a fact-finding technique. It is, however, important that this reception be in keeping with management's personnel point of view, since this first contact may go a long way toward answering the applicant's unspoken question, "Is this a good place to work?"

tion of "discrimination,"[1] since congeniality of work associates is as legitimate an item for policy decision as is technical ability. In fact, a candidate may be "undesirable" for a routine job because he has too much education or intelligence to be contented and acceptable on a work team where there is a current vacancy.

If the applicant seems to be a likely candidate, the preliminary interview should conclude with reassurance about the various tests to be taken (if any are used). It should be made clear that tests are administered to determine just how good the candidate is and where his special abilities lie, rather than to trick him into making mistakes. Tests are so commonly regarded as mantraps, that workers almost always need reassurance on this point. When the preliminary interview precedes the filling out of the application blank, some explanation may also be offered about the blank itself.

2. *The Application Blank.*—If properly designed, the application blank has the following advantages for many kinds of work:

   a. It constitutes a simple test as to the candidate's ability to spell, to write legibly, and to answer factual questions rapidly and accurately.

   b. Combined with material gathered later during testing, it gives the employment manager a line on the candidate before the main employment interview begins.

   c. Some candidates find it easier to think out the answers alone than if the same questions were asked during an interview.

   d. It gives the candidate assurance that his desire for work and some of his qualifications are on record with the company.

But these advantages are to be realized only under certain conditions. The application blanks should conform to the following pattern:

   a. They should be brief, in order not to discourage workers who are unaccustomed to doing much writing.

   b. They should contain only items that, according to company experience, are correlated with job success. It follows from this that each company should develop its own application form, preferably after studying blanks used by other companies.

---

[1] Many companies modified their application forms, hiring procedures, and personnel practices after the establishment of the Federal Fair Employment Practice Committee (FEPC) as a war agency under Executive Order 9346. This agency was set up "to promote the fullest utilization of manpower and eliminate discriminatory employment practices." Many states have subsequently enacted antidiscrimination laws. In order to conform with the spirit of these laws, management must make sure that no applicant will be discriminated against because of his race, color, or religion,

c. They should not contain any questions that might tempt a candidate to answer dishonestly. For instance, the question why the applicant left his last job is preferably put to the former employer.

3. *Investigation of Previous Employment History.*—By checking the information given on the application blank and that gained from other sources, the employment manager has an opportunity not only to double check on facts but also to get a line on the applicant's candor and accuracy.[1]

4. *The Physical Examination.*—Before the physical examination is made, special reassurance should be given that, like other tests, it is used to help both the applicant and the company rather than to spy out weaknesses.[2] It should be recognized, however, that the company must protect its employees against the risk of infection from communicable diseases and itself against the risk of claims for compensation from individuals who are afflicted with disabilities such as hernia, for instance. The medical examination should be both general and thorough. If no company doctor is available, it may be given by any qualified physician who has adequate knowledge of the company's job requirements. Data disclosed by examination and questioning may be supplemented, if necessary, by X rays and laboratory tests. The findings should be carefully recorded so as to give a complete medical history, the scope of current physical capacities, and the nature of disabilities, if any. All information should be kept confidential.

5. *Employment Tests.*—Before a given company decides whether or not to use employment tests, the following general questions should be answered:

a. Is top management prepared to spend the money required in developing tests that are well suited to the specific company and in hiring the experts needed to administer them? Tests are comparatively new

---

[1] Letters of recommendation are not discussed here, since they seem not to be a sound device for getting reliable information. The writers are usually more concerned with avoiding disagreeableness than in stating their considered opinion or describing their experience with the candidate. When previous employers are consulted, it is desirable to do so over the telephone or, if necessary, by calling on them. For an excellent article on "Past Employment-reference-inquiry Forms," see HUNT H. UNGER, *Personnel*, Vol. 20, No. 6, pp. 357–368, 1944.

[2] For example, according to a report by Ethel M. Spears in the *Conference Board Management Record*, July, 1945, approximately 80 per cent of the epileptics in this country are capable of doing industrial work, and about 80 per cent of this group are actually employed. Discriminating placement is important, however, especially in the subgroup having periodic epileptic seizures. These individuals should not be assigned to work at heights, around moving and unprotected machinery, or at jobs where, if they fell, they might suffer from burns. Information on the employment of epileptics may be obtained from The National Association to Control Epilepsy, New York, N. Y.

tools in industry. No adequate estimation of their worth can be made in a given company until considerable evidence has been collected and correlated with its job specifications resulting from job evaluation, production standards, employee rating, and labor turnover. This kind of work cannot properly be done by amateurs. Such tests can actually be misleading unless expertly administered and diagnosed.

b. Does everyone concerned recognize the limitations of tests, and will their pitfalls be avoided? Test results are not guarantees of performance. Special dangers to be avoided are the suppositions that a single brief test can provide significant results and that standard tests are necessarily useful for a given company's requirements.

c. Are supervisors ready to accept tests as an improvement in hiring procedure? Unless department heads believe that tests are worth experimenting with, they will probably not support test findings. In that case, tests will neither promote line and staff collaboration nor reduce labor turnover.

If, knowing all these limitations, line management from the top down wants to cooperate with the personnel administrator and the safety director in experimenting with tests, the results may be of great value.

a. As a measurement of the extent to which an applicant's abilities and disabilities fit or unfit him for job demands, in order to eliminate from hazardous occupations those who seem to be "accident-prone."

b. As a check on reported experience.

c. As a basis for objective comparison between applicants.

d. As an aid in setting up standards for employment procedure such that predictions can be traced, checked, and progressively improved.

There has been considerable experimentation with tests of numerous kinds. What is their reliability and validity in the sense that test results consistently measure what we wish to measure? In the selection of hourly rated workers, mechanical, clerical, and trade tests have proved to be most satisfactory. Tests of this type are generally classified as *performance tests.* They are a refinement of the work-sample technique and are used to measure what an employee actually can do.

For factory jobs, management is concerned not only with what an employee can do but also with his safety. Jobs differ according to their rate of accident liability, *i.e.,* as to whether or not there are special job risks. People differ according to their accident-proneness; *i.e.,* in an unselected group, whatever the job, some individuals have a disproportionate number of accidents. For the safety of accident-prone persons and for the sake of others who work with them, it is important to keep these individuals away from jobs where the rate of accident liability is high, especially if this rate is associated with a high rate of accident severity. In order to protect workers, there has been considerable experimentation with tests to appraise accident-proneness. In relation to skilled work, it has been possible to measure one factor that has considerable prediction value—hand-eye coordination. Those who do well in tests of hand-eye coordination have a lower accident rate and a higher rate of productive efficiency than those who do badly.

In relation to unskilled work, this factor seems not to have the same validity, and no tests have yet been developed that enable advance predictions of accident-proneness among unskilled workers.

Performance tests in general are subject to the limitation that other factors are responsible for a large percentage of job failures. The general level of intelligence is one other item about which the employment manager needs information. Thus another group of tests is used to forecast an employee's ability to learn. Such *aptitude tests* are more difficult to validate, since they are used to forecast future performance after training. Furthermore, they usually measure general ability, which is expected to be applied to particular jobs. They are also open to the objection that differences in background may account for differences in test results. When a battery of tests is used, something about intelligence can probably be deduced, although it is sometimes doubtful whether the results are as pertinent to the job situation as data to be gained by careful interviewing. It should in any case be noted that test objectives must be formulated with care. Our objective is not always that of finding individuals who demonstrate superior ability. Sound placement is as important as selection. For instance, in placing routine workers, especially for repetitive factory jobs, the most intelligent candidates are not necessarily the most acceptable. Study of employees who are making good on the job now open usually shows that people with a specific level of intelligence, not always the highest, are most successful. On that same job, an employee who has much more or much less intelligence is liable to boredom or overstrain. Furthermore, since he is to work in a group whose regular members have one general level of intelligence, he will more easily be assimilated as a teammate if his intelligence is at about the same level. If he gives evidence of superior intelligence, fellow employees are apt to deride him as a "brain truster" or "quiz kid."

It is generally known that interest and ability to get along with other people are important factors in job success. With this in mind, psychologists have devised a third group of tests to measure the more complex aspects of *temperament and personality*. When used as a supplement to performance and aptitude tests, they have a negative value in weeding out candidates who have the required skills but are likely to become misfits because of personal conflicts or maladjustments.[1]

However, even in the case of so-called "normal" and able people, the employment manager still needs most of all to know about each job applicant: *Will* this person do all that he *can?*

In hiring workers who are expected to fill or to prepare themselves for skilled jobs, a tentative answer to this question is usually sought in the main employment interview. In regard to applicants for unskilled and semiskilled jobs, judgment on this matter is made only by the first-line supervisor during the probationary period.

6. *The Employment Interview.*—In many companies, this interview is the only tool used in selection. In all companies, it is a valuable one when carried out with skill and care. Pitfalls to be avoided by the interviewer are

  a. Thinking that in one brief interview anyone can make a complete and reliable diagnosis of a person's character or clearly forecast his future achievements.
  b. Overselling the job or the company on the basis of what is offered to exceptional employees. For the average worker, this inevitably leads to disappointment.
  c. Being so familiar with job and company requirements, or having repeated them so often, that many points are carelessly described or even omitted.
  d. Being unduly influenced by trivial mannerisms or by resemblance and dissimilarity to other people whom the interviewer likes or dislikes.
  e. Assuming that the interviewer's uncorroborated judgment is more valid than any or all other evidence gathered about the candidate.
  f. Assuming that the sole function of the interviewer is to accept or reject the candidate. Every type of interview can succeed as a human experience if courtesy is preserved throughout. If a candidate must be rejected at the end of this talk, courtesy is of special importance, because this one interview may determine the applicant's opinion of the company. It may also play a part in

---

[1] The whole field of personality tests needs development and doubtless will be carried further. If industry cooperates intelligently with psychologists, it should be possible to obtain results that are of considerable value in the selection and follow-up of employees. At the present time, personality tests are useful to the employment manager not primarily as a substitute for the diagnostic skills used in interviewing but chiefly because they give clues that often lead to significant insight when followed up in the employment interview.

conditioning his attitude toward other companies and toward his own future.

In order to avoid these risks, the employment interviewer should be personnel-minded and have certain other qualifications. He should be skilled in interview techniques, be able to talk and understand the language of the majority of applicants, be thoroughly familiar with the company's range of job opportunities and with the wages paid for similar jobs in local industry, and be a perennial student of local labor conditions, labor policies, relevant legislation, and current developments in his own industry. For these reasons, the main interview should usually be conducted by the employment manager himself, who presumably has superior qualifications in all these areas.

The primary function of this main interview (when used in conjunction with the other techniques described above) is to complete or to correct the picture whose outlines have been blocked in by the other selection procedures. Details of personality are filled in during an interview by frankly depending on the personal impressions that, by the use of objective standards and tests, have been subordinated during other pre-employment procedures.

Conducting the Employment Interview.—Much of what was said about interviewing in Chap. 6 applies to the employment interview. But planning can be more definite when it is known in advance what the subject matter will be than when the direction of talk cannot be predicted.

In preparing for this interview, the employment manager may either use a check list or merely go over in his mind the material already gathered about the applicant. He will also want to do some preliminary thinking about the job for which this individual seems best fitted. Such preparation enables the employment manager to make a tentative schedule, mental or written, of the topics to be covered during the interview according to the order of importance and the sequence in which they can most easily be introduced. He also thinks out in advance the kind of observation that it seems most important to make, either because of inconsistencies in data previously gathered or because there are indications of unusual qualifications or possible disabilities.

During the interview itself, the employment manager has in mind certain questions that he usually does not put directly to the applicant. For instance, he may be interested to know: Why is this person applying for work in this company? What values does he expect to get here besides money? Will his needs and values fit in with what we can give him? What seem to be his job qualifications? How will he work out on the job? What are his potentialities? Is he a stable person?

Using such mental questions as guides, a progressive evaluation can be made of information obtained during the interview, correlated both with data previously gathered about this person and with knowledge of company practice and specific jobs. Some of these judgments are obviously more difficult to make than others. For instance, in interviewing an applicant for the job of telephone operator, it is easy to decide whether or not she has a "good voice" but far more difficult to judge her emotional stability.

Some of the necessary information is obtained by asking direct questions. In doing this, the interviewer should exercise some caution.[1] The questions should be stated in words whose meaning will be clear to the applicant—*i.e.*, insofar as possible in terms of the individual's context of experience. Second, inquiries should not be put in the form of leading questions, *i.e.*, suggesting a specific answer. For instance, the question, "How do you feel about the work I have outlined?" is preferable to "Don't you think the work I have outlined is interesting?" Trick questions should never be used. They often confuse and antagonize the applicant. Thus they are out of keeping with the relation into which management wants to enter with every employee, beginning with preliminary contacts. Other precautions to be observed are that questions should be asked one at a time and not be so rapid or so numerous as to confuse the applicant. All should be pertinent to the work situation.

This last point needs further comment. Sometimes questions are relevant to the work situation though not directly connected with the job itself. For instance, if a married woman is applying for a job, the interviewer needs to know whether she has young children and, if so, what arrangements can be made for their care. Experience shows that no mother should undertake to work on the night shift if she is entirely responsible for the care of young children during the whole day. When such a situation is revealed during an interview, tact is needed to help the applicant understand that it is a sense of responsibility toward workers and not indifference to their needs that prevents management from employing a person who would inevitably be subjected to overstrain.

During the interview, the employment manager may come to feel that the candidate, though a desirable person, is not likely to succeed in the job for which he has applied and has been tested. In this case, the employment interview is an opportunity to steer the candidate toward another job in which he may excel. The aim here is, if possible, to make assets out of liabilities by matching some special lack or idiosyncrasy with a specific

[1] *Cf.* DRAKE, FRANCIS S., *Manual of Employment Interviewing*, Research Report No. 9, American Management Association, New York, 1946.

company condition.[1] For example, if hearing is not a necessary job qualification, a deaf person may satisfactorily be used in a noisy place. Again, a person who is shy and introvertive may not mind working on a single-machine job or on the "graveyard" shift. In a large Eastern corporation, it was found that a special type of inspection caused headaches and eyestrain to people who had inadequate muscular control or farsighted vision, but not to nearsighted people. Thereafter, nearsighted girls or women were steered toward this work.

An important step to be taken with likely candidates, either in this interview or at some other time before placement, is to give an accurate picture of job requirements and company standards. In most companies, some explanations are offered during the employment interview about what the company expects from its employees.[2] During talk about the job, it may be possible to predict whether a given applicant will find his work monotonous. Monotony is often spoken of as though it were a feature of the job itself, but actually it describes an individual's attitude toward a job. When candidates during selection can be steered away from the type of work that seems to them monotonous, time and nervous strain are saved at the stages of placement and follow-up.

If for any reason the interviewer concludes during the conversation that the applicant cannot be accepted, a tactful but clear statement of this fact should be made. It is tempting to let the rejected applicant leave without putting into words the unpalatable truth. But it is kinder to reject an applicant promptly than to allow him to realize gradually why he has received no word about the job for which he is waiting. The interviewer should also give the ground for the rejection if he thinks there is a reasonable expectation that this will be used constructively by the applicant.

Even when the interview confirms the favorable impression gained from other material, the applicant is not definitely accepted as a regular worker at this point. He is only classified as apparently desirable. This tentative judgment needs to be confirmed by actual tryout and approved by the supervisor who will be responsible for the candidate's work if he is accepted at the end of the probationary period. Thus the successful employment interview is followed by introducing the candidate to his future supervisor, who, if he decides to accept him, will show the new employee

[1] In this connection, see the excellent handbook, *Selective Placement for the Handicapped*, U. S. Employment Service, U. S. Government Printing Office, Washington, D. C., 1945.

[2] This step is part of induction and is discussed in Chap. 12.

his workplace, acquaint him with his fellow employees, and explain exactly what the job requirements are.

PLACEMENT: AN EXPERIMENTAL DECISION

Placement has an experimental element, but for routine workers it is a decisive step and should consist in matching what the supervisor has reason to think the new employee can do with what the job *demands* (job requirements), *imposes* (in strain, working conditions, etc.), and *offers* (in the form of pay rate, interest, companionship with others, promotional possibilities, etc.). It is not easy to match all these factors for a new worker who is still in many ways an unknown quantity. For this reason, the first placement usually carries with it the status of probationer.

If the company is unionized, probation is specifically defined as a trial period, usually 1 to 3 months, at the end of which period the worker who makes good becomes a regular employee. During this time, the union will usually accept without question management's decision to discharge an unsatisfactory probationer. But, once a worker has achieved the status of a regular employee, management can discharge only for cause. It is therefore obvious that the supervisor who authorizes the transition from probationer to regular employee makes a decision that is of great importance to management.

THE QUESTION OF INTERIM PLACEMENTS

If there is no current opening that seems suitable for a specific worker, some companies seek to hold a desirable employee by offering temporary placement in any available job no matter how unsuitable. The excuse made for such a sacrifice to expediency is that the candidate is placed with the company and may be transferred to the desired position as soon as an opening occurs. But, from the viewpoint of employment policy, such placement is ill-advised, because it leaves too much room for misunderstanding and for development of individual and organizational instability. The following is a case in point.

A likely looking boy applied for the opportunity of becoming a machinist apprentice. Unfortunately, the class was full and the next one was not due to start for 6 months. In the meantime, the boy was placed as a helper to an elderly rough grinder who had been with the company for 20 years and who therefore was presumably a well-satisfied and stable employee. A month later, the boy was slated for discharge on the ground that he was uncooperative and slovenly in his work. Only during an exit interview was the root of the difficulty uncovered, so that the new employee could be spared the humiliation of having failed on his first job. During the interview, it was brought out that the worker whom the boy was helping had jeered at his aspirations to make something of himself and scoffed at the idea that the company would actually train him as an apprentice. He assured the boy that the talk of training was only " a come-on-game." "Why not get wise to yourself? I used to think I could make something of myself, too. And look at me! What have I got to show for 20 years of faithful service?" Exposed to such defeatism and without the encouragement that he should have received in follow-up interviews, the boy had become discouraged and demoralized. After the talk, he was placed as a helper to a more satisfied worker and was reassured at intervals until the time came for him to start his apprentice training.

Although interim placements can, of course, be more skillfully handled than this one, they are unsound in principle because they ask too much of everyone concerned. Marking time is always a strain, the ill effects of which are usually communicated to others in the work group. Normally, the worker is placed on the job for which he is thought fit and for which a requisition was made. If he proves satisfactory after adequate induction, training, and probation, he is accepted as a regular employee.

Summary

Modern hiring methods are an excellent illustration of the way in which policy thinking can determine procedures for typical situations and yet leave room for adaptation to special cases and for unique conditions.

The broad purposes of top management can be an effective force at the work level only when hiring procedures are centralized. Dignified and effective recruiting builds a list of qualified individuals who within a reasonable period can expect to be seriously considered for employment in the company. Fairness to all applicants and management's general aim for every employee can be achieved by the use during selection of various techniques to assess relevant individual differences. When a variety of selection methods is used by experts, the applicant's skill, potentialities, and personality are more likely to be fairly appraised than when they were assessed only by the old-line foreman at the gate. Especially valuable in selection is the main employment interview, which should be planned, conducted, and evaluated by an expert.

The key management representative during an initial placement is the first-line supervisor, whose responsibility it is to determine which probationers are acceptable as regular employees.

When recruitment, selection, and placement are all seen as steps toward an enduring employment relationship and are progressively improved by subsequent evaluation of successes and failures on the job, labor turnover can be kept at a low figure, and new employees can rapidly come to feel a sense of membership in the company community.

During these initial hiring procedures, as well as in the follow-up and development of workers, the activity of the first-line supervisor is important for good personnel relations. He may have started as a regular worker and been gradually promoted to the management level, or he may have been hired expressly as a candidate for this supervisory position. In any case, his qualifications and preparation for the job are so important that we devote the entire next chapter to a consideration of his selection and training.

Chapter 11

Selection and Training
of Supervisors

Foremen are not really the forgotten people of industry,
many of them might be more aptly described as the confused and uninformed members of management.

AMERICAN MANAGEMENT ASSOCIATION[1]

A large part of the success of any personnel program depends upon the
first-line supervisors who are called upon to apply personnel policies and
procedures in their dealings with subordinates. Helping to select and
train supervisors is therefore an important function of the personnel administrator. It is one of the ways in which he does his job with and through
line management.

To be most effective, supervisory training should be directly related
to the needs and policies of the organization rather than being based
primarily on general information, which makes up the subject matter of
canned training courses. Good training helps supervisors actually to be
management representatives and to share in management functions by
making suggestions on policies that are not clear to workers and by
learning to administer the policies that are in force.

CONFUSION OVER THE SUPERVISOR'S JOB

The responsibilities of a first-line supervisor have changed so much and
so rapidly during the last twenty-five years that there is at present considerable confusion as to just what his job actually is. Before discussing
methods of supervisory selection and training, therefore, we must first be
clear as to what a modern foreman is supposed to do. This, however,
is not an entirely simple inquiry, since managements disagree as
to what the supervisor should do and what his position actually

[1] *The Development of Foremen in Management*, p. 9, Research Report No. 7, American
Management Association, New York, 1945.

is.[1] The difference of opinion derives partly from diversities in the nature of the product made or service rendered and the type of worker employed. But a more fundamental source of confusion is that the job itself is still in transition. In many firms, it is stuck somewhere along the road between the job of an old-line foreman and the complexly interrelated position of a representative of modern management.

What Is the Supervisor's Function?

Most companies have grown beyond the notion that a foreman is a sort of subcontractor running an independent unit, with authority to hire and fire his own workers and to handle them in any way he thinks best. But, in many firms, the duties of first-line supervisors have not yet been entirely geared in with all the functions performed in the same area by staff technicians. Sometimes these experts forget their role and usurp part of the authority that should go with the responsibilities of being a foreman. This makes many supervisors feel that they are expected just to do a lot of paperwork and to be kicked around by everyone; in other words that the job now carries with it less prestige than when it was simpler. Other foremen, insufficiently aided by staff technicians or improperly trained in working with them, feel that being a supervisor is impossibly complicated, a task too difficult for any one man to perform.

In both cases, the supervisor's conviction that his position is unrewarding prevents his developing the sense of unity with other management representatives that should be exemplified in all management activity, and especially at the level where management comes into closest contact

---

[1] The American Management Association made a survey in 1944 of about one hundred concerns, leaders in their respective fields, to ascertain the status and function of their foremen. The following data were obtained:

"Hiring.—In two-thirds of the companies replying, the personnel department interviews and selects new employees, while the foreman has final say; but in one-third, the foreman has no voice in hiring.

"Discharge.—Foremen have some say in discharge, but only in one-tenth of all cases can they discharge without any consultation.

"Pay Increases and Promotions.—These must almost always be approved by other authorities.

"Discipline.—In only one-tenth of all cases do foremen have complete charge of discipline.

"Grievances.—Discussion with the foreman is generally the first step in the grievance procedure, but the extent to which he settles grievances is not clear. A small sample in the automotive-aircraft industries shows that this may range from 45 to 80 per cent.

"Policy Making.—Only 20 per cent of the companies replying held policy meetings with foremen."

The Development of Foremen in Management, p. 9, Research Report No. 7, American Management Association, New York, 1945.

with workers. And this lack of unity must be blamed squarely on those top executives and personnel administrators who have not clearly analyzed what the modern supervisor's duties and responsibilities should actually be.

Some of the current confusion on this question is revealed by a lack of uniformity in terminology. Does the term "supervisor," for instance, refer to the hourly rated foreman who works on the floor with the men or to the salaried foreman who spends most of his time directing the work of others?[1] Has the foreman, or first-line supervisor, actually crossed the invisible but real line between workers and management? Or is he caught halfway in a sort of "no man's land" such that he can feel a genuine sense of membership neither with management nor with workers?

Unfortunately, in many companies the first-line supervisor is in this uncomfortable position. He is conscious of being neither fish, flesh, nor fowl and of receiving no powerful support from anyone. The feeling that he must protect his own interests has recently been expressed in the formation of foremen's unions.[2] Management usually resents this union as an indication of disloyalty on the part of supervisors. But it is more realistic to recognize it merely as a symptom of insecurity that would not manifest itself if the supervisor were treated as a genuine management representative.

The status of foremen's unions has changed as a result of the Labor-management Relations (Taft-Hartley) Act of 1947. Supervisors are no longer protected by law in their efforts to join unions and bargain collectively, and in Section 2(11) a supervisor is defined as:

any individual having authority, in the interest of the employer to hire, transfer, suspend, lay off, recall, promote, discharge, assign, reward, or discipline other employees, or responsibly to direct them, or to adjust their grievances, or effectively to recommend such action if in connection with the foregoing, the exercise of such authority is not of a merely routine or clerical nature but requires the use of independent judgment.

This definition would presumably exclude leadmen, straw bosses, etc., but there will probably be disagreement in individual cases.

Unions also are divided on this question. According to most of them,

---

[1] In this book, we use interchangeably the terms "foreman" and "first-line supervisor." We think he should be a salaried official for reasons that we shall give below. His relationship to other employees is well defined in the article by DOMINICK and CRAWFORD, "The Foreman Expresses His Training Needs," *Personnel*, Vol. 21, pp. 19–30, 1944. The term "foreman," as used in the Radio Corporation of America plants, refers to *the supervisor in charge of a recognized section of a manufacturing department. He supervises assistant foremen and working group leaders and, through them, the other employees in his section. He reports to a general foreman or a superintendent who is responsible for two or more manufacturing sections.*

[2] For a detailed discussion of this problem, see *The Unionization of Foremen*, Research Report No. 6, American Management Association, New York, 1945. Also of great interest in this connection is the *Report and Findings of a Panel of the National War Labor Board in Certain Disputes Involving Supervisors*, Sumner H. Slichter, chairman, Washington, D. C., Jan. 19, 1945.

the foreman is a member of management and not a worker. If a foreman has been promoted from the ranks, he usually ceases to be acceptable as a union member.[1] Furthermore, most unions restrict him from performing productive work. On the other hand, in a few unions (as in the building trades and printing), foremen are admitted to membership in the union of rank and file workers.

NEED FOR CLEAR THINKING

All these differences of opinion and divergences of practice could not flourish so strongly if top management everywhere had developed a clear-cut policy as to the supervisor's status, duties, and pay. In our opinion, the conception of an hourly rated foreman is a contradiction in terms. If a foreman is to be anything more than a group leader, straw boss, or leading hand, he should be put on salary and regarded as a genuine management representative. When he is accepted as such, it is not difficult to bring his job up to date by thinking logically about what should be his duties, responsibilities, and area of authority, and where his activities should be coordinated with those of staff technicians.

An analysis of what the job itself calls for is most useful if begun by making a composite picture of what the foremen in different companies actually do. One of the authors carried out this project over a period of years. Observations in a number of firms were supplemented by discussions in foreman-training courses about the difficulties that supervisors encounter. In this way, a detailed analysis of the modern supervisor's job was evolved and periodically revised. The specific duties for which foremen are properly held responsible may be classified as in Table 1.[2]

[1] In some unions, the foreman is allowed to keep his union card in order to retain his status as a member if and when he should be put back into the ranks. Other unions have sought to make it impossible for a foreman to retain or accumulate his seniority rights. This attitude has contributed to the foreman's feeling of insecurity.

[2] Similar conclusions were reached as the result of a survey made in plants of the Radio Corporation of America. By breaking down the job into broad areas, it was found that the average foreman's workday was divided among the following activities:

	Per Cent
Meeting production schedules	29
Human relations	14
Quality control	11
Cost control	9
Methods	8
Personnel functions	7
Tools, equipment, and machines	6
Materials and supplies	6
Working conditions	5
Other activities	5
	100

With minor differences, superintendents and foremen agreed on this analysis. Dominick

TABLE 1.—RESPONSIBILITIES OF FIRST-LINE SUPERVISION [1]

Duties of foremen	*In collaboration with* staff technicians or	Union representatives	*Delegated to* assistant foreman or	Group leader	*Involving* technical skill	Skill in human relations
A. GETTING OUT PRODUCTION						
1. Requisitioning and issuing materials, tools, etc.						
2. Planning work and assigning jobs						
3. Supervising to maintain flow of production						
4. Follow-up of production schedule						
B. INSPECTING AND TESTING PRODUCT FOR QUALITY						
5. Inspecting incoming material						
6. Inspecting output						
7. Fixing responsibility for poor quality product						
8. Attending to salvage and repair of poor quality product						
9. Distributing repair jobs for balance and economy						
C. COST CONTROL						
10. Keeping accounts						
11. Promoting cost reduction—checking overtime requirements						
D. MAINTENANCE OF PLANT AND EQUIPMENT						
12. Maintaining cleanly and orderly conditions. Housekeeping						
13. Maintaining tools and equipment in efficiency						
E. IMPROVING EQUIPMENT AND METHODS						
14. Experimenting with tools and equipment						
15. Studying processes and methods to effect improvements						
F. MAINTAINING COMMUNICATION						
16. Making and transmiting records and reports						
17. Interpreting management to workers						
18. Interpreting workers to management						
G. HANDLING HUMAN RELATIONS						
19. Selecting workers to be hired						
20. Inducting new workers						
21. Training novices						
22. Analyzing jobs for job specifications						
23. Rating men for qualifications						
24. Recommending pay raises, transfers, and promotions						
25. Maintaining discipline						
26. Adjusting friction between employees						
27. Handling employee complaints						
28. Securing and evaluating suggestions						
29. Nominating and training understudies						
H. ASSURING SAFETY AND HEALTH						
30. Maintaining safety measures						
31. Safeguarding health						

[1] The use of this table as a teaching device in training experienced foremen will be discussed on p. 151.

Obviously, in such a complex job, the supervisor should not be held responsible for *doing* all these things himself. His responsibilities should be subdivided into *thinking*, *doing*, and *cooperating* with other people. His thinking consists of planning, observing, analyzing, and evaluating. What the foreman actually does varies according to the number and ability of those assigned by higher management to work with him. Aside from giving orders, holding interviews, and writing records and reports, the foreman should be able to do his job by collaborating with other people. This *collaboration* consists in delegating and consulting.[1]

Supervisors are both born and made; in other words, selection *for* certain qualities and training *in* certain attitudes and skills can greatly contribute to supervisory success. If selection is to be in line with the principles of modern management, it must be more than the old-fashioned method of merely telling an aggressive and technically qualified employee to stop doing production work and to start directing others. Such casual selection, combined as it usually is with little or no training and with inadequate notification of workers and other supervisors as to the new promotion, meant that the new foreman started with a severe and unnecessary handicap. Under such circumstances, only an exceptional man could make good. The many who failed found themselves in the unsatisfactory position of having lost face to such an extent that they usually preferred to leave the company. Such action had an unfortunate effect on other employees and brought home to management the wastefulness of haphazard selection. It became apparent that a double loss was sustained. Not only had management failed to acquire a new foreman, but it had also lost an outstanding mechanic.

IMPROVED METHODS OF SELECTION

Such unsatisfactory experiences have convinced many managements that it would be more efficient to look outside the company for supervisory material among college-trained men and to hire them as promotional candidates. When combined with an adequate training program, this method of selection has obvious advantages. However, its great weakness

---

[1] See CAREY, H. H., "Consultative Supervision and Management," *Personnel*, Vol. 18, No. 5, pp. 286–295, 1942.

and Crawford, *op cit.* This, of course, is the experience of one company under wartime conditions. In other companies and in peacetime, there would be at least minor differences, almost certainly including greater emphasis on cost. Nevertheless, our observation in a variety of other concerns over a number of years indicates that the RCA picture is fairly representative.

See also McGREGOR, DOUGLAS, "The Foreman's Responsibilities in the Industrial Organization: A Case Study," *Personnel*, Vol. 22, No. 5, pp. 3–11, 1946.

is that ambitious and qualified employees become disgruntled if there is no possibility of their working up from the ranks. Recognition of this fact leads to the conclusion that what is needed for efficient selection is a careful survey of available material both inside and outside the company and a clear-cut policy as to the order and method by which selection is to be made. The personnel point of view suggests that any promising candidates already in the company's employ should be considered before outside recruiting is undertaken.

When candidates for the position of supervisor are selected from within the company, the choice is usually made by one of the following methods:

1. Appointment of understudies by supervisors or by higher management.

2. Recommendations by the personnel department after initial screening.

3. Nominations by present supervisors and final selection by a committee.

This last method has been recommended by the Training Within Industry Division of the War Manpower Commission[1] and seems to combine the advantages of other methods without incorporating their weaknesses. Before the selection process is set in motion, responsibility should be assigned to one operating or personnel official who will carry it through all stages. He should be assured of the complete support of top management and, if possible, of all other management representatives.

Steps in the Selection Process

The recommended steps may be outlined as follows:

1. *Starting the Program.*—When top management has decided to start looking for supervisory ability in the company, a meeting of all management representatives, including present first-line supervisors, should be called to outline the general approach. Such a meeting should be conducted by a member of top management who stresses the policy of planning for the future. It should also be pointed out that the selection program in no way endangers the job of present supervisors. In fact, if all supervisory ability is discovered, those with limited capacity can be used to assist present supervisors by acting as understudies or assistants. Lastly, it should be explained that the success of the selection program depends largely on the judgment of present supervisors.

[1] *How to Select New Supervisors*, Training Within Industry Bulletin Series, Bulletin No. 4-E, Bureau of Training, War Manpower Commission, Washington, D. C., April, 1943. See also *Personnel*, Vol. 20, No. 2, pp. 66–79, 1943.

2. *Getting Nominations from Present Supervisors.*—Nominations may or may not be preceded by consultation with key workers and union representatives, although the ability to make himself acceptable to his fellow workers is a point in the candidate's favor. On the other hand, being disliked by union officials should not be considered as a bar to promotion. The choice of nominees should recognize existing informal relationships and ability as indicated by employee rating or objective records of performance. Supervisors should know whether or not some of their workers have demonstrated a knack of planning work and are sought out for advice and help by fellow employees.

3. *Getting Information about Candidates.*—Discussion with supervisors who made the nominations should be held by the management representative responsible for the program and usually elicits many new facts and the reasons for the judgments stated. The discussions are fact-finding interviews, not debates. At their conclusion, some names may be withdrawn and others added.

It is essential that each nominee be judged not only as a technician and an intelligent, reliable individual but also on the evidence of his ability to get along with people.

Importance of Human Relations.—Experience shows that the capacity to handle people is primary among a supervisor's qualifications. As a sub-leader, he will need to collaborate with others who exercise various functions and operate on various levels. In direct line relationships, he will need an objective attitude toward the whole process of taking and giving orders as well as toward collaborating with other supervisors on his own level. Moreover, special skill will be required if he is to avail himself to the full of all that various staff experts have to give. Finally, considerable understanding is needed to work effectively with union leaders.

4. *Rough Screening.*—The personnel records for all candidates still under consideration should then be screened by the selection committee. This process should emphasize current performance and should weigh the nominator's recommendation against all other factors revealed by the nominee's record. Such an objective scrutiny tends to preclude the influence of favoritism.

5. *Giving Information to Candidates.*—At this point, all remaining candidates should be told by a company executive what is being planned. It should be explained that not all will be accepted but that it is a compliment to be tried out. "Someone thought you would make a good supervisor." The job of supervisor should be clearly outlined, with emphasis both on its headaches and on its rewards. Some candidates may indicate that they "do not wish to run."

6. *Testing and Interviewing Candidates.*—All nominees still in the running should now take various kinds of tests. Simple practical tests are needed to show, among other things, how the candidate can handle the type of paperwork that is an essential part of a supervisor's job. And personality tests are often administered in the attempt to appraise a candidate's qualifications in the important area of human relations.

But, for supervisors, as for other promotional candidates, results from this type of test have not hitherto shown a significant correlation with success on the job.[1] Individual interviews have proved more successful than tests as a means of appraising a candidate's qualifications and trainability in the field of personnel relations. If interviews are used in conjunction with tests, information obtained during the talk often throws new light on test data and may elicit new facts.

7. *Reviewing the Candidate's Qualifications.*—The selection committee now reviews all the information about each candidate. Any promising person with whom someone on the committee has not already talked should be interviewed at this stage. In case of doubt, some candidates may be observed on the job. Unanimous decisions on each person are desirable. If complete agreement cannot be reached, it is probably wiser to drop the name from the active list. Rejected candidates are entitled to a full explanation.

8. *Final Selection of Trainees.*—According to the amount of supervisory material currently needed, and the training facilities available at the time, the committee now makes up a list of trainees. Desirable candidates not included in such a list constitute a reserve pool for future consideration. However, care should be taken to avoid raising hopes that cannot soon be satisfied. Unless a reasonable proportion of this group can be given supervisory training within 6 months or so, and unless every member eventually will be given an opportunity for training, the whole selection program is likely to become unpopular with employees.

When all these steps have been taken, management does not emerge with a candidate who, after training, will certainly be promoted. All that is known at this stage is that each person seems to be a good bet. How shall management train him so that his current abilities and latent assets may be developed to such a point that he can be useful as a supervisor?

Training for Future Supervisors

A program to select supervisors is of little use unless followed by adequate training. Nowadays it is generally recognized that this training

[1] For a contrary opinion on this question, see an article by F. H. Achard and F. H. Clarke, "You Can Measure the Probability of Success as a Supervisor," *Personnel*, Vol. 21, No. 6, pp. 353–373, 1945.

should be carefully planned. The difficulty with old-fashioned training on the job was that it inevitably varied in different parts of the company, because it consisted in the casual absorption of what each supervisor's immediate superior said and did. Obviously such training could never lead to uniform practice by all first-line supervisors or enable them to feel and act like representatives of a management team led by the chief executive. In order to achieve this objective, all supervisory training in the company must be planned by one person in collaboration with the president, who should give the program his continuous and serious support.

Granted that supervisory training should be planned, the major questions to be decided in each company are: (1) Shall there be any training for candidates before they undertake the responsibilities of a supervisor? (2) What areas shall training cover? (3) How long shall it continue? (4) How shall training be given? (5) Who shall be the teacher?

If the personnel point of view is accepted, the supervisor has so much to learn that, in our opinion, it is important for him to get a head start by beginning his training before he actually takes on his new job.

Preparation for Candidates

1. *Technical information.*—Presumably every candidate for a supervisory position has superior technical ability. But, before making him responsible for the work of others, management should be sure that he has a sound working knowledge and all necessary information about the technical features of his job (operations, machines, tools, methods, etc.).

2. *Information about the company.*—Before he can be an interpreter of management, he should also develop understanding of company purpose and of the policies and procedures from which rules and regulations logically derive. This part of his training covers material that management would like to go over with every employee in a comprehensive course, if there were sufficient time and interest. It includes information about

    a. Company history, development of products and processes, and major turning points in the company's growth.

    b. Organizational structure. (This can be clearly shown by organizational charts.)[1]

---

[1] It is essential to efficiency that every management representative or, for that matter, every employee, should know what the organizational structure is. Yet, even in comparatively well managed companies, there is often considerable confusion on this point. This is revealed by such simple questions as "Who is your chief?" "To whom do you report?" It also manifests itself in the perennial problem of by-passing or short-circuiting of authority. An excellent article developing this and other points has been written by Col. E. W. Reilley, "Organizational Planning for Executive Development," *Personnel*, Vol. 22, No. 2, pp. 84–93, 1945. The article contains a useful check list for diagnosing organization problems.

c. Major policies of top management and the procedures by which they are implemented, especially policies and procedures for handling personnel.

d. Aims and future plans of management.

In addition to such information, there should be discussion of

e. Possibilities and value of collaboration between all employees in the company, with particular reference to problems and opportunities for cooperation between people who perform different functions in the same organizational unit.

3. *Training for line responsibilities.*—This includes preparation for

a. Giving and receiving orders.[1]

b. Understanding the proper relationships between authority and responsibility. (Functions to be performed, power to make decisions to go with functions.)

c. Reading and writing reports.

d. Understanding the requirements of formal organizational procedure and the functions and relationships of all types and levels of management.

All these topics call for further training on the job, since few men at the supervisory level, or any other, reach a point where they cannot improve their understanding and skill as leaders and interpreters of higher management.

Placement

Several points need to be considered. Whenever possible, a new supervisor should be placed under a superior who will be willing to accept sponsorship and take responsibility for giving further training on the job. It is helpful, furthermore, to place the new supervisor in a department where he is familiar with personnel and operations. However, effective coordination is promoted if the new supervisor is routed through several

---

[1] *Cf.* PIGORS, PAUL, and FAITH PIGORS. *Understanding as a Condition of Success in Order-giving*, Industrial Relations Associates, Inc., Cambridge, Mass., 1945.

"Every efficient instance of order-giving contains the following phases, however they may vary in scope and pace:

"1. *Comprehending* the situation as to

  a. What the need is; *b.* what, therefore, must be done; *c.* who should act; and *d.* what kind of order shall be used.

"2. *Preparing* the receiver to put the order into effect.

"3. *Presenting* the order to the receiver.

"4. *Verifying* the reception of the order.

"5. *Action* by the receiver towards meeting the need.

"6. *Checking* to test the success of action and its results.

"7. *Evaluating*, to form considered opinions as to the functioning of both agents throughout the process."

related departments for a year or so, before being transferred to his original department for a permanent assignment.

SPECIFIC TRAINING FOR PRESENT SUPERVISORS

The most effective training for present supervisors is that in which the judgment of men who are experiencing problems on the job is pooled and developed. For this purpose, actual case material is needed. After a class is well launched, it is usually not difficult to get the men to bring up actual cases for discussion. But, at the outset of a course, a preliminary step is to find some other method of centering attention on relevant facts. The list of duties presented on page 144 has proved useful for this purpose. If mimeographed copies are distributed, the following steps may be taken in class.

1. The supervisors check and discuss their duties, being invited to add anything not already listed. This discussion brings out variations in the foreman's job according to the specific activities of his department and section. Obviously the variations are greater if the class is made up of supervisors from different companies.

2. Next the supervisors fill in the spaces according to which duties are performed in collaboration with staff technicians or union officials. This phase of the discussion will bring out points of friction, which can lead to an exploration of appropriate steps to facilitate line and staff contacts.

3. Supervisors then check the duties that can be delegated to an assistant or group leader. This step gives each member food for thought, whether or not he has an assistant, because it clarifies the nature of the different tasks. Thinking along this line usually leads to a consideration of the question: How does one effectively delegate authority?

4. Next the group marks each responsibility with a "T" or "H" according to whether the skill it calls for is primarily technical or human. This step usually proves something of a stickler but is worth the trouble because it soon leads the group to the discovery that both kinds of skill are needed in most areas of their job. Furthermore, this phase of the discussion almost invariably produces interesting case material about unexpected human complications that were found to be associated with technical features of the supervisor's job.

After some such method has been used to focus supervisors' attention on their manifold duties and responsibilities, the group can profit by a methodical exploration of the four major areas of their job. The aim here is to develop

1. *Technical Mastery.*—This means acquiring greater understanding and more facts about methods and processes, including such matters as

time and motion study, technical training of new workers (with special attention to efficient and safe practices), methods of computing pay (especially incentive rates, if any), cost and quality control, job evaluation, etc. Included in this area may be practice in other paperwork such as making concise and clear-cut reports of various kinds.

2. *Skill in Planning.*[1]—This means learning how to think ahead about both the technical and nontechnical features of the foreman's job. For an intelligent person, experience is a good teacher of technical planning. But learning can be greatly speeded up if members of the supervisory group pool their experience under the guidance of a stimulating discussion leader.

Thinking ahead about nontechnical matters, such as giving workers advance notice of changes and watching their current performance with an eye to their development and to the company's future needs, is another area of planning in which supervisors can profit by experience and study.

This nontechnical planning and the technical instruction mentioned under point "1" both reach over into a third area.

3. *Skill in Human Relations.*—In one sense, this skill may be said to cover all the features of the foreman's job, since he depends for results so largely on other people (workers, staff experts, his superiors, as well as union leaders).

In relation to workers, the first-line supervisor needs to acquire skill in teaching (how to explain clearly, to win acceptance of efficient and safe methods, to check on understanding and to follow up, in order to be sure that new methods become steady habits, etc.). Other skills needed by the supervisor in directing workers are learning how to size up people (for selection, placement, and merit rating), to build communication as a bridge for understanding (in discussion groups, order giving, interviewing, the complaint procedure, announcing changes, etc.), and to time his own contribution in order giving, explanation, or the introduction of a change in routine in such a way that his activities synchronize well with the pace of people and of events.

The foreman also needs continued training in ways to cooperate with

---

[1] An outstanding contribution of the Training Within Industry group during the Second World War was the development of training programs for the skills universally needed by supervisors: (1) skill in leading (Job Relations Training), (2) skill in planning (Job Methods Training), and (3) skill in instructing (Job Instruction Training). In addition, each supervisor needs to know his job technically and to have a clear understanding of company policies and organization and of his own responsibilities. This knowledge, said TWI, must be acquired locally in each firm. See appendix to Chap. 11, the Job Relations Training Program of the TWI, pp. 498 to 502.

staff experts and with other supervisors at various levels. And he must learn to work effectively with union leaders. In short, the supervisor needs to become personnel-minded and adept at dealing with people. He should learn how to act as a member of the management team and how to develop team spirit among his subordinates.

4. *Skill in Interpreting and Administering Policies.*—Before he becomes a supervisor, he will, according to our program, have a sound general knowledge of what a policy is. But this logical knowledge needs to be supplemented by practical skills in understanding specific policies and in applying them to daily work situations. Experienced supervisors can profit even more than beginners by full discussions of personnel policies. When discussions in foreman-training courses indicate that any existing policy needs reformulating, the necessary changes must be put into effect promptly, if supervisors are expected to retain interest in policy talk.

How Long Shall Training Continue?

The discussion of what supervisory training on the job should be indicates our opinion of how long it should go on. For best results, it should be continued as long as supervisors are on the job, and something like it should be extended to all higher levels of management. There are two reasons for this:

For one thing, as stressed in the TWI program, education in technical and human leadership is not something to be learned by heart and kept in a notebook. Rather it is something to be constantly developed by a combination of practical experience and group thinking. Once a supervisor has been "bitten by the bug" of self-education, he will want to go on learning how to handle his job better; and alert supervisors, young and old at all levels, will want similar training. For this reason, a foreman-training program should not be inaugurated unless management is prepared to offer it to all. When every supervisor may sign up for a course, none can feel sensitive because he was left out.[1]

In the second place, it is important for younger foremen to know that all supervisors and executives have been trained along the same lines. For instance, unless it is generally known that the same ideas about leadership are held at all levels, supervisors may feel that they cannot apply their

[1] An interesting side light on the foreman's perpetual preoccupation with prestige was given in one company shortly after the beginning of an experiment with foreman training. Each member of the first course was given a zipper notebook in which to keep the mimeographed course material. Shortly thereafter, almost all the other foremen in the plant came to work equipped with similar notebooks, in which they actually carried their lunches.

newly acquired skill (what they have learned) because their own superiors do not handle personnel problems in the same way.[1]

How Should Specific Training Be Given?

The decision that a training program is to be offered to all supervisors both potential and present does not mean that training must necessarily be given to everyone in exactly the same way. For instance, questions as to the length, time of day, and frequency of meetings may well be answered differently according to whether members of the course are candidates, newly appointed supervisors, or experienced men. If meetings are held in the evening, the candidates have an opportunity to demonstrate their ambition by attending on their own time. But supervisors on the job should, if possible, be trained on company time. When meetings are in the evening, they may perhaps run to 2 hours in length, with a break in the middle, since members usually feel that a shorter period merely "spoils a good evening" without offering a sufficient substitute for recreation. Another advantage of a 2 hour period is that the break gives a chance for informal discussions that sometimes prove of greater value than a lecture, and it may serve to reanimate discussion in the larger group. But, when training is on company time, it may not be convenient to have supervisors away from their work for such a long period.

In relation to the frequency of sessions, beginners need to meet more often than foremen taking refresher courses or doing advanced thinking. A break of over 2 weeks tends to disrupt continuity.

The question of homework perennially divides students and teachers; but, in support of the pupil's position when he is already an experienced foreman, it may be argued that his most valuable homework can be done in the plant while he carries out his normal duties. Written homework for experienced foremen should certainly be kept to a minimum, since these men are usually overworked even when they are given no additional tasks of a theoretical nature. Beginners can profit by doing more work out of class, especially when it is practice in the kind of assignment called for by their job.

---

[1] This point is stated in another way by Douglas McGregor. "If you reward people for adequate, skillful handling of men in your organization, they will become adequate, skillful handlers of men. If you punish them for it or ignore their attempts in that direction, they will not. That is a simple and obvious fact. But as we examine our own companies and our own practices, it appears that we have been ignoring it. We must see to it that the man who develops skills is rewarded, and I don't mean merely with money." From "Re-evaluation of Training for Management Skills," in *Training for Management Skills*, Personnel Series No. 104, American Management Association, p. 21, 1946. This article contains a number of other excellent suggestions on supervisory training.

All these differences, in addition to the variety of subject matter and approach needed by different groups, suggest that the question: "Who should conduct foreman-training courses?" also has more than one answer.

Who Should Be the Teacher?

Advanced students can usefully teach each other. For this reason, experienced foremen learn much from the discussions that are an essential feature of so many foremen's clubs or associations, particularly when the foremen's group is made up of supervisors from different companies, so that problems are varied and experience may be pooled. If there is no foremen's association in the community and no foreseeable opportunity of there being one, good results may be obtained by regular panel discussions attended by supervisors within the company. These discussions may be led by a general foreman or by the supervisors themselves.

But, when foreman-training courses are given to understudies and assistants, they need to be directed by someone who has experience in teaching and who is more conscious than experienced supervisors usually are of the kind of problem that baffles a beginner. In each company where training for beginners is offered, management must decide who the instructor or instructors should be.

Opinions differ as to whether it is better to have such courses given by people outside the company or by insiders. Qualified outsiders presumably have a wider knowledge than most company officials of general conditions and typical problems. But they necessarily know less than an alert insider about the specific and unique features of the company.

In regard to technical matters concerning the beginning supervisor's own work, or in areas where he needs to collaborate with various specialists, it is certainly useful to have the appropriate company experts conduct lectures or demonstrations. In this way, relevant information is given, acquaintance with company personnel is promoted, and specific company procedures and practices can be explained. It should be kept in mind, however, that all such talks on special subjects need to be discussed in advance with the person who is in charge of the training program as a whole. Experience has shown that many practical people, when asked to give a lecture, talk about anything but their day-to-day experience. Sometimes they surpass the most dry-as-dust academician in presenting a dull and theoretical account of what they assume to be the principles of their specialty. Other experts discuss concrete facts but entirely omit the general principles by which the supervisor can build many special kinds of fact into the system of knowledge essential to complete mastery of his job. Unless the various talks are unified by bringing the subject matter of each lecture into line with the course as a whole, the educational results are apt to prove disappointing.

The Personnel Administrator as Teacher

If the personnel administrator is equal to his general assignment in keeping track of current conditions and typical problems as well as of specific and unique features in the company situation, he is a logical person to conduct supervisory training courses. Futhermore, such an assignment gives him a vital opportunity to work toward a better understanding and consistent administration of personnel policies. He may be expected to be informed about training methods and presumably is a good teacher. If he is not up to date on these matters, the discussion of current problems during the course should certainly prove instructive to him. Moreover, the course itself may dovetail with his other work by giving him a chance to discuss delicate questions in an impersonal manner and to indicate the policy requirements that call for certain procedures. Some foremen who cannot readily accept individual instruction can absorb new ideas when they are given out to a whole group.

Summary

The processes of selecting candidates for supervisory positions and of planning and administering a training program are excellent examples of adult education at its best.

Top management and the personnel administrator begin by clarifying their own ideas as to the job of a modern supervisor. When top management is clear as to what it intends the job to be, the specific task of selecting and training candidates should be delegated to experts who exercise their special skills in conformity with management policy as to general methods. Thus it is a policy decision whether the selection of supervisors shall be from within the company, insofar as possible. But line officials, in cooperation with specialists from the employment department, make all specific decisions at each step in the selection process.

Experienced supervisors should share both as teachers and as students in the selection of new candidates for this position. They should be able to tell the personnel administrator and higher management what the job itself calls for, and they should know which employees show promise as leaders. In conferences with committee members, supervisors have an opportunity to learn more about top management's personnel point of view. A similar collaboration between different types and levels of management helps to make a success of the training program. Present supervisors can tell the training director what skills they use, what they wish they had not had to learn the hard way, and in what areas they feel the need of more training. The exchange of such information before and during a training program sets up a second circular process of education. By studying training needs and trying to fill them, the training director (and through him presumably top management also) learns more about what the job of supervisor is and how people can most effectively be trained to succeed in it.

If the training director is not the personnel administrator, the latter must keep his ear to the ground and apply for his own benefit what is learned during the course. As a perennial student, he is in a good position to profit by this knowledge whether he acquires it indirectly as an auditor or directly by the process of teaching the courses and learning from his own students.

When the personnel administrator is also the person in charge of the supervisory training program, perhaps his greatest contribution can be to communicate his own consciousness that he does not and never will know all the answers. If he can impart this attitude to the supervisors, they will have learned lesson number one in the personnel point of view. This will be peculiarly valuable when the supervisors themselves act as teachers in training new workers or collaborate with specialists who carry out this training.

Chapter 12

Employee Induction and Training

Training is not something that is done once to new employees—it is used continuously in every well-run establishment. Every time you get someone to do work the way you want it done, you are training. Every time you give directions or discuss a procedure you are training.

C. R. DOOLEY[1]

The value to any organization of well-planned employee induction and training is evident if we consider the question: What can a good program accomplish? First, through induction, the new employee is given information about the organization, its policies and regulations. This should be done in such a way as to help him feel at home quickly. Second, the new employee is instructed in the requirements of the specific job that he is to perform, so that he can as rapidly as possible meet standards for quantity and quality production and thus increase his earnings.

Third, training enables present employees to acquire more and greater skills, thus increasing their versatility for transfers and their qualifications for promotion. Fourth, if employees are properly trained, accidents, spoiled work, and damage to machines and equipment are reduced. Fifth, training helps employees to adjust to new methods and processes that are introduced from time to time. Finally, good training reduces dissatisfaction, absenteeism, and turnover, because it helps both new and experienced employees to use to the full their individual capacities.

These benefits cannot be realized, however, unless the line organization, beginning with the chief executive, is convinced of the importance of systematic training and unless employees themselves believe that they will benefit. If the training program is to get good results, employees must

[1] "Training within Industry in the United States," *International Labour Review*, Vol. LIV, Nos. 3-4, September-October, 1946, p. 161.

want to learn and supervisors must *want* to teach. Supervisory training is thus a prerequisite for an effective training program.

Furthermore, the training program will fail if recruitment and selection of new employees is poor, if new employees are told certain things about company policies and later discover them to be incorrect, if jobs are improperly analyzed for training purposes, or if transfers and promotions are made regardless of employee efforts to learn new skills. As in all personnel procedures, success in induction and training depends upon the effectiveness of other parts of the personnel program.

RESPONSIBILITY FOR INDUCTION AND TRAINING

The first step in establishing an induction and training program, once top management has been fully committed to its support, is to assign specific responsibilities. The responsibility for final results clearly rests with line management—with supervisors in the department in which employees are to be trained. Since the supervisor is responsible for the production of his department, he is also clearly responsible for the proper induction and training of the employees he will supervise. He may have assistance in this, but he cannot escape the responsibility.

In most large and medium-sized organizations, however, it has been found advisable to place staff responsibility for the induction and training program as a whole in the hands of a specialist. This person may be the personnel administrator or a training director who is either in a separate department or (preferably) subordinate to the personnel administrator. Unless there is a staff man primarily concerned with induction and training, the program is likely to be neglected by line officials who are confronted with what seem to be more urgent problems.

For example, in some firms new employees are hustled from the employment office to their new jobs without so much as a word about the company for which they are going to work. If the foreman is busy when they report for work, as he usually is, the new employees are assigned to some of the "older hands" for training. The results are frequently those experienced by a woman worker who doffed bobbins from a spinning frame in a textile mill. After 6 months, she quit and explained to an interviewer:

When I came to work they put me with an older doffer. She was a fast worker and told me to watch how she did it. I thought I saw what she did and started in on my own. But for 6 months I guess I've been doing it the wrong way. Yesterday the boss bawled me out for grabbing the bobbins near the top, but nobody ever told me that this was the wrong way and made the yarn run together. So I'm getting through.

If there had been a training director in this firm, it would have been his responsibility to determine this and other training needs of the organization, to work with the line supervisors in developing a program to fit these needs, to coordinate the training activities in different departments, and to check results. He would not have relieved the supervisor of responsibility for actual training, but, as a staff man, he would have helped him to perform his function better.

At times, line responsibility for training may seem to conflict with the long-range objectives of a training program. For example, in one company, the superintendent thought that a foreman would be tempted to use trainees on actual production work when he was short of operators on particular machines, before the trainees were ready to handle regular jobs. Consequently, he issued an order that the instructor, not the foreman, was to decide when trainees were to be assigned to production work. This overlapping of responsibility might have been avoided by convincing the foreman of the long-run value of training new workers properly and of avoiding the unsettling effects of giving them full work assignments before they were ready.

Induction as a Part of Training

Before a newly hired employee is trained in the company for a specific job, he should be welcomed as a new member of the organization. The first day of employment is long remembered by most people. Initial impressions and information count heavily in later attitudes toward the job and the company. Proper induction is therefore an integral part of the training process. By helping new employees to feel at home more quickly, it enables them to get the full benefit of specific job training.

A friendly welcome to the organization is not the only purpose of good induction, however. An equally important objective is to give the new employee accurate and useful information about the company, the employee services it offers, and the personnel policies that will affect him as well as all other employees.

Experience with well-planned employee-induction programs in industry, in government, and in the armed services is so favorable in terms of subsequent employee satisfaction and performance that no organization, except possibly a very small one, can afford to omit this procedure from its personnel program. A good induction program has three parts:

1. Introductory information given informally or in group sessions in the personnel department.

2. Further information given by the new employee's supervisor in the department about departmental facilities and requirements.

3. A follow-up interview several weeks after the employee has been on the job, given by either the supervisor or a representative of the personnel department, to answer further questions that the new employee may have and to repeat some of the earlier information for emphasis.

The following summary outline, based in part upon an extensive field survey of induction programs for factory employees,[1] is illustrative of the kinds of information that should be provided in well-planned induction to any organization:

1. In the personnel department—introductory information given by a staff representative:

   a. The company—its history, development, organization, management, products, and type of industry.

   b. Personnel policies—what the new employee can expect of the company and what the company expects of him.

   c. Terms of employment; general disciplinary rules and procedures.

   d. Employee activities and services, such as benefit plans, off-the-job activities, self-improvement opportunities.

This information may be included in an attractively prepared and interestingly written employee handbook, given to every new employee. The oral presentation can then be based on this handbook, which the employee will read later.

   e. Company or plant facilities, such as cafeterias, parking lots, day nurseries, etc.

   f. Community facilities (of interest to new residents).

   g. The job—general remarks about the department, its organization and personnel, type of work, hours, wages, and opportunities for promotion.

   h. In unionized firms, the union with which the firm has a contract, whether union membership is required for employment, grievance procedure, etc.

2. In the department where the new employee will work—further information given by the supervisor:

   a. Introduction to other subordinate supervisors in the department, under whom the new employee will work.

   b. Departmental rules and regulations; safety measures.

   c. Tour of department to show (1) relation of employee's job to others in department and (2) departmental facilities such as washrooms, lockers, drinking fountains, bulletin boards, etc., which are provided for employees.

[1] YEOMANS, GEORGE H., "The Induction of New Factory Employees," *Personnel*, Vol. 19, pp. 390–398, 1942.

    d. Description of job—its duties, standards, safety on the job, hours, wage rate or incentive and method of computing pay, workplace, tools, use and care of equipment. (This phase merges with actual job training.)

    e. Introduction to fellow workers, with possible assignment of new employee to a "sponsor" with whom the new man may feel freer to talk and ask questions. In unionized firms, the new employee may be introduced to the union steward.

3. Follow-up interview—conducted several weeks later either by a representative of the personnel or training department, or by the departmental supervisor, preferably the latter, who

    a. Answers questions that the new employee has about his relationship with the company, its policies and procedures.

    b. Repeats some of the earlier information about company policies, disciplinary rules, etc.

    c. Checks on the employee's interest in voluntary group insurance or other voluntary employee services or activities.

    d. Conducts the employee on a tour of the plant, so that he may understand better the relationship of his job and his department to other jobs and departments.

    e. Checks on success of initial job placement and subsequent job training, with a view to greater improvement or possibly to transfer to another job if this seems desirable.[1]

To sum up, the whole induction program should be directed toward giving the new employee a sense of "belonging" to the organization. Much of the success of subsequent training and performance depends on good induction, and failure is measured in dissatisfaction, poor work, and labor turnover.

TYPES OF EMPLOYEE TRAINING

The types of employee training best suited to a specific organization depend upon a number of factors, such as skills called for in jobs to be filled, qualifications of candidates applying for jobs, and the kinds of production problems confronted by the firm. Although it is important that the training program be developed to meet specific needs, the personnel administrator or training director should also be familiar with the whole range of training as practiced in other firms and organizations so that he can recommend for his company the program best suited to its needs.

[1] For some actual examples of follow-up interviews that resulted in interdepartmental transfers, see Chap. 14, Transfer, Downgrading, and Layoff.

Various types of employee training and their relative advantages may be outlined as follows:

1. *Public Vocational-school Training or "Refresher Courses."*—These may be arranged by the training director in cooperation with public- or trade-school authorities, to provide training for prospective employment applicants in shop mathematics, blueprint reading, welding, steam fitting, etc. In some cases, this type of training precedes employment, although it may be geared to the needs of a specific company. In other cases, training outside the plant may supplement on-the-job or vestibule training in the plant.

2. *Apprentice Training.*—This is desirable in industries like the metal trades which require a constant flow of new employees who expect to become all-round craftsmen. Since the training program is long and requires continual supervision, this method of training is expensive. Standards are rigid and are defined in an apprenticeship agreement that, in unionized firms, involves union acceptance. Furthermore, after the long period of apprenticeship is completed, there is no assurance that the man will remain with the firm that trained him.

3. *Vestibule Training.*—This type of training is used primarily when large numbers of workers must be trained quickly, as during wartime, although it is also helpful as a preliminary to on-the-job training. New workers are trained for specific jobs on special machines in a separate part of the plant. In some cases, an attempt may be made to duplicate as closely as possible the actual workroom conditions, but one of the advantages of vestibule training is that it permits more emphasis on teaching the best method than on getting production. Furthermore, the trainees have an opportunity to get accustomed to plant routine and recover from their initial nervousness before going onto actual production jobs.

The artificial atmosphere usually associated with this type of training, however, may actually increase the adjustment problem when trainees go into the shop. In one company, the vestibule school became increasingly different from the manufacturing department it was supposed to duplicate, because the school lagged behind the shop in manufacturing technique and equipment. Trainees who had been constantly helped by the teacher missed his encouragement when they moved into the shop, and they became easily discouraged. The foreman had to retrain these workers, yet pressing production demands forced him to leave them alone much of the time, thus increasing their sense of failure. Many quit voluntarily. Management finally decided to assign staff instructors to do training on the job, and eventually the vestibule school was discontinued.

One firm succeeded in meeting this difficulty by making the vestibule training period relatively short (about 1 week); the instructors in the vestibule school then visited trainees on the job during the succeeding weeks. The continued interest and encouragement of their former instructors helped the trainees to do better work, yet it did not interfere with the responsibility of the departmental foreman to offer encouragement during the same period.

4. *On-the-job Training.*—In contrast to vestibule, or off-the-job training, the new worker is assigned in this type of training to a machine or workplace in the shop. He is instructed by an experienced employee, a special instructor, or his supervisor. Effective on-the-job training depends primarily upon qualified trainers. Without them, it is simply the old haphazard practice of putting new workers with "old hands" who may have neither the inclination nor the ability to teach the newcomer properly. The case of the doffer cited earlier can be multiplied many times.

With competent instruction, however, this type of training may be most effective for rapid training of large numbers of unskilled and semi-skilled workers. It was the method by which, during the Second World War, millions of persons, many of whom had never been in the labor market before, were trained to do thousands of different jobs in war plants. The value of adequate on-the-job training was one of the war's great lessons in personnel administration.

DEVELOPING A TRAINING PROGRAM

It is impossible to recommend a training program that would be equally good for every company, because there are so many special features in each organization to which the program should be adapted. A small company with relatively unskilled employees obviously needs a less elaborate training program than a firm manufacturing a variety of intricate products with the aid of many skilled and semiskilled workers. No organization, however, has the choice between training and not training; most new employees have to be trained, and present employees often must learn new skills and processes. The choice is between haphazard or misdirected training and carefully planned, systematic training.

Training is also needed where there is a special problem interfering with production, such as excessive turnover among new employees, considerable absenteeism, a high accident rate, excessive spoilage of work, or a serious shortage of adequate replacements for a given job. The training director can fit the training program to the needs of the line supervisors by discussing their problems with them and studying records of production, quality, costs, labor turnover, absenteeism, accidents, etc. Usually supervisors are glad to talk about their problems and anxious to have help in solving them. A training program developed in this way is bound to have the support of supervisors, because they recognize its usefulness to them and therefore do not regard it as just something that a personnel administrator or training director thinks would be helpful in a general way.

Once training needs have been determined, the training director in consultation with the line officials involved should consider the following points: (1) who is to be trained, (2) the content of the training program, (3) who is to do the training, and (4) when, how long, and where it should be done.[1]

Finally, as the program is put into operation with the support of top management, and as experience regarding it accumulates, the results should be checked and evaluated. Has production increased? Were former training periods reduced for certain jobs? Are new workers able to reach expected earnings more quickly? Are there fewer accidents? Is there less spoilage and less damage to machines and equipment? Have turnover rates been reduced? Answers to these questions,[2] applying to the same or comparable groups of workers before and after the new training program, will indicate the degree of its success and perhaps suggest changes that would make training even more effective.

How a Training Need Was Met

The steps in developing a training program are illustrated in part by the experience of a cotton-goods mill in establishing a "loom-fixers' school." Supervisors of the weaving departments had felt that the old method of training loom fixers was not getting sufficiently good results. It was traditional in the industry for "learner fixers" to pick up what they could by working with older men. All the old-timers had learned this way, yet the supervisors had difficulty with them when new types of looms were introduced or when it was necessary to make transfers to different types of loom for production reasons. The old-timers lacked versatility and frequently had no adequate understanding of the way in which a loom functions.

---

[1] These points are stressed in the program development part of the Training Within Industry program, which reached many thousands of new training directors during the Second World War. See Dietz, Walter, "Spotting Training Needs," *Manpower Review*, Vol. 12, pp. 11–13, 1945; and also in *The Training Within Industry Report*, 1940–1945, Chap.16, War Manpower Commission, Bureau of Training, Training Within Industry Service, Washington, D. C., September, 1945.

[2] For further suggestions, see C. H. Lawshe, "Eight Ways to Check Value of Training Program," *Factory Management and Maintenance*, Vol. 103, p. 117, 1945.

This company lacked a training director, but the superintendent and the employment manager, with the supervisors' help, established a loom-fixers' school—one of the first to be set up in any 'textile firm. Various types of looms in different stages of assembly were put in a special room, and a loom expert, who was also an excellent teacher, was secured as the instructor. Weave-room supervisors urged their older loom fixers, as well as learners, to attend classes before or after their shifts. In addition, difficult problems in fixing looms were brought to the school by loom fixers and worked out with the assistance of the instructor.

The results were excellent. Many men took the courses each year, spurred on by the prospect of more rapid promotion. Supervisors reported that their loom fixers were better trained and more versatile in meeting new types of mechanical problems. New men learned loom fixing more quickly than had been thought possible, because in the school they were able to take apart and reassemble a loom under the guidance of an expert instructor.

Only one instructor was needed in this school, and he proved to be an excellent teacher. Not every organization is so fortunate in meeting specific training needs, however. No matter how well the training program looks on paper, it cannot succeed without competent instruction.

TRAINING TECHNIQUES

A knowledge of training techniques is important for the success of a training program. If instructors do not know how to teach their subject or job, it makes no difference how sound the content of the program is. One of the major training functions of the personnel department, or its training section, is to provide qualified trainers. Experienced workers or leadmen may be selected to do this training, and supervisors themselves should be taught this skill.

Teaching is a skill—and an art—that can be learned, as thousands of key workers and supervisors discovered during the Job Instructor Training (JIT) sessions conducted in war industries by the Training Within Industry Division of the War Manpower Commission.[1] The simple but basic methods used in the JIT program should be the core of any effective training program.

[1] This excellent program, consisting of five 10-hour sessions, was developed in 1940 by Glenn L. Gardiner, vice-president of the Forstmann Woolen Company, and a group of New Jersey men, under the general direction of C. R. Dooley, of Socony-Vacuum Oil Company, and Walter J. Dietz, of Western Electric Company, who set up the Training Within Industry Program in 1940. Job Instructor Training was giv to more than a million supervisors and key workers in war industries.

Before the actual training begins, the instructor must get ready to instruct. The JIT program suggested four steps:[1]

1. *Have a timetable.*—How much skill do you expect the trainee to have, and how soon? This gives both the trainees and the instructor a series of goals at which to aim.

2. *Break down the job.*—List the principal steps. Job description and analysis are a necessary preliminary to training. The working sequence of operations should be listed, and even the exact motion sequence may be useful. "Key points," such as special knacks of doing an operation, quality requirements, safety and health precautions, and factors requiring careful judgment on the part of the operator, should be listed. Experienced workers may think they "know their job by heart," but usually they omit important points in the first listing. Consequently, a written job analysis is usually necessary if training is to be efficient.

3. *Have everything ready.*—The right equipment, materials, and supplies. This is an important preparatory step, so that there need be no delays when actual training begins.

4. *Have the workplace properly arranged.*—Just as the worker will be expected to keep it.

The instructor is now ready to begin the actual training process, which was divided into four steps under the JIT program:

1. *Prepare the worker.*—Put him at ease. Find out what he already knows about the job. Get him interested in learning the job by explaining its relationship to other jobs and to the company's product. Place him in the correct working position.

2. *Present the operation.*—Tell, show, illustrate, and question carefully and patiently. Stress the key points as listed on the job breakdown sheet. Instruct clearly and completely, taking up one point at a time—but no more than he can master.

3. *Try out performance.*—Test the trainee by having him perform the job. Have him tell and show you what he does; have him explain the key points. Ask questions and correct his errors. Continue until you know he knows how to do the job. "If the worker hasn't learned, the instructor hasn't taught."

4. *Follow up.*—Put the trainee on his own. Designate to whom he goes for help. Check him frequently and encourage further questions. Get him to look for key points as he progresses. Be sure he understands the *reason* for his job and its relationship to other jobs in the department or plant. As he acquires skill and understanding, taper off the extra coaching and finally close your follow-up.

[1] Some of the wording is that used by TWI; some is the authors'.

No person who has been through the JIT sessions will forget the application of these principles in the tying of the "fire underwriter's knot," as presented in the first session. The demonstration began with the leader's "telling" one of the group members, who acted as trainee, how to tie the knot. When asked to do it himself without further instruction, the trainee, of course, bungled the job. He was also unable to tie it after one rapid demonstration by the instructor, who stood facing the trainee. Finally, after putting the trainee in the proper position, the instructor tied the knot slowly and explained each step as he did it, stressing key points. He then asked the trainee to perform the job in the same manner. Only then was the average trainee able to tie the knot quickly himself; and having been trained in this manner, few ever forget how to tie the knot.

TRAINING AS A CONTINUING FUNCTION

The four steps in job instruction are the essence of good teaching technique, distilled by training experts for successful industrial practice. Many firms benefited tremendously during the war from the instruction that their supervisors and leadmen received in training techniques, but the benefits were usually in proportion to the attention given by line and staff officials to the continuing application of these techniques.

Training should not be thought of as something that is given once to new employees and then forgotten. Training is the very essence of management, for it is showing someone else how to do a job that might otherwise not be done, or be done wrong. It is therefore a continuing management function.

Most supervisors need assistance in making full use of job breakdowns as an aid in training. This assistance can be given by the training director and his staff. It will be welcomed, however, to the extent that line supervisors accept the need for training in specific situations. Here, as pointed out earlier, is a real opportunity for the training director to develop a training program that is designed to help supervisors solve specific production problems and to meet new situations created by changes in technology and processes.

SUMMARY

Employee induction and training are important procedures in building an effective work team that will reach a high level of productive efficiency. They are not separate from the job of getting out production but are a part of that job and hence a responsibility of line management. Generally, however, a staff man—a training director or the personnel administrator—should have the broader responsibility for developing the training program in the light of the needs of the organization and in co-operation with the line officials. He can also assist in developing instructors who have a grasp of sound training techniques.

Both induction and training are closely related to other parts of the personnel program, such as recruitment, selection, job analysis, employee rating, promotion, and transfer. The success of training is measured by subsequent performance on the job, and one method of assessing job performance is by an employee-rating procedure. Training is also a means by which employees can prepare themselves for better jobs. In the next chapter, we shall turn to a discussion of employee rating and promotion.

Chapter 13

Employee Rating
and Promotion

> Whether a formal rating plan is adopted or not, manage-
> ment is constantly rating employees. . . . In the absence of
> precise records of performance and ability, management
> must rely solely on the supervisor's opinion of the relative
> worth of an employee. . . . Haphazard, careless, or biased
> decisions on matters of layoff and promotion may be more
> injurious to employee morale and efficiency than are rigid
> seniority rules. For this reason, progressive employers have
> introduced formal ability rating plans as an aid in reaching
> more objective and unbiased judgments respecting the
> relative competency of individual employees.
>
> FREDERICK H. HARBISON[1]

When an employee has been selected, hired, placed, inducted, and
trained for a particular job, he is entitled to know from time to time how
he is measuring up to expected standards of job performance. His supervisor is responsible for giving him this information. The prospect of advancement is also important to most new employees. They want to know
what they can do to improve their performance and to prepare themselves
for better jobs. A sound promotion policy is therefore a vital part of the
personnel program, and an acceptable employee-rating plan may be an
important aid in the administration of this policy.

Some form of systematic employee rating has been adopted by many
organizations as a means of telling employees how they are getting along
on their jobs and of selecting candidates for promotion to better jobs.
Rating is also useful as a check on the success of recruitment, selection,
and placement procedures. In this chapter, we shall first consider the

[1] *Seniority Policies and Precedures as Developed through Collective Bargaining*, Princeton
University, Industrial Relations Section, Princeton, N. J., 1941, p. 42.

elements of a workable employee-rating plan and then turn to a consideration of promotion policy.

What a Good Rating Plan Does

Informal employee rating, which is simply the comparison of one employee with another, takes place whenever a supervisor says, "I think Bill's a better man than John, so I'm going to promote him." What are the objections to this kind of informal rating? One difficulty is that, without systematic information, regularly gathered and periodically reviewed with the worker, it is hard for a supervisor to be fair. Moreover, it is impossible for him to prove that he is fair. And employees have no satisfactory basis on which to build their expectations. The charges of favoritism and the inevitable disappointments that ensue have a bad effect on personnel relations.

Formal employee-rating plans have been developed to reduce the element of favoritism and snap judgment in personnel decisions. They are widely used by government agencies and in private industry where management is vitally interested in building a loyal and efficient group of employees. The principal advantages of a good employee-rating plan may be outlined as follows:

1. It provides for uniform and systematic judgments by supervisors of the performance and conduct of each employee over a period of time, in advance of the need to make decisions concerning these employees.
2. It gives supervisors a record of progress or difficulties, which they can discuss with each employee, commending good work, pointing out deficiencies, and suggesting possibilities for improvement.
3. It provides comparable information that can be used in selecting employees for promotion or for individual merit wage or salary increases and, where performance is a factor to be considered, in selecting employees to be retained in downgrading and layoff.

Employee rating is not a substitute for objective records of output, quality, piecework, or incentive earnings, and other concrete data that indicate relative employee performance. Rating is essentially subjective and therefore cannot be exact. But it is based on pooled judgments periodically rendered by supervisors when each employee is compared, one factor at a time, with every other employee in the same work group. These results are certainly better than the individual judgments and hasty opinions that might otherwise be used.

But the reliability and accuracy of employee rating are not sufficiently great, in our judgment, to warrant basing individual merit wage or salary increases solely on numerical rating scores. This is probably the most common single use of employee rating, yet worker and union opposition to this practice is growing.[1] Factors such as "quantity" and "quality" of output have a more understandable relation to earnings than do "reliability," "attendance," or "cooperativeness." The latter factors are clearly more important in deciding whom to promote or to retain than in deciding what wage rate or salary to pay.

DEVELOPING AND ADMINISTERING A RATING PLAN

Should the personnel department consider the development and administration of an employee-rating plan as one of its exclusive functions? The answer is clearly no. Like so many other parts of the personnel program, employee rating is ultimately a line responsibility, to be met with the assistance of the personnel administrator and his staff. Moreover, almost any plan will be worthless if it lacks the support of top management, if raters are poorly trained or unconvinced as to its value, if discussion of ratings with employees is badly handled, or if ratings are not honestly used for the purposes intended. These and other difficulties often prevent the successful operation of an employee-rating program. They may be avoided if the personnel administrator takes the following steps:

1. Secures full agreement of line management on the need for a formal employee-rating plan and on the purposes for which it will be used. The proposed use of the plan controls the choice of the type: (a) point system with weights for each factor, (b) nonpoint system with a chart or form listing the factors to be rated, or (c) the rank-order method, when each supervisor rates only a small number of employees and divides them into groups.

2. Studies plans of other companies and existing literature on the subject, to develop a plan best suited to the needs of the particular company.[2] Complicated plans should be avoided, and, in our judgment, point

[1] See *U. E. Guide to Wage Payment Plans, Time Study, and Job Evaluation*, p. 90, United Electrical, Radio, and Machine Workers of America, CIO, New York, 1943. This union and a number of others have pressed in contract negotiations for "automatic progression" of individual rates within rate ranges on particular jobs, on the basis of length of service rather than "merit."

[2] Excellent suggestions on employee rating and actual plans from a number of well-known companies are found in *Employee Rating*, Studies in Personnel Policy No. 39, National Industrial Conference Board, Inc., New York, 1942. For a good description of the development of a successful employee-rating plan in the Atlantic Refining Company, see R. S. DRIVER, "A Case History in Merit Rating," *Personnel*, Vol. 16, No. 4, pp. 137–162, 1940. Pitfalls in rating plans and how they can be avoided are discussed by JOSEPH TIFFIN, Merit Rating: Its Validity and Techniques, in *Rating and Training Executives and Employees*, Personnel Series No. 100, American Management Association, New York, 1946.

systems are open to criticism for this reason. Ratings in not more than five classes, such as A, B, C, D, and E, are preferable, because points and numerical weights suggest a degree of accuracy that is not possible in subjective employee rating.

3. Enlists the cooperation of supervisors in drawing up the rating form, including discussion of factors to be used, weights and points (if any) to be assigned to each factor, and uniform descriptions or instructions to be followed. To repeat, the final responsibility for rating should rest with the line organization.

4. Makes sure that the purpose and nature of the rating plan are explained to those who will do the rating (first-line supervisors and department heads) and to those who will be affected by the rating. For example, where there is a union, there should be full discussion of the proposed rating plan with union representatives, and subsequently all employees should be informed of it.

5. Provides or secures careful training of the raters, in order to get unbiased, uniform rating of all employees. "Progress in rating," according to the training director of a company with successful employee rating, "will be almost directly proportionate, at least in the early stages of the program, to the amount of intelligent effort expended to improve the ability of the individual raters."[1]

6. Achieves line and staff coordination and mutual checking of ratings, in order to get consistency and uniformity of rating within and between departments. In a large metal-trades company, there was much employee dissatisfaction because, in one department, a point rating of 75 was "excellent," whereas it took 90 in another department to be considered excellent. Coordination of raters, through group discussions with the personnel administrator and superintendents, can help to minimize such discrepancies.

7. Arranges for periodic discussion of ratings by the supervisor with each of his employees. Good points should be stressed, failures pointed out, and better performance encouraged.[2] If these interviews are poorly handled, much harm can be done. Unless there is adequate discussion of ratings with employees, the plan may be regarded as a "black list" by employees. Every employee has a right to know from his supervisor how he is getting along. To tell him in a manner that will make him want to do better is a real challenge to every supervisor.

[1] DRIVER, R. S., "Training as a Means of Improving Employee Performance Rating," *Personnel*, Vol. 18, pp. 364–370, May, 1942.

[2] See ARMSTRONG, T. O., "Talking Your Ratings," *Personnel*, Vol. 20, pp. 112–115, 1943.

8. Recommends careful use of the ratings in selecting employees for promotion to better jobs, as discussed later in this chapter.

9. Provides for challenge and review of ratings through the complaint and grievance procedure if employees or their union representatives are dissatisfied with management's decisions.

Promotion and Upgrading

With a well-administered employee-rating plan, management is in a better position to develop a sound promotion policy. What is a promotion? If an employee is moved from the second shift to the preferred first shift on the same job, or if he is moved into a room where working conditions are better though other features of the job are the same, has there been a promotion—or a transfer?

We shall consider that a *promotion* is the advancement of an employee to a better job—better in terms of greater responsibilities, more prestige or "status," greater skill, and, especially, increased rate of pay or salary. Better hours or better location or working conditions may also characterize the "better job" to which an employee is promoted. Not all these are combined in every promotion, however.

Upgrading is a related term that was widely used during the war as skilled labor shortages became acute. Upgrading is the movement of an employee from a less skilled job to a more skilled job within the same organizational unit. It is "the method that leads workers upward in the pyramid of organization"[1] and in this sense is a small-scale promotion. When a second-class machinist is upgraded to the job of a first-class machinist, he has also been promoted. Both upgrading and promotion are ways of developing and recognizing the talents of employees within the organization, instead of filling skilled and responsible positions from the outside.

Promotion and upgrading should be distinguished from *transfer*, which is the movement of an employee from one job to another on the same occupational level and on about the same level of wages or salary. No appreciable increase or decrease in duties and responsibilities is involved, although there may be a change in their specific nature. Transfers and transfer policy are discussed in the next chapter.

Seniority and Ability in Promotions

The most important policy question in promotion is the relative significance of seniority and ability. There is an increasing tendency, espe-

[1] *Upgrading*, Bulletin No. 2, Training Within Industry Branch, Labor Division, Office of Production Management, Washington, D. C., August, 1941.

cially in unionized firms, to give more weight to seniority in making promotions because of the great importance that workers attach to length of service. This raises two basic questions: Is the employee with the longest service necessarily the best? If workers automatically qualify for better jobs by accumulating seniority, will there be any incentive for new employees to improve their performance?

The answers to these questions, particularly the second, are so generally in the negative that management should stress ability above seniority in promotion. No supervisor can get effective results through people if he is limited in his opportunity to make the best use of each person's capacities. Promotions should be fairly and capably used by management to place on each job the most competent and productive workers available. Promotions should be a reward to encourage those employees who make a successful effort to increase their knowledge or skill and who maintain a high level of productivity. When seniority is made the sole basis for promotion, it becomes a strait jacket. Seniority should be considered, but only when the qualifications of two candidates for a better job are, for practical purposes, equal.[1]

Management will not be able to win acceptance for this kind of promotion policy, however, unless it succeeds in establishing confidence in the fairness of its procedure for selecting the employee to be promoted. The difficulties are especially obvious in unionized firms. Certainly, one of the reasons for the demand for strict seniority in promotions was the abuse by some managements of the privilege of selecting the best man. Too often, this was influenced by personal acquaintance, favors performed, and recent events—rather than by objective records of performance or by a systematic subjective procedure for rating employees.

Clearly, management needs these records and procedures if it is fairly to administer a promotion policy based upon employee ability. The only way that management can meet increasing union demands for straight seniority in promotions is to insist that ability be considered as the most important factor and then to demonstrate its fairness and objectivity by selecting for promotion those employees who, on the basis of performance records and employee rating, are clearly superior to their fellow em-

---

[1] Evidence that unions have begun to question the wisdom of seniority as the sole factor in promotions is found in a report by a special union committee on the internal problems of the Brotherhood of Papermakers, AF of L, *Labor Unrest and Dissatisfaction*, pp. 47–50, Albany, 1944.

The adverse effects of seniority on efficiency are described by DAN H. MATER, "A Statistical Study of the Effect of Seniority upon Employee Efficiency," *Journal of Business of the University of Chicago*, April, 1941, pp. 169–204.

ployees.[1] This means that, in most cases, slight differences in ability should not be considered.

A personnel-minded management is willing to go more than halfway to meet the union on this difficult question. For example, one company, operating under a union agreement that retained management authority to make promotions on the basis of ability, nevertheless instructed its supervisors to consider the senior employee first when a promotion was to be made. If the senior employee was clearly unqualified for the job, as evidenced by records of performance and other information such as attendance, safety record, etc., the supervisor could then promote a more capable junior employee. He was asked, however, to make a full report to the superintendent on his reasons for not following seniority. If the superintendent approved this departure from the seniority principle, he sent the report to the personnel administrator, who, in turn, notified the union of the reasons for promoting the junior man. If the supervisor had a reasonable doubt about the qualifications of the employee with greatest seniority, he was instructed to put the employee on the job for a temporary trial period of 6 weeks. This procedure tended to minimize the number of complaints about promotions.

Problems in Determining Seniority

If seniority is to be given some weight in promotions, however, the problem still remains: How is an employee's "seniority" determined? We have been using the term as if seniority were a readily definable and measurable factor, but this is possible only if certain basic questions are first answered. (1) What is the seniority unit—occupation, department, plant, or company? (2) Within this unit, how is seniority to be computed, and when is it broken?

Occupational or job seniority is likely to be more logical as a basis for promotion to a better job when there is a functional relationship between the two jobs. If the choice is between an employee who has been on a certain job 2 years and with the department (or plant or company) for 15, and an employee who has been on the job 10 years and with the department (or plant or company) for 12, the latter is likely to feel that he is "next in line" for advancement to a more skilled and related job. Occupational seniority, however, tends to restrict mobility within the or-

---

[1] In the agreement between a union and a large automobile manufacturing firm, the following clause appeared: "In the advancement of employees to higher paid jobs when ability, merit, and capacity are equal, employees with the largest seniority will be given preference." The impartial umpire (arbitrator) under the agreement ruled in a series of cases that seniority should be disregarded only where an employee with less seniority stands "head and shoulders" above the employees with greater seniority.

ganization and may be less appropriate for certain other purposes, such as transfer and layoff.[1]

Computation of seniority, or length of service, within the seniority unit can be made in several ways. An employee's seniority can start when he is first employed in the company (or in the plant, department, or job), regardless of subsequent transfers, layoffs, leaves of absence, etc. Or these interruptions may be deducted to compute a net length of service. Another possibility is to compute seniority from the date when the employee was *last* hired. This would be his length of *continuous* service, although in practice exceptions are often made for interruptions due to temporary layoffs and leaves of absence. Occupational seniority is usually broken with transfers to a different job, and all types of seniority are broken when an employee quits or is discharged.

Increasing emphasis on seniority in personnel decisions requires that management, with the assistance of the personnel administrator, establish clear policies on these questions. In unionized firms, they will obviously be negotiated with union representatives. In either case, when decisions have been reached, the seniority of each employee should be computed and posted, so that employees can be informed of their relative seniority standings, and any errors corrected before the seniority lists are actually used.

OTHER POLICY ELEMENTS IN PROMOTION

In addition to emphasis on ability and decisions on seniority, there are other elements of a sound promotion policy. The personnel administrator should bring these to the attention of top management in policy formulation and to the attention of line management in policy administration. A few of these elements are

1. A statement of management's intention that higher paid and better jobs will be filled by advancement from within, whenever possible, rather than by hiring from outside the organization. Obviously, the statement will be worthless if it is not faithfully practiced.

2. Encouragement for supervisors to permit capable employees to leave the department or plant if better opportunities are available elsewhere. If a good man is held back, he is not likely to remain a satisfied employee.

3. Establishment of lines of progression—ladders of promotion—within the organization. It is desirable to use job analysis to develop a

---

[1] See later discussion in Chap. 14. The seniority unit and other problems in determining and administering seniority policies are ably discussed in FREDERICK H. HARBISON, *Seniority Policies and Procedures as Developed through Collective Bargaining*, Princeton University, Industrial Relations Section, Princeton, N. J., 1941.

chart showing basic job requirements (in ability, experience, formal education, etc.) and how each job leads to another. Employees need to know what is expected of them on higher rated jobs in order to prepare themselves for advancement.

4. Line responsibility for making promotions, with the advice and assistance of the personnel department in a staff capacity. The supervisor should initiate promotions, which should then be subject to approval by his immediate superior in the line organization. This serves as a check on the fairness of promotions and ensures that the policy will be consistently administered. Joint responsibility of management and the union, however, is neither a wise nor a workable procedure.

5. Provision for employee or union challenge of a particular promotion, within the limits of the promotion policy and the union agreement. Some firms have taken the position that "questions as to the correctness of management's selection will be heard by management but will not be arbitrable." Where management has demonstrated its fairness over a considerable period, it may be possible to secure this type of provision in union negotiations, but ordinarily a management that has consistently adhered to a sound promotion policy should have little to fear from a commitment to arbitrate grievances about promotions.

Two allied procedures that are important for the success of a promotion policy are:

1. Posting of openings for promotions, so that interested employees may apply within a specified period, usually several days or a week. If possible, the opening should be posted and the candidate selected before the job actually becomes vacant. If the job is temporarily filled by an employee who is subsequently advanced to the job permanently, the other applicants are likely to feel that the posting procedure is a farce.

2. Provision for training as a means or preparation for promotion. Special on-the-job training, vestibule schools, night classes, or vocational courses should be available.

Handling Promotions and Demotions

The actual handling of promotions by line officials offers the personnel administrator an excellent opportunity to develop understanding and acceptance of management policy. In his contacts with supervisors, he can emphasize the importance of skillful policy administration.

Employees should be fully informed as to ladders of promotion, as to how they can prepare themselves for advancement, and as to what will be expected of them on the higher rated jobs. In selecting candidates for promotion, there should be careful review of any objective records of performance and of employee ratings. The man to be promoted should not be selected casually or on the basis of something that happened last week. Senior employees who have been by-passed in the selection of a better man are entitled to an explanation of the reasons, as are union representatives when the organization is unionized. People have a right to know in advance about the changes that will affect them, even if the results for them are negative. Employees who are unable to handle more skilled jobs should not be falsely encouraged.

Sometimes employees who have been promoted fail to make good. The supervisor has the opportunity here to give a fair trial and then to explain the reasons for subsequent demotion. An example of skillful handling of a case involving both promotion and temporary demotion is the experience of Peter K., who was first hired in 1937 as a cloth trucker in the weave room of a textile mill. He proved to be an able and willing worker, and a year later the supervisor promoted him to the job of "warp man," which consisted in putting full beams of warp yarn in a set of looms. This job is ordinarily a steppingstone to the job of loom fixer, which is the most skilled job in the mill, and Peter was subsequently promoted first to "learner fixer," then to "fixer." As a loom fixer, however, Peter did not get along well. He was poor at detecting loom troubles, thus causing a lot of lost time for the weavers, who complained and always seemed to be at odds with him. He became morose and tended to blame the weavers rather than himself for his trouble.

During this period, the supervisor talked with Peter on a number of occasions, pointing out the importance of cooperating with the weavers and offering to help him learn to detect loom troubles more quickly. Very little improvement resulted, however. In July, 1943, Peter was called into the supervisor's office, and, in the presence of the union steward, he was told that the poor condition of his section of looms and his inability or unwillingness to get along with his weavers made it difficult to retain weavers and battery hands in the section and that, therefore, it was necessary to demote him to "spare fixer," which carried a lower rate of pay. He was further told that, if he could improve his work, he might get another trial as a loom fixer.

A year later, the supervisor did give him another trial on a different section of looms. His relations with the weavers were better, but mechanical difficulties still bothered him; and, in May, 1945, he was again demoted after a long talk with the supervisor, who, again in the presence of the union steward, explained the reasons for the change. Peter accepted this without resentment and subsequently improved considerably, often going out of his way to help others. When an assistant supervisor was absent because of illness or vacation, the supervisor began to use Peter to assist the others; and, with this encouragement, Peter rapidly improved to the point where the supervisor was ready to promote him to the next opening as assistant supervisor.

Under careful, patient handling, this worker had found a job on which he was making the best use of his ability and contributing the maximum to the organization. He might have been embittered and sullen in his work; instead he became a useful, satisfied employee. This is personnel administration at its best.

Note that, in this case, the union did not participate directly in the administration of the promotion policy. But a union representative was present when action was taken, and this was an important factor in avoiding grievances over the changes made.

Disputes over Promotions

When a management decision on promotion is disputed, however, the resulting discussions with labor representatives offer a further opportunity to achieve understanding. If management itself has departed from established policy or lacks adequate reasons for its action, the conference may still be a fruitful one if errors are admitted and adjustments made. On the other hand, if, after investigation, the promotion appears to be fully justified, reasons can be more thoroughly explained, records produced, and the consequences of a departure from sound policy pointed out.

In one dispute over a promotion, for example, the union representatives argued that management had unfairly ignored seniority in selecting a younger carpenter's helper for promotion to the job of "outside carpenter." Management maintained that the younger man was more competent and that the older man (sixty-five years of age) was physically unable to do the work because his eyes were poor and he had once fallen off a ladder when assigned to temporary outside work. Unfortunately, it was not until the dispute had advanced to the last stage of the grievance procedure— between top management and the regional officer of the union—that management convincingly stressed the point that, in by-passing the older man, it was also protecting him by not putting him on a job in which his own safety and that of others would be endangered.

Disputes over promotions that cannot be resolved should, as we have pointed out, be submitted to arbitration. Willingness of management to let an impartial umpire review the soundness of its decision, within the limits of established policy, may itself be convincing evidence to the union that the decision was sound, as was the case in the example just cited.

When management's position is weak, this should be admitted and corrective action taken before the arbitration stage is reached.

SUMMARY

In this chapter, we have stressed the importance of a systematic employee-rating plan as an aid in telling employees how they are measuring up to expected standards of performance, and in making personnel decisions. Rating of employees is a line function that can be performed with the advice and assistance of the personnel department. Periodic discussion of ratings with employees is one of the most important parts of a sound rating program. If the rating has been well done, the supervisor has an opportunity in these discussions to demonstrate the fairness of his judgments and to encourage better performance.

Employee rating and objective records of employee performance are essential features in promotion, which should be made primarily on the basis of ability. Management will not be able to meet the growing union demand for straight seniority in promotion, however, unless it can demonstrate that its personnel judgments are fair. Few things destroy the will to work as surely as the conviction on the part of employees that "pull" and "influence" win the best jobs.

Clear, consistent policies, fairly administered, are equally important for transfer, downgrading, and layoff. These are discussed in the next chapter.

Chapter 14

Transfer, Downgrading, and Layoff

Since no one knows where he will stand when layoffs come, it is understandable why seniority provisions in union contracts remain of interest to large numbers of wage earners. While it is but human for managements faced with acute problems of accelerating production to become impatient with the complexities of seniority provisions, their significance to the individual worker and their possible contribution in releasing incentive cannot be disregarded without impairment of good industrial relations and efficient operations.

J. Douglas Brown[1]

Like promotion, transfer is a method used by management to place employees in positions where they will contribute their best efforts to the organization. If a newly hired worker is assigned to a certain job and left there despite his desire to transfer to a different kind of work or to advance to a better job, he will not be a satisfied employee. His resentment will probably express itself in reduced work effectiveness and perhaps in formal complaints. When better job opportunities are available outside the organization, his dissatisfaction is frequently registered in labor-turnover statistics.

Every organization, therefore, needs sound policies of transfer as well as of promotion. The personnel administrator should be prepared to make recommendations for these policies and to help line officers administer them effectively. He should also make sure that these policies are supported by other features of the personnel program. For example, careful job description and analysis are needed to establish the avenues of transfer

[1] Foreword to *Seniority Policies and Procedures as Developed through Collective Bargaining*, Princeton University, Industrial Relations Section, Princeton, N. J., p. IV, 1941.

and the ladders of promotion. Sound procedures of selection and placement are required to prevent an excessive number of subsequent transfers.
Systematic training of employees and supervisors helps to prepare workers
to make transfers and to be promoted and enables supervisors effectively
to administer the respective policies.

Downgrading and layoff, as operations decline, also call for clear-cut,
consistent policies. Should an employee be laid off or downgraded to a
lower rated job? On what basis should layoffs be made? Should advance
notice of layoffs or dismissal pay be given? These are some of the questions
that we shall consider in the latter part of this chapter.

Types of Transfer

Before turning to a discussion of requirements in transfer policy, it is
worth while to distinguish among the different types of transfer. Transfers
differ in terms of (1) the unit within which each takes place and (2) the
purpose for which each is made. The transfer unit may be the work group
or section, the department, the plant, or the entire company when there
is more than one plant. The nature of the operation or the industry has
an important bearing on the appropriate unit for transfer. For example,
interdepartmental or interplant transfers are easier to arrange and require
less retraining if job skills are roughly comparable in each department or
plant than if the work is entirely different.

When we consider transfers from the standpoint of their purpose, five
types may be distinguished, although these are not always mutually
exclusive.

1. *Production Transfers.*—These are transfers from jobs in which labor
requirements are declining to jobs in which they are increasing or in
which vacancies have occurred through separations. This type of transfer
is made to avoid layoffs on one job at the same time that workers are
being hired for a similar type of work. Production transfers are an essential
part of a program to stabilize company employment, and they require
some form of centralized employment control. The personnel department
may act as a clearinghouse through which all layoffs and hirings are
funneled. In some cases, production transfers may of necessity be to less
skilled jobs.

2. *Replacement Transfers.*—These are similar to production transfers
in their intent—*i.e.*, to avoid layoffs among present employees. However,
in replacement transfers, a long-service employee is transferred to a similar
job, usually in another department, where he replaces or "bumps" an
employee with shorter service. A replacement-transfer program is used
when all operations are declining and is designed to retain the long-service

employees as long as possible. Examples of this type of transfer are found in two cases appended to earlier chapters, The Effect on Work Teams of Labor Turnover and Internal Mobility (Chap. 8) and A "Personal" Complaint (Chap. 9).

3. *Versatility Transfers.*—This type of transfer is for the purpose of providing management with a more versatile work force. These may be used as preparation for production or replacement transfers. The versatility transfer is also necessary for flexibility of operation in a small shop where there is not enough work on a particular job to keep a man busy. A small gear plant, for example, had to use its milling-machine operator on a number of other jobs; in fact, he practically had to be an all-round machinist.

Another use of this type of transfer is in the development of "flying squadrons" of specially trained workers who can handle peak needs on a variety of jobs. This is partly an employment-stabilization device, to avoid short-term hires, and partly a means of training future supervisors by giving the trainees experience in a variety of operations and situations.

4. *Shift Transfers.*—Where there is more than one shift, transfers may be made from one shift to another on the same type of work. Generally, transfers are from the late shifts (the second and third) to the day (first) shift. Many workers dislike a second-shift assignment, because it interferes with their participation in the afternoon and evening life of the community. Others object to the third shift because it requires a reversal of the normal processes of working and sleeping. Yet there are always some people who have special reasons for preferring the second or third shifts to the first. For example, a mother may prefer second-shift employment, if her husband already works on the first, so that someone is at home with the children during most of the day. These human aspects of multiple-shift operations are discussed in greater detail in Chap. 18.

5. *Remedial Transfers.*—This type of transfer is made for various reasons primarily concerning the *person* on the job. Initial placement may have been faulty, or the worker may not get along with his supervisor or with other workers in the department. He may be getting too old to continue on his regular job, or the type of job or working conditions may not be well adapted to his present health or accident record. If the job is repetitive and monotonous, the worker may have gone stale and would benefit by transfer to a different kind of work.

One of the key principles of good personnel administration is the treatment of employees as individuals, within the framework of broad policies. Remedial transfers offer an excellent opportunity for the personnel department, working with line supervisors, to practice this principle, as the following examples illustrate.

EXAMPLES OF REMEDIAL TRANSFERS

A large textile company introduced a formal induction program for new employees in 1944, and an important part of this program was the follow-up interview with the new employees after their first 6 weeks of employment. In a number of cases, remedial transfers were recommended by the personnel department and made with the approval of the supervisors concerned. The result of these transfers in better placement and improved employee morale is shown in the following excerpts from the interview reports. These reports also indicate certain faults, such as poor initial placement, in the personnel practices of the company.

ROSE B.—Was a doffer at No. 1 Mill, where conditions had her nerves badly upset. We transferred her to the spinning room in No. 2 Mill, where she finds everything and everyone much different—particularly the supervision, because, when the work does not run right, the boss goes out of his way to see that she does not become upset. She expects her boy friend home very soon after 3 years overseas and has asked to go out at that time to get married. But she says she will not quit her job, definitely not.

JOHN S.—This fellow did not like his job because it was inside work. Talked with his foreman, and he said it was O. K. to transfer him to the yard, which we did. Found out later that his health was poor and he should work out in the fresh air. Saw him today, and he said he was feeling better and liked his new job.

ELMER W.—Transferred from boiler house, as he could not work on the third shift because of family reasons. He had experience as a machine tender in Dept. B, so was transferred there to the second shift. He likes his new hours, as he can be at home during the first part of the day. Because of his experience, he is more valuable as a machine tender than as a helper in the boiler house.

CHARLES C.—Could not stand dust in Dept. B, and, as he had a medical slip from his doctor, we transferred him to the south storehouse. He is getting along fine now and likes his job. We had to transfer him, or he would have gotten a release to leave the company.

LOUIS A.—In Dept. E, he worked on piece rates, and that made him very nervous. Before he came here, he had worked outdoors for many years. So we transferred him to the yard, and he likes it very much. The work does not make him nervous, and he is used to it.

HARRY Y.—Since he lives out of town, he had to come on the 7 P.M. bus and wait around until his shift began at 10 P.M. to start work. He told me he was going to quit because of his transportation problem. I checked with other departments and found him a job from 7 P.M. to 10 P.M. in Dept. B. He works there

3 hours and then goes direct to his work in Dept. K. This arrangement is satisfactory, as he earns more money and does not waste so much time.

ANDREW C.—After discharge from the Army, this man went to work in Dept. F but was out sick for a long time and could not return to work in this department because of physical condition and type of work. Transferred him to Dept. A, and he now states that his new work is much better for him. We found out this man is suffering from stomach ulcers and is under treatment.

TRANSFER POLICY

The examples just given indicate the wisdom of having a procedure whereby an unsatisfactory placement may be corrected. If the responsibility for interdepartmental transfer is left with the individual foreman, his workers may hesitate to ask for transfers out of the department. Or some foremen may be more lenient than others, or they may recommend transfer to get rid of poor workers rather than attempting to improve them or discharging them. Without a policy, there are no bench marks to follow in making other types of transfer, such as production and replacement transfers.

A systematic transfer policy, therefore, is needed to get uniformity of treatment throughout the organization. In formulating this policy, information and decisions are needed on the following points:

1. *The circumstances under which transfers will be made.*—Are operations in different departments sufficiently alike to permit production and replacement transfers? What other types of transfer should the organization encourage?

2. *Responsibility for initiating and approving transfers.*—Should the first-line supervisor have the entire responsibility, or should his decision be subject to review by his immediate superior or by the personnel administrator?

3. *Jobs to which transfers will be made*, as shown by job description and analysis. How much retraining, if any, will be required, and how much time should a transferee be given to demonstrate that he can satisfactorily perform the new job?

4. *The area or unit over which transfer will take place.*—Should transfers be made between departments, divisions, and plants, or only within one subunit? When an employee is transferred, does he carry his previous seniority credit with him, retain it for a temporary period, or lose it altogether?

5. *Basis for transfers*, when two or more persons desire transfer to the same job or same shift. Should seniority (length of service) be the sole determinant, assuming minimum capacity to handle the job? Or should

skill or competence be the deciding factor? What importance, if any, should be given to marital status and dependency?

6. *The rate of pay* to be received by the transferee on the job to which he is transferred. Under what circumstances should he get the rate on his previous or regular job (assuming it is higher), and when should he get the rate of the new job (assuming it is lower)?

To make dogmatic statements on these points is hazardous, since a transfer policy, like other personnel policies, should be tailored to fit the particular organization. However, the personnel administrator can be of assistance to top management in policy formulation if he is familiar with similar policies developed by other comparable firms and is aware of certain pitfalls to be avoided as well as the broad aims to be achieved.

Most firms need, at one time or another, all the types of transfer we have discussed. These transfers should either be initiated by the immediate supervisor or recommended by the personnel department, subject to review, if disagreement exists, by a higher line officer. There may be a temptation for a new personnel administrator to want this authority for himself, but he would then be assuming line responsibilities that are beyond his proper sphere.

Whether transfers are to be made only within departments, or between departments, divisions, and plants, depends largely on the similarity of operations and how much retraining is necessary. If the transfer unit is too wide, *e.g.*, in replacement transfers, excessive bumping of shorter service employees will be necessary, particularly where seniority is the sole basis for transfer. To avoid this, the transferee may be required to possess the necessary ability to do the job or to demonstrate his competence within a short trial period. As in promotions, records of employee performance and an employee-rating plan are of great assistance to management in making these transfers. If interdepartmental or interplant transfers are used as a means of keeping experienced employees in the organization, it will be necessary to adopt some form of plant-wide or company-wide seniority so that experienced employees do not lose accumulated rights if they are later returned to their former jobs. This is one of the thorniest questions in the whole seniority problem.

Finally, in a production or replacement transfer to prevent layoff or in a remedial transfer to correct faulty placement, the transferee should ordinarily get the rate of pay on the new job, not that of his previous job. The same is true of shift transfers, which are ordinarily desired by employees who wish to get on a preferred shift. When transfers are made to accommodate management and to balance operations, as in many versatility and some shift transfers, the transferee should be paid his old rate or the new rate, whichever is higher.

Skill in Handling Transfers

In addition to advising on policy formulation, the personnel administrator's greatest contribution to a sound transfer program is in making recommendations for the solution of specific transfer problems that are brought to his attention and in helping the parties affected to understand the reasons for the proposed transfer. Here, as in other personnel problems, he can help supervisors in "getting down to cases," in considering the "facts"—the claims of each side, the attitudes displayed, and the characteristics of the individuals or groups involved. He helps the supervisor, the employees, and their union representatives to view the problem both in its policy aspect and from its person-centered aspect. His recommendation, though conforming to the general limits of the transfer policy, is designed to fit a specific case.

For example, suppose an employee requests a transfer from the second to the first shift because she has small children who must be looked after during the daylight hours. The supervisor may ask the advice of the personnel administrator. The latter listens sympathetically, but he cannot consider the request solely upon an individual basis. He must bring out the policy requirements in shift transfers. On what basis are transfers made to better shifts on the same job or within the same department? If he recommends making an exception for this case, no matter how deserving, will there be a flood of demands from other workers for exceptional treatment? If the transfer cannot legitimately be made, does the employee understand why not? Will any other expedient meet her case? Perhaps she can be transferred to another department that has only one shift and needs labor. The effect this will have on her seniority standing is another matter that needs to be understood and administered in terms of policy requirement. Perhaps no immediate solution can be found, but at least the problem has received sympathetic consideration, and presumably the worker has achieved a better understanding of management policy. And perhaps consideration of the workers' individual needs may, in the aggregate, convince management of the desirability of broadening the personnel program in some such way as by developing a company-sponsored day nursery, for instance.

When a recommendation or decision in a transfer case is disputed, the personnel administrator has the further opportunity to help the parties understand the aims of a transfer. A replacement transfer, for example, moves people from certain jobs and departments to other jobs and departments. The readjustments may be difficult, making demands on the patience of the foreman, union representatives, and workers in the department to which the transfer is made. There is need for someone to explain the policy involved, the adjustments called for from all concerned, and the mutual advantages of the transfer. As a specialist in human relations, the personnel manager is presumably well equipped to perform this task. The case for Chap. 9, entitled A "Personal" Complaint, is an illustration of this point.

DOWNGRADING—OR LAYOFF?

Replacement transfers sometimes involve downgrading. As operations decline, it may be possible to avoid laying off the more skilled employees by downgrading them to less skilled and lower rated jobs. Is this a good policy, or should workers who cannot be transferred to equally good or better jobs be laid off?

Opinions differ on this question. If a skilled employee is downgraded to less skilled work and paid the lower rate on that job, he may become disgruntled—especially if he is likely to remain long on the lower paid job. This may occur when technological changes permanently displace skilled workers. If equally good jobs are not available within the company to which these employees can be transferred or for which they can be retrained, layoff is usually better policy than permitting permanent dissatisfaction to develop in the work force.

But the degree of dissatisfaction felt by workers who have been downgraded depends to a large extent upon the availability of other job opportunities in the community. If there is widespread and substantial unemployment, employees may prefer lower rated jobs with their present employer to the uncertainties of a glutted labor market. When jobs are plentiful outside, downgraded employees may leave voluntarily. Their chief reasons for remaining would be the expectation that they might soon be upgraded to their old jobs and the realization that in leaving they would lose seniority rights and other accumulated employee benefits.

Whichever policy is adopted, it should be explained to all employees before it is put into effect, and it should be consistently followed. Reasons for individual decisions on employees to be downgraded or laid off, when job performance is considered, should be given to those affected.

USE OF RATING IN DOWNGRADING AND LAYOFFS

Determining competence and performance through employee rating is clearly more important for promotions and transfers than it is for downgrading and layoffs. In unionized firms, seniority is generally accepted as the major factor in downgrading workers to less skilled jobs as operations decline and in making layoffs or recalling employees to work after a layoff. Many nonunion firms also give considerable weight to seniority in downgrading and layoff, although here management obviously has more discretion in selecting employees to be retained.

But, when management does not follow strict seniority in downgrading and layoff, it needs some sound procedure for determining the relative competence of employees. Snap judgments and biased opinions will be just as unsatisfactory in layoff as they are in promotion. A formal employee-rating plan provides informed judgments, reached in advance of the need to make personnel decisions; and it is therefore more likely to win employee acceptance.

Experience with a rating plan in a unionized plant is illustrated by the following statement from the manager of industrial relations in a firm using employee rating in layoffs:[1]

In our case the union officially does not have much use for our plan. In our (contract) clause we say seniority will prevail if the man can do the job. We do not talk ratings, we do talk about the man's progress, and we use the (rating) form as a means of analyzing prior to talking. I can assure you we don't win all the cases! It has been interesting, however, over the past couple of years whenever there has been a problem, to hear the union president, business agent, or steward asking to bring out the progress form and let's look at the record! So you see, we have a plan which has become a pattern and generally accepted.

We have found in our experience that we have been able to take action in cases of layoff, demotion, etc., because we have a record built over a period of time. The man knows it each time the rating is made and so does the union steward, so that, when it becomes necessary to take action, all parties are pretty much in the position of knowing where the individual stands.

Employee rating may also be helpful in making demotions based on unsatisfactory performance, even when operations are not declining. After adequate warning, given by the supervisor when he discussed periodic ratings with the employee, workers who cannot meet reasonable job standards should be weeded out and assigned to less skilled jobs that they can handle, or discharged for incompetence.

FORMULATING A LAYOFF POLICY

Nearly every organization, at one time or another, is faced with the necessity of laying off employees for lack of work. Some layoffs are temporary and expected by employees in the nature of the job. These can be planned for and are not so serious. When changes in operations or a

[1] Letter to one of the authors.

decline in business necessitate permanent layoffs, however, the problem is more difficult.

In both types of layoff, but especially in the latter when long-service employees will be affected, there is need for a definite layoff policy. The cold written notice in the pay envelope that "your services are no longer required," or the casual word from the boss, "I guess we don't need you any more after tomorrow," will not suffice. Such methods are destructive of employee morale—not only for those dismissed but for those who remain, wondering whether their turn is next.

Granting the need for a sound policy, its formulation is not easy because of various possible alternatives and the conflicting demands of security and efficiency. The major problems that must have the full consideration of top management in formulating a layoff policy are:

1. *Will hours of work be reduced before any employees—or certain groups—are laid off?* It is common to lay off probationary (new) employees first and, after this, to reduce hours. But experience during the depression demonstrated the undesirability of excessive worksharing. When workers were getting only 2 or 3 days of work each week, nearly all were dissatisfied. From the standpoint of the individual firm, it is better to lay off the junior employees in order to give the remaining senior workers at least 4 days (or 32 hours) of work a week. Generally, however, some work sharing should precede the layoff of employees (excluding probationers) who have seniority standing, and union contracts frequently spell out the procedure to be followed.

2. *What factors shall determine who will be laid off first?*—As we have seen, seniority is increasingly accepted as important and, in many cases, is considered as the sole factor.[1] Some union contracts, however, provide

[1] The strong desire of employees for recognition of length of service and for a definite order in layoffs is met in some firms with a policy of strict seniority in layoffs. Efficiency is then protected by (1) careful selection when new employees are hired, (2) weeding out clearly incompetent employees by discharge, and (3) promotion on the basis of ability. But there is no simple answer to this problem. During the war, the National War Labor Board permitted regional boards to order seniority as the basis for layoff either when skill and ability were "equal," as between two employees, or when they were merely "sufficient" for the job. The majority opinion in a notable case contained the following observation:

"Under a provision granting seniority only where skill and ability are equal, seniority may be rendered well-nigh meaningless by the employer's insistence that his judgment may not be questioned. Conversely, a union can very seriously handicap an employer under a clause qualifying seniority only by ability to do the work if it fails to recognize that wide differences in proficiency are a legitimate consideration in layoffs and still more in promotions. Neither of these qualifications any more than any other provision in a union contract will work satisfactorily unless there is good will on both sides and an earnest desire to make the contract work." *In re Holtzer-Cabot Electric Company and United Electrical, Radio and Machine Workers of America, Local 214 (CIO).* Case No. 111-6021-D, Oct. 18, 1944 (made public Nov. 11, 1944). *War Labor Reports,* Vol. 19, p. 396.

that consideration also be given to skill and ability, physical fitness, and family status [1] Layoff policies in nonunion firms generally include all these factors and also, when the firm is dominant in a small community, take into consideration whether or not the employee is a local resident. Another alternative to straight seniority in layoffs is to exempt a certain percentage of the ablest employees, usually 10 or 15 per cent, in each job classification from the application of seniority rules. This group of clearly "exceptional" employees may be retained regardless of seniority, and the others laid off on a straight seniority basis. If management has freedom in making promotions on the basis of ability, however, perhaps it would be well advised to follow straight seniority in layoffs (when ability is adequate for the job) as a means of providing a greater degree of employment security to long-service employees.

3. *How should seniority be determined?*—This involves two points, as we have seen in Chap. 13: (*a*) the seniority unit—occupation, department, plant, or entire company; and (*b*) interruptions in length of service that might abrogate seniority rights. The first problem is particularly troublesome; for, whatever decision is reached, someone is likely to consider it unfair. For example, if long-service employees are transferred from another department to avoid laying them off, considerable training may be necessary, and the younger workers they displace may be resentful because "outsiders" are taking their jobs. On the other hand, a narrow departmental or occupational unit will lead to layoffs of long-service people in one department while employees with short seniority who are fortunate enough to be in a stationary or expanding department are retained. The second problem requires decisions on whether seniority is broken by transfers, layoffs, and extended absences due to illness, family problems, etc.

POLICY CHANGES: AN ILLUSTRATION

The difficulties involved in formulating a satisfactory layoff policy and the need for flexibility are illustrated by the experience of an electrical-goods manufacturing firm during the 1937-1938 recession. Before it was necessary to make mass layoffs, each layoff was considered as an emergency situation that could be dealt with only on its merits. The only aspect of

[1] In plants where labor relations are good and the union is not worried about its "security," a flexible layoff policy works well. Furthermore, workers are likely to have diverse interests that are recognized by such a policy. This was found to be the case in a study of layoffs and layoff policy in a large manufacturing firm in 1937. See McGREGOR, DOUGLAS, "The Attitude of Workers toward Layoff Policy," *Journal of Abnormal and Social Psychology*, Vol. 34, pp. 179-199, 1939; or MACLAURIN, W. RUPERT, "Workers' Attitudes on Work Sharing and Layoff Policies in a Manufacturing Firm," *Monthly Labor Review*, Vol. 48, pp. 47-60, 1939.

policy that had been developed before 1937 was general agreement between management and the union that no workers would be laid off before a 4-day work week (32 hours) was reached.

During May, 1937, when layoffs appeared imminent, union officials tried repeatedly to get management to state some general principle or rule of thumb that could be applied to all cases. Management felt unable to commit itself. It admitted that there was justice in the demand that preference be given to long-service employees but insisted that the criterion of ability also be used in determining the order of layoff. Union officials, on the other hand, demanded that layoff be according to strict seniority.

When the meaning of seniority was considered, however, a number of questions arose. What should be the seniority unit—company, plant, department, or occupation? How should length of service be computed— from the date of first employment regardless of interruptions, total time actually employed, or from date of last employment? Conferences between union and management representatives enabled them to reach initial agreements on these questions. The basis of seniority was first established according to service in the local plant. Length of service was computed from the date of first employment excluding interruptions.

But, as layoffs increased, the union's demand for plant seniority became increasingly difficult to administer. Replacement transfers between departments were made, frequently in the face of opposition from foremen who had to break in the new employees. When the matter was discussed on a case basis, even some union representatives were not positive that strict plant-wide seniority was best. On one occasion, a general foreman and a union steward (representing the winding section) were discussing seniority policy. The steward, who was a skilled winder, had insisted that straight plant-wide seniority was the only fair rule to follow, but the general foreman answered:

GENERAL FOREMAN: Well, I wonder. Let's take another instance. We all know how hard it is to get good winders. It takes 11 weeks to break in a girl at an average training expense of $300. And experience has shown that only two out of every five girls make good winders. Knowing all that, we certainly wouldn't want to touch our winding group during a layoff even if they all had short service.

UNION STEWARD (*quite excited and with sudden conviction*): That's true and certainly makes me look like a sap. . . . Say! . . . As a matter of fact, you can't even depend on transferring a winder from some other department. Gosh, we've had winders come out of the refrigeration division, and they were no good to us at all.

GENERAL FOREMAN: Well, that's what I mean when I say that ability must be taken into account.

UNION STEWARD: Sure. But just the same, when it comes to assemblers and bench hands, then we have another story.

GENERAL FOREMAN: That's true, and if you'll look into it, you'll find that we've laid them off according to length of service.

UNION STEWARD: Well, that's the way it should be done.

As business declined further after the fall of 1937, however, both management and the union modified their attitudes. Small orders began to replace mass production, and management needed versatile workers rather than those with specialized skills. Frequently, these were the workers with the longest service, and management became more willing to accept plant seniority as the criterion.

When most of the short-service workers (those under 5 years' service) had been laid off, union officials were confronted with pressure from the 5- to 10-year groups in one division whose security was threatened by a possible transfer of long-service employees (10 years and over) from other divisions. Disputes over interdivisional transfers involving long-service workers also became difficult to handle, since stewards in each division knew either about the qualifications of the man to be transferred or about the requirements of the job to which he was to be transferred but seldom about both. During the last stages of the layoff, therefore, union officials ruled out requests from their members for complicated interdivisional layoffs. It became evident that policies ought to be flexible enough to meet changing conditions.

OTHER FEATURES OF LAYOFF POLICY

In formulating layoff policy, consideration should be given to still other questions. Should leaves of absence or advance hiring commitments be given to key workers whose services will be needed within the foreseeable future? Should advance notice of layoff be given? Or would pay in lieu of notice, or some form of dismissal compensation, be preferable? What part should exit interviews play in the layoff program? What should be done to place laid-off workers with other firms in the area?

Advance hiring commitments offer another means of cushioning the shock of layoff. Under a straight seniority policy, the last worker laid off is the first one recalled, and to some extent this removes the uncertainty in the question, "When shall I get back to work?" But management should be able to do more than this. Commitments are made in advance for materials and equipment; why not for keymen? To the degree that it is possible to estimate future labor requirements following a temporary curtailment or shutdown, it should be possible to specify certain dates on which groups of key workers will be rehired.

When permanent layoffs are necessary, they should be planned in advance so far as possible, in order to give adequate notice to the employees affected. Steelworkers at one mill bitterly remembered the cold formal notice that they found in their pay envelopes on a Saturday stating that "effective Monday, your services will no longer be required." At least 1 week's advance notice of layoff should be given, and a longer notice to long-service employees. Some firms fear that this will result in a "slowing down" during the last week and consequently prefer to give a week's pay in lieu of notice. If a slowdown occurs, however, it is an evidence of poor morale that no layoff policy will cure.

Dismissal compensation is provided by a relatively small number of firms,[1] but every company should consider the possibility of some compensation for permanent displacements caused by technological change, shutting down of less efficient plants, etc. The amount of compensation should vary with the employee's earnings and length of service, and it should be regarded as a payment to which a permanently displaced worker is entitled as a consequence of the loss of his job.

Exit interviews, usually given when employees leave voluntarily, may also be useful during a layoff. In one large wartime ordnance plant, laid-off workers were asked how they had liked their jobs and were given an opportunity to discuss with a sympathetic listener any special problems. This had a good effect on the company's public relations in the community as well as on personnel relations in its other plants.

Finally, each company should make an effort to place laid-off workers with other firms in the community. The first approach should be through the public employment service. In planning layoffs, each company should notify the service as far in advance as possible of the probable number of employees who will be laid off on an approximate future date in each job classification. The personnel administrator should stress the broad obligation that his company has in working closely with agencies in the labor market that are seeking to place workers in new jobs. As we said in Chap. 10, the public employment service can become an effective clearinghouse for workers and jobs only when it is fully used by employers and job seekers.

EMPLOYMENT STABILIZATION

Although some layoffs are inevitable in certain industries, no organization should neglect serious study of how it can minimize layoffs by

---

[1] Dismissal-compensation plans for 160 companies are reported in *Dismissal Compensation*, Conference Board Reports, Studies in Personnel Policy No. 50, National Industrial Conference Board, Inc., New York, 1943. Only 10 of the 160 firms had accumulated reserves for this purpose; the others made payments out of current income. For a comprehensive discussion of the subject, see EVERETT D. HAWKINS, *Dismissal Compensation*, Princeton University Press, Princeton, N. J., 1940.

employment-stabilization methods. The experience of many pioneering firms in various industries has conclusively demonstrated that seasonal and intermittent unemployment can be reduced by management action. The personnel administrator should acquaint himself with the methods that have been successfully used to stabilize employment in other firms; and, in cooperation with line executives, he should carefully consider what can be done in his own firm.

Many of the personnel procedures we have already discussed are essential in a program to stabilize company employment. A centralized hiring and placement process is needed to avoid the wasteful practice of hiring workers in one department while they are being laid off in another. Replacement transfers and production transfers can also be used to avoid this, and workers should be trained to do several jobs so that they can be transferred rather than laid off. Some work sharing is also necessary and desirable, if not carried too far.

Firms with seasonal sales have sought to even out their production by manufacturing standard products for stock during the slack periods or by standardizing or simplifying their line of products so that manufacture for stock becomes feasible. Other firms have stimulated off-season orders by advertising and by increased sales efforts that tap new markets or change the buying habits of consumers. Some particularly ingenious companies have developed side lines or fillers that diversify their line of products and provide orders sufficient to maintain factory employment on a more even keel throughout the year.

An important stimulus to employment stabilization is the current drive for a guaranteed annual wage. This is discussed in a later chapter in connection with other methods of wage payment, but here it should be pointed out that few firms will be able to offer a guaranteed annual wage unless they first successfully stabilize employment on a year-round basis for a greater number of their employees.

Summary

Transfers are used for a number of purposes in a well-rounded personnel program: to retain long-service workers as production requirements change or decline, to develop versatility in workers, to permit movement between shifts, and to remedy unsatisfactory placements. Policies must be developed to cover these types of transfer and to meet such other issues as the basis on which transfers shall be made and the location of responsibility for making them.

Policies are also needed for downgrading and layoff. Seniority is an increasingly important factor in downgrading and layoff, but this raises difficult questions that must be answered in a policy statement. What is the seniority unit? How is seniority computed? Other features of layoff policy, such as reducing hours of work before layoff and giving advance notice of layoffs, must also be considered. It is the concern of the personnel administrator to bring these issues to the attention of top management in formulating and administering policies and to assist the company in reducing the need for layoff by employment stabilization.

Downgrading and layoff have sometimes been used as disciplinary measures, and in some firms "layoff" is frequently confused with "discharge." A clear distinction should be made, however, because discharge and disciplinary measures are usually with prejudice to the employee. We shall consider the features of a constructive disciplinary policy in the next chapter.

Chapter 15

Discipline and Discharge

Until human nature attains greater perfection, the fullest
measure of individual freedom of action can be realized
only within the framework of an *expressed* discipline. In the
social situation, this takes the form of laws; in industry, it is
manifest in standards. Firmness in securing conformity in
both instances is wholly consistent with our democratic
approach. *But the requirements must be fair, the reasons behind
them must be clear, and, insofar as possible, they must be arrived
at cooperatively.* This is the road to self-discipline; this is the
aim of a wise leadership.

AMERICAN MANAGEMENT ASSOCIATION[1]

Every organization needs the kind of discipline that is present when
subordinates willingly carry out the instructions of their superiors and
abide by established and known rules of conduct in the organization.
Some managements still believe that they can establish discipline solely
by punishment or by threats, though this view is not widely held today.
Authoritarian methods lose their effectiveness in time, and meanwhile
irreparable damage is done to employee morale.

Good discipline is the result of constructive, positive leadership, exercised within the framework of a clear, consistent disciplinary policy. An
important task of the personnel administrator is to assist in the formulation of such a policy and to guide supervisors in putting it into practice.

WHO NEEDS DISCIPLINE?

The need for a disciplinary policy should be considered with reference
to which groups in industry need disciplinary treatment. Experience
shows that the majority of employees in most organizations sincerely want
to do what is expected of them when they come to work. They have been
conditioned by their previous experience in the family and in school to

[1] "Constructive Discipline in Industry," *A.M.A. Special Research Report*, No. 3,
p. 36, 1943.

198

accept leadership and to follow reasonable rules and instructions when these are explained to them. If the basic conditions that make for good discipline are present in the organization, therefore, this large group of employees will seldom "break the rules." In other words, they are self-disciplined.

Another form of self-discipline exists when there is good teamwork. It is not unusual to find the members of an effective work group exercising disciplinary pressure on one of their number who fails to measure up to expected standards of conduct and workmanship. Of course, this pressure may also be exerted to keep down unusual performance in terms of high output. The discipline of a well-knit group can work in either direction.

But, in every organization, there are a few employees who, for various reasons, fail to observe established rules and standards, even after having been informed of them. In periods of extreme labor shortage, the number of these employees is apt to increase. If these offenders "get away with" violations, the morale of others in the work group is seriously weakened. Furthermore, some individuals who are just on the border line of being in this group are likely to be encouraged to engage in similar practices.

A disciplinary policy embodying definite penalties is needed for this minority of the work force, who, if unchecked, would spread dissatisfaction and poor conduct throughout the organization. But, if the disciplinary policy contains no more than rules and penalties, it will fail to promote the self-discipline of the larger group.

FOUNDATIONS OF CONSTRUCTIVE DISCIPLINE

The two aims of a disciplinary policy—(1) to provide the framework within which self-discipline can develop and (2) to take prompt action against the unruly minority—are not conflicting. It is possible to provide for both in a policy that includes the following elements:

1. A clear and reasonable list of plant rules, with uniform penalties for their violation.
2. Instruction of all employees in what is expected of them, in terms of both observance of plant rules and established standards of job performance.
3. A procedure for telling employees how well they are meeting job standards and rules of conduct.
4. Careful investigation of the background and circumstances of each case before taking disciplinary action, when apparent breaches of conduct or expected performance do occur.

5. Prompt, consistent application of disciplinary measures by the employee's immediate superior, when guilt has clearly been established.

Further discussion of each of these basic requirements in the following paragraphs will bring out the nature of a constructive disciplinary policy.[1]

FORMULATING PLANT RULES

What is the first step in developing a disciplinary policy? Rules alone will not bring good discipline, but certainly a clear-cut list of reasonable rules of conduct in the plant is needed. Employees cannot be expected to meet standards of conduct unless those standards have been clearly defined in advance. Yet this fact is overlooked by those managements which insist that, since it is impossible to anticipate everything that will occur, each offense "should be considered on its own merits." But, without uniformity of definition, the same offense is almost certain to get different treatment at different times and in different departments. On the other hand, too many rules will inevitably lead to nonobservance of some and nonenforcement of others. Rules alone will not bring good discipline.

In formulating plant rules, participation of the line organization should be encouraged by the personnel administrator and by top management. Since first-line supervisors will be responsible for administering the disciplinary policy, they especially should be asked to make suggestions on what should be included. The list resulting from these discussions and suggestions will therefore be tailored to fit the needs of the particular company.

In unionized firms, should formulation of plant rules be a matter for joint discussion with union representatives? Many union contracts provide that workers may be discharged "for just cause," and, either directly or by implication, they recognize management's right to promulgate reasonable rules for the operation of the plant. It is not necessary to take sides on the controversy over "management prerogatives" to assert that in most cases it is a wise practice to discuss any proposed change in personnel policies with the elected representatives of employees.

In considering plant rules, the discussion can be on an informational and educational rather than a bargaining level. When union officials know in advance about proposed additions or changes in plant rules and the reasons for them, they are likely to accept as "reasonable" the same rules

---

[1] For excellent discussions of tested disciplinary policies, see *Constructive Discipline in Industry* (based on a study of 58 representative companies), Special Research Report No. 3, American Management Association, New York, 1943; and M. J. MURPHY and R. C. SMYTH (of Bendix Radio Division of Bendix Aviation Corporation), "Discipline: A Case Study in the Development and Application of a Discipline Procedure," *Factory Management and Maintenance*, Vol. 103, No. 88, pp. 97–104, 1945.

that, if unannounced and unexplained, might be condemned as "unreasonable." Furthermore, if the union officials do not accept or understand any proposed change, there is a good chance either that the point questioned needs revision or that it will prove difficult to administer.

The kinds of plant rules that have been developed in this manner are illustrated by the experience of one company that formulated its disciplinary policy after discussions with supervisors and union representatives. The following list is not intended to be complete, and the offenses are not arranged in the order of their seriousness:

> Using liquor on the premises; drunkenness.
>
> Fighting or attempting to injure others (aggressor only).
>
> Stealing from company or from any employee.
>
> Falsifying time cards and production records.
>
> Immoral behavior.
>
> Unauthorized possession of weapons.
>
> Engaging in a strike or group stoppage of work of any kind, slowdown, sabotage, picketing, or failure to abide by the terms of the union agreement or by the award of the impartial arbitrator.
>
> Willful destruction of company property.
>
> Insubordination or willful disobedience in carrying out reasonable requests of the supervisor.
>
> Gambling and bookmaking on the premises.
>
> Refusing to accept job assignments.
>
> Unexcused absence for a period of 3 consecutive working days without notification of the supervisor or the employment department.
>
> Inefficiency, i.e., failing to do the amount and quality of work that was expected of the employee when he was hired.
>
> Defacing company property.
>
> Violation of safety rules.
>
> Occasional unexcused tardiness and absenteeism.
>
> Horseplay and practical joking.
>
> Smoking in prohibited areas.[1]

TYPES OF DISCIPLINARY ACTION

Just as employees are entitled to know plant rules and the reasons for them, so they have a right to know the approximate consequences of violations. If consistency of treatment is to be achieved and charges of favoritism and discrimination are to be avoided, a set of standard penalties should be formulated to accompany the list of plant rules. This set of penalties need not be followed to the letter; in fact, it cannot be if the special circumstances surrounding each disciplinary case are to be given any

[1] For a more complete list, based on policies in 15 representative companies, see *Constructive Discipline in Industry, loc. cit.*

consideration. But it can serve as a guide to supervisors and to employees of the action that should be taken when *like* cases occur.

Disciplinary action generally includes some or all of the following penalties, when the facts have been established and guilt is clear:

1. Oral warning or reprimand.
2. Written or official warning.
3. Disciplinary layoff or suspension for specified number of days.
4. Demotion to lower rated or less desirable job.
5. Discharge.

In a set of standard penalties, the action to be taken depends upon two principal factors: (1) the seriousness of the offense, and (2) whether this is the first, second, or third offense.[1] Except for those offenses which are considered serious enough to require immediate discharge, some form of warning is usually the appropriate action for a first offense. The effectiveness of a skillfully given oral reprimand often surprises the hard-boiled, old-type supervisor who has been accustomed to "give a man a few days off to think it over" when some minor offense has been committed.

Disciplinary layoffs, in fact, have probably been used too readily, especially in periods of labor surplus. One old-time supervisor admitted this in discussions leading to the formulation of a new disciplinary policy, when he said, "The fellow you lay off is often glad to take the time off, and in the meantime you've lost the services of one of your regular hands. And, if he isn't glad for the loaf, he's sore at you when he is allowed to come back."

Demotions are also a questionable form of disciplinary action, except where there is failure to meet established job standards. Demotion or downgrading to a former less skilled job is appropriate when a man has clearly failed to make good on the job to which he has temporarily been tried out. But, once the trial period has passed and the employee continues on the higher rated job, the wisdom of subsequent demotion for poor performance is open to question. If the employee fails to improve after adequate warnings and constructive criticism, discharge may be a preferable action in order to avoid leaving permanently dissatisfied employees in the organization. As in nearly all cases of disciplinary action, however, discharge should be the last resort.

INFORMING EMPLOYEES OF DISCIPLINARY POLICY

Whatever specific rules and appropriate penalties are adopted by the organization, the personnel administrator should insist that employees

---

[1] For such a list used in one company (Atlantic Refining), see H. W. JONES, "The Discipline Problem," *Management Record*, Vol. 4, pp. 1–5, 1942.

be clearly informed about them. How can this be done? In unionized firms, some of this information may be included in the discipline-discharge clause of the union agreement. Usually, however, such a clause is concerned with establishing the right of the employee to have his case heard if he thinks he has been unjustly disciplined or discharged, and seldom does it spell out in detail each plant rule and the consequences of violations.

It is therefore necessary for management, or the union and management jointly, to provide this important information to all employees in some other manner. Bulletin-board announcements are sometimes used, but they suffer from the coldly formal nature of much bulletin-board material. A better and more widely used medium of written communication is the employee handbook, in which a section can be devoted to summarizing or listing the rules of conduct, the reasons for them, and the penalties that will be used for violations.

Supplementing the handbook are two oral means of informing employees about disciplinary policy. First is the induction program. In this, a representative of the personnel department or the supervisor (preferably the latter) can tell new employees about the important rules of conduct and performance, as listed in the employee handbook. Second, as a part of the later follow-up or in answer to questions, the supervisor can make a further explanation of new rules or of those which were not clearly understood before.

Changes in plant rules, which are necessary from time to time, should also be explained orally by supervisors, since bulletin-board announcements are not sufficient. There was general agreement among supervisors in one firm, for example, that such explanation was necessary when the management decided to "tighten up" on the practice, which had been more or less condoned in past years, of letting employees bring liquor into the plant during the Christmas and New Year season.

Although explanations by the employee's immediate supervisor are part of a good disciplinary policy, the personnel administrator frequently has an opportunity to clarify and promote employee (and union) understanding of the reasons for certain rules and the need for disciplinary action. When he participates, as a staff man, in discussions of employee grievances involving discipline, for example, he can explain the particular rule, the nature of the alleged violations, and the consequences of permitting the violation to go unheeded.

In one firm, a skilled employee with 5 years' seniority was discharged for bringing liquor into the plant, drinking it, and offering it to other employees. When the union business agent protested the discharge, the personnel administrator called his attention to previous warnings for the same offense and pointed out the danger to employee safety of permitting such a practice to continue in the vicinity of high-speed machinery. The union thereupon dropped the case.

A Procedure for "Talking It Over"

Constructive discipline should be supported by some procedure for telling employees periodically how they are meeting job standards and requirements, and talking over first and subsequent violations of plant rules. Some violations are serious enough to require immediate discharge for the first offense, but most are not. Experienced supervisors know that, when the facts of a violation have been clearly and objectively established, there is a real opportunity to point out the consequences of repeated violations and to suggest possibilities for improvement.

An employee-rating plan, as we have seen, provides one systematic method of reviewing employee progress on the job, pointing out strong and weak points and suggesting ways to improve. One factor to be rated in many plans is conduct. And if minor violations have occurred during the period covered by the last rating, a review of these is properly a part of the assessment of the employee's progress on the job. The emphasis, however, should be on improvement, not criticism; and good conduct and performance should be praised.

When a new man was hired for a staff position in one firm, the general manager told him, "If you don't get bawled out once in a while by me, you'll know you're doing all right." It is not surprising that 3 years later this man commented, "No one has ever told me that I'm doing a good job here. I don't really know how I stand, and I guess I don't amount to much here."

"Bawling a man out" is seldom an adequate disciplinary measure. If done in front of other employees, it is likely to be greatly resented by any high-spirited employee. Instead of trying to improve, such people are likely to want "to get back at the boss." Hot tempers and sharp words lead to hasty and ill-considered decisions, which are always damaging to good discipline.

A Situational Approach to Discipline

Constructive discipline is more concerned with causes and explanations of breaches of conduct than with punishment. It is difficult for the supervisor to suggest ways for an employee to improve if he is ignorant of the reasons for his misconduct. Thus, the person-centered approach should complement policy thinking about discipline. A personnel administrator can help the line organization in both branches of this positive approach.

When a breach of discipline occurs, just as when a machine breaks down, an alert supervisor investigates the reasons. Why did the employee act as he did? What company policies are involved, and were they clearly understood? Has the employee's past record been spotty, or is this his first offense? Are there any contributing factors, such as ill health, family troubles, or another unsettled grievance, which may explain his action? A talk with the employee is necessary to bring out some of these points; others may be obtained from employee records and sometimes from discreet inquiries of fellow employees.

Failure to get all the background facts can lead to ill-advised disciplinary action, often with serious consequences. This point was driven home to the half million wartime supervisors who received instruction in Job Relations Training through the Training Within Industry program. They were told of the case of Joe Smith, who was absent from work the day after a general wage increase. His foreman concluded that he had taken the day off; and, since this was not the first time, he decided to lay Joe off for a week when he returned. Later, another foreman asked him why he had been so rough on Joe and explained that the whole department knew that Joe's father had been in an automobile accident that day and that Joe had to look after him. He told a neighbor to tell his foreman why he could not be at work, but the neighbor had forgotten to do so. When he appeared for work, he assumed that his foreman knew the whole story. The foreman got in the first word, however, and Joe had no further chance to explain.

One supervisor in a JRT session told a similar experience involving a tardy employee. The man's record had not been too good, and he had been warned by the foreman. One night he arrived for work an hour late and found in place of his time card in the rack a notice to report immediately to his foreman. The foreman was not at his desk, so the man waited there for him. Several employees passed by, and he told them why he was late. In the meantime, the foreman was out in the department and getting hotter every minute about the employee's tardiness. When he returned to his desk, he discharged the employee at once and marked "chronic tardiness" on the dismissal notice. The rest of the employees thereupon walked out, in protest against what they considered unjust action. Those employees who had talked to the tardy one had passed the word around that, just as he was leaving his home to come to work, the telephone rang and he had to rush to the hospital to give a blood transfusion to his wife, who had undergone an operation the previous day.

In both cases, a simple question, giving the employee a chance to explain, would have avoided the damage that was done by unjust treatment. But many breaches of discipline are not so easily explained. Rational and logical explanations may not always be forthcoming. In interviewing an employee, the supervisor often has to probe more deeply to get at hidden causes or motivations. Skillful interviewing is needed, not in a spirit of cross examination, but in an effort to understand *why* the employee acted as he did. Objective facts in themselves seldom provide the answer; sentiments and feelings are frequently at the root of breaches in discipline.

The interview itself may bring improvement of performance and conduct, even though the supervisor does not ask leading questions and does not take subsequent action. With a sympathetic listener, a "problem employee" may get something "off his chest," see his own errors, and suggest his own means of improvement. The resulting change is likely to be more effective and more lasting if the employee brings himself to accept it than if he is told by his supervisor what to do.[1]

Taking Disciplinary Action

When it is clear that disciplinary action should be taken in a specific case, who should do it? Delegation of this responsibility to a staff officer, such as the personnel administrator, weakens the position of the supervisor and gives the personnel man authority that he should not exercise. Clearly, therefore, the employee's supervisor should discipline him. This does not mean that the first-line supervisor's action in a disciplinary case should always be final, with no review by others in the organization. But it is desirable that the supervisor have the initial responsibility for taking corrective action, principally by "talking it over" with the offending employee and pointing out what will be done if the offense is repeated.

The disciplinary policy adopted by the organization, with a list of plant rules and appropriate penalties, will, in general, govern the action that the supervisor should take in each case. Some administrative discretion is needed to fit the penalty to the particular case, of course, but interdepartmental consistency and avoidance of favoritism require uniform treatment, within very narrow limits, of *similar* offenses.

[1] *Cf.* Chap. 6 on Interviewing. The effectiveness of the nondirected interview in bringing corrective action has been demonstrated in psychoanalysis and in employee counseling. See Rogers, Carl R., *Counseling and Psychotherapy*, Houghton Mifflin Company, Boston, 1942. Serious and deep-rooted cases of employee maladjustment, of course, cannot adequately be handled by supervisors. They should, if possible, be referred to a psychiatrist for diagnosis and treatment, especially if the firm wishes to retain the employee.

The *way* in which disciplinary action is taken by the supervisor, however, is often more important than *what* is done. One supervisor can reprimand an offending employee so that the man will not resent it and will try to improve; whereas another's manner, tone of voice, and facial expression are such that he is disliked and even feared by his subordinates. The oral reprimand, given in private for the first offense, is part of the "talking it over" procedure, and each supervisor should learn how to develop its constructive opportunities.

Subsequent violations are met in many companies by written warnings. But, again, the manner in which these are handled is important. One grievance in an electrical-equipment firm, for example, involved a foreman's method of filling out warning notices. A girl employee had objected to being given a different job assignment, when other less experienced girls were allowed to remain on the same job. She complained to the shop steward; and when they approached the foreman, he pulled out a warning-notice pad and started to fill it in. He refused to discuss the case with the steward and continued to fill out two warning notices against the girl for "refusal to cooperate." When the case was taken to top management, the warning slips were disallowed.[1]

The written warning should be prepared only after a talk with the offending employee.[2] It should not, in any way, be used as a black list or as a means of "getting" particular employees.[3] Sufficient copies of the written warning should be made so that one can be given to the offending employee, one to the personnel administrator, and one to the union in unionized firms, and one can be retained by the supervisor for his own records.

Forewarning union representatives that certain employees are liable to be disciplined more severely if performance or conduct is not improved will help to reduce the number of disciplinary layoff and discharge cases

[1] For further details, see PAUL PIGORS and ALFRED D. SHEFFIELD, Union Action on a Prejudiced Foreman, *Case Studies in Industrial Relations*, Series 3, Sect. 7, Addison-Wesley Press, Inc., Cambridge, Mass., 1944.

[2] For description of successful procedures, see MURPHY and SMYTH, *loc. cit.;* E. G. MICHAELS (Vick Chemical Company), "The Warning Interview," *Personnel*, Vol. 21, pp. 105–106, 1944; and ARTHUR K. BRINTNELL (Allis-Chalmers Manufacturing Company), "How Our Discipline Board Dispenses Justice," *Factory Management and Maintenance*, Vol. 101, pp. 104–105, 1943. The latter describes a four-man board to which foremen refer disciplinary cases.

[3] This is a bad personnel practice from any standpoint, but, in addition, any discriminatory use of disciplinary procedures runs the great risk of involving the company in union charges of violating Sect. 8(3) of the National Labor Relations (Wagner) Act of 1935. This section states that it is an unfair labor practice for an employer "by discrimination in regard to hire or tenure of employment or any term or condition of employment to encourage or discourage membership in any labor organization."

taken up through the complaint procedure. For example, the personnel administrator of one firm notified the union business agent that a male worker had been warned by the foreman about using abusive language toward women employees in the department. The business agent checked the facts and found them to be true. Two weeks later, when the employee was discharged for continued and excessive swearing, the union declined to press the case for the offending employee.

Advance notification does not mean, however, that union representatives ought to participate jointly with management in taking disciplinary action. Such a procedure would weaken management's responsibility for discipline and place union officials in a position where they could not really "represent" their members.

A final point on the way in which good discipline is administered is the necessity for prompt action, once the facts of guilt have been established. This does not mean that action should be taken hastily or in the heat of emotion. Talking it over and getting the facts will give both the supervisor and the offending employee a chance to "cool off." But when the supervisor has decided what action is necessary under the established disciplinary policy, he should take this promptly. Indecision, or passing the buck, will weaken the supervisor's ability to get good discipline in the future.[1]

DISCHARGE AS A LAST RESORT

At one time, discharge was used more frequently than it is today. For example, the discharge rate in a large rubber-products manufacturing company was between 12 and 25 per cent of the total pay roll during the years 1920 to 1928, when the foreman had unquestioned power of discharge. By 1937, the discharge rate in this company had fallen below 2 per cent. Industry in general has followed the same pattern.

This change is partly a result of the growth of unions, which have provided a means of challenging the former absolute right of the foreman to dismiss an employee. But, on its own initiative, management has increasingly recognized the drastic nature of discharge and has sanctioned its use only for the most serious and habitual offenders.

From the employee's standpoint, discharge is drastic, because it destroys his seniority standing with the firm and lessens his chances of securing new employment if the prospective employer learns the reason for leaving his last job. Since it reduces his chances of earning a livelihood, further-

---

[1] An excellent check list for foremen to follow in disciplinary cases, based on the Job Relations Training four-step method of handling a case, is found in FRANCES SPODICK, "Making Foremen Discipline Conscious," *Personnel*, Vol. 20, pp. 339–342, 1944.

more, it may affect his personal equilibrium and family relationships. Some offenders admittedly deserve such a drastic penalty, but fairness requires that employers resort to it only when all other methods of bringing improvement have failed. Moreover, the list of offenses requiring immediate discharge for the first violation should be as short as possible, covering only the most serious offenses, such as intoxication or smoking in hazardous locations.

If the penalty of discharge is frequently and haphazardly used, there is also a loss to the employer. A "separation"—whether it be a quit, a layoff, or a discharge—represents a loss of time and money spent in hiring, training, and supervising the employee. If the discharge is patently unjust and not rectified, it may seriously affect the morale and performance of other employees in the group. Finally, if discharge is used too frequently, it may lose its effectiveness as a penalty, just as any form of punishment will fail in its object if indiscriminately used.

An extreme illustration of the misuse of discharge is the case of Albert Prestorato, an experienced heeler in a firm manufacturing canvas footwear. In 1915, the department had been having trouble with "started heels," which were frequently caused by improper hand rolling but might also be brought about by atmospheric conditions or improper mixing of cement in another department. The department superintendent brought pressure on his foremen to eliminate this defect, and one of the foremen who had been raked over the coals relieved his annoyance by taking it out on his workers. He threatened, "The next man who has any started heels is fired. That's all."

The next 50 pairs of shoes with the defect were traced to Prestorato, who had been in the department 10 years and was one of the best men. Although the foreman probably realized that the trouble was not wholly Prestorato's fault, he feared that he would lose face if he did not carry out his threat. Prestorato was discharged; but, since he was a valuable man, the foreman hired him back the next day. Unfortunately, Prestorato was unaware of a company rule that any discharge automatically broke a man's record; and, in 1930, when he claimed 25 years' service and eligibility for an extra week's vacation, he discovered that his continuous-service record dated only from 1915.

In every organization, however, there are some employees who cannot fulfill minimum job requirements or who will not follow instructions or obey reasonable rules of conduct. When other more constructive measures have failed, these employees must be weeded out by the discharge procedure, just as a bad apple must be taken from the basket to prevent the others from spoiling. A definite discharge procedure is therefore a necessary part of a personnel program.

ELEMENTS OF A DISCHARGE POLICY

What are the essential elements of a good discharge policy? Most of the following list is equally important for other types of disciplinary action, and it is repeated here for emphasis.

1. A clear and known list of reasons for discharge should be prepared.
2. The supervisor should have the initial right to discharge employees from his department but not from the company. His action may be reviewed by or require the approval of his immediate superior. Persons discharged from one department may be transferred to another department, with the permission of the supervisor of that department.
3. Upon notification of discharge, the employee should leave the company's premises immediately, even though he has the right of appeal. Failure to do so promptly and in an orderly manner should in itself be ground for discharge, regardless of the merits of the dispute.
4. A review procedure should be provided, both as a check on the supervisor's action and to give the employee the opportunity to present his case if he thinks he has been unjustly treated. In a unionized firm, this is furnished by the complaint and grievance procedure. Exit interviews may also be helpful.

SUMMARY

Good discipline in an organization is secured by positive and constructive measures, rather than by punitive methods such as disciplinary layoffs and discharges. Plant rules are necessary, of course, in order to encourage self-discipline and to punish the few chronic violators. The rules should be formulated clearly, with appropriate penalties, and should be made known to all employees. Enforcement should be uniform and consistent, and violations should be handled promptly when guilt is clearly established.

But rules alone are not enough. Constructive discipline requires a procedure for telling employees periodically how they stand and talking over with them any breaches of established rules. Emphasis should be placed on suggestions for future improvement, rather than exclusively on the employee's failure to measure up to expected standards of job conduct and performance. A person-centered approach to disciplinary problems is needed as an aid to understanding the reasons for misconduct and helping to correct it.

Finally, the manner in which disciplinary action is taken is extremely important, and many line supervisors need assistance in developing this skill. Part of the personnel administrator's responsibility for good discipline lies, therefore, in helping these line officials to improve their handling of disciplinary problems. The personnel administrator is also concerned with assisting top management in the formulation of a clear, consistent disciplinary policy and in bringing his influence to bear in support of its positive aspects.

A more congenial line of policy thinking is that of suitable rewards in the form of wages and salaries. But this area of management responsibility also presents its own problems. These will be discussed in the next two chapters.

E. WAGES AND HOURS

Chapter 16

Wage Policies and
Wage Administration

> The experience of the National War Labor Board is that
> the lack of a reasonable balance within the rate structure
> of a particular plant can frequently be highly destructive
> of employee morale and, therefore, of production.
>   GEORGE W. TAYLOR[1]

In some firms, good wages have been overemphasized as the key to
peaceful personnel relations. The one-sidedness of this view has been properly criticized by those who, like members of the Western Electric research group, have pointed out that workers are not motivated solely by
financial incentives. But without a fair wage policy and consistent
internal wage relationships, the personnel program will be faced with
insurmountable difficulties. The various aspects of wage and salary
relationships therefore have a vital bearing on the success of the whole
personnel program.

RELATION OF WAGES TO THE PERSONNEL PROGRAM

If the general level of wages and salaries in the organization is too low,
relative to other comparable firms, it will be more difficult to attract and
hold qualified personnel. But recruitment is not the only phase of the
personnel program in which wages and salaries are important. A good
promotion policy requires that earnings on each job be related to the
value of the job. Furthermore, the establishment of these sound internal
wage and salary relationships is necessary to avoid the dissatisfactions
that would otherwise develop over inequalities between similar jobs.
Finally, methods of wage payment, and particularly the manner in which

[1] "Michigan and Wisconsin Lumber Companies Case," as reprinted in the *War
Labor Reports*, Vol. 9, p. 499, June 8, 1943.

an incentive wage plan is handled, also affect the ability of management to get effective results from people.

The personnel administrator, therefore, is vitally interested in the kinds of wage and salary policies and procedures that are to be used. As an advisor to top management in policy formulation, and as one who assists the line organization in developing and utilizing effective procedures, the personnel administrator is concerned with the following aspects of the wage and salary question:

1. The general level of wages and salaries in the firm, as compared with levels in competing firms in the area or in the industry.

2. Wage and salary administration in (a) establishing and maintaining proper internal relationships between the earnings on each job and (b) advancing individuals within rate ranges.

3. Methods of wage payment, by time or by output; the characteristics of a sound wage-incentive plan; and getting employee acceptance of changes in output standards.

Wage and salary levels, internal relationships, and methods of payment cannot be left to chance or to the uncertain forces of the labor market. Competition of employers for labor and of laborers for jobs is not sufficient, except in periods of severe labor shortage, to equalize wages for jobs of comparable skill even within a local labor market.[1] And competition cannot establish proper rates and differentials for jobs that are found in only one or two firms. Finally, labor-market forces have relatively little effect on the methods of wage payment and their administration.

In this chapter, we shall consider, first, the various factors that should be taken into account in determining the general level of wages in the firm and, second, the procedures that have been developed in sound wage and salary administration. Methods of wage payment, the requirements of a good incentive wage system, and getting acceptance of changes in output standards are discussed in the following chapter.

THE GENERAL LEVEL OF WAGES

Four principal considerations affect the determination of and changes in a firm's general level of wages: (1) wages paid for comparable work by other firms in the labor market or in the industry, (2) financial condition of the firm, (3) cost of living, and (4) governmental regulation, such as minimum wage laws. Whether wages are determined unilaterally by the firm or in joint negotiation with a union, these factors must first be

[1] MYERS, CHARLES A., and W. RUPERT MACLAURIN, *The Movement of Factory Workers*, pp. 72–74, John Wiley & Sons, Inc., New York, 1943.

thoroughly explored in management conferences in which the personnel administrator should sit as an advisor. [1]

Wages paid for comparable work by other firms in the labor market or in the industry is probably the most important single factor affecting a firm's general wage level. Many firms attempt to follow a policy of paying the "going wage" in the community for their particular jobs or some "average" of going rates. In some industries, such as woolen textiles, the wages paid by firms in the same industry in other localities are considered more important than wages paid by other industries in the local labor market. [2] A few firms consciously adopt a policy of paying better than the community or industry average, in order to attract superior workers, and these firms are considered the "wage leaders." When a decision is reached on which of these alternatives is most desirable to follow in the particular firm, the policy should be stated in written form in the employee handbook or other publication.

A pronouncement is not enough, however. Periodic surveys of wages and salaries paid by local firms in the same industry must be made in order to keep practice in line with policy. This is true whether or not the firm considers itself a "wage leader" or a "wage follower."

MAKING WAGE SURVEYS

Systematic wage surveys, which are frequently conducted by leading firms or by employer associations, usually include the following steps:
1. Selection of firms to be included in the survey.
2. List of key jobs, common to all firms selected.
3. Detailed descriptions of these jobs, so that valid comparisons can be made. (Job description and analysis are discussed in a later section of this chapter.)
4. Questionnaires or, preferably, individual visits to each firm, to secure accurate wage and salary data on jobs that are essentially similar. These data include hourly rates or earnings, weekly earnings, hours worked, shift premiums, method of wage payment, etc., since the content of the term "wages" often varies in different firms.
5. Compilation of the wage and salary data for each job, showing the mean or arithmetical average, the median, and the range of rates

[1] For fuller discussion see, SUMNER H. SLICHTER, *Basic Criteria Used in Wage Negotiations*, The Chicago Association of Commerce and Industry, 1947; and JOHN T. DUNLOP, "The Economics of Wage-Dispute Settlement," *Law and Contemporary Problems*, Vol. XII, No. 2, Spring, 1947, pp. 281–296.

[2] The problem facing companies with branches in different localities is particularly difficult. Should the same rate be paid for the same jobs in each branch, regardless of location, or should the rates in each branch be geared to the local community? Partly as a result of union pressure, an increasing number of firms have adopted uniform company-wide wage scales, because they are, as one employer said, "easier to defend."

paid, and the supplementary wage data listed in 4. The data may also be reported by companies, labeled A, B, C, etc.

In collecting and compiling wage and salary information, it is very important that the data refer to jobs with essentially similar content and that for each job the data are essentially comparable. In other words, it is downright misleading to learn that Firm A pays "machinists" $1.00 an hour and Firm B pays $1.25, when further investigation would reveal that Firm B's machinists do their own setup work and are paid on an incentive basis, while machinists in Firm A do no setups and receive only an hourly rate. Clearly, *two* different jobs are involved, and they should not be compared. Yet this is often what happens when an executive in Firm A telephones to one in Firm B "to find out what you're paying machinists."

Wage and salary data must be collected systematically and carefully if they are to be useful in helping to determine a firm's general level of wages and salaries. Furthermore, detailed data will be helpful in explaining to employees or union representatives *why* machinists in Firm B receive more than in Firm A. The personnel department in many firms performs a real service in making these periodic wage surveys.

OTHER FACTORS AFFECTING WAGE LEVELS

The range of wage rates that usually exists for comparable jobs, however, permits a company to consider the other factors affecting the general wage level that were outlined earlier. In unionized firms, of course, the general wage level is a matter for negotiation with union representatives, though the same factors are usually considered. Where unions are firmly entrenched in an industry and are seeking or have secured industry-wide agreements, the tendency is toward equal wage rates (hourly or piece) for the same jobs in all firms. This is particularly likely where jobs are standardized in content throughout the industry, although industry-wide bargaining does not always lead to uniform wage scales.[1]

The financial condition of the firm, or its "ability to pay," will determine whether it can afford to be liberal as compared with other companies, or whether it must pay about what the lower paying firms offer and possibly use other means to attract and hold labor. "Labor productivity" (output per man-hour) affects a firm's financial condition, but seldom if ever can it be measured objectively enough to be a factor in actual discussions or negotiations over the general level of wages. Nonetheless, increased labor productivity is the ultimate basis for increases in real wages. Money wage increases that cannot be absorbed by the lower unit costs resulting from

[1] See LESTER, RICHARD A., and EDWARD A. ROBIE, *Wages under National and Regional Collective Bargaining, Experience in Seven Industries*, Princeton University, Industrial Relations Section, Princeton, N. J., 1946.

greater output per man-hour will eventually be offset by increases in the cost of living, although this will occur in different degrees in different industries.
If labor productivity is equal to that in comparable firms, this fact is likely to be reflected in the wages paid for comparable work in the area or in the industry. If it is higher or lower than that in comparable firms, and this can be demonstrated, there are strong reasons for paying a higher or lower level of wages. But this will be reflected in the financial condition of the firm and thus in its ability to pay a given level of wages.

Financial condition is also a function of managerial efficiency, however, and there is serious doubt whether nonlabor economies that a superior management is able to effect should be the basis for a substantially higher level of wages, or whether wasteful management practices should be the basis for paying lower wages. Some unions in 1945 to 1946 sought to make "ability to pay" an important factor in wage negotiations, but the issues were not squarely faced. Should a firm in which management (not labor) is more efficient than the average pay higher wages, and should a firm in which management (not labor) is less efficient than the average pay lower wages? Generally, the large national unions are reluctant to subsidize an inefficient management by accepting lower than standard wage scales, although in the past they have made concessions in marginal firms when job security was involved.

When management relies on financial condition and ability to pay in union negotiations, however, it must be prepared to present factual information on costs, prices, and profits to buttress its position. The personnel administrator can bring his influence to bear in urging top management to put forward honest and factual reasons for its ability or inability to meet salary and wage requests of its employees, whether unionized or nonunion. It is no longer possible, nor was it ever wise, to keep employees in the dark about the financial condition of the enterprise of which they are a part. In recent years, companies have published "financial statements for employees." These are a step in the right direction, but they may not be sufficiently detailed if financial condition is an important factor in wage determination.

Changes in the "cost of living" as reported by the U.S. Bureau of Labor Statistics[1] or by the National Industrial Conference Board, Inc., should

---

[1] The BLS index is now more accurately labeled as a "Consumers' Price Index for Moderate-income Families in Large Cities." The NICB index is also now called a "Consumers' Price Index," or, more formally, an "Index of Quoted Retail Prices for Consumers' Goods and Services Purchased by Moderate-income Families." The wartime controversy over revision of the War Labor Board's "Little Steel" wage formula showed that the term "cost of living" means different things to different people. It is especially important in wage negotiations to talk in terms understood by everyone.

also be considered in making changes in a firm's general level of wages and salaries, particularly upward revisions. If money wages and salaries fail to keep pace with the prices of living necessities, employees soon become disgruntled over the increasing difficulty of making ends meet. Firms that have been most successful in avoiding this sort of discontent have been leaders in making wage and salary increases in periods of rising retail prices. If a company has a policy of following the leader in wage changes, the cost of living factor will usually not be an independent factor.

Finally, *state and Federal minimum-wage laws* place an absolute lower limit on the level of wages and salaries that can be paid by any firm subject to these laws.[1] As a service to management, the personnel department must keep informed on how the firm is affected by these laws, as well as about changes in the "cost of living." Financial condition will obviously affect the ability of a firm to pay above the legal minimum, but no company can expect good personnel relations if it makes no effort to pay the majority of its employees more than the minimum. The president of one firm failed to understand this simple truth when he protested that "we have always treated our employees fairly, because we have always paid them the minimum wage required by laws."

During wartime and in emergency periods, governmental action may affect a firm's wage level even more directly. Orders of the National War Labor Board, and subsequently the National Wage Stabilization Board and Fact-finding Boards, had a tremendous effect on wage-level changes in the war and postwar periods.

Internal Wage and Salary Relationships

Important as is the firm's general level of wages, the relationship of wages and salaries paid on different jobs within the firm is still more important for good personnel relations. Employees may be disgruntled if workers in a firm across the street or in another community are earning more money, but more serious dissatisfactions are likely to arise over inequities within the firm. Possibly with some exaggeration, the National War Labor Board in one case observed:

There is no single factor in the whole field of labor relations that does more to break down morale, create individual dissatisfaction, encourage absenteeism,

---

[1] The principal Federal laws are the Fair Labor Standards (Wage-Hour) Act of 1938, under which the 40 cents an hour minimum wage became effective before 1945; and the Public Contracts (Walsh-Healey) Act of 1936, under which the Secretary of Labor specifies minimum wages to be paid in various industries that have contracts with the Federal government. A number of states also have laws under which a commission may order minimum wages to be paid.

increase labor turnover, and hamper production than obviously unjust inequalities in the wage rates paid to different individuals in the same labor group within the same plant.[1]

The truth in this statement is evident to anyone who has talked with wage earners and salaried employees. If Bill is earning less money than Jim on a job that he firmly believes is more difficult or more skilled than Jim's, he is dissatisfied and cannot do his best work. Wage differentials are a mark of social status in the factory organization; and if they do not correspond with the relative significance of jobs as employees view them, the worker's sense of fairness and justice is outraged.[2]

When management uses haphazard methods to set rates for different jobs in the plant, inequalities are bound to arise. Today one rate is "pulled out of the air." Tomorrow some official says, "Well, I guess this job's worth about 75 cents." Then, perhaps, a superintendent learns that the X Company is paying riveters 95 cents an hour, so one job rate is changed without making corresponding changes in the rates on related jobs. Or an employee on a particular job kicks loudly, and he is given a raise to keep him quiet. Gradually, a chaotic wage structure develops, with destructive effects on employee morale.

How can this be avoided? An increasing number of firms, particularly during the war, have found that a formal job-evaluation procedure can reduce these inequalities to a minimum by establishing proper internal wage and salary relationships.

Job Description and Analysis[3]

Before attempting to evaluate jobs, however, it is necessary to know what a worker does on each specific job and the demands, in terms of such factors as skill, effort, and responsibility, that the job makes upon the worker. This is job description and analysis, and it is basic to successful wage determination as well as to other parts of the personnel program. We have already seen that good job descriptions are needed in selection and

[1] National War Labor Board, West Coast Airframe Companies case, Mar. 3, 1943, *War Labor Reports*, Vol. 6, p. 594. Majority opinion, written by William H. Davis, chairman.

[2] The Western Electric studies brought this out clearly. See ROETHLISBERGER, F. J., and W. J. DICKSON, *Management and the Worker*, pp. 575–576, Harvard University Press, Cambridge, Mass., 1940; also BAKKE, E. WIGHT, *The Unemployed Worker*, p. 11, Yale University Press, New Haven, 1940.

[3] Much of the following is based upon the excellent *Training and Reference Manual for Job Analysis*, prepared by the Division of Occupational Analysis and Manning Tables, Bureau of Manpower Utilization, War Manpower Commission, Washington, D. C., June, 1944. The division also prepared a shorter *Guide for Analyzing Jobs*, Washington, D. C., February, 1944. See also *Job Descriptions*, Studies in Personnel Policy No. 72, National Industrial Conference Board, Inc., New York, 1946.

placement, training, transfer, upgrading, and promotion, and in making wage surveys. We shall see that they are also helpful in a safety program and as a partial basis for time studies in connection with wage-incentive plans.

Brief, informal job descriptions consisting of a few sentences may be useful for certain purposes, but generally a more detailed study of each job is necessary in job evaluation. This process requires skill, time, and patience if it is to be done correctly. In many firms, job descriptions and analyses are prepared by staff specialists, who must first explain their purpose and methods to departmental supervisors and then obtain, through observation, discussion, questions, and rechecking, the information that they need. Their reports should be reviewed and approved by the supervisor of the department involved and, in unionized firms, by union stewards. Since job description and analysis are fact gathering and securing agreement of informed people on job factors, some firms have encouraged participation by the union. In any case, workers should be interviewed at their jobs, and their representatives should be consulted in the process of preparing job descriptions and analysis.

Distinguishing "a job" may not be easy, for what appears to be one job may actually be several. "A job may be defined as a group of positions [each requiring the services of one individual] which are identical with respect to their major or significant tasks."[1] When the job analyst by observation and questions has determined the limits of the particular job as it now exists and has noted its title, he prepares a description, preferably chronological, of the tasks performed on the job. The complete descriptions should adequately explain *what* the worker does, *how* he does it, and *why* he does it. For example, the summary of a detailed job description of engine-lathe operator first class might be the following:

Sets up lathe (what): Carefully examines blueprints (what) to determine the dimensions of the part to be machined (why), using shop mathematics (how) to calculate any dimensions (what) not given directly on the prints (why) or to calculate machine settings (why).

As an aid to further analysis, the percentage of total time spent on each task or part of the job can be indicated.

The next step is analysis of the basic factors of the job that distinguish it from other jobs. The analyst here attempts to evaluate the degree of difficulty of the work performed, and this later serves as the bridge between job description and job evaluation. Each organization regards certain job factors as important—the factors that it "is paying for" when it hires a man to perform a specific job. Job analysis should be geared to these factors, especially if the later evaluation is to be in terms of job factors. A fairly

---

[1] *Training and Reference Manual for Job Analysis, op. cit.,* p. 7.

common set of job factors is skill, responsibility, physical effort, mental effort, and working conditions.[1] All this analysis, together with the job description, can then be reported on a "job specification" for each reported job.

ELEMENTS OF JOB EVALUATION

After a careful, detailed description and analysis have been prepared of each job in the organization, the evaluation process can begin. Job evaluation is a systematic method of appraising the worth or value of each job in relation to other jobs in the company. It cannot be completely accurate, since it depends upon the judgments of the evaluators. But these are informed judgments based upon detailed studies of the jobs and comparisons of their contents, and for this reason relative evaluations are likely to be much more reliable than haphazard determinations. Furthermore, job evaluation rates the *jobs*, not the *men and women* on the jobs, which, as we have seen, is the task of *employee rating*.

Job evaluation is used to determine the relative compensation of salaried jobs as well as of hourly rated jobs, although usually the list of factors is somewhat different. For example, "responsibility for confidential data" might be used in evaluation of the former, but not the latter. One method of job evaluation is to rank all jobs in their order of difficulty or importance and then to assign them to broad job classifications. The principal methods, however, are (1) point rating and (2) factor comparison,[2] although some

[1] For a different list, see *Training and Reference Manual for Job Analysis, op. cit.,* pp. 18–52. This includes responsibility, job knowledge, mental application, dexterity, and accuracy, listed as "performance factors"; and the additional "selection factors" of experience, training, physical demands (such as physical activities, working conditions, and hazards), and worker characteristics required on the job. If too many factors are used, however, job analysis and subsequent job evaluation become too complicated. Studies show that, in practice, ratings are often controlled by a few factors and that a simple list of factors will yield about the same results as a more complicated system. See LAWSHE, C. H., JR., "Studies in Job Evaluation: II. The Adequacy of Abbreviated Point Ratings for Hourly-paid Jobs in Three Industrial Plants," *Journal of Applied Psychology,* Vol. 29, No. 3, pp. 177–184, 1945.

[2] For a full discussion of these methods, see EUGENE J. BENGE, SAMUEL L. H. BURK, and EDWARD N. HAY, *Manual of Job Evaluation,* Harper & Brothers, New York, 1941. The book is devoted largely to the factor comparison method. Another excellent review of the problems encountered in job evaluation is *Principles and Application of Job Evaluation,* Studies in Personnel Policy No. 62, National Industrial Conference Board, Inc., New York, 1944, which contains brief papers by experts in the field and the report of a panel discussion. See also C. C. BALDERSTON, *Wage Setting Based on Job Analysis and Evaluation,* Monograph No. 4, Industrial Relations Counselors, New York, 1940; A. L. KRESS, "How to Rate Jobs and Men," *Factory Management and Maintenance,* Vol. 97, pp. 60–65, 1939 (discusses the "degree" plan developed for the National Electrical Manufacturers' Association and the National Metal Trades Association); and the two studies by JOHN W. RIEGEL, *Wage Determination* and *Salary Determination,* Bureau of Industrial Relations, University of Michigan, Ann Arbor, 1937.

plans combine features of both. No one plan can be recommended as best for every firm. The development of a suitable plan in a given company requires careful preliminary thought and discussion by a management committee or a management-labor committee, with the advice of the personnel administrator.

After job factors have been selected and jobs described and analyzed in terms of these factors, the usual steps in a point-rating plan of job evaluation are as follows:

1. Assigning "weights" in terms of total points (or "degrees") to the factors, so that, for example, "skill" may have a maximum of 90 points, while "physical effort" is assigned a maximum of only 50. Sometimes the factors are subdivided, as in "responsibility for tools and equipment" and "responsibility for materials and products."

2. Selecting from 15 to 25 "key jobs," including representative unskilled, semiskilled, and skilled jobs on which there are a fairly large number of workers. These jobs are usually wellknown and easily identified by employees and supervisors. They constitute the "yardstick" against which the other jobs are later measured.

3. Evaluating the key jobs by assigning points to each factor. This is the heart of the evaluation process, because the point totals for each factor for each job should represent the best judgment of the evaluation committee on the *relative* importance of each factor in job *A* as compared with job *B*, job *C*, etc. In some plans, this step is shortened by deciding which "degree" (first, second, third, etc.) of a factor is appropriate, and each "degree" then carries a fixed number of points.[1]

4. Evaluating all the other jobs, department by department, in relation to the evaluations already placed on the "key jobs." When the number of jobs is large, the evaluation must constantly be checked by reference to a growing catalogue that lists for each factor which job has been assigned the most points or highest degree, which second, third, etc. In this way, the *relative* character of the evaluation process is maintained.

5. Determining a "wage curve" by means of a wage survey of the key jobs. The curve (which may be a straight line) is based upon the present rates paid on those key jobs whose rates are in line with those paid by other firms in the labor market or in the industry. It is derived from a scatter diagram of points whose coordinates represent (1) rate paid and (2) point-evaluation total, for each key job.

[1] For good descriptions of the installation of point plans using "degrees" for each factor, see M. J. MURPHY and R. C. SMYTH, "Job Evaluation by the Point Plan," *Factory Management and Maintenance*, Vol. 104, pp. 137–148, 1946; and F. H. JOHNSON, R. W. BOISE, JR., and D. PRATT, *Job Evaluation*, John Wiley & Sons, Inc., New York, 1946.

6. Interpolating from the curve the single rates (or rate ranges) for other jobs, considered either singly or in groups called "labor grades." (For piecework or incentive jobs, the curve gives the base rate.) Assuming that job rates above the curve are lowered to the curve and that job rates below are raised to the curve, the decreases and increases, weighted by the number of employees on each job, should roughly cancel out, leaving the total pay roll unchanged. Job evaluation is not a method of increasing or decreasing total pay roll; rather, it is a procedure for distributing a given pay roll among various jobs in accordance with their relative skill and difficulty.

7. Putting the new rates into effect, by raising job rates below the curve, but not reducing present incumbents on jobs whose present rates are above the curve. By transfers and upgrading, or as job contents change, or through turnover as new employees are hired at the proper job rates, these above-the-line present-incumbent rates will gradually be eliminated. This process may be a lengthy one, however, giving rise to many complaints. A better method is to put the results of the job evaluation into effect at the time of a general wage increase. Then it may be possible to achieve a balanced wage and salary structure immediately by not raising, or raising in less amounts, the rates of employees on jobs that have been overpaid according to the evaluation.

8. Continuing administration of the program, by analyzing and evaluating changed jobs and new jobs to establish rates that will bear a proper relationship to the rates on existing jobs. If existing rates are challenged, reevaluations should be made. Job evaluation must be kept up to date if it is to be worth while. This will also involve periodic wage surveys to assist in keeping key job rates in line with prevailing or "market" rates for similar jobs.

ADVANTAGES OF JOB EVALUATION

A well-developed plan of job evaluation has clear advantages in achieving a more rational and consistent internal wage and salary structure. If key job rates are carefully kept in line with market rates on similar jobs, the firm's general wage level will also be more satisfactory. Finally, and most important, when there are a number of jobs that are peculiar to the firm, job evaluation provides a means of determining rates for these jobs that will be consistent with rates on jobs that are more common in the community or industry.

These wage-setting advantages of job evaluation are clear, but the "administrative" purposes or advantages of job evaluation have not received enough emphasis.[1] They may be outlined as follows:

---

[1] These purposes are stressed and ably discussed by E. ROBERT LIVERNASH, *An Analysis of Job Evaluation Procedures*, Chap. V, unpublished doctoral dissertation, Harvard University, Cambridge, Mass., 1941.

1. Specializing and centralizing the process of determining wage differentials—in the job-evaluation committee and the staff analysts assisting it.
2. Securing agreement among the various management officials in the organization, and in unionized plants the union representatives, on the question of proper wage and salary differentials.
3. Establishing a frame of reference for the settlement of grievances over individual rates and for negotiations with the union over internal wage differentials.
4. Developing machinery for systematically reviewing job rates as job contents change with technological and process improvements, or as variations occur among market rates for particular jobs.

LIMITATIONS AND PROBLEMS OF JOB EVALUATION

Although job evaluation does have clear advantages over haphazard procedures of wage determination, its proponents and practitioners have sometimes overlooked its limitations. It is inaccurate to claim scientific exactness for the results of job evaluation. No judgment, however well informed, is exact in a scientific sense, yet some managements have maintained that the rates set by job evaluation should not be open to question or discussion by union representatives.

Another limitation of job evaluation is that jobs of equal content in terms of the usual factors may not necessarily be of equal attractiveness to workers. For example, it is not uncommon to find that one job in a plant is more or less of a "blind-alley" job, whereas another is recognized by workers as a steppingstone to a better job. Yet the two jobs may be equal in terms of skill, responsibility, physical effort, mental effort, and working conditions. Traditionally, the rate on the blind-alley job may have been higher than on the other, yet a job-evaluation program can upset this relationship and create a new kind of inequity.

Career prospects outside the company are also important.[1] Some jobs are highly specialized in a particular firm, whereas others develop skills that are marketable in other firms and industries. Despite similarity in job content, it may be necessary to pay more for the first type of job than for the second in order to attract and hold capable workers. The same comment can be made with respect to two jobs, equal in content but different in continuity of employment. It is traditional, for example, that maintenance carpenters in a factory get steadier employment than construction carpenters outside, and the higher hourly rates of the latter generally

[1] This point and other equally important limitations are discussed by ROBERT TILOVE, "Functions and Limitations of Job Evaluation," *Personnel*, Vol. 22, pp. 206–214, 1946.

reflect this important difference. In short, unless the results of job evaluation approximate in practice the relative social evaluations that workers place on the jobs, dissatisfactions are apt to be created by the system itself.

Inflexibility and too great reliance on internal standards of job comparison are other limitations of job evaluation. In some labor markets, the supply and demand for a particular type of labor or occupation have an important bearing on the rates paid, and a job-evaluation plan that seeks to determine wage differentials largely on the basis of factors and points, without reference to market rates, is likely to breed opposition, especially in unionized situations. This difficulty can be minimized if the plan has a relatively large number of key jobs which are related to market rates and if changes are made in job rates on these key jobs as market rates change, regardless of changes in job content. A simple plan is likely to be more flexible, and flexibility is vital if market forces are important.[1]

If the market rate that must be paid on a certain job to attract and retain good workers is much higher than the job-evaluation system would justify, it may be better to make this job an "exception" and have it recognized as such by everybody. Juggling points to "justify" a high rate, which has been done in some cases, is less defensible; although a "balancing factor" may be added to the standard factors to take into account these variables.[2] Obviously, in isolated labor markets and in certain types of firms where jobs are unique, this problem of adjustment to market forces is not so great.

In view of these limitations, common sense more than devotion to "a system" is needed in the development and application of job evaluation. Its principal usefulness is in relating rates on jobs that are more or less specialized in the particular firm to the established or market rates on jobs that are common to the industry or the area.

Two other problems in job evaluation should be mentioned, and they are particularly important in unionized plants. First, as we have seen, the process of job evaluation may result in the *reduction* of some job rates, as well as in the increase of others. This is to be expected if a greater internal consistency is desired in a previously chaotic wage structure. Even though the rates of present incumbents on those jobs are not reduced, and even though the new lower rate is to be paid only to new employees, the idea of any rate reduction is opposed by some unions. Failure to understand and accept the principle of job-rate reductions, as well as increases, however, will eventually result in "an out-of-line" rate structure. This is particularly

---

[1] This point is discussed more fully by LIVERNASH, *op. cit.*, Chap. V.

[2] GOMBERG, WILLIAM, "A Collective Bargaining Approach to Job Evaluation," *Labor and Nation*, Vol. 2, No. 1, pp. 51–53, 1946.

likely when changes in job content result from technological or process changes. A simplified job should carry a lower rate, relative to unchanged jobs, and the gains from technological change should be shared with *all* workers through general wage increases rather than only with particular workers on the affected jobs.[1]

Second, in unionized plants, management must accept realistically the fact that rates on important or key jobs will be negotiated with the union and not determined precisely by factors and points under a formal job-evaluation system. In fact, this very process of negotiation may give the plan the flexibility that it needs with reference to market forces and the social evaluations of workers. In saying this, we do not intend to minimize the danger that unions may bring pressure for job-rate changes that would unbalance the rate structure.

ADVANCING INDIVIDUALS WITHIN RATE RANGES

When, by job-evaluation, rate and salary ranges are established instead of single rates for each job, as is frequent where jobs are grouped in broad labor grades or classifications, some procedure must be established for advancing the hourly rates of individuals within these ranges. In other words, if the rate range for class A machinists is $1.10 to $1.25 an hour, how can John Jones, who now receives $1.10, get a higher rate within the range?

There are two bases for making individual increases within rate ranges, merit and length of service. The latter is subject to the same objection that has been made against seniority as the sole factor in promotions; the reward for superior performance is reduced or eliminated. However, if merit is to be the sole or major factor in making individual increases, decisions ought to be based on something more reliable than the supervisor's offhand opinion.

Most firms faced with this problem have adopted an employee-rating plan, which was discussed in Chap. 13. A poorly conceived and poorly adminstered rating plan, however, will be but a slight improvement on haphazard judgments. And if the fairness of merit increases is widely questioned, it may be expected that employees and their union representatives will press for automatic length-of-service increases or single rates for everyone on the job.

Faced with a demand for length-of-service increases to the top of each rate range, some companies have negotiated a compromise that recognizes

[1] For further discussion of this point, see Chap. 17, p. 242; GOMBERG, *op. cit.*, pp. 52–53. For an opposite view, see SOLOMON BARKIN, "Wage Determination: Trick or Technique," *Labor and Nation*, Vol. I, No. 6, pp. 24–26, 1946.

the advantage of partial recognition of seniority and yet retains a merit incentive. Under this plan, increases to the mid-point of the range are made automatically on a length-of-service basis, and increases above the mid-point are made on a merit basis.

RATES ON "WOMEN'S JOBS"

The matter of "women's rates" is also a problem in wage administration. Should women be paid less than men on the same jobs? Job evaluation helps to answer this question. If the content of the job as performed by women is identical with the content of the job as performed by men, there should be no difference whatever in their rates. Discrimination on the basis of sex, in other words, has no place in good wage administration. [1] But, if certain adjustments are made in the job to accommodate women employees, such as special lifting devices, etc., then the rate should be based on the job content as evaluated in relation to the content of other jobs. In this sense, "women's jobs" may carry a lower rate than "men's jobs."

RESPONSIBILITY FOR WAGE AND SALARY ADMINISTRATION

Who should participate in the job-evaluation program? Should it be strictly a management responsibility, handled by a job-evaluation committee composed solely of job analysts or of selected line officials? Or should employee or union representatives be included on the committee, with equal voice in all decisions?

In attempting to answer these questions, it may be stated that, to be effective, a job-evaluation program must have the support and understanding not only of top management but also of supervisors and employees and, in unionized plants, of union representatives. The program must be simple, therefore, and explained carefully to all who will be affected. It cannot be regarded solely as a management prerogative. Employees may participate in job analysis by being asked to describe their own jobs, as we have seen, and supervisors must certainly be represented on the evaluation committee or be present when the jobs in their departments are evaluated. Secrecy and highly technical hocus-pocus in job evaluation are bound to arouse suspicion and outright opposition.

[1] Many union agreements provide for "equal pay for equal work" in an attempt to prevent discrimination in wages between men and women on comparable jobs. Some states, including Massachusetts, have also passed laws requiring equal pay for equal work, designed to eliminate this discrimination. Within a given plant, the principle can be defended; but, if it is applied more broadly to all firms in an industry, other questions arise. What is "equal work"? Should financial condition or the local labor market have no influence on rates paid for similar jobs in different localities?

Whether union representatives should participate directly and have joint responsibility for determining relative job rates and for putting them into effect is a moot question. Some unions take the position that they should be consulted on the basic principles of the plan and that they should be kept informed of each step. But they oppose full joint participation, because this puts union representatives in the position of having to argue against their own constituents if union members subsequently object to rates set under the plan. These unions prefer to retain their position of critics and present complaints against specific results of the program.[1]

On the other hand, joint union-management job-evaluation committees have been successful in a number of firms where relationships were already good. One of the pioneers in job evaluation has summarized his experience as follows:

After fifteen or sixteen years of working with job evaluation, I must say that my philosophy is that success depends not only on selling the program to employees but also upon the extent that employees believe in it. That belief is greatly enhanced by the opportunity to participate. . . .Employee participation may consist, for example, of interviewing the employee at his place of work; he has a pride in his job. It may consist of bringing in shop stewards on an equality with the foremen to committee meetings; it may consist of bringing in the leaders of the union on an equality with top management.[2]

The responsibility of the personnel department for wage and salary administration is largely an advisory and service responsibility. The personnel administrator or job analysts on his staff may train and assist the evaluation committee in its work, but they should not perform a line function in actually evaluating jobs and setting proper rates. Continuing administration of the program should also be a committee responsibility, assisted by the personnel department in calling attention to new and changed jobs.

When wage administration involves individual merit increases within rate ranges established by job evaluation, it is also important that the

[1] As an example, see *U. E. Guide to Wage Payment Plans, Time Study, and Job Evaluation*, pp. 77–85, United Electrical, Radio, and Machine Workers of America, CIO, New York, 1943. However, a local of this union participated jointly with management in a successful job-evaluation program; see ANDREW J. PERCIVAL and GLENN B. GROSS, "Job Evaluation—A Case History," *Harvard Business Review*, Vol. 24, pp. 466–497, 1946. For another example, with somewhat different results, see NICHOLAS L. A. MARTUCCI, "Case History of a Joint Management-labor Job Evaluation Program," *Personnel*, Vol. 23, No. 2, pp. 98–105, 1946.

[2] BENGE, EUGENE J., Employee Participation in a Job Evaluation Program, in *Principles and Application of Job Evaluation*, p. 7, Studies in Personnel Policy No. 62, National Industrial Conference Board, Inc., New York, 1944.

personnel department should not usurp line authority. In one firm, for example, all increases within rate ranges had to be approved by the personnel department, and foremen soon acquired the habit of telling an employee who sought a raise, "Well, Fred, I'd like to give one to you, but it has to have the O.K. of the personnel department, and they've been turning me down lately." The proper role of the personnel department should be to assist the foremen in developing and administering an employee-rating plan on which individual merit increases may be based. But each foreman should have the authority to make these increases, subject to the approval of his own superior in the line organization.

SUMMARY

Two principal aspects of the wage question have been discussed in this chapter: (1) determination of the general level of wages and (2) internal wage and salary relationships. The first is an important top-management responsibility; and, in unionized firms, periodic negotiations with union representatives are necessary. The second also requires the attention of line officials, with the personnel department acting as a service and advisory agency in securing the job descriptions and analyses that are necessary for thoroughgoing job evaluation.

Four factors are important in the determination of the general level of wages and changes in it: (1) wages paid for comparable work by other firms in the community or in the industry; (2) financial condition of the firm, particularly as affected by managerial efficiency and labor productivity; (3) "cost of living"; and (4) state and Federal minimum-wage laws and governmental wage orders. The personnel department is expected to keep informed as to these factors and especially to assist management in making periodic wage and salary surveys.

Internal wage and salary relationships have a tremendous effect on employee morale, and some systematic method of determining differentials between jobs is needed to avoid a chaotic wage and salary structure. Increasing use is being made, therefore, of job evaluation, though sometimes its basic limitations are overlooked.

The wage aspect of personnel administration also involves methods of wage payment, including incentive plans, and getting employee acceptance of new output standards. These are considered in the next chapter.

Chapter 17

Methods of Wage Payment; Output Standards

> There are many wage incentive plans that are successful
> because the employers are carrying out the basic principle
> of consultation with their employees. These results are by-
> products of this cooperation rather than the direct result of
> time study and rate setting. The plan is working primarily
> because the employer has as a background the respect and
> loyalty of the employees. If this kind of relationship is lack-
> ing, it matters little how well worked out the plan is, it will
> fall short of the results expected of it.
>
> CARROLL E. FRENCH[1]

Technical problems in developing and administering various methods
of wage payment have received considerable attention, particularly from
industrial engineers. These problems are certainly important, and trained
industrial engineers are needed; but the personnel aspects of wage-payment
methods have too often been neglected in practice. In fact, it is no exaggeration to say that the human problems involved in getting employee
acceptance of new methods of wage payment and new output standards
are both more important and more difficult to solve than the technical
problems of developing and establishing these methods and standards. It
is encouraging to note, however, that the better industrial engineers today
are often as aware of the human problems as are personnel administrators
and that this is particularly true of the new generation of engineers.

THE PERSONNEL ADMINISTRATOR'S ROLE

In many firms, rate setting is such a specialized function that it is
delegated to a separate department, known as the "industrial engineering,"
"standards," or "rate" department, which often has full authority to

[1] Discussion of *A Psychologist Looks at Wage Incentive Methods*, by RICHARD STEPHEN
UHRBROCK, Institute of Management Series, No. 15, A.M.A., 1935, p. 31.

establish new methods of wage payment, new output standards, and new rates under existing plans. When this happens, the line organization has lost one of its responsibilities, and, as in the case of merit increases, the opportunity for buck-passing is great.

Friction between the technically trained men in the rate department, on the one hand, and foremen and employees, on the other, may be inevitable, but it can be somewhat reduced by good organizational practice. Changes involving methods of wage payment should have the approval of the foreman or of one of his superiors in the line organization. The principal function of the rate department, as a staff or service department, should be to provide the line organization with the technical assistance necessary in establishing new piece or incentive rates and new methods of wage payment. A control function may also be exercised, to ensure consistent practice, but it is better for this to be done through the line organization.

The rate department is often separate from the personnel department, but this does not mean that the personnel administrator has no concern with these matters. A badly conceived and poorly administered wage-payment plan can disrupt personnel relations. Similarly, output standards that are set capriciously and changed without notice or explanation will destroy morale and fail in their objectives. As the quotation at the beginning of the chapter suggests, the best technical plans will be worth little unless good personnel relationships have already been developed.

An understanding of the different methods of wage payment and of the circumstances in which each is appropriate is a part of the equipment that the personnel administrator must bring to his job. He should also know the requirements of a good wage-incentive system and some of the procedures that have been successful in winning employee acceptance of output standards. As a staff man, he can influence other staff men, such as the industrial engineers who take the time studies and set the standards, and help them to avoid errors that result in employee opposition to the whole program.

BASIC METHODS OF WAGE PAYMENT

Methods of wage and salary payment fall into two basic groups: (1) payment on the basis of time—by the hour, day, week, month, or year; and (2) payment on the basis of output—by the piece, or by time spent in completing a piece or a "unit."[1] Hourly rates or salaries are the most

---

[1] An example of this is the well-known Bedaux, or "point," system, in which output is measured in time units instead of in pieces completed. The amount of work per minute, together with allowances for fatigue, etc., is called a "B," or a point. Sixty B's, or points, constitute the standard or task hour, and 80 points are considered the average for experienced operators.

frequently used types of payment on the basis of time, and straight piece rates or some other form of wage-incentive plan in which time rates may be combined with payment on the basis of output "above standard" are the usual methods of payment by output. Both piecework and other types of incentive plans may be either "individual" or "group" and, in some cases, even "plant-wide."

The relative advantages of each of the two basic methods of wage payment may be summarized in terms of the circumstances or situations under which each is to be preferred.[1]

1. Payment on a time basis is more satisfactory when
    a. Units of output are not distinguishable and measurable.
    b. Employees have little control over the quantity of output, or there is no clear-cut relation between effort and output, as on some machine-paced jobs.
    c. Work delays are frequent and beyond employees' control.
    d. Quality of work is especially important.
    e. Supervision is good, and supervisors know what constitutes "a fair day's work."
2. Payment on the basis of output is more satisfactory when
    a. Units of output are measurable.
    b. A clear relation exists between employee effort and quantity of output.
    c. The job is standardized, the flow of work is regular, and breakdowns few or, if many, consistent.
    d. Quality considerations are less important than quantity of output, or at least are uniform and measurable.
    e. Supervision is poor, or supervisors cannot devote enough attention to individual performance.

Clearly, then, payment on the basis of output (wage incentive) is not best under all circumstances. Even where basic conditions seem to favor it, a wage-incentive system needs to be carefully considered before it is introduced. *It is not a panacea for poor morale and low output.*

EMPLOYEE ATTITUDES ON WAGE INCENTIVES

When management concludes that some form of wage incentive is desirable, engineers are usually called in to advise and assist in the installation of a plan. The technical aspects of the installation receive considerable attention; and, if a system appears to be sound technically, some managements assume that employees should accept it without protest.

---

[1] For a fuller discussion of these differences, see SUMNER H. SLICHTER, *Union Policies and Industrial Management*, Chap. X, Brookings Institution, Washington, D. C., 1941.

They forget, however, that a system that depends upon human effort requires for its success more than a knowledge of mathematics and engineering. It is necessary not only that such a system *be* fair but that employees *believe* it to be fair. They have an almost uncanny ability for devising ways to "beat the system" once they have made up their minds that it is not in their interest to cooperate.

Technical specialists are often unwilling to accept as facts to be reckoned with the attitudes and sentiments of employees toward time study and wage incentives. Yet, since the success of these methods depends upon employee acceptance, the personnel administrator should help the technical men to discover workers' attitudes in a specific situation and to take them into account in the installation. The person-centered approach is useful in this field as in all other situations where people are at work.

Employee attitudes toward time study and wage incentives differ from firm to firm, but some of the fairly prevalent beliefs held by workers may be outlined in general terms:[1]

1. A belief that many wage-incentive plans are so complicated that even the experts cannot explain them. As one worker said, "Nobody ever told us how those standards were figured or how we figure our pay. Sometimes we get different pay for the same work, so I don't think they (the engineers) know what it's all about either."

2. A conviction that standards are set unfairly, by using fast workers, juggling allowances, underrating "effort," and selecting the shorter times to be used in computing the standard. Most employees know very little about the mechanics of time study, but isolated instances and even hearsay about poor time study are likely to convince them that the whole process is "hocus-pocus" designed to confuse and injure the worker. An operator in the dyehouse of a textile finishing plant complained, "I've worked as hard as I can and I'd just like to see the foreman or the time study man do it any faster, like they say you can." Restudy of the job revealed that some mistakes *had* been made in the original study.

The approach and methods used by time-study engineers are also frequently resented. For example, workers in one metal-trades plant complained about a time-study man in the following words: "If trouble develops in Building 20, the help know just where to put their finger on it. Jamieson, the timester, is certainly a wonder at creating said trouble. The help are not against a fair time study, but when a time-study man steps in and tells the operator how to run his machine and which hand to

[1] Some of these beliefs, of course, are the basis for union policies on wage incentives. See *U.E. Guide to Wage Payment Plans, Time Study, and Job Evaluation*, United Electrical, Radio, and Machine Workers of America, CIO, New York, 1943.

use and that he wants more speed, then it is time for the union to step in and take a hand. The union did, and we hope that Jamieson realizes that he is only a timester and not a gang boss."

3. The fear of a rate cut and "speed-up" if good earnings are made after a rate is established. Sometimes this belief is held even though workers can cite no actual instance when it has occurred; they have just "heard about" it. Yet the statement that "they'll cut your rate" is a powerful deterrent to increased output and a justification in workers' eyes for restriction of output by pegging it at some fixed figure.

4. A belief that workers are treated as a commodity, that their opinions and feelings do not count when the time-study man comes around. Because of this and other beliefs, there exists among working people a profound distrust of certain types of industrial engineers who are also called "efficiency experts," "systemizers," and many less flattering names. In one instance, where time-study men were members of the same union as production employees in a large electrical-goods manufacturing plant, a union official nevertheless described these fellow union members as "birds who sit on their fat fannies all day and figure out how to cut our rates."

When such attitudes exist, it is shortsighted to ignore them or brush them aside as "illogical" or "unreasonable." Obviously, the personality and approach of the specialists who perform the technical aspects of the installation are very important, and management must exercise great care in selecting and training these experts. Equally important, however, is the adoption by management of policies and procedures designed to modify these attitudes in workers and to minimize their natural fears.

REQUIREMENTS OF A GOOD WAGE INCENTIVE SYSTEM

From the record of experience in installing and administering wage-incentive systems, it is possible to list some of the requirements for success. The ability of management to meet many of these requirements will depend upon the background of the company's personnel and labor relations.

1. Discussion of the need for a wage-incentive system with the supervisors and employees who will be affected, and an explanation of the proposed system, *before* installation begins. In unionized firms, this means consultation with union representatives and then, in cooperation with these representatives, further explanation with individual employees on the job. Changes are more likely to be accepted if people are told about them in advance, and acceptance may be even more wholehearted and a better plan may result if both supervisors and employees have an op-

portunity to suggest improvements in the plan, which then becomes partly "their" plan.

This was the experience when a new wage-incentive system was introduced on the tenter (drying) frames in a bleachery. The proposed system was discussed in detail with the supervisors and the union representatives, and the latter, in turn, talked it over with the men affected. Before the plan was finally put into effect, it had been improved by their suggestions. The new incentive then operated without a hitch, in contrast with the constant bickerings and misunderstandings that led to a spontaneous walkout under the previous plan.

2. A wage-incentive system must be simple and understandable to the employees. They should not have to be mathematicians or "slide-rule artists" in order to figure their pay. Complexity is one of the basic drawbacks in many of the wage-incentive systems that have logical appeal to some engineers. If the worker cannot understand how his pay is figured, the incentive is largely wasted.[1]

3. The job or jobs must be standardized, to determine the "one best way" of performance at the present time. This may involve motion study and work simplification *before* a standard and rate are set on the job and the training of qualified operators in the use of the prescribed standard method, in which delays and interferences are at a minimum. If the job is timed and a rate set beforehand, short cuts are soon discovered, the rate becomes known among workers as a "loose" rate, and earnings either rise out of line with other jobs or the operators "take it easy" and peg production to avoid detection.

4. The standard of output (the "task"), on which incentive earnings are based, must be determined by competent time-study methods or from records of past performance if there have been no significant changes in job methods and the job has been standardized. Time study is generally the more satisfactory procedure, but it involves a number of judgments or "guesstimates," and the validity of its results depends as much on these as on the actual stop-watch readings.

For example, judgments are involved in the following: (a) selecting the person to be timed—"the normal qualified operator," (b) determining the conditions under which the time study is to be made, (c) deciding how many studies to make, (d) selecting the "element" times to

---

[1] Some types of wage-incentive plans meet this requirement; others do not. For detailed descriptions of the various types, see J. K. Louden, *Wage Incentives*, John Wiley & Sons, Inc., New York, 1944; and Charles W. Lytle, *Wage Incentive Methods, Their Selection, Installation, and Operation*, rev. ed. The Ronald Press Company, New York, 1942.

get a "cycle" time for one complete operation, (e) rating the "effort" or "performance" of the operator being timed, and (f) making allowances for fatigue, personal time, and unavoidable delays.[1] Technical competence, good judgment, and integrity are usually not enough to ensure that time studies will be successful, however. Practitioners are needed who also have the knack of explaining what they are doing and gaining the confidence of the persons affected. A time-study man who has previously worked on various jobs in a department, therefore, is likely to be more acceptable than a technically trained person who has had little or no work experience. A few firms have also been successful in reducing the mystery and suspicion of time study by providing for the training of union time-study stewards, who can then work with management in arriving at an agreement on the time required to do a specific job.[2] Some unions also train their own time-study specialists.

5. An hourly (or "base" or "standard") rate should be established for each job on incentive pay, preferably by job evaluation. This rate should be guaranteed on an hourly or daily basis, or there should be some sort of payment for "waiting time" caused by delays beyond the control of the operator. When the method of payment on a job is changed from a time to an output basis, the time rate is usually the guaranteed rate. It is expected that operators will earn, on the average, 10 to 25 per cent more than the guaranteed rate, depending upon the type of work. Piece rates or bonus rates are set with this objective in mind.

6. Earnings above standard or "task," as set by time study or records of past performance, should be in direct proportion to the increase in output above standard. Variable relationships at different levels of output are confusing and therefore undesirable. Paying the worker 100 per

---

[1] The variation in time study results that can occur is illustrated by the example of a simultaneous time study made by 11 men. One set a standard 11 per cent above the average for the group and another set a standard 12 per cent below the average—a spread of 23 per cent. After a series of training conferences, in which emphasis was put on training in effort rating, the variation was reduced to 9 per cent. BARNES, RALPH M., Is the Rate of Output Right? in *Incentives for Management and Workers*, p. 15, Production Series No. 161, American Management Association, New York, 1945.

An excellent discussion of the limitations of theory and practice in time study, especially from the union viewpoint, is WILLIAM GOMBERG (Director, Management Engineering Department, International Ladies Garment Workers Union, AF of L), "The Relationship between the Unions and the Engineers," *Mechanical Engineering*, Vol. 65, pp. 425–430, 1943.

[2] An example is the experience of the Murray Corporation of America, Detroit. See *Production Standards from Time Study Analysis by Labor and Management*, Local No. 2. United Automobile Workers of America and the Murray Corporation, Detroit, 1942; and "More Pay = More Production. Murray Corporation of America Proves It at the Ecorse Plant," *Fortune*, Vol. 28, pp. 139*ff*., 1943.

cent of what he produces above standard ("100 per cent sharing") is also generally preferable, because workers are usually unable to understand and tend to resent plans (such as the old Bedaux system) in which earnings above standard are shared between supervision and employees. However, 100 per cent sharing is not always desirable; for, on a particular job, the output may vary because of factors beyond the workers' control, and the wide variations in earnings that occur under 100 per cent sharing may be the source of friction between operators. A high base rate and a relatively small premium that represents less than 100 per cent sharing may be preferable under these conditions.

7. There should be a clear system for inspecting, counting, and recording the output of each individual or group, and results should be posted daily, if possible, so that employees know just what they have produced.

8. After standards and rates have been established, they should be guaranteed against changes, *except* when there are substantial changes in methods, materials, or equipment. Thus, higher than average earnings, due to the superior skill or ingenuity of certain employees, should never be the occasion for an increase in the standard and a reduction in the rate. But if changes introduced by management are responsible for increased earnings, the standard and rate *must* be revised to prevent inequalities from creeping into the system. They should be revised, however, only to the extent that equipment, methods, or materials have changed. Fairness in this respect is essential to success with incentive-wage administration.

9. There should be careful follow-up and checking to see that standards are maintained or exceeded or, if they are not, to determine the reasons. Failure to meet standards and reach expected earnings may not be the fault of the employees. Management may be to blame because of improper training, poor equipment, or unequal flow of materials, and these possibilities should be investigated first.

10. Employees should be encouraged to use the complaint procedure promptly when they think that conditions under the new standard and rate are not right. As we have pointed out earlier, the complaint procedure is not only a "safety valve" for employees but also an aid to management in spot-lighting difficulties that require attention before they develop into major problems in labor relations.

11. The incentive plan should cover all workers whose jobs can be adapted to the incentive method of payment. Otherwise, dissatisfaction will result among those workers who do not have an opportunity to participate in the higher earnings possible under an incentive plan. There may also be complaints among indirect workers, such as maintenance and service employees, who are paid hourly rates and yet have to work

harder because of the increased output under the incentive system for production workers.[1] In some cases, difficulties arising under incomplete coverage have led to group and plant-wide incentive systems.

GROUP AND PLANT-WIDE INCENTIVES

Individual incentives are still the most widely used type of incentive plan; but, when it is difficult to measure individual performance, group and sometimes plant-wide incentive plans may be more appropriate. Furthermore, as an alternative to individual incentives, group piecework or group bonuses for output above an established standard have the following advantages:

1. Individual members of the group do not bear the whole loss if they happen to get a job with a "tight" rate or a job that requires more care than the average because of special technical difficulties.
2. Charges of "favoritism" in the assignment of "fat" and "lean" jobs are therefore less likely to occur.
3. Each member of the group has an incentive for training new members and helping the others, since individual earnings depend upon the total output of the group, apportioned according to hourly or base rates.

The principal drawback in group incentives is the obvious one that the relationship between *individual* effort and output is not direct. Another is that, if standards are based on past performance rather than on careful time studies, it is difficult to distinguish between increase in output due to methods changes by management and increases due to increased skill and effort on the part of employees. These objections are even more pertinent in the case of plant-wide incentives.

During the Second World War, plant-wide incentives were adopted for various reasons. In some cases, as in the rapidly expanding aircraft industry, there was not sufficient time to set standards and rates on individual jobs, and a plant-wide incentive, which tied bonus earnings to increases in physical production per worker above a defined standard,[2] offered a rough opportunity to stimulate greater output. In other cases, plant-wide incentives provided a method of compensating indirect

---

[1] For fuller discussion of this point and other aspects of wage-incentive administration, see a field study of 21 firms and 5 national unions by ARNOLD O. PUTNAM, *Administration of Wage Incentives*, pp. 93–95, unpublished master's thesis, Department of Business and Engineering Administration, Massachusetts Institute of Technology, Cambridge, Mass, 1947.

[2] As an example, see F. T. KURT, The Grumman Aircraft Plan, in *Practical Uses of Wage Incentives*, Production Series No. 150, American Management Association, New York, 1944; and National War Labor Board, Case No. 13–285, Sept. 14, 1943, II, p. 322, *War Labor Reports.*

workers, who were frequently paid hourly rates, for the added effort required from them when plant production increased.

In a small plant with a fairly standardized product, a plant-wide incentive system can help to develop real team spirit. If the product is subject to frequent technological changes, the plan may be a method of sharing with all employees the gains from technological changes by leaving the standards unchanged. If this is done, a plant-wide incentive probably resembles profit sharing more than it does individual or group incentive, although employees will share in the gains from better methods even if there are no profits. In a competitive situation, when competitors do not have the same type of incentive plan, this may be a distinct hardship.

In any incentive system, whether it be individual, group, or plant-wide, management must face the fundamental question: Will the incentive plan actually stimulate greater production and employee earnings, so that both gain; or will it be the occasion for misunderstandings, friction, decreased production, and lower morale? The basic job conditions that exist, the background of labor relations, and the manner in which the incentive system is introduced and administered will be important factors determining the answer to this question.

GETTING EMPLOYEE ACCEPTANCE OF NEW OUTPUT STANDARDS

When a wage-incentive system is first installed, output standards must be set, as we have seen. Furthermore, when new machines are introduced, methods changed, and materials altered to get better quality or to meet competition, standards and rates on jobs paid on an individual or group incentive basis must also be changed if inequalities are to be avoided. Getting employee acceptance of these changes is often one of the most difficult problems in the whole field of personnel administration and labor relations. When there is a technological change, the fear that the new machine or method will destroy a skill, resulting in demotion or layoff, is added to the fears already mentioned in our earlier discussion of workers' attitudes toward wage incentives.

The personnel administrator may be called upon to guide management in securing from employees the cooperation that is necessary if strife is to be avoided. The record of spontaneous strikes and violence against new machinery, because of the fear of "speed-up" or displacement, is an example of what can happen if insufficient attention is given to the human aspects of laborsaving and the new output standards required.

Some guiding principles emerge from the experience of companies that have been more successful than the average in securing employee acceptance of new output standards resulting from changes in machinery, methods, or materials. These may be briefly summarized:

1. As in the installation of a new incentive plan, there should be advance consultation and explanation, with employees and their representatives, concerning changes under consideration and the probable new output standards that will result. This consultation should take place well in advance of the change, and there should be full discussion of competitive conditions and other reasons that make the new arrangements desirable and necessary. In general, employees are more inclined to accept changed assignments willingly if they know *why* these are necessary. Furthermore, the experience of some firms and the findings of research studies on the operation of democratic work groups suggest that technological changes and new output standards will be accepted more willingly if workers actually participate in the *determination* of these changes.[1]

2. If possible, guarantee against layoffs by advance planning of transfers and retraining employees who may be displaced by the change. In cases where this is not possible, advance notice of layoff should be given, and dismissal compensation should be provided.

3. Timing of the change so that it does not coincide with declining business and wage reductions, and gradual introduction so that displacement is minimized through normal turnover, transfer, and retraining.

4. Careful advance preparation and standardization of the new job and all auxiliary operations, so that, when a standard is set, it can be attained without additional strain on the worker, and so that the proposed rate will yield equivalent earnings for the same effort.

5. Explanation of the procedure to be used in setting the new standards and rates.

6. Establishment of a tentative or preliminary standard and rate for a definite trial period, during which operators will be guaranteed either their average straight-time hourly earnings in some past period or their (lower) base rate. A full guarantee of previous earnings protects operators against losses that are the result of mechanical or similar difficulties during the trial period; but, if cooperation is poor, this guarantee may cause the operators to take it easy and not give the new standard a fair trial. A better plan may be to provide a flat bonus or guarantee in addition to actual earnings under the new tentative rate, thus leaving some incentive.

[1] Employee participation in technological change has developed under union-management cooperation in production problems, which is discussed in Chap. 21. For significant experimental evidence on getting democratic group decisions in setting new production goals, see the report of the experiment by Alex Bavelas and Kurt Lewin in NORMAN R. F. MAIER, *Psychology in Industry*, pp. 264–266, Houghton Mifflin Company, Boston, 1946.

7. At the end of the trial period, review of all the data with employees and their representatives, for the purpose of reaching an agreement on output standards. Responsible union representatives can be helpful here, as they were in one firm when employees slowed down on a newly introduced machine. After reviewing the data with company representatives, the union business agent convinced the workers that they should give the new output standard a fair trial. The result was that the new standard proved to be a fair one and yielded earnings that were in line with those on jobs of comparable skill and difficulty.

8. Finally, if agreement cannot be reached, the matter should be submitted to arbitration, like any other unsettled grievances, with the understanding that both parties will abide by the arbitrator's decision.

SHARING THE GAINS

As a means of getting acceptance of these changes, it has been suggested further that employers should be willing to share with the employees affected the resulting gains, as shown by lower unit costs. This prospect would certainly make the proposed change more acceptable to the particular workers, but it overlooks the possibility that the change may be vitally necessary to meet competition through lower prices.

However, if the gains add initially to profits, there is the further question of whether the employees who happen to be on the changed jobs should be the only ones to share in technological progress. Favoring these employees with increases in their earnings may win their acceptance more easily, but it may also put their earnings "out of line" with the earnings on other jobs of equal skill and difficulty. In this case, one personnel problem is met by creating another.

This dilemma should be frankly faced. It requires full discussion with employees and union representatives in an effort to secure understanding of policy requirements. Several alternative solutions are open. Savings from technological change and increased output standards can be generalized through plant-wide increases or general improvements for all employees. A plant-wide incentive or an annual bonus plan or formal profit-sharing arrangement may also be worked out. Profit sharing has been advanced as a means of identifying the interests of workers and management more closely and encouraging joint cooperative efforts. Does this latter plan answer the problem?

THE PLACE OF PROFIT SHARING

Profit sharing has had a long history, not only in this country but abroad, although it is still not widely used. Plans differ in details, but a common feature is periodic employee participation in profits, usually above a specified minimum, on a percentage basis. Distribution among individual employees is then usually on the basis of their regular earnings.

Some strong advocates of profit sharing maintain that, if workers have a stake in the earnings of the enterprise of which they are a part, they will redouble their productive efforts, avoid wastes that raise costs, and do everything they can to boost sales. In some instances, these results seem to have occurred.[1] The experience with profit sharing in many companies, however, has been unfavorable, and at least 60 per cent of the plans established for wage earners have subsequently been discontinued.[2]

The incentive value of profit sharing is questionable, for most workers apparently tend to regard periodic payments or bonuses based on profits as "so much gravy." Workers in one large firm with a profit-sharing plan stated to an interviewer that the annual distribution had no effect on their effort or output during the year, largely because they could not see any direct relation between their individual work and company profits. Furthermore, when profits declined as general business conditions became worse, they resented the drop in profit-sharing bonuses to which they had become accustomed.

A few firms have experimented with sharing profits in the form of issuing stock to employees, and some have encouraged employees to purchase common stock in the company, usually at prices below the market. As in the case of profit sharing on a cash basis, many employee stock-ownership plans have subsequently been dropped. When stock prices fell drastically in the depression, employees lost faith in this form of extra incentive compensation and in the management that sponsored it. In short, there has been relatively little success with the effort to make employees "entrepreneur-minded" through profit sharing or employee stock ownership. Apparently other methods are needed to identify the workers' long-run interests with those of the specific firm.

This mutuality of interest might be developed under a type of profit sharing that is combined with genuine employee participation in a joint program to reduce costs and increase production. One unpublicized example which bears watching is the experience of a small firm manu-

[1] Perhaps the most publicized plan recently has been the Lincoln Electric Company's "incentive" plan, which has a profit-sharing arrangement as its central feature. See J. F. LINCOLN, The Lincoln Electric Company Incentive Plan, in *Industrial Engineering for Better Production*, pp. 34–48, Production Series No. 153, American Management Association, New York, 1944.

[2] STEWART, BRYCE M., and WALTER J. COUPER, *Profit Sharing and Stock Ownership for Wage Earners and Executives*, p. 49, Industrial Relations Monograph No. 10, Industrial Relations Counselors, Inc., New York, 1945.

facturing oil-storage tanks. In this company, employees through their C.I.O. steelworkers' union actually participate in making suggestions that will reduce costs and increase production and profits, and the union committee is given full information about the company's production problems and its cost, price, and profit situation.[1] Profits are shared equally under the plan between employees and the owner-manager, and payments are made monthly to enhance the incentive effect.

One episode illustrates the effect of this plan. Welders used to draw waiting-time pay when there was a shortage of materials on their jobs. At a meeting of the production committee, a member who was a welder suggested that welders help unload freight cars to get materials more quickly, and this was done, with consequent increased production, lower costs, and more profits to share. Initial results under the first two years of the plan indicate a substantial increase in the money amounts represented by the owner's and the employees' shares of profits, despite no increase in prices. It is too early, however, to draw any final conclusions on the plan's success and general applicability.

Annual-wage and Guaranteed-employment Plans

As in the case of profit sharing, there is a long but limited experience with annual-wage and guaranteed-employment plans. The three most widely publicized plans (Proctor and Gamble Company, Nunn-Bush Shoe Company, and the George A. Hormel Company) grew out of the effort of enlightened managements to provide greater employment and income security for their employees. Organized labor has now made the "guaranteed annual wage" one of its major objectives, and a number of existing plans have been developed in collaboration with union representatives.

Experience with annual-wage and guaranteed-employment plans suggests that they can be successfully introduced in a particular firm when (1) sales or production are not subject to violent seasonal or cyclical fluctuations or when stabilization efforts (as outlined at the end of Chap. 14) are feasible; (2) the guarantee is limited to certain groups of employees or to a certain number of hours or weeks of employment per year; (3) the background of employee-employer relations has been good and the plan can be jointly developed. When these conditions are met, greater income and employment security for wage earners are possible, resulting, in turn,

---

[1] For a fuller discussion of union-management cooperation on production problems, see Chap. 21. The experience of this company is summarized by Joseph Scanlon in *Adamson and His Profit-Sharing Plan*, A.M.A. Production Series No. 172, 1947.

in less resistance by employees to technological changes and cost-reduction programs, and in greater employee productivity.

In view of the increasing interest in these plans, every firm should study the feasibility of providing more regular employment[1] and formalizing this in an annual wage or employment guarantee. Labor is almost the only factor of production for which management does not make an advance commitment covering a future period of time. The consequences of making labor a "fixed" cost rather than a "variable" cost are great, but this is one of the challenges that management and personnel administration must face squarely in the years ahead. The alternative, which may be the only possible one for most employees, is increasing dependence for greater security upon government support.

Summary

Methods of wage payment, and particularly the installation of wage-incentive plans, have frequently been the special concern of industrial engineers. The human problems that arise in connection with wage-incentive plans and changes in output standards, however, are so important that the personnel administrator should be able to help in these matters. He should be familiar with the different circumstances under which time and output methods of payment are appropriate and with the requirements of a good incentive system, and the problems involved in introducing new output standards. With his skill and experience in similar situations, he may be expected to contribute an answer to the key question: How can employee acceptance be secured?

This question can never be answered in terms of money alone. The cooperation of workers is also to be secured by showing them that management is genuinely concerned in helping to solve their problems. One of the best ways to demonstrate this is by setting up hours of work and, when necessary, shift assignments that do not create avoidable difficulties for workers. This important subject will be discussed in the next chapter.

[1] See Chap. 14 for a discussion of employment-stabilization methods.

Chapter 18

Hours of Work and Shifts

Except for short periods, a considerable extension of the usual hours of work does not result in a sustained proportionate increase in output. The high production level which follows the introduction of overtime soon gives way to a pace which the worker feels he can safely maintain over a longer period. Rest periods keep production at higher levels, short multiple shifts are better than long shifts, and 1 day's rest in 7 is essential.

MAX D. KOSSORIS[1]

Effective utilization of labor in modern industry makes it necessary for employers to develop definite work schedules. Every organization must make specific policy decisions on the length of the workday and workweek, the number of shifts, rest and meal periods, holidays and vacations.

In considering work schedules, management is concerned first with policies that will meet the technical requirements of the organization. If the production process is continuous, for example, or if the investment in machinery and equipment is high, relatively long hours of operation will be appropriate for technical reasons. But human requirements must be integrated with technical needs. How long can individuals be expected to work per day and per week before their total output declines because of fatigue, illness, and accidents? Are the proposed work schedules compatible with what workers hope to get out of life in the way of recreation, family relationships, and association with friends? What personal problems of the workers, as groups and as individuals, should be taken into account in scheduling work assignments?

The human problems of work schedules, which are sometimes overlooked by managers in their concern for as full operation of available machinery and equipment as possible, should be the special province of the personnel administrator. In recommending policies and in helping to

[1] "Hours and Efficiency in British Industry," *Monthly Labor Review*, Vol. 42, p. iii, June 1941.

administer them, he should keep in mind the need of the enterprise for maximum production at lowest cost and the need of the employees for work schedules that will be most satisfactory to them. Perhaps it is unnecessary to add that these two needs are not always conflicting.

Optimum Hours

Some industries must be operated continuously, day and night, for technical reasons or because the public requires uninterrupted service, as in the case of public utilities. When this necessity does not exist, the decision on the number of hours per day and per week to operate the present productive facilities of an organization will depend upon (1) the demand for the product or service relative to existing plant capacity and the investment it represents, (2) the availability of additional labor or the willingness of present employees to work longer hours, (3) Federal and state legislation on hours of work, and (4) union contracts regulating hours of work. Within this framework, the decision on the length of work schedules for individual workers will be affected primarily by judgments on the optimum workday and workweek. What are the optimum hours of work for human beings?

No general answer can be given to fit all work situations; for the optimum workday and workweek vary according to the mental and physical effort required by the particular job, the working conditions, the capacity and temperament of the individual worker, his incentives for working, the kind of supervisor he has, and the congeniality of his fellow workers. For example, normal, healthy workers in a friendly, well-supervised work group with strong incentives for high output can perform light assembly operations in a comfortable workroom for longer hours than can older workers doing heavy disagreeable physical labor paid by the hour in an industry such as the foundry industry. Most workers, furthermore, can endure relatively long hours for occasional periods, but few can sustain an effective performance for long hours over a considerable period of time.

Experience with long working hours in this country during the Second World War indicates that "on the whole, the 5-day week and the 8-hour day are more efficient than a work schedule with longer hours."[1] When a

[1] Kossoris, Max D., "Studies of the Effects of Long Working Hours," (Part 2) Bulletin No. 791-A, p. 2, Bureau of Labor Statistics, U.S. Department of Labor, Washington, D. C. 1944. This conclusion was based upon 12 careful studies in various types of metalworking industries. See also *Health and Efficiency of Workers as Affected by Long Hours and Night Work: Experience of World War* II, Division of Industrial Relations, Women in Industry, and Minimum Wage, Department of Labor, State of New York, August, 1946.

sixth day of 8 hours or less is added, there is some loss in hourly efficiency, and it is seldom that more than a 46- or 48-hour week should be recommended in factory work. Furthermore, 1 day of rest in 7 is considered essential.[1] Longer hours may bring greater total weekly output, but at the expense of lower hourly efficiency, increased absenteeism, and more accidents. Finally, as the British discovered after the debacle at Dunkirk in 1940, very long hours of work may actually decrease total weekly output.[2]

This experience should be carefully considered by the individual plant in establishing the length of the workday and workweek under varying labor-market conditions. Some experimentation will undoubtedly be necessary to determine what is the optimum workday and workweek for any particular firm. During the Second World War, for example, shortages of labor forced some firms to change from three shifts of 46 to 48 hours a week each to two shifts of 10 hours a day each, working 5 days a week for a total of 50 hours. New workers could be recruited who were accustomed to a 5-day week, and week-end absenteeism was reduced, especially for married women workers who had home responsibilities. These gains were somewhat offset, however, by the increased fatigue, absenteeism, sickness, and accidents that resulted from the longer workday.[3]

TRENDS IN WORKING HOURS

As in the case of wage determination, the experience of other comparable firms in the industry or in the labor market should be taken into account in setting schedules of working hours. Surveys of current practice are helpful, and data on actual average weekly hours worked in various industries are published monthly by the U.S. Department of Labor and the National Industrial Conference Board, Inc.[4]

The general trend of working hours in industrial countries has been downward over the past century, partly because progressive employers

[1] See recommendations of eight wartime government agencies in "Recommended Hours of Maximum War Output," *Labor Information Bulletin*, U.S. Department of Labor, Vol. 9, p. 203, 1942; also *Optimum Hours of Work in War Production*, Princeton University, Industrial Relations Section, Princeton, N.J., 1942.

[2] KOSSORIS, MAX D., "Hours and Efficiency in British Industry," *Monthly Labor Review*, Vol. 42, pp. 1337–1346, 1941.

[3] The BLS study found that "the primary effect of this lengthening of daily hours for workers on the day shift, when the 5-day week is maintained, is to wipe out the midweek spurt in efficiency during the third and fourth days of the week." KOSSORIS, MAX D., Bulletin No. 791–A, p. 2. During peacetime, of course, firms in many states would be prevented by state maximum-hours laws from employing women and minors as long as 10 hours a day and after certain hours.

[4] See issues of the *Monthly Labor Review* and *The Conference Board Management Record*.

recognized the inefficiency of long hours, but more often because legislation and collective action by wage earners have constituted strong forces in the direction of shorter hours. Labor unions in this country have sought the 10-hour day, then the 8-hour day, and now the 6-hour day or 30-hour week. Many states have prescribed maximum hours of work for women and placed limitations on night work in certain industries or occupations employing women. The Federal Fair Labor Standards Act of 1938 establishes the 40-hour week as the standard workweek for all except executive personnel in industries involved in interstate commerce, which has been broadly defined by the courts. However, there is no absolute limitation on working hours; the only requirement is that hours worked above 40 must be paid for at one and one-half times the regular rate of pay.[1]

PAYMENT FOR OVERTIME WORK

The requirement that premium rates be paid for work above 40 hours a week also applies in the case of firms holding government contracts to work beyond 8 hours a day and is, in a sense, a public expression of socially desirable hours of work. To be sure, this expression was partly a result of depression conditions, when a penalty on overtime work was designed to spread available employment. Wartime labor shortages, however, did not result in any modification of these limitations, and the 8-hour day and 40-hour week at straight-time rates are now standard practice in most industries except purely local ones. Collective-bargaining agreements between employers and unions have further strengthened this practice and, in some cases, specified the payment of overtime rates after only 35 or 36 hours a week.

Furthermore, under an increasing number of these collective-bargaining agreements, Saturday and Sunday work is compensated at time and a half and double time, respectively, regardless of whether or not the employee has worked 40 hours. Again, this is an expression of the undesirability of work at times that are generally regarded as days of recreation and rest. When public convenience or necessity demands that work be done on Saturdays and Sundays, the payment of higher rates can be considered as a legitimate bonus.

The payment of premium rates for work beyond 8 hours a day and 40 hours a week, and for Saturday and Sunday work, is desirable from another standpoint. It is difficult to recruit workers for these schedules

---

[1] Fair Labor Standards Act of 1938, Sec. 7 (a) (3). See bulletins of the Wage and Hour Division of the U.S. Department of Labor for interpretations of this section. The same requirement applies to firms with Federal government contracts under the Public Contracts (Walsh-Healey) Act of 1936.

except in periods of great surplus, and premium rates serve, therefore, as a means of attracting the necessary labor. The same is also true of work on late shifts, as we shall point out later.

Some firms not covered by the Federal law or union agreements continue a practice on overtime work that has little to recommend it. They ask employees to work overtime in rush periods and later compensate them with days or hours off after the rush is over. Most employees want full-time work on a normal working schedule, but this practice, in effect, forces them to accept irregular hours without extra compensation.

RESPONSIBILITY FOR SCHEDULING HOURS

When management, with the advice of the personnel administrator, has determined the hours of work per day and per week, it faces the further responsibility of scheduling the hours to be worked by different groups of employees. Frequently, in order to achieve or maintain balanced operations, it is necessary for some "bottleneck" department to work longer than others; or, for production reasons, management may be forced temporarily to reduce the hours of work in certain departments as an alternative to layoffs.[1] It is good practice here to tell the employees affected in advance about the proposed change in working hours and the reasons for it. In unionized concerns, this notification will involve discussions with union representatives.

Arbitrary and unexplained changes in work hours will not secure full cooperation of employees any more than will arbitrary actions on other personnel matters. Some managements resent the necessity of discussing these changes in advance with employees and their representatives as an encroachment on "management's prerogatives," but this is shortsighted. Not only have employees a legitimate concern about the hours they are expected to work, but as human beings they have a right to know in advance about changes that will affect them. It is only common sense for management to treat people in this manner.

An example of how advance explanations will gain cooperation in accepting changes in working hours and assignments is the case of a new supervisor in the carding room of a textile mill. This man was employed after a bitter strike had ended, and he had inherited from his predecessor what was described as "a hell of a department." In the past, it had been customary in this department for the operators to stop their machines at 8 o'clock each Saturday morning and spend the remainder of their time until noon cleaning the machines, alleys, ceilings, etc. On Friday afternoon, shortly after the new supervisor had arrived, he discovered that the

---

[1] This question was discussed in Chap. 14.

supply of cotton strands or "sliver" produced by the cards was very low; and he knew that, if this situation was not remedied, other machines in the department that processed the sliver would have to be stopped. Explaining this to the men, he asked them to run their cards until noon Saturday.

Shortly afterward, the union business agent stormed into the office and demanded that the order be changed. Rather than bristling at this challenge, the supervisor listened patiently while the union representative "blew off steam" and then explained why he felt it was necessary to ask the men to run the machines longer than they were accustomed to do. He asked, "Do you want to see other machines in this department shut down and men sent home because there is no sliver from the cards to keep their machines running? Do you want to see this shortage spread into the spinning room and weave room and then have other people laid off for lack of work?" Confronted with these questions, the union representative cooled off; and, with the supervisor's promise that the men would not also be held responsible for the cleaning on the same day, he accepted the change in assignment without further protest. Later, he told the supervisor, "Anything you want to do after this is all right with us—you're fair and on the level."[1]

It is part of the personnel administrator's job to develop and encourage in line officials this kind of skill in handling changes in hours assignments, which, as in the above case, may also involve changes in work assignments.

Another problem concerns fair assignments of overtime work when there is not enough for every worker. If overtime is paid for at premium rates, many employees welcome this additional income and actively seek more overtime work. Equal division of the available overtime among those requesting it is the fairest policy and the only one that will preclude charges of favoritism.

When overtime work is necessary, a schedule should be prepared and posted listing the overtime assignments for each employee. Employees

[1] This case had an interesting sequel, which is something of a commentary on old-time management attitudes. After the episode, relations between the supervisor and his employees became increasingly cordial. One day he was called in by the general manager, who said, "You'll have to stop going to the drinking clubs with your help." The supervisor vigorously denied that he had done this and stated that he would resign in the face of such a false accusation. This reply flustered the general manager, who had evidently been accustomed to bully his supervisors. He pleaded for a reconsideration and said, "I didn't mean it that way." "Then why did you say it?" asked the supervisor. "Well," the general manager replied, "I thought you must be doing something like that, because there has been so little trouble in your department, and your help seem to be so friendly with you."

then know clearly when they are expected to work longer than normal hours, and they can plan accordingly. In a stitching room, for example, considerable confusion and dissatisfaction resulted from the practice of asking the girls in the morning whether they wanted to work overtime the same afternoon. Many complained that their recreational plans were often upset by this practice. Dissatisfaction was eliminated by the posting of definite schedules.

SHIFT OPERATIONS

Adding another shift is one alternative to lengthening the hours of work for present employees if it is necessary to expand output. Shift operations, however, may also be necessary for other reasons. The availability of additional labor and state laws governing hours and night work will also determine the feasibility of extra shifts in periods of high production, such as during the Second World War. But, even when these conditions are not present, continuous-process industries, such as steel and chemicals, must operate around the clock.

There are several possibilities in scheduling extra shifts:

1. Two shifts with two crews, working 8 to 10 hours each day, 5 or 6 days a week. This is frequent when only a second shift is needed to meet output requirements or where it is difficult or impossible to recruit workers for a third shift.

2. Three shifts with three crews, working 40 to 48 hours a week, with a week-end "blackout"—i.e., a shutdown during part of Saturday and all of Sunday. This was perhaps the most frequent multiple-shift schedule found in war plants during the Second World War.

3. Three shifts with four crews, staggered on different days of the week in successive weeks to give different "days off," or rotation of the shifts to cover a large part of the 168 hours in a week. There may also be three full shifts assigned to fixed days of the week, with a short week-end "swing" shift. [1]

4. A shorter shift, usually 4 hours, for part-time workers who would otherwise be unable to work. During the Second World War, "victory shifts" in the afternoon or early evening were popular with housewives, high-school students, and many professional men who wanted to contribute their bit to winning the war as well as to supplement their regular incomes.

[1] For specific illustrations of various possibilities, see PAUL PIGORS and FAITH PIGORS, *Human Aspects of Multiple Shift Operation*, Series 2, No. 13, Chap. 1, Department of Economics and Social Science, Massachusetts Institute of Technology, Cambridge, Mass.; also, *Shift Schedules for Continuous Operation*, Princeton University, Industrial Relations Section (Industrial Relations Digests, 15), Princeton, N.J., May, 1943.

In scheduling more than one shift, decisions must be made on the hours when the shifts shall begin. If the first shift starts as late as 8:00 A.M. and, with a half hour for lunch, ends at 4:30 P.M., workers are spared the inconvenience of early rising and difficult transportation in getting to work on winter mornings. But their afternoons are lost for recreation, and the second-shift crew gets home from work well after midnight. This is especially likely if daily shifts are longer than 8 hours each. Some first shifts start as early as 6:00 A.M., but workers complain about "getting up in the dark," and the second-shift crew must work all afternoon even though they do get home at a reasonable hour at night. These difficulties have led most firms on multiple-shift operations to break the shifts within a half hour of 7:00 A.M., 3:00 P.M., and 11:00 P.M. This arrangement is possible if shifts are no more than 8 hours long.

CHARACTERISTICS OF DIFFERENT SHIFTS

Each shift has its own characteristics, which must be appreciated by line officials and by the personnel administrator if problems arising under shift assignments are to be met successfully. What situations are created for employees by the different shifts?[1]

First (Day) Shift.—The first shift is almost universally preferred by employees because it is the only one that fits into the traditional pattern of work, rest or recreation, and sleep. Nevertheless, some workers prefer later shifts for a number of reasons. Supervision is closer, and the pace of work is generally faster on the first shift, and the easygoing type of worker may therefore wish to avoid it. Working mothers may also prefer second-shift work if their husbands already work on the first shift.

Second (Afternoon or "Swing") Shift.—Work on the second shift conflicts squarely with the routines of family living and with late afternoon and evening recreation. The married male worker on a second-shift schedule from 3:00 to 11:00 P.M., for example, may want a later breakfast than children or other workers in the household who are accustomed to rising earlier. The midday meal for children at school may be too early for the male worker, who usually wants something to eat before he goes to work. With the exception of the noon hour, the father seldom sees his older children during the week, for they are at school before he awakes and asleep when he returns home from work at night. And his wife is faced with an evening at home alone; for, except on the day off, evening recreation is out of the question for the second-shift worker.

---

[1] Much of the following is taken from a report on extensive research in the human aspects of shift problems by one of the authors. PAUL PIGORS and FAITH PIGORS, *op. cit.*, especially Chap. III.

Opportunities for a night out "with the boys" or at a social club are also restricted.

Single workers on the second shift complain particularly about the loss of afternoon and evening recreation. Few movie theaters, for example, are open during the morning when the second-shift worker has his leisure hours, and also there are few good radio programs at this time. Dances and parties are missed, as are adult education classes, which are generally held in the evenings. Beginning the day with leisure and ending with work does not appeal to many persons. With the exceptions mentioned earlier, probably most of the "contented" second-shift workers are those, especially older workers, who have become resigned to this schedule because they do not expect much fun out of life anyway.

Third (Night or "Graveyard") Shift.—Workers assigned to the third shift face a reversal of the normal sequence of working, sleeping, and eating. The third-shift worker's "day" is other people's night, and he must try to sleep when the community is going about its daily tasks. As one worker said, "It's hard to live a night-shift life in a day-shift neighborhood." Furthermore, normal eating habits are upset. The night worker generally eats when he comes home from work in the morning before he goes to bed; then he may have his "breakfast" when he awakes sometime in the late afternoon. Finally, if he has to be at work by 10:30 or 11:00 P.M. and must travel a considerable distance, his opportunities for evening recreation are almost as limited as for second-shift workers. The psychological and physical adjustments necessary for night work are therefore considerable.

Additional problems may face the night worker on the job. His opportunities for a hot meal at work around 2:00 A.M. may be poor unless there is an all-night cafeteria or lunchroom. Technical services provided by maintenance crews, nurses, child-care centers, and the personnel department are frequently poorer on the night shift than on the other shifts, and the same is often true of supervision. In fact, the night-shift worker sees his department head only if the latter arrives for work as the night shift is leaving. As in the case of the second shift, there are some workers who either prefer the night shift for personal reasons or who seem to be resigned to it; but most workers hope eventually for transfer to an earlier shift.

Meeting Shift Problems

An important responsibility of the personnel administrator is helping management to make second and third shifts as attractive as possible. Various methods have been used at different times, principally the following:

1. Premium pay for late-shift assignments, such as 7 cents an hour more for the third shift and 5 cents for the second.
2. Cooperation with community officials and local businessmen in providing child-care centers, morning and late evening recreation, better schedules on public transportation systems, and evening hours in banks, stores, beauty parlors, etc.
3. Improving in-plant services on the late shifts, such as cafeterias, nursing, supervision, and even some of the services listed in 2.

Workers on these late shifts have many personal problems arising from the necessary adjustments, and these require sympathetic consideration. Supervisors, therefore, need to be especially competent and understanding; yet all too frequently, they are new and anxious to get onto the day shift themselves. Here is another challenge and opportunity for the personnel administrator. Working through the supervisors, he must demonstrate that management is concerned with the problems that late-shift assignments create for workers.

Another type of problem arising under shift operations is intershift conflict. When each crew uses the same tools and machines, the previous crew may not leave work in proper order or the machines in proper condition. Undesirable jobs or duties are left for the next shift, and this process can become progressively worse unless it is checked at the start. If supervision is overlapped at shift-change time, much of this "buck passing" can be prevented. Each conflict, however, is a product of local factors, such as employee attitudes, method of wage payment, composition of the work groups, etc. But intershift cooperation is possible, as the following comment by a union executive board member in a large machinery plant indicates:

I'm on group incentive in the B Works now, and we're well satisfied with it. It all depends on the group you're with, and how you work it. We're a bunch of old-timers on the day shift, and we've put some old-timers on the night shift to see that they play ball. The foreman cooperates with us—he even comes down and talks over his production problems with us, and we help him meet his schedules. All the fellows in the group have to pull their weight, or we let them know about it. That's the trouble with a lot of groups—there's too much dead weight, too many fellows letting the other guy do the work while they just come along for a free ride.

Rotation of shifts is sometimes used as a means of meeting the objections of workers to late shift assignments. Although it seems fair in principle, in practice rotation often creates problems of its own. Workers find it difficult enough to adjust to one of the late shifts, but physiologically it is even more difficult to keep adjusting to *changes* in shifts, especially if they are frequent. If rotation of shifts is practiced, the changes should not be more often that once every 4 weeks, and preferably not more than every 2 or 3 months. A 48-hour break between changes is also desirable.

When shifts are rotated, the principle of seniority in shift assignments is violated. Many union agreements establish seniority as the basis for transfer from the night shifts to the day shift, and this is a simple, understandable method of making shift assignments and transfers. Workers may be more willing to accept temporary late-shift hours if they know that their turn for daywork will come. But the same principle frequently results in staffing the night shifts with inexperienced people, and it gives management no opportunity to consider genuine personal and family requirements in assigning workers to various shifts. Under a rigid seniority system, for example, a worker who cannot do nightwork for reasons of health or of home responsibilities is not able to get a transfer to the day shift on the basis of these special circumstances. It should be possible in unionized firms to bring cases deserving of special treatment to the attention of union representatives and to work out a mutually acceptable solution within the framework of broad policies.

REST AND MEAL PERIODS

One day off for rest and recreation in every 7 has already been mentioned as part of a desirable hours' policy. Designated rest periods within the working day may also be beneficial, although the number and frequency depend upon the type of work and characteristics of workers involved. As in the case of optimum hours, each firm must experiment on this question, in the light of the general experience that, for women workers in repetitive work, at least two 10-minute rest periods per 8-hour day (in addition to the meal period) are beneficial to total output.

Naturally, most workers take some time off during the workday; and piece rates or other forms of incentive wages set by time-study methods typically allow a certain percentage of time for rest or personal time. The adequacy of these rest periods taken at the option of the worker must be weighed in the particular situation against the desirability of regularly scheduled rest periods.

A meal period of 30 minutes or longer is now standard practice in many industries and needs no defense or elaboration. Scheduling of meal periods for different groups of workers, to avoid crowding in canteens or cafeterias, is an obvious responsibility of supervision but one not always carried out.

PAID VACATIONS AND HOLIDAYS

Vacations with pay have been traditional for office workers, but wage earners have begun to enjoy them on a wide scale only within the past decade. Union pressure, supported by War Labor Board directives, accelerated the trend during the war.

Eligibility requirements are common. Usually a worker must have been employed in the company for a certain length of time in order to qualify for a vacation with pay, and the length of the vacation may vary with his years of service. The amount of pay he receives is frequently computed as a percentage of his earnings in the preceding year or as the equivalent of forty times his regular hourly rate of pay. The desirability of paid vacations for wage earners is obvious. Everyone needs a complete change from work routines at least once a year in order to do his best work; and, even during wartime, such a change was recommended.[1] Vacations without pay, as in an indefinite layoff period, are not conducive to peace of mind. From another standpoint, paid vacations are being increasingly regarded as something earned by past performance, so that pay in lieu of vacations was frequent during the war when labor was scarce and plant shutdowns costly.

Management has the responsibility of scheduling vacations, either all at one time or on a staggered basis to avoid stopping operations completely. Clearly, workers entitled to vacations should be notified of the scheduled period well in advance, so that they may make their vacation plans.

As with vacations, there is an increasing trend toward paid holidays, which are frequently granted as a result of negotiation with unions. When wage stabilization during the Second World War limited general wage increases, many unions sought and won "fringe" adjustments such as paid vacations and paid holidays. Local and industry patterns were thus established. The value of paid holidays for wage earners may be questioned, though they have long been enjoyed by salaried white-collar workers. The principal problem of a given firm is one of consistency. If competitors in the area or in the industry are giving paid holidays to wage earners, failure to do so may be a serious cause for dissatisfaction. As in the case of paid vacations, there should be eligibility requirements for paid holidays. Regular attendance at work is encouraged if employees must be on the job the day before a holiday and the day following in order to be eligible for holiday pay.

SUMMARY

Personnel aspects of work schedules that require policy decisions by management include (1) length of the workday and workweek per employee, (2) payment for overtime and for Saturday and Sunday work as

[1] See recommendations of eight government agencies in 1942, *Labor Information Bulletin*, U.S. Department of Labor, Vol. 9, pp. 2–3, 1942.

such, (3) the number of shifts and the hours when they start, (4) making night shifts as attractive as possible, (5) fixed *vs.* rotating shifts, (6) basis for shift assignments and shift transfers, (7) desirability of scheduled rest periods, and (8) paid vacations and paid holidays.

The personnel administrator may be expected to bring to policy discussions and policy formulation a familiarity with practice in other comparable firms in the local labor market and in the industry. He can also bring to line officials a better understanding of the human problems of long hours and multiple shifts. And, as in the administration of other policies affecting personnel, the personnel administrator can stress to top management and to supervisors the importance of advance explanation and consultation when changes from established practice are necessary.

If management accepts the responsibility for providing good working conditions and setting up humanly satisfying work schedules, has it any further obligation toward employees? This question is discussed in the next chapter.

F. EMPLOYEE SERVICES AND PROGRAMS

Chapter 19

Services for Employees

"Welfare" is not something apart from the job—not something that is bestowed or withheld at the will of the employer. Rather it will be recognized that "welfare" in the view of the personnel administrator is represented by provisions, treatment, and rewards that are to the mutual advantage of both the employer and the employee.

WILLIAM J. BARRETT[1]

When the personnel program thus far described is effectively administered by a technically efficient management, personnel relations should be good. But there are few human relationships that cannot be improved. Many employers have set up employee service programs with this in mind. Other managers doubt the wisdom of such a course. Yet no one denies that workers, like the rest of us, have human needs that they cannot meet without help from someone. The key question about an employee service program therefore is: Are these needs any concern of management; and, if so, is a service program worth the cost?

Opinions differ on both these points. In working toward an answer that will be appropriate for his own company, the chief executive, in consultation with the personnel administrator, may begin by examining the services that are customarily offered to employees.

THE SCOPE OF EMPLOYEE SERVICES

A fully rounded service program is planned to meet needs in three areas of the worker's life; on the job, off the job but in the company, and outside the company in the community at large. It includes facilities and advice for promoting (1) health and (2) safety,[2] provisions for (3) conveniences (such as coatrooms, locker space, and rooms for rest and lunch),

---

[1] "Employee Welfare," Lecture given at Special Industrial Relations Course, Massachusetts Institute of Technology, February 9, 1942.

[2] These two services are discussed in more detail in the following chapter because of their special importance.

260

(4) education and information, (5) a greater measure of economic security (by such mechanisms as retirement funds, various forms of insurance, credit unions, and profit sharing), (6) recreation (as a constructive use of leisure time), (7) counseling in connection with personal and family problems, and (8) community interests (civic and humanitarian).[1]

Some of these needs seem rather remote from the worker's job. Therefore, many executives have felt that it would be simpler and cheaper to rule out all of them as beyond the scope of management's appropriate interest. But this position is no longer tenable. Legal requirements for safety and health and for various forms of insurance now compel the employer to think about some of his workers' needs, whether he wants to or not. Baldly stated, therefore, the practical question as it appears to many employers today is: Shall I do more than the law requires, and, if so, why?

Should Management Offer Extra Services?

Employers who do not care to exceed legal requirements usually justify their position in one or more of three ways:

1. Family and community problems are of no concern to management.
2. "Coddling" workers only weakens them and makes them dependent.
3. Welfare activities are an unwarranted extravagance for an economic organization.

A different position is adopted by a few employers who think that welfare work is good advertising and also a method of buying the gratitude and loyalty of employees. Of course, they would not state their attitude so crudely, but actually a welfare program seems to them a transaction that should be cheap at the price. In practice, however, bargaining on such a low level rarely works well in human relations. When employees feel that there is a string tied to every service, they are apt to respond not with gratitude and loyalty but with resentment. This often puzzles employers who naively think they can, by benevolent paternalism, control the workers' motivation.

The personnel point of view suggests a third position. Management should offer employee services, not because they have to, not only within legal limits, and not as a camouflaged form of bribery, but because such services are in line with the whole personnel program.

The chain of reasoning is as follows: Every worker is a whole person,

---

[1] Discussion in this chapter centers on the general problems connected with the fundamental question as to whether or not services should be offered. For this reason, a detailed discussion of these services is out of place here. Appendix 19, Summary of an Employee Service Program, pp. 503–510, gives a systematic presentation of typical service activities.

not only while he is on the job but wherever he is, throughout the whole 24 hours of each day. When any person has a serious problem to which he cannot satisfactorily adjust, his preoccupation is likely to affect both his productivity and his morale. Management depends for success on the efficiency and stability of workers, as well as on their support of the principle of mutual responsibility, both while they are at work and in their attitude toward the company at all times. It is, therefore, to management's advantage to provide plant conditions that are satisfying both on and off the job and to give each employee whatever help can properly be offered in meeting his personal problems.

This line of thinking embodies a twofold principle of leadership. In sustaining those upon whom he depends, a leader maintains himself. In developing those through whom he works, a leader strengthens himself. This is closely allied to another sociological principle, namely, that a sound human relationship can be maintained only between parties both of whom are willing and able to do more than meet minimum requirements. Mutual responsibility is characteristic of people who work together to promote a single group purpose.

The importance to management of applying and developing the principles of leadership and of mutual responsibility is now generally recognized in regard to technical conditions and standards on the job. Management is expected, for instance, to set up good working conditions and to provide high-grade tools and equipment. In return, workers are expected to meet quantity and quality standards of production and to maintain a responsible attitude toward their work.

The same principle of mutual responsibility is equally valid and is being applied with increasing frequency in relation to human factors in the work situation. An employment process such as that described in the previous chapters embodies management's sense of responsibility toward the worker's needs for security and development in his job. These needs are anticipated in such ways as (1) the formation of congenial work teams, (2) the provision of high-grade supervision, (3) arrangements for recognition of ability by merit rating, upgrading, and promotion, (4) stabilization of employment by such mechanisms as production scheduling and transfers, and (5) training to bring out latent capacities as revealed in employment tests.

By an extension of the same principle, it can be seen that employee services are logical complements to work requirements. Management can fairly expect a high standard of efficiency from employees whose energies are not being wasted in combatting unnecessarily adverse conditions.

But if an employer decides to offer services in this spirit, he still needs to answer to his own satisfaction the three objections commonly brought forward against such a program. Examination of them indicates that these objections are all founded on misapprehensions. First, a service program need not take over family or community functions. Its aims should be to supplement rather than to supplant existing services. Second, helping workers need not be "coddling." Legitimate services, wisely administered, can strengthen all concerned—employees as individuals, the company as a whole, and the local community. Third, a service program need not subject a firm to financial strain. Indeed it can save money for the company.

How Should Services Be Offered?

To be successful, services should be planned by competent policy thinking and administered in ways that are technically and humanly efficient. A personnel administrator who measures up to his job should be able to convince line management on the following points:

1. Employee services can properly and usefully be offered by management only in a sound mutual relationship.
2. Services will weaken employees if organized as handouts.

A service can be offered with propriety and accepted with dignity only between people who respect each other. Of course this can be done most easily and satisfactorily between friends. For this reason, employee services are natural in a very small business. Here the connection between human needs and work efficiency is obvious to the owner-manager, who knows all his workers in daily association. When the chief executive has a friendly relationship with every employee, there is no need to set up a formal program of services to be administered by someone representing management. It is natural for the owner-manager to offer help and advice when one of his fellow workers is in difficulty. And it is easy for a worker to accept such assistance when he knows that the give and take of the mutual relationship is such that he can make good the deficit in other ways.

The handicap under which the owner-manager of a very small business suffers is that employees are likely to appeal to him personally, if they want money, for instance; and it is difficult to refuse a person whom one knows and likes. Obviously, it is easier to give Joe the loan he wants than to determine whether or not he will really benefit by receiving it. But suppose Joe is a well-paid employee who would have no trouble in meeting his bills if he had not exceeded his income by betting on the dogs? The owner-manager may not know this or take the trouble to find out. But the fact remains that Joe does not deserve financial assistance and will probably only go from bad to worse if he gets it with no questions asked. Moreover, in a small work force, other employees know the facts and watch to see how the owner-manager will act. To say that he has neither the training as a social worker nor the time to delve into case histories does not absolve a giver of gifts from the obligation to use his kindness constructively.

INTEGRATION WITH THE PERSONNEL PROGRAM

In a large company, services and benefits can be administered by people who specialize in human relations. Of course, this advantage is useless unless personnel relations are sound. They cannot be as informal as the relation that exists between an owner-manager and his very small work force. But if the company has a comprehensive system of personnel policies, ably administered by line management and fostered by the personnel department, someone knows when an employee is in trouble. Moreover, all employees are aware that, when they encounter serious difficulties for which they cannot find a solution, they can apply to line management or to the personnel department for advice and help. In a large organization, it may take longer to reach a decision, because the personnel representative and the employee may meet as strangers. But this can be remedied by interviewing and various forms of check-up, including a talk with the first-line supervisor, who should have a sound understanding of all his men.

The one condition that makes the rendering of services useless is the failure of other parts in the personnel program to manifest management's respect for employees and to convince workers that management is fair and humane. When mutual confidence is lacking, the attempt to offer services is almost certain to cause a further deterioration in the relationship.

For instance, suppose management tries to protect its workers by requiring them to wear safety shoes. This type of shoe is usually heavy. Unless properly fitted, it can be extremely uncomfortable and in any case feels less sympathetic than an old pair of sneakers. If workers do not trust management's judgment, therefore, many of them refuse to bother with safety shoes. Instead of attempting the education that is necessary in such a situation, some companies provide safety shoes free of charge in order to ensure that employees will wear them. This practice usually accomplishes something tangible, but it often arouses the suspicion and resentment that management should be primarily concerned in dissipating. Employees who doubt management's purposes readily conclude that the order about safety shoes is "just a publicity stunt or some other phony idea." "They're only using us" or "They do it because they get a kick out of it" are other comments that reveal this state of mind. Workers with this attitude naturally feel no gratitude to management for the gift of shoes. And because people easily undervalue what they have no share in paying for, these workers are apt to be careless with the new item of company-supplied property. At worst, they may even sell the shoes and brazenly apply for another pair on the ground that the first pair was lost. Management naturally resents such practices. Yet anger at the workers' dishonesty is irrelevant to the basic issue. "These—won't cooperate even when we try to help them" is a cry not infrequently heard from managements who have failed to put over some employee service.

In such ways, an unsatisfactory relationship easily goes from bad to worse if services are pushed as handouts between people who distrust each other. In order to promote the fundamental aims of strengthening individual workers and the whole company, it is wise to limit a service program in at least three ways.

LIMITATIONS FOR MUTUAL PROTECTION

No service should be included unless
1. It is to the long-term advantage of both management and workers.
2. It is defensible on economic grounds.
3. Workers can and will have a share both in planning and in the cost of upkeep by expending their time, money, or skill.

The first condition means that management would not, for instance, undertake to handle a serious case of mental illness. Even if the company employed a qualified psychiatrist, it would not pay management to offer the amount of treatment required for such a case or to employ the maladjusted person during treatment. Management's obligation would be satisfied by referring the case to a competent specialist or community agency and making suitable arrangements for leave of absence or termination of employment. Similarly, if an employee is unable to pay his bills, it is unwise for management to meet this situation by just giving him money, however great his need. Such behavior is unsuitable in a business relationship and tends to pauperize the employee.

Conversely, no item should be included in the service program primarily because it is a temporary convenience to management. To reduce profits and thereby to dodge high taxes, to bribe workers in a tight labor market, or to impress the public by making a display of benevolence—none of these is a legitimate reason for initiating an employee service. Many legitimate services that were undertaken by managements during the Second World War had some or all of these effects as by-products. But, if these results were actually management's aim, the program will be curtailed or eliminated as the situation changes.

When unusual profits are no longer in the picture, management will carry on employee services with greater ease if it has previously limited its program in the second respect—by thinking in terms of cost. This consideration sounds more hard-boiled than it actually is, when we take into account both direct and indirect costs of such factors as ill health and mental strain. These result in lowered productivity, increased absence, accidents, and undue personnel mobility, to say nothing of the tensions they impose on supervision and other members of a work team. Ideally, each service should be self-supporting in the long run. Certainly the program as a whole should pay for itself.

The third limitation, as to the workers' share in planning and upkeep, is necessary to implement both the principle of mutual responsibility and also management's aim to strengthen workers. Unless workers have a share in the service, they are likely to be uninterested in benefitting by it, or they may misunderstand and even resent it. The best way to ensure a continuance of employee interest is to initiate a service only when employees believe in it enough to want a share in planning and administering it. In certain services, like recreation or any system for supplying food, for instance, the whole burden of administration can sometimes be shouldered by employees. In a large plant, management may wish to supply a recreation director or nutritionist. But, in small companies, the workers themselves often administer their own cafeteria and plan their recreation to suit themselves.

AN EXAMPLE OF OVERDEPENDENCE ON MANAGEMENT

In the field of recreation, it is peculiarly unfortunate to encourage employees in overdependence on management. This is doubly bad, because it paves the way for undue interference by the employer.

For example, in one company, a few employees came to the president to ask his approval in organizing a company baseball team. This seemed a good idea, and the president readily approved. They then asked if they could have an extension of their lunch hour in which to practice. Most of them lived far away, and they could never develop a team good enough to win for the company unless they could get together during the working day. This seemed a reasonable request, granting the premise, to which the president agreed, that it was important to win for the company. Then there appeared a further obstacle. They had no adequate equipment. Having become enthusiastic about the idea of his "winning team," the president also agreed to pay for new equipment. Soon afterward the team returned with an appeal for sweaters. These the president was more reluctant to buy. But he finally agreed when it was explained that it would be good advertising to have the company's name woven into the sweaters.

Unfortunately, after two games with local competitors, it appeared that the company team was unlikely to be a winner in the foreseeable future. Interest lagged from then on. When the next season opened, no baseball team was to be seen practicing in the company yard. The president went to the former captain and raked him over the coals for ingratitude, ending with the demand: "I paid out good money for all that stuff. Now, you boys had damn well better go out and play." [1]

For recreation, as in all other services, self-respecting workers will want their share of the expense to be large enough so that there need be no stigma of charity attaching to the activity. Even if, in a large company, there is a recreation director paid by management, there is much committee work to be done in setting up and managing all the different groups that represent the range of employee interest. The participation of workers in launching and administering a service not only increases their enthusiasm but also makes it possible to increase the scope of a service without involving management in undue expense.

WHICH SERVICES SHALL BE OFFERED?

After a chief executive has made the decisions necessary to cover the why and how of the service program, he is ready to consider the question: Which services shall be offered? Obviously the program should be related to the fundamental needs of people. What are these?

Human needs may be classified as general, specific, and unique. Certain kinds of problem are encountered by every worker at one time or another. These are associated with sickness, accidents, and advancing age. Therefore, management will want to include in any service program provisions for health, safety, and retirement; and, since recreation is a universal need, most companies that have any service program at all plan for recreation in one form or another.

In each company, there are also certain special problems that vary according to the nature of the work, the type of person employed, and the location of the plant. For instance, numerous special problems exist in continuous-process industries for workers who are employed on shifts that do not coincide with the normal working day. Again, a large plant in a small rural community creates a situation that imposes many specific problems not only for the workers but also for the local community.

The time factor is also part of the picture, since it affects both technical

[1] The same enthusiasm for a winning team or an outstanding company band has sometimes led management into the inconsistent practice of hiring as regular workers a good pitcher or a professional saxophonist, for instance, even though these people could not meet production demands.

and human aspects of the situation. No program can specifically provide in advance for all kinds of need. But it should be flexible enough to take on desirable new activities and to drop services when they become unnecessary. During the Second World War, for instance, alert personnel departments promptly initiated "share-the-ride" clubs, child-care programs, and other timely services to provide for special needs. Some of these may prove to be of lasting value, especially where they were soundly planned and administered; others have only a temporary usefulness for special conditions and have no permanent place in the program.

The postwar housing shortage, for example, has led many managements to offer direct assistance to employees who were harassed by their inability to find adequate shelter for their families. Furthermore, problems connected with housing have prompted some employers to modify their practice of freely transferring employees from one location to another. As the housing situation improves, this kind of service and special consideration will no longer be appropriate when the natural desire for freedom of choice is matched by diversified opportunity.

The same mental and administrative flexibility is needed to an even greater degree if the program is also to be geared to the needs of certain special kinds of employees or even to the unique needs of individuals. Whether management should attempt to help employees with special needs is a matter on which people differ sharply. Those who believe that fairness consists in identical treatment for everyone fear the effect of offering a special service to one or a few employees. But, if these services are part of a personnel program that itself is geared to meet individual differences, there need be no fear of employee resentment when special solutions are offered for unique cases. The danger of misunderstanding can be removed at the outset if a suitable policy is made clear before the program is set up. Management expects to provide different services for various people according to special needs. Fairness to all is preserved because

1. Any person in a similar situation can receive similar help.
2. Each person beset by a problem that interferes with his emotional stability is entitled to ask for any help that management can justifiably offer.

Special Services

For instance, child-care service during the war was one of the most expensive and difficult services that management has ever undertaken to render. Only with the aid of local or government agencies could it be adequately administered. Unquestionably, it paid for itself, because only in this way could many married women employees with small children continue their attendance. But certainly few, if any, men in these same companies were receiving an equal amount of help. This fact probably did not arouse resentment anywhere, because it was obvious that men were not faced with the same problem.

In other cases, the difference in need is less clear. In regard to certain kinds of medical treatment or special help with family problems, for example, it is not always easy for employees to understand why one worker should receive more help than another. But the principles remain the same; and if employees know and share these, they can readily accept differences in procedure. Of course, it is easier for employees to believe in management's fairness and good intentions if the same qualities are demonstrated in all other parts of the personnel program.

Beyond the policy decisions of why, how, and which services shall be rendered, there remain other questions that test management's understanding of its own situation, of its relation to workers and to the community, as well as of the various features of the time factor. Some of the relevant questions differ in each company in every year. Others need to be asked about any service before it is actually launched in any company. A few of these questions will illustrate the kind of thinking that needs to be done.

OTHER QUESTIONS TO BE ASKED

1. *Is the projected service planned along generally valid lines?*—For instance, if management is undertaking a counseling service, it is well to consult during the planning stage with experienced psychiatrists and social workers as well as with counselors in other industrial organizations. In this way, management can learn by the experience of others and avoid incorporating in the new service any features that are generally unsound.

2. *Is the projected service well planned to meet the specific need for which it is being undertaken?*

   a. Is there a long-term need felt by a significant proportion of employees in this company at this time?

   b. Have the people who feel the need been well represented among those who planned the service? Or is this just a project of one enthusiast or unrepresentative group?

It is unsound to launch a new kind of service on the mere assumption that workers should welcome it because, in a general way, it is "a good thing." In one company, the president concluded that industrial workers are starved for beauty. He determined that the aesthetic longings of his employees should be satisfied. Unfortunately, he felt it unnecessary to consult with them as to how this worthy impulse could best be carried out. He had shrubs and flowers planted on the company grounds, and the lawns were made into a "thing of beauty." Of course, this meant that employees could no longer sit or walk on the grass, but what of that? In numerous other ways, he beautified the plant inside and out. The last touch was to place boxes with geraniums in every window. Shortly thereafter his employees went on strike. The president was more grieved and bewildered than angry when he heard the perhaps metaphorical statement of their grievance: "We just couldn't stand those damn geraniums."

3. *Is this company the most suitable agency to provide this service?*

    a. Is the service consistent with our other policies and procedures? For instance,

        (1) Has it preventive value?

        (2) Will it work not *around* but *through* line management, strengthening not weakening it?

    b. Is the same service already available in the community?

    c. Would it be better for our workers to provide additional facilities for it here?

    d. Will it weaken or strengthen the community to have us provide this service?

    e. Can we do it as well as, or better than, a community agency?

        (1) Have we, or can we rapidly acquire, the necessary experience to administer it?

    f. Can we get the community to undertake this service?

4. *Is this a good time to initiate the service?*

    a. Are our workers ready for it? Or should we have to promote it by high-pressure salesmanship or even launch it without the voluntary participation of workers? For instance, profit sharing is a useful service if workers want it. But union leaders may oppose it, because they fear it will undermine their influence and lead to "loss sharing." In that case, management should not attempt it until union leaders become convinced of its value.

    b. Can we and/or the workers assume the burden (in time and money) of launching it now without abandoning our principle of economic self-sufficiency for the service program? Suppose a new group-insurance plan would have to be started on a noncontributory basis if it were undertaken at this time. It might be expedient for management and convenient for workers to administer it in this way. But, since this is an unsound policy, from the point of view of mutual responsibility, the plan had better be deferred until workers can pay their share.

    c. Have we, or can we get, the space, facilities, and equipment to provide adequately for the need? It is a mistake to initiate a service under such adverse conditions that it cannot be satisfactorily administered. If it is inefficient or has to be abandoned, more harm than good has been done.

5. *Can both management and workers reasonably expect to maintain their share in the service?*—Are the company president, the management representatives immediately concerned, and workers themselves sufficiently interested to stand behind the service after the novelty has worn off? Or is this just a temporary romantic impulse?

It is, of course, impossible to predict in every case whether a service will prove worth the cost in time, effort, and money. But, if the question is carefully considered, it can usually be answered on the basis of experience. It has proved useful to set up conditions for certain services such that employees are likely to ask themselves: How much do I want this? In one company, for instance, a provision of this sort was made for first-line supervisors who wanted to develop themselves and win promotion by taking evening courses in a local college. Experience shows that as many as 50 per cent of the people who optimistically enroll in such courses drop out before the end. The reasons for this are usually loss of interest; inability to meet requirements in time, energy, and application; or transfer, change of job, etc. Knowing this, management agreed to repay the tuition fee only after the course had satisfactorily been completed. This ruling properly divided the risk of investment between management and the worker. The company assumed the financial burden only when the employee had invested the time and effort to complete the course successfully. Moreover, when a supervisor was told of this ruling, he was likely to think twice before embarking on a project that would test his mental and physical energy at the end of the working day and cost him money if he did not put it through.

In another company, the same general aim was promoted by a different method. If a supervisor seriously wished to develop himself as a technician or for an executive position, management felt that he was entitled to assistance. But, before embarking on a training program, he was given the opportunity of an interview with a top-flight man in a position similar to that which he hoped to reach. This meant that his own personal and technical qualifications were reviewed by an expert. He also got a preview of the difficulties he might expect to encounter both on the way up and after he had arrived. Unless he showed promise and serious purpose, he received no further aid from management in a project that was judged to be a romantic impulse rather than a realistic ambition.

When top management and the personnel administrator keep their share of participation within due limits and maintain an experimental attitude toward the service program, they help to ensure that services will be useful and appropriate. To follow through on this same purpose, the personnel administrator should watch each service after it has begun to operate to make sure that it is working out as planned. It may be that the original purpose miscarries; if, for instance, the person in charge of administering the service does not actually represent management's purpose to serve employees.

In one company, an employee store was set up. But after a short time it was learned that workers had ceased to patronize it. Investigation revealed that this was the fault of the old pensioner who had been put in charge. He had run the store to suit himself. Being a man with a chip on his shoulder, he did not behave courteously to his customers and would not take the trouble to find or order what they wanted. In his opinion, the employees were getting a break by being allowed a generous discount on seconds and should be satisfied to take what they could get. But since the employees were rugged individualists and the time was before the Second World War, they saw no reason why they should patronize a store where courtesy and service did not prevail.

If, however, services do work out as planned, they can play an important part in developing and uniting all participating members into a strong community of stable people.

OPPORTUNITIES OF A SERVICE PROGRAM

Each employee service has its specific objectives. These can be seen at a glance when a whole program is drawn up in tabular form, as presented in the Appendix to this chapter. Aside from these, what are the mutual advantages to be gained from the whole service program?

MUTUAL ADVANTAGES OF A SERVICE PROGRAM

To the Employee	To the Employer
Heightened morale	Greater productivity and therefore lower unit cost
	More team spirit
Greater sense of well-being	Reduction in absence, tardiness, accidents, and complaints, and in undue personnel mobility
Fewer causes for dissatisfaction	
	Better personnel relations
Better relations with management	Lower costs in hiring and training
Maximum job security and increased earnings	Opportunity to work constructively with employees
	Occasion to explain and demonstrate company purposes and policies
Opportunity for constructive participation	Opportunity to improve public relations by
Greater understanding of a company's policies and purposes	a. Working with local community leaders
More information about local facilities and agencies and better knowledge in the community of the employee's needs as a person	b. Strengthening local service groups
	c. Making known the good purposes and practices of the company

SUMMARY

The point of view presented in this chapter may be summarized in the following service policy:

Management depends on workers as partners in the joint enterprise and as fellow members of the company community. It therefore wishes to do its share in supporting the principle of mutual responsibility by helping its employees to help themselves in meeting their fundamental needs.

With the aim of doing this in a way that endangers neither the company's financial status nor the employee's self-respect, the service program shall be subject to the following limitations:

1. Each service shall be to the long-term advantage of both management and workers.
2. Each service shall be expected to pay for itself in the long run.
3. For each service, workers shall have a share in planning and in the cost of upkeep—in money, time, or effort.

When a service program is planned and operated along these lines workers can see that each item in it is, humanly speaking, good business and not philanthropy. In this way, workers share in the advantages to which they are entitled as members of a well-ordered community. Only legalistically can such services be referred to as "benefits." Policy thinking of a high order is needed to establish and maintain a service program that is both technically and humanly efficient. And no personnel administrator should ever indulge in the notion that such a system is finished and that he can just sit tight and administer it "as is." In the constantly evolving situation, he should keep looking ahead. In view of his diagnosis of existing needs and activities, he can see what changes should be introduced. And, by watching incipient trends, he can learn to anticipate new needs before they become causes for dissatisfaction. New problems call for new solutions. These should, however, be in line with enduring policies. New phases in union-management relations offer new opportunities and new challenges. What people wanted or needed yesterday is not necessarily what they want or need today. And tomorrow is something else again. A realistic understanding of current situations and a sense of timing tell the personnel administrator when to introduce and when to withhold suggestions for a new service. He knows that to wait is not necessarily to give up and that poor timing may spoil good planning.

Understanding of human nature in general teaches him that long-run purposes can be sustained only by inner motivation. Therefore, he does not make the mistake of overselling any service. And, in thinking about each new item, he bears in mind the principle of mutual responsibility.

If an important share in planning and administering a service can be taken by employees, so much the better for all concerned. And when these planners and leaders can be found among employees whose routine work does not call for planning and initiative, the personnel administrator is helping management to round out these people's lives in an important respect.

Understanding of the specific company's situation and of top management's central purposes helps the personnel administrator to know which employee needs can be met to mutual advantage and how this can best be done. Individual interviews sharpen his focus on personal needs and widen his view of company opportunities to help employees in ways that strengthen them as people, while also strengthening the company as a whole and the community at large.

Among the many services that management can render, none is more important to all concerned that those which contribute to health and safety. These will be discussed in the next chapter.

Chapter 20

Employee Health and Safety

> The outstanding lesson to be drawn from a study of the
> progress of safety accomplishment is undoubtedly that the
> present accident waste is almost wholly needless. This waste
> . . . can be largely eliminated if only we can bring about
> the application of informed, safety-minded common sense
> to the day-by-day work in the multitude of establishments
> that constitute American industry.
>
> ROLAND P. BLAKE[1]

The personnel point of view suggests that employee health and safety
are major concerns of management. And they are closely connected. The
accident record is a significant index of individual health, both physical
and mental, as well as of the quality of supervision and the level of teamwork. Moreover, accidents involving injury are connected with morale
both as cause and as effect. Thus, aside from the purely practical consideration that accidents and ill health reduce productive efficiency and occasion
irregularity of attendance, management is concerned with keeping the
accident rate at the lowest possible figure and health at a high level. An
active and practical program to promote health and safety is one of management's most effective means of demonstrating its continuing interest
in the welfare of every employee as an individual.

The general principles that govern activity in this area are, of course,
in line with other parts of the personnel-policy system. What are some of
the policies that may be expected from a personnel-minded management?

POLICIES FOR SAFETY AND HEALTH

The most general policy is top management's broad objective that
the plant shall be a safe and sanitary place to work. This policy is based
on the principle that, since management provides the plant and the work,
in order to make a profit, it is committed to do everything within reason

---

[1] BLAKE, ROLAND P., *Industrial Safety*, Prentice-Hall, Inc., New York, Preface, p. v.

to protect employees from the risks inherent in group living under industrial conditions and in the kinds of work offered.

Policies for both safety and health should stress prevention and education. Policy thinking along these lines is based on careful study of specific situations and individual cases.

In relation to safety, it should be management's policy to advocate constant and thorough analysis of specific company situations as well as of accident and injury records. This type of analysis[1] enables the safety director and line management to choose among safety standards, such as those developed by the National Safety Council, the U.S. Department of Labor, and the American Standards Association. The same study of specific situations leads to the development of homemade standards and rules. These are needed in every organization to cover special conditions and risks that can never be fully provided for in publications intended for general use.

The same line of thinking keeps the company doctor on the alert for specific health risks and interested in developing measures realistically adapted to promote the health of company employees.

In both areas, management's purpose can be promoted by a person-centered approach to special cases. A personnel-minded chief executive plans procedures that aim toward understanding of uncooperative or careless behavior. He knows that it is useless merely to tell workers or supervisors to be more careful, and often worse than useless to blame them for accidents or for behavior that risks their health. Unless it is possible for management to understand why the difficulty exists, useful remedies cannot be suggested.

In all these ways, situational thinking aids management in developing policies for health and safety. But a realistic understanding of human nature indicates that, no matter how sound and how well administered these policies are, there will always be accidents and a need for medical attention. In view of this, top management is obligated to establish clear-cut and uniform procedures, known to everyone, to assign responsibility

---

[1] It includes study of the company's safety record as compared with other companies in the same industry, examination of the company's frequency rate in different types of accident (such as falls, misuse of hand tools, burns, etc.), and consideration of the accident record of different departments according to the kind of work done and the quality of supervision provided, as well as the current levels of productive efficiency and teamwork (see Chap. 7). This line of exploration often reveals that fewer accidents result from the most serious risks, such as high-voltage wires, than from minor sources in connection with which both employees and supervisors are more careless. Many of the standard safety rules provide for this natural human tendency.

and to direct action when accidents occur or health requires attention. Such procedures may actually be formulated by the safety director and the company doctor, but they will probably carry more weight with line management if given out by the chief executive with the announcement that their acceptance constitutes company policy.

PLANNING FOR HEALTH

Policies planned especially for the company health program should implement management's purpose to serve employees for mutual advantage and to supplement and strengthen people in the community who are working toward the same end. These policies embody the recognition that education (*i.e.*, enlightened self-motivation) is stronger than enforcement or propaganda. The purpose not to abandon educational policies in favor of high-pressure salesmanship, showmanship, or even bribery is often severely tested in administering a health program. Often the people who most need service and care for ill health are the very ones who want it least. This is perhaps because their fear of undesirable consequences prevents them from asking for help. Experienced doctors and nurses, as well as competent personnel administrators, know that one cannot ram advice down people's throats. It is useful only when desired. What, then, can a company do to promote health for workers who do not ask for help?

A program that is feasible for every company and for each employee includes provisions to enforce minimum requirements, to maintain good conditions, to encourage sensible living, and to offer extra services. For instance, the general preemployment medical examination, extra tests for types of work that present special health risks, and sound placement are requirements that management can enforce. These are supplemented by provisions for sanitation, good ventilation, adequate lighting, optimum hours and nutritious food, if any food is provided in the company.[1] Management cannot ensure, but should encourage, healthful living by its workers. Sometimes the personnel counselor or the company doctor can suggest that exercise before or after work, and more sleep, will relieve

---

[1] In this connection, a realistic approach to human problems helps management to serve workers better. The question of between-meal snacks is one about which nutritionists and the majority of mankind seem not to agree. Nutritionists condemn eating between meals. But most of us go right on doing it. If workers are going to eat between meals, management can help by providing snacks that are simple, nutritious, hot, and sufficiently appetizing to compete with the rich cold food that workers often bring from home. For a survey of company practice concerning "snacks" and the use of dispensing machines, see *Office Customs: A Tabular Presentation of Practices and Facilities Affecting More than 260,000 Office Employees of 836 Companies in 75 Principal Cities of the United States and Canada* (*No. 1, The National Office Management Association, 1947, pp. 18–23*).

nervous tension. And, except in periods of genuine emergency, workers should be encouraged to enjoy the benefits of an annual vacation instead of earning double pay by working during the vacation period.

Within due limits, management can further promote employee health by encouraging workers to participate in a broader health program that includes an annual physical check-up, simple treatment, and perhaps also advice on general health. In line with the principles that apply to all services, management may decide not to have in the plant such specialists as a podiatrist, an oculist, or a dentist, for example. Usually it is wiser for the company doctor to refer patients to the family doctor, to local specialists, or to a clinic for special treatment.

An important service to be rendered here is the spread of understanding among workers of what the local medical facilities are and how they can be used. This helps to combat the unreasonable fears that prevail among workers about surgeons, hospitals, and clinics. In pursuance of this general aim of health education, a company not only works through its medical division and personnel department but also joins with others in the community who are trying to promote health. Courses in first aid and nutrition, health lectures, and films can be offered for this purpose. And industry can usefully cooperate with local agencies that offer free X-ray examinations to reduce tuberculosis and that work toward the elimination of social diseases.

ORGANIZATION FOR HEALTH

In setting up a health service, many firms have adopted the following "working principles" advocated by the American College of Surgeons.[1]

1. An organized plan.
2. A staff of qualified physicians, surgeons, and attendants.[2]
3. Adequate facilities.[3]

[1] *Medical Service in Industry and Workmen's Compensation Laws*, p. 3, American College of Surgeons, Chicago, 1938.

[2] In a small firm, most authorities agree that the part-time services of a doctor and the full-time services of an industrial nurse may be enough. The doctor may be either a local practitioner, giving a few hours a week to industry, or one whose full time is divided among several companies in the community. The former arrangement is preferable, since it strengthens the tie between a company and its local community.

The duties of an industrial nurse vary widely in different companies. In general, she can greatly aid management and the personnel department by using wisely the opportunities for interviewing that come her way. Most of the information she receives should be kept confidential. Especially if she is sent on home visits when employees are absent, her call should clearly be shown to be a part of the personnel program and not a form of camouflaged police work.

[3] According to the size of the company, these may include an emergency dispensary and first-aid facilities. Whatever facilities there are should, of course, be fully manned during all working hours.

4. A preemployment medical examination.
5. Efficient care of individual injuries and occupational diseases.
6. First aid and advice on medical problems.
7. Education in accident prevention and personal hygiene.
8. Elimination and control of health hazards.
9. Adequate and accessible medical records.
10. Adequate supervision for sanitation and health.
11. Ethical and cooperative relations with family physicians.
12. Use of approved hospitals.

To these the following might be added:

13. Referral of serious cases of maladjustment to competent pathologists.
14. Periodic consultations with the personnel department, and sometimes directly with line management, about special needs for transfer to a different type of work or another shift.
15. Occasional consultations with a family member to encourage a visit to a local practitioner or clinic. [1]

The medical division and the personnel department should work closely together to develop a program covering these services. If they receive the active support of line management, they can be of great value to industry.

In both health and safety, management should take the lead by showing a responsible attitude. But it is powerless to get optimum results unless employees lend their voluntary support.

ORGANIZATION FOR SAFETY

In the safety program, as in the health service, specific responsibilities are delegated to a number of technicians and to all line officials. Ultimately, every employee should be held partly responsible for his own safety and for that of other workers.

Thus, in one sense, safety is everybody's business. But, as a practical fact, everybody's business usually turns out to be nobody's business unless responsibility is formally centered in one person. Legally this person is the chief executive. But, even in a small firm, it is seldom feasible for the owner-manager himself to be continually occupied with matters of safety. Therefore, it seems preferable for small companies to employ a part-time safety consultant. In larger firms, it is usual to have a full-time safety di-

---

[1] The fact that employees often wish to bring family members to the company doctor is an encouraging sign of the latter's success in gaining their confidence. The question of whether or not to extend company services to family members is, of course, a policy matter.

rector, who may be either on the chief executive's general staff or a member of the personnel department. Whatever his title and whoever his direct superior, he needs to work closely with other staff and line officials. His qualifications, status, and duties are important points for top-management decision.

THE SAFETY DIRECTOR'S QUALIFICATIONS

It is essential that the safety director should be engineering-minded. If the safety program is to be effective, the director's competence as an engineer must be sufficiently outstanding to command the respect of the other engineers and line officials with whom he has to deal.[1]

But fully as important as his technical qualification is the requirement that the safety director should be personnel-minded. If he is to aid all types and levels of management and all employees to build safety into their habits of work and thought, he must be persuasive and versed in situational thinking. Like the personnel administrator, the safety director is a staff official who depends for his success largely on being an effective exponent of ideas that carry weight because they are valid and useful.

HIS PLACE AND FUNCTION

Unlike the personnel administrator, however, the safety director is usually empowered upon occasion to exercise direct line authority in departments other than his own. When, during an inspection tour, for instance, he sees some unsafe practice or hazardous condition that involves risk of serious injury, he can give orders to suspend operations. If he is wise, he will use this delegated authority only as a last resort. Whenever possible, he carries out his inspections accompanied by the supervisor in charge of that area. And he will not short-circuit the supervisor's authority by going over his head or by giving orders to the latter's sub-

---

[1] Yet safety directors are not always selected on the basis of this important qualification. What may happen when the safety director lacks technical competence is well summarized in the following statement: "Often a hurried search is made through the organization for an engineer who is not too valuable in the job he is holding, whereupon he is given the title of safety director and is told to get busy and reduce the accident rate. When the individual thus selected is suddenly placed in charge of safety activity with all an engineer's faith in mechanical devices, he sets about learning all he can about machine guarding. From books and catalogues of safety appliances he picks up the language of accident prevention and learns something about the use of goggles, safety helmets, and similar protective equipment. He attempts to cover every machine and worker in the plant with some sort of mechanical safeguard and pleads with the better paid production executives to cooperate with him. When the accident rate steadily increases, the harassed man then brings in some outside agency to conduct courses in first aid in order that injuries may result in nothing more serious than lost time." JUDSON, HARRY H., and JAMES M. BROWN, *Occupational Accident Prevention*, p. 155, John Wiley & Sons, Inc., New York, 1944.

DUTIES OF A SAFETY DIRECTOR

Responsibility for	Special Contact with
I. *Accident prevention by the promotion of safety*	
A. Checking plant layout, and designing and checking equipment, to ensure conformance with Federal and state standards as well as with recognized safety practices and company policies	Construction Engineers Drafting department
B. Supervising the purchase, testing, installation, and check-up of protective equipment and fire-fighting apparatus	Purchasing department Inspection department Cost department Methods department Fire department
C. Planning and establishing other measures of safety control, such as specific precautions based on surveys to determine special risks	Medical department
D. Supervising plant housekeeping as a factor in safety. This may include	Investigators from insurance companies and government agencies
1. Advising on regular and efficient systems of storage, maintenance, and cleaning	
2. Recommending assignment of responsibility for performance and follow-up	
3. Recommending adequate allowance for cost	
4. Developing systems for housekeeping inspection	
5. Advocating department rating for housekeeping	
E. Seeing that adequate safety inspections are made and reported. This may include	
1. Setting up special inspection committees	
2. Making occasional checks	
3. Helping to formulate procedures for regular safety inspection by line management, as well as devising and encouraging use of safety check lists	
F. Analyzing accidents. This includes	First-aid room
1. Examining the circumstances surrounding accidents in order to determine accident causes and types of risk by	Medical department Personnel department
a. Correlating and studying accident and injury reports	
b. Making special investigations	
2. Tabulating data and preparing reports on accident cost (direct and indirect)	Accounting department
G. Planning and administering safety education. This includes such matters as	Methods department Personnel department
1. Safety features in operating practices	Public relations department
2. Safety education for supervisors	
3. Safety training features in job instruction	Training director
4. Rules for safety and sanitation	Medical department

DUTIES OF A SAFETY DIRECTOR (Continued)

Responsibility for	Special Contact with
5. Person-centered approach to special cases	Key workers
6. Work with safety committees (preparing material, attending meetings, and follow-up)	
7. Individual or group conferences with anyone who has a safety problem to discuss	
8. Safety programs and campaigns	
a. Planning and using new safety devices	
9. Formation and direction of plant fire brigade	
H. Keeping up to date on such matters as standard accident codes; data given out by the National Safety Council; Federal, state, and municipal laws and ordinances concerning safety and sanitation	Private and public agencies concerned with safety and sanitation
II. *Procedures in injury cases*	
A. Helping to formulate, establish, and maintain accident procedure for major and minor injuries. This includes	First-aid room Medical department Hospital Insurance company
1. Investigating and reporting accidents	
2. Utilizing first-aid facilities	
B. Serving as a liaison official with private and government agents and investigators in connection with accident cases. This means	Public law-enforcement agencies and administrative commissions
1. Acting as company representative in compensation cases	Insurance company Corporation lawyer and other legal representatives
2. Corresponding with all interested parties in injury cases and maintaining appropriate files	

ordinates, except in cases of serious risk and then only if the same result cannot be achieved by getting the superior himself to give the necessary orders.

But, because he may have to give orders to line officials or to their subordinates, it is usually wise for the safety director to be a member of the chief executive's general staff. This gives him the necessary prestige and a direct channel of communication for the recommendations and reports that should be brought to the attention of the president or plant manager.

The duties of the safety director vary to some extent according to specific conditions. But a typical list indicates their general nature. The wide scope of his activity can be seen by correlating the various responsibilities with the persons who help to fulfill them. In connection with each item, the safety director has an opportunity to consult with the chief executive and with department heads, supervisors, union officials, or key workers. Other special contacts that need to be made in relation to specific duties are listed in the right-hand column of the preceding table.

The methods by which the safety director carries out these duties are developed in part from his capacity as an engineer and in part from his ability to get results through people. Technical knowledge, practical ingenuity, and sound common sense are essential qualifications in all phases of his work. But, if he is to use these qualifications to the full in promoting safety, he must also be a keen student and skillful teacher of the personnel point of view.

His primary function, like that of the personnel administrator and company doctor, is to prevent the development of unsatisfactory conditions. In one way or another, the first seven duties listed above contribute to this aim. The National Safety Council advocates as the essential steps for safety the three "E's"—engineering, education, and enforcement. To this an exponent of the personnel point of view would add *enlistment*. Neither education nor enforcement can be counted upon to control behavior along the lines suggested by engineering unless every person in the plant feels a genuine sense of enlistment in his special work team as well as in the company as a whole.

It would be out of place to include in this text a comprehensive discussion of all the safety director's duties. Most of them are amply covered in the existing and constantly growing literature on this subject. But accident analysis calls for special consideration here, because it is such an important application of situational thinking.

ACCIDENT ANALYSIS

The methods used in this area are the same as those typically employed by the personnel administrator. They consist in getting the *facts* (by correlating different kinds of information, by interviewing, and by studying trends as shown in a cumulative record), in examining typical features of specific situations with the purpose of uncovering causes, and in applying the person-centered approach to special cases. The safety director's function is to promote and apply management's safety policies and to lift everyone to the level of policy thinking. For this purpose, he examines all the facts he can gather in order to see what he can learn and teach that is of general validity. He tries to increase in himself and to spread among others an understanding of underlying causes.

What is an accident?—He begins by putting to himself and to all employees whom he teaches the key question: What is an accident? This apparently simple inquiry usually proves difficult to answer, because it is so generally taken for granted that an accident is something that necessarily costs blood or money or both. People recognize an accident when it results in material breakage and spoilage or in bodily injury. But they often fail to recognize essential characteristics of the accident itself. In one company, for example, all accidents that did not result in loss were considered as "near accidents."

The general preoccupation with extreme consequences, to the exclusion of causes, was vividly demonstrated in the experience of a safety engineer who conducted numerous accident-prevention conferences. Over a period of years, he obtained a striking uniformity of reaction from workers and minor supervisors when he asked the following questions:

1. Suppose a man is trying to put a screw into a window frame and the screwdriver slips. Is that an accident? To this question the immediate answer was almost invariably, no.
2. Suppose the screwdriver slips out of the slot of the screw and smashes the window pane without hurting the worker. Is that an accident? The answer to this question came more slowly and showed a slight increase in affirmatives.
3. Suppose the man hurts his wrist as the screwdriver goes through the window pane. Is that an accident? The answer to this question was a prompt and unanimous yes.

Concentration on results diverts attention from analysis of causes and is often expressed in a fatalistic attitude toward accidents as "acts of God," unpredictable and unavoidable features of industrial life. This attitude was clearly indicated in the following "definitions" of accidents made by minor supervisors during conferences on accident prevention: An accident is "something that sneaks up on you," "an unexpected event," or "something that goes wrong and can't be helped."

The safety director is committed to a more far-reaching analysis and to the view that the unforeseen is not necessarily unforeseeable. He therefore tries to define an accident in such a way as to bring out its typical characteristics. For this purpose, it is useful to develop a definition that centers attention on the accident process.

The Accident Process.—Recognition of the continuity of events indicates that an accident is not an isolated or arbitrary occurrence but part of a process in which some condition or mode of behavior leads to an unplanned result. This conception of the accident as an unplanned incident[1] emphasizes its important relationship to planful behavior. Each accident

---

[1] Many unplanned incidents have desirable consequences, such as accidental discoveries or inventions, for example, but in relation to personnel work and industrial safety, our concern is with unplanned incidents which involve risk or injury.

is one of a sequence of happenings which at some stage was probably subject to control. If proper adjustments had been made, the unplanned incident could have been prevented.

The accident process can, therefore, be thought of as a sequence of actions or occurrences, during which, for lack of some needed adjustment (in behavior, in mechanical operation, or in external conditions) there is likelihood of an unplanned incident.

Thus, the only sound feature in the prevailing preoccupation with results is the fact that the consequence is part of the process. But from the point of view of prevention and safety education, the center of interest in the accident sequence should be on what happens before, rather than on what happens during or after the accident.

And not only should accidents be studied as one moment in a larger segment of time but also as being one feature in a situation that includes more than one person and his immediate environment. The accident situation contains not only the victim and the tangible object or circumstances to which he is not safely adjusted but also all the people, feelings, ideas, and surroundings that make up his environment and experience. For instance, an accident may be occasioned by worry about something quite separate from the work situation or by the tension and preoccupation that are set up in one person when he sees another involved in an accident.

When we keep in mind this larger setting of accidents, both in time and in situational setting, we are in a favorable position to observe accidents in embryo, as it were, and so to nip them in the bud. In trying to do this, we need to concentrate primarily not on such statistical data as the severity rate of injury accidents but rather on what can be learned from the vast number of *noninjury accidents* that are usually ignored by management representatives in developing safety programs. The success of such a program is ensured when a safety director can convince both line management and workers of the necessity of studying that part of the accident process which precedes the accident itself, as well as the larger situation in which the accident occurs. And safety education is most effective when workers learn to cooperate by reporting and helping to analyze all noninjury accidents, each of which constitutes a potential safety hazard.

For the purpose of accident analysis, the safety director may begin his study by differentiating between mechanical and human causes (sometimes termed "accident sources" and "accident causes"). In this way, he can focus attention first on environmental and mechanical sources of accidents, for which management is primarily responsible. Afterwards he can study the states of body and mind that make different people, at various times, more or less safe in the same environmental circumstances. Even when an accident is occasioned by a mechanical risk, there may still be need to hunt further back along the chain of factors that produced the accident. If a worker was inattentive or failed to observe rules or to obey orders, why did this happen? Were the rules and orders clearly stated? Was there any check-up to find out whether they were understood? Had the worker failed in the same way before? If safety equipment was not used, why not?

Understanding and Helping People.—Exploration of the circumstances surrounding accidents may indicate that psychological factors deserve attention. In such a case, the person-centered approach is needed to determine what kind of strain or maladjustment has existed and whether the condition can be alleviated or remedied. Fears arising out of job insecurity, anger aroused during labor disputes, tension growing out of an assignment to an uncongenial work team or due to the pace of work, boredom because a job seems monotonous—all these accident-causing attitudes are at least partly within management's control.

A person-centered analysis of individual accident cases and their causes may also contribute to policy thinking about accident prevention. Analysis of typical features found in the situation of certain classes of employee suggests new needs for orientation, training, supervision, and work assignment. For instance, early in the Second World War, it was found that, in certain types of machine work, women's clothing, hair, and long fingernails involved special risks. By analyzing these risks, foremen and the safety director can progressively improve their understanding of accident causes and relay to higher management recommendations for more effective policies and procedures in accident prevention.

Direct and Indirect Costs.—Part of the safety director's work is the tabulation of costs with special emphasis on indirect costs, insofar as these can be estimated in connection with the chain of accident results. Indirect costs of injury accidents include such items as time lost to productive work (by injured employee, supervisor, and other workers), time spent by first aid or medical department, continuing cost of overhead during lost-time period, and cost of subsequent injuries occurring during an accident cycle. All these expenses and many more raise the indirect cost of accidents to a figure that averages four or more times the amount involved in such direct costs as the wage loss to the injured employee, medical expenses, and overhead cost of insurance and/or compensation. By tabulating and reporting these hidden losses and thus being more cost-minded than line management itself, the safety director may be able to make his point that unsafe conditions and practices are an extravagance that the company cannot afford.

SAFETY COMMITTEES

Much of the actual safety work in a large company is done by the safety director through committees. Even if he could carry on all the necessary activities himself, no personnel-minded safety director would attempt to do so, since this would greatly limit his opportunity of awakening and maintaining a widespread interest in safety.

The committee setup varies in different firms according to the size and specific conditions of the company as a whole and depending on top management's policies for safety. In a large plant, where the safety program includes all the policies discussed above, there will need to be at least two types of safety committee. Sometimes a third type also proves useful. All committees should meet frequently and regularly on company time.

There should be an interdepartmental committee composed of department heads and of which the safety director is a member. This makes it possible to pool the ideas and experience coming up from the supervisory level and to disseminate new ideas for accident prevention supplied by the safety director. If the plant manager is chairman of this committee, he has an opportunity to show his continuing interest in the program. Incidentally, his regular attendance at such meetings is one of the best ways to keep interest at a high level.

But, though the cooperation of this management group is vital, thinking about safety should obviously not stop at this level. In order to channel interest down toward the work level where most accidents happen, a second type of committee should be formed within each department, including all first-line supervisors and usually led by the department head.

Union officials or key workers may be members of such an intradepartmental type of committee, or they may belong to a third type of committee composed of management and employee representatives from various departments. When committee membership is rotated among workers who participate in planning for prevention and for accident procedures, they develop an interest in safety that is far stronger and more lasting than anything that can be whipped up by artificial campaigns.

Whether or not the safety director is a regular member of all these committees, he should keep posted as to the agenda discussed and conclusions reached. Part of his responsibility is to see that relevant material is fed to all safety committees and that decisions reached by them are put into effect.

HEALTH, SAFETY, AND OTHER PERSONNEL ACTIVITIES

The safety director depends for his success not only on the committees through which he largely functions but also on the effectiveness of the personnel program as a whole. The company doctor, too, finds that his work is impeded or forwarded by other personnel activities. If either of these staff officials is appointed in a company where there is no systematic personnel program, he usually has a hard row to hoe before he can get results. But when they undertake their duties in a firm where the personnel point of view is accepted and practiced at all levels, they find that much of the spadework for their own jobs has already been done. A glance at the various activities shows why this is so.

Selection of applicants contributes to health and safety when, by adequate testing, through preemployment physical examination and skillful employment interviewing, the unfit are rejected and those accepted are physically, mentally, and emotionally suited to fill current vacancies. Proper placement contributes greatly to health and safety, especially when idiosyncrasies such as accident-proneness or emotional instability are taken into account.

The importance for safety and health of adequate orientation by induction is not so generally recognized. Careful induction is needed not only for new workers but also for employees who have been transferred and thus have to make adjustments to a new work group and possibly to new working conditions. It is often a great aid to individual stability when an employee has been rehired after a considerable interval and thus needs to learn his way around again in the constantly evolving company situation.

The value of a thorough training program that incorporates safety methods for both workers and supervisors has already been discussed. Careful follow-up is needed to keep management informed as to the need for remedial transfers, upgrading, and other changes that protect workers from the effects of such factors as tension and boredom.

A well-planned personnel program is particularly important during the difficult conditions of a layoff and to meet special problems of downgrading, demotion, and discharge. All these difficult decisions should be carefully prepared for, demonstrably fair, and carried out with due notice and clear explanation. When this is done, there is less resentment among those directly affected and thus less risk of the emotional instability that undermines health and is a contributary cause of accidents. Hours of work and methods of pay affect employee health and morale and thus also play a part in safety.

DISCIPLINE AND SAFETY

Management policies and procedures in connection with discipline and employee participation are of special importance in safety work. The safety policy that emphasizes education rather than discipline is most effective when it can be superimposed, as it were, on a company situation where self-discipline, mutual confidence, and a sense of joint responsibility already exist. It is then in line with accepted attitudes and practice to assume that occasional infraction of rules is the result of misunderstanding or some other involuntary cause rather than willful disobedience. In safety programs, it has repeatedly been shown that blame fixing and disciplinary measures tend to reduce employee participation and to negate a central purpose of safety work. Merit rating for safety and badges or other awards for those with good safety records are far more effective measures of accident prevention than punishments, especially in an injury case when the victim has already been effectively punished by the situation itself.

The logical attempt to fix blame is apt to result in buck passing, distortion of facts, or withholding of information. It is therefore unwise to make this an official procedure except in the case of extreme or repeated offenders. Of course, chronic and apparently willful infraction of rules, especially when associated with risk to other people, has to be met by firm disciplinary measures. But, even then, it may on occasion be wiser to have the offender judged by a management-worker committee rather than in private by his immediate supervisor. Employee participation in a safety program may be lost by any disciplinary measure that suggests to workers the least hint of unfairness.

Both the possibility of winning a high degree of employee participation in accident prevention and the danger of imposing penalties for accidents were impressively demonstrated by the experience of a large eastern public utility. In this corporation, management had appealed to the workers to provide information about the slight errors and unexpected results in daily work routine that are not usually regarded as accidents at all. The employees responded enthusiastically and submitted brief notations of many such accidents. This opened to the safety engineer a valuable source of firsthand material that would otherwise have been untapped. The data provided clues for a causal analysis that enabled management to answer such vital questions as: Have our supervisors proper training, and do they evince a responsible attitude toward accident prevention? Are our workers adequately instructed and given the tools and working conditions that promote safety? Do the workers exercise reasonable caution in regard both to their own safety and to the safety of others?

As management took appropriate steps on this information, the frequency and severity of accidents progressively declined. Several departments established a no-accident record. Unfortunately, an operating vice-president with a mistaken conception of efficiency threw a monkey wrench into the works. Analysis of the workers' notes over a considerable period clearly showed that some of the men were "accident-prone" individuals. To safeguard company interest, therefore, the executive decided that it was more efficient to eliminate these "offenders." When this policy was put into effect by discharging a number of workers, word was passed along the grapevine, and employee cooperation ceased almost overnight.

Summary

This case provides ample evidence both of the value of employee participation in a safety program and of the need for consistency in policies and procedures to win and maintain it. The central policies for health and safety are prevention and education. These are specifically formulated and administered with the aid of technical experts. In large firms, responsibility is usually centered in a company doctor and a safety director, respectively. But each of these specialists depends for results on the cooperation of line management and on the genuine enlistment of employees.

In safety, especially, committees are an important feature of the program. It is through these committees that the ideas of the safety director become an effective influence throughout the company. In his role of specialist and teacher, the safety director has much in common with the personnel administrator. And the method of accident analysis, with its emphasis on the chain of events that constitutes the accident process, is typical of the personnel point of view.

Central to both health and safety programs is the aim to win the support of employees for purposes that benefit both management and workers. A suggestion system and labor-management committees can be important contributions to success in these programs, especially when actively supported by union officials. When employees can be enlisted in a company-wide program of cooperation, the benefit to all concerned is beyond anything achieved solely by management efficiency.

Such a program is necessary and practicable in regard to safety and health, which are obviously matters of employee interest. When employees have learned to cooperate with management concerning their own welfare, it is usually not difficult to get them to extend this attitude to problems that seem more directly to concern management.

Voluntary participation is, of course, merely a symptom of the team spirit that line management, aided by the personnel administrator, should continually be trying to build. When team spirit reaches a high level, all members are strengthened by the more than personal trust inherent in a unified team and are stimulated to greater efforts in support of the organization in which they feel a strong and continuing sense of membership. This attitude has incalculable values of an intangible nature. It also makes a striking contribution in purely practical affairs. In some companies, a surprising degree of productive efficiency has been achieved because the practical insight of workers has been geared in with management planning to solve production problems. It is to the interest of all managements to answer the question discussed in the next chapter: How can this be done?

Chapter 21

Employee Participation in Production Problems

Union-management cooperation to reduce costs, eliminate wastes, increase productive efficiency, and improve quality represents a practical program that provides workers with effective direct participation in the creative phases of management.

CLINTON S. GOLDEN and HAROLD J. RUTTENBERG[1]

Some of the most difficult and challenging problems in personnel administration center upon employee participation at the level of production. How can management get the wholehearted cooperation of employees in increasing productive efficiency, reducing waste and scrap, improving methods, conserving equipment and materials, and improving quality? Can the latent interest of employees in these questions be mobilized and utilized to mutual advantage? Does management really desire this kind of participation, or does it fear labor encroachment on management's prerogatives? If management is willing, how can cooperation be developed? These are the broad questions we shall consider in this chapter.

EMPLOYEE INTEREST IN PRODUCTION PROBLEMS

An older employee in the shipping department of a manufacturing plant once went to his foreman with the suggestion that more careful stamping of the destination on cartons would help the crew that was loading those cartons on freight cars. He said that the stencil used was poorly designed and that often the shippers could not tell quickly where the carton was to be sent. This resulted in delays and in occasional misrouting. The reply he got from his foreman is unfortunately not infrequent in industry: "Look here, Tom, if you guys would just tend to your work instead of thinking up ways to make it easier, you'd be better off. Problems

[1] *The Dynamics of Industrial Democracy*, Harper & Brothers, New York, 1942, p. xxvi.

292

like that are my worry, not yours." When the foreman later told the superintendent about Tom's "sticking his nose into things that don't concern
him," the superintendent agreed that Tom was "just a troublemaker"
and was "always trying to find fault because he thought he should have
been made assistant foreman last year when we promoted Bill Simpson."

These management officials failed to appreciate that the average employee, especially if he has worked on a job for some time, is likely to know
more about its details than anyone else, even the supervisor. If he is
reasonably intelligent, he has some ideas on how the job might be done
more simply or efficiently. Workers on incentive wages, for example, frequently discover short cuts that management did not foresee when the job
was first set up. Even in the absence of a monetary incentive, if a worker
enjoys doing his job well, it is a challenge to him to discover ways of
doing it *better*.

Once such an employee is rebuffed, however, he is likely to keep his
ideas to himself. In other instances, employees may hesitate to make suggestions that might result in a cut in piece rates, an extension of work
assignments, or accusations by fellow employees that they are "company
stooges." Or their experience may have been that a suggestion made to
foremen was later put into effect without due credit being given to the
suggestor. The foreman himself may think the suggestion is good but may
fear higher management criticism of his own failure to think of it first.
"You should have spotted that yourself without having one of your help
point it out" is a sure way to discourage the foreman's interest in promoting a flow of productive ideas from the work force.

Good supervision, with understanding and support from top management, can informally stimulate and reward employee suggestions. But it
is the experience of many firms without an organized program to encourage presentation that these ideas are more likely to remain bottled up at
the work bench and at the office desk. This suppression not only results
in the loss of good suggestions on ways of improving efficiency but also
breeds dissatisfaction and poor morale. Tom, the shipper, may be a
"troublemaker" because his supervisors are unwilling to admit that he
has some good ideas. In any case, he does not go about his work with much
feeling of satisfaction. Perhaps he wants to make his job easier, but it is
equally possible that he would get a kick out of helping to solve a problem
and seeing his idea accepted and put into effect.

EMPLOYEE SUGGESTION SYSTEMS

Many companies have established employee-suggestion systems as a
means of stimulating and utilizing the interest of their employees in production problems. During the Second World War, suggestion systems

were widely adopted in the drive sponsored by the War Production Board "to get ideas for Uncle Sam."

Experience with these systems varied. In some instances, they were carelessly drawn up and poorly administered, as in the case of a cotton mill with a thousand employees. This firm reported that it had "a rather simple suggestion procedure, consisting of a locked mail box at our main gate. We did not issue any formal instructions, rules, or regulations but posted a notice over the box that serious suggestions would be welcome and acted upon." The number of suggestions received "was comparatively small. . .a few silly ones, a few grievances, and some rather practical ones."

Some suggestion systems, however, are better planned and more successfully operated. It is not unusual to find the percentage of accepted suggestions between 25 and 35 per cent, and nearly 300 out of every 1,000 employees submitting suggestions.[1] To reach this level of employee participation, it is necessary to meet the following requirements:[2]

1. *Top management must wholeheartedly support the suggestion system*, not just tolerate it. This means willingness to recognize employees as sources of ideas that may be valuable to the organization rather than simply as subordinates from whom constructive suggestions are not be be expected. Furthermore, when such suggestions are made, top management should regard them as a credit to the employee's foreman rather than as a reflection on his ability to run his department. Foremen will be cool toward the suggestion system if they feel that they will be criticized for failing to think of an idea submitted by one of their workers.

2. *Employees must be clearly informed of the kinds of suggestion wanted and even as to the specific problems on which management seeks help. Rules under which the system will operate must also be clearly explained and publicized.*—In one firm, suggestions were considered if they concerned one of the following groups:

    a. Increase in production, including work simplification, with equal or better quality.

    b. Improvements in quality.

    c. Improvements in manufacturing, handling, packing, shipping, and clerical methods.

    d. Improvements in tools and equipment.

    e. Reduction in cost of maintenance.

    f. Prevention of accidents and fires.

    g. Reduction of waste.

[1] HENDRICKSON, ALBERT W., and AUDREY E. HEUSSER, "Analysis of Suggestion Award Practices," *Factory Management and Maintenance*, Vol. 103, No. 5, pp. 110–12, 1945.

[2] *Cf. Suggestion Systems: A Brief Survey of Modern Theory and Practice*, National Association of Suggestion Systems, Chicago, 1944.

Another company, through attractive posters in a certain department, asked for specific suggestions on how to reduce the large number of "seconds" coming from that department. Thinking was thus directed to specific departmental production problems.

3. *Awards for acceptable suggestions should be monetary and on the liberal side.*—If it is not possible to measure probable savings, a minimum cash award should be paid for any suggestion adopted. Nonmonetary awards may be used, such as certificates and pins, but by themselves they are usually not enough to stimulate many individual suggestions. (The effect of illiberal awards is discussed more fully later).

4. *All suggestions should be promptly acknowledged, and, if suggestions are subsequently rejected, the reasons should be explained to the suggesters.*—Many suggestion systems have failed because reasons for rejection were not adequately given and suggesters became disgruntled. There can be real educational value in explaining why a particular suggestion cannot be used and in encouraging the suggester to improve his suggestion or to direct his thinking along different lines. This may be difficult when suggestions are submitted anonymously and identified only by serial numbers, but it is not impossible to work out. Reasons for rejection may be listed and suggesters with specific serial numbers invited to meet with designated individuals for an explanation. Personal contact in making explanations is always better than formal rejection slips.

Examples of inept handling of suggestion awards and rejections are unfortunately not difficult to find. For instance, one employee made a suggestion and received a form letter stating that his suggestion was being considered. Later he was notified by another form letter that it was rejected as being "impractical." About 6 months after that, he saw the change he had suggested being put into effect. He wrote a letter asking what had been done with his suggestion but received no reply. This experience thoroughly discouraged him, and he refused to make any more suggestions. He thought the foreman or some "higher-up" had modified his suggestion and taken the credit for it. This may have not been the case, but the important fact is that he *thought* so, and nothing was done to explain the situation. Possibly, as in another case, the conditions had changed, and the suggestion then became practical to adopt. In any event, the suggester was entitled to an explanation. The educational value of a suggestion system is one of its greatest benefits.

WHO SHOULD ACT UPON SUGGESTIONS?

Central to the issue of genuine employee participation in production problems is the question of who should act upon suggestions. Perhaps more suggestion systems are operated by management alone than with the aid of a joint committee composed of representatives of employees and management. It is not infrequent to find a "suggestion secretary"—a management official—who handles the details of the system, and a management committee that takes action on suggestions received.

A suggestion system operated exclusively by management personnel may be more "efficient," in the sense that investigations are made by trained plant engineers or methods men, and decisions are usually reached more quickly. On the other hand, in some cases, there may be buck passing, delays, and even favoritism. But, even assuming that these do not exist, some advantages of a joint procedure are lost when management takes the sole responsibility for discussing and acting upon suggestions.

When employee representatives are members of the suggestion committee, they have an opportunity to learn about the various production processes in the plant as a whole and to see their interrelationships. They learn how to evaluate suggestions and to understand a variety of production problems. Furthermore, rank and file employees are likely to have greater confidence in the fairness of the suggestion procedure if their representatives are on the suggestion committee.

Much depends, of course, on the type of employee representatives elected to the joint committee. It may take time to develop men with talent and responsibility. But this is a valuable opportunity for management to share certain types of information with employees and to develop understanding of the mutual problems confronting management and labor. If management stops short of encouraging participation of employees in the process of deciding upon suggestions, the suggestion system is likely to retain an air of paternalism—a means of "passing out a few extra bucks to the boys in the shop."

An Example of a Joint Suggestion Committee

During the war, after extensive joint study and discussion of various plans, management and union officials in a large manufacturing firm set up a joint suggestion system. The superintendent acted as ex-officio chairman of the suggestion committee and each week assigned the task of investigating different suggestions to pairs of management and labor representatives. They reported back at the next meeting, and only rarely were they in disagreement. Management's initial fear that the labor representatives would "gang up" to push through all suggestions proved to be unfounded, for usually the joint committee's action was unanimous. The labor representatives learned what kinds of suggestion were needed and which ones were most valuable. As the superintendent said later, "We discovered some real talent among the labor members that we didn't know existed."

The weekly meetings, furthermore, kept the superintendent better informed on minor details around the mill that otherwise might have been overlooked. The result in some cases was an improvement in managerial efficiency. For example, an award was made for a suggestion that "an oilcan be put under the motor that is suspended from the ceiling and that runs the blower for the warper. This will keep the oil off the floor and eliminate the danger of slipping." A similar suggestion was made in another department, and, to avoid further duplication, the superintendent ordered the maintenance department to cover all such cases as well as other specified similar situations that a labor member of the committee suggested.

Another result was that foremen who were ineligible for awards discovered that, through the suggestion system, they could get things done on which they had failed to get action in the past through other channels. They "tipped off" workers on suggestions that might be submitted. The interest and support of the joint committee for a worth-while idea proved to be just the spur needed to get action. As a regular procedure, this has undesirable policy implications, but it did expose a weakness in the previous method of getting action on departmental improvements.

This suggestion system was temporarily suspended by joint agreement at the end of the war, as the quality and quantity of suggestions declined. One explanation of this decline was the fact that the industry is characterized by highly automatic and standardized operations, and the number of opportunities for making production suggestions is more limited than in a new, developing industry or in one performing unstandardized operations. Nevertheless, the labor representatives urged continuance of the joint committee on a somewhat different basis, because they said it had given them a better understanding and appreciation of the company's production problems than they ever had before.

LIMITATIONS OF A SUGGESTION SYSTEM

Despite the success of many employee-suggestion systems, there are limitations that preclude full-fledged employee participation in production problems by this method. First, the appeal to the self-interest and self-satisfaction of the individual worker may in some cases weaken rather than strengthen team spirit. For example, an employee in an electrical-products firm won a $400 award for a suggestion that eliminated six men. The informal attitude of his group was that "anyone who helped management find a way to eliminate someone else from his job was a 'no-good'." Fellow workers therefore confronted the suggester with the demand that he use his award money to give a party for the department. He did so reluctantly, and no more suggestions were received from that department.[1]

A second limitation, which is usual, though not inevitable, is the widespread niggardliness of awards, which has a dampening effect on the submission of suggestions. To many workers, management appears to be unwilling to share fairly the savings made by suggestions. A common practice is to pay 10 per cent of the first year's net savings. It does not take the worker long to figure out that this leaves nine-tenths of the first year's net savings to the company, plus *all* savings in later years. Occasionally awards are even less generous, as in an oil company that paid a sliding scale of awards ranging from $5 for suggestions with an estimated annual saving of $100 to $100 for those with an estimated annual saving of $9,000. A more generous method is to base awards on estimated gross savings or to pay higher percentages of net savings. At least 25 per cent appears to be warranted, despite the costs of running the suggestion system and paying awards for intangible suggestions.[2] When savings cannot readily be estimated and the suggestion is a minor one, a minimum award of $5 is preferable to small token awards. If the award for any accepted suggestion is too small, it will backfire, as did a check for 99 cents received for a safety suggestion by an employee who said, "I felt like throwing it in their faces."

Another example of the effect of niggardly awards in a suggestion system is the case of a master mechanic in the lathe department of an aircraft-parts company.[3] Production delays on a vital wartime product had resulted from the melting and fusing of aluminum waste in the tool bits used on the lathes. The methods department had assigned an engineer to study the problem, but he had been unable to find a solution. One day, however, the master mechanic successfully contrived a tool that combined two bits into one, thus eliminating the space between the bits that had caught the molten-aluminum waste. This new bit enabled operators to increase their efficiency 50 per cent. After discussion with his fellow workers, the mechanic decided to share his discovery with them secretly rather than to submit it through the company's suggestion system. The group felt that awards equal to 1 month's savings were inadequate,

---

[1] Cited in GOLDEN, CLINTON S., and HAROLD J. RUTTENBERG, *The Dynamics of Industrial Democracy*, pp. 274–275, Harper & Brothers, New York, 1942.

[2] The Lincoln Electric Company, of Cleveland, Ohio, pays awards of 50 per cent of the first year's net savings. LINCOLN, J. F., The Lincoln Electric Company Incentive Plan, in *Industrial Engineering for Better Production*, p. 37, A.M.A. Production Series No. 153, 1944.

[3] See PIGORS, PAUL, and FAITH PIGORS, *Work Group Ownership of an Improved Tool*, Addison-Wesley Press, Inc., Cambridge, Mass., 1944.

especially if increased incentive earnings could be maintained over an extended period. Furthermore, the mechanic feared that, once the tool became company property, layoffs of group members might result, or output standards and piece rates might be changed. The foreman learned about the new tool after it was put into use, but he decided to let the men handle it in their own way. The methods engineer also heard about it but was unable to persuade the master mechanic to reveal it or to submit it through the suggestion system.

This example also illustrates a third limitation of a suggestion system. In this firm, the men were not encouraged to submit their ideas directly to their own supervisor, who under other circumstances might have worked with them in the solution of a mutual production problem. Instead, they were asked to submit their idea through the suggestion-box system. Thus, in effect, the employees were invited to by-pass their supervisor and to offer their proposal to a group of people presumed to be more impartial and more competent to evaluate the suggestion. Admittedly, the absence of these qualities in some supervisors has led to the establishment of the suggestion-box system, but the question may be asked: Is it better to by-pass the supervisor or to help him develop attitudes and procedures that will enable him to stimulate suggestions directly from his own subordinates? In well-run suggestion systems, foremen are consulted before a suggestion affecting their department is adopted, but this does not squarely meet the criticism that a procedure has been established, operating independently of the supervisor, for encouraging and even acting upon suggestions from his employees.

MEETINGS WITH SUPERVISORS ON IMPROVING EFFICIENCY

This third limitation of the suggestion system has been avoided by a procedure developed during the war by officials of the Federal Social Security Board.[1] The procedure has since spread to other governmental offices and to some private business offices; and it is adaptable to almost any type of operation. Using the principles of Job Methods Training developed by the Training Within Industry Bureau of the War Manpower Commission, a trained leader instructed *all* employees in each department, not just the supervisors, "how to find a better method"[2] of doing their own particular jobs.

[1] See POWELL, OSCAR M., "Adjusting Administration to Wartime," *Social Security Bulletin*, Vol. 6, p. 409, 1943; CHASE, STUART, *Men at Work*, pp. 77–88, Harcourt, Brace and Company, New York, 1945; and HALL, MILTON, and WILLIAM P. MALLARD, (Training Division, Social Security Board), "Making Employer-employee Cooperation Practicable," *Personnel*, Vol. 22, pp. 237–247, 1946.

[2] HALL and MALLARD, *op. cit.*, p. 242. The instructions to employees were as follows:

In group meetings, employees were then encouraged by their supervisors to submit proposals for consideration by the group. Supervisors themselves were commended by their chiefs when they successfully encouraged subordinates' ideas, and employees were assured against loss of jobs or salary reductions as a result of improvements. Furthermore, no financial awards were given; recognition and credit by higher officials and the feeling that everyone in the group was cooperating seemed to be enough incentive to encourage the submission of ideas. The machinery for approval consisted in passing the suggestion along to the line official who had authority to act on the problem, although all approvals and disapprovals (with reasons) were sent to the top official, as a means of giving recognition and avoiding arbitrary action at lower levels.

The essence of this plan is the democratic work group and the team spirit that can be developed in the section meetings on improvements, especially when the participants have some training in methods study. Employees are encouraged to work *with* their supervisors, instead of *around* them. In one of the first groups to use this plan, methods improvements

---

How to Find a Better Method

Step I—*List all details* of the operation.
1. *List everything* you or others do by the present method.
2. Make explanatory notes about the details as necessary.

Step II—*Challenge* (question) each detail.
1. Apply these questions:
   Why is it necessary: Does it serve a useful purpose?
   Where should it be done?
   When should it be done?
   Who should do it?
   How is the best way to do it?
2. Question the
   Materials, equipment, forms, storage, office layout, workplace, safety, housekeeping.

Step III—*Develop* the better method (in cooperation with others).
1. *Eliminate* unnecessary details.
   Watch especially for unessential routing, reviewing, and checking.
2. *Combine and rearrange* details.
   Find a better *place*.
   Find a better *sequence*.
   Use the right *person*.
3. *Improve* the manner of doing necessary details.
   Substitute better equipment, materials, forms, etc., use *preprinted and prepared in advance* materials when practicable.
   Pre-position equipment, supplies, and papers at the *best places* in the *proper work area*.
   Let *both hands* do useful work; use devices for holding.
4. *List* the details of the new method.
5. *Write* up your proposal.
   Give it to your supervisor.

were adopted that were expected to increase productivity by 15 per cent, but output actually increased by twice this percentage. The explanation seemed to be that members of the group had increased their own will to work by participating in the development of changes that, under other circumstances, they might have resisted and resented. Genuine employee participation of this sort in solving production problems is a key that can unlock the door to still greater output.

Joint Labor-management Committees

Another means of developing this participation is through joint labor-management production committees. During the Second World War, these were encouraged by the War Production Board in the hope that employee participation could be secured in increasing war production.[1] The activities of these committees were varied. They tackled many purely wartime problems, such as transportation pools, war-bond sales, blood donations, and excessive absenteeism. In some cases, they were largely "window dressing," devoting their attention to slogans, pep rallies, and posters. This was frequently the fault of management, which sometimes viewed the committee idea with suspicion as another means of giving labor more influence and power. Also, labor representatives sometimes failed to keep grievances and matters of collective bargaining out of the discussions.

In cases where joint committees operated successfully, top management and union officials wholeheartedly sponsored the plan and brought production problems to the committee meetings for discussion and solution. Often a suggestion system was jointly administered by the committee, as in the example described earlier in this chapter. At other times, suggestions were brought to the committee meetings by members who had canvassed their departments prior to the meeting. Discussion stimulated still other ideas from the committee members themselves.

For example, in a chemical firm with highly technical processes, joint departmental production committees, composed of AF of L union representatives and supervisors representing management, discussed current and potential bottlenecks and ways to eliminate them. Proposals offered by committee members were of this sort: a pump with greater capacity should be substituted for the present pump, an emergency tank should be provided to supplement the present tank, a specific coil is often air-bound and

---

[1] For an excellent account, see W. ELLISON CHALMERS, "Joint Production Committees in United States War Plants," *International Labour Review*, Vol. 47, pp. 22–45, 1943; also CHASE, *op. cit.*, pp. 28–29. Instructions to plant committees are found in several War Production Drive publications, of which one of the best is *Production Guide for Labor-management Committees: Ways of Handling Production Problems*, War Production Drive Headquarters, War Production Board, Washington, D. C., 1945.

should be redesigned to speed the flow of chemicals through it, or a pipe should be inserted into a still to free accumulated air. More than one-third of the committee's time was spent in discussing modifications of or additions to current equipment. Other matters frequently discussed were stowing and stores, control, layout or change in position of machines, tool control, interdepartmental relationships, and routine of work.

Discussion on this plane was possible, because it was based on a foundation of amicable labor relations. Two years after the union had organized this chemical plant, union leaders could say, "We were no longer regarded by management as a bunch of rabble rousers, looking for trouble." By the time the joint production committee was established in 1942, each side had respect for the feelings and problems of the other. Labor and management were ready to sit down together in a cooperative effort to increase war production. The patriotic motive was undoubtedly strong, as it was in many other committees, but it would have been worth little without the background of mutual understanding and respect.

UNION-MANAGEMENT COOPERATION

Wartime labor-management production committees were not an innovation. The idea sprang largely from the earlier experience with union-management cooperation, especially in the railroad, clothing, and steel industries.[1] One of the first experiments was in a shop of the Baltimore and Ohio Railroad, where in 1923 a joint committee of machinist and shop craft unions and management representatives discussed ways of reducing waste and improving productive efficiency so that work would not have to be contracted out, as it had been in the past because of the high costs in the shop. The plan spread to other shops, and in 18 years of operation, the joint committees on the Baltimore and Ohio considered 32,000 suggestions, of which 86 per cent were adopted.[2] There were no individual awards, but the men gained through greater job security and better working conditions made possible by the lower costs and greater output. Furthermore, the experience of these joint committees resulted in

[1] See SLICHTER, SUMNER H., *Union Policies and Industrial Management*, pp. 393–597, Brookings Institution, Washington, D. C., 1941, for detailed discussions of these plans. The experience in the steel industry is described by two men who took part in it, Clinton S. Golden and Harold J. Ruttenberg, of the United Steel Workers of America, CIO, in their book, *The Dynamics of Industrial Democracy*, pp. 233–291, Harper & Brothers, New York, 1942. A brief summary of union-management cooperation is found in S. T. WILLIAMSON and HERBERT HARRIS, *Trends in Collective Bargaining: A Summary of Recent Experience*, pp. 130–141, The Twentieth Century Fund, New York, 1945.

[2] WILLIAMSON and HARRIS, *op. cit.*, p. 134. Compare this with the 25 to 35 per cent acceptance rate in suggestion-box systems operated by management alone.

greater understanding by the men of the problems of the railroad and in an improvement of morale and union-management relations generally.

In this experiment with union-management cooperation, it was the unions that took the initiative. The same was true in the steel industry, where technologically backward firms faced with bankruptcy agreed to try union-management cooperation when it was proposed by the union as a means of saving the company and the jobs of the union members. Research and planning committees, composed of four representatives of management and four of the union, were established with joint subcommittees in each department "to solicit from the employees in their departments suggestions designed to increase efficiency, reduce production costs, and eliminate wastes, [and] to adopt those that are considered practical and feasible . . . ."[1] Management and labor were to share the benefits through regularized employment, better working conditions, increased earnings, lower costs, and presumably higher profits. In practice, the effect of cooperation in most cases was to enable marginal firms to continue to provide jobs and pay the union scale of wages. Workers became cost-conscious, however, as management brought cost information to the committee meetings. Furthermore, they derived both personal and group satisfaction from making suggestions on production problems in these meetings and from seeing their ideas adopted. As in the railroad experience and in some of the joint labor-management production committees during the Second World War, labor and management began to understand and solve their mutual problems in a new spirit.

CONDITIONS FOR SUCCESSFUL UNION-MANAGEMENT COOPERATION

It is clear from the preceding discussion that union-management cooperation on production problems can succeed only under certain conditions. These may be briefly outlined:

1. *Top management must fully accept the union and genuinely welcome its assistance in solving production problems.*—Without an assured status, a union cannot reasonably be expected to give up some of its restrictive rules and practices. Furthermore, if management is jealous of its "prerogatives" and fears that the union "wants to run the company," the atmosphere necessary for cooperation will be difficult to develop.

2. *As an aid to understanding, management should state clearly what its problems are, with supporting information on costs, sales, prices, and profits or losses, when such information is pertinent to the problems at hand.*—Unless this informa-

---

[1] From "Proposal for Union-management Cooperation," made to various steel companies by the United Steel Workers of America, CIO, GOLDEN and RUTTENBERG, *op. cit.*, pp. 259–261.

tion is shared, the understanding necessary for genuine cooperation is unlikely to be developed.

3. *Union leaders must carefully explain the purpose of union-management cooperation to rank and file members and keep them regularly informed of progress made and difficulties encountered.*—If this is not done, the men and women in the shop may later repudiate the labor committeemen as "management's boys."[1]

4. *Gains from union-management cooperation must be equitably shared, not only in the economic sense through job security and good earnings, but in terms of prestige and recognition.*—Management cannot reasonably expect that labor will continue to suggest changes if these changes result in demotions and layoffs. Nor can it expect a free flow of ideas if it is reluctant to give credit for them. On the other hand, labor cannot expect management to join it in a cooperative undertaking, if labor insists on appropriating all the gains through increased wages or shorter hours or if it fails to make a genuine effort to understand management's problems.[2]

In the past, these conditions for successful union-management cooperation appear to have been met principally in crisis situations. Firms facing bankruptcy or serious competition from more efficient companies or from nonunion firms have grasped union-management cooperation as a last straw when it was proposed by the union.

SUMMARY

Why should the initiative usually come from the union side? Have profitable and well-run enterprises anything to gain from sharing production and cost information with their employees, whether unionized or nonunion? Do they benefit by encouraging employee and union participation in the discussion and solution of problems?

We believe that these questions can be answered affirmatively, in the light of experience with suggestion systems, the Social Security Board experiment, and labor-management production committees during the Second World War. These programs, particularly the latter two, have helped to develop still further the team spirit that is necessary for the

---

[1] Something like this happened in the joint research on extended work loads, undertaken by management and union leaders in the Naumkeag Steam Cotton Company, Salem, Mass., between 1927 and 1933. For details of this interesting episode, see SLICHTER, *op. cit.*, pp. 532–559; and R. C. NYMAN, *Union-management Cooperation in the "Stretch-out,"* Yale University Press, New Haven, 1934. See also a problem encountered in the case for this chapter, The Scrap Campaign (An Experiment in Union-management Cooperation.)

[2] Sharing of gains from union-management cooperation is ably discussed by IRVING KNICKERBOCKER and DOUGLAS McGREGOR, "Union-management Cooperation: A Psychological Analysis," *Personnel*, Vol. 19, pp. 520–539, 1942.

successful functioning of any organization. They are built upon the recognition by management of two points: (1) that most employees have ideas on ways of doing their jobs better and (2) that most employees get increased satisfaction from their work if they are given an opportunity to make positive contributions and see them accepted.

When there is a union in the picture, the challenge to management and to personnel administration is more evident. How can this representative unit be developed into something more than a collective-bargaining agency whose leaders dispute with management over the relative shares to be distributed to workers and stockholders? Part of the answer lies in union-management cooperation on production problems, which can help to increase the total net income of the enterprise by increasing efficiency, reducing waste, and improving quality.

In the past, unions have usually been more willing to share this responsibility for productive efficiency with management than management has been to admit unions into this kind of partnership. But, if managements want responsible unions that understand the problems of the enterprise and help it to prosper, they must be willing to share information with union representatives and to take the initiative in setting up the machinery for genuine cooperation in solving production problems.

CONCLUSION

Chapter 22

In Short: The Personnel
Point of View

A profession is an occupation for which the necessary
preliminary training is intellectual in character, involving
knowledge and to some extent learning, as distinguished
from mere skill; which is pursued largely for others, and
not merely for one's self; and in which the financial return
is not the accepted measure of success.

JUSTICE LOUIS BRANDEIS

Personnel administration is still a young profession—so young that its
name has not even yet been generally agreed upon. Because it is still in
the formative stage, all of us who follow this profession have an opportunity to share in setting its aims and standards. If you have not already
decided what you think these should be, you may be helped to do so in
agreement, or disagreement, with the following key questions and capsule
conclusions.

WHAT IS PERSONNEL ADMINISTRATION?

Personnel administration is a basic management function. Unless it is
effectively carried out, technical efficiency is inadequate to achieve enduring organizational success. Problems of personnel should not be thought
of as something separate from technical problems. Both are parts of a
single situation that needs to be understood and dealt with by line officials,
beginning with the chief executive. Effective management gets results by
winning cooperation. This is personnel administration. It means developing teamwork.

Of course, the president is the captain of the management team. As
such, his responsibility for personnel administration is no less because he
has delegated a share of it *to* you as his personnel administrator. After he
has appointed someone to represent him in this field, he actually has more
responsibility. Now he is responsible *for* you and *through* you in relation to

his other employees. Thus, unless the personnel point of view is his as well as yours, you can never be a completely effective exponent of it in his company.

YOUR PLACE ON THE MANAGEMENT TEAM

If you are lucky, you will have found from the outset that your chief executive recognizes the importance of your job. Then you will have a chance to help in planning personnel policies before executive action is taken. And, strengthened by top-management support, you will probably receive cooperation from all other members of the management team, both line and staff.

But you may find yourself in a company where this is not the case. Your president may not be truly personnel-minded. Do you notice that, when you give your point of view on personnel policies, you are the still small voice of conscience to whom no one listens? Even so, you need not be unduly discouraged. Many other personnel men have found themselves on the same spot. Not all of them have remained there. Above all, do not yourself accept your job at its current valuation, if this is a low one. Keep looking for new ways to prove to management at all levels that your work is important to them.

In selling your program to management, you must not forget to be cost-minded. For private industry, a major objective is to make a profit. This means keeping costs below income. On numerous occasions, you will be asked: How much will this proposal cost, and what benefits shall we get from it? Although personnel administration is to be tested in human values, it must also justify itself in terms of dollars and cents. In presenting your recommendations, you should not hesitate to talk in these terms and to point out indirect and long-range costs as well as direct and short-range expenses.

Even if you are not titled and treated as vice-president, see to it that you think and talk like one. Never allow all your time and energy to be spent in wrestling with details, however urgent. See them and treat them as part of a larger pattern, and find time somehow to think along policy lines about major issues. When your chance comes, be sure you are ready to take it and to demonstrate to other management officials the validity of the personnel point of view. Through you this point of view should in time penetrate the whole management structure. When it does, your job will have proved to be as important as any in the organization.

LINE AND STAFF RELATIONSHIPS

But remember the limitations of your role as a staff official. Never give orders to the line. Rely instead on the power of ideas. Make sure, however, that your ideas are known and are such as to carry weight. Since your aim is to build cooperation, see to it that you practice what you preach. In some organizations, there is tension and frustration instead of a high degree of cooperation between line and staff officials. It is part of your job to help eliminate such barriers to efficiency. Do your best to prevent any gap or obstruction in the vital channel of communication between your department and the line officials upon whom the company must depend for good personnel relations.

The acid test of your success is the extent to which your ideas are actualized in the behavior of your colleagues. If you do your job well, every line official will be working with and for you. Although your own contribution will then not be conspicuous, you should not worry about that. If your chief executive is worth his salt, he will value you all the more because you have the ability to get a large part of your work done by others. In any case, it is poor personnel work to blow your own horn. It has been said that one cannot both do things and get the credit for them. Do things. Let others get the credit. They will be all the more enthusiastic about your ideas.

Your Part in Labor Relations

If these ideas are good enough, you can be influential in the field of labor relations. For one thing, you can help to set the tone of management-union negotiations. Try to convince top management that unions can be useful to the company, *e.g.*, when regarded as a check on management's thinking about personnel. Employers who are reasonable and fair need not fear to be challenged as to their purposes. And management should be ready to take the initiative in developing constructive relationships with the union.

Help management to be realistic about unions. They are here to stay, and they should be accepted, not only in the kitchen as workers but also in the parlor as equals. Management fights a losing battle when it concentrates on safeguarding its prerogatives. These can never be guaranteed by a clause in the union contract. They can be kept only when they are earned. Progress in personnel relations lies in developing mutual interest between management and workers and in making common cause. Help top management to take and hold this line in union negotiations, but remember that contracts are worse than useless unless they are supported by daily action at the work level.

Long-term results in labor relations depend on a soil-building program. This work has to be done by the first-line supervisors. Help them to build sound management-union relations from the ground up, by their daily conduct toward workers and union officials. The supervisor's basic rule should be to respect the worker's rights under the law (the shop law of the union agreement) and to see that the workers respect management's rights under the same law.

UNDERSTANDING THROUGH SITUATIONAL THINKING

It is part of your job to help the first-line supervisor learn how to get and how to weigh the relevant facts, both technical and human, upon which his judgments must be based. Help him to see that human facts are subtle, elusive, and variable. In human relations, we rarely meet the so-called "plain" fact. Even an objective event is bound to affect people in different ways and will often seem quite different even to the same person at different times. Thus every point of view—yours, even ours—is only a *point* of view on the whole arc of human understanding. Get other angles and more evidence. Get around, as far as you can. Be flexible. Look for meanings beneath "unreasonable" words. Get perspective by setting up a time frame. Try to understand feelings by seeing the inside picture. Then get outside and look at the situation objectively. Examine sentiments in the light of principles. Help others to do the same.

In building understanding for yourself and others, you have several different kinds of responsibility. Top management may need to be reminded that policies are for people and that people respond better when treated not as we think they *ought* to feel and act but rather as they *do* feel and act. Fine policies are dynamite unless realistically formulated for specific situations and unless they allow room for discretion in border line cases.

Policies also need to be clearly explained, wisely interpreted, and consistently applied. Supervisors need help in showing workers why policy requirements are more important than purely personal pleas. There are exceptions to all rules. But policies should be broader than rules. If many special cases cannot be handled within policy patterns, there is something wrong with the policies. Find out what it is, and try to get it fixed.

Be concerned with long-term principles more than with short-term results. Principles are related to people in personnel policies. Be sure that you and all concerned understand the principles that apply to the specific company situation at the time. Be sure also that you know what a genuine policy is and how existing policies are actually working out. Although you have no final word on policy making, you should be top management's key adviser on all policies for personnel. See to it, therefore, that your policy thinking is sound in theory and useful in practice.

If new evidence at any time makes present policies seem unrealistic, help management to adapt its thinking to current situations. See that workers understand the reasons for the change. To take up a new position is not necessarily inconsistent. Every living thing is constantly changing, people most of all. If management's thinking remains stationary, it will inevitably get out of touch with reality, which continually moves along and will leave a rigid mind high and dry—aground on the barren reef of theory.

GETTING DOWN TO CASES

Do not keep your understanding bottled up inside your own mind. Take it out where it is needed, and put it to work. When you apply it to actual situations, you will make mistakes. Everyone is entitled to make a mistake, but try not to make the same mistake twice, and see that the errors you do make are put to some use. Learn from them, and help others to do so too.

When you hear reports of "hopeless" misunderstandings or incompatible opinions, get down to cases, and see if you can reconcile the differences. Try to get inside the situation and learn the whole story bit by bit. Check and weigh the facts. Determine the issue. Look for a solution that integrates basic needs. But avoid like the plague the temptation to go it alone in planning for the future. Do not emerge onto the scene with the results of solo thinking, crying, "Boys, here it is!" The boys will be more likely to agree with your answer if they have helped to work it out.

It is your responsibility to get each tentative solution for a human problem examined in the light of current data on technical requirements and policy implications. But you should not indulge in this fruitful exercise alone. It is wiser to let others in on it. Perhaps what they learn in this stage will help to prevent misunderstandings next time.

If by group thinking you can evolve a hopeful solution, do not spoil it by poor timing. "There is a tide in the affairs of men. . . . ." There is also an ebb. There are certain developmental stages when action is most fruitful. But, at other times, the pace of events is too rapid for intervention.

When you have finished doing what you can in any given case, you have still not finished with the case. Write up the course of events, and then think how you might have done better. Before you finish, draw the line clearly in your own mind between what you understand and what you do not. Afterward, keep the case record on file. And do not forget to go back to the file when fresh evidence throws new light on what was obscure before.

INTERVIEWING

When in search of understanding, do not suppose that you need either always think alone or do all the talking. To create understanding by and between people, there will be need for interviewing. While doing this, remember that for each person what counts most is not what *you* say but what *he* thinks and feels. Learn to prepare for an interview so that both participants can make the most of it. Learn to listen, and help him speak his mind. When he is talking, you may both get new light on what he is asking of the situation and on what the situation is asking of him. Use your imagination to evoke meaning, and use your pencil to pin it down. When an interview is over, amplify your notes, and evaluate both the experiment in human relations and the gain in understanding. What happened? Was new insight achieved? How can you do better next time?

The Level of Teamwork and Morale

Your ability to understand should be matched by your readiness to examine the facts. Never indulge in wishful thinking. How stable are the individuals and the groups in your company? Your organization is certainly not just "one big happy family." What is it? Is it merely an aggregate of people held loosely and temporarily together by economic interest? Or is there a sense of united purpose and common membership? Is there more of this feeling in some sections than in others? Have you any real work teams? If so, where? How were they built? How are they maintained? Think about this. Give credit where credit is due and help where help is needed.

For instance, study the data on attendance, labor turnover, transfers, and promotions. Is the current rate of personnel mobility strengthening the organization as a whole and building the morale of individuals? Or is it undermining teamwork? Who is leaving the company? Why? From which departments? What is labor turnover costing the company in money and in human values? Could the transfer policies be more wisely formulated and more skillfully administered? Are employees satisfied with the possibilities and actualities of promotion? Whatever the answers to these questions, presumably you cannot be pleased with all the facts you find. But such figures always give food for thought to those who are hungry to learn. And, if you get a new view of some situation after you have assimilated a pile of statistics, do not be satisfied to stop there.

Learning from Complaints and Grievances

Often you can get useful insight by studying employee dissatisfactions and the methods by which they are being handled. What kinds of complaint are you getting? And where are they coming from? How does the complaint and grievance procedure in your company work? Is it aimed to suppress squawks, to appease troublemakers, or to disclose dissatisfactions? Part of your job is to see that there is a definite and simple procedure, known to all, and that it can function fast. Try to convince management that, if a complaint is made officially, it is an opportunity and not just another headache. When dissatisfactions are frankly brought into the open, the first step has been taken toward clearing away the underbrush of misunderstanding that impedes progress toward good relations.

Help line management to learn the trick of listening to what speaks *in* workers (*e.g.*, resentment, jealousy, hurt pride, insecurity, or fear) when they present complaints, as well as to what they speak *about*. Study complaints yourself. Sometimes they are eye openers. In that case, open your eyes and look hard, even if this means seeing your own department and the company in an unattractive light. If there are complaints that cannot be settled short of arbitration, this fact may have to be scored up as a failure. But it need not be a sterile failure. How can such a breakdown be avoided next time? What does the arbitrator do that you did not or could not do yourself? Wrestle with this question, and do not let go until you win new insight.

Building and Maintaining Work Teams

The whole employment process is of major concern to your department and to the line officials whom you serve. Are you satisfied with the way in which situational thinking is being applied in every phase? Is everything being done that can be done to build and maintain stable work teams?

Recruitment should be both dignified and effective in attracting a suitable number of qualified employees. Placement should be a preliminary decision for routine workers and part of a continuing experiment for promotional candidates. Discriminating selection *among* candidates, on the basis of clearly defined policies, protects management from the charge of irrelevant discrimination *against* applicants. Your department should set an example for other staff experts by the way in which it works with supervisors to make a success of these initial hiring procedures. Does it?

A keyman in the formation of effective work teams is the first-line supervisor. Try to make this not just an empty statement in your company but a fact that can be thought about with pride. Do not be afraid to prove that what the first-line supervisor does, day in and day out, counts for more in personnel relations than what the president says at the annual picnic.

Help top management to select foremen for their skill in human relations as well as for their technical efficiency. Train them in the personnel point of view. Learn about their problems on the job. Show them that people can go on learning as long as they are alive. If you and they pursue your education together, personnel relations are bound to improve.

HELPING WORKERS TO MAKE GOOD

Another vital person in the employment relationship is the worker himself. Help him to recognize that his ability to do the job will largely determine his status. Seniority need not be accepted by management as the only standard for decisions on promotion, transfer, downgrading, and layoff. But management need not fear to give seniority due weight when the earlier steps of recruitment, selection, induction, and training have been taken with care.

Sound procedures of induction and training are essential in helping workers with what they need to feel, to know, and to do. As part of the job of getting out production, these activities are the responsibility of line management. But, as personnel administrator, you can help in developing induction and training programs that fit the company situation. You may also assist in training the instructors who actually do the teaching. Unless this teaching is effective, both technical efficiency and success in personnel relations are inevitably limited.

Employee rating, of which each worker is informed in regular follow-up interviews, is an essential procedure for mutual understanding and for the maximum development of employees. When the worker knows where he stands with management, he can adjust his expectations and behavior accordingly. Employee rating also helps management to make sound decisions on promotion. When careful ratings replace snap judgments on employee performance, management, workers, and union leaders can find more solid ground for agreement.

A personnel administrator should also be allowed to help top management with its policies and procedures for transfer, downgrading, and layoff. Established avenues of transfer should be soundly built into the organizational structure and generally known. Lack of clarity in this area tempts workers to assert that management's professed aims to make the most of ability are "just a lot of hooey." Decisions for downgrading and layoff are difficult both for management to make wisely and for unions to accept. Only on the basis of clear-cut policies, consistently and constructively administered, can both sides be sure that all are treated fairly.

Procedures of discipline and discharge also test management's success in applying the personnel point of view. The personnel administrator has not succeeded in his job if line management fails to understand that daily discipline should be maintained within each work team, and chiefly by self-discipline on the part of every employee. Such inner discipline should be encouraged by a constructive discipline policy and supplemented by a few simple rules that are promptly and consistently enforced.

When a worker has to be discharged, every management representative who has regularly dealt with him should look at the record and examine his own memory in search of clues as to what went wrong. Was he ever the right man in the right job? Was his follow-up adequate? A skillfully conducted exit interview may throw light on these points. Or management may never learn why it failed in getting this man to cooperate. Was it perhaps that he did not know what was expected of him in time to adjust to the requirements? If so, try to use this failure to some purpose by showing management that workers need to have notice and explanation of changes in work routines, in personnel, and in rates of pay.

Other procedures, closely related to the employment process, are of equal interest to the personnel administrator.

Earning a Living and Making a Life

For instance, it is up to you to give top management the personnel point of view about wages and salaries. These are not all that employees work for. But money matters. It is both prestige and groceries. Levels of wage rates should be related to those paid by other comparable firms in the community or in the industry. The cost of living, the company's financial status, and government wage orders must also be considered. It may be difficult to make the necessary job evaluations and to set up an internal salary and wage structure that meets all requirements and clearly represents existing job relationships. But the principles are easy to explain. See that every interested worker understands them as well as the facts of his own case. If union officials want to participate in the early stages of job evaluation, so much the better. If not, see that they at least are given an opportunity to understand the aims and methods.

When you talk money to the chief executive, show him that you can be cost-minded. But, if you are a skillful exponent of human values, you may also be able to persuade him, if necessary, that penny pinching is an extravagance in personnel relations.

If your company has an incentive system, how well does it work? Do employees understand the why and how of output standards? Does the system step up production or keep it down? If it results in gains to the company, are these gains fairly shared with the workers? Does the incentive system divide or unite work groups? Does it convince workers that management values effort, or do they think it is just a device to cut rates? Are time-study men regarded by the rank and file as villains, as necessary evils, or as technicians with an understanding of human problems? The personnel administrator should know the answer to these questions and should bend his efforts to see that the answers are right.

Many of us find that earning a living to some extent interferes with making a good life. Try to reduce the conflict between these two needs for personnel in your company. Evaluate for line management the human aspects of hours and shifts, but do not yourself underestimate technical requirements. It is not hard to plan schedules solely with a view to meeting production demands. Nor is it difficult to adjust one worker's schedule to fit his personal situation. But such adjustments, if made for many people, produce chaotic group schedules. And, if made for some people and not for others, they easily lead to unfairness. Can you help top management better to integrate all relevant needs and to achieve technical and human efficiency by situational thinking?

Schedules should be planned on the basis of total patterns of work and living in which all basic factors are seen in relation. Since each company operates not in a vacuum but in a community, both the company and the community may need to make adjustments. You may be able to supply constructive suggestions that will reconcile differences.

If late shifts are necessary, try living on these schedules yourself, and be sure that you know what it would mean to your wife and children if you had to keep it up. Reproduce this picture for those who plan the schedules, and remind them that two-thirds of each worker's life is lived outside the plant.

The Test of Personnel Relations: Mutual Responsibility

It is sometimes hard for operating management to remember that every worker is a whole person and that a serious problem in any area of his life inevitably reduces his total efficiency. It is your job as personnel administrator to remind the chief executive that the workers' problems are in part his problems. It therefore makes sense for management to offer appropriate assistance when employees have difficulties that they cannot meet alone. This does not mean doing things *for* people, so much as thinking and acting *with* them. It means helping them to help themselves and to make intelligent use of plant and community facilities. It also means being realistic and not romantic, going in not for spasmodic do-good-ism or Utopian experiments but rather for long-run mutual responsibility in a working relationship.

By an employee-service program, management can show that its professed belief in responsibility is neither hot air nor just a one-sided demand on workers. Services depend for success on mutual responsibility. Management should participate with employees in planning an all-round program to meet human needs. Workers should participate with management in administering and paying for the program.

Health and Safety

Mutual responsibility between line management and workers is nowhere more essential than in regard to health and safety. As personnel administrator, you, too, have a great responsibility here. In studying the frequency rate of accidents and the current health data in the firm, you should be willing to shoulder your share of the blame. What more could you have done to help prevent accidents and sickness?

For instance, ask yourself what do the safety records and the results of the accident-prevention and health programs show about the success of your department. If top management is not sufficiently personnel-minded to have developed the necessary policies, you may be partly to blame. If operating executives are not sufficiently interested in their subordinates to be constantly mindful of their health and safety, you have not been a successful exponent of the personnel point of view. If the safety director and the company doctor do not come to you for advice, you are missing a valuable opportunity for cooperation. If union officials are not invited to take part in safety discussions and in planning for health, the personnel point of view has not proved fully effective in labor relations. And if workers must often be punished for willful infractions of rules for safety and sanitation, your department has fallen down on the job of selecting the right kind of person to join the company community.

Engineers have shown how greatly their knowledge, skill, and experience can contribute to safety. Doctors have done much to build successful health programs in industry. But neither of these specialists can do the whole job alone. How much are you doing to help the good work along?

Employee Participation in Production Problems

But perhaps your employees participate in these services and not in solving production problems. If so, why? Is it primarily because management does not want their participation in this area? In that case, what are you doing to correct such a shortsighted and unconstructive attitude? Workers always have ideas about their jobs. The question is whether these ideas are being used to "beat the system" or to step up production. People normally like to make suggestions in order to improve conditions and gain prestige. If management is not getting ideas from employees, it is probably the fault either of the organizational structure or of the personnel program as a whole.

By and large, people want to have a share in solving their own problems. If workers and union officials do not take an interest in company problems, it is perhaps because they have the notion that these difficulties are no concern of theirs. This attitude does not spring from nowhere. But such a sign of cleavage between workers and management is not hopeless. It is a challenge. What can you do to meet it? Can you do anything to make democracy a reality in your own firm? If daily work life in your company approaches the ideal democrary, you will have reached the millennium where every citizen does his share in making community living a success.

The Will to Understand and to Believe

You are not, of course, responsible for building a Utopia. But all personnel men are obligated to go on trying and to interest others in this absorbing occupation. Thoreau said, "Gnaw at your own bone: bury it, unearth it, and gnaw it still." Your "bone" should be the conviction that people can understand each other if they will and can work together more effectively when they do. You will never get all the marrow out of this bone, because you will never reach the point where you know all the answers.

But do not be discouraged. Keep at it. And let neither your own failures nor the mistakes of anyone else convince you that the personnel administrator's job is not worth doing. It is all the more worth doing because it can never entirely succeed. Keep on learning and believing that there is a fair solution to every human difference. You cannot hope always to find it, but in any event you should keep on believing. You must believe in people, in principles, and in your profession. You must also believe in yourself. Unless you do, how can you ask others to rely on you?

Part II

CASE ILLUSTRATIONS

THE CASE METHOD

Extensive experience in using cases for teaching has shown us some of the common difficulties met by students who work with this type of material. These difficulties we have tried to avoid by developing a new method of case presentation.

One difficulty frequently found in case material is that the situation described is unrealistic. This may be because, in order to illustrate one point, the case has been oversimplified, or a few "facts" have been added or even altered. To avoid such unrealism, we have tried accurately to record all the key facts in the episode described. Nothing has been invented to make the case seem more logical. Similarly, in any observed sequence of events, nothing has deliberately been left out because it complicates the situation.

As an aid in visualizing the specific setting of each case, we have usually included a brief description of the company background, although, of course, all names of persons and of organizations have been disguised. In some cases, we have also given a brief résumé of previous events whose effects are reflected in the situation immediately under consideration.

Because there has been no pruning of relevant data, each case is true to life in that it presents more than one issue. In fact, often the first and most difficult task for the student is to get a clear conception of what the central problem is. This gives an opportunity for training in situational thinking. In order to leave full scope for developing this skill, we have refrained in most cases from giving our own interpretations of the first-hand data presented. In our opinion, case material is less valuable when the writer's judgments are intermingled with objective facts. Of course, no case can be presented with perfect objectivity. The selection and arrangement of facts inevitably represent the writer's viewpoint. But we have at all times attempted to keep this subjectivity to a minimum.

However, if experienced students are presented with a complex case situation, they are apt to find it almost bewilderingly lifelike unless they are given some help in how to think about it.

Such help we have tried to supply in two ways. First, in order to suggest the central issues that are illustrated in each situation and to relate case material to the subject matter discussed in the chapters, we have written a general introduction for each case. Without some such guide, we have found that novices are apt to be handicapped by one of two difficulties. Either they become intrigued with the human story and, losing sight of policy implications, identify themselves with one side or the other; or, in the effort to be impartial, they try to hold in their minds simultaneously all the data given. But, if this is attempted without any frame of of reference, it is impossible not to be swamped by the mass of detail.

Second, at key points, we have interpolated sample questions for discussion. These are labeled to suggest specific and general areas that need to be thought about. Advanced students may benefit by formulating other questions that would bring out different features.

Our reasons for not putting all the questions together at the end of each case are as follows: First, the groups of questions serve to divide each case into manageable units so that students can assimilate the facts piecemeal. Second, this division of an evolving situation into phases serves to emphasize the developmental stages and turning points at which certain kinds of thinking are appropriate. Lines have sometimes been numbered to aid both the student and the teacher in quickly locating passages that are to be considered in discussing detailed developmental questions. Obviously, an understanding of these subordinate questions enables the student to make a more satisfactory answer of the general summary questions.

In our own classes, we have never used all these cases in any one term. And at different times, by looking at the same material as through the eyes of a different management representative, we have emphasized different implications. In such ways, and by combining these cases with other kinds of class assignment (field work, analyses of management procedures such as employee rating, job analyses, etc.), one can avoid a stereotyped use of this material.

Whether or not teachers and students who use this material agree with our method of presentation, we hope that the cases may prove useful. For advanced students and for personnel workers, these cases will best serve our purpose if they stimulate in readers the desire to write cases from their own experience in personnel relations. The ability to analyze and to systematize one's observations is the end toward which all cases written by other people are only a means. No case writer can give to anyone else that sense of immediacy and challenge to insight that comes from field experience. It is to be hoped that many more personnel workers will engage in the absorbing task of recording firsthand observations and assembling them into cases, of which there can never be too many for use in understanding, teaching, and evaluating the principles and practices of personnel administration.

A Need for Policy Thinking

(Deborah Larkin)

Introduction

When the personnel administrator approaches a problem situation, he should make sure that his suggestions for solving personal difficulties fit into the larger pattern of policy requirements.

The treatment described in the following case clearly illustrates what happens when activity is confined to checking facts and trying to arrange for personal adjustments, without planning and pretesting the solution in view of company-wide policies. The fact that this case was only one fragment of a large-scale situation, which included many similar cases, made especially urgent the need for inclusive understanding. Yet because the personnel administrator did not take a broad view, he missed the chance to use a current difficulty as a step toward permanently improved understanding all around.

This case also illustrates what may happen when staff officials in the personnel department accept responsibility for decisions that should be made by line officials.

What was the immediate problem, and how was it handled?

The Problem: What shall be done about a transferred inspector with long service who insists that she should have preference for a first-shift assignment?

Characters:

Miss Deborah Larkin, inspector, forty-eight years of age.

Mr. Oviedo, business agent of the union.

Mr. Avery, supervisor, industrial relations.

Mr. Dunstable, interviewer, women's employment.

On July 8, 1937, the business agent, Mr. Oviedo, called Mr. Avery on the telephone and asked for an interview, saying that he was bringing with him an employee who deserved special consideration because of her long service. A meeting was arranged.

I. THE MEETING

1   OVIEDO: Mr. Avery, I thought this was a worthy case to bring to your attention, and I wish you would listen to her complaint. (*to Miss Larkin*)
Will you tell Mr. Avery your story?

   LARKIN: Well, I worked in A-29 as a tester for 15 years, and I was always
5   on the first shift. When I heard that motors were going to Cleveland,[1]
I was worried and asked whether I might be transferred. I asked my
foreman, and he said he would see what he could do. It wasn't going to
be easy, because A-29 was shutting down within 2 weeks, and we were
all going to be laid off soon. A little later, the foreman told me to go over
10   to the employment department. There they told me I had to take a
second-shift job. I didn't know what else I could do, so I took it. Now
I've been working for the last 3 weeks on the second shift in the refrigerator
department. I don't like the second shift, and I don't believe I'm getting
proper treatment, because I've been here 15 years, and I think I ought
15   to have some pick of my job. I live alone with my sister at home, and she
works in a restaurant down the street. She works in the afternoon and
late at night. This makes it hard for us to keep our house clean, and I
like to work on the first shift because I can be home while she is away.

   AVERY: Let me call Mr. Dunstable [interviewer, women's employment]
20   and see what he has to say. (*Telephones Mr. Dunstable, who comes in*) Do
you recall Miss Larkin, Mr. Dunstable?

   DUNSTABLE: Yes, certainly. (*to Miss Larkin*) How do you do?

   LARKIN: How do you do?

   AVERY: What information have you got on Miss Larkin's case?

25   DUNSTABLE: About 3 weeks ago, Mr. Hobbes [foreman, Department A-29]
came to my office with a layoff list to tell me that a number of girls with
long service were going to be laid off. He asked if I couldn't place them
in the plant before the actual layoff. I told him I would do my best. An
hour later, Miss Larkin came in to ask what I was going to do for her.
30   She said I had to do something because she had such long service. I told
her I would do all I could but that it would take a little time for me to
look around and see what kind of work we could put her on. She said
she wouldn't consider any other job than a test or inspection job, that
she knew of plenty of places where I could put her, and that there were
35   plenty of girls in other departments with less service whom I could lay
off in order to give her the preference she deserved. I told her I would
look into the situation and let her know. Three different times that day
she came to see me, asking what I had done. Each time I let her know

---

[1] Management had decided to transfer its small-motors division to Plant No. 11.
This project displaced 1,058 workers. Eighteen of these elected to follow their jobs to
the new plant. The others decided not to change their residence. Of this number,
292 employees had 10 years or more of service.
534 employees had less than 10 years but more than 3 years of service.
214 employees had less than 3 years of service.

that, so far, I hadn't had a chance to do anything but would attend to
40   her case as soon as I could. I told her she needn't worry, we would keep
her on where she was until a job had been found. We did keep her on
in the department for more than a week. I finally made a place for her
as inspector on the second shift by laying off a junior who had been with
us only a short time. She took that job, but every day since that time she
45   has been in to see me about a transfer to the first shift. It is difficult to
find her a job at the same rate of pay on the first shift, because she's not
so speedy as the other girls. I've offered her several other jobs on the
first shift, as bench worker or assembler, but she won't take them because
they are production jobs.

50 LARKIN: There are plenty of other girls on that shift who have less service
than I, and I don't see why you can't transfer one of them and put me
in her place.

AVERY: We are doing all we can for you, Miss Larkin. After all, you haven't
lost a single day's work in this transfer, and we made sure that your new
55   job was at the same rate of pay. This shows that we are giving every
consideration to your service record that we can. Furthermore, we are
going to find a place on the first shift for you. Only you must realize that
for several reasons this is not so easy. In the first place, you definitely
limit the possibilities by specifying the type of work you want. Secondly,
60   you cannot expect that the foreman should jeopardize production by
releasing highly efficient girls who have learned to work together in his
department.

LARKIN: Well, anyway, Mr. Dunstable didn't tell me of any other jobs on
the first shift.

65 DUNSTABLE: I am sorry you take that attitude, Miss Larkin. But if you will
recall, I showed you three jobs on the first shift. One of them was as
bench worker; the others were assembly jobs.

OVIEDO: Miss Larkin, I think this is all beside the point. I am certainly
convinced that management is trying to place you. And please, don't
70   let us waste our time. I have plenty of other cases where people have
not been so fortunate as you have been. They are losing time and money
by this transfer and would gladly take any job. Mr. Avery has told you
that he will continue to try to place you on the first shift, and I certainly
don't want him to fire anybody to do this.

75 LARKIN: Well, please do everything you can, Mr. Avery, and do it quickly,
will you? I want very much to get on the first shift.

AVERY: I'll do everything I can, Miss Larkin. I suppose you wouldn't be
interested in taking a job as charwoman on the first shift? We can make
a place for you in the office building.

80 LARKIN: Certainly not. I couldn't consider that.

AVERY: Well, give us a few weeks to turn around in. Come in to see me
Monday, July 26. Will that be all right?

LARKIN: Oh, yes, indeed.

QUESTIONS ON THE MEETING

1. *On person-centered and policy-centered thinking*
   In the business agent's presentation of the case to Mr. Avery, what wording suggests that he regarded it as an individual difficulty rather than as a sample problem calling for policy thinking? (lines 1 to 2)

   a. If you had been in Avery's position at this point, how might you have attempted to clarify the situation?

2. *On communication*
   What key statements made in Miss Larkin's speeches need to be checked as to their factual accuracy? (lines 4 to 18, 50 to 52)

3. *On employee attitude*
   a. What two lines of argument does Miss Larkin use to "prove" that she should get what she wants? (lines 14 to 18)

   b. What do you consider to be the merits of each?

4. *On fact finding*
   a. Why would you approve or disapprove Avery's method of checking facts? (lines 19 to 21)

   b. What kind of statement should, in any event, have preceded this fact-finding activity?

5. *On the role of staff officials*
   a. Assuming that Dunstable's report is accurate, comment on his handling of the situation at that time. (lines 29 to 49)

   b. How could he have clarified the situation?

   c. For what reasons was it ill-advised for Mr. Avery to promise Miss Larkin a position on the first shift? (lines 57 to 58) Consider
   (1) Organizational requirements
   (2) The stage of fact finding reached at that point.

   d. Comment on the content and tone of Mr. Avery's final remarks. (lines 77 to 79, 81 to 82)
   Why would you approve or disapprove of his giving a definite date?

6. *On union attitude and responsibility*
   a. What change in the business agent's attitude is indicated by his speech? (lines 68 to 74)

   b. What does it suggest as to his thoroughness in getting down to cases before he sponsored this complaint?

SUMMARY QUESTIONS

1. *On a personnel administrator's responsibility for policy thinking*
   a. How would you have handled this meeting if you had been in Avery's position?

   b. After the meeting, what things should Avery have done before making any recommendations on this case ?

2. *On union responsibility for policy thinking*
   What would you have done at this meeting if you had been the business agent?

II. The Employment Interviewer's Report

July 21, 1937
Deborah Larkin

Industrial Relations
Mr. J. Avery, *Supervisor*

1   On the case of Deborah Larkin which you asked for a report on, I have
talked today with Mr. Masters [foreman, Department L-50] concerning
her case and have the following explanation to offer as to why it is impossible
at the present time to transfer her onto the first shift.

5   She is on a job especially suited for her, as it is a simple meter-reading
occupation on the stators in Department L-50. Mr. Masters does not feel
he could transfer her to any other type of work, and on the particular job
on which she is working the two girls on the first shift both have more than
5 years' service on that same occupation. In Mr. Masters's estimation, both
10   girls on the first shift are more valuable to him, and he could not legitimately
transfer one of them to the second shift without endangering production.

Mr. Masters has gone over this with Miss Larkin and has absolutely
guaranteed that, the first opening on any occupation for which she might
be suitable, he will place her immediately.

15   Under these circumstances, I cannot see how we can be of any assistance
to her at this particular time unless we can place her on a bench job on
some easy occupation.

H. N. Dunstable
Employment Department

Questions on the Report

1. *On a personnel administrator's role*
   a. What problems does this report present to Mr. Avery?
   b. If you were in Mr. Avery's position at this point, how would you explain
      the situation to Miss Larkin?

III. Interview with Miss Larkin

July 22, 1937. Miss Larkin in Avery's office

1   AVERY: Miss Larkin, we must come to some definite understanding on your
      case. You have had more consideration than any other employee, and
      yet you continue to make trouble.
   LARKIN: (*fumbling for her handkerchief*): Oh, Mr. Avery, you're not angry
5   with me, are you?
   AVERY: Well, I'm not exactly pleased. You agreed to give us time to turn
      around in to find you a job on the first shift. But, instead of living up
      to this agreement, you make matters worse by appealing to everybody
      in sight to do something about your situation.
10   LARKIN (*in tears*): I don't know what you mean, Mr. Avery.
   AVERY: I mean just this—your case has bobbed up in this office every single

day since we came to our agreement, July 8. You have talked to four
people since you've been up here—Cameron [president of the union],
Oviedo, and two shop stewards. If there is something that is not clear
15   to you, why don't you come to us?

LARKIN: I didn't want to bother you.

AVERY: Why bother them? Besides, by talking to them you bother both
them and me. Naturally, they have to take some action, and the only
way they can do that is to come to this office. And it isn't as if we are
20   neglecting your case entirely. We gave you all possible consideration,
because we appreciate that you have 15 years of service. We even fired
a boy to make a place for you.

LARKIN: Fired?

AVERY: Yes, we fired a junior to give you your present job. And your foreman
25   has absolutely agreed to place you as soon as he can find a job for which
you are suited. Why don't you give him a chance?

LARKIN: I do.

AVERY: I beg your pardon. You're not helping us a bit by misrepresenting
your case to the shop stewards.

30   LARKIN: Oh, I didn't do that.

AVERY: Well, you certainly had Dunstable on the spot by telling one of the
shop stewards that he was not taking any interest in your case. What
do you expect the shop steward to do when you tell stories like that?
He naturally comes right to this office to find out why nothing has been
35   done. More than that, you told Mr. Cameron that we didn't even want
to give you the charwoman job on the first shift. Now you know that
this isn't true. You can have the charwoman job right now. I didn't
stress the charwoman's job, because I knew you wouldn't like it. Cleaning
toilets is different from what you have been doing before.

40   LARKIN: Oh, I wouldn't mind cleaning the toilets for office people, so long
as it isn't in the shop.

AVERY: All right. I am ready to transfer a woman from the office building
in order to give you the job.

LARKIN: Oh, no, I have no right to ask that.

45   AVERY: Well, you have 15 years of service. You have a right to get preference.

LARKIN: Well, I don't know. I'll wait till Monday.

AVERY: I think that's the best thing. If you will only wait a little while, I am
sure we can find a place for you. Mr. Masters has promised. . . .

LARKIN (evidently anxious to be gone): Yes, he was very nice to me, and I'm
50   sure. . . .

AVERY: Well, give him a chance. Your best bet is in the refrigeration department, because the work there is steadier than anywhere else.

QUESTIONS ON THE INTERVIEW

1. On a personnel administrator's role
    a. Why do you agree or disagree with Mr. Avery's approach? (lines 1 to 52,

especially lines 1 to 3, 6 to 9, 17 to 22, 28 to 29, and 31 to 39)

b. Why do you suppose he now adopts a method that differs so radically from his earlier approach? (see Sec. I)

2. *On interviewing*

a. What is accomplished during this interview?

b. Do you think Miss Larkin had really accepted her situation at this point? (line 49) Give reasons for your opinion.

QUESTIONS ON THE CASE AS A WHOLE

1. *On a personnel administrator's opportunities for service*

If the case had been presented to you at the stage when it first reached Mr. Avery, how would you have proceeded from then on? (Consider facts to be checked, people to be talked to, policy implications to be evaluated, current decisions, and recommendations to be made for the future.)

2. *On employee understanding*

How much do you think Miss Larkin's understanding of her situation grew during the period of case treatment?

3. *On union responsibility in a complaint case*

What would you say is the union's responsibility in such a case?

a. In what respects was it carried out?

b. What more might the union have done?

Case for Chapter 6

Planning for Interviews
(The Bakers' Helpers)

INTRODUCTION

The following case illustrates the need for planning interviews and includes a sample outline for this purpose. In the two letters (at the beginning of The Assignment), statements are made about facts, events, and agreements. Evidences are also given of feelings. All these data were used as leads by the consultant,[1] who also built on what he already knew about the company and about the people concerned. On this basis, he worked out a plan for verifying "facts," both objective and subjective, and for supplementing his partial knowledge of the situation.

The plan given as part of the case need not be accepted as the only possible one for this situation or even as the best. A useful exercise for the reader will be to use this plan as a springboard, after reading the letters. What questions would seem more fruitful? In what other ways could the schedule have been improved?

The method used to gain understanding in this case is that described in various ways in Chaps. 4 to 6. Interviewing here serves as a means of "getting down to cases," which is in itself a practical application of the ideas contained in "situational thinking."

Like any other real case, this one also throws side lights on points other than the central problem. For this reason, the case may also be used as an illustration of Chap. 9 on Complaints and Grievances.

The People Concerned:

HENRY MORGAN, president, Morgan Brothers Bakeries.

DAVID SAMSON, manager of the Salem plant.

FREDERICK MURRAY, production supervisor.

GUSTAV SVENSON, foreman of bakers.

OLE HANSON, union president.

ANDREW McCANNON, secretary, Local 280.

---

[1] Sometimes owners of small concerns are of the opinion that they cannot afford a full-time personnel administrator. They may find it convenient to retain the services of a consultant in personnel relations, who is called in as need arises. This arrangement is seldom entirely satisfactory, since the personnel administrator is most useful when

ANGUS McCULLOCH, shop steward
THE "BOYS," Bill and Jack.
JOHN ANDERSON, consultant.

I. THE ASSIGNMENT

On Oct. 10, 1940, John Anderson, a consultant in labor relations, received the following letter from the secretary of a local union:

BAKERY AND CONFECTIONERY WORKERS
INTERNATIONAL UNION OF AMERICA
LOCAL UNION No. 280

Wednesday, **Oct. 9, 1940**

1 Hello John:

Here we go again. Mr. Samson called us over and talked of the excessive amount of overtime. We agreed that it was wrong to have a competent baker picking up bread from the carrier at $1 per hour. We went further
5 and said a boy should be hired to clean and grease roll pans.

Our final say was one *boy* on the pick-up, and one *boy* on pans.

Mr. Murray hired two friends of his, sick of the conditions in the *M & M* Bakery (a nonunion concern).

These men are about thirty years old. One of them is a bruiser, weighs
10 about 200 pounds, and from their comments on men and methods—their comments are caustic—they are top-notch bakers.

The men in the Salem plant are on edge, what in H— is coming off! I've had more earaches on the phone in two days than I've had in a month.

I am enclosing a copy of a letter I sent Henry. Samson got a copy at the
15 same time.

What in H— is wrong with Murray? I don't believe Henry knows anything about it. I'll be home Saturday morning. Give me a ring if you have anything.

Sincerely,

ANDREW McCANNON

The following is a copy of the enclosure:

BAKERY AND CONFECTIONERY WORKERS
INTERNATIONAL UNION OF AMERICA
LOCAL UNION No. 280

Wednesday, Oct. 9, 1940

Mr. Henry P. Morgan, *President*
Morgan Bakeries
Boston, Mass.
Dear Sir:

We agreed with Mr. Samson that, as work was increasing in the Salem
20 plant, *boys* should be hired for roll-pan greasing and picking up bread.

---

he can prevent difficulties and when he can utilize his intimate knowledge of plant conditions to aid management in building and maintaining sound personnel relationships. As an "outsider" skilled in the personnel approach, however, the consultant may bring a fresh viewpoint to a troublesome situation.

The boys hired by Mr. Murray are friends of his, are thirty years old, and from their comments on the methods used in the plant are really wonderful bakers. The comments on your personnel in the plant are not conducive to harmony.

25   We have boys in Salem looking for work, and we fail to see why it was necessary to bring men from the *M & M* Bakery in New Hampshire to do boys' work.

We recognize that you and Mr. Samson have done a lot for us down here in Salem, but this introduction by Murray of disruptive elements must

30   be brought to your attention.

Are these men, hired where only boys are needed, being paid boys' wages? If so, there is something wrong, because we had difficulty finding competent bakers. If not, why are they introduced?

Sorry to trouble you, but if I don't we shall both be in trouble.

35   Yours respectfully,
                                        ANDREW McCANNON
                                        Secretary, Local 280

The same morning that the above communication was received, President Morgan called the consultant on the telephone, referring to his copy of the letter and urging that as soon as possible the consultant should look into the situation.

QUESTIONS FOR DISCUSSION

1. *On interpretive analysis*
   a. Note the tone of each of the two letters.
      (1) Is it what one would expect in the existing relationships?
      (2) What can be inferred from it about the special nature of the relationships in this case, between the union secretary and the consultant, and between the union secretary and the president of the company?
      (3) What is evident about the union secretary's state of mind at the time?
2. *On a complex complaint situation*
   a. What three accusations are made of faults committed by local management?
   b. What more far-reaching causes for dissatisfaction with the motives and actions of local management are implied? (Consider the statements made in lines 9 to 10, 16 to 17, and 21 to 22.)
3. *On planning for interviews*
   If you had been the consultant, how would you have planned to get the whole story of which only the union side is given in these letters? (Answer before reading further in the case.)

II. THE CONSULTANT'S PLAN

In planning how to set the stage for interviews in such a situation, the interviewer needs to think clearly about specific objectives. The consultant started with three of these: (1) The statements of fact made by the business agent had to be verified and amplified. (2) The implications had to be investigated so that these fragments could be fitted into the total pattern of the trouble situation. (3) The attitudes of all concerned had to be learned in order to discover what feelings had contributed to make the situation what it was and which of them were continuing elements to be dealt with. In view of these objectives, therefore, the consultant had to make several decisions before trying to arrange for interviews.

What more did he need to know?—Careful study of the letters enabled the consultant to reach a working hypothesis. At this point, he had to be clear in his own mind as to what he knew, as to what he did not know, and as to what he needed to find out.

In order to make a complete report to the president, the consultant needed to be fully informed about the following key topics:

1. The hiring agreement at issue.
2. The circumstances under which the "boys" were hired.
3. Attitude of the foreman (Svenson) toward this situation.
4. Attitude of the regular employees toward the "boys."
5. Attitude of the "boys."
6. Union attitude toward local management.

Who could tell him?

1. Which of the people directly concerned could check the key statements made about the hiring situation?
2. What people must be seen to fill in the blanks left by vague implications?
3. Who could complete the picture by revealing the feelings that are an integral part of the situation?

The consultant decided in advance on only the irreducible minimum of people who must be seen. He knew that subsequent developments always broaden the field of inquiry.

In what sequence was it advisable to seek the interviews?—Organizational propriety indicated that, in both company and union, interviews should be held first with top officials and from then on be planned to follow the line of authority down to the worker. This procedure not only satisfies the demands of courtesy but strengthens organization and makes it easier for the respective officials to cooperate. By allowing each superior to make the necessary arrangements to interview his immediate subordinate, the consultant made it possible for him to plan the interview with the least interruption to production and also gave him an opportunity to reassure the subordinate that he should feel free to tell all he knows and do all he can to help unravel the difficulties.

The consultant was now ready to prepare a schedule of questions and a list of people to be seen.

TABLE 1.—SCHEDULE OF SAMPLE QUESTIONS TO INVESTIGATE
A MULTIPLE COMPLAINT

What do I need to Know?	Who Can Tell Me?

1. *The hiring agreement at issue*
   a. What was the agreement?
   b. How was it reached?
      Was it formal; in writing?
      Was it informal; an oral agreement?
   c. When was it made?
   d. Is it consistent with the existing union contract with
      the company?
	Mr. Samson, manager of
	   Salem plant
	Mr. Hanson, union
	   president
	Mr. McCannon,
	   secretary, Local 280

2. *The hiring circumstances*
   a. What is the standard hiring procedure in the local
      plant?
   b. Who hired the "boys"?
      If it was Murray, why did Samson allow this?
      Were they, in fact, friends of Murray?
   c. On what date were they hired?
   d. For what position?
   e. What was their starting rate?
   f. Pertinent employment data: age, previous experi-
      ence, etc.
   g. If the facts are as stated, why overlook the local
      labor market and bring in people from New
      Hampshire? Why hire men for boys' work?
   h. Did management discuss the hirings with the union?
   i. Were the "boys" properly inducted?
	Mr. Samson, manager
	   of Salem plant
	Mr. Murray, production
	   supervisor
	
	Mr. Svenson, foreman
	   of bakers

3. *Attitude of the foreman toward the situation*
   a. Are the men "on edge"?
   b. Who seems to be at fault?
   c. Have the "boys" done satisfactory work?
	Mr. Svenson, foreman
	   of bakers

4. *Attitude of the regular employees toward the "boys"*
   a. Are the "boys" acceptable to the work group?
   b. If the "boys" are not already union members, will
      they be acceptable to the local?
   c. What objectionable "comments" did the "boys"
      make?
      Under what circumstances?
	Mr. McCulloch, shop
	   steward
	Key bakers

5. *Attitude of the "boys"*
   a. Why did they take these jobs?
   b. Are they satisfied?
      With the jobs?
      With the rates of pay?
	The "boys"

TABLE 1.—SCHEDULE OF SAMPLE QUESTIONS TO INVESTIGATE
A MULTIPLE COMPLAINT (Continued.)

What do I need to Know?	Who Can Tell Me?

c. What are their expectations with regard to upgrading, pay raises, promotions, etc.?
 d. Did they, or are they planning to, apply for union membership?
 e. What remarks have they made to which regular employees might object?
 Have they bragged about
     Their friendship with Murray?
     Their competence as bakers?
     The superiority in methods of the M & M
     Bakery?
	The "boys"

6. *Union attitude toward local management*
 a. Have union-management relations been satisfactory in the past?
 b. Why is the union suspicious of Murray?
 c. What does the union fear?
	Mr. Hanson, union
	   president
	 Mr. McCulloch, shop
	   steward
	 Sample union members

This list of questions is not exhaustive but calls attention to areas that need to be explored. In the course of the interviews, other questions suggested themselves.

QUESTIONS FOR DISCUSSION

1. *On the form of interview schedules*
   Criticize the form of the above schedule. What other arrangement could you suggest?
2. *On the use of interview schedules*
   What possible dangers are inherent in the interviewer's reliance on such a schedule of questions? How can these dangers be avoided?

III. THE INTERVIEWS

The interviews took place as scheduled and were completed by Tuesday, Oct. 15. To give a detailed report of all that was said and revealed would involve an enormous amount of repetition and much material irrelevant to the immediate situation. For these reasons, we merely give a résumé of the relevant data obtained.

RÉSUMÉ OF INTERVIEW MATERIAL

1. *The Hiring Agreement.*—Local 280 of the Bakery and Confectionery Workers was a craft organization and had a union shop contract with Morgan Brothers. Their chief interest lay in protecting skilled bakers.

However, to promote productive efficiency in a highly competitive business, the local union leaders were glad to cooperate with management by permitting the introduction of "one or two boys" as helpers. Since their membership consisted entirely of skilled bakers, the local had no candidates for the helpers' jobs and merely assumed that management would fill these places from the Salem labor market.

The specific hiring agreement was oral. On Wednesday, Sept. 15, 1940, upon the request of Mr. Samson, the union committee (president, secretary, and shop steward) had met in the plant manager's office and informally discussed the need of freeing skilled bakers for their proper work. Nothing said at this meeting was committed to writing by either party.

2. *The Hiring Circumstances.*—Ordinarily, the plant manager did all the hiring. In this instance, he had allowed Murray to hire the "boys."[1] This was done on Monday, Sept. 30. The men were hired to perform boys' work at a starting rate of 45 cents.

The men were thirty and thirty-two years of age, respectively, experienced bakers, formerly employed at the *M & M* Bakery.

This unusual hiring situation came about for the following reasons. Both men had previously been working with Murray when he was production supervisor at the *M & M* Bakery. During the autumn, they contacted him at Morgan Brothers, asking if he could do anything to help them find a job in or near Boston because their wives were dissatisfied with living in the country. The production supervisor thought he could do the smart thing and satisfy everybody by offering these men helpers' jobs at the Salem plant.[2] The men took these jobs to please their wives, no doubt hoping that they would soon be able to reestablish themselves as bakers. They were put to work without due explanation either to them or to the regular employees.

3. *Attitude of the Foreman.*—The foreman confirmed the fact that the regular bakers were "on edge" and showed resentment against the "boys." On one occasion, he had reprimanded the "pick-up boy" for taunting the bakers. The "boy" had held up a finished loaf, exclaiming, "Do you guys call this *bread?*"

The "boys" met minimum requirements but were evidently not keen on their work and wasted time trying to engage bakers in conversation.

4. *Attitude of the Regular Employees to the "Boys."*—The regular employees were startled to see men doing boys' work. Since there had been

[1] The manager was vague in his explanation as to the reason for making an exception here. It seemed unwise to press the question.

[2] He disavowed any friendship for these men, insisting that their employment was a good way of "killing two birds with one stone."

no explanation either from management or from the new employees, the bakers speculated about this unusual situation. As they learned that the "boys" were competent bakers from the *M & M* Bakery (an unorganized plant) and "friends" of Murray, they put two and two together. They concluded that management was "trying to pull a fast one" by introducing these men as "labor spies" and aimed to use them to replace bakers who had incurred the production supervisor's displeasure. In view of all this, the "boys" were entirely unacceptable as fellow employees or even as potential union members. In fact, a meeting had been called with the objective of "black-balling" these men if and when they applied for membership in accordance with contract agreements. Specifically, the bakers objected that these men were looking for trouble, by bragging about being friends of Murray and about their own superiority as bakers. The bakers repeated the incident described by the foreman but specified no other "caustic comments."

5. *Attitude of the "Boys."*—Bill and Jack, the new employees, confirmed Murray's account of their reasons for taking these unskilled jobs. They professed themselves satisfied with the work and the pay and said that, of course, they expected to stay and to join the union and hoped eventually to be employed as bakers. It seemed to them surprising and unfair that the regular bakers should be so antagonistic. When questioned about the alleged taunt, the "pick-up boy" retorted, "For Pete's sake, can't these boobs take a joke?" According to their testimony, no other comments had been made about their friendship with Murray, their own skill as bakers, or methods used at the *M & M* Bakery, which could conceivably have annoyed the other men.

6. *Union Attitude toward Local Management.*—According to the union officials, management-union relationships had been entirely satisfactory until Murray came to the plant. All along he seemed unsympathetic to the workers' interests and was regarded as a driver, concerned only with speeding up production.[1] His previous connection with a nonunion plant was another strike against him. When he "began bringing in" his nonunion friends, workers feared that these men were the entering wedge of a campaign to undermine the union.

QUESTIONS ON THESE FINDINGS

1. *On the union's complaint*
    a. Has the union cause for complaint? If so, what?

---

[1] Murray was the first to hold the newly created job of production supervisor. Since this kind of innovation always tends to rouse resentment in workers, they usually feel antagonistic to the man who holds this position unless care is taken to give him a good start.

    b. What informal arrangement seems to have been the occasion of trouble?

    c. Whose poor judgment does this reflect?

2. *On possibilities for action*

    a. How serious does the situation seem to be at this point?

    b. Why do you think similar situations need or need not recur in this company?

3. *On employment policy*

    a. In what way did the production supervisor, Mr. Murray, violate sound hiring policy?

    b. Comment on his placement of the new employees.

    c. What evidences, if any, are given of formal induction, and why was it especially needed in such a situation?

4. *On Employee attitudes*

    a. How might one explain the unacceptable behavior of the "boys"? (Consider what you know about defensive reactions of persons in similar situations.)

    b. Why might the response of the regular bakers have been expected?

    c. Why might union leaders have been tempted to make the most of Murray's ill-advised activity?

QUESTIONS ON THE CASE AS A WHOLE

1. *On opportunities for a personnel consultant*

After analyzing the interview material, what recommendations would you have made to the president if you had been Mr. Anderson?

    a. Consider the opportunities for private interviews. With whom and by whom would you suggest that these be held? What subject matter should be covered?

    b. Would it seem likely that any joint conferences would be helpful; among what officials, for what purpose?

    c. What specific action would you recommend that management might take with regard to the "boys"? Who should take it?

The Effect on Work Teams of Labor Turnover and Internal Mobility

(Work Group No. 7)

INTRODUCTION

The situation of Work Group No. 7, from Aug. 1, 1937, to Aug. 1, 1938, may at first glance not seem typical. Much of the personnel mobility was specifically occasioned by the nation-wide depression going on at the time. But, in a broader sense, the experience of this group is normal. Personnel mobility in this case, as in so many others, was determined also by company policies, by the development of a new product, and by the interdependence of all parts of the company that were affected in different ways by the same union agreement. But if change had not been occasioned by these factors, it probably would have been brought about by something else. Change of a sufficiently radical nature to produce extensive personnel mobility is a constant factor in such a dynamic situation as American industrial life.

Study of the data given below shows that higher management lacked much of the information needed for adequate policy making. Insiders (like group leaders, union officials, and the foreman, not to mention the workers themselves) certainly knew far more than is recorded here. But this knowledge was never put to full use. Therefore, the superintendent had little conception of what was going on below the surface or of the reasons why workers in Group No. 7 felt and acted as they did. If a personnel administrator had been asked to study the circumstances and to make recommendations, he would have needed to begin with a thorough situational analysis that would have included a comprehensive program of interviewing. The material thus obtained certainly should have thrown more light on the differences in thinking that to some extent separated

341

management and workers and on the forces that at first balked management efforts to set up an effective work team. Lacking such inside information, we can only speculate about the reasons for some of the manifestations described here and note that management's freedom of action was greatly limited both by circumstances that it recognized as beyond its control and by forces of whose existence management was not even aware.

Incomplete though it is, the available information gives us considerable insight into the effect of personnel mobility on a small group. The case also illustrates our point that, for each subunit in an organization, internal mobility in the form of transfers in and out has an effect similar to labor turnover on the company as a whole. Furthermore, it throws into relief the fact, so frequently overlooked, that no subgroup can be established and maintained as though it were an isolated unit, untouched by what is going on in the company as a whole and in the larger community.

The activities here described also provide some insight into the conditions that promote or hinder development of effective work teams. Some of the facts given and questions asked relate to this inclusive objective as well as to the narrower field of personnel mobility.

Starting from bald, over-all statistics of personnel mobility and productive efficiency, we have broken down these figures in order to identify the workers who were moving about and who produced for management with a degree of efficiency that varied according to the current situation of the work group and the changing attitudes of its members. When one knows who the people were at all times, how rapidly they moved in and out of the group, and why, one is able to answer such questions as

1. Did the rate of personnel mobility described here allow for the development of the relationships and attitudes that promote teamwork?
2. Which management policies and activities may have helped to develop team spirit?
3. In what ways was management's policy thinking and understanding of workers inadequate to promote management aims?

In looking toward the answers to these questions, we may begin our study of Work Group No. 7 by a brief survey of its specific setting.

COMPANY BACKGROUND

Plant No. *X* of the National Manufacturing Company in Springfield, Mass., produced a variety of electrical appliances such as domestic refrigerators, small motors, small motored appliances (fans, vacuum cleaners, etc.), and air-conditioning units. Each group of products was manufactured in a separate division. Of these four divisions, three were established operating units, making standardized products. The air-conditioning division alone was a new departure at this time, a small experimental unit making their product to order.

Work Group No. 7 was part of the machining section and turned out valve plates and bearings for air-conditioning units. This work was done on drill presses. The operators also did grinding on side-plate covers and end valves. Both activities were classified as nonrepetitive.

The interrelation among Work Group No. 7, the machining section, and the air-conditioning division was as follows:

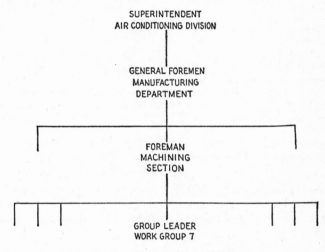

DIVISIONAL EMPLOYMENT POLICY

In January, 1937, the superintendent in charge of the air-conditioning division had a definite employment policy that for some months he was able to put into effect. This policy was to requisition relatively young men, with the necessary skills and flexibility, who might be expected to become increasingly expert in this line of work. Since he was primarily interested in skill and flexibility, his policy in regard to age was expressed chiefly as a negative preference: "Don't send me any old-timers who have grown up with small motors and are set in their ways." He had no objection to the rehiring of qualified former employees and a few specially recommended transferees from other divisions.

EMPLOYMENT DATA

Available statistics on the distribution of workers according to length of service were calculated at the beginning and middle of each year.

These figures give a general indication of the initial results of the superintendent's employment policy for the air-conditioning division as a whole.

TABLE 1.—DISTRIBUTION OF PRODUCTIVE WORKERS IN THE AIR-CONDITIONING DIVISION ACCORDING TO LENGTH OF SERVICE IN PERCENTAGE OF THE TOTAL WORK FORCE. JANUARY AND JUNE, 1937

Service groups	Jan. 11, 1937		June 11, 1937	
	Number	Percent	Number	Percent
0 to 5...............	79	85.0	148	80.9
5 to 10 years...........	11	11.7	23	12.6
10 to 15 years...........	2	2.2	8	4.4
15 to 20 years...........	1	1.1	3	1.6
20 to 25 years...........	0	0	1	0.5
	93	100.0	183	100.0

In relation to similar data for older divisions, these figures represent a large proportion of short-service employees. In management terminology, the new division, made up of relatively young, ambitious workers who were given an opportunity to help develop a new product, was "all set to go places."

Work Group No. 7, as a subunit in this division, was developed in accordance with this general policy. Beginning in January, 1937, this work group was gradually expanded from 6 employees to 26 at the following rate:

TABLE 2.—ACCESSIONS TO WORK GROUP NO. 7.

JAN. 1, 1937 TO AUG. 1, 1937

Jan. 1, 1937	total number of employees:				6
Feb. 1, 1937	"	"	"	"	10
Mar. 1, 1937	"	"	"	"	13
Apr. 1, 1937	"	"	"	"	14
May 1, 1937	"	"	"	"	18
June 1, 1937	"	"	"	"	22
July 1, 1937	"	"	"	"	24
Aug. 1, 1937	"	"	"	"	26

Standard employment records concerning these 26 workers provide the following data:

TABLE 3.—EMPLOYMENT DATA, WORK GROUP NO. 7.
AUG. 1, 1937. TOTAL NUMBER: 26

No.	Occupation	Age	Length of service	Nationality	Residence
1	Drill-press operator	23	Less than 1 year	Polish	Westfield
2	Drill-press operator	28	1 to 2 years	American	Russell
3	Drill-press operator	39	1 to 2 years	German-American	Springfield
4	Drill-press operator	29	1 to 2 years	French	Willimansett
5	Drill-press operator	37	2 to 3 years	Irish-American	Chicopee Falls
6	Drill-press layoutman, group leader, and shop steward	46	4 to 5 years	American	Springfield
7	Drill-press operator	26	4 to 5 years	English	Springfield
8	Drill-press operator	30	1 to 2 years	French	Holyoke
9	Drill-press operator	25	0 to 1 year	French American	Northampton.
10	Drill-press operator	31	2 to 3 years	Polish	Chicopee Falls
11	Drill-press operator	29	4 to 5 years	American	Chicopee Falls
12	Assembler	35	13 to 14 years	English	Springfield
13	Assembler	25	4 to 5 years	German	Springfield
14	Assembler	35	0 to 1 year	French	Bondsville
15	Lathe operator	27	0 to 1 year	American	Palmer
16	Packer	46	1 to 2 years	American	Ludlow
17	Drill-press operator	35	1 to 2 years	Scotch	Springfield
18	Drill-press operator	22	1 to 2 years	American	Springfield
19	Drill-press operator	30	1 to 2 years	American	Springfield
20	Drill-press operator	51	2 to 3 years	Lithuanian	Westfield
21	Drill-press operator	21	4 to 5 years	Polish	Wilbraham
22	Surface grinder	51	13 to 14 years	American	Springfield
23	Gas welder	53	1 to 2 years	American	Springfield
24	Drill-press operator	23	3 to 4 years	American	Chicopee
25	Drill-press operator	19	2 to 3 years	Polish	Ludlow
26	Drill-press operator	22	3 to 4 years	American	Springfield

SUPERVISION

Each group in the machining section was under the direct supervision of the section foreman. In addition, each of these subunits had its own group leader. Management expected the group leader to build and maintain group morale. It was his function not only to integrate his group but to be a link between it and other groups and to act as contact man for production schedulers, inspectors, and other staff technicians.

The group leader also taught newcomers their job and helped them, as well as older employees, to acquire the most efficient work habits. His technical responsibilities included seeing that the group had as steady a flow of work as the business situation permitted and that it was adequately supplied with necessary piece parts and raw materials. He was also responsible for such paperwork as checking order specifications and reporting the number of units finished by the group.

In the minds of his fellow group members, the group leader's most important activities were those dictated by operational requirements.

At this time, Group No. 7 was led by Ted Martin (operator No. 6 in Table 3), who was also a shop steward.

QUESTIONS FOR DISCUSSION

1. *On personnel mobility and teamwork*
   a. What influence, if any, do you think the rate of expansion shown in Table 2 (page 344) might have on group unity and the development of teamwork?
   b. In view of the impending business recession and the fact that some older divisions were already compelled to lay off operators owing to lack of work, why do you think it was or was not a good policy to requisition so many young employees? (See Table 3, page 345.)
2. *On group composition and teamwork*
   a. What do you notice about the age distribution of group members?
   b. What inferences would you make from your observations? (See Table 3.)
   c. What would be your opinion as to the effect on group unity of the fact that almost all the workers have short service?
   d. What significance, if any, would you attach to the residential distribution listed in Table 3?
   e. What bearing on teamwork would you attribute to the variety of nationality shown in Table 3?
   f. Taken together, what might be the cumulative effect on group unity of all the factors recorded in Table 3?

PERIOD OF REPLACEMENT TRANSFERS

During the year, Aug. 1, 1937, to Aug. 1, 1938, the foreman's freedom of choice in selecting operators according to the policy laid down by the division superintendent was increasingly circumscribed. There were two reasons for this. On one hand, the depression had begun to affect operations in the air-conditioning division so that it could no longer expand, and, beginning in September, 1937, layoffs became increasingly necessary. The resulting diminution of the work force can be traced in the Chart on page 348. Secondly, the air-conditioning division was asked to absorb by replacement transfers (bumping) long-service employees who had been laid off in other divisions owing to lack of work. Consequently, like other work groups in the air-conditioning division, No. 7 was subjected to an influx of long-service employees. This procedure was adopted in accordance with a union agreement to give employment preference to qualified workers with long service (length of service being calculated on a plant-wide basis) and involved laying off short-service workers. This meant that the air-conditioning division was now being increasingly manned by the very "old-timers" whom the superintendent had at first intentionally excluded.

DISTRIBUTION OF PRODUCTIVE WORKERS IN THE AIR-CONDITIONING DIVISION ACCORDING TO LENGTH OF SERVICE. IN PERCENTAGE OF THE TOTAL WORK FORCE. JANUARY AND JUNE, 1938

Service groups	Jan. 14, 1938		June 17, 1938	
	Number	Per cent	Number	Per cent
0 to 5 years............	63	51.6	19	31.2
5 to 10 years	21	17.2	8	13.1
10 to 15 years............	18	14.8	17	27.8
15 to 20 years............	16	13.1	12	19.7
20 to 25 years............	4	3.3	5	8.2
	122	100.0	61	100.0

The altered situation for the air-conditioning division as a whole, in the first 6 months of 1938, is again reflected in the over-all statistics on the distribution of workers according to length of service.

QUESTIONS FOR DISCUSSION

1. *On teamwork and length of service*
   a. What do you notice in comparing the number of short-service workers employed on June 17, 1938, with that employed in January, 1937?
   b. What do you observe about the relative size of the long-service groups on these two dates?

PERSONNEL MOBILITY IN WORK GROUP NO. 7

The change from a large majority of short-service workers to a membership entirely made up of long-service employees was produced by an

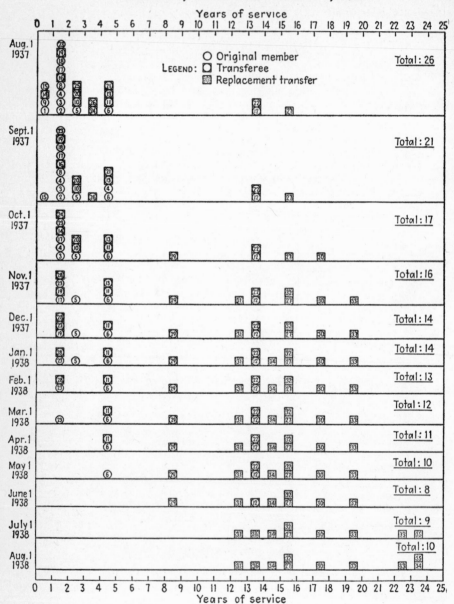

PERSONNEL MOBILITY IN WORK GROUP 7
AUGUST 1,1937 THROUGH AUGUST 1,1938

internal labor turnover of 100 per cent in Work Group No. 7 during the year under study.

The standard employment data for these transferees, No. 27 to No. 40, are as follows:

TABLE 5.—WORK GROUP NO. 7. EMPLOYMENT DATA CONTINUED.
SEPT. 1, 1937 to AUG. 1, 1938

No.	Occupation	Age	Length of service	Nationality	Residence
27	Drill-press operator	40	15 to 16 years	French	Chicopee Falls
28	Blanchard grinder	37	1 to 2 years	American	Shutesbury
29	Drill-press operator	32	8 to 9 years	American	Ludlow
30	Drill-press operator	41	17 to 18 years	American	Chicopee Falls
31	Drill-press operator	34	12 to 13 years	Italian	Springfield
32	Borematic-machine operator	46	15 to 16 years	American	Springfield
33	Drill-press operator (and group leader,	42	19 to 20 years	French-Canadian	Springfield
34	Assembler	45	14 to 15 years	Scotch Canadian	Springfield
35	Hand-milling-machine operator	45	23 to 24 years	French Canadian	Chicopee Falls
36	Turret-lathe operator	42	13 to 14 years	American	Chicopee Falls
37	Chucking-machine setup	54	22 to 23 years	American	Chicopee Falls
38	Borematic-machine operator	49	22 to 23 years	American	Chicopee Falls
39	Milling-machine operator	60	23 to 24 years	Scotch	Chicopee Falls
40	Drill-press operator	40	16 to 17 years	French	Springfield

QUESTIONS

1. *On group development*
   What is happening to Work Group No. 7?
2. *On group composition*
   a. In regard to group composition, what significant facts do you notice in studying Table 5?
   b. At various stages during this year, what different influences do you think these facts might have on employee relations in Work Group No. 7?

PHASES IN GROUP DEVELOPMENT

In the process of this radical transformation, Work Group No. 7 passed through four clearly defined phases. Each of these has special features, presents unique problems, and is reflected in a different degree of productive efficiency.[1]

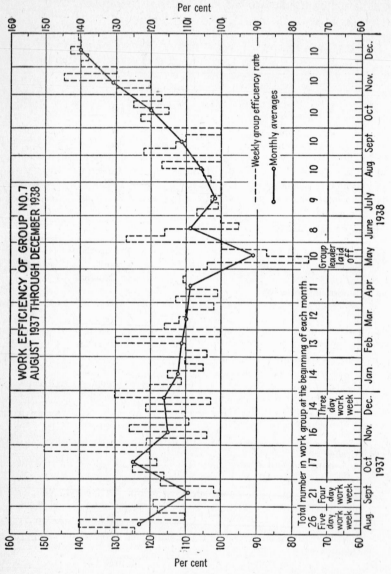

[1] The workers were on group piecework. The 100 per cent line on this Chart indicates the guaranteed base rate. Indexes above this line are incentive earnings; indexes below the 100 per cent line are "fall-downs" and indicate a "red variance in the foreman's labor account." That is to say, whenever group efficiency dropped below

A detailed history of each of these phases would be a book in itself if we had all the relevant information. As it is, we can gain some insight by studying available data.

Phase 1—Aug. 1, 1937, *to Dec.* 1, 1937.—At the beginning of this phase, the work group had reached peak expansion. As indicated by the employment data given in Table 3, it was a rather heterogeneous aggregate of semiskilled and skilled workers, showing wide differences in age, nationality, and locality of residence. It was composed of four elements: the original members of the work group and their leader (operator No. 6), employees who were rehired, transferees from other operating divisions, and one replacement transferee from the small motors division.

As judged by the efficiency rate, group productivity was unsteady, showing extreme weekly fluctuations. The general average was around 117 per cent.

Phase 2—Dec. 1, 1937, *to Apr.* 1, 1938.—During this period all but 6 of the original 23 short-service workers had been laid off. The entire phase was characterized by friction between two cliques and a slowly declining trend in weekly group efficiency.

Phase 3—Apr. 1, 1938 *to June* 1, 1938.—At the beginning of this phase, only two of the original group members remained; worker No. 11 and the group leader No. 6. Worker No. 11 was laid off in April.

The group leader, No. 6, who had never been accepted by the replacement transferees, now had no one to support him, except the foreman. In order to force the removal of the group leader, the workers engineered a "fall-down."

The consequences for productive efficiency in May can be seen on the Chart (page 350).

This resort to direct action proved successful. Group leader No. 6 was laid off and was replaced as group leader by No. 33. From then on, the long-service workers were the only element in the group.

Phase 4—June 1, 1938, *to Jan.* 1, 1939.—In this phase, for the first time, Work Group No. 7 was a fairly homogeneous work team unified by mutual acceptance of their group leader whom they liked and respected. During this phase, productive efficiency for the group showed an upward trend with a tendency to level off at about 140 per cent.

In passing through these four phases, Work Group No. 7 was subjected to numerous adjustment problems. Some of these were as follows:

Changes in Length of Work Week.—From Jan. 1, 1937, to Apr. 1, 1938,

---

100 per cent, management actually lost money, since the workers were paid according to a guaranteed base rate. An important part of a foreman's duties consisted in preventing "red variance in the labor account."

there were several changes in the length of the work week. At the beginning of 1937, Group No. 7 worked full time, 6 days a week. On June 1, 1937, the schedule was reduced to a 5-day week. On Sept. 1, 1937, there was another drop to a 4-day week; and beginning Dec. 1, 1937, for a period of 4 months, the group worked on a 3-day-week schedule. After that, the amount of work slowly increased. The reaction of group members to these changes is expressed to some extent in their attitude toward work sharing.

Attitude toward Work Sharing.—In August, 1937, it was apparent to the superintendent that contraction of operations in the air-conditioning division would be inevitable owing to the general business recession. In discussions with union leaders, it was decided that the employees should be given an opportunity to express their opinion as to how this difficult situation could best be met. The superintendent was interested in promoting security of employment. For this reason, he was willing as an initial step to accept a slight reduction in productive efficiency if the workers should prefer work sharing among all to the layoff of some employees. The following ballot was used:

ATTENTION: MANAGEMENT SUGGESTS THAT..5..PEOPLE
BE LAID OFF FROM YOUR GROUP

—*—

How shall this be arranged?

	Yes	No
1. Maintain present work force by accepting lower group percentage.	____	____
2. By layoff	____	____

3. How many people shall be laid off from your group?

1	2	3	4	5
—	—	—	—	—

August, 1937

A worker voting for option No. 1 agreed to accept lower weekly earnings in order to divide a smaller amount of work among the same number of employees. With the exception of operators No. 12, No. 22, and No. 27, the group unanimously favored this form of work sharing. For a few weeks, the majority decision was put into effect.

Early in December, 1937, a similar employee poll resulted in a complete repudiation of work sharing through lower group percentage.

QUESTIONS

1. *On factors that divide work teams*
   a. What obvious reasons would operators 12, 22, and 27 have had for opposing a policy of work sharing in August, 1937?
   b. What reasons could you give to explain why other employees in Work Group No. 7 should in December, 1937, reverse the stand they took in August? (Consider the increasing number of replacement transfers and changes in the length of the work week.)

SYMPTOMS OF GROUP INSTABILITY

All these changes in the composition of Work Group No. 7, the amount of their weekly take-home, and the length of the work week, naturally produced tensions. Some resulting dissatisfactions were forcefully brought to management's attention in two significant ways.

Complaints about Group Leader Martin. (No. 6)—Early in October, 1937, complaints about the group leader were made to the foreman in charge of the machining section. These complaints came from operators No. 11, No. 12, and No. 22, all transferees. The charges were that Martin was not doing enough productive work and that he not only spent too many hours keeping track of records but that, in his capacity as shop steward, he also wasted time talking to other workers in the section.

When the foreman investigated these complaints, he found that the group leader had recently failed to be reelected as a union representative and therefore was no longer active as a shop steward. In view of this finding, the foreman was inclined to regard all complaints made about the group leader as unfounded and merely the result of a critical attitude of the transferees.

During December, 1937, the dissatisfaction with group leader Martin became increasingly pronounced. Complaints came, as before, from operators No. 11, No. 12, and No. 22. It was apparent, however, that these men were strongly supported by other workers who had entered the group from the small motors division. These men urged that the present group leader should be replaced by one of their subgroup of transferees from small motors. The most popular candidate was operator No. 33, a newcomer in Work Group No. 7, but well known to the older men who, like him, came from the small motors division.

From December, 1937, to March, 1938, complaints continued to be presented against group leader Martin. It was now specifically charged that he was incompetent and unable to perform the operations called for by his occupational classification. The foreman continued to ignore these complaints, insisting that the older men "had it in for the younger men."

Resort to Direct Action.—In May, 1938, the oppositional attitude against group leader Martin came to a head and expressed itself in direct action. When the complainants found early in May that they got no satisfaction and that the foreman persistently ignored their grievance, they put their heads together and engineered a "fall-down" (see chart on page 350) to call management's attention to their dissatisfaction. When the foreman investigated this situation, he found that an excessive amount of defective work could be traced to faulty layout for which group leader Martin was responsible. As a result of this finding, Martin was laid off, and operator No. 33 was appointed group leader in his stead. This man was an exceptionally able worker who had the complete confidence of the group.

QUESTIONS

1. *On symptoms of group instability*
   What indications are given during the first two phases that Work Group No. 7 was not a unified work team effectively promoting company purpose?
2. *On supervisory responsibility*
   a. Why do you agree or disagree with the foreman's action on the complaint made in October, 1937?
   b. What action could the foreman have taken at this time to promote group equilibrium despite unavoidable difficulties resulting from excessive personnel mobility?
3. *On employee complaints*
   Can you suggest any reason why the complaint should shift from an allegation that Martin did not spend enough time on productive work to a charge that he was incompetent? (*Cf.* pages 353 and 354; see also Chap. 9, Complaints and Grievances)

QUESTIONS ON THE CASE AS A WHOLE

1. *On employment policy*
   Comment on the superintendent's employment policy.
   a. In view of the company's commitment to plant-wide seniority and in the face of impending layoffs, what difficulties should he have foreseen?
   b. What other policy might he more wisely have adopted?
2. *On factors making for stability or disunity*
   Taking the case as a whole, what features in the history of Work Group No. 7 tended to promote stability? What features made for disunity?
3. *On the nature of groups*
   Contrast the various meanings in which Work Group No. 7 is used. What advantages and disadvantages attach to the use of the term "group" in these different ways?
4. *On layoff policy and measures for building work teams*
   Using the experience of Work Group No. 7 as a typical example, what recommendations could a personnel administrator make when layoffs are to be administered?

Case for Chapter 9

A "Personal" Complaint

(George Poole and John Bowditch)[1]

INTRODUCTION

One of the most striking facts demonstrated in this case is the need for situational thinking. Unless the component elements in a complaint situation are sorted out and seen in their proper perspective, treatment can be of surface problems only. The underlying difficulties are actually obscured if, as in this case, the false impression is gained that the complaint has been successfully handled. The situation described below at first appears to consist only in a single complaint made by a shop steward about a worker (in itself a rather unusual situation). In the course of talk, however, it is revealed that there are a number of different causes for dissatisfaction felt by various people.

The need to sort out and to investigate these related difficulties, as well as to prepare the way for necessary readjustments, illustrates such other points as

1. That employee complaints may throw light on first-line supervision and on management policy as well as on the feelings of workers and on working conditions.
2. That complaints may become grievances against the union as well as against management.
3. That a complaint in which facts and sentiments are intermingled is especially difficult to verify and to handle.
4. That complaints may offer an opportunity for a gain in understanding both by people directly involved and by others who are concerned with the same general principles or affected by the same general kind of difficulty.

These various features of a complaint situation, and the kind of

[1] For an analysis of this case from a different point of view, see PAUL PIGORS and ALFRED D. SHEFFIELD, *The Foreman and Friction among His Men* (The Case of Inspector Bowditch), pp. 1–12, Addison-Wesley Press, Inc., Cambridge, Mass., 1944.

understanding called for, are brought out in three phases of a conference attended by the following people:

Persons directly concerned:

JAMES AVERY, personnel director.

DAVID SIMPSON, foreman of inspection department.

JOHN BOWDITCH, inspector (by transfer).

GEORGE POOLE, shop steward, inspection department.

CASE BACKGROUND

In the fall of 1937, the National Manufacturing Company moved its small motors division to Plant No. 11 in Cleveland. This laid a great burden on its employment department in Plant No. 10 to make new placements for employees thus thrown out of work. The employment manager, however, took seriously the plant policy of making "replacement transfers" whereby employees of longer service escaped layoff by being placed on jobs in other departments.[1] With the cooperation of foremen in all divisions of the plant, he was thus able to transfer most of the workers who had seniority of at least 3 years.

Among the men thus kept at work was John Bowditch, who had had 6 years as operator of a Jones and Lamson chucking machine—a skilled job. He was transferred to inspector work; and, since this put him into a staff department, he liked the prestige of his new position and was anxious to "make good" in the technical and clerical tasks that it presented. Unfortunately, this proved difficult—as will appear in the dialogue that follows.

One unusual feature of the situation was that the inspectors, as well as the production workers, were members of the union. Ordinarily, an inspection department would not be unionized, since staff technicians seem too closely identified with the interests and point of view of management.

In Plant No. 10, however, each department and hourly rated occu-

---

[1] Chiefly as a result of the Larkin case (see Case for Chap. 4), management had formulated the following policy:

The workers who were displaced by the transfer of the small motors division were to be grouped and treated as follows:

A. Employees having service of 10 years or more (292) were to be transferred to positions in other divisions and as far as possible placed on jobs that guaranteed weekly earnings comparable with those received in the small motors division.

B. Employees having less than 10 years but more than 3 years of service (534) were to be placed on service-work and day-work occupations. This meant that their weekly earnings were slightly reduced.

C. Employees with less than 3 years of service (214) were to be laid off.

pation was represented by an industrial union (an affiliate of the United Electrical and Radio Workers of America, CIO).

I. The Appeal

On Dec. 16, 1937, at 2:30 P.M.,[1] Poole came to the industrial relations office with a formal complaint card and asked the secretary whether he could talk to Mr. Avery. The secretary arranged an immediate interview.

1 POOLE: Mr. Avery, I've a complaint to make. I think we ought to get Mr. Simpson over here.

AVERY: Wait a minute, Mr. Poole, let's see first what the complaint is. Maybe Mr. Simpson ought to handle it out there.

5 POOLE: Well, here's the story. We have a fellow there that makes a lot of mistakes—bad ones, too, in the count of material. As a matter of fact, groups have complained that they were short in their pay all because they didn't get credit for work they had performed. I've talked this over with Mr. Simpson several times, and we've agreed that the man is not fit

10 for this type of work. He came to us on a transfer and really isn't an inspector anyway.

AVERY: Well, just as I thought, Simpson can handle that. If the man is not fit to do the job, the foreman should send him back to the employment department.

15 POOLE: I know all that, but this fellow got personal.

AVERY: What do you mean "personal"? If it is just a private matter between you and him, I'm not interested in mixing up in any personal fights.

POOLE: Well, it isn't personal in that sense. The fellow came to me and wanted to know whether I was for him or against him. He said it was my duty

20 as representative to back him up. I asked him if he belonged to the union. He said, "Sure." As a matter of fact, he hasn't paid any dues for 7 months, and this automatically drops him from the union. Not that it makes any difference to me, you understand. If he was in the right, I would have backed him up, and if he's wrong, I wouldn't. So, knowing that he

25 couldn't handle the job, I told him I couldn't do anything for him. Then this fellow folded his hands (*illustrates by clasping his hands*) and said, "Well, you wouldn't do anything for me anyway because you and the foreman are just like this." Now, I don't think a fellow ought to be allowed to talk that way, accusing me and the foreman of being in collusion. I think

30 he ought to be dropped from the department for behaving like that, or at least he ought to apologize.

AVERY: Well, Poole, I don't see why I should get mixed up in any dog-fights. I still think this matter should be settled between you and the fellows and the foreman right in the shop.

---

[1] The hour indicates that Poole came soon after his outburst in the foreman's office, mentioned on page 362 (line 20).

35 POOLE: But Simpson won't do anything about it. He says this is personal and has nothing to do with production. Wouldn't it be a good thing to get him over here?

AVERY: No. I'll tell you what I'll do, though. I'll call Simpson on the phone and ask him why he can't settle this matter out there. It's part of his job,
40 and he ought to attend to it. (*calls Simpson on the telephone*) This is Jim . . . Avery, industrial relations. Say, I have one of your men up here. I guess you know what it is all about. Why can't you settle this affair out there?

SIMPSON (*over the telephone*): Well, we have. But this matter with the shop steward is personal, and I think it ought to be settled over in your office.
45 I'd like to come over and bring this fellow, Bowditch, with me.

AVERY: Well, all right. If you want to, come right over.

QUESTIONS ON THE "APPEAL"

1. *On complaint and grievance procedure*
   a. What do Poole's opening remarks (lines 1 to 2) indicate as to his sense of his organizational position and of Avery's function?
   b. What do you suppose is Mr. Avery's purpose in making this suggestion? (line 4)
   c. Why do you agree or disagree with Avery's stand at this point? (lines 33 to 34)
2. *On types of complaint*
   a. According to the classification of types of complaint (Chap. 9, page 108), what kind of complaint is made by Poole about Bowditch? (lines 9 to 10) Give reasons why this sort of complaint can or cannot appropriately be made by a shop steward.
   b. What kind of complaint is being made here? (lines 15 to 31)
3. *On personnel relationships*
   a. What new light is thrown on the complaint situation by this last remark? (lines 10 to 11)
   b. What seem to be the two meanings of the word "personal"? (lines 15 to 19)
      (1) If Avery had been correct in interpreting Poole's use of this word, why would you, or would you not, share his opinion that such matters are none of his business?
4. *On union relations to a delinquent dues payer*
   a. If you had been in Avery's position, what mental notes would you have made when Poole made this statement about his attitude toward Bowditch as a union member? (lines 20 to 24)
   b. What seems to be Bowditch's grievance as quoted in Poole's speech? (lines 25 to 29)
   c. If Poole is reporting facts accurately (lines 28 to 29), would this be ground for discharging Bowditch?
   d. Would there be any conceivable reason for Poole to change the stand that he took at the beginning of the interview? Explain.
   e. Do you think Avery's answer (line 46) represents a change of mind on his part?

(1) Does it contradict what he says in line 38?

(2) What would be your comment on this technique of handling Poole and Simpson?

Summary Questions

If you were the personnel administrator, how would you, after the "appeal," analyze the complaint situation and your responsibilities to the people concerned?

A. Which of the two complaints made by Poole about Bowditch do you think most influences Poole's attitude?

B. If a personnel administrator takes part in such a situation, what sort of role should he play, and what could he usefully and appropriately do? Consider the fact that a responsibility to do something may mean

1. Taking decisive action oneself.

2. Helping the person who can appropriately act to see the full significance of the situation before making a decision.

3. Stimulating and directing "group thinking" between several persons who need to agree on appropriate action.

C. What, if anything, could be done at this point by situational thinking? Comment on the relevance, if any, of the points discussed in Chap. 4. Consider the complaint as

1. A quarrel between two people.

2. A difficulty between a worker and his union representative.

3. A difficulty arising out of a transfer from one status and occupation to another.

4. An adjustment problem involving group stability.

5. An opportunity to help a union representative in getting a better conception of (*a*) his own responsibilities, (*b*) the role of the personnel administrator, and (*c*) the appropriate relationship between line and staff officials.

II. The "Conference"

1   The foreman brought Inspector Bowditch into the personnel director's office. There was an exchange of greetings between Simpson and Avery and between Avery and Bowditch, but no communication among Simpson, Bowditch, and Poole. Bowditch seemed worried and
5   ill at ease. He kept shifting his weight from one foot to the other and twisting his cap in his hands. Poole stood with his back to Bowditch and facing Avery who was seated at his desk. Simpson was sitting next to Avery.

Simpson (*to Avery*): I thought you ought to know all sides of this story, so I
10   brought Bowditch with me. After I tell what I know, Mr. Poole can pick up from there.

We took Mr. Bowditch from the small motors knowing that he wasn't an inspector and that it was our job to try and make him one. He had 6 years of experience as a J. and L. operator and was entitled to some con-
15   sideration. He is an excellent machine man but keeps on making clerical mistakes. We have talked to him about this, but he didn't improve, and finally we decided that he wasn't the man for an inspector's job and that he ought to get back to the machine. So I went to the employment department and told Kendricks [employment manager] that he would have
20   to take him back. At the present time, we are merely keeping him on until the employment department finds a more suitable job for him. That's the story so far as I'm concerned. Mr. Poole can pick up from here.

AVERY: I've already heard Mr. Poole's story, but I haven't heard what Mr. Bowditch has to say.

25 BOWDITCH: Well, I suppose I did fly off the handle, but this whole change has kind of upset me. And after all, what was it that Mr. Poole said to me? I didn't get all of it, but it sounded like, "We can't be bothered with a bunch of . . . ." I didn't get the rest.

POOLE: Well, I don't recall saying anything like that. But Mr. Bowditch in-
30   sulted me, and I think he ought to apologize. He hasn't any business to talk to the fellows about me being in collusion with the foreman.

BOWDITCH: Who did I talk to?

POOLE: Well, I guess you didn't talk to anybody that I know of, but you told me to my face that the foreman and I were just like this, which makes
35   it even worse.

BOWDITCH: Well, I guess, I said a little more than I should have. I get excited easy.

POOLE: Well, you have no business to say these things. You are new in the department, and you don't even know me.

40 BOWDITCH: That's true. That was the first time I ever saw you.

POOLE: That's just it, and all the more reason why you shouldn't say such things. You don't know what you're talking about.

BOWDITCH: No, I admit I was in the wrong and I apologize.

POOLE: O.K. I'll accept the apology and am willing to forget what happened.
45   I guess that settles everything.

AVERY (to Simpson): That's that. But I still don't see why this couldn't have been settled out in the shop. There's no reason for coming here.

POOLE: Well, Simpson didn't want to take any action because this was a personal matter.

50 SIMPSON: I thought it best that Mr. Avery should know about this. But I think it's all settled now and we shouldn't take up any more of his time. (Poole and Bowditch leave the office)

QUESTIONS ON THE "CONFERENCE"

On employee attitudes

1. *a.* What reasons could you give for Bowditch's apparent nervousness at the beginning of the conference?

b. What is revealed (lines 25 to 28) about Poole, about Bowditch, and about the clash between them?

2. *On complaint and grievance procedure*

   a. Why would you approve or disapprove the foreman's action in bringing Bowditch to this conference?

      (1) What do you think was his motive in doing so?

   b. What has been "settled" at this point? (line 46)

      (1) Name the various factors that you think contributed to the settlement of the quarrel between Poole and Bowditch.

   c. Why do you agree or disagree with Avery's statements (lines 47 to 48)?

   d. What do you suppose that Simpson thinks has been accomplished during this conference? (line 52)

3. *On interpreting an employee complaint*

   What light is now thrown upon Poole's complaint that Bowditch is not fit to work as an inspector? (lines 12 to 22)

Summary Questions

1. *On underlying dissatisfactions*

   What issues remain unsettled and unexplored in this situation?

   a. Do you think similar occasions for friction are likely to arise again between the same or other parties? Give reasons for your opinion.

2. *On staff leadership in a complaint case*

   What was accomplished by Avery at the one point where he exercised the sort of leadership to be expected of a personnel administrator (by calling on Bowditch instead of Poole)?

3. *On complaint and grievance procedure*

   If you had been the personnel administrator, what would you have tried to accomplish in this conference? Consider the following points:

   a. Simpson and Poole want Avery to settle a quarrel.

   b. Avery might properly expect something more of them. What?

   c. What additional facts should have been brought out here?

III. The Interview

(Simpson starts to follow his men)

1   Avery: Just a minute, Simpson. Don't you think it would have been wise if you had handled this question in the shop, even if you do consider it personal? You could have handled it by suggesting to Bowditch that, though you didn't want to interfere with personal matters, you could not
5   allow this kind of friction in your department and so it would be well for him to apologize to Poole for the remark made.

    Simpson: I suppose so. But that little tiff was nothing. You know this fellow Bowditch isn't as bad as he's painted. I don't want to be too hard on him and see him lose his job. He has a wife and children and owns his
10   own home. After all, Poole knew we had no intention of keeping this fellow as an inspector. There's a note on Kendrick's [employment

manager] desk right know, reminding him to find a machine job for
Bowditch as soon as he can. I felt if I could only stall this thing along for
a while, everything would be all right. I'm sorry this came up.

15 AVERY: The whole thing is, if you don't settle these questions in your shop,
how can the men look to you as the natural person in authority? What did
Poole get here that he couldn't have got from you?

SIMPSON: Well, for one thing, he had cooled off quite a bit. You should have
seen how he carried on in the shop. He came to my office just before
20 2 o'clock, banged his fist on my desk, and demanded that Bowditch be
sent out of the department. I told him I wouldn't take action until I
knew what this was all about. Poole then told me that Bowditch had
insulted him and that he wasn't going to stand for it. He even brought a
witness along to testify to what Bowditch had said. I still refused to fire
25 Bowditch because it was understood that he would leave anyway as soon
as we find him another job. Poole then said, "If you refuse to do anything
about it, I'm going higher up." So I told him, "If that's the way you feel
about it, I'm going along." I called your office at that time, but you
weren't in. Poole hung around for a while and finally sent away the
30 fellow who was willing to come along as a witness on his own time.

You see, I thought the whole thing had really nothing to do with what
Bowditch had said. My opinion is the shop steward was riding Bowditch
because he hadn't paid his dues. This is what happened. Bowditch talked
to Poole and said, "As a union representative you ought to fight for me
35 rather than against me." Then Poole reminded him that he hadn't paid
his dues and so he didn't belong to the union any longer. After that
Bowditch took the stand that Poole should at least leave him alone. He was
able to handle his own grievance. It was at this point that Poole told him,
"Sure, I'll leave you alone. We can't be bothered with a bunch of . . .
40 (unprintable language)." Then, when Bowditch got mad, Poole told him,
"Why don't you . . . (unprintable language)." That's the whole story and
that's why I took the stand that this quarrel was personal and had nothing
to do with the shop.

AVERY: What sort of mistakes did Bowditch make in his work?

45 SIMPSON: Oh, mostly clerical. You see, inspectors have to have quite a varied
background. They must have good mechanical ability, but they also must
have good clerical ability. Bowditch is a crackerjack of a machine man,
but he gets rattled easy when it comes to clerical work. Several times he
credited one group with the work of another group. For instance, day
50 before yesterday, he credited group 130 with 40 hours of work when the
work had actually been performed by group 110. Mistakes like this happen
sometimes to other inspectors, especially around 2 o'clock when the inspector is in a hurry to finish all the work on hand.[1] But Bowditch

---

[1] As the shift ended, the men would crowd forward with their pay cards, on which
the inspector had to enter:
The number of pieces the operator had completed.

makes more mistakes than the others and doesn't seem to learn by ex-
55 perience. He keeps on making the same mistakes. Then there is another
trouble. There is no doubt that Bowditch had "crashed the gate." He
wasn't an inspector and came to us on a transfer while other inspectors
were still out of work.

AVERY: Yes, I suppose that was bad.

60 SIMPSON: Sure, it was. It placed Bowditch in a difficult position. The poor
fellow had one strike against him already.

AVERY: Say, I wonder if we could have avoided some of these difficulties if
we had given Bowditch one of our clerical tests before putting him on that
job. Would you mind if we gave him a test now, just to see how he would

65 come out?

SIMPSON: Not at all. Go right ahead. Only let me talk to Bowditch first so he
won't get worried.

Bowditch volunteered to come to the employment department and let one
of the interviewers administer a *clerical ability test*. He obtained the following

70 score:

Accuracy: Superior.

Speed: Average.

QUESTIONS ON THE INTERVIEW

1. *On staff and line relations*
   Why do you suppose that Avery chose this time to follow up this point?
2. *On supervisory responsibility for handling complaints*
   What comments would you make on Simpson's qualifications as a leader as
   revealed by his remarks made during this interview?
   a. "That little tiff was nothing."
   b. ". . . stall this thing along . . . ."
   c. (Poole, a worker) "banged his fist on my desk and demanded . . . ."
   d. "My opinion is the shop steward was riding Bowditch."
3. *On complaints and grievances*
   What was Bowditch's complaint and what was his grievance? (line 41) Consider
   his grounds for dissatisfaction.
   a. That the work group was prejudiced against him from the outset.
   b. That neither the shop steward nor the foreman did anything to protect him.
4. *On employment procedure*
   a. What do you think of Avery's suggestion? (lines 62 to 65) What about its
      timing?
   b. Comment on the foreman's reaction to this suggestion.

The number of pieces rejected (calling for added clerical notes on cause of defect).
The total to be approved in the pay-credit column.
Simpson mentioned an instance of what might happen. In checking up on one in-
spector, he found a card with the credit figure wrongly entered. The inspector said,
"Oh, I guess somebody talked to me while I was making out the card." Later, man-
agement took steps to ease the congestion at the end of the shift.

1. *On evaluating evidence*

What facts brought out during this interview suggest that there were extenuating circumstances in connection with Bowditch's errors, which should be considered on his behalf?

2. *On supervisory responsibility toward a newcomer*

In your judgment, what responsibility does a foreman have when his subordinates are prejudiced against a newcomer (as Simpson admits when he says, "The poor fellow had one strike against him already.")?

   a. If you think that a foreman has any responsibility at all in such a situation, what might he appropriately do? What sort of action would certainly be inappropriate and useless?

QUESTIONS ON THE CASE AS A WHOLE

1. *On dissatisfactions*

In view of all that you *now know* about the complaint situation, what causes for dissatisfaction seem to have existed, who felt them, and how should each have been handled?

2. *On complaint and grievance procedure*

Comment on the complaint procedure in this case as carried out by management and union representatives.

   a. To what extent does the procedure exemplify the features listed in Chap. 9, pages 111 to 112?

   b. In your opinion, does the behavior of the officials concerned indicate a need for training?

   c. Apply to this case the four test questions suggested in Chap. 9 as Criteria of Success in Handling Complaints and Grievances.

      (1) Was the case handled so as to bring out its full significance to the parties directly involved?

      (2) Was the incident closed with a sense of satisfactory adjustments in regard to the specific complaint?

      (3) Did the solution also provide for an advance of understanding by the persons directly involved, and perhaps also for a spread of understanding among people not immediately concerned?

      (4) Would the solution increase production?

3. *On conference technique*

If the meeting reported in Sec. II had been directed by Avery as a genuine conference, what might each participant have gained in understanding of his share in making a success of management's transfer policy?

   a. Consider the following potential benefits to workers of this policy:

      (1) That it retains good workmen who would otherwise be laid off.

      (2) That it respects seniority as a claim on stability of employment.

      (3) That it affords opportunities for retraining that give men versatility.

      (4) That it gives men new job openings.

   b. If these benefits are to be realized, what difficulties would normally have to be overcome by what kind of effort from what people?
4. *On interviewing technique*
   a. What reasons can you suggest why a personnel official may in this sort of case tend to use the interview method for handling it rather than the conference method?
   b. Even if the decision reached as to Bowditch would be the same, whether reached through interview or through conference, just what might Poole and Simpson gain from a conferring experience here that would result less well from interviewing? (Give the reasons, as lying in the different relationships in two kinds of contact between minds.)

Case for Chapter 10

Need for Effective Employment Policies and Procedures.

(Anton Kuczinsky)[1]

INTRODUCTION

The events described here and the possibilities that are revealed are typical of what used to happen in many companies. Policies for selection and placement were not carefully formulated, and the procedures needed to implement them were inadequate. There is no evidence of skillful interviewing, of any selection testing, of thoughtful placement, or of effective follow-up. Because of these weaknesses, the company failed to develop the latent abilities of an intelligent, ambitious, and loyal worker, who, in spite of certain idiosyncrasies and tensions, was potentially a valuable employee. One of the most depressing features is the amount of time, effort, and good will wasted on both sides through lack of situational thinking. What the result of skillful employment practices might have been in this case cannot, of course, be known. But certainly they would have represented a gain over what did happen.

I. BACKGROUND AND EARLY JOB HISTORY

Anton Kuczinsky, born June 25, 1905, in Warsaw, Poland, was the youngest of five children. In 1910, his parents came to America and settled their family in Chicopee Falls, in the heart of a Polish community. Anton successfully passed through the local public schools, completing

[1] As an illustration of problems and opportunities discussed in the text, we have divided this case into two parts, Part II being used in connection with Chap. 19. In both parts of the case, our understanding is limited by the absence of material that would be contained in a full employment record. Tantalizing though this is, it is useful because it vividly illustrates the value of adequate record keeping.

Part II gives the end of the story begun here. The social waste entailed in an accumulation of opportunities missed by all concerned could, in part, have been avoided by an effective personnel program initiated at the outset of this factory worker's connection with the company.

in 1918 the eighth grade of grammar school. He was eager to pursue his education and, encouraged by his father, entered high school, but at the beginning of his second year his father died. In 1920, his mother married again so that, in accordance with Polish tradition, there should be a man at the head of the family. This effort to reestablish normal home life was not so successful as she had hoped. Friction developed. The stepfather was particularly critical of Anton and insisted that he should go to work. The mother completely subordinated herself to her husband. Anton's only confidante at this period was his teacher, to whom he confided that he was lonely and unhappy. "No one cares whether I live or die."

At the age of sixteen, Anton left school and found his first job with the National Manufacturing Company (Nov. 21, 1921) as a material handler. He worked in Department A–42 of the small motors division and earned 25 cents an hour, base pay. In the next 18 months, Anton made steady progress, and his earnings increased as follows:

> Aug. 21, 1922, rerate........... 28 cents (standard time)[1]
> Nov. 6, 1922, rerate........... 30 cents
> Jan. 22, 1923, rerate........... 35 cents

On May 7, 1923, he left the company with a notice, giving as his reason for wanting to leave that he was "dissatisfied." Within a week, however, he sought reemployment and on May 15 was rehired as a winder in Department A–49 of the small motor division. His hourly base rate was 34 cents.

After about 6 weeks (June 23), Anton again quit—with a notice, but giving no reason. On June 26, he was again rehired, this time as a bench hand in Department A–42 of the same division. His new hourly rate was 36 cents.

On July 11, 1923, foreman Matheson discharged Anton, giving the following reason: "This man has been warned about throwing material at people—which is dangerous and a great annoyance to other workers. But he will insist on doing it."

Under the heading, Remarks by Employment Department, employment manager Kendricks made the following notation: "Do not rehire this boy, as he had all the chances to make good and will not."

QUESTIONS FOR DISCUSSION

1. *On the forces affecting employee attitudes*
   To what factors in Anton's life situation might one attribute the major difficulties that prevented his making a good adjustment as a worker?

[1] The figures for hourly rates given throughout this case are *base rates* for "incentive earnings," which are higher than the rates might otherwise suggest.

2. *On placement*

In view of what might have been learned about Anton in an employment interview, what do you think of his first placement, for 18 months, as a material handler?

3. *On exit interviewing*

What gains might have accrued to Anton and to the company from a skillful exit interview at the time of his first quit?

4. *On rehiring*

What information might an employment manager try to give and to obtain, and what kind of understandings might he attempt to reach, when a former employee (in good standing) requests to be rehired for the first time?

5. *On supervisory training and shop discipline*

   a. In view of the disposition to "horseplay" common among young fellows, how should a foreman be prepared

      (1) To prevent this type of behavior?

      (2) To deal with it when it appears?

   b. If the foreman did not consider behavior like Anton's as ground for discharge, what other treatment would have been open to this official?

6. *On exit interviewing following a discharge*

   a. If you had been the employment manager, what might you have expected to gain by interviewing either Anton or his foreman on or after July 11, 1923?

   b. In such a case, do you think an interview with Anton would be easier before or after he left the company? Give reasons for your opinion.

II. Two More Placements and Two More Quits

A 4-year gap in Anton's employment record followed this discharge. On Aug. 17, 1927 (at the age of twenty two), he was rehired as a bench hand (hourly rate 36 cents) and went to work in Department D-50 of the feeder section. Employment manager Kendricks made the following notation on Anton's previous quit slip: "I am going to give this young man one more chance to make good, and I think he will." On Mar. 16, 1928, Anton informed his foreman, Mr. Poole, that he wished to leave the company's employ.

On May 2, he again applied for reemployment and was set to work in Department G-50 as a punch-press operator at 40 cents an hour. On Sept. 4, he quit again—this time without a notice. Two months later (Nov. 8) he applied for reemployment and went back to work in Department G-50 on the third (or night) shift as a punch-press operator at 45 cents an hour. After 3 months, however, his new foreman, Mr. Davis, discharged him, making out the following quit slip: "Services of Anton Kuczinsky not desired after Feb. 5, 1929. Reasons: Not satisfactory. Too much sleeping."

Anton thereupon asked his old foreman, Mr. Poole, to intercede. The latter's efforts were successful, and Mr. Kendricks penciled the following note on Anton's quit slip: "Mr. Poole sent this young man to the office and says he thinks 'this young man has learned a lesson.' O. K. to rehire."

Nevertheless, for the time being, Anton was not offered any opportunity for employment with the company. There is a gap of $4\frac{1}{2}$ years in his record. During this time, he worked in other concerns.

QUESTIONS FOR DISCUSSION

1. *On employment policy and practice*
   a. (Anton's reemployment on Aug. 17, 1927) Would you necessarily disapprove of this reversal by the employment manager of his former decision? (Give your reasons.)
   b. What techniques might have been practiced and what understandings reached that would justify giving such an employee another chance?
   c. What sort of information should have been secured and recorded when an employee returns after four years away from the company?
2. *On employee attitudes*
   a. What significant sign is given on Sept. 4, 1928, of a deterioration in Anton's attitude toward the company?
   b. In Mr. Kendrick's place, what would you have attempted to do about this on or before Nov. 8, and what would you have said to Anton when he again asked to be rehired?
3. *On a shift problem*
   a. Is "too much sleeping on the night shift" a typical or unique kind of problem?
   b. What do you know about Anton that might aggravate this tendency?
   c. If you had been the night-shift foreman, what would you have done before discharging an employee for this offense?
4. *On responsibility for remedial effort*
   a. When a foreman takes enough interest in an employee of uncertain worth to intercede for him,
      (1) How can management use this interest for the employee's fuller benefit?
      (2) What opportunity does it open for staff and line cooperation?

SUMMARY QUESTIONS

1. *On rehiring and wage administration*
   a. What is revealed about the company's rehiring policy by the various wage rates received by Anton on the different occasions when he was rehired?
   b. In view of the natural tendency in certain employees to shop around, what wage policy would you recommend for rehiring this type of employee?
2. *On employment policies*
   In what ways might the company desirably have helped an employee like Anton with the following typical needs:

    a. Assessment of his mechanical ability and aptitudes.

    b. Vocational guidance and training.

    c. Orientation in the company through understanding of his place in the group, of company policies, and of sound organizational procedures.

    d. Periodic follow-up to inform him of his standing, both technical and human?

3. *On opportunities for teamwork*

    a. Who else, besides staff and line officials, might have helped Anton to develop a sense of belonging to the organization?

    b. In what way might this have been done?

4. *On situational thinking*

How could the various kinds of situational thinking usefully have been applied to this case?

The Old-Line Foreman

INTRODUCTION

The following case illustrates a foreman's need for training both as a subordinate in the company organization and as a management representative dealing with the union organization. As a subordinate, he should have a sound understanding of organizational procedure. But management cannot reasonably expect that this "organization sense" will develop spontaneously in each official. And the independent type of person often selected as management representative is especially apt to need training along these lines. No less essential for the first-line supervisor's success is the capacity to understand, administer, and explain company policies. Training for this proves an especially good investment when a foreman deals with the union in connection with complaints.

The episode and meeting reported here illustrate the kinds of problem that inevitably develop when a foreman's training in organizational procedure, in policy thinking, and in the personnel point of view has been neglected. In this case, the foreman was brought in as an expert from an outside firm, and higher management apparently forgot that technical competence alone is not enough to ensure a man's success as leader and follower in a new organization. Unsound practices and attitudes were here allowed to develop and to persist until a management-union clash resulted.

In the situation that arose, it is easy for an outsider looking back to see how major responsibilities could have been more adequately met by

1. Higher management.
2. A first-line supervisor.
3. A personnel administrator.
4. Various union officials.

CASE BACKGROUND

Until 1932, Plant No. 10 of the National Manufacturing Company had purchased from a nonunionized outside supplier all aluminum die castings for its home appliances. In that year, however, the production of food mixers and vacuum cleaners increased to such an extent that management decided to manufacture these parts in its own plant. As it happened, the outside supplier was ready to retire from business at about that time. He therefore proposed that the National Manufacturing Company should take over his foreman, Mr. Halsey, and several of his skilled operators. This seemed convenient for the management of Plant No. 10 which had no supervisor or operators specially trained for a die-casting department.

The organization of the new department was as shown in Fig. 1.

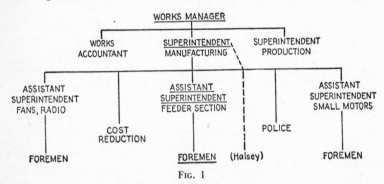

FIG. 1

Mr. Morse, superintendent of manufacturing, was put in charge. Since he had no practical experience with die-casting, he delegated to the foreman, Mr. Halsey, full authority to set up his own organization. This meant that Mr. Halsey was empowered to hire his own people, buy his own machinery, and in every way assume full charge of the new department in order to set it up on a going production basis. Whenever he felt in need of advice, he was to report directly to the superintendent.

Mr. Halsey proved to be a die caster of unquestioned ability and a man of independent character. The latter attribute would immediately have created problems in a department more closely allied to the main organization than his own. As it was, the practical convenience to higher management representatives of having a man in the new department who could "go it alone" blinded their eyes to the human problems that were bound to develop from his methods and attitudes. Mr. Halsey showed no great respect for such of the company rules as interfered with his convenience. For example, he smoked when and where he chose and left the plant whenever he wished. There was evidence that he was somewhat fond of alcohol, which influenced his behavior but not his competence. His previous experience in handling foundry workers, who are on the whole a "rough bunch," had developed his tendency to use coarse language and harsh methods. In the similar setting of the die-casting department, his firm hand and technical ability enabled him to get results. Therefore, he was never reprimanded. And apparently he received no instruction in company policies toward the union.

In the spring of 1934, local management changed hands, and the plant was reorganized. The position of superintendent in charge of manufacturing was abolished, giving place to five divisional superintendents, one for each line of product. Under the divisional superintendents, there were general foremen. The foundry and die-casting departments, as well as the carpenter and pattern shop, were placed under one of these general foremen, Mr. Hermiston, who reported to Mr. Rankeillor, superintendent of the feeder division. Mr. Halsey was now one of the five foremen who reported to Mr. Hermiston. The resulting official organization was as displayed in Fig. 2.

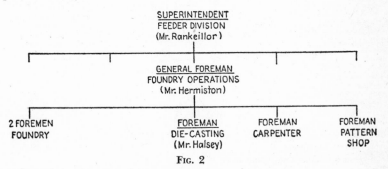

FIG. 2

Mr. Hermiston was of Scottish ancestry, thirty five years of age, deeply religious, and an ardent prohibitionist. His previous work history was of a clerical nature; he had been a cost clerk for the foundry before he was promoted to general foreman.

Mr. Halsey ignored his new supervisor and went about his business as before. Mr. Hermiston naturally objected to this but decided not to make an issue of the situation, hoping that Mr. Halsey could gradually be brought to cooperate. No one interviewed Mr. Halsey about the new organization, of which he was apprised only by a routine intraplant letter. In spite of Mr. Hermiston's efforts to overlook Mr. Halsey's independent behavior, the situation came to a head on Apr. 15, 1937, when the business agent of the local union presented a written complaint to Mr. Avery, the industrial relations supervisor, stating that foreman Halsey had refused to recognize the shop steward in his department.

THE MEETING

On Apr. 16, 1937, a meeting was held in Mr. Avery's office, the following men being present:

Union:

> Mr. Cameron, president of the union.
> Mr. Oviedo, business agent.
> Mr. Walker, die-casting cleaner and shop steward.

Management:

> Mr. Rankeillor, division superintendent.
> Mr. Hermiston, general foreman, foundry operations.
> Mr. Halsey, foreman, die-casting department.
> Mr. Avery, supervisor of industrial relations.

1   Avery: Gentlemen, I have called you together this morning for the purpose
of discussing a complaint. (*to the business agent*) Would you like to open
the meeting, Mr. Oviedo, or do you wish me to?

Cameron: I think you should read the complaint, Mr. Avery.

5   Avery: All right. (*reads*)

COMPLAINT REPORT

Name: John F. Walker	Department: F–10
Address: 654 South Street	Badge: No. 20
City: ——————	Home Phone: 6-5357

10 *Complaint:*

The above-named individual has been elected by his department employees as a shop steward. On Apr. 7, 1937, he went to Mr. Halsey, the
foreman, to ask him about increasing the ventilating equipment in the department, claiming that there was not enough ventilation for the machine
15 operators. He wanted to know if something couldn't be done about it. The
foreman, Mr. Halsey, would not accept Mr. Walker as a representative
of the union and, using abusive language, told him to go about his business.
We ask that a meeting be called in your office with Mr. Halsey and Mr.
Walker in order to clear up this situation.

20   (signed) Oviedo, *Business Agent*

Avery: Mr. Halsey, inasmuch as this complaint is against you, have you
anything to say?

Halsey: Plenty, this guy, Walker, here, doesn't realize that the gang is
kidding him. They haven't got anything to kick about. All this stuff he
25 is bringing up is old stuff. We've gone over it before with the other
representative. That representative was sick of the job and gave it up,
so the gang decided to elect this squirt because nobody else wanted
the job. This fellow doesn't know anything about the department.
He's only been there 3 months. He's only a kid and doesn't know
30 what it's all about. I haven't got time to rehash this all over again.[1]

---

[1] With due allowance for Mr. Halsey's informal style, the facts of the situation
were as stated here. Some of the older foundrymen had indulged in a rather crude

OVIEDO: It's *our* job to decide whether Mr. Walker is qualified to represent his people or not. They have elected him, and that's all there's to it. The reason that we called this meeting is to find out why you won't recognize him as a representative and deal with him as other
35   foremen in the plant deal with their representatives.

HALSEY: Well, he might be a representative to you, but as far as I'm concerned he don't represent . . . (indecent language). He's not qualified to talk about anything that happens in my department, and I haven't got time to waste on him. He brings up all this stuff and nonsense just
40   so he can be a big shot.

AVERY: I wonder, Mr. Halsey, whether you are acquainted with the setup in our whole plant. You know that each department has a shop steward. These employee representatives are privileged to take up complaints with our foremen. It seems to me that you would have used better judg-
45   ment if you had recognized Mr. Walker as the elected representative and discussed the problem with him. All you would have to do is to sit down with him for a few minutes and discuss any complaints he may bring to your attention. Furthermore, you could have advised him that you had gone over these matters with the former shop steward and that
50   they had been closed to the satisfaction of all concerned. You should have told Mr. Walker that we were not installing new ventilating equipment in the die-casting department because it is shortly to be moved into a new building where the latest and best equipment is to be installed. If you had told Mr. Walker those things, I am sure we should not be here
55   today.

WALKER: I didn't know anything about what the other shop steward had brought up and would have been satisfied if Mr. Halsey had at least talked to me decently.

HALSEY: Don't give me any of that stuff. Don't tell me that you don't know
60   nothing about what the other representative has done. You're not kidding me, Walker, you've been out there long enough to know that the ventilating problem was brought up before.

CAMERON: Mr. Avery, I don't believe we are getting anywhere. I think that you or Mr. Rankeillor should tell this fellow what he's got to do.
65 AVERY: Well, what d'you say, Mr. Halsey? Do you think we can work this all right in the future? Mr. Walker is the chosen representative of his fellow employees. Let's see if we can't pull together from now on. What d'you say?

HALSEY: All right.
70 AVERY: Let's give Mr. Halsey and Mr. Walker a chance to get together on this. If they can't reach a decision, we shall meet again. (to *Mr. Walker*)

---

sense of humor by getting Walker to complain to Halsey about a matter that they knew was no longer a live issue.

Do you now understand the ventilating situation, Mr. Walker?

WALKER: Yes, I do.

AVERY: If anything else comes up, will you take care of it with Mr. Walker,
75   Mr. Halsey?

HALSEY: Yes, I will.

QUESTIONS FOR DISCUSSION

1. *On higher management's responsibility toward a first-line supervisor*
   a. By what acts and omissions toward Mr. Halsey did higher management contribute to his failure?
   b. Management has special responsibilities toward a supervisor who has gone through situational developments as Mr. Halsey did. How might these responsibilities be discharged and by what company officials?

2. *On specific work settings as an element in problem situations*
   a. What influence on Mr. Halsey's language, attitude, and behavior would you attribute to his specific work setting in a foundry?
   b. How much understanding would you expect to find at the outset between two men, one of whom is at home in a foundry, while the other has a clerical work history?
   c. Would you say that adequate mutual understanding could or could not have been developed between people of such different work backgrounds? Discuss the problems involved, and indicate how Mr. Hermiston might have talked to Mr. Halsey in an effort to develop better understanding.

3. *On a foreman's competence*
   a. To what extent would Mr. Halsey's personal defects count as disqualifications for his position as foreman in an independent foundry or as a management representative in one section of a large modern manufacturing organization?
   b. What understanding had he been encouraged to form as to his status in the company?

4. *On union responsibility*
   a. Judging by Halsey's first answer to Mr. Avery's first question (lines 23 to 30) how well "briefed" does Walker seem to have been?
   b. What union officials have failed in meeting their responsibilities when an issue of this sort is made the subject of an official grievance? What responsibilities, and to whom, have not been met? (Consider the functioning of the complaint procedure and the dignity of a representative system.)
   c. Does the business agent adequately answer Halsey's challenge as to Walker's qualifications by saying, "They've elected him and that's all there is to it". (Give reasons for your opinion.)

5. *On the responsibilities of a personnel administrator*
   a. How might Mr. Avery have been more constructive in the situation
      (1) Before the official complaint was made?
      (2) After the complaint was registered and before the meeting?
      (3) During the meeting?

Consider the following points:

He allowed Mr. Hermiston and Mr. Rankeillor to remain silent throughout the meeting. What position in the matter does this, by implication, assign to them?

How appropriate are his concluding remarks? ("Let's give Mr. Halsey and Mr. Walker a chance to *get together on this*. If they can't *reach a decision*, we shall meet again.")

Has the group been dealing with a *disagreement* between the two men? If the failure of relationship between them continues, should it be dealt with by reconvening this group? Why or why not?

b. If you had been in Mr. Avery's position after the meeting, what more might you have attempted to do with and for

(1) Mr. Hermiston.

(2) Mr. Halsey.

(3) Mr. Cameron.

Case for Chapter 12

Learner Spinners

INTRODUCTION

The following case illustrates the kind of problem that can be met, in part, by induction and training. It also brings out the role of the personnel administrator (or training director) in helping supervisors and higher line management to solve production problems. Finally, it shows the relation of induction and training to other parts of a well-rounded personnel program.

CASE BACKGROUND

In February, 1943, the supervisor of the spinning room of the Beecroft Mills (manufacturers of cotton-textile products) told the vice-president in charge of manufacturing that he needed more learner spinners on the third shift. He said that he was losing spinners faster than new applicants were being sent to him and that, unless something was done, he would not be able to meet production schedules because he was already short of experienced spinners. The vice-president then asked the personnel administrator to look into the problem and give him a report on what should be done.

The personnel administrator first studied the departmental labor-turnover reports and then asked his assistant to make a special tabulation. He found that of 11 learner spinners hired between Dec. 1, 1942, and Feb. 19, 1943, only 3 remained. Furthermore, he learned from his employment interviewers that girls applying for work did not want to go into the spinning room as learners.

Next, the personnel administrator talked with the foreman of the spinning room and his assistants. Then he interviewed the union stewards and, individually, about 10 different spinners on the first and second shifts. These included younger girls who had started on the third shift as learner spinners, older women who had been spinning for some time, and girls who either were now working on bobbin machines (which removed the remaining yarn from used bobbins) or had learned to spin after starting on the bobbin machines.

THE REPORT

After these interviews, the personnel administrator again discussed the problem with the supervisor of the spinning room and then prepared his report for the vice-president. The following are the significant portions of this report:

1. Learning to spin is a difficult job initially for the average young girl, and the first several weeks are a particularly difficult time. A learner is apt to be discouraged easily if too many "ends (of yarn) go down" for one reason or another, and she is unable to "piece up" these ends as rapidly as she should. A certain amount of nervous tension is involved; and, when combined with a new job, night work, and the inevitable noise and dust of the spinning room, discouragement may lead to quitting the job. This is especially apt to happen under the present labor-market conditions, when the alternative to sticking to a job is no longer unemployment. If a girl feels she can get another job elsewhere, she is not so likely to put forth that extra effort to overcome the initial discouragements of learning to spin.

2. Teaching and supervising learner spinners on the third shift, therefore, require more patience than ever before. Mistakes must be pointed out carefully and corrected sympathetically. It is significant to note here that all the girls interviewed who had started on the third shift had been taught how to spin by one of their relatives. Some said that, if it had not been for the patience of these relatives and the encouragement given by them, they would have quit their jobs long ago.

3. If learner spinners say they are discouraged and want to quit, this should not be accepted as a fact, but instead a real effort should be made to discuss their work with them and to encourage them to "stick it out." If third-shift girls still want to quit, the foreman has asked that they remain until 7 A.M. so that he may also discuss their problems with them. [Note that this procedure fits very well into the "exit interview" program.]

4. When new learner spinners are first hired, they should be referred by the employment interviewer during the day to the spinning-room supervisor, before they report for work on the third shift at 11 P.M. This will give the supervisor an opportunity to explain the initial difficulties and discouragements that are likely to be involved in learning to spin. A "pep talk" of this sort should prepare the new girl for some of the difficulties she will first encounter on the job.

5. Frame assignments for learner spinners are increased faster than the girls feel they are able to handle them. There seems to be a tendency for the assistant foreman on the third shift to get out production at the expense of adequate training of learners. The common-sense observation here is: Ask the new girl whether she thinks she can do it, and give her every encouragement to try to handle more sides; but do not force her to take more than she thinks she can handle. Otherwise, discouragement will result, and production will suffer in the long run.

6. Physical conditions on all shifts should be made as attractive as possible, within the limitations of the nature of the work (noise and dust seem inevitable)

and governmental restrictions on new plumbing equipment. One thing that could be done, however, is to provide somewhat better dressing facilities in the various spinning rooms, similar to what is now available at the end of Mill No. 7. The young girls who are spinning seem to feel that they are unable to come to work in street dresses, since there is no place where they can conveniently change to a work dress, and after work, back to a street dress.

7. A final point concerns the initial wage differential between new learner spinners and girls on the bobbin machines. The latter job is clearly much less difficult, but the starting rate is 47.5 cents an hour. Within a few weeks a girl can earn the top rate of 51.9 cents an hour. The newly hired learner spinner, on the other hand, starts at the learner rate of 42.5 cents; and, although she goes up at least 2.5 cents every 2 weeks before reaching the piecework base rate of 55 cents, she continues for at least 6 weeks to earn less per hour than the bobbin-machine girl.

The reaction of some girls was: "Why try to learn to spin if you can make more on the bobbin machine?" Of course, in the long run, the spinners do make more money on piecework, but workers frequently think of the immediate future, especially when their friends emphasize the present differential. Furthermore, if a girl starts on the bobbin machine and later learns to spin, it is the practice in the department to guarantee her at least her hourly rate on the bobbin machine while she is learning to spin. Thus the newly hired learner spinner starts at a lower level, as compared with newly hired bobbin-machine girls and as compared with learner spinners who transfer from the bobbin machines.

It may not be practicable to revise the learner spinners' rates, especially if other learners are not similarly treated. However, one suggestion is this: In order to encourage learner spinners to "stick it out" and to pay them at least as much per hour as bobbin-machine girls if they do, it might be possible to make a retroactive payment of the difference upon completion of the learning period. In other words, a learner spinner might be told that, if she stayed on the job and really learned to spin, she would be paid a sort of "bonus" at the end of the learning period. This payment would amount to the difference between her actual hourly earnings during the first 7 or 8 weeks (when she earned less than the bobbin-machine girls) and the actual hourly earnings of the bobbin-machine girls during the same period. At most, this would not amount to more than $16 per girl, probably less; and, if it served to keep only a few girls from quitting, it might be worth while. It is only a suggestion, however, and not a recommendation.

QUESTIONS FOR DISCUSSION

1. *On training and induction*
   a. What were the "training" aspects of this problem? Was the personnel administrator successful in spotting training needs?
   b. Describe how a good induction program might have reduced the turnover of learner spinners.
   c. The personnel administrator did not recommend a definite training program for learner spinners. On the basis of his findings, what type of program,

if any, should he have suggested? (Relate your answer to the four points on page 165 of Chap. 12.)

d. Many of the points in the report deal with the *manner* in which learners should be taught, rather than with the actual content of the training program. Why do you think the personnel administrator stressed this aspect of training?

e. When the report was made, the supervisors in the mill had not yet been given the Job Instructor Training program. In what way would this have helped the spinning-room supervisor in solving his own problem?

f. Was better induction and training the answer to the supervisor's problem?

2. *On the personnel administrator's role*

Comment on the manner in which the personnel administrator investigated this problem, and on the value of this method of meeting a personnel problem.

3. *On personnel activities*

What other features of a good personnel program were involved in this case?

4. *On line responsibility*

If the vice-president agreed with the personnel administrator's report, what action should he have taken?

Case for Chapter 13

Factors in Promotion Policy
(Selection of a Head Lift-truck Operator)

INTRODUCTION

In unionized plants, it is difficult to settle the question: Shall seniority or ability be the governing factor in making promotions? Even when management does secure a contract clause providing for ability as the primary factor, there remain many problems of day-to-day administration. Some difficulties may be eliminated by careful wording of the policy statement or of the contract clause, but differing interpretations are still possible, as in the case here reported. Can management decide immediately which of several candidates is the most competent for a better job, or should it give the senior man an opportunity to show whether he can perform the new job capably?

Besides the main issue of defining and weighing seniority and ability, the difficulties described in this case also illustrate other points, such as

1. A need for employee rating and job evaluation.
2. A typical opportunity for preventing dissatisfaction and a need for improved policy thinking about a complaint before it develops into a grievance.
3. The unfortunate results of "horse trading" in a problem involving a policy issue.
4. The inefficiency resulting from poor coordination among line officials and from confusion as to the proper role of a staff expert.

CASE BACKGROUND

The company in which this case arose had an agreement with a CIO union that provided that

When an employee is promoted to higher skilled or higher paid jobs in the same department which have a functional relationship, the promotion shall be made upon the basis of seniority, provided the employee is qualified and competent to

382

fill the position. Competency shall be considered a large factor. When such promotions are made by management on grounds of qualification and competency to perform the work required, without regard to seniority, the union and the employee or employees with higher seniority than the employee promoted shall be entitled upon request to a statement of the reasons for disregarding seniority, and the matter shall be arbitrable.

Other relevant clauses were

Seniority shall be by job classifications, and shall be based upon length of continuous service in each job classification. Periods of layoff shall not interrupt continuous service.

An employee shall lose all seniority rights if he or she (a) quits or terminates his or her employment or (b) is discharged.

On Apr. 12, 1945, the Wister Corporation purchased two fork-lift trucks for use in loading and unloading materials and finished goods in its warehouse. This purchase was part of a program to improve material handling in which the company had the advice of a consulting traction engineer. When the trucks arrived, the plan was to use one on the ground level to unload boxes from freight cars onto pallets (wooden platforms into which the fork fitted for lifting) and then to move the pallets full of boxes to the elevator. On an upper floor, another fork-lift truck would be driven into the elevator to pick up the pallets and move them to a storage area where they could be piled for later use.

With these lift trucks, the men were able to handle materials more efficiently and quickly than by the former hand-trucking method. Several similar trucks were already in use in the warehouse and in other parts of the plant, and at least 12 men had operated these trucks at one time or another. At this time, there was no problem of labor displacement, because drafting of men for the armed services had made male labor extremely scarce. There was no opposition on the part of the warehousemen to the new trucks. In fact, they welcomed these mechanical aids that lightened their jobs. Most of the material handlers were anxious to have an opportunity to operate these trucks. The skill required to drive a lift truck was similar to that needed in operating an automobile, since it had a clutch, gear shift, accelerator, brake, and gasoline engine.

I. THE NEW JOB AND THE PROMOTION

When the new trucks were received, Samuel Soluka, the foreman of the warehouse, assigned one of his men, John Fortineau, to get them ready for operation. When the consulting engineer arrived to supervise the new system of handling, Fortineau and another warehouse employee,

Earl Chadwick, were asked by the foreman to operate the new trucks temporarily. Chadwick was a new employee and had to be shown how to operate this type of truck. Fortineau, however, had operated one of the trucks before and was quick to grasp the ideas of the consulting engineer and the additional instructions that were given.

The engineer was so favorably impressed by Fortineau's intelligence and ability that he requested the plant superintendent, James Allerdice, to assign Fortineau to the special job of head lift-truck operator. This job was created at the request of the consulting engineer. He felt that, in his absence, it was necessary to have someone be responsible for seeing that the trucks were properly used. When promoted to this job, Fortineau received a pay raise of 5 cents an hour. He was expected to check on all points of the work, such as piling boxes straight on pallets, the number of pallets on hand, proper sizes of pallets, and care of the two new lift trucks.

At this time, no one except Fortineau and Chadwick was asked to operate the new trucks. And no one except Fortineau was given the opportunity to try out for the new job of head lift-truck operator. However, several other warehouse employees had considerable experience in operating such trucks. The relevant parts of the work histories of these various men were as follows:

1. John Fortineau (thirty-nine years old)
First employed in company (Dept. B).................. Mar. 2, 1925
Quit... May 9, 1925
Rehired, Dept. C.................................... Oct. 19, 1926
Quit... Jan. 15, 1927
Rehired in warehouse............................... June 29, 1933
Quit... Aug. 19, 1933
Rehired in warehouse............................... Feb. 21, 1934
 (Served as a general warehouse hand, trucking cartons and cases on the main floor for shipping. General all-round man; has been gang leader)
Quit to go into taxi business...................... Dec. 7, 1940
Rehired in warehouse............................... Mar. 12, 1942

2. Andrew Conté (thirty-three years old)
First employed in company (Dept. B).................. June 6, 1927
Discharged... June 30, 1927
Rehired in warehouse............................... July 19, 1933
Quit... Jan. 6, 1934
Rehired in warehouse............................... Feb. 20, 1934
Laid off temporarily because of slack work.......... Feb. 1, 1936
Recalled to work................................... Feb. 13, 1936
 (Served as general warehouse hand, and for last 4 years has marked location slips on cartons for shipment)

3. Edward Paradise (forty-two years old)

First employed in company, in warehouse............... **May 18, 1927**
(Served as general warehouse hand, and, after Fortineau
quit in 1940, he was made gang leader. Worked with
and supervised three men in loading and unloading
trucks, loading cars, and working on the shipping floor.
Also has done some labeling. Continuous service in the
warehouse since date of first employment)

On the seniority list, which was prepared by job classifications in
accordance with the union agreement, these three men and others appeared as follows:

Edward Paradise (gang leader)............................. Dec. 7, 1940
William Cassidy (general warehouse man).................... Aug. 15, 1944
Andrew Conté (location slip marker)....................... Feb. 8, 1941
John Fortineau (general warehouse hand).................... Mar. 12, 1942
Louis Watkins (general hand in yard)...................... Apr. 4, 1944
Thomas Coté (general hand in yard)........................ Mar. 26, 1945
Leo Lamb (machinery mover)................................ June 25, 1944
Arthur Dumont (machinery mover)........................... Nov. 9, 1944
Albert Teriault (helper on auto truck).................... Sept. 7, 1943
Kenneth Altman (helper on auto truck)..................... Oct. 27, 1944
Earl Chadwick (general warehouse hand).................... Jan. 10, 1945

QUESTIONS FOR DISCUSSION

1. *On administration of a promotion policy*
   a. Should the promotion policy apply to this case? Give your reasons.
   b. Assuming that the promotion policy as stated in the union agreement is
   applicable, what would have been the proper procedure to follow in selecting
   a man for the new job?
   c. Do you see any difficulties in determining which man has the greatest
   seniority?
   d. On the basis of the information presented up to this point, whom would
   you have selected, and why?
2. *On the role of a consultant*
   a. Comment on the activity of a consulting engineer in selecting an employee
   for advancement to a better job.
   b. What would you have done if you had been the consulting engineer?
3. *On the data necessary for decision making*
   What further information would management need to have before making a
   sound decision in such a case?
4. *On a foreman's duties and responsibilities*
   What implications for the foreman's status as a management representative has
   the episode described in Sec. I?

5. *On placement*
Consider the placement of Chadwick as temporary lift-truck operator, and give your reasons for or against the proposition that this was a satisfactory step for management to take.

II. The Grievance

1   On May 7, 1945, Mr. Evans, labor relations director of the Wister Company, received the following letter from the business agent of the union:

Dear Mr. Evans:
The following matter was brought up at a meeting held by employees
5   of the warehouse. The major complaint of all the workers is that they cannot see clearly why John Fortineau was given a job with a higher rate when he had very little seniority. There are workers with much more experience and greater seniority than he had, and yet they were not given the opportunity to go on as lift-truck operators. Not only was Fortineau
10 given a lift-truck operator's job, but he was also classified as head lift-truck operator.
The union is requesting that a conference be held for this particular matter, because of the fact that the workers are very much disturbed by this procedure. May I hear from you at your earliest convenience?
15   Very truly yours,
                (*signed*)   John B. Coté
                      Business Agent, Local No. 215

After a brief investigation of the case, Mr. Evans replied on May 11, 1945, as follows:

20 Dear Mr. Coté:
John Fortineau was appointed head lift-truck operator on the strength of his outstanding qualifications and demonstrated competency to perform the work required. The characteristics, aptitudes, and abilities of the available men were given due consideration at the time of this ap-
25 pointment. Fortineau was the unanimous choice of the management and the consulting engineer, Mr. Collins, who has been employed by the company to supervise the installation of the new lift trucks.
Management takes issue with your statement: "There are workers with much more experience. . . ." It is management's position that this was
30 a proper appointment substantiated by the facts.
                          Very truly yours,
                (*signed*)   A. D. Evans

This reply failed to satisfy the union business agent, who took the case to the vice-president of the company. On the advice of the labor-
35 relations director, the vice-president refused to reconsider the deci-

sion and agreed with the union to take the case to arbitration. At this point, the company attorney was called in to assist in preparing a brief to support the company's position. He asked for an opportunity to review the case with company officials who were familiar with the

40 facts. A meeting was arranged the next day in the office of the labor-relations director, with the following persons present:

D. K. Jackson, company attorney.

A. D. Evans, labor-relations director.

James Allerdice, superintendent.

45 Samuel Soluka, foreman of the warehouse.

The meeting opened with a statement by the company attorney:

Jackson: I asked for this meeting, gentlemen, because, if we are going to win this case at arbitration, we have to be absolutely sure of our facts and of our position. If we are weak, we'd better find it out now rather

50 than have the arbitrator tell us. Now, I have read the material that Mr. Evans gave me about the case, and some further questions have occurred to me. First, as between Fortineau, Conté, and Paradise, did their last jobs have any "functional relationship" to the new job that was created and to which Fortineau was promoted?

55 Evans (to Soluka): I guess you'd better answer these questions, Sam, because you know more about the specific facts of this case than anyone else.

Soluka: Well, the general warehouse work and experience in gang leading that Fortineau had was a help in this new job. Conté's job of marking

60 location slips has no relationship with this new job, though he has a good sense of general warehouse work. Paradise's job as a gang leader and his general warehouse experience was good, the same as Fortineau's.

Jackson (taking notes): All right, now what about the physical strength of these three men, their eyesight, quickness of operation of automo-

65 biles, and other specific evidence of qualifications?

Soluka: All three are strong men—they have to be to work in the warehouse. Fortineau has good eyesight and is an expert at handling automobiles because he had his own taxi for a while. He has a good appearance; he is neat and a quick thinker and talker. He is steady at

70 work. Conté has good eyesight and drives a 1½-ton truck around his farm. His appearance is good; he is fairly neat and a fairly quick thinker and good talker. He is a steady worker, too. Now Paradise is good, too. His eyesight is good. I don't know how he handles automobiles, but he drives his own. He is neat and has a good appearance,

75 maybe is not so quick a thinker, but he is a steady worker.

Jackson: Did these two fellows who might be considered eligible for the job have any opportunity to demonstrate their qualifications?

Soluka: No, because at the time I didn't know there was to be any new job out of it. As I told Mr. Evans, Fortineau did a fine job right away

80   of handling the fork-lift truck and grasped the ideas of the engineer,
     Mr. Collins, who was showing him what to do and the way he wanted it
     done. He showed an intelligence about the work that took the engineer's
     notice, and the engineer requested of Mr. Allerdice that John Fortineau
     be appointed to see that this work went along as he, the engineer, had
85   laid it out, during the times that he was not in town.

ALLERDICE: That's right. Mr. Collins thought that Fortineau would be just the
     man for this special job and asked me to make him sort of a special
     assistant to him. So we created a new job and called it head lift-truck
     operator. I agreed on Fortineau because he has always been a good
90   worker and has shown a real interest in his work and has made many
     constructive suggestions. His attitude is good too. He's not always
     complaining about something, and I don't think he gets along very
     well with the union steward in the warehouse, who is also the president
     of the union.

95   SOLUKA: Yes, about 2 months ago, my assistant foreman, Al Bandeau,
     asked Fortineau to put up cards showing carload lots and arrange
     the cases. There were about four cases not placed just right, and he
     asked another fellow to help him move them. The steward heard him
     and went over and told this other fellow he need not do anything
100 Fortineau told him, because Fortineau was no boss. He seems to have
     it in for Fortineau.

JACKSON: Well, we are treading on thin ice when we bring up things like
     this. But you think Fortineau is the best man?

SOLUKA: He was excellent for the job, and his capabilities have been proved.
105 He can converse intelligently with the engineer about the work and all
     in all is, I think, much better than anyone else in the warehouse that
     I might have got. We were not making a choice for this job at the time
     Fortineau was put onto this work, because, as I have said before, I
     didn't know any new job was in the making. But, if I had, I think that,
110 all things considered—capabilities and personalities—John Fortineau
     is the best man for the job.

JACKSON: Could either Conté or Paradise have handled it?

SOLUKA: Well, I guess they could have done it. Maybe Conté was entitled
     to more conscious consideration for the job than he got, because I think
115 well of him. He's younger than Fortineau, though. Recently, Paradise
     has felt aggrieved because he was not considered, and I'll have to
     admit he's a pretty good man. But I still think Fortineau is better.

JACKSON: Have these other two run lift trucks?

SOLUKA: Yes, both Paradise and Conté have run the first trucks that we
120 got before these new ones came.

JACKSON: Ordinarily, when there is an opening on a better job, how do
     you go about filling it?

SOLUKA: We look at seniority and capabilities.

JACKSON: Did you consider seniority here?

125   Soluka: No, because as I told you I didn't know there was going to be a
         new job at the time.
      Jackson: Does the new job involve any supervisory duties?
      Soluka: Yes, the man must have in mind the whole operation from the start
         in the freight car to the end where the boxes are piled up in the ware-
130   house.
      Jackson: Well, could we consider it a real supervisory job? Our position
         would be stronger if we could say that this case came under Paragraph
         D of the seniority clause of the union agreement. (Reading) "Promo-
         tions of employees to jobs outside the bargaining unit (for example,
135   to assistant foreman), shall be at the sole discretion of management,
         shall not be restricted in any way by seniority, and shall not be the sub-
         ject of a grievance, dispute, or arbitration hereunder." What about it?
      Evans: I'm afraid we couldn't claim that, could we, Jim?
      Allerdice: No, the job is not really a supervisory job. It's paid by the
140   hour, furthermore, and has been listed on the department job list as a
         nonsupervisory job.
      Evans: I think our strongest argument is that under the union agreement
         management has the right to consider competency as a large factor
         in making promotions. We are not bound to follow seniority alone.
145   Jackson: Well, that gives me about all the information I need. Frankly,
         this case isn't as strong as I thought it was at the beginning, but I'll
         see what I can do to work up something for the arbitrator. We have
         four other cases going to arbitration, and maybe we can win some
         of them.

QUESTIONS FOR DISCUSSION

1. *On interpretive analysis*
   a. On what evidence do you think the union business agent is basing his
      statement in line 7?
   b. What appears to be the union's interpretation of the promotion clause of
      the agreement?
   c. Evaluate Mr. Evans's letter in the light of the information presented in
      Sec. I of this case.
2. *On the role of a labor-relations director*
   a. Comment on Mr. Evans's position in the grievance procedure.
   b. Should Mr. Evans have taken a more active part in preparing the case for
      arbitration? If so, what should he have done?
3. *On evidence for decision making*
   a. What would be the implications of the two possible answers to Mr. Jack-
      son's question? (lines 52 to 54)
      (1) Which answer would support management's contention?
      (2) Which answer would support the union's position?
   b. Evaluate the evidence given by Foreman Soluka on the relative qualifi-
      cations of the three men. (lines 58 to 62 and 66 to 75) What other informa-
      tion would have been helpful in this case?

    (1) Which of the facts stated are relevant to this issue?

    (2) Which, if any, justify management's decision?

    (3) Which, if any, justify the union's contention?

  c. Why do you think Mr. Jackson rejected (lines 102 to 103) the evidence given (lines 86 to 101) by superintendent Allerdice and foreman Soluka? Do you or do you not agree that this is a valid objection?

  d. What is the importance of the information that is brought out so late in the discussion? (lines 112 to 117)

  e. Would you agree with Mr. Evans that the argument mentioned in lines 142 to 144 is the "strongest argument" management has in this case? Compare his statement with his earlier letter to the business agent (Sec. I).

  f. Do you share Mr. Jackson's feelings about this case (lines 145 to 147)? Why or why not?

4. *On administration of a promotion policy*

  a. Should Mr. Conté and Mr. Paradise have been given an opportunity to demonstrate their qualifications for the new job of head lift-truck operator? Why or why not?

  b. Comment on superintendent Allerdice's reasons (lines 86 to 94) for favoring Fortineau for the new job.

  c. In the light of the statements made in lines 121 to 128, what consideration, if any, should have been given to seniority in this case? What is the seniority of these three men?

5. *On promotion policy*

Do you or do you not think it is wise to include in the union agreement such a provision as that mentioned in lines 133 to 137? Give reasons.

6. *On top-management action on a grievance*

What would you recommend that top management should do at this point?

7. *On the foreman as a management representative*

Comment on the relative prominence given to the foreman:

  a. When the decision to promote Fortineau was made.

  b. During the subsequent meeting.

    (1) What effect is this sort of inconsistency likely to have in the long run on a foreman's prestige and on his loyalty to higher management?

    (2) How well does the foreman show up during the meeting? On what evidence do you base your opinion?

    (3) If the foreman had made the decision himself, what evidence is there that he might have decided differently, and what advantages did he have that the superintendent lacked?

III. The Informal Settlement prior to Arbitration

Arbitration of this case and four others was scheduled for July 25, 1945. Prior to the hearing, however, the president of the company arranged to meet with the regional director of the union in an effort to settle some of the cases. He also had a number of other matters he wanted to discuss with the representatives of the national union, and he thought this would be a good opportunity to "trade off" some of the weaker cases for others that were of greater concern to the company.

In preparation for this meeting, he asked the company attorney and the labor-relations director to give him a memorandum summarizing briefly the strong and weak points of each case from the company's standpoint. He also requested the attorney, the vice-president, the superintendent, and the labor-relations director to be present at the meeting. The union was represented by the regional director, another representative of the national union, and the local union business agent.

At this meeting, the president and the regional director agreed on a settlement of this case as well as on the other four that were in dispute. Three of them were settled in favor of the company, two in favor of the union. None was taken to arbitration. The memorandum of agreement contained the following paragraph:

In the head lift-truck operator case, it was agreed that Paradise be given a reasonable trial in the position. John Fortineau may be permitted to retain his present rate and is named as an assistant to a supervisor. His rate in this position is to be a "present incumbent" rate. It was agreed that this disposition of the case settles all questions relating to the head lift-truck operator.

Paradise was given a trial period on the new job, and he performed it to the satisfaction of the warehouse foreman. Fortineau's new position was "created" to save him (and management) the embarrassment of his return to a lower rated job. He continued, however, to be of real assistance to the foreman, relieving him of many minor details.

QUESTIONS FOR DISCUSSION

1. *On labor-relations policy*
   a. What do you think of the wisdom of the president's proposal to "trade off" some grievance cases against others?
   b. Was it wise to invite the superintendent and labor-relations director to this meeting?
2. *On decision making*
   In the light of previous information, subsequent developments, and policy requirements, do you think that the agreed upon settlement was the best possible solution of the case at this stage of developments? What weaknesses did it contain?

QUESTIONS ON THE CASE AS A WHOLE

1. *On promotion policy*
   a. Discuss the relative advantages and disadvantages of two types of promotion policy: (1) one in which seniority is reviewed first and the senior employee is given a trial period in which to demonstrate his ability, or (2) one in which

management considers ability first and makes its selection without a trial period. Under what conditions would the second type of policy be feasible?

b. Can you suggest any desirable improvements in the promotion policy as stated in this case?

2. *On related procedures*

In a case of this sort, how can "competency to do the job" be established clearly enough to convince the union, the other employees, and, if necessary, an arbitrator that management's selection is right?

3. *On labor-relations policy*

As a general policy, would you advise that management discuss a proposed promotion and the reasons for it with a union steward or business agent *before* the promotion is actually made? Why or why not?

4. *On responsibility for executive action and/or policy thinking*

In view of the promotion policy as stated in the union agreement, how would you have handled this case if you had been (*a*) the warehouse foreman, (*b*) the superintendent, or (*c*) the labor-relations director?

Difficulties in Rating Employees

(Pierre Renault)

INTRODUCTION

The following case illustrates various weaknesses of informal employee evaluation and shows the need for a sound rating system as a meeting ground for management representatives, union leaders, and workers. Without such a system, the foreman here presented had to shift his ground for criticism of a worker and finally to reverse his announced decision to lay the man off. If this decision had been based on valid and relevant facts, which had previously been discussed with the worker, the foreman would not have found himself in such an awkward predicament.

During the hearing, "talk that gets somewhere" is impeded by the lack of previous performance records, of verifiable data, and of regular follow-up interviews that would have kept the employee posted as to his standing. In the course of discussion, flaws in techniques are revealed on both sides—in management policy and administration and in union policy and technique. Unfortunately, such weaknesses are not unique but are typical of management and union representatives in many companies, large and small.

Subsidiary points illustrated in this case are the opportunities offered and techniques needed in a complaint case, at the first and second levels.

CASE BACKGROUND

Pierre Renault was forty-two years of age and a skilled mechanic. Since 1926, he had worked as wireman on radio panels at one of the National Manufacturing Company's subsidiaries and on Jan. 6, 1936, was transferred to the local plant to work on test equipment. He was a member of the United Electrical and Radio Workers of America, CIO, and the next year he was elected department representative.

Work in the test-equipment department was of a highly skilled and technical nature. Mr. Carter, the foreman of test equipment, was an outstanding technician and spent most of his time on the design and installation of apparatus and fixtures used for testing. Employees regarded him as somewhat of a genius at invention, and it was considered a privilege to be associated with him. But, since his work required frequent contacts with factory supervisors and many conferences with development engineers, Mr. Carter spent much of his time outside the department.

Mr. Carmichael, Carter's young assistant, was actually the working foreman, supervising the employees, distributing work assignments, and so on. He had graduated with honors from a well-known technical school and was exacting in his requirements. He found it hard to get along with employees and prior to his appointment as assistant foreman had worked in the department as instrument construction and repair man. He did not go out of the plant during the strike, and it was generally known that he hated to deal with the union.

On Sept. 17, 1937, Pierre Renault's name was put on the layoff list. He filed a complaint with the union, charging discrimination and stressing the fact that a man named Parkman, doing similar work, had only 4 years' service and was still being employed. Mr. Cameron, president of the union, forwarded the complaint to the personnel administrator and requested a hearing.

The Meeting

A meeting was arranged for Sept. 21, at which the following people were present:

Joseph Carter, foreman.

George Carmichael, assistant foreman.

Mark Cameron, president of the union.

Pierre Renault, test-equipment construction work.

James Avery, supervisor of industrial relations.

1   Cameron: I think I'll open the meeting, since I asked for it to be called. Mr. Renault here has 11 years' service and is being laid off. What I want to know is why he should be the one to go when Parkman, who is doing the same kind of work, has only 4 years and 8 months. I suspect
5   that Renault has been laid off because he is a union representative.

Carter: Nothing of the kind. Renault's layoff is due to lack of work in the department. There's been no discrimination. The story simply is this: productive labor has dropped considerably, our department is a part of overhead, and we can't afford to be top-heavy. Renault is one of five
10   others who are being laid off.

Cameron: That's beside the point. I know that. I want to know why Mr. Renault's service isn't considered. He has 11 years, and we know there are other fellows in the department who have only 4 years. I understand

that Mr. Carmichael says Renault isn't as good a worker as the other
15   fellow. We want him to prove it.

CARTER: As far as I'm concerned, seniority doesn't enter into the picture.
I must run my department as efficiently as possible. Mr. Renault has
been a good worker for us, but he is limited. He isn't versatile enough
to do any kind of a job that has to be done. He lacks analytical ability,
20   which is most important in our work. My department is dropping down,
and I must keep only versatile men who can do a variety of jobs thoroughly and quickly. I had to let Renault go, because Parkman is a better
trained man and can do a better job. He's only thirty years old, but his
training at the Bliss Electrical School makes him particularly valuable.
25   He can follow a job through 100 per cent and has done so every time.
Renault, on the other hand, can't follow drawings any too well, and it
takes him 3 hours to do a job that Parkman can do in 1. I don't say that
he is loafing intentionally, but his mind just doesn't seem to work as
fast as Parkman's. Besides, Renault's not as careful as he might be. When
30   he does finish a job, there are apt to be "bugs" in it.

CAMERON: Well, it seems kind o' funny you have to bunch up all these
criticisms at this time when we have a layoff. Why hasn't Renault been
told of this before?

CARTER: While the department was running well, I saw no reason why I
35   should complain. I was satisfied to keep him on in spite of his deficiencies.
So long as we had plenty of work to select from, I could make good use
of him. But I can't pick and choose a man's work now. He just has to
be able to do anything that comes along. That's why I kept Parkman.
He has the analytical ability that is needed to diagnose trouble quickly.
40   In fact, this young fellow has come along so well that he can do a better
job diagnosing trouble than I can.

CAMERON: You've got to be more specific if you want to talk to us. The
works manager said himself that seniority counts if a man can do
the work. We believe that Renault can do his job, and we insist that he
45   be kept. There's more behind this than you know, Mr. Carter. We've
been watching your department for a long while.

RENAULT (to Carter): When did I ever fall down on any job?

CARTER: I wouldn't say exactly that you fell down on any job. You're all
right if you have all the time in the world and aren't given work that
50   requires analytical ability. All I know is that, the last time you made a
test fixture for the refrigeration department, we were criticized because
the cost was twice as high as on a similar fixture that Parkman made.

RENAULT: Well, nobody ever said anything to me about that. I've always
55   worked faithfully and have done what I was told to do. When I worked
at the other plants as a wireman, I had to do more complicated work
than I have to do here. And no one had any fault to find. As a matter of
fact, it was Parkman who got fired because he couldn't make the grade.

CARMICHAEL: Oh, I know all about that. Parkman just couldn't get along
60   with the foreman down there. He's been all right here and has been
stepping right along. In my opinion, he is twice the man Renault is.

CAMERON: Oh, he is eh? Well, you needn't talk, Carmichael, we know you.
You've always bucked the union. We believe that Renault's in the right,
65   and we're going to fight for him to the limit.

AVERY: Now let's keep personalities out of this, Mark. Let's stick to the
issue. All we've got to find out is whether or not Renault can do the
work as well as Parkman.

CAMERON: That doesn't mean a thing. He's got seniority, and we stick to
70   that.

AVERY: Well, ability comes first. Seniority counts, provided a man has the
ability to do the work. You know that's the clause in the contract.

RENAULT: I claim that I can do all the work that is required.

CARTER: No one disputes your claim. You can do the work all right, but
75   you can't do it as well as Parkman. And I can't be expected to run my
department efficiently if I can't select the best men to do the job.

CAMERON: Well, this doesn't get us anywhere. If we can't settle the case
here, we're prepared to take it to top management.

AVERY: If you mean by that remark that a settlement not in your favor isn't
80   a settlement, you'd better take it to top management right now. My job
is to see that all the cards are on the table and that every man is treated
fairly. After all, it's up to Mr. Carter to decide whether or not he wants
to keep this man.

CAMERON: All we're interested in is the fact that Renault has 11 years
85   service and that he can do the work.

AVERY: True enough, but Renault's been with Carter only 2 years, and we
all know that the work he did before was not at all similar to ours. I can
only agree with Mr. Carter that a foreman's job is to run his department
90   efficiently, in a slack period as well as in a boom. Naturally, when his
work is dropping down, he's going to keep the ablest fellow.

CARTER: Well, I'll tell you what we'll do, gentlemen. I'd be willing to take
95   Renault back if he will buckle down to business, not kick every time he's
assigned some work, and just begin to realize that his ability means
something to him from the standpoint of keeping his job as well as
seniority. I don't want to get involved in a squabble, but Mr. Renault's
got to learn that 11 years of service with the company and membership
100   in a union do not guarantee him the opportunity to stall on the job.

AVERY: Well, how is that with you fellows?

CAMERON: That's O.K. with me.

RENAULT: Me, too.

AVERY: I'm willing to go along with this, too, provided Mr. Renault fully
105   understands what was said. (to Renault) And, Mr. Renault, that doesn't
mean the foreman is going to watch you like a hawk in an endeavor to
find an excuse to fire you. Neither do we expect you to go back to the

department with an "I-told-you-so-attitude." That's not going to help
the situation at all. All it means is that now you have an opportunity to
110   prove to these gentlemen what you can do.

QUESTIONS FOR DISCUSSION

1. *On employee rating* (lines 14 to 16)

By implication, what is the company policy for rating ability? Comment on
this policy.

2. *On a foreman's understanding of rating policy*

   a. Comment on Mr. Carter's statement. (lines 16 to 17)

   b. What are the four criticisms he makes to justify his layoff of Renault? (lines
17 to 30)

   c. Discuss the relevancy of these judgments.

3. *On follow-up for employee rating*

   a. Why do you think the union president is or is not justified in the criticism
he makes of the foreman? (lines 31 to 33)

   b. What do you think of the foreman's rebuttal? (lines 34 to 41)

4. *On the need for consistency between management representatives*

   a. Comment on the foreman's position when a union president can make a
remark such as that in line 43 about seniority. [Compare Carter's first
statement (line 16) with his shift of ground after line 48.]

   b. What evidence is given during the hearing that Cameron is correct or
mistaken in his understanding of management policy?

5. *On the need for consistent and verifiable statements*

   a. Compare the foreman's remark (lines 48 to 50) with his previous criticisms
of Renault.

      (1) Which former criticism seems now to be contradicted?

      (2) Which criticism is now omitted, implying that it does not really count?

   b. Comment on the foreman's phrase, "all the time in the world."

      (1) Why is this kind of remark peculiarly unfortunate when made by a
management representative in such a situation?

   c. Comment on the usefulness of the assistant foreman's contribution when he
says that Parkman is "twice the man Renault is." Could such a judgment
be verified?

6. *On employee understanding of management policy on ability*

Comment on the relevance of the various points made by Renault in his own
defense. (lines 54 to 58)

7. *On discussion leadership*

   a. How constructive are the directives (both positive and negative) given by
the personnel administrator? (lines 66 to 68)

   b. How clear is Avery's statement of policy? (lines 71 to 72) Note the subsequent evidence, if any, of increased understanding by the disputants.

   c. If you had been in Avery's position at this point, how would you have
attempted to lead the discussion? (Note the need for policy thinking, for
correcting undesirable attitudes in regard to past, present, and future

relationships, and for eliciting statements of a type that will enable the members to get somewhere in thinking together.)

8. *On statements affecting policy*
   a. Compare the judgment and statement (lines 74 to 76) with the criticism of Renault made in lines 28 to 29.
   b. If you had been in the union president's position, what conclusions would you have drawn by this time about the foreman's attitude and ability?

9. *On union policy in a complaint case*
   If you had been in Cameron's place at this point (lines 77 to 78), would you, or would you not
   a. Have reached the same conclusion?
   b. How and on what grounds would you have expressed it?
   c. Comment on Cameron's diagnosis of the conference and the expression of his decision.

10. *On staff responsibility in complaint procedure*
    a. Do you or do you not agree with Avery's position? (lines 79 to 83)
    b. What three policies does he here express?

11. *On the "settlement" of a complaint involving employee rating*
    Comment on the decision stated by the foreman in lines 94 to 100.
    a. How well does it reflect policy thinking?
    b. How consistent is it with the criticisms previously made of Renault? (Note the new criticism, lines 95 to 96.)
    c. What does it do to clarify the basic issue that will certainly recur in other cases of this sort?
    d. For which side is it a "victory"?

12. *On a personnel administrator's responsibility for policy thinking*
    In Mr. Avery's position, what would you have said after Mr. Carter's compromise solution?

QUESTIONS ON THE CASE AS A WHOLE

1. *On management policy*
   What difficulties inevitably arise when management policy on ability is of the type that seems to have been in existence here?

2. *On conflicts in interpretation of "ability"*
   How can you reconcile the conflict of interest implied in management's insistence on comparative ability as the key factor in employee rating and the union's insistence on the key factor being ability to meet agreed upon minimum requirements?

3. *On discussion leadership by a staff official*
   At what points during the hearing, and in what ways, could Mr. Avery have exercised a more effective leadership?
   a. Comment on the fact that he did not open the meeting or attempt to check Cameron's rudeness and assert his leadership at such points as lines 42 and 69, or clarify the points of disagreement or adequately explain how

management determined "relative" differences in "ability" or carry the talk through to a solution that resolved basic differences.

   b. At what two points before Foreman Carter offered his solution did Mr. Avery exercise authority, and with what results?

4. *On union attitude toward staff and line officials*

What seems to be Cameron's attitude toward Mr. Avery, Mr. Carter, and Mr. Carmichael?

   a. Which remarks point this up?

   b. To what extent, and for what reasons, do you think it is justified?

   c. In view of all the situational factors, how might a union president have handled this case differently to reach a more constructive solution?

5. *On supervisory responsibility for leadership*

What opportunities for helping an employee to improve his performance and understanding did Mr. Carter miss before and during the hearing?

   a. How would he have been helped by an adequate layoff policy and employee rating procedure?

Case for Chapter 14

When Should a Remedial Transfer Be Made?

(Elsie Varda)

INTRODUCTION

It is not always possible to say when a remedial transfer should be made. The decision must rest upon the facts of the particular case, brought to light by person-centered situational thinking, and within the framework of the company's transfer policy. Even then it is possible for management officials to disagree as to the right course. Some may emphasize the desirability of settling this particular case to the satisfaction of the employee chiefly concerned, whereas others may stress the "bad effect" that a proposed method of settlement may have on other employees. Since any solution is likely to be looked upon as a "precedent," a fair policy, consistently adhered to, is important.

I

In his mail one morning in May, 1945, the personnel administrator of the Beecroft Mills received the following letter from one of the business agents of the local CIO union:

Dear Mr. Merriam:

Elsie Varda, who is a burler (inspector and mender) in the mill, asked her foreman for a transfer from burling sheets to burling blankets on the same shift. She says burling sheets is too hard for her, and she has a doctor's statement to prove it. There is an opening on blanket burling, and she has seniority for the job, but her foreman refuses to transfer her. Can you look into this and let me know what the story is?

Sincerely yours,

(*signed*) James Costa
Business Agent, Local 217

The personnel administrator, believing that this was a routine request for information, telephoned the foreman of the department (Mr. Carson) and then wrote the business agent that the foreman sympathized with Miss Varda's problem but that he could not transfer her without "upsetting the whole department."

The personnel administrator thought no more about the matter until Miss Varda herself appeared at his office a few days later, at the end of her shift. The following conversation took place:

1   Miss Varda: I came here to find out whether you had an answer to my problem yet. Didn't the union write you about it?

   Mr. Merriam: Yes, but was I supposed to have an answer? I wrote the union—Mr. Costa—that the foreman sympathizes with your problem, but
5   that he doesn't feel he can do any more without upsetting the department.

   Miss Varda: Well, I did go to the union, but I didn't think they'd do much for me. I pay my 25 cents dues every week, and what do I get? All I want is a transfer to blanket burling. I'm not well. I have a lame back. The doctor says it's "sacroiliac" and I must not do the work I'm on.
10   Here is his statement. (*shows it to Mr. Merriam*)

   Mr. Merriam: Did you show this to the foreman and talk with him?

   Miss Varda: Yes, and I'm tired of talking with him about it. He has all kinds of reasons why I should stay where I am. Can't a person get any consideration around here? I'm not well, and nobody will do a thing
15   for me. (*sobs hysterically*)

   Mr. Merriam: Well, I'll talk to Mr. Carson [the foreman] and see what the story is. Maybe we can do something. You come back tomorrow afternoon at 3 o'clock, and I'll have an answer.

Questions

I

1. *On the nature of a complaint and grievance procedure*
   In what ways does Mr. Costa's letter meet, or fail to meet, the requirements of appropriate procedure in presenting a grievance?
2. *On handling an employee request*
   a. Why do you think that the personnel administrator assumed that Mr. Costa's letter was "just a routine request for information"?
   b. If you had been in his position and had received such a letter, how would you have gone about checking the key facts?
   c. What further information did the personnel administrator need?
   d. After getting the facts, what action might the personnel administrator have taken in addition to writing to Mr. Carson?
   e. What opportunities for improved understanding are offered by this "request?" Include in your answer

(1) Names or positions of the people who seem to be in need of understanding,

(2) The areas involved.

3. *On interview technique*
In what way might Mr. Merriam's interview techniques have been improved?
(Consider both the general objective of interviewing and the specific purpose
of this talk.)

4. *On a staff official's role*
Comment on Mr. Merriam's closing remark. (lines 17 to 18)

II

As soon as Miss Varda had left his office, the personnel administrator
called the foreman again on the telephone:

1   MERRIAM: Hello Carson, this is Merriam. Elsie Varda, one of your workers,
was just in my office, and she wants a transfer because of a lame back.
I talked with you about this a few days ago, and I thought we had it
settled then, but she still wants her transfer. Can't you handle it some
5   way?

CARSON: That's not the real reason she wants a transfer. Any doctor can
fill out a slip saying anything. The fact is she has been slipping on her
work, and we're tightening our standards on sheet burling. She has
to run a lot of her goods through twice because of rejections, and she
10   just wants to get onto blankets where we aren't so strict.

MERRIAM: Can't you put her on blankets anyhow? She has more seniority
than some of the other first-shift girls who are now on blankets.

CARSON: No, that would upset the whole room, as I told you before. We
usually fill first-shift openings on sheet burling from among sheet burlers
15   on the second shift and first-shift openings on blanket burling from among
the blanket burlers on the second shift.

MERRIAM: But this girl is listed under "burlers" on the seniority list we gave
the union, and she has 10 years' continuous service. There was no distinction among types of burlers on that list.

20 CARSON: I know. We didn't want to have too many separate seniority classifications. But we've always done it differently on burling, and I don't
see any reason for making a special exception in this case. If we do,
then every time a sheet burler gets tired of her job, she'll want to change,
and she'll be entitled to do it. Now they have to stick where they are.
25   It just wouldn't work. She understands this. I told her all about it several days ago. She's just trying to see how much she can get from you
and from the union after she got a "no" from me.

MERRIAM: Well, I was impressed with the story of her lame back. I asked
our nurse here about "sacroiliac," and she says it can be very painful.

30 CARSON: But it would be just as painful on blanket burling. She'd have to
lift more rolls of cloth. Anyhow, I offered to give her a blanket job on

the second shift, if she wanted it. Why don't you tell her *that* when you see her again, and tell her that we'll give her a leave of absence from her first-shift sheeting job so that, if she wants to come back to it after
35   a few months, she won't lose her seniority by going on blankets.

MERRIAM: All right, and suppose she wants another job in another department where she can sit down more?

CARSON: That's O. K. by me. I'll give her a release. She isn't such a good worker anyhow.

The personnel administrator then checked with the employment department and learned that there was a "sitting down" job in another department to which the girl might be transferred. He was prepared to tell her this the next afternoon, but she did not show up at the specified time.

QUESTIONS

1. *On staff and line relationships*
   What are the implications of Merriam's question? (lines 4 to 5)
2. *On supervisory responsibility in a complaint case*
   What do you think of Carson's suggested solution? (lines 31 to 35)
3. *On determining seniority standing*
   What seems to be the difference in the methods used by Merriam and by the foreman in determining seniority? (lines 17 to 19, 20 to 25)
4. *On transfer policy*
   a. What features of the company policy on transfer are brought out by foreman Carson?
      (1) What about his final comment? (lines 38 to 39)
   b. What do you think of the suggestion made by Merriam in lines 11 to 12 and 36 to 37?
   c. How well versed in policy thinking does foreman Carson seem to be?
   d. In the light of this conversation, what basic transfer-policy questions have to be clarified before there can be any satisfactory settlement of this case? (lines 11 to 39)
5. *On a personnel administrator's role*
   a. How well prepared was Mr. Merriam to discuss Elsie's request when she was scheduled to return to his office?
   b. What further steps might he have taken at that time to prepare himself more adequately?

III

Since Miss Varda failed to keep the appointment and sent no further word, Mr. Merriam let the matter drop in the midst of other problems. But one morning, about a week later, he sat in on a grievance conference between the representatives of the union and top management. Among other matters, the case of Miss Varda was brought up by the union as "unsettled." After hearing the union's side of the case, the vice-president turned to the superintendent and asked him to look into the matter and "settle it."

Following the meeting, the personnel administrator talked with the superintendent and told him what he knew of the case and what had been done. He expressed an opinion that the girl had a legitimate reason for requesting a transfer to what she considered less arduous work and that her job seniority on burling entitled her to an opening on a different type of burling on the same shift. He pointed out that the foreman's offer of a transfer to another job in another department would mean the loss of seniority on her burling job, since the union contract provided only for job seniority.

On the basis of these considerations, the superintendent decided to approve the request for the transfer. He went to the foreman and told him that he should make the transfer, "at least for a while to see how it works out." When the foreman began to object that it would upset the whole department, the superintendent pointed out that the seniority list for burling made no distinction between sheet and blanket burling. He also asked the foreman whether, in a similar case, if a good weaver on one type of loom wanted an opening on another type of loom and had the seniority for it, he would permit the transfer. The foreman admitted that he would do so, and the superintendent replied that "this case is no different."

The final comment of the foreman was that "it will still create a lot of trouble." Consequently, 2 months later, the superintendent and the personnel administrator were interested to hear the foreman admit that "she's working out O. K. on the other job, and there's been no flare-up in the department because of it."

QUESTIONS

1. *On the nature of a complaint and grievance procedure*
   a. When was Miss Varda's case made the subject of an official complaint?
   b. Does the procedure seem to have been clear to all concerned?
   c. In what ways might the procedure have been improved?
      (1) Was the personnel administrator wise in "letting the matter drop" when Miss Varda failed to keep her appointment?
2. *On transfer policy*
   a. Were the questions of transfer policy (raised in the previous episode) adequately discussed and understood before action was taken?
   b. What appears to be the company's transfer policy?
3. *On relevant facts*
   a. Is the opinion expressed by Mr. Merriam (Sec. III, par. 2, page 404), relevant to the issue?

    b. What are the facts that need to be brought out here?

    c. Why do you think Elsie Varda wants a transfer? (Consider lines 1 to 10 in Sec. II.)

4. *On the role of a personnel administrator*

    a. Why was it necessary to bring the superintendent into this case? Could not the personnel administrator have handled it himself?

    b. Comment on the parts that the personnel administrator and the superintendent took in this episode.

5. *On the difficulty of evaluating medical evidence*

    What light is thrown on Elsie's complaint about her back by the fact that she makes good on blanket burling?

6. *On labor relations*

    How can you account for the fact that the trouble anticipated by the foreman did not develop?

QUESTIONS ON THE CASE AS A WHOLE

1. *On getting down to cases*

    Suppose that the personnel administrator had made a real effort "to get inside the situation" when the case was first brought to his attention. How might he have been expected to handle it differently?

2. *On policy thinking*

    In what way, if any, could this case have been used to get better understanding on the part of the foreman of the desirability of remedial transfers?

3. *On supervisory leadership*

    a. What seems to have been foreman Carson's attitude toward Elsie Varda?

    b. In what ways might he have been more helpful in this case?

4. *On a foreman's attitude toward company policy*

    When a foreman is convinced that a company policy is unworkable in his department, what courses of action are legitimately open to him?

Case for Chapter 14

Problems in Downgrading

Anna Petruska

INTRODUCTION

The following complications are apt to ensue during downgrading when a foreman has been weak in the exercise of his leadership responsibilities and when company policies and procedures were not clearly stated or understood. Management and union officials disagree as to the standard according to which an ineffective employee should be judged. False issues are raised and further confuse those management officials who are inexperienced in policy thinking. Time and energy are wasted without developing genuine understanding. Top management finally overrules the first-line supervisor without taking any steps to make the most of the educational opportunities that the situation has presented.

BACKGROUND

It was part of the established procedure at the Beecroft Mills that foremen should report to the personnel office any episodes that in their opinion might subsequently be raised by the union as complaints or grievances.

I

On Oct. 4, 1945, Mr. Merriam, the personnel administrator, received the following report from the general foreman of the weaving department:

GENERAL FOREMAN'S REPORT OF CONVERSATION
WITH EMPLOYEE

Name: Anna Petruska
Occupation: Weaver
Department: Weaving
Date: Oct. 3, 1945
DETAILS OF CONVERSATION:

This weaver is no good, so I intend to overlook her seniority and keep her as a spare weaver. Here are some complaints:

Oct. 2, 1945.—Ethel Wolcheck complained that her work is in bad shape every time Anna Petruska works on her set. She showed me misdraws and selvage threads pulled off harnesses and drop wire. Last week she was caught starting two looms without finding pick, making cracks in cloth. She is no good as a weaver.

(signed) Andrew Bennett, *Second Shift Foreman*

I have had her on several sets, and she is no weaver.

(signed) John Trudeau, *General Foreman*

We had her weaving on Florence Gann's set on second shift on Sept. 15, and Mrs. Gann complained the very next day to me that she had found several errors in the work.

(signed) John Trudeau, *General Foreman*

All our weavers have been told and shown how to find pick.

(signed) John Trudeau, *General Foreman*

In the next mail, Mr. Merriam found an official grievance report by the union business agent:

TEXTILE WORKERS UNION OF AMERICA
AFFILIATE OF THE CIO
GRIEVANCE DATA

Date: Oct. 4, 1945

Local No. 801
Name of Member: Anna Petruska
Shop: Beecroft Mills   Dept: Weaving
Steward: Rene Dumais   Business Agent: Fred Cullinane
Nature of Grievance: Seniority
Dear Mr. Merriam:

The above-named person was taken off her work as a weaver and placed on jobs, such as spare weaver or battery hand. This person has been weaving for quite a length of time, and the foreman making a change of this kind certainly overlooked seniority. Therefore the union is asking for a conference on this matter at your earliest convenience.

Signature of Member: Anna Petruska
Signature of Steward: Rene Dumais

Mr. Merriam then called the general foreman and arranged for a conference the next afternoon at the foreman's office. The following were present:

JOHN TRUDEAU, general foreman, weaving.
FRED CULLINANE, business agent, Local 801.
ANNA PETRUSKA, weaver who raised the grievance.
MR. MERRIAM, personnel administrator.

1 MERRIAM: Well, Fred, you asked for a conference on this grievance. Here is your grievance report. Just why do you think we "overlooked seniority"?

CULLINANE: Because this weaver had more seniority than any of the other weavers on the second shift. When she was transferred to the second shift
5   on Sept. 10 because there was not enough work on the first, she was not given a regular weaver's set of looms. She has been a weaver since Aug. 30, 1941, according to the seniority list here, and there are five other second-shift weavers with less seniority. But they are still on their sets, and she was made a spare weaver.

10   TRUDEAU: But she's not a good weaver. We have had a lot of complaints from other weavers and from loom fixers who have had to work with her. Just last week she deliberately disobeyed my instructions, and I caught her starting two looms without first finding the pick. She is just no good as a regular weaver.

15   MRS. PETRUSKA (*interrupting*): Oh, so I'm no good now. I work all right during the war. I make good work for the Army and Navy. I'm a good weaver then. Now when the war is over I'm no good. Mr. Trudeau, you're a damn liar!

TRUDEAU (*controlling himself*): Just a minute. Didn't I tell you the right way
20   to start looms about 6 months ago when you first started them the wrong way?

MRS. PETRUSKA: Yes, but that's just a little thing.

TRUDEAU: No, it isn't. When you do that, you spoil the whole width of the cloth.

25   MRS. PETRUSKA: Well, it still ain't nothing. And those other weavers have it in for me. So do the loom fixers. Why, last winter a loom fixer kicked me.

TRUDEAU: You didn't tell me anything about it. Anyhow, those other weavers say that when you are working on their sets there are a lot of damages and the work is poor. And you can't deny that you didn't follow my in-
30   structions about starting up looms. (*Mrs. Petruska shrugs her shoulders*)

CULLINANE: That may be, Mr. Trudeau, but you should have disciplined her at that time, last week. You have no right to change her job classification just because she fails to carry out orders or does unsatisfactory work. Our contract covers that.

35   MERRIAM: What clause of the contract is involved?

CULLINANE: Right here, Art. II, Sec. 3: "All layoffs in each job classification shall be made in the order established by the seniority list upon the basis of 'last in . . . first out'." [He did not read aloud the rest of the clause: "Provided, however, that in layoffs and recalls competency to do the
40   work may be considered a factor by the employer. When the employer departs from seniority on grounds of competency, the union and the employee or employees with higher seniority shall be entitled upon request to a statement of the reasons therefor, and the matter shall be subject to arbitration."]

45   MERRIAM: I don't see how layoffs are involved here at all. Mrs. Petruska was not laid off. She was just transferred back to the second shift, and when she failed to carry out instructions, Mr. Trudeau kept her on spare work.

CULLINANE: That's not the way we see it, and I'm going to take this case higher. Management just can't ignore seniority.

50 MERRIAM: Excuse me a minute, I'd like to talk with Mr. Trudeau a moment. (*they step out of the room*)

MERRIAM: Why didn't you suspend or discharge that woman when she disobeyed your instructions last week?

TRUDEAU: I probably should have, but she has to make a living same as I,
55 and I thought I'd give her something to do even though I didn't put her on a regular set of looms.

MERRIAM: Well, all right, let's go back. (*on returning*) It's quite apparent that this case involves a matter that will have to go to higher management at the next stage of the grievance procedure. We can't even agree on the
60 facts now.

At the conclusion of the conference, Mr. Merriam wrote the business agent a formal letter stating that he agreed to take the case to the next step—between the business agent and regional director of the union, on the one hand, and the vice-president of the company, on the other.

For his own notes on the case, Mr. Merriam jotted down the following:

At no time has Mrs. Petruska complained about the Sept. 10 transfer from the first to the second shift.

After going onto the second shift, Trudeau assigned her to no particular job. She worked at a variety of jobs: spare weaver, battery hand, etc., wherever Trudeau put her.

About 6 months ago, all weavers were given instructions as to the correct method of starting up a loom. During the last week in September, Trudeau caught her disobeying these instructions and starting up several looms in a way that caused cracks and damaged the cloth on several looms. This disobedience on her part was known to the shift foreman and can be corroborated by further evidence. It was only when Anna Petruska was reprimanded for improper starting of looms and for spoiling cloth in consequence, that she complained. Prior to this event, she made no complaint regarding being moved from the first to the second shift. In consequence of this, the union argues, not that she should not have been penalized for disobedience and infraction of rules, *but* that, because of her seniority, she should not have been assigned to spare weaving, plugging batteries, and other odd jobs instead of being left on her regular job classification as a weaver.

It is my opinion that, if any error in procedure occurred, it was in management's failure to discipline Mrs. Petruska by means of a layoff or suspension at the time she was apprehended in disobeying instructions and willfully damaging cloth. Hence, the irrelevance in Mr. Trudeau's association of Mrs. Petruska's infraction of rules with the change in her seniority. Seniority should have been excluded from the framework of any penalty imposed on her for infraction of rules. The punishment imposed does not seem to "fit the crime." As a spare weaver she would still do poor work and damage the cloth.

He also asked the employment department to give him a record of Mrs. Petruska's employment.

Re: Anna Petruska—Weaving

July 7, 1920	Hired	As scrubber	Weaving
Aug. 28, 1920	Quit	On account of children going to school	
Sept. 6, 1922	Hired	As general hand	Cloth room
Sept. 30, 1922	Quit	Didn't like the work	
Nov. 20, 1922	Hired	As weaver	No. 10 Weave
Mar. 3, 1923	Quit	Reason unknown	
Apr. 21, 1931	Hired	Machine girl	Cloth room
		Laid off and rehired in weaving department while employment office was closed	
Aug. 30, 1938	Quit	On account of illness	
Apr. 26, 1939	Hired	Battery hand	Weaving
Feb. 27, 1945		Claims that loom fixer kicked her. Neither nurse or Doctor could find any evidence of this	
Aug. 3, 1945		Ill with sinus trouble Aug. 3 to Sept. 9	
Sept. 10, 1945		Transfer to second shift	

QUESTIONS FOR DISCUSSION

1. *On complaint and grievance procedure*
   a. What do you think of the desirability of foremen notifying the personnel director in advance of episodes that may lead to formal complaints presented by the union?
   b. Describe the role that the personnel administrator has assumed in the handling of this grievance, and compare it with the proper function of a staff man in a well-administered grievance procedure.
2. *On interpretation and application of personnel policies*
   a. What do you think of the union's contention (line 36) that the layoff clause of the contract is involved in this case? Does the paragraph in the contract that was omitted in the reading by the business agent throw any light on the handling of this case by the foreman?
   b. What do you think of the personnel administrator's suggestion that disciplinary action should have been taken at the time when the employee disobeyed instructions? To what extent are the problems of discipline and downgrading related here?
   c. On the basis of your understanding of the case thus far, what changes, if any, would you make in the personnel administrator's notes stating his tentative conclusions?
3. *On an employee's work history*
   From the facts presented, what would you conclude about the work record of Mrs. Petruska? What bearing, if any, does this have on the problem?

4. *On line authority*
   a. Why do you think the shift foreman was not invited to the meeting?
   b. What advantages might there have been if he had been?
5. *On defining the issues*
   a. What are the issues?
   b. Whose responsibility is it to clarify the issues?
6. *On supervisory responsibility*
   Consider the various statements made by the general foreman. To what extent does he throw light on the situation?

II

During the next day, Mr. Merriam had an opportunity to reflect further on the case. Some points failed to fit together, he thought. The weaver did not make a complaint until she was bawled out by the shift foreman when she started the looms incorrectly. Why? She apparently did not object to the transfer, and yet the union alleged that the contract had been violated. Was not the business agent simply using an unrelated clause in the contract to strengthen a weak case involving a disciplinary question?

Mr. Merriam was not satisfied that he could answer these questions, so he arranged to see the general foreman again and, at the latter's suggestion, invited the mill superintendent, Mr. Collins, to join them. For Collins's information, Merriam reviewed the case briefly and then continued:

1   Merriam: The thing I don't see is this—why didn't Mrs. Petruska complain to you or to the union when you moved her to the second shift on Sept. 10 and put her on spare work?

    Trudeau: Well, I told her that I had to move somebody back because we
5   had too many weavers on the first shift, and since she was the youngest [had least seniority], she was the one. She didn't object to that.

    Merriam: And, when you didn't give her a regular weaver's set on the second shift, you told her it was because she was a poor weaver, didn't you?

10   Trudeau: No, not exactly. She said to me, "Mr. Trudeau, what are you going to give me?" I told her, "I don't know what I'll be able to give you. Right now I'll put you on spare work." She didn't complain then, even though she earns less on spare.

    Merriam: But you didn't really tell her that she would not get a regular set?
15   Trudeau: No, I guess I didn't. I felt she wasn't a very good weaver—we'd had complaints about her work all along—and I didn't want to take those other second-shift weavers off their sets. They're good weavers, and she isn't.

    Merriam: Let's see how much seniority they had. (*looking at seniority list*)

20   Well, one of them started as a weaver the same time as Mrs. Petruska on
      Aug. 30, 1941, two started in October and two in November. There
      isn't a great difference in seniority between them.
      TRUDEAU: That's right, and those others are better weavers. Mrs. Petruska
      is a poor weaver on No. 62 [a type of cloth being woven on the second
25   shift], and she admits she can't handle wide looms. On the narrow
      looms, the weavers I've got now on the second shift are better weavers.
      MERRIAM: How can you prove that they are better?
      TRUDEAU: Well, they just are. I know they are. And I'll bet their loom
      efficiencies (according to which they are paid) are better.
30   COLLINS: I've been listening to all this, and it strikes me that we'd have
      saved a lot of headaches if we'd had an employee-rating plan like the
      one we were discussing some time ago. If we could show that this weaver
      was slipping over a period of time and that she received a number of
      warnings, then we'd be in a much stronger position. As it is, we don't
35   have this, so about all we can do is get some efficiency figures on all
      these weavers. You'd better dig those out, John, before we turn this case
      over to the V.P. [vice-president].
      TRUDEAU: O.K., but I don't know whether they'll show the difference. Loom
      efficiencies can be different for a lot of reasons, and it may not be the
40   weaver's fault. But I'll see what I can find.
      MERRIAM: Now, I want to ask some more questions. Let's review just what
      happened after that. You transferred her to the second shift on Sept. 10.
      Then what happened?
      TRUDEAU: Well, on Sept. 15 I put her on Florence Gann's set, as I wrote
45   on my report. Mrs. Gann was out, and we had to fill her place. When she
      came back, she kicked to me about the condition of her looms—said
      there was a lot of bad work. Then, on Sept. 17, 18, and 21 (looking at
      time sheets), she was put on Ethel Wolchek's set when Ethel was out
      for a few days. Later, Ethel complained to Andy Bennett, the shift
50   foreman, about the poor work. The next day—that was Sept. 22—Andy
      reprimanded Mrs. Petruska and showed her the damages she caused.
      MERRIAM: Did he say anything to her about keeping her on spare weaving
      because she was such a poor weaver?
      TRUDEAU: I can't say. All I know is that he wrote on the slip I put in my
55   report to you.
      MERRIAM: Now, what happened when you caught her starting up the looms
      the wrong way—disobeying your instructions? That was on Sept. 28,
      wasn't it?
      TRUDEAU: Yes, I was right in my office, and, since she was working near by,
60   I saw it. I rushed right out and stopped those two looms, and I bawled
      her out plenty. I told her she would never be a good weaver, and I was
      keeping her on spare weaving and would not give her a regular set
      because she was so poor. I said that other weavers had complained about
      her work, too.

65 MERRIAM: You should have suspended her right there, but what happened
   next?

TRUDEAU: Well, the next Tuesday—that was Oct. 2—she came to me with
the first-shift steward (there isn't any on the second shift), and she asked
me why she wasn't being given a regular set of looms. I told her again

70 that it was because she was not a good weaver. I guess she must have
gone to Cullinane [the business agent] after that. I wrote my report to
you the next day.

MERRIAM: I see. Now the facts fit together a little better. You really
didn't tell her that she would not get a regular set of looms on the second

75 shift until you bawled her out last week for starting looms the wrong way?

TRUDEAU: I guess you're right.

MERRIAM: So her complaint wasn't because she was bawled out but because
she thought she should have a regular set of looms. And Cullinane is
saying that, under the contract, we have got to push people back and lay

80 off according to seniority.

COLLINS: Well, even if that layoff clause does apply, it still says we can
depart from seniority on the grounds of competency. Isn't that what we
did?

MERRIAM: I suppose we could say that. But what evidence do we have to

85 support it? How does she compare with those other weavers that have
less seniority?

COLLINS: John will get that information, and we'll turn it all over to the
V.P. But I certainly wish we had an employee-rating plan. Then we
might have avoided all this.

90 MERRIAM: One other thing. Isn't the punishment—or the downgrading to
spare work—a poor solution? Isn't she just as likely to make the same
mistakes when she is a spare weaver?

TRUDEAU: Not so much. On spare work, she just helps the other weavers.
She can't do as much damage as she can if she has a whole set of her own.

95 I needed weavers during the war and I kept her on, but now I have
more than I need, and I don't see why I should put back better weavers
for her. I told her, though, that she had to earn a living same as me,
and I would give her spare work instead of putting her out on the street.

MERRIAM: Well, I guess we have everything—except those loom efficiencies.

100 Let me know when you have them.

QUESTIONS FOR DISCUSSION

1. *On handling downgrading and shift transfers*
   What should the foreman have told Mrs. Petruska when she was transferred to
   the second shift on Sept. 10? (lines 1 to 22)

2. *On seniority*
   (lines 16 to 22) Four of the five second-shift weavers had slightly less seniority
   than Mrs. Petruska. In the light of the union contract, is this point of any
   importance?

3. *On the need of employee rating*
   (lines 30 to 32) If loom-efficiency figures are available, is there any real need for an employee-rating plan, as the superintendent suggests?
4. *On handling cases of unsatisfactory work.*
   a. (lines 44 to 51) When regular second-shift weavers complained about Mrs. Petruska's work on their looms, in their absence, what should have been done?
   b. (lines 65 to 66) Would you agree with the personnel administrator that Mrs. Petruska should have been suspended immediately when she started up the looms the wrong way?
5. *On personnel policy*
   a. (lines 90 to 98) Assuming that the weaver was inefficient, what do you think of downgrading or demotion as a method of handling inefficient workers?
   b. Give reasons for or against the view that layoff, or discharge for incompetence, would have been preferable.

III

It proved difficult to compute the "efficiencies" of the weavers concerned, and instead the general foreman furnished Mr. Merriam with comparative piecework earnings. Mrs. Petruska had lower earnings than the other weaver with equal seniority but greater earnings than at least one of the regular second-shift weavers with less seniority.

A few days later, the union brought this grievance, along with several others, to the next stage of the grievance procedure—a meeting with the vice-president. The international representative of the union presented the union's argument:

1   INTERNATIONAL REPRESENTATIVE: In this Petruska case, we agree it was all right to put her back to the second shift when there was not enough work on the first, but she should have bumped a younger weaver. The shift transfer was the wrong time to say she was a poor weaver. The foreman
5   should have laid her off earlier if she was inefficient.
    VICE-PRESIDENT (*to Mr. Merriam, the personnel administrator*): Was she downgraded at the same time that she was moved back to the second shift for lack of work? Is that the story?
    MERRIAM: Yes, that's essentially what happened, as I told you yesterday.
10   But Mr. Trudeau felt he was within his rights.
    VICE-PRESIDENT: Well, possibly. But generally I think it's bad practice. (*turning to the international representative of the union*) I agree with you on this case. We'll assign Mrs. Petruska to a regular set of looms on the second shift and downgrade the youngest one to spare weaving. If she can't make
15   good, then that's another matter.

QUESTIONS FOR DISCUSSION

1. *On top-management action in a grievance case*
   a. Why do you think the vice-president made the decision he did? (Lines 11 to 15)
   b. Would you agree with it? Why, or why not?
   c. What objections are there to reversing a foreman's decision?
2. *On opportunities for improving personnel procedure*
   How might the vice-president and the personnel administrator use this case to improve the company's procedure in handling inefficient employees?

Case for Chapter 15

Discharge for "Insubordination"

(Irene Mason)

INTRODUCTION

Sound disciplinary action can be taken only within the framework of a constructive disciplinary policy. In the case here reported, a clear-cut policy, well formulated and soundly administered, might have prevented the discharge of Irene Mason. Thus, as in so many other instances, constructive discipline would have been of value both to management and to the worker.

Furthermore, the situation is typical in that the central issue was beclouded in the minds of the participants by other aims and preoccupations. For instance, the problem of dealing with the case of "insubordination" was complicated for management by its concern with educating an old-line foreman. Another complicating element in the situation was the presence of a newly organized union.

Thus a case that at first seems to center on the question of discharge for cause can fully be understood as an evolving situation only by considering all the following points:

1. The elements of a constructive disciplinary policy.
2. The kind of disciplinary action to be taken by line officials.
3. The constructive opportunities for union participation in securing good discipline.
4. The relation of good discipline to supervisory training and to higher management's relations with foremen.
5. The need of building and maintaining respect for management's authority.
6. The need for policy thinking in personnel and labor relations.

BACKGROUND OF THE CASE

The Winston Mill was a small woolen-textile factory that had been a family business for more than 50 years. It had never employed more than 150 workers. During the depression of the thirties, financial difficulties resulted in absorption by a large New England textile firm. The Winston Mill became a branch plant, although in practice the local manager was given considerable authority in handling day-to-day problems. There was also an assistant manager who took care of the office, the accounts, and some of the purchasing; and a superintendent who scheduled production, gave instructions to department heads, and handled disciplinary problems. There was no personnel administrator and no employment manager. The superintendent handled the limited personnel functions, and informal relationships continued much as they had in the past.

There was one important difference, however. About a year prior to the episode described in this case, the Textile Workers Union, CIO, won an election conducted by the National Labor Relations Board and was certified as the exclusive bargaining agency for all production and maintenance employees. Contract negotiations began soon afterward; but, for a number of reasons, final agreement was delayed for more than 9 months. The union had not notified management of the selection of stewards, so that the formal grievance procedure specified in the contract was not yet operative when the events described below took place.

I. The Discharge

1   In April, 1945, Irene Mason had been employed in the mill for about 6 years. At this time, her job was that of cloth inspector. She had the responsibility for final checking of the cloth and was frequently in contact with various representatives of management. Irene had been

5 transferred to this job 2 years earlier, when another girl left. Then, according to the mill manager, "something happened to her." After a series of episodes in which she was reprimanded by the superintendent and by the assistant mill manager, she was finally discharged because she told the superintendent, Bill Smolokas, that he "didn't know what

10 he was talking about." According to the records, the reason for discharge was "insubordination."

    The episode leading to this discharge took place one Saturday morning. Earlier, the superintendent and the foreman had been given instructions by the mill manager in regard to pieces of cloth that

15 came through to the inspection table with too much "shive," or foreign matter, in the wool nap. He told them to send the pieces back to the napper (a machine that "naps" the cloth). Accordingly, Irene had been instructed to put aside such pieces and call the foreman or the superintendent for instructions. Not all these pieces had to be sent

20 back, and the judgment of the foreman or the superintendent was needed.

On this Saturday morning, one such piece came to Irene at the inspection table. Since the foreman was busy helping to repair a napper that had broken down, she called superintendent Smolokas. He looked
25 at the piece carefully and told her to put it aside to be sent back to the napper. In what he later described as a "sassy" tone of voice, Irene said, "You don't know what you're talking about." The superintendent made no answer to this, but laid the piece aside, went to the front office, and asked the mill manager to come and look at it. He did not
30 tell the manager what Irene had said but simply asked him what he would do with the piece. The manager said that it should go back to the napper. The superintendent then told him the rest of the episode, but nothing further was done about it that day. The manager later explained that he had wanted to talk to the foreman about Irene's con-
35 duct. Since the foreman was busy on the broken-down napper, the discussion was postponed until Monday morning.

On Monday morning, the foreman was still busy. It was not until Monday afternoon that the foreman, the superintendent, and the mill manager met to discuss the episode. Both the superintendent and the
40 manager felt that Irene should be asked to apologize for her remark to the superintendent and should also be transferred to a different job where she would not be in continual contact (and conflict) with management. The foreman said very little during this discussion.

On Tuesday morning, however, the foreman told the superintend-
45 ent that he did not think Irene would either apologize or accept a transfer. The superintendent wondered whether the foreman had discussed the whole matter with Irene in his car when he took her home the night before, according to their usual share-the-ride arrangement. However, the superintendent said nothing. The mill manager then
50 called Irene into the foreman's office and tried to convince her that she should apologize to the superintendent for saying that he did not know what he was talking about. This she refused to do, explaining that she had spoken "as she felt" and that she still was of the same opinion. The mill manager then said that, if she would not apologize, she would
55 have to leave the mill.

The manager sent a notice to the union office, as required by the new contract, stating that Irene had been "suspended" for "insubordination" and that within 7 days the suspension would become a discharge.[1] At the same time, he called the union office and told one of

[1] Article VII of the union contract stated: "No employee shall be discharged except for just cause—just cause to mean, among other things, inefficiency, insubordination, or persistent or serious infraction of rules relating to the health or safety

60 the assistant business agents the whole story. According to the man-
    ager, this business agent said that he thought the right action had been
    taken under the circumstances.

    The next morning, the head business agent of the union called the
65 mill manager for an appointment to discuss the matter. His attitude
    was quite different from that of the assistant business agent. He was
    incensed at Irene's discharge and threatened "to blow the place
    apart." The manager said nothing in reply to this, except that he
    would be glad to see him at 2 o'clock the following afternoon.

QUESTIONS FOR DISCUSSION

1. *On discharge for cause*
    a. Was Irene Mason's discharge justified?
       (1) For what cause was she discharged?
       (2) Did her behavior constitute insubordination?
       (3) What is insubordination?
       (4) If superintendent Smolokas had discharged Irene on Saturday morning,
           could he justifiably have alleged insubordination?
       (5) How might superintendent Smolokas have brought the issue to a head
           on Saturday morning?
    b. How much responsibility should the "home office" of a branch plant have
       in cases of this sort?
    c. What official should have the responsibility for discharge in this case?
    d. Is it advisable in a situation of this sort to discuss the case with the foreman?
       Why or why not?
2. *On disciplinary policy*
    a. Judging by the action described thus far, what can be said of the disciplin-
       ary policy here?
    b. Comment on the fact that superintendent Smolokas said nothing to Irene
       after her impertinent remark. (line 27)
       (1) Why do you think he acted as he did?
       (2) What bad effects are likely to follow such indecisive behavior by a
           management representative?
       (3) Comment on the validity of the manager's reason for postponing dis-
           cussion with the foreman of Irene's conduct. (lines 34 to 36)

---

of other employees, or to rules reasonably promulgated by management relating to the
actual operation of the plant, or engaging in a strike or group stoppage of work of any
kind, slowdown, strike, sabotage, picketing or failure to abide by the terms of this
agreement or by the award of an arbitrator."

    The suspension-discharge procedure was also specified in the contract. "A grievance
alleging such suspension is unjust or discriminatory must be mailed to the employer
within three (3) regularly scheduled working days of the union's receipt of the employer's written notice of the suspension and of the specific reason or reasons therefor.
If the employer specifically directs that such suspension shall not become a discharge,
the employee involved shall be given pay for all time lost by reason of the suspension."

    c. What instructions and orders relating to this episode were given to Irene?
(1) Did she disobey any of them? If so, which?

    d. Comment on the timing of top management's first step in disciplining Irene.

3. *On executive responsibility*

    If you had been the superintendent, what would you have said when the
foreman brought the "message" from Irene? (lines 44 to 46)

4. *On getting evidence to review a decision*

    On the basis of the information thus far presented, what points should be
checked further before the meeting with the head business agent of the union?

5. *On labor relations*

    How should management interpret and reply to a "threat" such as that ex-
pressed by the head business agent of the union?

II. Employee Discipline and Supervisory Training

1   The mill manager knew that he had had little experience in handling cases with a union, since the union had been officially recognized
for only a few months. Therefore, although he was busy with a number of other matters that he felt were more directly connected with
5 production, he decided to devote some time the morning before the
meeting with the union to getting the facts on the case. He sat down
with the assistant manager and with the superintendent to review all
the difficulties they had experienced with Irene Mason. During the
discussion, the manager did not review in any detail the problem that
10 was uppermost in their minds with regard to foreman Williams. But
they all recognized that it was an important element in the discharge
case. When the superintendent had been hired 3 years before, it was
with the understanding that he develop uniformity of practice
throughout the plant. Having come from the outside, his presence
15 was at first resented by many foremen. But gradually he won the re-
pect of most of them and had continuing difficulties with only a few.
Ed Williams, an old-timer, was one of these, and the superintendent
devoted considerable time to working with him in trying to improve
the standards and practices of his department. The superintendent's
20 desire to educate Ed Williams was his main reason for handling the
case as he had.

    The following facts were brought out in the course of the discus-
sion: Soon after Irene was placed on the inspection job, superintendent Smolokas noticed that she was talking and "kidding" with some
25 of the truckers who occasionally came past her work station. In his
judgment, both she and the truckers were neglecting their work, so he
went to Irene's foreman, Ed Williams, and asked him to check up on

this and stop the practice. In carrying out these instructions, Williams went over to Irene and said, "Bill says you should get back to
30 work. You're bothering the boys." At this remark, Irene walked out of the plant "in a huff." When she came back the next day, she was reinstated only after a private talk with the superintendent, who outlined what was expected of her on the job.

The "campaign to educate Ed Williams" had continued. Accord-
35 ing to superintendent Smolokas, Ed was "lax on details," such as record keeping, and he was "lax on handling the help." He was inclined to be easy-going, except where he formed definite opinions about someone. Apparently he often got these opinions from Irene, whom he drove to and from work in his car. (She was a "friend of the
40 family" and lived near his home.) Although they could not prove it, both the manager and the superintendent believed that the girl influenced the foreman against people whom she did not like. According to statements of present workers, several girls had left the mill "on account of Irene."

45 At various times, the superintendent had spoken to the foreman about his work, telling him that he must "tighten up" his management of the department. One day, Irene came to the superintendent's office and asked to see him. She opened the conversation with the statement, "Why do you pick on Ed all the time?" The superin-
50 tendent replied that, although he would be glad to discuss her work with her at any time, he could not discuss with her any problems that merely concerned the foreman. He said to her, "Go back to your work and mind your own business. Your job is inspecting, not acting as a nursemaid for Ed Williams. If Ed has any complaint, he should be
55 man enough to come to me himself and tell me." As Irene left office, she said something over her shoulder that sounded to the superintendent like "You damn Polak." So he added, "The next time you interfere in anyone's business you will be discharged." She then asked, "What is my job?" The superintendent again outlined her duties and
60 finally said, "I don't want you influencing Ed."

One morning about 6 months later, a temporary worker was sent home by foreman Williams at 9:30 A.M. because there was no more work for her that day. Later the same day, the office girl came back to the foreman's office to get his "O.K." on the girl's time card,
65 marked for 2½ hours. The foreman said he thought that the new "reporting-time" provision of the union contract applied in this case. (This clause provided 4 hours' reporting pay or work at the em-

ployee's regular rate of pay if there was insufficient work for an employee at the beginning of a day.) He thought that the girl should get
70   4 hours' pay.

Irene was working near by and was either called over by the foreman or came into the discussion on her own initiative (the facts are
not wholly clear). She sided with the foreman and insisted that the
girl's card should be marked for 4 hours' pay. This confused the office
75   girl, who had not been told about the reporting-pay provision, so she
called over superintendent Smolokas, who happened to be walking
past at the moment. She said, "Ed and Irene say we must pay this
girl 4 hours' reporting pay." Superintendent Smolokas then told foreman Williams that the reporting-time provision of the union contract
80   was not to go into effect until it had been approved by the Regional
War Labor Board; and, since this approval had not yet been received, the provision did not apply at this time. He then told Irene to
go back to her work, since the matter did not in any event concern
her. She did not go immediately, however, and continued to insist
85   that she was right.

At this point, another official had entered the discussion, Mr.
Forbes, the assistant mill manager, who was on his way to check up on
another matter, when he saw one of the girls from his office talking
with Ed, Irene, and superintendent Smolokas. The superintendent
explained the problem to Forbes and asked his opinion. The assistant
90   manager replied that the reporting-time provision was not yet in effect. He then turned to foreman Williams and added, "Ed, you let the
office handle things like that. I'll tell my girls when any new provisions apply. Furthermore, you shouldn't have let Irene get into the
discussion. It didn't concern her."

95   At this remark, Irene observed, "It's a free country, and I guess I
can say what I think is right if I want to."

"Your job is inspecting, not butting into other people's business,"
replied the assistant mill manager. "You have no right in this discussion. You're not a union representative."

100   He then called the foreman aside and told him that he was "off
base" on two points: (1) in his opinion as to the applicability of the
reporting-time provision, and (2) in permitting Irene to leave her
work and enter the discussion.

Shortly after the episode involving the temporary worker's time
105   card, Irene joined the union. When the union had first won bargaining
rights, Irene had been most outspoken against it. She said that she

could not see any benefit to be derived from it. It seemed that she reflected some of the feelings of foreman Williams, who had previously said, "I don't want the union telling me how to run my department."
110 Now, without any explanation to her fellow workers, Irene signed a membership card in the union. The "grapevine" reported that she had told several people that she was out to "get" superintendent Smolokas.

Another difficulty with Irene, preceding the one leading to her
115 discharge, occurred when she told Ed Williams that the girl on the second shift had not inspected her cloth properly. The foreman then told the second-shift girl (apparently without checking the facts), "Irene says you haven't inspected your cloth right." The second-shift inspector denied this and was much upset. When Williams later
120 asked Irene what she meant, she denied that she had said the girl was doing poor work. She said that she just meant that the work was not being done as well as she thought it should be done.

QUESTIONS FOR DISCUSSION

1. *On placement*
Since difficulties with Irene began soon after she was placed on the inspection job, what is indicated about her placement?
2. *On supervisory training by higher management*
   a. Comment on the methods used by higher management to "educate" foreman Williams on his responsibilities.
   b. What were the foreman's principal weaknesses?
   c. What could have been done about them?
3. *On line authority*
   a. Comment on superintendent Smolokas' handling of the situation when Irene accuses him of "picking on the foreman" (lines 47 to 60). If you had been in his place, what would you have said and done?
   b. As an example of line authority, what do you think of the superintendent's order to Irene (line 82) and of his neglect to follow through on it? (Consider it especially with reference to his previous warning, lines 57 to 58.)
   c. Evaluate the advantages and risks of direct intervention by a top-management official in a situation such as that described in the temporary worker's time card incident. (lines 86 to 103)
      (1) Should the assistant manager have talked to the foreman as he did? Consider the time and place as well as the tone and content of the remark.
      (2) How well does the assistant manager handle Irene?
      (3) Comment on the assistant manager's action in correcting the foreman at this point.

4. *On situational thinking*
   a. How might the episode involving reporting pay have been effectively used to secure better understanding and cooperation among the foreman, the higher officials, and Irene?
   b. Why is it important to determine whether foreman Williams brought Irene into the discussion, or whether she came on her own initiative? (lines 71 to 73)
5. *On reviewing a decision*
   a. In what way has the review of these earlier episodes shed additional light on the points you checked in question 1 at the end of the first section?
   b. Consider the wisdom of the discharge in the light of this additional information.
6. *On executive action in a grievance case*
   a. Did the mill manager go to unnecessary trouble in preparing for the conference with the union?
   b. Could he ordinarily expect to handle each grievance in this manner?
   c. Can you think of any reasons why he should have gone to extra trouble in this case?
7. *On decision making*
   Comment on the manager's timing in getting the facts in Irene's case.
8. *On the responsibilities of a foreman*
   a. Comment on foreman Williams's remark to Irene (lines 29 to 30).
   b. How should a foreman handle such a situation?
   c. What is likely to be the effect on a foreman's authority when a worker is reinstated by his superior officer without his appearing in the case? (lines 31 to 33)
   d. Comment on the foreman's action in dealing with the second-shift cloth inspector. (lines 114 to 118)
   e. What objections, if any, do you see in a foreman's sharing his car with a worker?
      (1) If you see any difficulties, how might these have been overcome?

III. The Grievance Meeting

Two days after Irene's discharge in May, 1945, the representatives of the union and the company met in the mill manager's office. The following were present:

Mr. Wilson, manager of the mill.
Mr. Forbes, assistant mill manager.
Mr. Smolokas, superintendent.
Mr. DuFresne, head business agent of the union.
Mr. Leboeuf, assistant business agent.

After the usual preliminaries and introductions (some of the men had not met each other before), the head business agent of the union "came to the point."

1　DuFresne: We came over to straighten things out about Irene Mason. You
　　can't just discharge a person for saying what she thinks. That's free speech.
　　Furthermore, she has been working for you for a good many years; she
　　must be a good worker.

5　Wilson: She is good when she sticks to her work. The trouble is that she
　　didn't mind her own business. But let's not argue before we have all the
　　facts. We have reviewed the case, Mr. DuFresne, but we should like to
　　to hear your side of the story first.

　　DuFresne (*glancing at a typewritten statement*): Well, she told me a lot of
10　things. There was this matter back a couple of years when she was told
　　not to bother the truckers. She tells me *they* were bothering her. Anyhow,
　　Mr. Wilson, you know as well as I do that, if people work next to each
　　other, they will talk. You can't fire them for that.

　　Then there was the time she was told to go back to work and mind
15　her own business when she gave her opinion about the 4 hours' reporting
　　pay. She says the foreman called her over and that the talk was near her
　　workplace, where she could have heard everything anyway. Now, she
　　was wrong about the reporting pay being in effect, but she was just
　　saying what she thought was right, when the foreman asked her.

20　　　And now last Saturday. She expressed her opinion again, and
　　probably she shouldn't have said what she did. But she didn't refuse to
　　do the work, and you can fire a person for insubordination only if he
　　refuses to do the work. If one of my office girls says I'm wrong about
　　something, I don't fire her. This is a democratic country, where every-
25　body has a right to express an opinion. Well, that's all I have. There just
　　aren't sufficient grounds for discharge.

　　Wilson: Now, we've looked into the case, as I said, and our information
　　doesn't check with yours at a lot of points. There were at least five times
　　in the last 2 or 3 years when we had trouble with Irene. [He then re-
30　counts the four episodes outlined in Sec. II and the discharge episode
　　described in Sec. I.]

　　DuFresne: Well, if she caused that much trouble, why didn't you discharge
　　her before? Why didn't you fire her when she called Mr. Smolokas that
　　insulting name?

35　Forbes: Because we were trying to convince her that she was in the wrong
　　and should change her ways. We were short of help, and we wanted to
　　hold onto her. She was a good worker, except for that.

　　DuFresne: Well, I can't help what she did before. She was discharged—or
　　suspended—on Tuesday for something she did Saturday, and I say what
40　she did Saturday, and refusing to apologize for it, is not reason enough
　　for discharge. If she isn't put back on her old job with back pay, I'm
　　going to take the case to arbitration. And I don't think any arbitrator
　　will rule against me on this case.

　　Wilson: We discharged her Tuesday because it was the last straw. All these
45　other episodes are important as background. We did offer to move her

to a different job where she wouldn't cause so much trouble, but she refused.

DuFRESNE: I'm not interested in another job for her. I want her back in her old job. She came to the union with her grievance, and we're going to 50 do something for her, even if we have to go to arbitration. I told her I thought she had a good case and would go to bat for her, and I'm not going to let her down. What d'you think would happen to the union if I didn't do something about cases like this?

FORBES: Well, Mr. DuFresne, just what will happen here if we put her back, 55 supposing we do? Will that help anything? There is a clash of personalities here that just can't be remedied. We've tried enough times, but it won't work. She'll do the same thing again.

DuFRESNE: What I want you to do is to give us a chance to show how the union can help you. If you put this girl back, I'll call her in and have a 60 good talk with her. I'll tell her that, even though this is a free country, she shouldn't express opinions that don't involve her, especially if they are insulting to management. I'll tell her that she is expected to do her work.

SMOLOKAS: Well what if she does the same things all over again, as she will? 65 If it is wrong for her to do them then, why isn't it just as wrong for her to do them last Saturday and before? I don't understand the difference.

DuFRESNE: The difference is this. You have given the union the chance to see what it can do to straighten this girl out. Then if she doesn't come around, we won't go to bat for her again. I'll tell her it will be her last 70 chance.

FORBES: But why should you do that? Isn't that management's job? Do we have to depend on the union to discipline our workers?

DuFRESNE: You can do whatever you like. But we want a chance to show you that we can be helpful, too. Why, the other mills in this town tell 75 us if they are having trouble with certain people—acting up or loafing too much—and I call the people in if they are union members and ask them what the story is. If they admit what the mill has told me, I tell them that they will have to turn over a new leaf if they expect to get any help from the union. If their stories don't agree, we go right down to the 80 the mill and get the thing straightened out before it goes too far. If you had called me about this girl when the trouble first started, maybe all this could have been avoided.

WILSON: Well, you know that we didn't have a union here until last year, and we don't have much experience with one. Why, we don't even know 85 who the shop stewards are in each department. But we were talking this morning about the angle you mentioned. I think in the future when we have trouble with anyone in discipline, Mr. Smolokas should call the union office about it, so that you know the story before it is necessary to take action.

90 DuFRESNE: That would be fine. We want to help. But what about this case? What are we going to do—go to arbitration?

WILSON: I don't know yet. Suppose you give us a chance to talk it over—to discuss what you have offered to do about her. Then I'll get in touch with you by tomorrow morning at the latest.

95 DuFRESNE: That's all right with me. I want to do the right thing, and I think you do, too. And I'll send you a list of the shop stewards that have been appointed in each department.

After the meeting adjourned, there was further discussion among the three management officials. They agreed that, if the case went to 100 arbitration, the foreman would probably be called upon to testify, which might weaken the company's position. This company had no experience with arbitration and wanted to avoid it on a case that was not "airtight." On the other hand, the officials felt that their case was strong enough so that they might reinstate the girl on her old job 105 without back pay. The loss of pay would be something of a penalty for her actions, they reasoned, and, furthermore, the "talk" that the the union business agent had agreed to give her would strengthen their position later if she persisted in her actions.

The assistant manager wondered whether the union business 110 agent would back down if management told him that it would not change its position and would carry the case to arbitration. The manager and the superintendent, however, felt that this challenge might be hazardous, since they were convinced the union would carry the case to arbitration.

115 The manager then called the union office and told the union business agent what the company was prepared to do. The offer was accepted, and there was no argument over the denial of back pay. The business agent assured the manager that he would have a talk with the girl the next morning.

120 After reporting this conversation to his colleagues, the manager suggested that they call in the foreman the next day and "have a talk with him." He also said that the superintendent should tell Irene when she came to work that "bygones would be bygones" but that she was expected to do her work and "mind her own business."

QUESTIONS FOR DISCUSSION

1. *On defining an issue*
   a. Why do you think the head business agent's statements (lines 1 to 4, 9 to 26 and 38 to 43) are or are not helpful in clarifying the issue?
   b. How well does Mr. Wilson, as a management representative, bring out the central issue? (lines 5 to 8, 27 to 31, and 44 to 47)
   c. At what point in the discussion, and by whom, is the issue clearly stated? What advantage of this clarification is taken by the parties to the dispute?

    d. If you had been at this meeting as a personnel administrator, what might you have said to clarify the issue at the outset?

    e. What subjects discussed were irrelevant to the central issue?

2. *On discipline as a management responsibility*

    a. As a matter of management policy, is the union's proposal (lines 58 to 63 and 73 to 82) acceptable? State reasons for your opinion.

        (1) What dangers to management's authority does it contain?

    b. Comment on Mr. Wilson's statement. (lines 85 to 89)

        (1) Are management's intentions made clear?

        (2) What possibilities for future difficulties in labor relations does this statement contain?

3. *On managment and union attitudes toward arbitration*

    a. Should management have "stuck to its guns" and taken the case to arbitration?

    b. What would have been the gains and losses in terms of plant morale and relations with the union?

    c. How good is management's case? Make a brief outline of management's contentions, and list supporting evidence.

    d. Why do you think the union was determined to take the case to arbitration? What commitments were made to the discharged employee?

    e. How good is the union's case? Make a brief outline of the union's contentions, and list supporting evidence.

4. *On management's technique to correct a mistake*

    a. What advantages might there have been if the mill manager had frankly admitted that the discharge was a mistake and reinstated Irene with back pay?

IV. Foreman Training

On the morning following the conference with the union, the foreman was called in by the manager and "put on the carpet." He was told that his actions had placed the mill in an embarrassing position and that he must handle his department differently if he expected to keep his job. His relations with Irene were critized, and the foreman admitted, "Maybe that's true." According to the manager, he took his reprimand, "like a great big kid that had had a spanking." He agreed he was "all wrong" and said that he "would try to do better."

The superintendent had a talk with Irene before she went to work, pointing out that "we will start with a clean slate, but you are expected to do your work and mind your own business." Irene said nothing. During the first week after her reinstatement, she was surly, but this attitude gradually changed. One day about 2 weeks later she came to the superintendent's office voluntarily to say that she realized that she had been "loafing on the job" and that her actions had hurt the work of the department, bringing criticism on the foreman.

After this confession, Irene "settled down," according to the superintendent, and "she is almost like her old self before all this trouble started." But the difficulties with the foreman continued; and, 8 months after the discharge episode, he was replaced by a new foreman. Irene continued to do her work well under the direction of this new supervisor.

Six months later, no further difficulties of this nature had been experienced with the union. Relationships improved; and, in negotiations for subsequent contracts, the attitude of the business agent was friendly and reasonable.

QUESTIONS FOR DISCUSSION

1. *On line authority*
   a. Comment on the manager's technique in criticizing foreman Williams.
   b. What could have been done to help the foreman?

QUESTIONS ON THE CASE AS A WHOLE

1. *On labor relations*
   On the basis of the facts presented above, what recommendations would you make for management action to develop sound labor relations?
2. *On a personnel program*
   What features of a fully rounded personnel program might have helped Irene to find her place more quickly?
3. *On supervisory training*
   a. What seem to have been the weaknesses in "the campaign to educate" foreman Williams?
   b. Which officials might have contributed in what ways to improve this "training program?"

Case for Chapter 16

A Dispute over Alleged Inequities

(A Wage Complaint by Finish Polishers)

INTRODUCTION

Remarks made in the course of the meeting here reported provide insight into the attitude toward wage rates held by workers, union officers, and a personnel administrator. As the argument proceeds, the following points are among those illustrated:

1. The difficulties that arise when it is assumed that two jobs with the same name are necessarily identical in content.
2. The importance attached by workers to wage differentials.
3. The significance to workers of various kinds of job factors.
4. The key position of a foreman in relation to understandings and misunderstandings about pay.
5. The use of clichés by both management and union representatives as a poor substitute for adequate preparation.
6. A disguised complaint used by workers to present what seems to them a more acceptable ground for complaint than the circumstances with which the real dissatisfaction is associated.

This case may be called a "tempest in a teapot." As such, it is typical of many misunderstandings that arise in industry. Not all complaints can be so easily disposed of as this one was. But every complaint can be used (although this one seems not to have been) as an index of employee morale, supervisory ability, and the success of top-management policy.

CASE BACKGROUND

In 1937, the National Manufacturing Company had a wage schedule in which all occupations were listed and defined. Each occupation had a base rate, which listed the minimum and maximum of wages paid. The employees called this base rate a "bracket." For example, the base rate for a rough polisher was 55 to 59 cents per hour. A finish polisher received 59 to 66 cents per hour. This wage schedule was originally set up in negotiation between management and employee representatives after a study of the interrelationships between occupations. Asking for an increase in a bracket was tantamount to asking for a general raise in this occupation. Reviewing a rate card meant considering the wages of an individual in any given occupation.

The company had a signed agreement with the United Electrical and Radio Workers of America, CIO, which provided that each department or occupation have one representative. For instance, there was one union representative for the rough polishers and another for the finish polishers. In meeting with management, each of these representatives was allowed to bring with him, if he so desired, a workman from his group.

On Jan. 13, 1937, Mr. Cameron, president of the union, submitted a written complaint from the polishers of department G-24 and asked for a meeting with management.

The industrial-relations director replied that a meeting could be held on Jan. 14, 1937, and would be attended by the foreman and the employee representatives of department G-24.

THE MEETING

On Jan. 14, 1937, the meeting was held in the office of the industrial-relations director, Mr. Avery. Those present were:

MR. CAMERON, president of the union.

MR. O'ROURKE, foreman, department G-24.

MR. JAMES, finish polisher and union representative.

MR. CARLSON, finish polisher.

MR. SMITH, rough polisher and union representative.

MR. JONES, rough polisher.

MR. AVERY, industrial-relations director.

The following conversation took place:

1 AVERY: I have here a complaint from the union that I would like to read for the benefit of all those present:

    We, the polishers of department, G-24, feel that the foreman is not rating the men properly in his department with respect to their oc-
5 cupation. In view of this, we would like to go over the present brackets for an increase in them.

                                        (*signed*) Cameron, *President*

    Mr. Cameron, inasmuch as you brought the complaint, have you anything to add?

10 CAMERON: No, not particularly, but these men feel that they are not
treated right in the matter of rating and that they should get more
money for their work because it is hard work, dirty and wet, and they
have to buy more clothes than the average worker in the rest of the
plant.

15 O'ROURKE: I believe these men are earning good money regardless of
their base rate, and that there's nothing to kick about. In the matter
of clothing, I should say that extra wear and tear is one of the accepted hazards of the occupation. As long as I have been in the same
game (and that is over 30 years), that hazard has been taken into
20   consideration in the bracket of the job.

SMITH: Nevertheless, Mr. Avery, we don't feel that we're getting paid
what other polishers in the community are getting. We feel we should
be given more consideration.

JAMES: That's right. I know a number of the employees of the Electrical
25   Appliance Company and know for a fact they're getting more money
than we are, despite the fact they don't do the high type of work we do.

JONES: I've been a finish polisher all my life, and I'm getting the rate of
a rough polisher.

AVERY: That may be true, Mr. Jones, but remember we pay for the job
30   and not the man. For instance, we might have a toolmaker, and, just
because we haven't got a toolmaker's job for him, he might have to
run a drill press. Obviously it would not be fair to pay him a toolmaker's rate on this job.

CAMERON: Yes, I agree with Mr. Avery. That is our policy. The rate carries
35   the job and not the man.

O'ROURKE: If I had enough finish polishing work I should be glad to
give it to you, Mr. Jones. On the other hand, I'm interested in keeping you working and don't want to send you home when I don't have
finish polishing work to do.

40 CAMERON: I think that's understood by all of us. But how about the point
that Mr. James and Mr. Carlson brought up . . . how about giving some
consideration to an increase in rates?

AVERY: It is a policy of our company to pay at least the prevailing rate
in the community for similar work. I believe we are following that
45   policy; in fact, we're paying not only the prevailing rate, but more.

CARLSON: I don't believe it. I know a man who lives next door to me who
gets as much as a dollar an hour.

AVERY: That may be true, Mr. Carlson. There may be a special reason
why his company is paying him that rate. He may be paid for special
50   ability. But on the average, we are paying more than anyone else in
the community for similar work. I have a chart here that shows the
earnings of workers in similar occupations in various companies. This
is proof that we are paying more for polishing work than anyone.

JAMES: Well, who are these companies you're talking about?

55 AVERY: I'm sorry, but I'm not privileged to give you the names of these companies. But they are companies in this community that employ more than 200 people and have work similar to ours.

CAMERON: I don't believe we care what is paid in this community. We're only interested in our own people. And we want a bracket increase.

60 AVERY: I'm sorry, Mr. Cameron, but we can't grant a bracket increase at this time. I'm not interested in increasing any brackets that will disturb our present wage schedule. For me to satisfy one group would only bring another group down on my neck.

CAMERON: Why couldn't we go over individual rates in this department
65 and see if we can't do something for somebody?

AVERY: I've no objection to this if it is all right with Mr. O'Rourke. He knows the men better than I do, and it is his prerogative to raise men within the brackets according to their ability, any time he sees fit. And I believe he's been doing that. How about it, Mr. O'Rourke?

70 O'ROURKE: You bet.

SMITH: Well, he hasn't been doing it. And I don't think he's fair the way he hands out raises or classes his people.

AVERY: I wouldn't say that, Mr. Smith. This is the first time I've had a complaint of Mr. O'Rourke or his department, and Mr. O'Rourke's
75 been with us for more than 15 years. You must remember that we can't hit a home run every time we go to bat. All I say is, if Mr. O'Rourke has talked to you and told you the reason why he couldn't give raises and been fair about it, I don't see why you have cause to complain.

CAMERON: Why can't we look over the rate cards?

80 O'ROURKE: I'm willing to go over them if Mr. Avery wants to.

AVERY Why don't we? (*calls for the rate cards of department G-24. The secretary brings them and the group goes over each card. In the process of doing this, Mr. James picks out the card of Mr. Wilson, a fellow workman. He hands it to the foreman*)

85 JAMES: How do you account for this fellow, Wilson, being a finish polisher?

O'ROURKE: He isn't a finish polisher. He's an acid dipper.

JAMES: Well, his card here classes him as a finish polisher.

O'ROURKE: There must be some mistake.

JAMES: Well, there isn't, and you signed the card.

90 O'ROURKE: I don't know how that happened, but anyway, he's not a finish polisher.

CARLSON: You're damn right he isn't. But he was told he was, and he thinks he is. And our men are sore about it, see? They say, if Wilson is a finish polisher, then we're silversmiths.

95 CAMERON: Well, is that what's bothering you fellows . . . that this Wilson here is called a polisher and isn't?

CARLSON: Yeah, he happens to be a friend of O'Rourke here and he's been bragging about it for weeks. And our fellows say that, if Wilson is getting paid as a finish polisher, we ought to have more money.

100   CAMERON: Mr. Avery, I think they're right, don't you?

AVERY: If it is true that Wilson gets the pay of a finish polisher, I think the men have a cause for complaint, But as Mr. O'Rourke says, there must be some mistake. Let me see that card. . . . (*examines card*) Why, it says right here that the boy is getting the pay of an acid dipper, and
105   that's . . . .

SMITH: Let me see that card . . . . If this is so, we haven't got much to kick about. We thought he was getting a finish polisher's money.

AVERY: Well, according to this card, he isn't. His classification as a finish polisher was a mistake. Does that settle everything?

110   JAMES: As far as I'm concerned.

O'ROURKE: Well, and I want to tell you fellows that Wilson is no special friend of mine. I do happen to have known him before he was employed here, but I treat him just the same as I do you. I didn't know that Wilson was doing any bragging. I do wish that you fellows would
115   come to me first instead of bringing me on the carpet with Mr. Avery.

AVERY: Well, Mr. Cameron, I think this is all straightened out, don't you?

CAMERON: Yes, I believe it is.

AVERY: Before we adjourn, I should like to add for the information of all that you should feel free at any time to see me if anything is bothering
120   you. On the other hand, we expect that you have and will continue to have confidence in your foreman and will discuss matters with him first.

SMITH: Well, if he shows a willingness to talk with us, I'm sure we'll be
125   glad to talk to him.

AVERY: How about it, Mr O'Rourke?

O'ROURKE: Well, I've always done that. I believe there was a little misunderstanding here.

CAMERON: Well, let's adjourn and forget it.

QUESTIONS FOR DISCUSSION

1. *On union policy*

Comment on these remarks as statements of a union wage policy. (lines 58 to 59 and 64 to 65). In what situations do you think that the union president would be likely to take an opposite position?

2. *On a personnel administrator's responsibility*

    a. If you had been in Mr. Avery's position at this point (lines 66 to 69), what would you have said, and why?

    b. Why do you, or do you not, think this a wise procedure in this situation? (lines 81 to 84)

    c. If you had been in Mr. Avery's position here (line 129), what would you have attempted to do?

3. *On union responsibility in handling grievances*

    a. This statement (lines 95 to 96) suggests that the union president here gets a new insight into the real cause of the polishers' dissatisfaction. What has he failed to do before presenting the complaint?

b. What does this remark (line 100) indicate about the president's approach to the complaint situation?

c. (lines 106 to 107) What does this suggest about the union representative's investigation of the complaint situation prior to the meeting?

4. *On interpreting employee complaints*

What are the various grounds for dissatisfaction voiced in these speeches? (lines 85 to 89, 97 to 98, and 124)

QUESTIONS ON THE CASE AS A WHOLE

1. *On wage policy*

Outline the company's policies on the general level of wages and wage inter-relationships as they emerge from this discussion. Can you suggest any improvements?

2. *On wage administration*

   a. Who appears to have the responsibility for wage administration in the company?

   b. Would you suggest any changes?

   c. Suppose that Wilson actually had been paid as a finish polisher. What should have been done?

3. *On a complaint and grievance procedure*

   a. From the standpoint of a good complaint and grievance procedure, how might the case have been better handled?

      (1) By management: What important weaknesses are revealed at two levels of management?

      (2) By the union: What omissions and errors are exemplified in the statements made by union representatives and by the union president?

4. *On complaints as an index*

What insight could be gained from the various complaints here presented?

A Dispute over Rates on Three Jobs

(Wilshire Shoe Company)

INTRODUCTION

The following case illustrates some of the problems confronting a management when wage rates on specific jobs are in dispute, especially in a unionized situation. Unions frequently apply the pragmatic test in adopting those arguments which best support their current demands. In this case, the union business agent is making an understandable effort to get "equal pay for equal work" in all plants in which the union is the bargaining agency. Confronted by this position, the employer is making an equally understandable objection to paying the same rates in a country town as in an urban labor market. The union business agent, representing only one group of workers, is interested only in their wages and not in the entire wage structure of the plant. But the company president must think in terms of his total labor costs, and he is genuinely concerned about the ultimate effect of piecemeal increases.

BACKGROUND OF THE CASE

In April, 1945, the Wilshire Shoe Company employed about 350 workers in the manufacture of Army shoes. Production of shoes for the armed services was its regular line of business, supplemented in peacetime with work shoes and police shoes. The company was located in a small country town about 35 miles from a larger city in which a number of shoe companies were located. For many years, a shoe workers' union, which was an amalgamation of 14 locals of the various shoe crafts, had represented the shoe workers in the city. In 1942, following a consent election, it won bargaining rights for employees of the Wilshire Shoe Company, and this was one of the few firms outside the city that the union had succeeded in organizing. General wage changes and other matters affecting all employees were negotiated by the top officials of the amalgamated craft union with this company and with a manufacturers' association in X City. But all grievances and requests for changes in job rates affecting a particular craft were handled separately by the business agent of the craft union involved.

The case here reported took place early in 1945, beginning with a meeting between the business agent of the Goodyear operators' local and the president of the company. The business agent had made an appointment to discuss a grievance on wages for the crafts he represented.

I

After the usual preliminaries, the business agent stated his case:

1   BUSINESS AGENT: A couple of days ago, the Goodyear operators asked me to come up and hear their gripe. I talked to them a little while ago, and they tell me they can't earn as much as operators do in X City. I looked at their earnings slips, and this seems to be true. So I'm asking an ad-
5   justment of the piece rates on welting, rounding, and Goodyear stitching, so that they can earn just what they would in X City, which is about $1.27 an hour.

COMPANY PRESIDENT: Well, I'd want to check their actual earnings here first, but you know, we've been all through that question before. This
10   little company just can't pay the city rates and stay in business. We aren't competitive with the city companies, and we aren't in that labor market.

BUSINESS AGENT: But you're making the same kind of shoes those companies are making for the Army now. We're not talking about dress
15   shoes or police shoes or work shoes; we're talking about Army shoes. I don't see why our members here, who pay the same dues and belong to the same union, should get less money than they do in the city for doing exactly the same work on the same type of shoe.

COMPANY PRESIDENT: I repeat, we just can't pay the city rates, and we
20   never have in the past. The X City companies have continued to make some dress shoes during the war, and they took this Army business on to help cover their overhead. They don't care too much what rates they have to pay on Army shoes, because the business is all gravy to them and is temporary. But it's different with us. We will go on making
25   Army shoes after the war, and our competitors in other parts of the country already pay lower rates than we do. How can we keep in business? We've already given a lot of increases during the war. Since December, 1940, they've totaled about 40 per cent.

BUSINESS AGENT: Oh, you'll do all right. But let's get back to the main
30   point. We should get the city rates here, because our membership pays the same dues in both places and should get the same pay for the same work.

COMPANY PRESIDENT: Have you checked how many jobs here pay more than the city rates? I know we have some. Our wage structure isn't what
35 it should be, I'll admit, but I've urged you union people to join me in a real job-evaluation or wage-classification program, so that we do the fair thing for everyone, not just for a few people who happen to kick the most. Maybe some of our rates ought to be raised and some ought to be reduced. But we can't keep on making a few increases here,
40 and a few more increases there, and expect to stay in business. Do you know that last year [1944] we lost money—our losses were half as great as our profits the year before? And it was all due to increased labor costs.

BUSINESS AGENT: How can that be? We haven't had any general increases
45 in the last year.

COMPANY PRESIDENT: Well, the War Labor Board ordered us to give paid vacations, and you remember there were several other cases in the other crafts that resulted in retroactive adjustments. And we've had to transfer skilled operators to less skilled jobs at their higher rates to keep a
50 production line going when labor was scarce. We've also had to pay some overtime for the same reason.

BUSINESS AGENT: Well, maybe so, but the companies in the city are making money and you must be too, even though you say you had a net loss this year.

55 COMPANY PRESIDENT: Our accounts are audited, and I don't know how else to convince you that these are the facts. I'm willing to let any impartial person look at them to verify what I say. Furthermore, I think we must pay at least as much as any other shoe firms in small towns in this area outside of the city. That's a high-rate place, you know.

60 BUSINESS AGENT: That's because we've raised wages for our people there, and members of the local here should get the same rates as members of the local in the city.

COMPANY PRESIDENT: I'm not willing to concede that, but let me check the actual earnings of our operators here and also what some of the other
65 shoe firms outside of the city pay. I'll get in touch with you in a week or so.

BUSINESS AGENT: All right, but I'd like to get this thing settled pretty soon. The men are dissatisfied.

QUESTIONS FOR DISCUSSION

1. *On wage policy*
   a. What factors should influence the determination of this company's general level of wages? Have they been adequately considered in the discussion between the company president and the union business agent?
   b. What assumptions are implicit in the union's claim that the same rates should be paid on the three jobs in the city companies and in this company? (lines 4 to 7, 13 to 18, and 30 to 32)

c. Is it important to make a wage survey of other shoe plants outside the city? Why or why not?

2. *On job evaluation*

What would be accomplished by the company's suggestion that a job-evaluation program be introduced in the plant? (lines 33 to 40)

3. *On wage negotiations*

What do you think of the manner in which the company president presented information on his inability to meet the increases requested? (lines 39 to 43)

4. *On grievance procedure*

Is there anything unusual in the way in which this grievance was presented by the union? How do you account for this procedure?

II

During the next week, the company president telephoned executives in three other shoe firms, two located in another small town 20 miles away and one larger firm located in a medium-sized city 50 miles away. He asked them what piece rates they were paying welters, rounders, and stitchers in the Goodyear room, and he then tabulated the following information:

Goodyear operators	Company A	Company B	Company C	Average A, B, C	Wilshire	X City
Welters	$0.3630	$0.3444	$0.2880	$0.3318	$0.3333	$0.3600
Rounders	0.2178	0.2220	0.1680	0.2026	0.2361	0.2402
Stitchers	0.5929	0.6202	0.5400	0.5844	0.5139	0.5701

He also asked the paymaster to compute the average straight-time hourly earnings of the operators on each job during the third quarter of 1944. These were reported as follows:

Welters .... $1.2952 an hour
Rounders .... $1.1394 an hour
Stitchers .... $1.1027 an hour

Only one of the firms that the President telephoned could give him quickly the average hourly straight-time earnings figures for these jobs, and this firm reported that, for the current week in 1945, stitchers' earnings averaged $1.23 an hour and rounders' earnings averaged $1.34 an hour. He did not consider that these figures provided a fair comparison, however, for the particular company was one noted for very efficient production and high piece-rate earnings. Further study of his own pay-roll figures also revealed that the average hourly straight-time earnings of individual operators in the third quarter of 1944 fell between the following ranges:

> Welters ....$1.2367 to $1.5443
> Rounders ....$0.9005 to $1.3012
> Stitchers ....$0.8899 to $1.4284

These figures, he thought, showed that individual operators could earn well above the X City average of $1.27 an hour on these three jobs.

Finally, the president asked the paymaster to check the location of the homes of present employees, to determine whether any came from the city and its suburbs. He received the following report:

> Live in town...........................156
> Live in town or adjacent towns...........249
> Live within 11 miles of town..............322
> Live in X City area.....................None

When the union business agent returned a week and a half later, the company president showed him the figures that he had collected and maintained his original position that he could not pay the city rates. He added that there was no train or bus service between the city and the small town in which the Wilhsire Company was located, and consequently they must be considered two separate labor markets. As for other communities, he felt that Wilshire rates and earnings compared favorably, on the whole, and that he could not agree to an isolated increase for one craft. He again urged that the union join him in beginning a job-evaluation program or some other procedure to determine proper wage relationships and "what would be fair labor costs for this type of business."

The union business agent put a different interpretation on the figures. He argued that "only the welters were earning their rate" (city rate) and that the piece rates of the rounders and stitchers should be increased to enable them to earn at least $1.27 an hour. He again repeated his argument that union members should be paid the same rates for the same work regardless of where the plants were located.

Unable to reach an agreement in the dispute, the parties agreed to submit it to arbitration.

QUESTIONS FOR DISCUSSION

1. *On wage policies and administration*
   a. Could there have been any improvement in the method used in making the wage survey?
   b. Is there any significance in the figures showing the location of the homes of Wilshire employees?

   c. Suppose that you were the personnel administrator in his company, how would you have suggested to the company president that the case be handled, in terms of both the data needed for reaching a decision and the manner in which the problems of the company should be presented to the union representative?

2. *On differentials in earnings*

   What might explain the wide variations in earnings of individual operators on the same jobs? Do you agree with the company president's conclusions based on these data?

3. *On getting down to cases*

   As an arbitrator, what would have been your decision on (*a*) whether the company should pay the city rates, and, if not, (*b*) what rate should be paid on the three operations? Give your reasons.

Case for Chapter 17

Difficulties with an Incentive System

(May Anson and Susan deMille)

INTRODUCTION

This case illustrates a situation that often results when incentive pay is used. Workers here saw their interests as being significantly opposed to management's purposes. Team spirit within the work unit was not used to advance mutual interests. Instead, production was pegged at a level well below that which could be reached by able workers. And the most efficient group members to some extent carried the less able by "trading points." Management and workers frequently regard this practice from diametrically opposed viewpoints, one party seeing it as dishonest, the other considering it as an expression of group solidarity.

The circumstances described also illustrate the unfortunate results of avoidable misunderstandings and lack of insight among workers, and between workers and management. A newcomer to the department precipitated trouble for two other employees because the "point" system had not been adequately explained to her, either by a management representative or even by a union official, from the worker's point of view. A more fundamental difficulty arose because policies and procedures for the incentive system had not convinced workers of management's understanding of job demands and of what constitutes a fair reward for effort. Moreover, there is some indication that management was not wholly aware of the difficulties at the root of the workers' "misconduct." Pegging of production must have been an established practice in the company. Yet there is no evidence that, before the episode here described, management had attempted to tackle this fundamental issue.

CASE BACKGROUND

The following incident occurred in the press department of the National Manufacturing Company. Three employees were discharged for

442

alleged misconduct in connection with the company's wage-incentive system, which was a "point" system. The discharged employees appealed to their union board to get the penalty commuted to something less severe. The steps taken are here given as they appeared in the union records.

I. APPEALS OF THE THREE DISCHARGED WORKERS

1. *Statement of May Anson*

May 20, 1943

1 On Friday, May 14, 1943, I worked on Press No. 9 on a job with a standard 31. There was a lot of production put out ever since I have been in the place. I have heard from different people not to pass in more than 1,000 points on one job.

5 Hearing this from various girls that I worked with, I passed in 990 points. What was left of the work some girl took. I do not know who the girl is. I was called up to Mr. Helford's office [department head] and questioned. Edward [night setup man] told me to pass in 990 points. I did exactly what he told me.

10 When I was up in Mr. Helford's office, I tried to protect Edward and did not tell Mr. Helford that he had told me to pass in so many but said that I did it on my own account. That is all, and I lost my job for a single reason.

Not knowing that the standard was 31,[1] I had been working right
15 along trying to make my night's work, thinking that the standard was 11. When I found out the standard, I immediately stopped working. I left the points there and did not care who took them or where they went. Before I knew it, I was called up to the office.

I have only 3 weeks' service in the press department and do not know
20 much about it. I have worked since September in the instrument department as a repair operator.

2. *Statement of Susan deMille* (operator and shop steward)

May 20, 1943

On Friday, May 14, 1943, May Anson worked on Press No. 9. At
25 10:30 P.M. a girl working Press No. 10 called me to fix her air (compressed-air nozzle to blow a completed piece out of the matrix.) While working there, I asked May how she was doing. When she said she had done 5,500 (pieces), I said, "You're doing fine. You've got 1,080 points made."[2]

---

[1] "A standard 31" means here that 31 hundredths of a minute is the standard time for one piece, so tha 3.226 pieces score one point. In order to achieve a score of 1,000 points, therefore, it would be necessary to put out 3,226 pieces a day or about 400 pieces an hour. This standard was obviously based on a "loose" time study, since May made almost three times as many as this (see the following footnote).

[2] Susan deMille is making a rough estimate on the basis of three pieces to one point, or three pieces a minute. Since May supposed that she had to turn out 9 pieces a minute (actually 9.016 pieces) even to make standard time (which she supposed to be 0.11 minutes a piece), the score for 5,500 pieces according to her figuring would have

She immediately went to our setup man and asked him what to do.
30 He said to take so many and leave the rest. He was going to give them to
a third-shift girl. When I heard about it, I went down to our setup man and
said, "You can't give a third-shift girl those points. They read the indicators between shifts, and you will get into trouble and so will she because
they will prove she did not make those points on the third shift."[1] I knew
35 he would get it and so would the new girl, May.

I had a miserable job that night, and the setup man knew it. He
did not tell me to take the points, but just said, "Sue, you had a lousy job
tonight, didn't you?" So, to help me out in my night's points and with no
idea of stealing, I took the points.
40 The work had been done, the pieces were there, and the points would
be of no value to the first- or third-shift girls.

3. *Statement of Edward Barr* (setup man)

May 20, 1943

It was about quarter to eleven last Friday night. I was very busy
45 getting ready for the third shift, when the Anson girl came to me and said
she had made way over her points. She gave me the number of points, but
I don't remember how many. I said, "Turn in (so many) and go see Sue
deMille." Sue came to me and said, "Don't leave them on the third shift.
Indicators are checked before the third shift comes on." She was talking
50 to the Anson girl, so I kept right on with my work.

Monday night about 6 o'clock I was called to Mr. Helford's office
and was asked if I knew anything about it. I said no. Mr. Helford went on
to explain that a person should make as many points as he could. We talked
on a while, and he said he would discharge the person who got those extra
55 points when he found out who it was.

That was all I heard until tonight (Thursday) at 3 o'clock when he
read me what the two girls had said. The only thing I told him was that
it was not the truth.

Data Added by the Business Agent (Offered orally and not in the office record)

60 Time studies on work in this department had not been performed with
equal adequacy. On some jobs, the resulting computations were "loose"

---

been 611 points, and she would have thought that she had to make about 3,500 more
pieces (or a total of 9,000) in order to turn in the number agreed upon among the girls
as the top limit. Because of this mistaken impression, she had exceeded the standard
to such an extent that, if she had turned in her true score (1,708 points), management
could no longer have ignored the absurdity of the situation. The operation would
almost certainly have been restudied and a higher "standard" set. This would, in
effect, cut the rate (increasing the number of pieces to be turned out both below the
standard and for each incentive point). When May's error was pointed out, she gave
away 718 points and turned in a score of 990.

[1] Indicators were read between shifts, and the total recorded by all machines on a
certain job was compared with the number of pieces reported by all operators on the
job on each shift. Separate counts were not made for each operator and each machine
on each shift.

(probably estimated), making a high rate of output easy. On others they were "tight," making a good rate hard to accomplish. It was a "loose" study that had enabled the newcomer to roll up her "excess" points, and probably
65 a "tight" study that had given the shop steward a hard run of work for the day.

QUESTIONS FOR DISCUSSION

1. *On union and management responsibility*
   What negligence on the part of the foreman and shop steward is indicated here? (lines 3 to 6) What difference would there probably have been in the actions here described if May had been "properly instructed" (from the company standpoint and the union standpoint) when she first entered the department?
2. On *interpreting statements*
   a. Do you think this is an accurate quotation of Susan's remarks to May? (lines 26 to 28) (Give the reasons for your impression.)
   b. In view of what happens, how would you interpret Susan's reference to her job as "miserable?" (line 36)
   c. What important item of Susan's statement is here omitted? (lines 44 to 50) Would this omission make you inclined to disbelieve Susan on this point?
   d. According to his own statement, on what count is the setup man involved in this incident?

II. NOTICE OF THE EXECUTIVE BOARD TO MANAGEMENT OF THE CASE FOR JOINT CONFERENCE

May 21, 1943

After hearing the complainants' stories with respect to their discharge and hearing a subcommittee's report after talk with management officials, the executive board wishes, on behalf of those discharged, to protest the severity of the punishment for the alleged crime.

QUESTIONS FOR DISCUSSION

1. *On union attitude*
   a. What difference as to union attitude in regard to the guilt of these employees can be made from this statement?
   b. What light does the expression "alleged crime" throw on the union's attitude toward the incentive system?

III. THE BOARD'S REPORT OF ITS CONFERENCE WITH MANAGEMENT

Case of: May Anson
Susan deMille
Edward Barr (setup man)

May 21, 1943
Dept. Head: Helford

Mr. Chesley [division superintendent] read from a report of the case from Mr. Helford. It was to the effect that a setup man on another shift had reported a poor condition on the job and involved Mr. Barr [complainant]. It was evident that, as a result of this other setup man's action, they were watching operators on the second shift.

The report showed that shop steward deMille had testified that girls gave each other "pieces" at the end of the shift and that they tried not to turn in over 1,000 points per shift.

Mr. Chesley was at first adamant, claiming that they would not condone any operator's taking payment for work she did not perform.

We argued against management's strict interpretation, saying that they, more than the operators, were responsible for the pieceworkers' slant on these matters. After we had criticized their severe attitude on this case, Mr. Chesley said he would not make a final decision without a talk with Mr. Helford and would let us know before 5:00 P.M. tonight.

About 2:30 this afternoon he called and said that, after reviewing the matter with Mr. Helford, they had agreed to let the three take the rest of the week off and come back on the job Monday, May 24.

They would talk with the group.

QUESTIONS FOR DISCUSSION

1. *On employee attitude*
   What difference in allegiance is to be inferred between Mr. Barr and the other setup man here quoted?
2. *On management policy*
   a. Why do you suppose management decided to commute the original sentence?
   b. On what grounds would you approve or disapprove the change in decision?
   c. Who should conduct the talk with the group? Why?
   d. If you were responsible for this "talk with the group," what would you say?

QUESTIONS FOR DISCUSSION ON THE CASE AS A WHOLE

1. *On discipline*
   a. Do you consider discharge too severe a penalty for any of the offenses committed in this case?
   b. What penalty, if any, would you have imposed on each of the offenders if you had been in Mr. Helford's position?
2. *On management opportunity for constructive action*
   Was anything done in the course of this case to improve conditions and relationships so that, in the future, the incentive system could be made to work to everyone's advantage?
3. *On policy thinking*
   What would you do to remedy the situation and prevent the recurrence of similar incidents?
4. *On management-union cooperation*
   a. If management should decide to consult with the union before making a final judgment on cases of this sort, what advantages and disadvantages might be expected?

b. What other kind of joint discussion as to the issues involved would probably be helpful to all concerned?

5. *On union attitude*

Comment on the following statement of a union official in this case on the matter of trading "points": "Tight and loose time studies are to the workers' pay what under- and overestimates of production costs are to the company's profit. When the company finds its costs on a contract turning out above estimates on some items and below on others, it simply offsets the unexpected losses with the unexpected gains—not correcting its bill to the customer. A work group does much the same when it lets the points lost through a 'tight' study by one member be made good by points gained through a 'loose' study by another."

Case for Chapter 17

Recommended Policy on Technological Changes

(Conestoga Woolen Mills)

INTRODUCTION

One of the central problems of management is how to win employee acceptance of the technological changes that constantly take place in a dynamic industry. Changes in output standards and work loads, dilution of skills, demotion, transfer, and sometimes layoffs are associated with technological changes, and these account in large part for the traditional opposition of workers to the introduction of new machines and processes.

In his capacity as a staff advisor, the personnel administrator has an opportunity to urge the adoption of policies and procedures that will help to overcome this resistance to technological changes. One set of recommendations is reported below.

CASE BACKGROUND

In order to meet competition and to provide customers with the types of woolen goods they wanted, frequent changes in machinery and work loads were necessary in the Conestoga Woolen Mills. In the past, these changes had encountered resistance from employees, and in 1942 this resistance was crystallized through a union that secured bargaining rights with the company. A personnel administrator was employed about this same time, and one of his first assignments was to prepare a set of recommendations to the president on the procedures to be followed in the introduction of new machinery and changes in work loads.

He submitted the following memorandum in May, 1942:

RECOMMENDED POLICY TO COVER INTRODUCTION OF NEW MACHINERY AND CHANGE IN WORK LOADS

At your suggestion, I am outlining below the procedures that I think should be followed during the period when new machinery is being introduced or where work loads or rates are being changed.

Procedures Recommended:

1. *Include* the personnel administrator in the final discussion before contract for purchase of laborsaving machinery is made, so that the future effect on employees will receive adequate consideration.

2. *Time* laborsaving machinery purchases, wherever possible, so that employees eliminated may be absorbed into other departments. Consider dismissal-compensation cost as part of the cost of new machinery.

3. *Introduce* laborsaving systems and machinery slowly, step by step, so that employees may adjust themselves gradually to the change and in this way avoid a dangerous cause of labor unrest.

4. *Inform* the union business agent and the department grievance committee of the purchase long enough before the machinery arrives at the plant to allow adequate plans to be made to take care of those employees eliminated and to consider rate adjustment if necessary.

5. *Explain* frankly to the grievance committee how the laborsaving system or machinery will affect them, and discuss the plans that have been made to safeguard them from unemployment, the objective being to gain their cooperation and agreement.

6. *Describe the procedure* for analyzing the new or revised job by means of a thorough study of the job, and gain the union's cooperation to arrive at dependable results covering the skill, responsibility, mental application, and physical effort required on the job as well as any changes in working conditions. Before the new rate or work load is placed in effect, the study should be discussed frankly with the union so as to indicate the company position and gain the understanding of the employees affected.

7. *Establish a preliminary rate* based on the employees' average earnings during the previous 3 months and flat increase per hour. This should be agreed upon by the company and the union for a reasonable trial period not to exceed 3 months, within which time the requirements of the job may be more fully studied, and necessary adjustments in work loads may be made by mutual agreement as soon as possible.

8. *At the conclusion of the trial period,* the company and the union will review the additional facts that have been gathered and will make a sincere effort to reach an agreement on a new rate that will be satisfactory to both parties. If they cannot agree on a new rate, the question will be submitted immediately to arbitration as provided in the contract. The rate finally set by the arbitrator shall be retroactive to the end of the trial period when the requirements of the job were finally established.

Company Plans to Protect Employees Displaced:

The management should formulate certain definite plans, *in advance*, to protect those employees who are being either laid off or transferred to other jobs. The only way that this can be done effectively is through long-term planning and close cooperation between the departments and with the union. The following plans are suggested to protect the employee:

1. Absorb displaced workers on equivalent jobs without the loss of seniority,

through transfer to other parts of the mill where openings are available as a result of labor turnover.

2. Provide the employees to be displaced with advance notice, so as to permit them to be retrained for other work to which they may be transferred later on. Hire temporary employees in this other work.

3. Provide advance notice of termination to those being laid off so as to afford them a chance to look for another job. Set up a preferential hiring list in our own company, and assist them in finding work elsewhere, if possible.

4. Study all requirements on the new job before setting rates—skill, responsibility, mental requirements, physical effort, and working conditions.

5. Set up adequate quality control of material in previous operations so as to protect employees from an overload when the work is not running well.

6. The new machinery should be manned by the employee with the greatest seniority in that occupation, provided that he is qualified to run the machinery satisfactorily after a fair test.

7. Consider dismissal compensation to be paid at the time of layoff in order to supplement unemployment compensation or lower earnings in another job, so that the employee may receive his normal earnings for a reasonable period of adjustment.

Conclusion:

If the above procedure meets with your approval, I would suggest that a meeting of the superintendents should be called immediately to discuss the matters presented above, so that the final procedure agreed upon may be put into practice immediately.

WILSON CAFFREY
Personnel Administrator

QUESTIONS FOR DISCUSSION

1. How well are the personnel administrator's suggestions designed to overcome the fears and resistance that normally accompany technological change and the new output standards that result?
2. What additions or modifications would you suggest in this memorandum, both in terms of desirable policy and in terms of the most convincing arguments for this approach in handling such changes?
3. In what ways are the various factors of situational thinking (technical considerations, people, principles, and the time element) reflected in these recommendations?

Need for a Service Program

(Anton Kuczinsky — Part II)

INTRODUCTION

This case gives more of the story whose beginning is given as the Case for Chap. 10. The three episodes here presented high light the needs felt more or less acutely by most industrial workers. Anton's case is an especially instructive example, because of the number and variety of openings it presented for management to help an employee help himself. If a well-rounded service program had met the challenge of his situation, he might have solved both the clash of loyalties that kept him out of the union and the various other difficulties that were too much for him to handle alone.

It is tempting to speculate what certain types of service might do for a person like Anton. For instance, a well-administered health and safety program would probably not only have been of practical use to him but might also have led the way to the kind of counseling of which he was evidently in great need.

If he had also participated in a well-planned recreational program, he might have developed his rather meager team spirit, relieved his emotional tension, and found an outlet for his desire to be a leader.

Further opportunities for education would surely have been both a pleasure and a practical benefit to him.

Help in achieving a greater measure of economic security would probably have given him a continuing reassurance and might have tided him over the layoff period.

Finally, if he had been encouraged to use up some of his surplus mental and emotional energy in the pursuit of civic and humanitarian interests, the results might have been of benefit to all concerned.

I. THE STRIKE AND SOME OF ITS CONSEQUENCES

A 4-year gap in Anton's employment record followed his discharge on Feb. 5, 1929. During this period, Anton sought and found employment with other companies, but no record of this experience is available.

On Sept. 14, 1933, Anton, now twenty-eight years of age, was reemployed by the National Manufacturing Company as a punch-press operator at 45 cents an hour. He went to work in department A-19 of the small-motor division. Soon afterwards there occurred an event of importance for Anton. A majority of the workers organized into a union and voted to go out on strike when management refused to recognize its negotiating committee. Anton did not join the union and was one of the few workers who returned to work at the company's request before the strike was settled. The reason he gave for refusing to join the union was that he hated to be represented "by fellows who are ignorant and bossy."

Union officials and such members as had daily work association with the "unorganized" workers disliked the latter and, after the favorable settlement of the strike, treated them rudely and in other ways made their work relationships difficult.

Up to this time, Anton had a perfect no-accident work record, but, beginning Nov. 3, 1933, he was involved in a series of small accidents. Thus

> Nov. 3, 1933: Cut finger left hand
> Nov. 20, 1933: Cut finger right hand
> Dec. 19, 1933: Cut thumb right hand
> Feb. 17, 1934: Lacerated third finger left hand
> Mar. 28, 1934: Lacerated back right hand

Each of these injuries required treatment in the first-aid department but otherwise involved no lost time.

On Apr. 23, 1934, Anton qualified as a die setter (a skilled job) and was given a 5-cent increase. On Dec. 12, he was reclassified as a setup man and punch-press operator.

On Apr. 3, 1935, Mr. Avery, supervisor of industrial relations, received the following report from the local police captain:

Police Report:

At 7 A.M., Lieutenant Riley received a telephone call from H. Anderson, assistant foreman, A-19, to come down to that department at once as there was trouble going on. Lieutenant Riley upon arriving found that two of the employees had been having some dispute and that one of them, Anton Kuczinsky, a setup man in A-19 (check 713), had struck the other employee, Stanley Demerski, a die setter in A-19 (check 975) in the mouth, cutting part of the mouth, which required half a dozen stitches (taken care of by Dr. Daley). I understand that Kuczinsky had asked Demerski for some papers pertaining to his work. Demerski said he didn't have the papers. Kuczinsky then remarked that he would like to punch Demerski in the jaw and then did punch Demerski in the mouth. Demerski made no attempt to fight back. From what I have learned, there seems to have been trouble or feeling between these two men because Kuczinsky worked all during the strike and is not a union man. H. Anderson (assistant foreman) made out a quit slip for Kuczinsky. Mr. Cameron, president of the union, who was in A-19, spoke about arresting Kuczinsky, but this could not be done unless the employee who had been assaulted went along and signed the complaint. (He was not willing to do this.)

(signed) Captain L. Rawlins

On the same date, foreman Conrad (department A-19) sent in the following quit slip to the employment department:

Services of Anton Kuczinsky are not desired after Apr. 3, 1935. Reasons: This man had put in notice to get through Friday. Wednesday he had an argument with the lineman which resulted in Kuczinsky striking him.

Investigation of the case by the employment interviewer led Mr. Avery to affirm the foreman's discharge.

Under the heading "Remarks by Employment Department," Mr. Kendricks wrote:

Never rehire in the plant unless Mr. Avery gives his approval first.

On Apr. 4, 1935, the works manager received a letter from Anton, which he forwarded to Mr. Avery with the recommendation that he use his own judgment. The letter read as follows:

Mr. E. L. Abbott   Apr. 3, 1935
General Manager
National Manufacturing Company
Dear Sir:

This morning occurred an incident of considerable consequence to me: I have been discharged for fighting. Following are some of the events leading up to the issue, and I leave you to render an opinion.

I am and have been aware all along that there exists a certain very rigid shop rule against fighting. And that awareness accounts for the year and a half that I have worked there. I got the job just 7 working days before the strike, but in those 7 days I laid the foundation of a deep enmity in the man I popped this morning. I voiced my views on the then impending strike, which, unfortunately, failed to coincide with his. I was against it. And, when I returned to work 4 days before the strike ended, upon the invitation of my foreman, his eyes turned upon me were not pleasant to see. In the beginning of our workaday relationship— after the strike—he was content to treat me with silent contempt, all of which was all right with me. But gradually he brought voice, manner, and words into play, till it was with the utmost difficulty that I restrained myself. Daily I was subject to slights, insults, and incivilities which nearly drove me frantic. I swallowed it all in the sweet name of peace. On several occasions I complained to the foreman, but I could get no satisfaction there. After all, I could not quote a single off-color word he used which might warrant official action. Naturally, I couldn't carry around a dictaphone and a camera with which to get evidence that his look and tone were offensive. The stock palliative became, "Try to keep out of his way."

But keeping out of his way was impossible in view of the fact that I depended on the output of his presses to supply work for my own. From time to time I simply had to have information relative to the job which only he could give. He never failed to take full advantage of these encounters. Where a " no" or "yes" or "maybe" might have sufficed, he instead resorted to loud denunciations of my temerity to question him on the subject. His attitude was so stupid and unreasonable that it left me helpless and speechless. You can't find words to answer the rantings of an imbecile. I used to walk away, my nerves in such a turmoil that I became dizzy and shaken. I finally resorted to threats—that if he continued these persecutions I'd wait for him outside the gate. This, if I had carried it out, might have simplified matters a great deal. But I'm not cold-blooded enough to wait hours for my revenge. I had but to laugh once and the storm in my soul was over. So this went on for months.

Then he grew bolder, convinced that I was only bluffing. Today he committed an outrage which no man worthy of the name could tolerate: He *snatched*, out of my hand, a sheaf of route cards I had picked off his truck, and was thumbing through, looking for a certain specific one from which to copy information I needed before returning them. I'd have been justified in slapping him down there and then, but didn't. I informed him that I had suffered my last indignity at his hands, that I would certainly "let him have it" the next time. He said, "Go ahead," and I did.

Now, after an interval of calm reasoning, I'm not so sure that I hadn't played directly into his hands. I wonder if he had not actually planned to goad me into an act which would cost me my job. There is no divining the working of a perverted mind, and it is just possible that he was willing to suffer momentary pain for the lasting satisfaction of seeing me disgraced.

Now the primary object of this letter is to point out to you the disadvantage to the National Manufacturing Company of dispensing with my services. I shall not here repeat what I already said to Mr. Kendricks. My claim to have saved the company thousands of dollars through improvements I made on the machines under my care can be verified easily. I further claim that those index presses cannot be operated efficiently without me. Those machines exact a peculiar treatment, a treatment such as is not readily found in the average die setter.

I think I have covered all the main points of my petition. I am aware, however, that you can scarcely be expected to reinstate me, assuming I have succeeded in convincing you of the justice of my act, over the heads of those who are more intimately concerned with the matter and its disposition. I can, at least, be an instrument in setting a precedent by which matters of a similar color can be dealt with a bit more equitably in the future. Would it not tend to discourage these morons if the price paid for their squelching were less—say a month's suspension without pay?

Sincerely,

(signed) Anton Kuczinsky

He was advised that his request would be considered. Meanwhile Anton left Springfield and went to New York City.

QUESTIONS FOR DISCUSSION

1. *On management's responsibility toward nonunion members*
   a. In such a situation, would you say that management has any special responsibility toward an employee in Anton's position? (Give your reasons.)
   b. If so, what officials might fulfill this responsibility?
   c. In what ways might it be done?
2. *On accidents as an index*
   a. In view of all the factors known to you about Anton's situation, what does his accident record from November, 1933, through March, 1934, seem to indicate about his state of mind at the time?
   b. What might management have done about it?
3. *On "getting down to cases"*
   a. Considering the previous history of Anton's case, comment on the choice of the employment interviewer to investigate the difficulties that culminated in the quarrel and discharge on Apr. 3, 1935.
   b. What official would be the natural choice for an investigation of such a case at this point?
   c. If you had been making the investigation, how would you have gone about it?
4. *On interpreting an employee communication*
   a. Comment on the fact that Anton addressed his letter to the works manager.
      (1) Why do you think he did so?
      (2) Was he unaware of the irregularity of such a procedure?
   b. What can one learn, and what is confirmed about Anton from this letter? (Note its wording, tone, and intention.)
   c. What light does the letter throw on the foreman's part in this affair?
   d. Apart from the unique context, would Demerski's behavior seem to constitute a serious offense between employees?
      (1) What type of complaint is this?
5. *On the personnel administrator's relation to policy on employee services*
   Comment on the timing of what seems to be Mr. Avery's first entrance into this case.
   a. What kinds of weakness might have been corrected if he had taken part earlier?
   b. At what point, and on whose initiative, do you think a personnel administrator might most usefully have cooperated in helping Anton to meet his difficulties?
6. *On a personnel administrator's responsibility and techniques*
   If you had been the personnel administrator at this juncture, what action would you have taken?
   a. If you were to "get down to cases" here, what situational factors would you consider, and which company officials would you interview?

II. Reemployment and Subsequent Difficulties

On May 8, 1935, Anton wrote the following letter to employment manager Kendricks:

May 8, 1935

Dear Sir:

I found New York not much to my liking, and so, after a month of it, I'm back. I debated long between seeing and writing you, and this letter is the result. I decided to write, knowing that my abilities in this branch of expression far exceed my talents as a conversationalist.

You can guess the purpose of this note: realizing that I "must" live and work round here, I find it hard to reconcile myself to the ordeal of working elsewhere than in the National Manufacturing Company. I therefore decided to probe and see if the gods of vengeance had not been appeased, and if they might not see fit to permit my return from exile.

In New York, I found that die setters are rated a dime-a-dozen, so to speak. And, while there appears to be a lively demand for tool and diemakers, I, of course, could not approach it. Another line of work for which the demand is equally great is that of screw-machine operating. Both of these were entirely outside my limited province. I tried at several offices to convince the powers that be of my aptitude for learning things mechanical, but failed. Experience—and that means years of it—is what New Yorkers want. Offers of a dollar an hour for screw-machine operators were common.

I was never more sharply brought up to realize how sadly neglected has been my education, how impotent a man can feel who has no worth-while trade. I might have accepted some offer of a job whose "second-best" character I might ignore, if only there had been some opportunity there to learn a respectable trade. Printers, bookkeepers, accountants, and artists can choose one of several schools; but, hard as I tried, I uncovered no agency there that will or can teach you mechanics.

It then occurred to me that I come from a town where facilities are abundant and perfectly suited to my ambitions—Springfield. Nowhere, I think, is opportunity to learn so abundant as here, where trade and business schools flourish. And no one perhaps, more than I, realizes that these advantages here go begging. At twenty-nine I am yet a young dog to learn new tricks, and, directly I am again settled, I shall make it a point of duty to enroll at Springfield Tech. Moreover, my enthusiasm to overcome the handicap of ignorance will advance me rapidly in the business of learning a trade. That trade is diemaking.

The first step is, of course, a job. And I'm not particular what manner of job it is, just so long as it pays my way till I have advanced far enough to begin my apprenticeship.

The second step is to prevail upon you to supply that job. I shall not again proceed to secure a position except through your office. Lest the above remark prove ambiguous I hasten to explain that this applies to the National Manufacturing Company.

I am confident that you will give this application the courtesy of your consideration, for which I thank you. There can be no doubt in your mind of my sincerity, I'm sure.

I feel myself, in a manner of speaking, under a cloud, and I therefore shall not inflict myself upon you without your consent and invitation. Can I hope to receive that invitation *soon?*

Sincerely yours,

(signed) Anton Kuczinsky

Mr. Kendricks sent this letter to the supervisor of industrial relations on May 10, 1935, with the penciled notation, "Mr. Avery, Please note." Mr. Avery ruled that Kuczinsky should have another chance, and on May 15 Anton was reemployed as a punch-press operator in department G-50 at 44 cents an hour, standard time.

In 1937 (Apr. 19), Anton was transferred to department A-35 (motorized-appliance division) as an assembler. No reason for this transfer was given. His hourly rate was 44 cents. On Apr. 26, Anton was transferred again to department A-37 (motored-appliance division) as a lathe hand, class B. This was a production transfer. His hourly rate was 59 cents standard time.

On May 17, 1937, Anton received his first vacation with pay. He was out 1 week, and on his return resumed his work as lathe hand. Another transfer took place on July 5, to department G-50, where he continued to be employed as a class B lathe hand at 59 cents an hour.

On Monday, July 12, 1937, Kuczinsky appeared in Mr. Avery's office dressed in his Sunday clothes. It was 8:30 A.M., and Anton had taken the day off to present his complaint. The following dialogue ensued:

ANTON: I'm very depressed this morning, Mr. Avery, and would like to talk to you about something.

AVERY: Sit right down, Anton, and let's see if I can help you.

ANTON: Well, you see, before I was transferred to the motored-appliance division, I was working in G-50; and, when I was there, I asked Mr. Hiller [general foreman] for a raise. He told me I couldn't get one, that I was lucky to have a job. I told him that I was one of the best operators he had and I feel I am. This happened back 3 months ago, and then the group I was working with was transferred to A-35. A week ago they decided to transfer this group back again into G-50. I've been working with Mr. Hiller only a week and am in trouble already. I think he has something against me, and it all goes back to my asking for a raise. This is the sort of thing that happens. Last Friday I was waiting for an assignment to work, and my lineman sent me to Mr. Poole [foreman]. I was waiting for him when Mr. Hiller came up very excited-like and hollered, "Scram! Come on, get going!" I didn't move, because I didn't think he meant me. Then Hiller came up and bawled me out. He wanted to know what in hell I was doing there. Didn't I know it was the height of impoliteness to stand around and stare at other people while they were working? I told him why I was there. This didn't make any difference to him. He just grunted and walked away.

A few minutes later I saw Mr. Poole and found there was no work in the department. Poole gave me a pass to go home. Then I went to Mr. Hiller for a furlough card.[1] Hiller asked me how long I wanted to stay out. I told him I didn't want to stay out at all but wanted a furlough card to see if I couldn't get a job in some other department. I told him I should like a furlough card for 1 week because I felt in 1 week the department would be going again full blast. Hiller gave me a furlough card. Then I went to see Mr. Kendricks at the employment office. Mr. Kendricks gave me a temporary job in the shipping department.

At quitting time Friday evening, I went back to G-50 for soap to wash my hands. There I met Mr. Darcey, my lineman, who stopped me and said, "Where were you today? I could have used you. Stick around. I can use you tomorrow." This made me glad, because it meant time and a half for overtime. I then went to Mr. Poole and asked him if the department was busy. Mr. Poole said, "Yes, we've got a sudden spurt." I asked him whether I could come in tomorrow and Mr. Poole said, "O.K." Then he wrote a pass for me to come in on Saturday. I put the pass in my shirt pocket and left the office whistling and feeling kinda happy.

While I was standing in front of the office for a moment, Mr. Hiller came along, stopped, and took the pass out of my pocket. He said, "You can't pull that kind of stuff around here." I said, "What do you mean, 'that kind of stuff'?" Hiller said, "Why you're supposed to be on furlough. Come into my office." So we went into his office. There he bawled me out again and said, "You've got to change your attitude around here. It's all wrong." I said, "What d'you mean by my attitude?" But he would not tell me and merely repeated the incident of Friday morning when he had to tell me to scram and not bother people by watching them work. Now, I had explained all that before, as I told you, that I was waiting for Mr. Poole. But, apparently, he paid no attention. That's what makes me think he has it in for me, and I believe he's felt that way ever since I asked him for a raise.

AVERY: Well, I wouldn't get excited, Anton. I'll look into this.

ANTON: Thank you, Mr. Avery. Sorry I took up so much of your time.

AVERY: Oh, that's all right, Anton, that's what I'm here for. Just go back to work and forget it. I'll talk with Hiller.

The next day Mr. Kendricks, in a talk with Mr. Avery, offered the following comment on Anton:

Physically, Kuczinsky makes a poor impression. He is undersized and high-strung. But on paper he can express himself well. He is quick-tempered but a good worker and works hard.

[1] This in effect puts the worker on a vacation basis, where otherwise he would have to reenter through the employment office.

I have followed him along ever since he came to us as a youngster. As a kid, he was quite fresh and full of pep. He was inclined to resent criticism from men and group leaders. He felt that he knew a lot and used better English than the average worker in the plant. He was quite touchy. I blamed that on his environment. He didn't have a happy home life and felt that no one gave a damn whether he lived or died. When he was a young boy, his father died. Then his mother married again. From what I've heard, the boy didn't get on well with his stepfather.

I rather like Anton. He is original and quite a reader. He has ambitions to become an assistant foreman or even a foreman. He never joined the union, because he doesn't want to be represented by the kind of man that gets elected as representative. He feels he has more brains than they. I always thought he had great possibilities and have urged him repeatedly to settle down and try to make something of himself. He certainly is a tough boy to handle, and I've often given him hell. But then, I enjoy tough cases.

One nice thing about him is that he is always willing to try. When he went to New York, he had to wash dishes for a living and had many tough experiences. He says he is willing to do anything so long as he can keep at work. To try him out, I recently offered him a temporary job loading freight cars. He took it.

We've given him more chances than most companies would, but I always believe, if you can salvage a man, you make a good loyal employee. He will feel that the company has done something for him. In this way, you can build loyalty and offset the radical element in the plant.

QUESTIONS FOR DISCUSSION

1. *On rehiring policy*
   If you had been Mr. Avery, how and why would you have acted on this letter?
2. *On employment policy*
   If you had been in Mr. Avery's place and had been convinced that Anton's story was essentially accurate, what would you
   a. Have said to Anton in the July 12 interview?
   b. Have done afterward?
   c. Specifically, how should a staff official proceed in handling such a case with the general foreman?
3. *On counseling technique*
   a. What do you know about Anton that would tend to make you hesitant to accept as facts all his accusations?
   b. Which statements bear the marks of authenticity? What makes them so convincing?
   c. In Mr. Avery's place, how would you have proceeded to check certain key statements made by Anton in this interview?
4. *On the employment manager's role in a service program*
   a. Comment on the various implications for a service policy made in Kendrick's statement.
   b. What is his conception of a staff official's function in a case where an employee needs help? Do you agree or disagree? Why?

III. Layoff and Recall

In the fall of 1937, there was a marked drop in productive activity, and many workers were laid off. On Dec. 6, Anton was transferred to D-68 (maintenance department) as a laborer. This was a day-work occupation and involved a derate to 55 cents. On Dec. 27, there occurred a slight increase in the activity of the domestic-refrigeration division. Anton was transferred on this date to department J-30 as a punch-press operator, hourly rate 55 cents.

Still another transfer took place Feb. 21, 1938, and Anton was employed as a class B assembler in department J-30, hourly rate 55 cents. His new foreman was Mr. Brewer, for whom Anton did satisfactory work.

On May 9, 1938, Anton received his annual week's vacation with pay with a notice that, after May 13, his services would be no longer required because of lack of work. On that day, foreman Brewer sent in Anton's furlough card to the employment department:

Assembler Kuczinsky: Services not required after May 13, 1938.

Reason: Reduction in force.

Recommend rehiring in same department and same job.

Remarks by Employment Department: Laid off. Lack of work. Good worker. Would rehire same occupation.

On Dec. 4, 1938, Anton (now at the age of thirty-three) wrote the following letter to the employment manager:

Dear Mr. Kendricks:

It is no exaggeration to say that I have reached a crucial period in my life. Stated simply, it means that my position in this vicinity is absolutely untenable unless I obtain work—and that soon. You can better understand the significance of this when I tell you that I am existing and have been for months past on the good will expressed in credits of those who dispense food and lodging. Between the two I am to date indebted to a sum well over $100.00. Spoken quickly, this may not seem much. But, when one considers the struggles of these good people to make ends meet, with business in general what it is, it's not to be wondered at if they have begun to provide these credits with less and less cordiality. I see the time not far off when it shall cease altogether.

From my accounts of adventures in New York, you may obtain a clue to the state of my feelings when faced with the necessity of returning there. I doubt that I shall survive another session on the Bowery. You can never realize what a terrific struggle it has been to overcome the consequences of the last one. There is a limit to the power of recuperation.

My object in writing you is simply to find out as definitely as possible where I stand. What are my chances of returning to work? When? I can hang on until the holidays. No longer. I feel I have as much right to a job as anyone else. I can look back at my years of association with the National Manufacturing Company with pride. They were pleasant for me, and, but for one or two unfortunate incidents for which I alone paid the price, they have been profitable for the company. On the basis of them, I base my claim to a right to work.

I learned only yesterday that my job in J-30 was given to another, a man with no experience whatever in that work. And thus was born my apprehension. I had counted on the seasonal upswing in refrigerator output to provide me with a job. That hope died.

Believe me, it will be a relief to know definitely whether it is to be yes or no. Even bad news is preferable to none at all. I can at least rouse my mind out of this apathy and begin once more to plan. This mental and physical inaction is driving me nuts. I repeat, I shall appreciate an early reply, be it good news or bad.

Yours sincerely,
(signed) Anton Kuczinsky

P.S. I use a pencil for better legibility.

To this letter, Anton received the following reply:

Mr. Anton Kuczinsky   Dec. 16, 1938
Chicopee Falls, Mass.
Dear Sir:

Your letter of recent date addressed to Mr. Kendricks has been turned over to the writer for attention.

We are at the present time bringing some of the long-service employees back to work but as yet have not got down to people with your service.

At such time, we will communicate with you and tell you to come in.

Very truly yours,
James Avery, Supervisor, Industrial Relations
(By) Thomas Burns, Assistant Employment Manager

Meanwhile, Anton Kuczinsky went to New York. On Feb. 14, 1939, he wrote the following letter to the supervisor of industrial relations:

The Biltmore Hotel
New York
Dear Mr. Avery:

I still cherish the promise that came with the letter you wrote me back in Chicopee Falls. I'm writing you now to ascertain whether or not you had called me. You see, I left the town as I told you I must; but I'm beginning to have doubts regarding the integrity of those I entrusted with the forwarding of my mail. They had proved themselves negligent in many instances in the past.

I get reports from time to time, and all seem very optimistic about conditions in the National Manufacturing Company. Only today I learned that the brother of a friend of mine was called back who has far less service than I. That among other things prompted me to sit down and dash off these lines to you.

I'd be very grateful if you would address the letter to me direct when and if my turn arrives to come back to work—at the address I'm about to give you. Anton Kuczinsky, 3509 12th Avenue, Astoria, Long Island.

On Mar. 13, 1939, the employment manager sent Anton the following by special delivery:

Dear Sir:

Please report to the Employment Department on Tuesday, Mar. 14, at 9:00 for an interview with the undersigned.

This letter will admit you to my office.

Kendricks, Employment Manager

Anton replied as follows:

Dear Sir:

I received a communication telling me that the long-awaited letter summoning me back to work has arrived. But, while I am very much pleased by it, I find that I cannot appear for an interview until Monday next, inasmuch as I feel obliged to work out a week's notice on the job I have now—operating an elevator at the Biltmore Hotel. Please extend the appointment until Monday, same hour, and oblige.

Yours truly,

Anton Kuczinsky

Letter to Anton Kuczinsky—special delivery:

Dear Sir:

We wish to advise you that the job we contacted you about was only labor work, and as we had to fill the vacancy immediately, we would advise you to continue at the Biltmore until we contact you again. The position as laborer would have lasted for only 3 or 4 weeks at the most.

Your present address will be kept on file, and, when we have something that looks steady, will notify you.

Very truly yours,

Kendricks, *Employment Manager*

On Mar. 17, 1939, the above letter was returned to the employment department marked: *Not claimed*.

QUESTIONS FOR DISCUSSION

1. *On layoff policy*

   Comment on the company's layoff policy as revealed in the abruptness of Anton's notice and the lack of any interview to soften the blow.

2. *On opportunities for rendering employee service*

   a. What opportunities for service does Anton's case present after he received his layoff notice?

   b. During the various stages of Anton's career, what advantages might the company have gained from offering a broad service program?

3. *On rehiring*

   a. In view of all the circumstances, do you think that Mr. Avery's note was suitable to the situation? (Give reasons.)

b. What would you have said or done if you had been in Mr. Avery's place at that time?

c. Comment on the letter sent to Anton on Mar. 13, 1939.

  (1) What do you think of the time allowed for him to report?

  (2) Why would you, or would you not, have recalled Anton for an opening of this sort?

Questions on the Case as a Whole

1. *On the interdependence of employment policy and a service program*
   In what ways might the company desirably have helped Anton at various stages?
   a. Which of his needs should have been met by regular employment procedures?
   b. Which other needs would have to be met by a service program? In what ways?

2. *On a policy for employee services*
   a. Give reasons for and against the view that management has a responsibility in helping a person like Anton adjust to his situation as an adult worker.
   b. If the company had offered a fully rounded service program to meet needs such as Anton's, what gains to itself might justify the program as good business?

3. *On community contacts for service*
   a. With what local agencies and institutions might the company have co-operated to help Anton during his industrial career as recorded in Parts I and II of this case?
   b. What part, if any, might the union have in maintaining community contacts for service to employees?

Case for Chapter 20

Safety in a Punch-press Department

(Human Difficulties with Protective Devices)

Introduction

This case illustrates a number of points made in Chap. 20 about accident causes and about essential features in a safety program. Study of the situation here described reveals many and varied weaknesses, including both mechanical defects and human attitudes.

Yet it should be noted that the National Manufacturing Company was a large industrial corporation, nationally known for its efficiency and far above the average in most features of its personnel program. The comments and questions included below are not offered in a spirit of criticism. Rather they are intended to bring out the complex nature of the problem itself and the importance of skill in dealing with people. Safety can never be achieved by concentrating on protective devices alone. Rather it is attained primarily by fostering among management representatives, workers, and union leaders the high morale and team spirit that contribute to efficiency and safety-mindedness.

In this case, analysis of the series of events that culminated in injury-accidents suggests that, among the many contributory causes, there were such varied items as

1. Top-management policies in regard to its system of pay and the method of handling labor relations.
2. The quality of supervision.
3. The behavior of a group leader.
4. Attitudes of workers.
5. Ideologies of a union president.

6. The overemphasis of a safety engineer on mechanical accident sources, and his neglect to analyze the physical, mental, and emotional factors that lead to accidents.

CASE BACKGROUND

The punch-press department of the National Manufacturing Company contained about 40 punch presses of various kinds and, on the average, employed about 100 punch-press operators (70 men and 30 women). The operators on the first shift started work at 6:15 A.M. and, with time off for lunch, worked till 3:00 P.M. Hours on the second shift were from 3:00 P.M. to 11:30 P.M.; on the third, from 11:00 P.M. to 7:00 A.M.

The punch press, particularly when applied to low-quantity or short-run production work, presented a serious accident hazard. In recognizing this high severity rate, management had impressed upon first-line supervisors and group leaders their responsibilities in regard to the workers' safety. It was the duty of the supervisors to see that the presses were properly safeguarded, that the operators were properly instructed, and that the safety rules of the company were enforced. Each group leader was expected to be a member of the safety patrol. It was his duty to see to it that the members of his work group were "safety-minded" at all times and to check on the use of safety guards or other protective equipment.

For certain types of work, a drop hammer rather than a punch press was frequently used, because it was a simpler and cheaper machine to operate. The forming operation accomplished in this way could also be done on a punch press, but a very large press would be required.

I. THE FIRST INJURY-ACCIDENT

1   On Jan. 7, 1936, the safety engineer, Mr. Hanson submitted the following report:

PRELIMINARY REPORT OF AN ACCIDENT

Operator: George Winslow, G-50, Badge No. 855, group leader and die setter
5 *Estimated extent of the accident:* Loss of first two fingers, left hand above second joint.
Hour of accident: Second shift, 9:20 P.M.
Machine in use: Drop hammer No. 9685.
Operation: Forming valve plates S No. 615243-D, 673 pieces, 70 per cent
10   complete.
Cause of accident: Defective machine and operator's carelessness.
Summary: Reconstructing the accident as closely as possible without contacting the operator, Mr. Winslow was running off a quantity of 673 valve

plates S No. 615243-D on Drop hammer No. 9685. With the work ap-
15 proximately 70 per cent complete, at 9:20 P.M., the weight lever that controls the clutch broke off, allowing the hammer to repeat when it reached
the top of its stroke. Mr. Winslow had been at this particular instant
placing a piece of work with his fingers, instead of using the tweezers, in
line with all established rules. When the hammer dropped, it cut off two
20 of the first fingers on his left hand. The hammer kept on repeating until
shut down by another operator.

It is interesting to note that this man is both a die setter and a group leader.
If he had not broken the company rule in regard to using tweezers, no serious
accident would have occurred.

25 I understand from Mr. Bowers, the previous safety engineer, that this
man had been previously cautioned on several occasions for his disregard of
company rules, as practiced both by himself and by members of his group.

Questions

1. *On situational thinking*
(line 7) Consider this accident in its temporal context, noting the shift assignment and also the time of day both in relation to a normal schedule of living
and in relation to the period covered by the work shift. From this analysis, what
can be inferred as a possible contributory accident cause?

2. *On causal analysis*
   a. (line 11) Comment on the second accident cause stated here.
   b. (line 22) What is the significance, in regard to accidents, of the fact that
   this man was a die setter?

3. *On employee evaluation*
(lines 26 to 27) What does this statement suggest as to the man's qualifications
as group leader?

4. *On accident prevention*
   a. What does this same statement imply about company standards of enlistment
   and enforcement?
   b. What, if anything, should have been done by the foreman in such a
   situation?

5. *On staff responsibility*
Why would you, or would you not, hold the safety engineer responsible for
knowing about the difficulty and suggesting the necessary action?

II. Investigation

1 During the investigation of this accident, the safety engineer found
that originally the drop hammer in question had been equipped with
a "sweep-motion guard." This appliance was designed to brush aside
the operator's hand whenever the hammer was used and the operator
5 failed to withdraw his hand from under the die.

However, the operator had frequently complained of the following inconvenience: He would withdraw his hand sufficiently to clear
the descending die, but not far enough to clear the sweep-motion
guard, designed to protect him from injury. As a result, he would
10   receive a smart rap on his knuckles or wrist. Operators regarded this
"punishment" as unnecessary and insisted that the sweep-motion
guard was more of a menace than a protection. Therefore, he and his
fellow workers repeatedly petitioned management to discard the
device. After some discussion, management agreed, on Jan. 15, 1935,
15   to remove the guard, basing its decision on the fact that the operator's
hands were still being protected through the use of tweezers. Nevertheless, with the automatic safety factor removed, it became absolutely
necessary that the operator should obey instructions as to the
use of tweezers and under no circumstances put his hands under
20   the die.

As indicated by the Winslow accident, this rule was not always
obeyed. Operators on incentive work were often tempted to cut as
many corners as possible in order to increase their output. For instance, in the operation of forming valve plates, according to regula-
25   tions based on time and motion studies, the operator was required to
pick up the unformed valve plate with his left hand out of the tray on
his left, *grip it with the tweezers in his right hand*, and insert it in the die
recess. He then tripped the hammer with his right foot. After the drop
hammer had completed its cycle, the operator was supposed to remove
30   the finished piece *with his tweezers*. He took it from the die recess and
tossed it into the tray on his right, at the same time picking up a
fresh piece with his left hand. He then repeated the whole cycle of
operations.

In order to gain time over the standard allowance, operators de-
35   veloped the habit of picking up an unformed part with the left hand
and placing it immediately into the die recess. This motion was
synchronized with the motion of the right hand, which picked up the
finished piece with the tweezers, tossing it into the tray. In this way,
two motions could be eliminated, thereby speeding up production
40   and increasing earnings. But, every time an operator placed his left
hand under the die, he risked a serious accident.

QUESTIONS

1. *On staff responsibility*
(lines 1 to 3) What inference would you make from the circumstance that

this fact seems to have been uncovered by the safety engineer only during the investigation, and after his original report?

2. *On mechanical safeguards*

(lines 9 and 10) Comment on the efficiency in human terms of this protective device. Why do you, or do you not, think that this unplanned result is a sufficient reason for discarding a device that was mechanically effective?

3. *On complaints as an index of employee morale*

(lines 10 to 12) What type of complaint is this? See Chap. 9.

a. What might it indicate about personnel relations?

4. *On accident prevention*

a. (lines 14 to 16) Comment on this decision by management

(1) In connection with management's engineering responsibilities in the safety program.

(2) As to its effect on personnel relations as a whole and, therefore, indirectly, on safety.

b. Comment on the investigation procedure as described here.

(1) In what ways would you think this investigation contributed to accident prevention in the future?

(2) What more should have been done?

5. *On staff responsibility*

(lines 14 to 16) If you had been Mr. Hanson, wnat might you have recommended to counteract the increased risks brought about by this decision?

6. *On the interrelation of personnel policies*

(lines 21 and 22) Taken in conjunction with the fact stated in Sec. II, lines 14 to 15, what share of responsibility does management seem to have had in motivation that led workers to the unsafe practice described in this paragraph?

III. Period of Preventive Work

1   For some time after the Winslow accident, the safety engineer experimented with mechanisms of various kinds that would safeguard this particular type of drop hammer and the punch presses. No satisfactory device was found. The drop hammer was removed from
5 service, and the work was transferred to standard punch presses.

    On Apr. 6 and 7, 1936, the safety engineer attended the annual New England meeting of the Massachusetts Safety Conference at the Statler Hotel in Boston. At this meeting, he heard about the Preston Positive Punch Press Safety Device, manufactured by the *Perry*
10 *Manufacturing Company* Inc., of Chicago, Ill.

    According to the prospectus:

The Preston device provides absolute safety because the operator's hands are removed from the danger zone by a *positive* action, which is independent of the personal equation or state of mind of the operator. Steel-cored cables
15 pull his hands away, and his own carelessness cannot cause an accident.

The diagram below illustrates how the device operates.

A fellow safety engineer who attended the conference told Mr. Hanson that he had just installed 17 of these devices and was pleased with the result. An employee in his plant had recently lost three 20 fingers, and, as a result of this accident, the workers were acutely "safety-conscious" and grateful for the company's effort to protect them.

Although the punch presses at the National Manufacturing Company operated on the two-hand trip principle, which seemed to

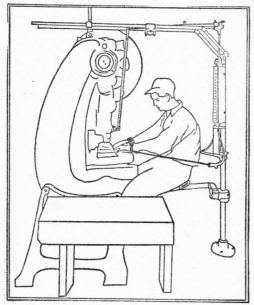

Fig. 1. — Preston Positive Safety Device.

25 provide adequate protection against any accident involving injury to hands or fingers, Mr. Hanson was convinced that it was worth while to try the new Positive Safety Device. Accordingly, on Apr. 22, 1936, at the meeting of the Feeder Section Safety Committee, Mr. Hanson called attention to this new safety device and explained in detail how 30 it functioned. He urged that one such device be installed as an experiment but met with considerable opposition on the part of Mr. Stahl, the foreman in charge of punch presses. This foreman had had some experience with the Preston Positive Safety Device at the Newark plant, where two of these devices had been installed. His 35 recollection was that management had experienced considerable

difficulty in getting workmen to operate punch presses that were so equipped. In view of the fact that the large Newark punch-press department had made no further installations of this type of safety device, the committee voted against Mr. Hanson's suggestion.

40   Following this meeting, Mr. Hanson corresponded with other National Manufacturing Company safety engineers, inquiring as to their experience with the Positive Safety Device. He found that it was not generally used.

The first opportunity for further constructive work in regard to
45   safety mechanisms on punch presses came about as the indirect consequence of safety work in another department.

On Jan. 28, 1937, at the meeting of the executive safety committee, Mr. Hanson suggested that glass guards similar to those used on tool grinders be developed for use by spot welders. This would
50   eliminate the need for goggles, which the workers disliked. He sent for samples of this glass guard device to the Perry Manufacturing Company, which specializes in safety equipment. Instead of sending samples by mail, the Perry Manufacturing Company directed its district salesman, Mr. Chester, to bring them himself. Mr. Chester
55   visited the plant on Feb. 4, 1937. During the conversation, Mr. Chester mentioned that he had been responsible for designing and installing the Positive Safety Device. Mr. Hanson told of his failure to get one of these devices installed and solicited the salesman's aid. He introduced Mr. Chester to Mr. Stahl, the foreman, who had
60   hitherto been opposed to the use of this device. As a consequence of this sales talk, Mr. Stahl agreed to give it a trial. The following arguments apparently convinced him.

Mr. Chester urged that it was in the foreman's interest to try the device. This absolute protection was on the market, and unless the
65   company gave it a fair trial, it would be open to the charge of negligence and lack of foresight. If an accident occurred and the punch-press operators learned that such a positive device existed, they might complain that their interests had not been properly protected.

As a result of this discussion, the Positive Safety Device was sent
70   for on Feb. 5, 1937.

In arriving at the decision to experiment with the Positive Safety Device, it was not considered advisable to talk the matter over with the operators or with the union representative. Referring to his experience at Newark, the foreman was of the opinion that it was
75   better not to consult the workers. He persuaded the safety engineer that once the device was installed and the workers saw that it provided

absolute protection, they would be satisfied. To experiment with the safety device, the foreman selected an odd-job press that would not interfere with line production. It stood near the aisle and had plenty
80 of free space around it to permit the installation of the device.

QUESTIONS
1. *On accident prevention*
    a. (lines 14 to 17) Comment on the wisdom of trying to develop safety by eliminating the human element. If this device could do it in one situation, would it, or would it not, contribute to the success of the whole safety program? Why?
    b. What important qualifications for his job are clearly demonstrated by the engineer during this period of preventive work?
2. *On the need of consultative supervision*
    (lines 74 to 78) What does this indicate about the leadership theories entertained by foreman Stahl?
3. *On line and staff coordination*
    a. Would you say that a foreman or a safety director should make the final decision in a case where they differ?
    b. Should top management's policies play a part here? Give reasons why you think they should, or should not.

IV. INSTALLATION OF THE POSITIVE SAFETY GUARD

1   On Friday, Feb. 26, 1937, the Positive Safety Device was installed, and Mr. Stahl notified the safety engineer. Mr. Hanson went to the punch-press department and gave the device a trial. After some final adjustments had been made, he was favorably impressed with the
5   way the guard functioned.

    A group leader was asked to try it. The group leader complied but refused to make any comments.

    Several punch-press operators were also invited to try the new harness but declined. Finally, Mr. DaCoste, an elderly employee,
10 consented to operate the press. He was of the opinion that the device would in no way interfere with his making standard time, but he would not agree that he could accomplish more work because of it.

    The experiment had not progressed far when Mr. Cameron, president of the union, appeared on the scene. Without trying the
15 device, Mr. Cameron requested that the mechanism immediately be discarded for the following reasons:
    1. The operator could not possibly be expected to submit to the "intolerable condition of being chained to his job."
    2. In case of emergency (fire, panic, etc.), the operator would not
20   be free to leave the machine.

3. Being chained to the machine, he could not avoid falling objects and so ran considerable risk of being injured.

4. The bracelet and chain would interfere with the operator's motion and make him less efficient.

5. The device was not actually foolproof, inasmuch as the chain might fail to function.

6. The use of such an automatic device would undo years of training with regard to safety. The operators had been cautioned, both by their supervisors and leaders, not to put their hands under the die and to use tweezers in handling the work.

7. The worker would be led into forming bad habits. The automatic device enabled him to put his unprotected hands under the die. Then, whenever he was transferred to another machine not similarly equipped, he would run the risk of hurting himself.

8. Finally, the present method of using tweezers and the two-handed trip principle was far superior to this new device, since the operator's hands were never allowed to go near the die.

The safety engineer tried to persuade Mr. Cameron that the new device should be given a chance by saying that

1. Theoretically, the worker was "chained" away from his job and not to it.

2. In emergencies, the "hand straps" could be released quickly by pressing clips.

3. There was sufficient slack to the cable to permit the operator to move a reasonable distance and to avoid any possible falling objects.

4. There was no restriction to the worker's movements once the device was properly adjusted.

5. Once the operator became familiar with the device, wear on the cable was negligible. Furthermore, periodic inspections would, of course, be conducted to check this device as well as any other part of the machine. There was no danger, therefore, that the device might fail to function.

6. True, workers were continually cautioned not to put their hands under the die, but the Winslow accident was evidence enough that such cautions were frequently disregarded.

7. In the event that the device proved successful, all presses would be so equipped.

8. The Perry Manufacturing Company had demonstrated that this new safety device guarded against lost time and was therefore more efficient than the tweezer and two-handed trip principle.

Despite all these arguments, Mr. Cameron insisted that the workers could not tolerate such a device and that it must be discarded.

65 After Mr. Cameron left the department, Mr. Hanson talked to the operators (especially the women) in order to get their reactions to the new safety device. They were uniformly of the opinion that they would be afraid to put their hands underneath the die and that they could handle the work faster by means of tweezers. They also

70 asserted that the use of tweezers enabled them to place the work better.

Mr. Hanson allowed the device to remain for 3 days in the hope that the workers might familiarize themselves with it. The workers, however, continued to refuse to operate the machine to which the

75 device was attached. And the union president reiterated his insistence that the new contraption be removed. In response to this situation, the safety engineer had the new device taken away.

On Mar. 4, 1937, Mr. Chester came to check the safety device and to inquire whether it had been found satisfactory. When he

80 learned that the device had been removed, he criticized Mr. Hanson for not calling him to "sell the device to the workers." Mr. Hanson referred him to the union president. Later, Mr. Chester reported that he had not been able to convince Mr. Cameron.

A week later, Mr. Chester appeared once more at the plant and

85 stated that his superior had urged him to try again. Mr. Hanson suggested a new method of approach: The salesman should attempt to convince the union president that this positive device was indispensable to the protection of the workers' safety and welfare. In order to protect the workers' hands, the president was in duty bound to

90 request management to install the new device.

After a conference that lasted several hours, Mr. Chester returned to the safety engineer's office, thoroughly convinced that there was no hope of installing the device.

QUESTIONS ON POINTS OF INTEREST

1. *On mutuality of interest*
   a. (lines 6 to 7) What does this suggest about the degree of identification of the group leader's interests with those of management?
   b. If you had been in Mr. Hanson's place at this juncture, what, if anything, would you have tried to do about this unsatisfactory feature of the work situation?
   c. (lines 8 to 9) Why would it always be important to change such an attitude, if possible?
   d. What would you have tried to do about it if you had been
      (1) The foreman?

(2) The safety director?

(3) The union leader?

2. *On union responsibility for safety*

(lines 13 to 14) In connection with question 1, *d*, (3) above, comment on the fact that the union president apparently "appeared on the scene" either on his own volition or in response to workers' complaints.

3. *On interpretive analysis*

(lines 17 to 37) Analyze and criticize this list of objections.

a. What are the five different grounds on which the new device was condemned?

b. What is your opinion as to the validity of each?

c. (lines 40 to 62) Comment on these counterarguments.

(1) Does each convincingly answer the corresponding objection?

(2) Can you give any reason why a purely logical statement, no matter how watertight its reasoning, might not be effective in this kind of situation?

4. *On staff responsibility*

a. If you had been in the safety director's place, how would you have met the situation after it had developed to this point?

b. (lines 72 to 77) Comment on this decision.

(1) How would such action be likely to affect the respect of workers for a safety director?

(2) What attitude in the union president did it encourage that would tend to make future labor relations in the company more difficult?

c. What seems to have been Mr. Hanson's primary motive in sending the salesman to the union president?

d. (lines 84 to 85) If you had been the safety director, why would you, or would you not, have permitted the salesman to try again? (Give and weigh arguments both for and against this further attempt to "sell" the union president on the positive safety guard. Do not take into account as a fact the outcome of the interview. It could not with absolute certainty have been predicted at the time when the decision had to be made.)

V. The Second Injury-accident

1   On Apr. 28, 1937, at 9:15 p.m. Mrs. Henrietta Perkins lost her left thumb and index finger while operating a 2½ Toledo punch press. The operator stated that she had some punchings in her left hand and was feeding the press with this hand when the press repeated

5 and crushed her fingers. She added that "the press was acting up since 9 o'clock, but the repairman was so busy that I didn't call him."

At the monthly meeting of the executive safety committee, May 27, 1937, the safety engineer made the following report:

Henrietta Perkins, department G-50. Traumatic amputation of left thumb

10 and left index finger.

Mrs. Perkins was operating a No. 2½ Toledo punch press equipped with air trips. She was performing a bumping operation on rotor laminations and had been working from 2:00 P.M. until the time of the accident, which was at 9:15 P.M., at which time she claims the press repeated and
15 cut off the thumb and first finger of her left hand.

In order to reconstruct the cause of the accident, Mr. Hanson operated the punch press for over an hour directly after the accident. During this time, the punch press could not be made to repeat under normal operating conditions. Based on the location of the two-hand trips, the position
20 of the parts of the fingers under the die, and the laminations being handled at the time, the following conclusion was reached:

Mrs. Perkins must have been feeding the laminations under the die with her left hand, holding the left air trip down with her left elbow.

At a later date, when Mrs. Perkins had sufficiently recovered, the
25 accident was reviewed with her, and she then agreed that she had been feeding the punchings under the die with her left hand but denied that she had been holding the air trip down with her left elbow. She stated, however, that it was possible that her left elbow accidently came in contact with the left-hand air trip. She stated,
30 furthermore, that she had been using her tweezers in her right hand, but using them only to lock some of the punchings when they went out of place under the die.

Questions on Points of Interest

1. *On causal analysis*
   a. (line 1) What do you notice about the time of day when this accident occurred?
   b. (lines 4 to 6) What three contributory accident causes were given here? (Two are stated and the third implied.)
   c. (lines 22 to 23) Why might this conclusion be invalid?
2. *On accident prevention*
   (lines 5 to 6) One of these causes is typical of situations prevailing at shift-change times. What could the foreman have done to prevent accidents at this time?

Question on the Case as a Whole

Do you think that permanent progress toward safety was made by the activities described in this case? Give reasons for your opinion.

Case for Chapter 21

The Scrap Campaign

(An Experiment in Union—Management Cooperation)

INTRODUCTION

The following is a brief account of changes, reactions, and mutual adaptations that took place within a company during a campaign to keep defective workmanship within normal limits. It shows how repressive discipline failed to solve the technical problem and aggravated the related human difficulties. Then management policy was changed so that cooperation was sought all the way down the line and especially with leaders of the recently organized union. This policy met with considerable success in reducing waste. But it also produced growing pains in unexpected places. Many of these could have been avoided if top management had been advised by someone skilled in personnel administration.

Developments during the campaign show the need for the situational approach in the following ways:

1. A new program of action and new attitudes in an evolving situation call for a reappraisal of policies and procedures, not only in the area where cooperation is sought, but throughout the whole personnel-policy system. New forces and new relationships make for new requirements. Because of this fact, some understanding person must be detailed to diagnose resulting stresses and strains and to interpret for line management the ways in which former policies are becoming inadequate.

When introducing innovations, consideration should be given not only to the immediate practical effects but also to the progressive influence on attitudes and expectations.

2. Responses to new demands and new policies vary according to the temperament, background, and company status of the participants. These individual differences should be evaluated in relation both to the requirements of the immediate program and to the long-run objectives of the enterprise as a whole. When understanding of this sort has been achieved

by the person-centered approach, it is easier for line management to appreciate in each problem area what are the necessary and feasible adjustments.

3. An appreciation of the time element is of primary importance in the direction of any far-reaching campaign. In the following case, management tended to overlook the continuity of experience by assuming that all workers would immediately respond favorably to liberalizing changes in policy. Actually, many employees who had previously been subjected to repressive discipline at first looked with suspicion on new arrangements even when these were intended to elicit their cooperation. Moreover, the rate of adaptation varied markedly in different individuals according to the way in which the evolving situation seemed to fit with their previous aims and expectations.

Evidently, better timing on management's part and more skillful policy thinking could have prevented many difficulties, as will be seen in the description of unexpected developments.

4. As cooperation spread during the campaign, management's technical proficiency could function more effectively. Instead of trying to "beat the system," workers now used their practical ingenuity to supplement management's technical knowledge and experience. By such teamwork, management was able to draw upon and to develop additional sources of strength.

Before describing the events of the campaign itself, it will be worth while briefly to summarize the technical and organizational background and to sketch a few earlier developments whose effects carried over into the episodes on which we wish to focus attention.

CASE BACKGROUND

The National Manufacturing Company, Inc., was an organization of international scope. The subsidiary plant No. 10, referred to in this case, manufactured electrical apparatus and was located in a New England city with a population of 100,000 and a plentiful supply of skilled labor. Nearly 80 per cent of the employees of plant No. 10 were American-born. Poles and French Canadians predominated among the male foreign-born group, Italians among the women. Of the younger employees, about 60 per cent were American-born children of Polish, Italian, and French-Canadian parents. A few of the older unskilled and semiskilled employees could neither read nor write English, but most of them had a grammar-school education. Skilled workers, such as tool and die makers, die setters and repairmen, welders, electricians, carpenters, and steam fitters, also had a high-school or trade-school education. Ninety per cent of the younger group (unskilled, semiskilled, and skilled) were high-school graduates or at least had several years of high-school training.

Early Organizational Structure.—Until 1934, the local plant was organized as shown in the chart below.

Personnel relations were a direct responsibility of the general and departmental foremen. The latter hired their own employees, forwarding their requisitions to the employment manager for notification, examination, and record. The discharge of employees and the rates of pay were also the responsibilities of these foremen, subject to the approval of the general foreman. The same was true of inspection. Each foreman was re-

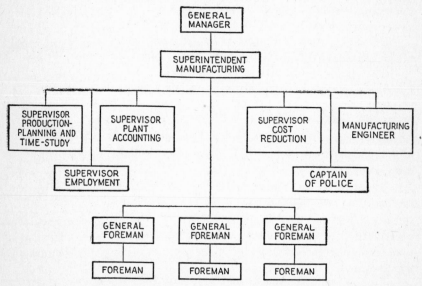

sponsible for the quality of products manufactured in his department. Sick benefits, pensions, and insurance were treated as matters pertaining to records and regarded as the responsibility of the accounting supervisor, who also acted as office manager. Suggestions were a function of the production-planning and time-study department, the members of which made up the committees to study and award suggestions from employees.

Unionization and Reorganization.—Lack of coordination of these various activities led to much dissatisfaction among employees and culminated in labor troubles. The employees organized an industrial union for the purpose of collective bargaining and in the fall of 1933 went out on strike to enforce their demands. The settlement of this strike brought with it a reorganization of management and the development of an industrial-relations department as a staff function. The position of the superintendent in charge of manufacturing was abolished. Instead, there were five divisional superintendents, one for each line of product. Under the divisional superintendents, there were foremen, or supervisors. In this way, company organization was more decentralized. At the head of the plant organization was the works manager.

The new management signed an agreement with the industrial union and worked in close cooperation with its officers. Union officials and elected departmental representatives met with management on the third Wednesday of every month to discuss policies affecting the plant as a whole. Upon request of either party, special meetings could be called. In the monthly meetings between management and the union, policies were formulated and published for the coordination and guidance of all divisions in such matters as wages, job classification, rates of pay, promotions, transfer, furlough, layoffs and dismissal procedure.

Industrial Relations.—The administration of policies was centralized in the new department of industrial relations. Routine complaints and matters concerning individual departments or occupational groups of workers were taken care of in daily conferences with the supervisor of industrial relations. A representation plan was set up, which provided one union representative for each department and occupation to discuss with management any problem that affected his group. When a union representative asked for a meeting with the supervisor of industrial relations, he was privileged to bring with him the complainant and a second worker from the department or occupation in which the complaint originated. The supervisor of industrial relations, in turn, saw to it that, in any discussion with the union representative, the supervisor of the department concerned was present.

I. The Problem of Scrap

Under both old and new managements, the problem of defective workmanship and materials had been a persistent difficulty, as reflected in excessive "45" charges.[1] The old management had relied chiefly on disciplinary measures to cope with this problem. If responsibility for defective work could be traced directly to an employee, he was discharged. In other cases, the entire group was charged for defective work and for the materials even on previous operations that they had not performed.

These repressive measures proved ineffectual. As pressure was applied, the scrap was squeezed out of the plant. Workman protected their earnings by hiding defective parts and smuggling them out of the factory.

[1] The expression was derived from the defective workmanship and general scrap account, which was numbered 545.

At one time, guards stopped the men as they were leaving the plant and searched each one. As soon as the workers in the line realized what was happening, they emptied their dinner pails and pockets of all incriminating scrap. The next day a large packing case was filled with defective parts picked up in the yard. This episode opened management's eyes and also helped to explain the large annual inventory loss that the company had been sustaining.

QUESTIONS FOR DISCUSSION

1. *On disciplin*
   a. Is it inherent in discipline that, whenever there is an infraction of a rule or a job standard, a superior must punish a subordinate?
   b. What kind of disciplinary measures other than those here described might have been more effective in dealing with the scrap problem?
   c. What forces besides external authority can be drawn upon to build discipline? (*Cf*. Chap. 15, Discipline and Discharge.)

II. NEW METHODS ARE TRIED

One of the first acts of the new works manager in 1934 was to revise company policy with regard to defective workmanship. It was announced that "the only deductions for defective work that will be made from bonus earnings will be replacing the defective operation or operations performed by the employee or the group." No charge was to be made for replacing material or for any operations previously performed by other groups or by individual operators. This more liberal policy brought a slight immediate improvement, but the problem of defective work remained a source of annoyance and expense.

Next the works manager instituted monthly meetings with division superintendents and staff members to discuss the problem of excessive 45 charges. Out of these meetings came many suggestions for attacking the difficulty.

One remedy tried was the introduction of inspection as a separate department. A chief inspector was added to the staff. He developed an efficient personnel and in different ways improved the status of inspectors and testers. The chief inspector also started an intensive educational campaign. In every department, "Bogie Posters" were displayed showing the monthly percentage for the plant. It was difficult to estimate the effect of such publicity. Several union representatives expressed the opinion that workers paid practically no attention to posters of this type. The statistical information was too remote from their everyday experience. If they did notice the high monthly percentages of scrap, they took the stand that it was up to the inspectors and testers to reduce such losses.

This may have been one reason why the chief inspector's campaign had no permanent effect. After a slight decrease, the defective charges again increased. It appeared that, unless something effective could be done, the average percentage for 1937 would be higher than it had been in 1936. The chief inspector urged that some means be found to enlist the cooperation of men and women at the bench. He was convinced that not only inspectors and testers but every worker in the plant needed to be educated as to the significance of the 45 account.

QUESTIONS FOR DISCUSSION

1. *On company policy*
   a. Comment on the revised company policy on deductions for defective work. Do you or do you not agree in principle with this modification of the former policy? Give your reasons.
   b. To what factors would you attribute the misunderstanding by workers of management's purpose in setting up an inspection department?
   c. In what ways might this misunderstanding and the resulting difficulties have been avoided?

III. UNION-MANAGEMENT COOPERATION

At this stage, management decided to attack the scrap question as an industrial-relations problem and to solicit union cooperation. The first step in this campaign was to "sell" the union officials. The union president and the business agent were at first inclined to be suspicious of this program. They feared that union representatives would be expected to act as spies, that employees who were responsible for defective work would be discharged, and that foremen would resent union participation in what was, after all, essentially a management problem. On the other hand, they could also see the advantages to the union in such cooperation. It offered an excellent opportunity to show how a responsible union could help management to attack a difficult plant problem. Furthermore, such cooperation would have the distinct advantage of acquainting union representatives and workers with management policies. After several meetings with the industrial-relations supervisor, the union leaders promised their support.

Planning the Campaign.—In planning the campaign, representatives of top management and top union officials favored propaganda as the most effective means of winning the workers' interest and support. But the industrial-relations supervisor succeeded in convincing the committee that propaganda without practical education would probably be ineffectual. In his own study of the problem, he had found, by analyzing statistics and following his analysis with observation and interviewing, that one department head had achieved a superior record for success in meeting this baffling problem. Mr. Wellman, superintendent of the motored-appliance division, had been able for over a year to keep his scrap account at a consistently low level. Interviews disclosed that he had been conducting weekly foremen's meetings to discuss the scrap problem and that union representatives in his division had also participated in these meetings. The industrial-relations supervisor was convinced that cooperation between union and management at the work level had been a significant factor in Mr. Wellman's success.

The Campaign Itself.—Accordingly, two of Wellman's union representatives, Messrs. Black and Moore, were selected by management to cooperate with the works manager and the supervisor of industrial relations as members of the planning committee. It was decided to adopt both a general publicity campaign and department discussion groups.

The publicity campaign was started off with posters of a mystery nature in order to arouse interest. The first poster placed throughout the plant was a huge question mark. This was followed by a poster with the statement: "U Should Be Interested." Each time a poster appeared, the union paper displayed the same message on each of its pages. All advertising space in the union paper was contributed by the union. Posters were changed once a week, and efforts were made to emphasize the part played by the union in this campaign. For instance, one poster put the question: "What Is the 45 Charge?" and urged each employee to "See Your Representative."

A specific date was advertised as the official start of the scrap campaign. On this day, several meetings were held with superintendents, foremen, and representatives of the different shifts. At these meetings, the works manager made the keynote speech in order to personalize the crusade against scrap as the "manager's campaign." Union representatives Black and Moore also addressed the groups and told of their experience in cooperating with Mr. Wellman to build up a scrap-minded department.

The next day, each foreman in the various departments held his own meeting in order to set up departmental scrap committees. These committees were composed of management and union representatives as well as key workers. The general procedure was simple and effective. Committee members gathered around a table that displayed samples of the scrap that had been collected in the department. The defective pieces were analyzed with the idea of locating the source of trouble and recommending methods of overcoming it.

Causal Analysis.—The effort to fix responsibility for scrap was developed into a careful system for determining not only *who* but also *what* was to blame. This analysis clearly showed that various factors not previously considered in connection with the 45 charge did in fact play a part in increasing it. First, union representatives found that faulty equipment, not always promptly repaired or replaced, was responsible for a considerable percentage of defective work. Second, errors in micrometer reading by new operators indicated that more effective training would undoubtedly reduce the amount of scrap. In another department, it appeared that more careful training and follow-up were needed in regard to efficiency of motion. Girls were pulling finished stators across the work bench instead of lifting them. This practice sometimes resulted in a short circuit if a nail or a metal part had become embedded in the bench surface.

Third, it became apparent that incentive pay was also a related factor. In one department, gouged shafts resulted from the practice of dropping them into the holder without first backing the grinding wheel. This practice saved time for the operators but sometimes resulted in scrap for the company.

Study of scrap in another section indicated that spot check by inspectors was letting through too much defective work and that a higher level of self-inspection by workers must be developed.

In the toolroom, it was found that unnecessary scrap resulted from the fact that not all drawings were always up to date. When obsolete drawings were used, the finished tool, even though perfect in workmanship, had to be scrapped, since it did not conform to the latest design. The toolroom foreman had repeatedly tried to convince the division superintendents that all drawings must be kept up to date. The superintendents, however, argued that they did not have sufficient funds to do this. They pointed out that drawings could not be kept up to date unless other draftsmen were hired. This the superintendents felt unable to do. After careful study of the costs involved, the union representatives asked for an interview with the budget director. This official promptly agreed that extra draftsmen be hired. Within a week, the 45 charge in the toolroom dropped from $800 to $20 a week. When rechecked 4 months later, it was still at the same level.

Activity of this sort was a significant element in progress toward the goal of reducing the 45 charge. But the enthusiastic enlistment of many workers and union officials produced unexpected problems both within the union and for management itself.

Questions for Discussion

1. *On unity of the employment process*
   a. Using as a guide the examples given of the kind of activity that led to scrap, trace the connection with features of the regular employment process.

b. What evidence is given that a more successful personnel program would have contributed to technical efficiency?

2. *On maintaining line authority*

    a. What essential organizational policy is threatened when union representatives ask a staff official to reverse a decision given by a line representative?

    b. How should the budget director have handled such a request?

IV. Unexpected Human Problems

Trouble within the Union.—For example, the activity of Black and Moore was an important factor in coordinating the campaign and was appreciated by management and by various committee members. However, it also aroused criticism among some of the employees. Rumors were started by a rival clique that these two had become "management men"; that they were trying to make a white-collar job for themselves; and that, now being "all dressed up, they had forgotten what it felt like to work at the bench." For a time, it seemed as if these rumors might disrupt the campaign.

Trouble between Individual Workers.—Throughout the campaign, the supervisor of industrial relations, or his representative, attended the various scrap meetings and analyzed the minutes. Many incidents called for the moderating influence of men versed in personnel relations. For example, during a scrap meeting where current defective apparatus was exhibited to the committee and subjected to a painstaking analysis, it often happened that employees responsible for scrap were brought from the bench into the committee room. At such times, feeling between workers often rose to such a pitch that it was difficult to prevent the meeting from degenerating into an inquisition. Employees who had become enthusiastic about the scrap campaign felt a natural desire to punish those who were found to be responsible for defective work.

Trouble for First-line Supervisors.—Another difficult feature of the scrap campaign was that foremen were frequently "put on the spot." Workers who had previously been put on the defensive when indiscriminately charged with primary responsibility for defective work now frequently resorted to the countercharge that management itself was by no means without fault. Group leaders and union representatives delighted in showing up a foreman by pointing out that some time ago he had been advised of a certain defect and its cause but that weeks had been allowed to pass without any action being taken.

Trouble for Staff Officials.—Various staff officials also came in for their share of criticism. For example, it was brought out that, when engineers made changes in design, some scrap resulted unless the work on obsolete parts was promptly stopped. This had not always been done. When this element in the problem was first brought to light, workers tended to feel that engineers were troublemakers with their new ideas.

Even the inspectors did not emerge unscathed from the searching analysis that went forward during and between meetings. It was discovered that some inspectors had developed a knack of using defective gauges. When these gauges were used by anyone else, mistakes almost inevitably resulted.

It was also discovered that, on some occasions, production chasers had insisted that they must have certain parts right away. In rush orders, they frequently would not wait for an accurate count of specified parts. Thus a whole week's order was frequently finished with the worker relying only on memory count. Sometimes this resulted in a surplus of unusable parts.

Such discoveries of poor teamwork led to improvement only after a certain amount of recrimination and hard feeling. Some of these feelings persisted even after the technical difficulties had been cleared up.

QUESTIONS FOR DISCUSSION

1. *On situational thinking*
   a. If you had been the supervisor of industrial relations at this point, what action would you have recommended to clear up the misunderstanding about Black and Moore?
   b. How and by whom might this manifestation of rivalry between union cliques have been prevented?
2. *On committee leadership*
   Which of the feelings displayed here by workers is to be encouraged, and how might the committee chairman have tried to redirect it so that it could operate as a constructive influence?
3. *On the position of the first-line supervisors*
   What measures might have saved foremen from being put in such an embarrassing position?
   a. Which of these was top management's responsibility?
   b. What could these subleaders have done for themselves?
4. *On the relations between staff officials and workers*
   a. What kind of thinking is called for by this typical attitude of workers toward staff officials?
   b. What measures might have promoted a better understanding of the aim and methods pursued by these officials?
   c. What management officials should have taken action to correct the technical inefficiencies that occasioned complaint?

V. Technical Success of the Cooperative Program

In the eyes of management, all these difficulties were more than counterbalanced by the practical results of the campaign. Every department experienced a lowering of the 45 charge. For the plant and its various divisions, this is graphically illustrated by the following charts:[1]

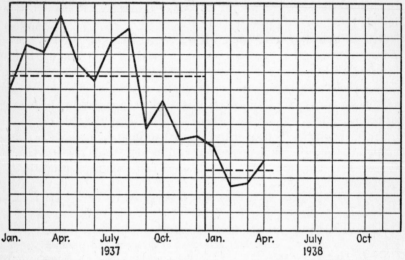

Jan.   Apr.   July   Oct.   Jan.   Apr.   July   Oct
            1937   1938

CHART A. — Local plant's 45 charge by months, expressed in dollars.

Chart A represents the total 45 charge for the local plant, expressed in dollars by months. The dotted lines show average values for the full year of 1937 and for the first 4 months of 1938. The general downward trend is to some extent affected by a decrease in productive activity.

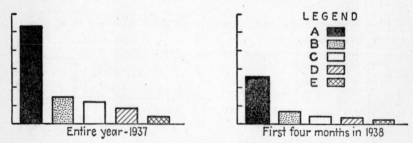

LEGEND

A
B
C
D
E

Entire year-1937   First four months in 1938

CHART B. — Divisional monthly averages of local plant's 45 charge expressed in dollars.

[1] The charts indicate relationships only. Actual amounts could not be given without disclosing confidential information.

The columns in Chart B show in dollars the average monthly charge for each division and thus indicate the distribution of these expenses by

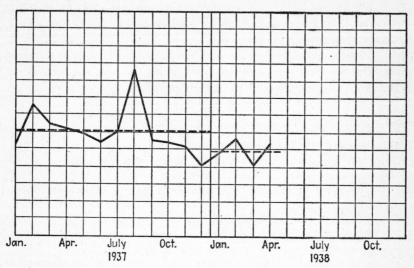

Jan. Apr. July Oct. Jan. Apr. July Oct.
1937 1938

CHART C. — Local plant's 45 charge in per cent of productive labor cleared in cost.

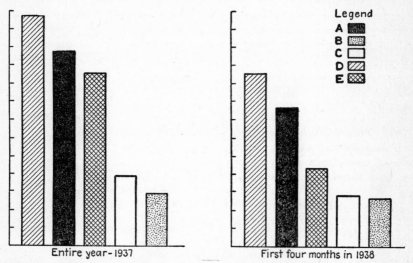

Legend
A
B
C
D
E

Entire year-1937 First four months in 1938

CHART D. — Divisional cumulative percentages of plant's 45 charge, in per cent of productive labor cleared in cost.

products. Here, too, the general downward trend is to some extent affected by the decrease in productive activity.

Charts C and D give the same information as A and B, respectively, but expressed in percentage of productive labor cleared in cost. This eliminates the effect of volume reduction and presents a picture of actual performance. In all charts, there is an observable downward trend.

Every department in the plant became thoroughly scrap-conscious and cooperated in improving the quality of the product and in reducing waste. The following letter sent out by the industrial-relations department calls attention to one example of such cooperation.

Dec. 3, 1937

Superintendents, Foremen,
and Chairmen of "45" Committees:

The "45" campaign committee of the power house has called to our attention, by way of reports, at various times since the "45" campaign got under way, many instances of windows being left open at the close of the shift. In some cases, the rain has blown in through the open windows, and considerable damage due to rust has been done to finished products.

The report of the power house this week listed approximately 145 windows that had been left open. Not only is the product damaged in this respect, but a severe loss of heat occurs, which naturally reflects seriously on our efforts to cut down waste.

Other instances that have been brought to our attention are truckmen leaving the doors open after passing through, rather than closing them, as they should.

Another item is air and steam leaks. These should be reported to the foreman of the department immediately so that proper repairs may be made with all possible haste.

It is my opinion that various "45" committees throughout the plant can aid materially in correcting these conditions, and we respectfully ask that you read this letter in your meeting and, if necessary, appoint a subcommittee to check into the situation in your various departments toward eliminating this particular phase of the waste, which is of great importance to our campaign.

We trust that, when we next have a report from the "45" committee of the power house, open windows, open doors, and steam and air leaks will show a material decrease. Needless to say, we anticipate your cooperation.

General Committee
(signed)   Endicott

Approved by: J. Avery

This appeal resulted in a 75 per cent improvement of the conditions.

VI. The Developing Situation

Fully as important in the long run as the reduction in tangible waste were the indirect results of the new attitudes and procedures developed during the campaign. Among other developments, the unofficial agenda at scrap meetings proved significant.

Unexpected Developments in Scrap Meetings.—While waiting for one of these meetings to start, or after official adjournment, a worker or union official would often seize the occasion to make some suggestion or complaint to a line official. Not all suggestions could be acted upon, but it was found valuable to have such an easy flow of communication.

For example, a committee member asked whether social activities in the evening could be made part of the company program, as they were at one of the other plants. On another occasion, a committee member brought up the fact that the employee discount at the company store was too small, since some company products could be bought cheaper in outside stores that featured cut-rate articles. At another meeting, a committee member who was working on the second shift asked whether anything could be done to make evening courses available to employees on the late shifts.

New Union Activities.—The new courses had been started at the request of the union. During the campaign, union officials had come to realize that a better understanding of management policies and practices was necessary to their own efficiency as leaders. In answer to their request, it was decided to give union representatives and group leaders a regular course in industrial management, covering such subjects as production control, inspection, and the keeping of records and accounts.

Incidentally, this innovation raised an immediate objection from first-line supervisors, who had never been given any formalized training. As management representatives, they naturally resented the fact that union representatives and group leaders were now receiving the benefit of this course. To meet such objections, management gave the same course to supervisors.

A further development, when union officials came to understand accounting methods, was their demand that the system be revised. They insisted, and were now able to demonstrate, that the current system of records and accounts did not adequately represent all the factors that went to make up the 45 charge. Without a more minute breakdown, the carelessness of workers received a disproportionate emphasis.

The system was revised so that it made a better record of all relevant factors. But naturally this was not done without some resentment in the accounting department, whose members felt that union officials had no business to interfere in such matters or to upset their traditional routines.

The question of "outside work" came up frequently at the 45 meetings and afforded management excellent opportunities to demonstrate the part played by defective workmanship and waste in increasing factory costs. If the discrepancy between inside and outside cost was too great, management subcontracted the work to outside suppliers. One way for the union to keep such work inside the plant was to reduce excessive 45 charges. As workers came to understand this, they cooperated heartily in an attempt to reduce waste, and in this way many items were brought back into the plant. Union officials, however, soon were dissatisfied merely with bringing work back. They requested an opportunity to consider what they might be able to do *before* any work was sent outside.

This eventually led to an elaborate procedure in which the supervisor of production planning (whose duty it was to schedule work throughout the plant, *i.e.*, place orders for work to be done in the plant or purchased outside) submitted to the industrial-relations director a list of items that were to be sent outside. The following information was supplied: name of part, style number, department in which the item was made, inside cost, and outside price. The supervisor of industrial relations then notified the union president and arranged for a meeting with the department representative, the departmental foreman, and a time-study man. This committee discussed all further details with reference to the item that was about to be purchased from outside suppliers. If the union could find a way to meet the outside competition, the work was kept inside the plant. There were numerous occasions, however, when sentiments complicated purely financial issues. For example, if the inside cost was only a fraction higher than outside cost, the union officials were disposed to ask, "Isn't it worth management's while to pay the slight difference in order to gain the workers' good will and cooperation?"

By and large, union officials became more management-minded. But sometimes they exceeded their authority, as when they ordered operators not to run a machine unless they were sure it was in perfect repair.

VII. Cooperation Is Dynamic

In all these ways, it was found that "something new had been added" when workers and union officials became genuinely enlisted in solving what had previously been regarded as a management problem. This new element enabled management to achieve a higher degree of technical success than would otherwise have been possible. It also served to keep management representatives, both staff and line, on their toes to make their own activity both efficient and fair. This indirect result in stepping up technical and human efficiency throughout the plant was even more significant in the long run than the successful solution of the problem as it had originally been conceived.

Questions for Discussion

1. *On communication*
   If there had been no need for a scrap campaign, how could management have

secured the same improvement in the channel of communication up the line? (See page 489, Pars. 2 and 3.)

2. *On training policy*

Comment on policy requirements that were overlooked when management introduced training for union officials on the first shift only. If you had been industrial-relations supervisor in this company at the time, in what order would you have recommended that such courses be instituted? What general-policy announcements should have been made?

3. *On union "interference" with management "prerogatives"*

Comment on the union's criticism of the current system of accounting for the 45 charge.

   a. What aspects of this situation might well be encouraged?

   b. What is unhelpful about the presentation of these ideas?

   c. What company officials should have handled the technical and human features of this evolving situation?

4. *On the scope of union activity*

   a. What difficulties might be anticipated when a union participates in decisions concerning the placing of work orders? (Consider the position and attitudes both of management and the union.)

   b. What participation, if any, is desirable in this area?

Questions on the Case as a Whole

1. *On situational thinking*

Using as illustrations the developments described in this case, show how a more skillful application of this multiple approach might have prevented many of the tensions that actually arose. (Consider the technical factor, people, principles and policies, and the time element.)

2. *On the principle of management responsibility*

Before inviting union participation in solving a technical problem, what steps should management have taken to ensure that its own activity was efficient to secure the desired end?

3. *On delimiting the extent of union participation*

Where should the line be drawn between joint responsibility for decision making and undivided management control? (Consider the functions and objectives both of management and of the union.)

Appendix to Chapter 4

The Western Electric Research Program

The Western Electric Research Program was a study of human problems in industry, carried on jointly by representatives of the Western Electric Company in Chicago and members of the Harvard Business School. It is a milestone in the development of personnel administration. Anyone who is seriously interested in personnel work as a profession should be thoroughly familiar with the work of this group.[1] And, as an illustration of person-centered thinking, this program is of peculiar interest. The detailed study of individual cases followed logically from the development of a policy to base a new training program on the unique features that together comprised the company's personnel situation. Throughout the study, progress in understanding was achieved by the interplay of general knowledge and insight into unique contexts. Understanding of tensions set up in areas outside the job enabled management to retain many normally good workers who would have been discharged if their behavior on the job had been made the sole criterion of decision.

This research program is especially significant, because the investigators allowed their center of attention to move, as new facts came to light, from primarily mechanical and physiological factors to the human element. The successive stages by which the inquiry developed were as follows:

At first, investigators carried out their experiments in the production departments and tried to test the effects on output of changes in a single

---

[1] ROETHLISBERGER, F. J., and W. J. DICKSON, *Management and the Worker*, An Account of a Research Program Conducted by the Western Electric Company, Hawthorne Works, Chicago, Harvard University Press, Cambridge, Mass., 1939; MAYO, ELTON, *The Human Problems of an Industrial Civilization*, The Macmillan Company, New York, 1933; WHITEHEAD, NORTH, *The Industrial Worker*, Harvard University Press, Cambridge, Mass., 1938; CHASE, STUART, *Men at Work*, Harcourt, Brace and Company, New York, 1941; Chap. 2, pp. 9–27, gives a popularized account of these experiments.

variable, such as light intensity. The results of these experiments were negative. Employee output went up during the test periods regardless of whether the value of illumination was increased or decreased. The observers concluded that, in a regular operating department, there were so many factors affecting the reactions of workers that it was impossible to evaluate any one by itself. Consequently, it was decided to put a small group of workers in a room apart from the regular working force, where their behavior could be scientifically studied.

However, the experiments with several such test groups showed that the logical approach of setting up a controlled experimental situation was not productive here. Even though there had been no alterations in work methods and materials, the investigators had unwittingly introduced a very significant change. The experimental situation was no longer that of a standard shop department but that of a small special unit that soon developed characteristics of its own. Observers quickly recognized that changes in the evolving social situation were more significant than the new experimental conditions that they introduced at various times. These social developments may be summarized under three headings: (1) development of a primary group, (2) development of social participation with an increased sense of personal dignity and status, and (3) improved relationships between workers and supervisors.

I. Development of a Primary Group [1]

In setting up the relay-assembly test room, for example, management had invited two experienced operators who were friends. These in turn had selected the other four operators needed for the experiment. Thus, from the outset, the work mates were congenial. As a result of the intimate work association in the small test room, they all became friends and spent their time together even outside the shop. This growing sense of solidarity in turn increased their efficiency as a work group. On occasions, when an operator was absent, the others voluntarily took over the task of maintaining the same level of group earnings. They were united for a common purpose, and there was a genuine spirit of friendliness.

[1] For a technical discussion of the contrast between primary and secondary groups, see CHARLES H. COOLEY, *Social Organization*, p. 23, Charles Scribner's Sons, New York, 1939. Durkheim's distinction between *solidarité mécanique* and *solidarité organique*, as well as Toennies's differentiation between *Gemeinschaft* and *Gesellschaft*, throw additional light on these structural differences from other angles. *Cf.* DURKHEIM, EMILE, *De la division du travail social*, Alcan (Librairie Félix), Paris, 1902; and TOENNIES, FERDINAND, *Gemeinschaft und Gesellschaft*, Curtius, Berlin, 1925. For an excellent comparative analysis, the reader may also refer to R. M. MacIVER, *Society: Its Structure and Changes*, Chap. IX, pp. 172–190, The Primary Group and the Great Associations, Richard R. Smith, New York, 1931.

II. Development of Social Participation with an Increased Sense of Personal Dignity and Status

Being an employee of a test group gave each operator a sense of importance. Higher supervisors and outside experts were greatly interested in these experiments, and the girls were treated with special consideration. Because their comments were considered of value, the girls were told in advance of contemplated changes. Furthermore, they were kept informed of the progress of the experiment. In short, they were treated as responsible employees whose feelings, attitudes, and opinions were not only of interest but of value to management.

The sense of dignity that grew out of such treatment and the realization that employees had something besides manual labor to contribute toward management enterprise was reflected in a change of attitudes and relationships. For example, one girl who had previously been considered as a troublemaker by her supervisors now showed herself as a leader, suggesting changes and criticizing procedures. Perhaps because of the new relationship established between operators and supervisor, the girl was enabled to offer her suggestions as a contribution instead of a criticism; and, in the test room, she was considered one of the most cooperative and responsible employees of the group.

III. Improved Relationships between Workers and Supervisors

In the test room, there was more supervision than there had been in the shop, since the operators were now under constant observation. But the *quality* of supervision was different. In many cases, the test-room observers showed their personal interest in the girls and their problems. They were friends rather than bosses and were constantly on the alert to detect and quiet any apprehension on the part of the operators.

For example, when it was found that production in the test room was much higher than output in the regular department, management planned to pay the test-room girls by the same "percentage" as was paid in the regular department, but once each month to pay the difference between the departmental percentage and their actual earnings in the form of a bonus. It was thought that this method would have a better psychological effect, since it would bring home to the test group the difference between their earnings and those of the regular department. But this failed to take account of the latent suspicions that so commonly exist in the minds of employees. When the girls were told of this plan, they volunteered the following opinions:

"Why do you want to pay us like in the department? Just so you can ball us up, I bet, and then we can't keep track of our record."

"We'll never get all the money." (When she was assured that there was no one else who would get it and as a joke was asked, "Who else could get it?" she quickly replied, "The bosses, I guess.")

Such frank statements, showing an unusual absence of restraint, give evidence of the superior quality of the new supervision, which was significantly characterized by the test-room operator who said of her supervisor, "Say, he's no boss. We don't have any boss."

A Program of Employee Interviewing

Evaluation of the observations made during these experiments suggested that workers have reserves of energy and ideas that normally go unused but can be brought into play when the social situation is satisfactory and when workers feel themselves a part of the management enterprise. If these benefits were to be extended to the company as a whole, it seemed clear that better supervision was needed in the shop. In order that a supervisory training program might be based on local conditions rather than on principles enunciated in textbooks, a preliminary program of employee interviewing was undertaken that should elicit facts and win the workers' participation. During this phase of the investigation, 21,126 interviews were held with operating, staff, and technical employees. But, in trying to determine the reliability of employee comments, the investigators again found themselves led away from a mechanical cataloguing of statistics toward a new way of thinking about human situations.

As the interviewing program went along, the investigators grew more skillful in evaluating the type of complaint in which fact and sentiment were intermingled. They realized that reference to the unique experience or context was essential to an understanding of employee attitudes and reactions. A case in point was that of a wireman (W-7) who was engaged in semirepetitive work. His work curve was divided by the investigators into five phases.

By correlating these work curves with interview material, the following significant relationships appear:

In an interview on Dec. 7 (see B in figure on p. 496), shortly after his output began to decrease, he complained that, although he was turning out more work then W-9, he was getting less money. This was the first time he had made this complaint, although the discrepancy between W-9's output and earnings was not a new discovery to W-7. Why then should it suddenly strike him as a grievance? The explanation seemed to lie in his social situation.

At the time of the first interview, W-7 was going with a girl who was self-supporting. He was thinking of marriage but wanted to increase his earnings first. At the time of the second interview, his girl was on shorter hours and was facing the possibility of a layoff which would mean her leaving Chicago and going home to North Dakota. This was very upsetting to W-7, since it confronted him with the necessity of making an immediate decision. Could he earn enough to support them both? At this crucial point in his life, his output curve began to go down, and his growing preoccupation probably accounts for the fact that the discrepancy between his earnings and those of W-9 now seemed to him to constitute a grievance. "The downward trend in W-7's output continued all during the period of indecision. Finally, on Jan. 7 (see *C* in the diagram), after sitting

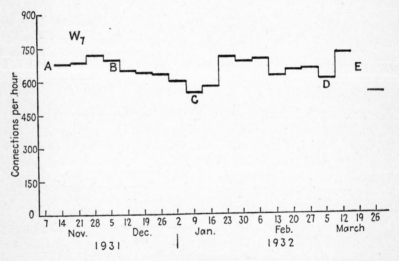

around most of the day and being unable to work, he announced his intention of getting married. He did so 2 days later. During the next week, his output curve started upward, and in the second week thereafter it reached its highest point up to that time. The conflict had been resolved."[1]

CONCLUSION

Study of numerous other cases indicated that work satisfaction not only increased an employee's work efficiency but also sustained him during domestic difficulties or other periods of stress.

In fitting these findings into a coherent whole, the investigators evolved

---

[1] ROETHLISBERGER and DICKSON, *op. cit.*, pp. 318–319.

a conceptual scheme for their new ideas about the worker and his complaints. Interpretation of these complaints called for study of all the major areas that make up a person's total life situation. These were explored not in a simple cause and effect analysis but as a network of interrelated factors that together form the basis for personal equilibrium or disequilibrium.

Appendix to Chapter 11

The Job Relations Training
Program of the TWI[1]

The value of a realistic approach in training supervisors was clearly demonstrated by the War Manpower Commission in its Training Within Industry Program during the Second World War.[2] Early in 1941, work was begun on how to help new supervisors with their problems in dealing with people. Considerable experimentation was necessary in various types of industry and at all levels of supervision, with men and with women who differed widely in educational and industrial backgrounds. From February, 1943, when the Job Relations Training course was released, to February, 1945, 425,000 supervisors were given this intensive coaching in the leadership principles of their jobs. All over the country, in small conferences, each group was taught how to build on its own experience. There was no textbook, only a small blue card that could easily be carried in one's billfold or vestpocket. One side of this card stated essential procedure:

HOW TO HANDLE A PROBLEM

Determine Objectives

1. *Get the Facts*
   Review the record.
   Find out what rules and plant customs apply.
   Talk with individuals concerned.
   Get opinions and feelings.
   Be sure you have the whole story

[1] *The Training Within Industry Report*, 1940-1945: A record of the Development of Management Techniques for Improvement of Supervision—Their Use.and the Results, pp. 330*ff.*, War Manpower Commission, Bureau of Training, Training Within Industry Service, Washington, D.C., September, 1945.

[2] C. R. Dooley of Socony-Vacuum and Walter Dietz of Western Electric were borrowed in 1940 by the government to serve as director and associate director of an industrial-training group. Under their leadership, the following four training programs were originated and launched on a national scale: (1) Job Instructor Training, (2) Job Methods Training, (3) Job Relations Training, and (4) Program Development.

2. *Weigh and Decide*
   Fit the facts together.
   Consider their bearing on each other.
   What possible actions are there?
   Check practices and policies.
   Consider objective and effect on individual, group, and production.
Don't jump at conclusions
3. *Take Action*
   Are you going to handle this yourself?
   Do you need help in handling?
   Should you refer this to your supervisors?
   Watch the timing of your action.
Don't pass the buck
4. *Check Results*
   How soon will you follow up?
   How often will you need to check?
   Watch for changes in output, attitudes, and relationships.
Did your actions help production?

The other side of the card gave an outline of leadership principles:

JOB RELATIONS
A Supervisor Gets Results through People
Foundations for Good Relations

Let Each Worker Know How He Is Getting Along
   Figure out what you expect of him.
   Point out ways to improve.
Give Credit When Due
   Look for *extra* or *unusual* performance.
   Tell him while "it's hot."
Tell People in Advance about Changes That Will Affect Them
   Tell them *why* if possible.
   Get them to accept the change.
Make Best Use of Each Person's Ability
   Look for ability not now being used.
   Never stand in a man's way.
People must be treated as individuals

This course was given by specially trained conference leaders, not to people who were hoping to become supervisors, but to supervisors already on the job. In 10 hours of basic training, the principles and procedures outlined on the card were explained and illustrated by the discussion leader. For instance,

1. *Get the Facts*
   Problems may come up because of something that happens at the moment,

but you need to get the whole background. Some of it will be made up of facts about the employee—his age, length of service, and experience on this job.

You will need, of course, to take into consideration both the plant rules and just "the way things are done here."

You may think you know the person quite well; but, if you are thinking of him as a "good fellow" or a "chronic kicker," you are not really looking at an individual person. You must regard him as a person who is different from his work partner and from every person in the department in every single aspect whether to a very slight or to a very great degree.

As a supervisor, you must know what that man thinks and feels about himself and the people around him. Find out what the man wants—is he able or willing to express it—and what does he think should be done? and why?

The experienced supervisor knows that he must also consider such other factors as health and working conditions that may be affecting the man.

If more than one person is involved, you must go through the same fact-finding steps for each person. Before you can plan what to do, you must be sure you really have the whole story.

2. *Weigh and Decide*

All these facts must be assembled and considered together. When all the factors are brought together, fitted in, and considered in the light of their relations to each other, the right answer almost "jumps out." The wise thing to do becomes clearer.

Certainly you, the man on the spot, are in the *best* place to know the *right* thing to do, for you have the most complete picture of the assembled facts. If you jump to conclusions, you make poor use of your strategic position. When you act without evaluating the whole situation, you are likely to have more difficult problems to handle later.

3. *Take Action*

Jumping to conclusions is an ineffective way to handle supervisory problems, but indecisive postponement is equally unfortunate. A supervisor cannot "pass the buck," or he, himself, will be by-passed.

However, it is not "passing the buck" to recognize after full consideration of the problem that there are some situations which you cannot handle yourself. You also make a decision and take action when you size up a situation as one on which you need help, or recognize one that is not within your own job to handle and see that it is passed on to the person who does have the responsibility and authority.

In any action, timing must be considered—the wrong "time" can make it the wrong thing to do.

4. *Check Results*

Since people are so different, since what worked before is not likely to work again in a somewhat similar situation, the supervisor may not always be sure that what he has done has been the most effective way of handling the particular situation. You must try to determine whether your action worked. If it did not, you must reexamine the whole situation and attempt to find what of importance you overlooked.

From the early days of the Job Relations Training program, there was considerable discussion as to the application of JRT principles to the problems of union shop stewards. In January, 1944, clearance was obtained so that union representatives were eligible for Job Relations Training courses. As a result, some 2,500 shop stewards received this instruction. Experimental work began on the development of an all-union version of the Job Relations Training program, called Union Job Relations. This was launched in January, 1945.

Throughout the Job Relations Training program, the discussion leader makes use of case illustrations. These are drawn from actual experience and help group members to bring out similar experiences and current difficulties. The following case is a good example of the way in which a conference leader focuses attention on the importance of getting all the facts and not jumping to conclusions.

THE CASE OF JIM BROWN

Wartime labor shortage had forced Bill O'Connor, a superintendent of a metal-products plant, to hire old Jim Brown, who for some years had lived by picking up odd jobs around town. Jim was a sociable fellow, somewhat slovenly, and fond of a drink "now and then." Everyone liked him, and Bill O'Connor took a special pride in helping Jim to steady down in a regular job. Jim started as a machine oiler in department B and, to everyone's surprise, took an immediate interest in his work. He did it acceptably and for 2½ months reported faithfully and promptly.

One day, a female shop clerk in department B slipped on the floor and broke her arm. When this was reported to the superintendent, he jumped to the conclusion that the girl had slipped on an oily spot probably made by old Jim's carelessness with his oilcan. Knowing that the old fellow was sensitive, he decided to caution him without specifically mentioning the accident. In order to make his point as clear as possible, he spoke to Jim the same afternoon while passing him in the shop, "Oh, by the way, Jim, I know I've mentioned this before, but please be careful about dropping oil on the floor. It makes it harder to clean, and then somebody might slip and hurt himself."

Jim nodded, and the superintendent walked on, well satisfied with his tactful approach. Next day he was surprised to learn that Jim for the first time had not reported for work. Nor did he come the following day.

At the end of the week, the girl in the main office reported that Jim had sent word that he was through.

Meanwhile the foreman in Jim's department found out why Jim had quit.

"Weren't you a little rough on Jim?", he asked the superintendent.

"Why, no, I was particularly tactful with him," Bill replied. "As a matter of fact, I thought I handled him pretty well. What's the trouble?"

"Well, Jim says you accused him of causing that girl's accident," said the foreman, "But the girl didn't slip on oil, you know. She slipped on a piece of wax paper."

Appendix to Chapter 19

Summary of an Employee-
service Program

It is difficult to tabulate all the interrelated items of an employee-service program according to a system that seems clear and satisfactory even to one person. Obviously, it is impossible to do so to the satisfaction of everyone. The following are some of the difficulties.

Since many of the typical service activities contribute in different ways to the employee's life, they should be listed under several headings. For instance, a company magazine should be listed under recreation if it contains the usual material about leisure-time activities. When articles on nutrition or hygiene are included, or notices of first-aid courses or about safety measures, the magazine also contributes to a health and safety program. Certainly it must be tabulated under education. It might well also be included under economic security if it contains any financial information and under community interests when editorials or reports are printed about money-raising campaigns, for instance. We have never listed a single item as many times as this but have sometimes included it in more than one service when it seems especially useful to think about it from more than one angle.

A second problem is the difficulty of pinning down a set of activities that is constantly shifting and of making a definite classification where there is such a wide range of practice. However, it is encouraging to remember that this difficulty is in part, at least, the worker's gain. Some activities that a few years ago were considered unusual benefits or services are now standard practice in leading firms. Other companies, through lack of money or of interest, lag behind. In a few years, it is to be hoped that personnel-minded executives will be able to standardize many procedures that are now considered only as desirable services and to include many new activities as regular services. Our classification is intended to represent a high level of practice in the present.

A third problem is the difficulty of making the lists sufficiently complete to be useful without being so detailed that they are complicated. We

503

have met this difficulty by listing under each heading a scattering of typical items. If the lists seem too scanty, they can be expanded by the reader.

I. RECREATION

The distinctive purposes that can be promoted by recreation are numerous and important. Health is among the most obvious. Sports, especially when they can be played outdoors, build physical health and provide an outlet for the energy not used in the many sedentary jobs of office and factory. Mental health is also promoted by any form of recreation that stimulates and refreshes mind and body, thus providing relief from a sense of job monotony. No less important are the less obvious values of group association, good sportsmanship, self-reliance, and the development of leadership capacity in sports, hobby clubs, or cultural activities.

Recreation also offers an easy opportunity for an employee to bring his family into association with the company members and their families. This is of special value to newcomers in a community, but it is always worth while, since in this way the employee can bring his two worlds into contact, thus integrating the two halves of his life. And the members of his family usually welcome the chance to meet the work mates who have only been names to them before.

Finally, well-planned recreation is to many people a new experience in the creative use of leisure. Commercialized amusements in America today have overdeveloped the natural tendency to passivity experienced by most people when they are tired. Many Americans are unused to thinking of recreation as a positive activity from which mind and body can gain refreshment. If the personnel administrator or recreation director, in cooperation with interested workers, can organize this service in genuinely "recreative" activities, it can contribute in important ways to physical and mental health as well as to enjoyment.

A. Typical Activities and Provisions.—Sports and games, hobbies and special interests, such as camera clubs, social clubs based on length of service, cultural activities, social and folk dancing, bands, choruses, dramatic groups, picnics, banquets and other special events, employee gardens and garden clubs.

B. Related Features in the Work Situation.—Formation of congenial work teams, opportunities for change and development, holidays, annual vacations, preemployment physical examination (information used to caution handicapped employees).

C. Management Representatives Specially Concerned.—Personnel administrator, recreation director, medical division, line executives.

D. Company Contribution.—Salaries of management representatives, loan of space, advice (about procedures and community facilities), direct financial aid, publicity (use of bulletin boards and public-address system, newspaper notices), motion-picture apparatus, services of the maintenance department.

E. The Worker's Share.—Participation in planning and administering, regular attendance, leadership of special groups, contribution of special talents, financial support and/or necessary labor.

F. Outside Contacts.—These include the National Recreation Association, Trade Union Athletic Association League of CIO and of A F of L, local YMCA, YWCA, YMHA, church groups, neighborhood centers and settlement houses, camps, private and civic amusement centers, public library.

II. Health and Safety (Including Nutrition)

The unique aims of this service are discussed in Chap. 20. They include protection and education for health and for safety, as well as prompt care for accidents and for incipient industrial diseases. If the company supplies any food, it should be nutritious as well as appetizing and served under sanitary conditions. In demonstrations and through the use of posters, the company can emphasize the importance for health of a balanced diet. This service protects the company and the local community by education, preventive work, and efficient treatment.

A. Typical Activities and Provisions.—Sanitation and other health measures, special physical examinations, first aid, elimination of mechanical accident sources, nutritious food and advice on nutrition, annual medical check-up, accident procedures, medical advice and treatment (both special and general).

B. Related Features in the Work Situation.—Preemployment medical examination, orientation, reasonable working hours, good working conditions, rest pauses, discriminating job and/or shift assignments, good housekeeping, annual vacation, investigation and control of special health risks and accident hazards, sickness and absence plans.

C. Management Representatives Specially Concerned.—Personnel administrator, doctor, industrial nurse, safety director, special inspectors, sports director, nutritionist, laboratory technicians, representatives of line management, engineers.

D. Company Contribution.—Cost of first aid, medical facilities, and supplies; salaries of medical division and safety director; expense of time spent by other management representatives; health- and accident-insurance premiums; cost of treatment; paid sick leaves, membership in National Safety Council; expense of clerical work (correspondence, records, etc.); time off for medical advice and/or treatment.

E. The Worker's Share.—Safety-mindedness in working methods and safety equipment, personal hygiene and sanitary habits, voluntary first-aid training, contributions to health-insurance premiums.

F. Outside Contacts.—Local boards of sanitation and health, local physicians, hospitals, clinics, Visiting Nurses' Association, Tuberculosis and Health Association, state and Federal agencies, National Safety Council, insurance companies.

III. Education and Information

The special advantages to be achieved by these services derive from the facts that understanding is essential to employee confidence, that knowledge is power, and that every alert worker has capacities other than those called out by routine work. A service for development is of the most potential value to those whose regular work makes no great demand on their mentality. People who have alert minds need to use them, and the company stands to gain if they do. New talent is sometimes discovered when useful inventions are developed by employees. This builds self-confidence in the inventors; serves as an outlet for their mental energy; and may lead to upgrading, promotion, or a change in job assignment. The gain from an educational service is not always immediately manifested by a new invention or improvement in a job method. But the dissemination of relevant general and technical information among employees is a valuable end in itself. It may also prove a means to technical progress in the future and a way of increasing employee understanding of company problems.

A. Typical Activities and Provisions.—Educational opportunities (such as are found in company classes and local schools), a technical library, help with new inventions, discussion clubs, book clubs, scholarship fund. Means of disseminating information, such as company magazine, financial reports (preferably mailed to homes), posters, charts, films, news releases, pay-roll inserts, reports on contract negotiations.

B. Related Features in the Work Situation.—Such employment procedures as orientation, testing, job training, placement, follow-up, merit rating, transfers, upgrading, promotion; also labor-management committees, suggestion system, patent assignments, employee handbook, explanation of policies, bulletin boards, management conferences.

C. Management Representatives Specially Concerned.—Personnel administrator, training director, librarian, patent attorney, engineers, time and motion experts, public-relations director.

D. Company Contribution.—Salary of training director, time of other management representatives, space and equipment for meetings and library, use of office facilities after hours, advice on procedures, information about local opportunities (including schools for children), expenses for attendance at technical conventions, membership in professional associations, subscription to technical journals.

E. The Worker's Share.—Planning, group leadership, regular attendance, and careful use of company property.

F. Outside Contacts.—Educational institutions (high schools, technical schools, colleges, adult education association), libraries, professional associations, patent office.

IV. Economic Security

Among the special objectives to be attained by this service, perhaps the most important is the habit of thrift. By encouraging employees to save, management can help them to look ahead and prepare both for the unexpected and for the inevitable expenses of the future. In this way, employees may spread their earnings and feel a reasonable peace of mind about what lies ahead.

Cooperation between management and workers in an insurance plan has mutual advantages of a practical nature. Group premiums are at a lower rate for each member, and workers who prepare for economic independence after retirement need not suffer the indignity of trying to keep a position that they know they can no longer properly fill. The company, too, stands to gain from the fact that the worker's old age is cared for. There is then no necessity to keep on an employee when advancing age prevents him from fulfilling job requirements. Younger employees who are ready for advance can thus move ahead.

Aside from old age, the unexpected jolts that come from accidents and illness are cushioned by insurance and savings.

A. Typical Activities and Provisions.—Insurance of various kinds (accidents, sickness, life, etc.), retirement or pension funds, thrift clubs, credit unions, stock-purchase plans.

B. Related Features in the Work Situation.—Union contract, wage and salary rates, dismissal pay, notice of termination of employment, policies for rehiring and layoff, annual-wage and guaranteed-employment plans.

C. Management Representatives Specially Concerned.—Personnel administrator, treasurer, accounting department, company lawyer, Medical division and safety director, production-scheduling department, line management.

D. Company Contribution.—Direct expense in premiums, salaries, and contributions; advice and information on Federal and state laws and insurance opportunities.

E. Worker's Share.—In planning, in administering, and in personal contributions.

F. Outside Contacts.—Insurance companies, Federal and state commissions and agencies, banks, local and national unions, hospitals, clinics, and local physicians.

V. CONVENIENCES

The practical advantages of a service that has a proper regard for employee conveniences are derived by both management and workers in time and therefore also in money. Anything that saves time for employees during working hours and promotes regularity and promptness of attendance obviously represents a gain to all concerned. Help with transportation, provisions for eating at the plant, and a company store are services that save time before and during the working day. The time saved for recreation or for work after hours is a direct gain for employees and a good investment for the company.

No less important than a saving in time is the less immediate gain to the company and to the worker from the increased orderliness that normally results when living arrangements in the plant are well planned and efficiently administered. This should also be reflected in improved housekeeping by employees.

Workers who appreciate the conveniences offered them usually repay management for this service, often unconsciously, by bragging about the plant setup, which is an effective form of advertising for the company in the field of public relations.

A. Typical Activities and Provisions.—Lockers, coatroom, washroom, rest room, lunchroom or lunch wagon, waiting room; arrangements for transportation, parking space, company-store or discount-purchase plan; provisions for installment buying, pay-roll deductions, cashing checks, help with income-tax returns, help with employee gardens.

B. Related Features in the Work Situation.—Housekeeping and maintenance, rules for regularity and promptness of attendance, staggered work and/or lunch hours, rest periods.

C. Management Representatives Specially Concerned.—Personnel administrator, construction engineer, safety director, medical division, attendants and cleaners, maintenance department, purchasing department.

D. Company Contributions.—Direct expenses for space, facilities, equipment, salaries. Information on local housing, transportation service, adequate planning.

E. *Workers' Share.*—In planning, upkeep, administration, and expense (*e.g.*, of cafeteria).

F. *Outside Contacts.*—Transportation companies, local eating places, banks, housing authorities, real-estate agents, caterers, local stores and and markets, child-care centers.

VI. PERSONAL AND FAMILY PROBLEMS

Anything that management can properly do to help employees with such difficulties has the special advantage of promoting individual and group stability. The peace of mind gained from settling, or adjusting to, a serious problem is important to each worker and therefore to the whole organization of which he is a member.

By sorting out the problems that vex employees, a personnel counselor can often open the way for use of the other services offered by management. And, by encouraging frankness, objectivity, and self-reliance, he can help workers to help themselves. These attitudes naturally carry over into the work situation and therefore benefit other members of a work team and thus help first-line supervisors with their responsibilities for leadership.

A. *Typical Activities and Provisions.*—Counseling for minor individual maladjustments, emergencies concerning health or money, vocational guidance, and character problems (*e.g.*, truant boy, wayward girl); legal aid, help with other special difficulties (invalid parents, handicapped child, need for rehabilitation).

B. *Related Features in the Work Situation.*—All regular interviews for employment, follow-up, and exit; minimum safety and health requirements; formation of congenial work teams; supervisory leadership; training program; complaint and grievance procedure.

C. *Management Representatives Specially Concerned.*—Personnel administrator, personnel counselors for men and women, employment department, training department, lawyer, medical department, first-line supervisors, accounting department.

D. *Company Contribution.*—Direct expenses for administration and provision of counseling services; loans (possibly without interest if repaid within specified period).

E. *Worker's Share.*—Realistic self-help.

F. *Outside Contacts.*—Social work agencies such as welfare societies, family aid, etc., visiting teacher and visiting nurse, YMCA, YWCA, YMHA, settlement houses, correctional and penal institutions, legal-aid bureau, prison association, church groups, hospitals and clinics, vocational schools, banks, camps, schools, housing authority, union welfare committee.

VII. Community Interests (Civic and Humanitarian)

A service that promotes these interests has special contributions to make for individual employees and for the company as a whole, as well as to the community. Employees should not have to feel a sense of conflict between such demands as earning a living and jury duty, for example. By allowing time off with pay, management can resolve the potential conflict for its employees. This also demonstrates management's sense of membership in the community where its plant is located. Lastly, in this way, and by allowing time off for voting, for instance, management actually strengthens the local community.

When campaigns for relief funds are encouraged in an industrial organization and the company also makes a generous donation, management shows its interest in broad humanitarian aims. An employer should, of course, avoid putting pressure on workers to contribute. Otherwise he lays himself open to the charge of using a humanitarian cause as a form of advertising. But, if workers themselves administer the campaigns, they have special opportunities for leadership and need not feel the sense of pressure that destroys the spirit of a "voluntary" gift.

A. Typical Activities and Provisions.—Absence with pay for jury duty, time off for voting, for Red Cross activities (including blood bank), for acting as witness, and for appearance before government boards. Leave of absence for union officials. Information and discussion on such questions as contributions to service and community funds and to special relief work.

B. Related Features in the Work Situation.—Recruitment contacts with local leaders, conformance with minimum requirements for safety and health.

C. Management Representatives Specially Concerned.—Personnel administrator, medical division, librarian, accounting department, and line management, especially the foreman.

D. Company Contribution.—Direct expense of company donations, cost of administration, advice, and information on procedure and available facilities, losses incurred in time off.

E. Worker's Share.—A responsible attitude toward civic and humanitarian needs, help in planning and administering activities, donations.

F. Outside Contacts.—Local, state, and national agencies in the humanitarian field; local courts; national and regional offices of unions; government commissions and boards; local civic groups.

Selected References

CHAPTER 1

What Is Personnel Administration?

APPLEY, LAWRENCE A.: *The Human Element in Personnel Management*, Pamphlet No. 4, Society for Personnel Administration, Washington, D. C., 1941.

————: "Management the Simple Way," *Personnel*, Vol. 19, No. 4, pp. 595–603, 1943.

BURK, SAMUEL L. H.: The Personnel Profession—Its Present and Future Status, in *Personnel Organization and Professional Development*, pp. 40–47, Personnel Series No. 74, American Management Association, New York, 1943.

DIETZ, J. WALTER: Organizing the Personnel Function of Management, in *Seventh International Management Congress Proceedings*, pp. 3–6, Personnel and General Management Papers, Washington, D. C., 1938.

————: This Thing Called Personnel Relations, in *New Responsibilities of the Personnel Executive*, pp. 3–8, Personnel Series No. 45, American Management Association, New York, 1940.

DIMOCK, MARSHALL E.: *The Executive in Action* (pp. 1, 92, 138, 153, 189, 204, 221), Harper & Brothers, New York, 1945.

EVANS, J. J., JR.: *A Program for Personnel Administration*, McGraw-Hill Book Company, Inc., New York, 1945.

LEWISOHN, SAM A.: *Human Leadership in Industry*, Harper & Brothers, New York, 1945.

McCORMICK, FOWLER: American Business and Its Human Relations, in *Industrial Relations and Social Change*, pp. 3–8, Personnel Series No. 106, American Management Association, New York, 1947.

NELSON, THOMAS H.: "Human Relations in Management," *Personnel Administration*, Vol. 7, No. 4, pp. 1–4, 1944.

NORTHCOTT, C. H.: *Personnel Management. Its Scope and Practice*, Sir Isaac Pitman & Sons, Ltd., London, 1945.

ROETHLISBERGER, F. J.: *Management and Morale*, Harvard University Press, Cambridge, Mass., 1941.

SPATES, THOMAS G.: *An Objective Scrutiny of Personnel Management*, Personnel Series No. 75, American Management Association, New York, 1944.

————: The Shifting Scene in Industrial Relations, in *The Status of Industrial Relations*, pp. 4–14, Personnel Series No. 32, American Management Association, New York, 1938.

URWICK, L.: *Personnel Management in Relation to Factory Organization*, Institute of Labour Management, London, 1943.

CHAPTER 2

The Place and Functions of the Personnel Administrator

AMERICAN MANAGEMENT ASSOCIATION: *How to Establish and Maintain a Personnel Department*, Research Report No. 4, New York, 1944.

————: *Personnel Organization and Professional Development*, Personnel Series No. 74, New York, 1943.

APPLEY, LAWRENCE A.: "Essentials of a Management Personnel Policy," *Personnel*, Vol. 23, No. 6, pp. 430–436, 1947.

511

————: *Functions of the Personnel Executive*, Bulletin No. 1, 3d printing, California Institute of Technology, Industrial Relations Section, Pasadena, Calif., 1946.

ARTHUR, GUY B., JR.: A Scrutiny of Personnel Practice, in *Measuring Results of Personnel Functions*, pp. 6–15, Personnel Series No. 111, American Management Association, New York, 1947.

ATKINSON, KENNETH B.: "A Personnel Man Looks at His Job," *Personnel Administration*, Vol. 7, No. 5, pp. 6–10, 1945.

BAKER, HELEN: *The Determination and Administration of Industrial Relations Policies*, Princeton University, Industrial Relations Section, Princeton, N. J., 1939.

BALDERSTON, C. CANBY: *Executive Guidance of Industrial Relations; An Analysis of the Experience of Twenty-five Companies*, University of Pennsylvania Press, Philadelphia, 1935.

BERGEN, HAROLD B.: "Fundamentals of a Personnel and Industrial Relations Program," *Personnel*, Vol. 13, No. 2, pp. 46–54, 1936.

BROWN, ALVIN: *Organization, A Formulation of Principle*, Hibbert Printing Company, New York, 1945.

DIMOCK, MARSHALL E.: *The Executive in Action* (Meshing of Line and Staff, pp. 99–105), Harper & Brothers, New York, 1945.

HOLDEN, PAUL E., LOUNSBURY S. FISH, and HUBERT L. SMITH: *Top-management Organization and Control* (Sec. 3, Staff Organization, pp. 45–49, Personnel and Industrial Relations Departments), Stanford University Press, Stanford University, Calif., 1941.

METROPOLITAN LIFE INSURANCE COMPANY, POLICYHOLDERS SERVICE BUREAU: *Functions of the Personnel Director*, New York, no date.

NATIONAL INDUSTRIAL CONFERENCE BOARD, INC.: *Organization of Personnel Administration*, Studies in Personnel Policy No. 73, New York, 1946.

————: *Written Statements of Personnel Policy*, Studies in Personnel Policy No. 79, New York, 1947.

NORTH, HAROLD F.: The Personnel Man's Functional Relationships, in *New Responsibilities of the Personnel Executive*, pp. 16–22, Personnel Series No. 45, American Management Association, New York, 1940.

NORTHCOTT, C. H.: *Personnel Management. Its Scope and Practice*, Sir Isaac Pitman & Sons, Ltd., London, 1945.

PRINCETON UNIVERSITY, INDUSTRIAL RELATIONS SECTION: *The Organization of a Personnel Department*, Industrial Relations Digests I, Princeton, N. J., 1941.

STEWART, BRYCE M.: *The Role of the Industrial Relations Executive in Company Management*, Industrial Relations Memos No. 62, Industrial Relations Counselors, Inc., New York, 1943.

TOOTLE, HARRY K.: *Employees Are People*, McGraw-Hill Book Company, Inc., New York, 1947.

URWICK, L.: *Personnel Management in Relation to Factory Organization*, Institute of Labour Management, London, 1943.

CHAPTER 3

Personnel Administration and Unions

AMERICAN MANAGEMENT ASSOCIATION: *Management's Stake in Collective Bargaining* Personnel Series No. 81, New York, 1944.

————: *Practical Techniques of Collective Bargaining*, Personnel Series No. 86, New York, 1944.

BAKKE, E. WIGHT: Labor and Management Look Ahead, in *Reconciling Labor and Management Philosophies*, pp. 9–25, Personnel Series No. 98, American Management Association, New York, 1946.

———: *Mutual Survival: The Goal of Unions and Management*, Interim Report No. 1, Labor and Management Center, Yale University, New Haven, 1946.

BROOKS, ROBERT R. R.: *When Labor Organizes*, Yale University Press, New Haven, 1937.

CHAMBERLAIN, NEIL W.: *Collective Bargaining Procedures*, American Council on Public Affairs, Washington, D. C., 1944.

CHEYFITZ, EDWARD T.: *Constructive Collective Bargaining*, McGraw-Hill Book Company, Inc., New York, 1947.

COMMITTEE FOR ECONOMIC DEVELOPMENT: *Collective Bargaining: How to Make It More Effective*, A Statement on National Policy by the Research and Policy Committee, New York, 1947.

EVANS, J.J., JR.: *A Program for Personnel Administration* (Chap. V, Personnel Administration, Sec. II, Contractual Labor Relations), McGraw-Hill Book Company, Inc., New York, 1945.

GARDINER, GLENN: *When Foreman and Steward Bargain*, McGraw-Hill Book Company, Inc., New York, 1945.

GOLDEN, CLINTON S.: Adapting Personnel Management Policies to Changing Labor Conditions, in *Personnel Management Policies*, pp. 73–80, Economic and Business Foundation, New Wilmington, Pa., 1945.

——— and HAROLD J. RUTTENBERG: *The Dynamics of Industrial Democracy*, Harper & Brothers, New York, 1942.

GREENMAN, RUSSELL L., and ELIZABETH B. GREENMAN: *Getting Along With Unions*, Harper & Brothers, New York, 1947.

HILL, LEE H., and CHARLES R. HOOK, JR.: *Management at the Bargaining Table*, McGraw-Hill Book Company, Inc., New York, 1945.

KNICKERBOCKER, IRVING, and DOUGLAS McGREGOR: *Union-management Cooperation: A Psychological Analysis*, Publications in Social Science, Series 2, No. 9, Massachusetts Institute of Technology, Department of Economics and Social Science, Cambridge, Mass., 1942. (reprinted from *Personnel*, Vol. 19, No. 3, 1942.)

MILLIS, HARRY A., and ROYAL E. MONTGOMERY: *Organized Labor*, Vol. III of *The Economics of Labor*, McGraw-Hill Book Company, Inc., New York, 1945.

NATIONAL ASSOCIATION OF MANUFACTURERS, INDUSTRIAL RELATIONS DEPARTMENT: *Preparing to Negotiate. A Discussion of Some of the Considerations Requiring Management Attention before Starting Collective Bargaining Negotiations*, Management Memo No. 2, New York, 1947.

PETERSON, FLORENCE: *American Labor Unions: What They Are and How They Function*, Harper & Brothers, New York, 1945.

———: *Survey of Labor Economics* (Chap. 19, Collective Bargaining), Harper & Brothers, New York, 1947.

PIERSON, FRANK C.: *Collective Bargaining Systems*, American Council on Public Affairs, Washington, D. C., 1942.

SLICHTER, SUMNER H.: *Union Policies and Industrial Management*, Brookings Institution, Washington, D. C., 1941.

SMITH, LEONARD J.: *Collective Bargaining*, Prentice-Hall, Inc., New York, 1946.

THE TWENTIETH CENTURY FUND: *How Collective Bargaining Works; A Survey of Experience in Leading American Industries*, New York, 1942.

U.S. DEPARTMENT OF LABOR, DIVISION OF LABOR STANDARDS: *The Foreman's Guide to*

Labor Relations, Bulletin No. 66, U.S. Government Printing Office, Washington, D. C., 1944.

WILLIAMSON, S. T., and HERBERT HARRIS: *Trends in Collective Bargaining; A Summary of Recent Experience* (Including the Report and Recommendations by the Labor Committee of The Twentieth Century Fund), The Twentieth Century Fund, New York, 1945.

YODER, DALE: *Personnel Management and Industrial Relations* (Chaps. XXI and XXII, Collective Bargaining), Prentice-Hall, Inc., New York, 1942.

CHAPTER 4

Situational Thinking

BAKKE, E. WIGHT: *The Unemployed Worker*, Yale University Press, New Haven, 1940.

BARNARD, CHESTER I.: *The Functions of the Executive* (especially Chap. 13, pp. 185–199, The Environment of Decision), Harvard University Press, Cambridge, Mass., 1938.

DOLLARD, JOHN: *Criteria for the Life History; With Analyses of Six Notable Documents*, Yale University, Institute of Human Relations, Yale University Press, New Haven, 1935.

GARDNER, BURLEIGH B.: *Human Relations in Industry*, Richard D. Irwin, Inc., Chicago, 1945.

HADER, J.J., and E.C. LINDEMAN: *Dynamic Social Research*, Harcourt, Brace and Company, New York, 1933.

HENDERSON, L.J.: "Physician and Patient as a Social System," *The New England Journal of Medicine*, Vol. 212, No. 18, pp. 819–823, 1935.

———: *Three Lectures on Concrete Sociology; Lecture* II. *The Social System*, Harvard University, Graduate School of Business Administration, Boston, 1937.

——— and ELTON MAYO: "The Effects of Social Environment," *The Journal of Industrial Hygiene and Toxicology*, Vol. 18, No. 7, pp. 401–416, 1936.

LEWIN, K.: *A Dynamic Theory of Personality*, McGraw-Hill Book Company, Inc., New York, 1935.

LINDEMAN, E.C.: *Social Discovery; An Approach to the Study of Functional Groups*, New Republic, Inc., New York, 1924.

MACIVER, R.M.: *The Contribution of Sociology to Social Work*, Columbia University Press, New York, 1931.

MORENO, J.L.: *Who Shall Survive? A New Approach to the Problem of Human Interrelations*, Nervous and Mental Disease Publishing Company, Washington, D. C., 1934.

PIGORS, PAUL, and FAITH PIGORS: *Human Aspects of Multiple Shift Operations*, Publications in Social Science, Series 2, No. 13, Massachusetts Institute of Technology, Department of Economics and Social Science, Cambridge, Mass., 1944.

ROETHLISBERGER, F.J.: *Management and Morale*, Harvard University Press, Cambridge, Mass., 1941.

SHEFFIELD, A.D.: *Social Insight in Case Situations*, D. Appleton-Century Company, Inc., New York, 1937.

WERTHEIMER, MAX: *Productive Thinking* (Introduction, Chap. IV), Harper & Brothers, New York, 1945.

CHAPTER 5

Getting Down to Cases

DEWEY, JOHN: *How We Think*, D.C. Heath and Company, Boston, 1933.

FELDMAN, HERMAN: *Problems in Labor Relations: A Case Book Presenting Some Major Issues in the Relations of Labor, Capital, and Government* (especially Appendix A, pp. 319–

333, Some Elementary Principles of Analysis and Their Application in the Study of Problems), The Macmillan Company, New York, 1937.

GARDNER, BURLEIGH B.: *Case Studies for Interviewing Methods and Techniques*, University of Chicago Bookstore, Chicago, 1944.

HENDERSON, L.J.: "The Practice of Medicine as Applied Sociology," *Transactions of the Association of American Physicians*, Vol. 51, p. 8, 1936.

———: *Three Lectures on Concrete Sociology; Lecture III. The Use of the Conceptual Scheme (in the Study of Cases)*, Harvard University, Graduate School of Business Administration, Boston, 1937.

HOSLETT, SCHUYLER DEAN, editor: *Human Factors in Management* (Manager Meets Union: A Case Study of Personal Immaturity, by Joseph M. Goldsen and Lillian Low), Park College Press, Parkville, Mo., 1946.

MAYO, ELTON: *The Social Problems of an Industrial Civilization* (especially Part II, The Clinical Approach, Chap. III, The First Inquiry), Harvard University, Graduate School of Business Administration, Division of Research, Boston, 1945.

PIGORS, PAUL, L.C. McKENNEY, and T.O. ARMSTRONG: *Social Problems in Labor Relations: A Case Book*, McGraw-Hill Book Company, Inc., New York, 1939.

ROETHLISBERGER, F.J.: "Social Behavior in Industry," *Harvard Business Review*, Vol. 16, No. 4, pp. 424–425, 1938. Reprinted as Chap. V, pp. 67–87, A Disinterested Observer Looks at Industry, *Management and Morale*, Harvard University Press, Cambridge, Mass., 1942.

——— and W.J. DICKSON: *Management and the Worker*, Harvard University Press, Cambridge, Mass., 1939.

ROGERS, CARL R.: *Counseling and Psychotherapy*, Houghton Mifflin Company, Boston, 1942.

WHITEHEAD, T. NORTH: "Social Relationships in the Factory: A Study of an Industrial Group," *The Human Factor*, Vol. 9, No. 11, pp. 3–16, 1935.

CHAPTER 6

Interviewing

AMERICAN TELEPHONE AND TELEGRAPH COMPANY, PERSONNEL RELATIONS DEPARTMENT: *An Interviewing Method, Outline of Certain Principles and Procedures Developed from the Harvard-Hawthorne Research*, New York, June 30, 1941.

———: *Personnel Counseling*, New York, Oct. 20, 1941.

ANDERSON, VICTOR V.: *Psychiatry in Industry*, Harper & Brothers, New York, 1929.

BAKER, HELEN: *Employe Counseling, A Survey of a New Development in Personnel Relations*, Princeton University, Industrial Relations Section, Princeton, N. J., 1944.

BINGHAM, WALTER V., and BRUCE V. MOORE: *How to Interview*, 3d rev. ed., Harper & Brothers, New York, 1941.

CANTOR, NATHANIEL: *Employee Counseling, A New Viewpoint in Industrial Psychology*, McGraw-Hill Book Company, Inc., New York, 1945.

DICKSON, WILLIAM J.: The Development of a Counseling Program (A Case History) (pp. 77–81, Western Electric Company), in *Addresses on Industrial Relations*, 1945, Bureau of Industrial Relations Bulletin No. 16, University of Michigan Press, Ann Arbor, 1945.

———: Employee Education and Counseling Programs, in *Understanding and Training Employees* (pp. 4–19, Western Electric Company), Personnel Series No. 35, American Management Association, New York, 1938.

GARDNER, BURLEIGH B.: *Case Studies for Interviewing Methods and Techniques*, University of Chicago Bookstore, Chicago, 1944.

————: *Human Relations in Industry* (Chap. X, Personnel Counseling), Richard D. Irwin, Inc., Chicago, 1945.

GARETT, ANNETTE: *Counseling Methods for Personnel Workers*, Family Welfare Association of America, New York, 1945.

————: *Interviewing, Its Principles and Methods*, Family Welfare Association of America, New York, 1942.

HIMLER, LEONARD E.: The Counseling Interview, in *Addresses on Industrial Relations*, 1945, pp. 63–74, Bureau of Industrial Relations Bulletin No. 16, University of Michigan Press, Ann Arbor, 1945.

HOSLETT, SCHUYLER DEAN, editor: *Human Factors in Management* (Part II, Sec. B, Facilitating Adjustments through the Counseling Method), Park College Press, Parkville, Mo., 1946.

————: "Listening to the Troubled or Dissatisfied Employee," *Personnel*, Vol. 22, No. 1, pp. 52–57, 1945.

McMURRY, ROBERT N.: *Handling Personality Adjustment in Industry* (Chap. VII, Handling "Problem" Employees), Harper & Brothers, New York, 1944.

MAIER, NORMAN R.F.: *Psychology in Industry* (pp. 409–416, The Counselor), Houghton Mifflin Company, Boston, 1946.

MOORE, HERBERT: *Psychology for Business and Industry*, 2d ed. (Chap. XIV, The Problem Employee), McGraw-Hill Book Company, Inc., New York, 1942.

NATIONAL RESEARCH COUNCIL, COMMITTEE ON WORK IN INDUSTRY: *Fatigue of Workers: Its Relation to Industrial Production* (Chap. IV, The Western Electric Researches; Chap. V, The Interviewing Method), Reinhold Publishing Corporation, New York, 1941.

OLDFIELD, R.C.: *The Psychology of the Interview*, Methuen & Co., Ltd., London, 1941.

ROETHLISBERGER, F.J., and W.J. DICKSON: *Management and the Worker*, Harvard University Press, Cambridge, Mass., 1939.

ROGERS, CARL R.: *Counseling and Psychotherapy*, Houghton Mifflin Company, Boston, 1942.

SHEPARD, JEAN L.: *Human Nature at Work*, Harper & Brothers, New York, 1938.

THOMAS, R.L., and JOHN H. MUCHMORE: "Getting Results in 'Problem Interviews'," *Personnel*, Vol. 21, No. 1, pp. 31–37, 1944.

U. S. WAR DEPARTMENT: *Personnel Counseling; Key to Greater Production*, Civilian Personnel Pamphlet No. 1, Washington, D.C., 1943.

WOODWARD, LUTHER E., and THOMAS A. C. RENNIE: *Jobs and the Man* (Chap. V, Practical Techniques in Industrial Interviewing and Counseling), Charles C. Thomas, Publisher, Springfield, Ill., 1945.

CHAPTER 7

Some Indexes of Employee Morale

ARENSBERG, CONRAD M. and DOUGLAS McGREGOR: *Determination of Morale in an Industrial Company*, Publications in Social Science, Series 2, No. 11, Massachusetts Institute of Technology, Department of Economics and Social Science, Cambridge, Mass. (In *Applied Anthropology*, Vol. 1, No. 2, 1942.)

BRADFORD, LELAND P.: "Basic Symptoms of Inadequate Supervision," *Personnel*, Vol. 22, No. 2, pp. 102–108, 1945.

————: "Building Employee Security," *Personnel*, Vol. 22, No. 4, pp. 215–221, 1946.

———— and RONALD LIPPITT: "Building a Democratic Work Group," *Personnel*, Vol. 22, No. 3, pp. 142–152, 1945.

———— and RONALD LIPPITT: "Employee Success in Work Groups," *Personnel Administration*, Vol. 8, No. 4, pp. 6–10, 1945.

BRODMAN, KEEVE: "Absenteeism, Working Efficiency and Emotional Maladjustments," *Industrial Medicine*, Vol. 14, No. 1, pp. 1–5, 1945.

————: "Rates of Absenteeism and Turnover in Personnel in Relation to Employees' Work Attitudes," *Industrial Medicine*, Vol. 14, No. 12, pp. 953–957, 1945.

EVANS, W. DUANE: "Statistics and Personnel Administration," *Personnel*, Vol. 23, No. 2, pp. 79–85, 1946.

GARDNER, BURLEIGH B.: *Human Relations in Industry* (Chap. I, The Factory as a Social System; Chap. XIII, Understanding Social Structure), Richard D. Irwin, Inc., Chicago, 1945.

———— and WILLIAM F. WHYTE: "The Man in the Middle: Position and Problems of the Foreman," *Applied Psychology*, Vol. 4, No. 2, pp. 1–28, 1944. Human Elements in Supervision: 1. Teamwork; 2. Two-way Communication; 3. Reciprocal Obligations; 4. Originating Action with Firmness and Decision, pp. 3–17.

HIBBS, RAY E.: *Absenteeism, Let's Solve It the Right Way*, North Star Woolen Mill Company, Minneapolis, 1944.

HOSLETT, SCHUYLER DEAN, editor: *Human Factors in Management* (especially, pp. 297–322, Psychological Studies of Employee Morale, by Arthur Kornhauser), Park College Press, Parkville, Mo., 1946.

JACKSON, JOSEPH H.: "Factors Involved in Absenteeism," *Personnel Journal*, Vol. 22, No. 8, pp. 289–295, 1944.

KORNHAUSER, ARTHUR W.: "The Technique of Measuring Employee Attitudes," *Personnel*, Vol. 9, No. 4, pp. 99–107, 1933.

KUNZE, KARL R., and RANDOLPH BRANNER: "Motivation and Absenteeism," *Personnel Journal*, Vol. 23, No. 2, pp. 69–72, 1944.

KURTZ, LeROY H.: "The Morale Function of the Executive," *Personnel*, Vol. 20, No. 4, pp. 202–219, 1944.

KUSHNICK, WILLIAM H.: "The Role of Psychology in Absenteeism," in *Proceedings, Seventh Annual Meeting, Industrial Hygiene Foundation of America*, November 10–11, 1942, Industrial Hygiene Foundation of America, Inc., Pittsburgh, 1943.

McGREGOR, DOUGLAS: *Getting Effective Leadership in the Industrial Organization*, Publications in Social Science, Series 2, No. 16, Massachusetts Institute of Technology, Department of Economics and Social Science, Cambridge, Mass., 1945. (Reprinted from *Advanced Management*, October-December, 1944.)

McMURRY, ROBERT N.: *Handling Personality Adjustment in Industry* (Chap. IV, Building Good Will and Morale), Harper & Brothers, New York, 1944.

MAIER, NORMAN R.F.: *Psychology in Industry* (Chap. 5, Morale; Chap. 16, Accidents and Their Prevention), Houghton Mifflin Company, Boston, 1946.

MAYO, ELTON: *The Human Problems of an Industrial Civilization* (especially Chap. 5, The Meaning of "Morale"), The Macmillan Company, New York, 1933.

NATIONAL INDUSTRIAL CONFERENCE BOARD, INC.: *The Problem of Absenteeism*, Studies in Personnel Policy No. 53, New York, 1943.

————: *Reducing Absenteeism*, Studies in Personnel Policy No. 46, New York, 1942.

POLITICAL AND ECONOMIC PLANNING: *Output and the Worker*, Planning No. 233, Apr. 20, 1945, London, 1945. (Reprinted in the United States by *The New Republic*, New York.)

PRINCETON UNIVERSITY, INDUSTRIAL RELATIONS SECTION: *Maximum Utilization of Employed Manpower*, Princeton, N. J., 1943.

SELLING, LOWELL S.: "A Psychiatrist Looks at Industrial Truancy," *Industrial Medicine*, Vol. 12, No. 4, pp. 189–201, 1943.

———: "Psychiatry in Industrial Accidents," *Industrial Medicine*, Vol. 13, No. 6, pp. 504–508*ff*, 1944. (Reprinted in *Advanced Management*, Vol. 10, No. 2, pp. 70–75, 1945.)

SOCIETY FOR THE PSYCHOLOGICAL STUDY OF SOCIAL ISSUES: *Industrial Conflict: A Psychological Interpretation* (Chap. 15, Methods of Measuring Industrial Morale, by Albert A. Blankenship), The Cordon Company, New York, 1939.

SPRIEGEL, WILLIAM R., and EDWARD SCHULZ: *Elements of Supervision* (Chap. VIII, Individual Differences, Group Attitudes, and Group Morale; Chap. XIV, Promoting Cooperation between Men and between Departments), John Wiley & Sons, Inc., New York, 1942.

STOCK, J. STEVENS, and HARRIET LUBIN: "Indices of Personnel Management," *Personnel*, Vol. 23, No. 1, pp. 6–16, 1946.

TIFFIN, JOSEPH: *Industrial Psychology* (Chap. 11, Accidents and Safety; Chap. 12, Attitudes and Morale), Prentice-Hall, Inc., New York, 1942.

U. S. DEPARTMENT OF LABOR, DIVISION OF LABOR STANDARDS: *The ABC of Absenteeism and Labor Turnover*, Special Bulletin No. 17, U. S. Government Printing Office, Washington, D.C., 1944.

———: *Auditing Absenteeism*, Absence Record Forms in Use by Representative Firms in War Industries, Special Bulletin No. 12-A, U.S. Government Printing Office, Washington, D.C., 1943.

———: *Controlling Absenteeism*, A Record of War Plant Experience, Special Bulletin No. 12, U.S. Government Printing Office, Washington, D.C., 1943.

VICTORIA UNIVERSITY COLLEGE, INDUSTRIAL PSYCHOLOGY DIVISION: *Industrial Absenteeism*, Report No. 1, Wellington, New Zealand, 1943.

WATSON, GOODWIN, editor: *Civilian Morale* (Part I: Theory of Morale, Chap. 1, The Nature of Democratic Morale, by Gordon W. Allport; Part IV: Morale in Industry), Houghton Mifflin Company, Boston, 1942.

CHAPTER 8

Labor Turnover and Internal Mobility

BRISSENDEN, PAUL F., and EMIL FRANKEL: *Labor Turnover in Industry, A Statistical Analysis*, The Macmillan Company, New York, 1922.

COOPER, JOSEPH D.: "Management Analysis and the Exit Interview," *Personnel Administration*, Vol. 8, No. 3, pp. 15–17, 1945.

DRAKE, CHARLES A.: "The Exit Interview as a Tool of Management," *Personnel*, Vol. 18, No. 6, pp. 346–350, 1942.

"Factory-labor Turnover, 1931 to 1939," *Monthly Labor Review*, Vol. 51, No. 3, pp. 696–704, 1940.

HIBBS, RAY E.: *Labor Turnover: It Can Be Reduced by Sound Methods*, North Star Woolen Mill Company, Minneapolis, 1944.

"Labor Turnover in Manufacturing, 1930–41," *Monthly Labor Review*, Vol. 54, No. 5, pp. 1193–1205, 1942.

MAIER, NORMAN R.F.: *Psychology in Industry* (Chap. 18, Psychological Factors in Labor Turnover), Houghton Mifflin Company, Boston, 1946.

MAYO, ELTON, and GEORGE F.F. LOMBARD: *Teamwork and Labor Turnover in the Aircraft Industry of Southern California*, Business Research Studies No. 32, Harvard University, Graduate School of Business Administration, Bureau of Business Research, Boston, 1944.

METROPOLITAN LIFE INSURANCE COMPANY, POLICYHOLDERS SERVICE BUREAU: *The Control of Labor Turnover*, New York, no date.

————: *The Exit Interview*, New York, no date.

MOORE, HERBERT: *Psychology for Business and Industry*, 2d ed., (pp. 51–54, The Cost of Labor Turnover), McGraw-Hill Book Company, Inc., New York, 1942.

MYERS, CHARLES A., and W. RUPERT MACLAURIN: *The Movement of Factory Workers, A Study of a New England Industrial Community*, 1937–1939, *and* 1942, John Wiley & Sons, Inc., New York, 1943.

ONARHEIM, J.I.: "Exit Interviews Help Us Check Personnel Policies," *Factory Management and Maintenance*, Vol. 102, No. 5, pp. 121–122, 1944.

SCOTT, WALTER D., R.C. CLOTHIER, S.B. MATHEWSON, and W.R. SPRIEGEL: *Personnel Management*, 3d ed. (Chap. XXXVI, Industrial Unrest, Working Conditions, and Labor Turnover), McGraw-Hill Book Company, Inc., New York, 1941.

SLICHTER, SUMNER H.: *The Turnover of Factory Labor*, D. Appleton-Century Company, Inc., New York, 1919.

TAFT, RONALD, and AUDREY MULLINS: "Who Quits and Why," *Personnel Journal*, Vol. 24, No. 8, pp. 300–307, 1946.

TEAD, ORDWAY, and HENRY C. METCALF: *Personnel Administration*, 3d ed. (Chap. XIX, The Measurement of Labor Turnover), McGraw-Hill Book Company, Inc., 1933.

U.S. DEPARTMENT OF LABOR, DIVISION OF LABOR STANDARDS: *The ABC of Absenteeism and Labor Turnover*, Special Bulletin No. 17, U.S. Government Printing Office, Washington, D.C., 1944.

U.S. DEPARTMENT OF LABOR, BUREAU OF LABOR STATISTICS: *Standard Procedure for Computing Labor Turnover*, Serial No. R. 487, U.S. Government Printing Office, Washington, D.C., 1938. (Reprinted from *Monthly Labor Review*, Vol. 43, No. 6, 1936.)

U.S. WAR DEPARTMENT: *Exit Interview; An Aid in the Control of Personnel Turnover*, Washington, D.C., 1943.

VITELES, MORRIS V.: *Industrial Psychology* (pp. 115–118, The Extent and Cost of Labor Turnover), W. W. Norton & Company, Inc., New York, 1932.

WALTERS, J.E.: *Personnel Relations, Their Application in a Democracy* (Chap. 8, Labor Turnover, Promotions and Transfers), The Ronald Press Company, New York, 1945.

WATKINS, GORDON S., and PAUL A. DODD: *The Management of Labor Relations* (Chap. XIII, Labor Turnover), McGraw-Hill Book Company, Inc., New York, 1938.

"What Makes Low Turnover," *Factory Management and Maintenance*, Vol. 101, No. 12, pp. 82–88, 1943.

YODER, DALE: *Personnel Management and Industrial Relations* (Chap. X, Industrial Unrest, pp. 270–282, Labor Turnover), Prentice-Hall, Inc., New York, 1942.

CHAPTER 9

Complaints and Grievances

AMERICAN MANAGEMENT ASSOCIATION: *Wage Adjustment and Grievance Policies* (pp. 9–16, Handling Grievances: A Case Experience, General Motors Corp., by H. W. Anderson; pp. 17–24). The Mediator Views Grievance Procedure, by E. H. Van Delden), Personnel Series No. 52, New York, 1941.

————: *Working with Unions—Grievance Procedures*, Personnel Series No. 57, New York, 1942.

BARKIN, SOLOMON: "Unions and Grievances," *Personnel Journal*, Vol. 22, No. 2, pp. 38–48, 1943.

GARDINER, GLENN L.: *How to Handle Grievances*, Elliott Service Company, New York, 1937.

HOSLETT, SCHUYLER D.: "What Is a Grievance?" *Personnel Journal*, Vol. 23, No. 9, pp. 356–358, 1945.

LAPP, JOHN A.: *How to Handle Labor Grievances, Plans and Procedures*, National Foremen's Institute, Inc., New York, Deep River, Conn., 1945.

PRINCETON UNIVERSITY, INDUSTRIAL RELATIONS SECTION: *Grievance Procedures*, Industrial Relations Digests IX, Princeton, N. J., 1941.

SELEKMAN, BENJAMIN M.: "Handling Shop Grievances," *Harvard Business Review*, Vol. 23, No. 4, pp. 469–483, 1945.

SPRIEGEL, WILLIAM R., and EDWARD SCHULZ: *Elements of Supervision* (Chap. VII, Techniques and Methods of Discovering and Adjusting Grievances), John Wiley & Sons, Inc., New York, 1942.

STEEL WORKERS ORGANIZING COMMITTEE: *Handling Grievances*, Pittsburgh.

U.S. DEPARTMENT OF LABOR, DIVISION OF LABOR STANDARDS: *Arbitration of Grievances*, by William E. Simkin and Van Dusen Kennedy, Bulletin No. 82, U.S. Government Printing Office, Washington, D.C., 1946.

————: *The Foreman's Guide to Labor Relations*, Bulletin No. 66, pp. 14–21, The Foreman and Grievances, U.S. Government Printing Office, Washington, D.C., 1944.

————: *Settling Plant Grievances*, Bulletin No. 60, U.S. Government Printing Office, Washington, D.C., 1943.

U. S. NATIONAL WAR LABOR BOARD: *Grievance Procedure Problems*, Research and Statistics Report No. 26, Washington, D.C., Aug. 30, 1944.

WESTERN ELECTRIC COMPANY, HAWTHORNE WORKS: *Complaints and Grievances; Supervisory Conference Material*, New York, 1942.

CHAPTER 10

Recruitment, Selection, and Placement

ACHILLES, PAUL S.: "Trends in Employment Procedures," *Personnel*, Vol. 19, No. 4, pp. 609–617, 1943.

AMERICAN MANAGEMENT ASSOCIATION: *Manual of Employment Interviewing*, Research Report No. 9, New York, 1946.

————: *Psychological Aids in the Selection of Workers*, by Edward N. Hay, G. W. Wadsworth, D. W. Cook, and C. L. Shartle, Personnel Series No. 50, New York, 1941.

AUSTRALIA, DEPARTMENT OF LABOUR AND NATIONAL SERVICE, INDUSTRIAL TRAINING DIVISION: *Hints on Interviewing*, Technical Publication No. 17, Melbourne, 1945.

AUSTRALIA, DEPARTMENT OF LABOUR AND NATIONAL SERVICE, INDUSTRIAL WELFARE DIVISION: *Selection and Placement of New Employees*, Bulletin No. 9, Melbourne, 1946.

BEAUMONT, HENRY: *The Psychology of Personnel* (Chap. III, Selecting Employees), Longmans, Green and Company, New York, 1945.

BENGE, EUGENE J.: *How to Prepare and Validate an Employee Test*, Proceedings of Institute of Management, No. 9, American Management Association, New York, 1929.

BENJAMIN, HAZEL C.: *Employment Tests in Industry and Business; A Selected Annotated Bibliography*, Princeton University, Industrial Relations Section, Princeton, N. J., 1945.

BENNETT, GEORGE K., and R. M. CRUIKSHANK: *A Summary of Manual and Mechanical Ability Tests*, Psychological Corporation, New York, 1942.

BINGHAM, WALTER V.: *Aptitudes and Aptitude Testing*, 4th ed., Harper & Brothers, New York, 1937.

—— and BRUCE V. MOORE: *How to Interview*, 3d rev. ed., Harper & Brothers, New York, 1941.

BRIDGES, CLARK D.: *Job Placement of the Physically Handicapped*, McGraw-Hill Book Company, Inc., New York, 1946.

BURTT, HAROLD E.: *Principles of Employment Psychology*, rev. ed., Harper & Brothers, New York, 1942.

COOK, DAVID W.: Psychology Challenges Industry, in *Advances in Methods of Personnel Evaluation*, pp. 33–50, Personnel Series No. 107, American Management Association, New York, 1947.

DRAKE, CHARLES A.: *Personnel Selection by Standard Job Tests*, McGraw-Hill Book Company, Inc., New York, 1942.

DRIVER, R. S.: "The Value of Psychological Tests in Industry," *Personnel*, Vol. 19, No. 5, pp. 656–664, 1943.

FEAR, RICHARD A.: Employee Selection for the Average Company, in *Rating and Training Executives and Employees*, pp. 3–13, Personnel Series No. 100, American Management Association, New York, 1946.

—— and BYRON JORDAN: *Employee Evaluation Manual for Interviewers*, Psychological Corporation, New York, 1943.

HAY, EDWARD N.: "The Use of Psychological Tests in Selection and Promotion," *Personnel*, Vol. 16, No. 3, pp. 114–123, 1940.

LAIRD, DONALD A.: *The Psychology of Selecting Employees*, 3d ed., McGraw-Hill Book Company, Inc., New York, 1937.

McMURRY, ROBERT N.: *Handling Personality Adjustment in Industry* (Chap. VIII, Factors in the Introduction of Scientific Selection Procedures; Chap. IX, Techniques of Employee Selection; Chap. X, How to Conduct the Selection Interview; Chap. XI, Interpreting the Findings), Harper & Brothers, New York, 1944.

MAIER, NORMAN R. F.: *Psychology in Industry* (Chap. 8, The Use of Psychological Tests in Industry; Chap. 9, The General Nature of Psychological Testing), Houghton Mifflin Company, Boston, 1946.

METROPOLITAN LIFE INSURANCE COMPANY, POLICYHOLDERS SERVICE BUREAU: *Personnel Records*, New York.

METROPOLITAN LIFE INSURANCE COMPANY, INDUSTRIAL HEALTH SECTION: *Physical Examinations in Industry*, Industrial Health Series No. 2, New York.

MOORE, HERBERT: *Psychology for Business and Industry*, 2d ed. [Chap. III, The Importance of Proper Selection; Chap. IV, Hiring the Worker; Chap. V, Testing the Applicant; Chap. VI, Special Ability Tests (Mechanical and Clerical); Chap. VII, Personality Tests], McGraw-Hill Book Company, Inc., New York, 1942.

MORGAN, HOWARD K.: *Industrial Training and Testing*, McGraw-Hill Book Company, Inc., New York, 1945.

NATIONAL INDUSTRIAL CONFERENCE BOARD, INC.: *Employment Procedures and Personnel Records*, Studies in Personnel Policy No. 38, New York, 1941.

——: *Experience with Employment Tests*, by Herbert Moore, Studies in Personnel Policy No. 32, New York, 1941.

OLDFIELD, R.C.: *The Psychology of the Interview*, Methuen & Co., Ltd., London, 1941.

POND, MILLICENT: "The Values and Dangers of Employment Testing," *Conference Board Management Record*, Vol. 3, No. 2, pp. 13–16, 1941.

PRINCETON UNIVERSITY, INDUSTRIAL RELATIONS SECTION: *Selection Procedures*, Industrial Relations Digests X, Princeton, N. J., 1941.

REED, ANNA Y.: *Occupational Placement*, Cornell University Press, Ithaca, N. Y., 1946.

ROBINSON, O. PRESTON: *Retail Personnel Relations* (Chap. V, Sources of Labor Supply; Chap. VI, Employment Procedure and Operation; Chap. VII, Employment Interviewing; Chap. VIII, Employment Testing), Prentice-Hall, Inc., New York, 1940.

SCOTT, WALTER D., R.C. CLOTHIER, S.B. MATHEWSON, and W.R. SPRIEGEL: *Personnel Management*, 3d ed. (Chap. V, The Employment Procedure; Chap. VI, Developing Sources of Labor Supply; Chap. VII, The Interview as a Tool of Personnel Management; Chap. VIII, Construction and Development of Instruments and Records; Chap. IX, Construction and Use of the Application Blank; Chap X, The Qualification Card), McGraw-Hill Book Company, Inc., New York, 1941.

SHARTLE, CARROLL L.: *Occupational Information, Its Development and Application*, Prentice-Hall, Inc., New York, 1946.

TEAD, ORDWAY, and HENRY C. METCALF: *Personnel Administration, Its Principles and Practice*, 3d ed. (Chap. V, Sources of Labor Supply: Chap. VI, Methods of Selection and Placement), McGraw-Hill Book Company, Inc., New York, 1933.

THOMPSON, LORIN A.: *Interview Aids and Trade Questions for Employment Offices*, Harper & Brothers, New York, 1936.

TIFFIN, JOSEPH: *Industrial Psychology* (Chap. 2, General Principles of Employee Testing; Chap. 3, Mental Tests and Mechanical Comprehension Tests; Chap. 4, Dexterity, Manipulative, and Achievement Tests; Chap. 5, Tests of Personality and Interest; Chap. 6, Visual Problems in Industry), Prentice-Hall, Inc., New York, 1942.

UHRBROCK, RICHARD S.: "Analysis of Employment Interviews," *Personnel Journal*, Vol. 12, No. 2, pp. 98–101, 1933.

U. S. WAR DEPARTMENT: *The Placement Interview*, Civilian Personnel Pamphlet No. 15, Washington, D.C., 1945.

VERNON, PHILIP E.: *The Measurement of Abilities*, University of London Press, London, 1940.

VITELES, MORRIS V.: *Industrial Psychology* (Chap. VIII, Basic Factors in Vocational Selection; Chap X, The Interview and Allied Techniques; Chaps. XI and XII, Standardization and Administration of Psychological Tests; Chap. XIII, Tests for Skilled and Semi-skilled Workers; Chap. XV, Tests for Office Occupations, Technical and Supervisory Employees), W. W. Norton & Company, Inc., New York, 1932.

WADSWORTH, GUY W., JR.: "Hiring for Better Labor Relations," *Personnel Journal*, Vol. 18, No. 2, pp. 51–60, 1939.

————: "The Use of Tests in Selection," *Personnel Administration*, Vol. 2, No. 6, pp. 1–8, 1940.

WATKINS, GORDON S., and PAUL A. DODD: *The Management of Labor Relations* (Part III, The Technique of Selection and Placement), McGraw-Hill Book Company, Inc., New York, 1938.

WONDERLIC, E.F.: "Improving Interview Techniques," *Personnel*, Vol. 18, No. 1, pp. 232–238, 1942.

YODER, DALE: *Personnel Management and Industrial Relations* (Chap. VI, Recruitment and Sources; Chaps. VII and VIII, Selection), Prentice-Hall, Inc., New York, 1942.

CHAPTER 11

Selection and Training of Supervisors

AMERICAN MANAGEMENT ASSOCIATION: *The Development of Foremen in Management*, Research Report No. 7, New York, 1945.

————: *Management Training for Foremen*, by executives of General Motors (H. W. Anderson and others), Personnel Series No. 78, New York, 1944.

————: *Planning Supervisory Development*, Personnel Series No. 96, New York, 1945.

————: *The Role of the Supervisor in Labor Relations,* Personnel Series No. 33, New York, 1938.

————: *Streamlining the Foreman's Job,* Personnel Series No. 73, New York, 1943.

————: *The Unionization of Foremen,* Research Report No. 6, New York, 1945.

AYERS, ARTHUR W.: "Selecting New Foremen and Supervisors," in *Proceedings of the Silver Bay Industrial Conference, 27th Year,* 1944, pp. 127–134, National Council of the YMCA's, New York, 1944.

BAVELAS, ALEX: *Role Playing and Management Training,* Publications in Social Science, Series 2, No. 21, Massachusetts Institute of Technology, Department of Economics and Social Science, Cambridge, Mass., 1947. (Reprinted from *Sociatry,* Vol. 1, No. 2, 1947.)

BECKMAN, R. O.: *How to Train Supervisors,* Harper & Brothers, New York, 1940.

BRADFORD, LELAND P.: "The Future of Supervisory Training," *Personnel,* Vol. 22, No. 1, pp. 6–12, 1945.

———— and RONALD LIPPITT: "Role-playing in Supervisory Training," *Personnel,* Vol. 22, No. 6, pp. 358–369, 1946.

BURNS MORTON, F. J.: *The New Foremanship,* 2d ed. rev., Chapman & Hall, Ltd., London, 1946.

CABE, J. CARL: *Foremen's Unions: A New Development in Industrial Relations,* Bulletin No. 65, University of Illinois, College of Commerce and Business Administration, Bureau of Economic and Business Research, Urbana, Ill., 1947.

CHAPPELL, GERALD G.: *Training of Supervisors,* Bulletin No. 10, California Institute of Technology, Industrial Relations Section, Pasadena, Calif., 1944.

DIETZ, WALTER: "Training New Supervisors in the Skill of Leadership," *Personnel,* Vol. 19, No. 4, pp. 604–608, 1943.

DORNSIFE, HAROLD W.: *Selection of Supervisors,* Bulletin No. 9, California Institute of Technology, Industrial Relations Section, Pasadena, Calif., 1944.

"The Facts About Foremen," *Factory Management and Maintenance;* Vol. 102, No. 9, pp. 82–92, 1944.

FERN, GEORGE H.: *Training for Supervision in Industry.* McGraw-Hill Book Company, Inc., New York, 1945.

GILBRETH, LILLIAN M., and ALICE R. COOK: *The Foreman in Manpower Management,* McGraw-Hill Book Company, Inc., New York, 1947.

HEINEMAN, ROBERT K.: "How We Know Management Is the Foreman's Business," *Factory Management and Maintenance,* Vol. 104, No. 9, pp. 96–99, 1946.

HERSEY, REXFORD: Problems in Selecting and Training Supervisors, in *Principles and Methods of Industrial Training,* pp. 20–32, Personnel Series No. 47, American Management Association, New York, 1941.

HOSLETT, SCHUYLER DEAN, editor: *Human Factors in Management,* (Part I, Sec. B, Training Leaders in Human Relations), Park College Press, Parkville, Mo., 1946.

INDUSTRIAL RELATIONS COUNSELORS, INC.: *Foremen's Unions,* Industrial Relations Memos No. 67, New York, 1944.

McFEELY, WILBUR M., and WILLIAM M. MUSSMAN: "Training Supervisors in Leadership," *Personnel,* Vol. 21, No. 4, pp. 217–223, 1945.

McGREGOR, DOUGLAS: *The Foreman's Responsibilities in the Industrial Organization: A Case Study,* Publications in Social Science, Series 2, No. 19, Massachusetts Institute of Technology, Department of Economics and Social Science, Cambridge, Mass., 1946. (Reprinted from *Personnel,* Vol. 22, No. 5, pp. 296–304, 1946.)

————: Re-evaluation of Training for Management Skills, in *Training for Management Skills,* pp. 17–22, Personnel Series No. 104, American Management Association, New York, 1946.

NATIONAL INDUSTRIAL CONFERENCE BOARD, INC.: *Communication within the Management Group*, Studies in Personnel Policy, No. 80, New York, 1947.

———: *Selecting, Training and Upgrading Supervisors, Instructors, Production Workers*, Studies in Personnel Policy No. 37, New York, 1941.

———: *Training Solutions of Company Problems: A. Programs Giving Special Attention to Development of Executive and Supervisory Personnel*, Studies in Personnel Policy No. 15, New York, 1939.

PFIFFNER, JOHN M.: "An Outline of the Supervisor's Job," *Personnel*, Vol. 23, No. 3, pp. 156–174, 1946.

PLANTY, EARL G.: "New Methods for Evaluating Supervisor Training," *Personnel*, Vol. 21, No. 4, pp. 235–241, 1945.

——— and WILLIAM McCORD: "The Scope and Organization of Supervisor Training," *Personnel*, Vol. 22, No. 4, pp. 222–229, 1946.

PRINCETON UNIVERSITY, INDUSTRIAL RELATIONS SECTION: *Selection and Training of Foremen*, Industrial Relations Digests VII, Princeton, N. J., 1941.

———: *Training the Foreman and the Shop Steward to Administer the Union Contract*, Selected References No. 7, Princeton, 1946.

RIEGEL, JOHN W.: *The Selection and Development of Prospective Foremen*, Bulletin No. 11, University of Michigan, Bureau of Industrial Relations, Ann Arbor, 1941.

ROETHLISBERGER, F.J.: "Foreman: Master and Victim of Double Talk," *Harvard Business Review*, Vol. 23, No. 3, pp. 283–298, 1945.

SCOTT, WALTER D., R.C. CLOTHIER, S.B. MATHEWSON, and W.R. SPRIEGEL: *Personnel Management*, 3d ed. (Chap. XXIII, Training the Executive and Supervisory Force), McGraw-Hill Book Company, Inc., New York, 1941.

SMITH, CHARLES C.: *The Foreman's Place in Management*, Harpers & Brothers, New York, 1946.

STEIN, H.F., H.F. RUSSELL, and JOHN W. RIEGEL: "How to Develop the Foreman as a Department Manager," in *Addresses on Industrial Relations*, 1945, pp. 17–24, Bureau of Industrial Relations Bulletin No. 16, University of Michigan Press, Ann Arbor, 1945.

SUTERMEISTER, ROBERT A.: "Training Foremen in Human Relations," *Personnel*, Vol. 20, No. 1, pp. 6–14, 1943.

TEAD, ORDWAY, and HENRY C. METCALF: *Personnel Administration, Its Principles and Practices*, 3d ed. (Chap. XII, The Training of Foremen), McGraw-Hill Book Company, Inc., New York, 1933.

U. S. WAR MANPOWER COMMISSION, BUREAU OF TRAINING, TRAINING WITHIN INDUSTRY SERVICE: *The Training Within Industry Report*, 1940–1945 (Chap. 14, The Development of the Job Relations Program), U.S. Government Printing Office, Washington, D.C., 1945.

UNIVERSITY OF MICHIGAN, BUREAU OF INDUSTRIAL RELATIONS: *Personnel Management in War Industries*, (V, Selection and Development of Prospective Foremen,) Vol. I, Bureau of Industrial Relations Bulletin No. 14, University of Michigan Press, Ann Arbor, 1943.

VEYSEY, VICTORY V.: *Selecting, Training, and Rating Supervisors*, Bulletin No. 6, California Institute of Technology, Industrial Relations Section, Pasadena, Calif., 1944.

YOUNG, ROSS: *Personnel Manual for Executives*, McGraw-Hill Book Company, Inc., New York, 1947.

CHAPTER 12

Employee Induction and Training

INDUCTION

FERN, GEORGE H.: *Training for Supervision in Industry*, (Chap. V, Starting a New Worker Right), McGraw-Hill Book Company, Inc., New York, 1945.

"Induction Procedures for New Employees," *Conference Board Management Record*, Vol. 1, No. 12, pp. 181–187, 1939.

METROPOLITAN LIFE INSURANCE COMPANY, POLICYHOLDERS SERVICE BUREAU: *Orienting the New Worker*, New York, no date.

NATIONAL INDUSTRIAL CONFERENCE BOARD, INC.: *Employment Procedures and Personnel Records*, pp. 50–54, Inducting New Employees, Studies in Personnel Policy No. 38, New York, 1941.

SCOTT, WALTER D., R.C. CLOTHIER, S.B. MATHEWSON, and W.R. SPRIEGEL: *Personnel Management*, 3d ed., (Chap. XXI, Introducing the Worker to His Job), McGraw-Hill Book Company, Inc., New York, 1941.

U. S. WAR MANPOWER COMMISSION, BUREAU OF TRAINING, TRAINING WITHIN INDUSTRY SERVICE: *Introducing the New Employee to the Job*, Bulletin No. 8, Washington, D.C., 1943. (Also in *Personnel*, Vol. 20, No. 1, pp. 15–22, 1943.)

U. S. WAR DEPARTMENT: *Orienting Your New Employee*, Washington, D.C., 1943.

YEOMANS, GEORGE: "The Induction of New Factory Employees," *Personnel*, Vol. 19, No. 1, pp. 390–398, 1942.

TRAINING

AMERICAN MANAGEMENT ASSOCIATION: *How to Establish and Maintain a Personnel Department*, Sec. 5B, pp. 51–66, Training and Education, Research Report No. 4, New York, 1944.

COOPER, ALFRED M.: *Employee Training*, McGraw-Hill Book Company, Inc., New York, 1942.

CUSHMAN, FRANK: *Training Procedure*, John Wiley & Sons, Inc., New York, 1940.

DODD, ALVIN E., and JAMES O. RICE: *How to Train Workers for War Industries*, Harper & Brothers, New York, 1942.

DRIVER, R. S.: "The Follow-through of Training," *Personnel*, Vol. 20, No. 3, pp. 130–137, 1943.

————: "Methods for Spotting Training Needs," *Personnel*, Vol. 21, No. 1, pp. 39–47, 1944.

HALL, MILTON: *Training Your Employees; Suggestions to Executives and Supervisors*, Pamphlet No. 3, Society for Personnel Administration, Washington, D.C., 1940.

KIRKPATRICK, FRANCES: "What TWI Has Learned about Developing Training Programs," *Personnel*, Vol. 22, No. 2, pp. 114–120, 1945.

MOORE, HERBERT: *Psychology for Business and Industry*, 2d ed. (Chap. IX, Training the Worker), McGraw-Hill Book Company, Inc., New York, 1942.

MORGAN, HOWARD K.: *Industrial Training and Testing*, McGraw-Hill Book Company, Inc., New York, 1945.

NATIONAL INDUSTRIAL CONFERENCE BOARD, INC.: *Quick-training Procedures*, Studies in Personnel Policy No. 26, New York, 1940.

————: *Selecting, Training and Upgrading Supervisors, Instructors, Production Workers*, Studies in Personnel Policy No. 37, New York, 1941.

————: *Training Solutions of Company Problems: B. Programs Giving Special Attention to Development of the Skill of Non-supervisory Production Employees,* Studies in Personnel Policy No. 18, New York, 1940.

————: *Training White Collar Employees,* Studies in Personnel Policy No. 36, New York, 1941.

PATTERSON, WILLIAM F., and M.H. HEDGES: *Educating for Industry: Policies and Procedures of a National Apprenticeship System,* Prentice-Hall, Inc., New York, 1946.

PLANTY, EARL G.: "Qualifications of an Industrial Training Director," *Personnel,* Vol. 21, No. 1, pp. 56–63, 1944.

SCHAEFER, VERNON G.: *Job Instruction,* McGraw-Hill Book Company, Inc., New York, 1943.

SCOTT, WALTER D., R.C. CLOTHIER, S.B. MATHEWSON, and W.R. SPRIEGEL: *Personnel Management,* 3d ed. (Chap. XXII, Training Workers), McGraw-Hill Book Company, Inc., New York, 1941.

TIFFIN, JOSEPH: *Industrial Psychology* (Chap. 7, Training of Industrial Employees), Prentice-Hall, Inc., New York, 1942.

U. S. WAR MANPOWER COMMISSION, BUREAU OF TRAINING, TRAINING WITHIN INDUSTRY SERVICE: *The Training Within Industry Report,* 1940–1945, U. S. Government Printing Office, Washington, D. C., 1945.

U. S. WAR PRODUCTION BOARD, LABOR DIVISION, TRAINING WITHIN INDUSTRY: *Job Instruction; A Manual for Shop Supervisors and Instructors,* U. S. Government Printing Office, Washington, D. C., no date.

WALTERS, J. E.: *Personnel Relations, Their Application in a Democracy* (Chap. 10, Personnel Training and Education), The Ronald Press Company, New York, 1945.

YODER, DALE: *Personnel Management and Industrial Relations* (Chap. IX, Training for Industry), Prentice-Hall, Inc., New York, 1942.

CHAPTER 13

Employee Rating and Promotion

EMPLOYEE RATING

DRIVER, R. S.: "A Case History in Merit Rating," *Personnel,* Vol. 16, No. 4, pp. 137–162, 1940.

HALSEY, GEORGE D.: *Making and Using Industrial Service Ratings,* Harper & Brothers, New York, 1944.

KNOWLES, ASA S.: *Merit Rating in Industry,* Bulletin No. 1, Northeastern University, College of Business Administration, Bureau of Business Research, Boston, 1940.

———— and ROBERT D. THOMPSON: *Management of Manpower* (Chap. VII, Merit Rating—Measuring Manpower Performance), The Macmillan Company, New York, 1943.

LYTLE, CHARLES W.: *Job Evaluation Methods* (Chap. 12, Merit Rating), The Ronald Press Company, New York, 1946.

MAHLER, WALTER R.: "Let's Get More Scientific in Rating Employees," *Personnel,* Vol. 23, No. 5, pp. 310–320, 1947.

MAIER, NORMAN R.F.: *Psychology in Industry* (Chap. 7, Measuring Proficiency), Houghton Mifflin Company, Boston, 1946.

NATIONAL INDUSTRIAL CONFERENCE BOARD, INC.: *Employee Rating,* Studies in Personnel Policy No. 39, New York, 1941.

PROBST, JOHN B.: *Measuring and Rating Employee Value,* The Ronald Press Company, New York, 1947.

RYAN, THOMAS A.: "Merit Rating Criticized," *Personnel Journal*, Vol. 24, No. 1, pp. 6–15, 1945.

SCOTT, WALTER D., R.C. CLOTHIER, S.B. MATHEWSON, and W.R. SPRIEGEL: *Personnel Management*, 3d ed. (Chap. XIX, Merit Rating), McGraw-Hill Book Company, Inc., New York, 1941.

SMYTH, RICHARD C. and MATTHEW J. MURPHY: *Job Evaluation and Employee Rating* (Part II, Merit Rating), McGraw-Hill Book Company, Inc., New York, 1946.

TIFFIN, JOSEPH: *Industrial Psychology* (Chap. 9, Industrial Merit Rating), Prentice-Hall, Inc., New York, 1942.

————: Merit Rating: Its Validity and Techniques, in *Rating and Training Executives and Employees*, pp. 14–23, Personnel Series No. 100, American Management Association, New York, 1946.

WADSWORTH, GUY W., JR.: Seniority and Merit Rating in Labor Relations, in *Advances in Methods of Personnel Evaluation*, pp. 22–32, Personnel Series No. 107, American Management Association, New York, 1947.

WALTERS, J. E.: *Personnel Relations, Their Application in a Democracy* (Chap. 7, Personnel Ratings), The Ronald Press Company, New York, 1945.

YODER, DALE: *Personnel Management and Industrial Relations* (Chap. XII, Service Ratings), Prentice-Hall, Inc., New York, 1942.

PROMOTION

BAKER, HELEN: *Company Plans for Employee Promotions*, Princeton University, Industrial Relations Section, Princeton, N. J., 1939.

BERGEN, HAROLD B.: "Developing Promotional Opportunities," *Personnel*, Vol. 15, No. 4, pp. 208–212, 1939.

HARBISON, FREDERICK H.: *Seniority Policies and Procedures as Developed through Collective Bargaining*, Princeton University, Industrial Relations Section, Princeton, N. J.,1941.

HILL, LEE H., and CHARLES R. HOOK, JR.: *Management at the Bargaining Table* (pp. 112–115, Promotions), McGraw-Hill Book Company, Inc., New York, 1945.

JOHNSON, W.C.: "Employee Participation in the Promotion Program," *Personnel*, Vol. 23, No. 6, pp. 425–429, 1947.

LIVINGSTONE, R.S.: "Policies for Promotion, Transfer, Demotion and Discharge," *Proceedings of the Silver Bay Industrial Conference*, 24th Year, 1941, pp. 82–89, National Council of the YMCA's, New York, 1941.

MOORE, HERBERT: *Psychology for Business and Industry*, 2d ed. (Chap. XI, Promoting the Employee), McGraw-Hill Book Company, Inc., New York, 1942.

NATIONAL INDUSTRIAL CONFERENCE BOARD, INC.: *Employee Procedures and Personnel Records*, (pp. 56–59, Transfers, Promotions and Salary Changes), Studies in Personnel Policy, No. 38, New York, 1941.

SCOTT, WALTER D., R.C. CLOTHIER, S.B. MATHEWSON, and W.R. SPRIEGEL: *Personnel Management*, 3d ed. (Chap. XII, Transfer, Promotion, and Discharge), McGraw-Hill Book Company, Inc., New York, 1941.

TEAD, ORDWAY, and HENRY C. METCALF: *Personnel Administration, Its Principles and Practice*, 3d ed. rev. (Chap. XV, Transfer and Promotion), McGraw-Hill Book Company, Inc., New York, 1933.

WALTERS, J. E.: *Personnel Relations, Their Application in a Democracy* (pp. 253–259, Promotions and Transfers), The Ronald Press Company, New York, 1945.

WATKINS, GORDON S., and PAUL A. DODD: *The Management of Labor Relations* (Chaps. XVI and XVII, Transfer, Promotion, and Dismissal), McGraw-Hill Book Company, Inc., New York, 1938.

YODER, DALE: *Personnel Management and Industrial Relations* (Chap. 15. Promotion and Transfer), Prentice-Hall, Inc., New York, 1942.

CHAPTER 14

Transfer, Downgrading, and Layoff

(For additional references on transfer, see the references for Chap. 13)

BUREAU OF NATIONAL AFFAIRS, INC.: *Collective Bargaining Negotiations and Contracts* (Contract Clause Finder, Vol. 2, Promotion, Demotion, and Transfer; Seniority), Washington, D. C., 1945.

DAVIS, H.A.: "The Transfer Problem," *Personnel*, Vol. 19, No. 6, pp. 722–726, 1943.

GOLDEN, CLINTON S., and HAROLD J. RUTTENBERG: *The Dynamics of Industrial Democracy* (Chap. V, Quest for Security), Harper & Brothers, New York, 1942.

HANAWALT, WILBUR R.: "Solving the Problem of Merit vs. Seniority in Layoffs," *Personnel*, Vol. 23, No. 6, pp. 405–409, 1947.

HARBISON, FREDERICK H.: *Seniority Policies and Procedures as Developed through Collective Bargaining*, Princeton University, Industrial Relations Section, Princeton, N. J., 1941.

HILL, LEE H., and CHARLES R. HOOK, JR.: *Management at the Bargaining Table* (Chap. VI, Seniority), McGraw-Hill Book Company, Inc., New York, 1945.

McGREGOR, DOUGLAS: *The Attitudes of Workers toward Layoff Policy*, Publications in Social Science, Series 2, No. 3, Massachusetts Institute of Technology, Department of Economics and Social Science, Cambridge, Mass., 1939. (Reprinted from *The Journal of Abnormal and Social Psychology*, Vol. 3, No. 2, 1939.)

MACLAURIN, W. RUPERT: *Workers' Attitudes on Work Sharing and Layoff Policies in a Manufacturing Firm*, Publications in Social Science, Series 2, No. 2, Massachusetts Institute of Technology, Department of Economics and Social Science, Cambridge, Mass., 1939. (Reprinted from *Monthly Labor Review*, Vol. 48, No. 1, 1939.)

NATIONAL ASSOCIATION OF MANUFACTURERS, INDUSTRIAL RELATIONS DEPARTMENT: *Seniority* (A Survey-study of Industry Practice and the Principles Governing Length of Service as a Factor in Employment Relationships), Management Memo No. 1, New York, June, 1946.

NATIONAL INDUSTRIAL CONFERENCE BOARD, INC.: *Curtailment, Layoff Policy, and Seniority*, Studies in Personnel Policy, No. 5, New York, 1938.

SLICHTER, SUMNER H.: "Layoff Policy," in *Addresses on Industrial Relations*, 1939, Bulletin No. 9, University of Michigan, Bureau of Industrial Relations, Ann Arbor, 1939.

————: *Union Policies and Industrial Management* (Chap. IV, Control of Layoffs—Union Policies; Chap. V, Control of Layoffs—Problems and Results of Major Union Policies), Brookings Institution, Washington, D. C., 1941.

DISMISSAL COMPENSATION

HAWKINS, EVERETT D.: *Dismissal Compensation*, Princeton University Press, Princeton, N. J., 1940.

NATIONAL INDUSTRIAL CONFERENCE BOARD, INC.: *Dismissal Compensation*, Studies in Personnel Policy No. 50, New York, 1943.

U. S. DEPARTMENT OF LABOR, BUREAU OF LABOR STATISTICS: *Dismissal Pay Provisions in Union Agreements, December*, 1944, Bulletin No. 808, U.S. Government Printing Office, Washington, D. C., 1945.

EMPLOYMENT STABILIZATION

FELDMAN, HERMAN: *Stabilizing Jobs and Wages*, Harper & Brothers, New York, 1940.

MINNESOTA AMERICAN LEGION FOUNDATION: *To Make Jobs More Steady and to Make More Steady Jobs*, St. Paul, 1944.

MYERS, CHARLES A.: *Employment Stabilization and the Wisconsin Act* (Chaps. 2 and 3), Employment Security Memorandum No. 10, U.S. Social Security Board, Bureau of Employment Security, Washington, D. C., September, 1940.

NATIONAL INDUSTRIAL CONFERENCE BOARD, INC.: *Reducing Fluctuations in Employment*, Studies in Personnel Policy No. 27, New York, 1940.

SMITH, EDWIN S.: *Reducing Seasonal Unemployment*, McGraw-Hill Book Company, Inc., New York, 1931.

YODER, DALE: *Personnel Management and Industrial Relations* (Chap. 19, Employment Stabilization), Prentice-Hall, Inc., New York, 1942.

CHAPTER 15

Discipline and Discharge

AMERICAN MANAGEMENT ASSOCIATION: *Constructive Discipline in Industry*, Special Research Report No. 3, New York, 1943.

ANDERSON, H.W.: *Management's Responsibility for Discipline*, California Institute of Technology, Industrial Relations Section, Pasadena, Calif., 1947.

BRINTNALL, ARTHUR K.: "How Our Discipline Board Dispenses Justice" (Allis-Chalmers Mfg. Co.), *Factory Management and Maintenance*, Vol. 101, No. 10, pp. 104–105, 1943.

CLEETON, GLEN U.: "The New Approach to Employee Discipline," *Personnel*, Vol. 16, No. 4, pp. 197–206, 1940.

GARDINER, GLENN: *How to Correct Workers*, Elliott Service Company, New York, 1943.

GIRDNER, WILLIAM: "Procedure on Discharges," *Personnel*, Vol. 14, No. 3, pp. 118–121, 1938.

HILL, LEE H., and CHARLES R. HOOK, JR.: *Management at the Bargaining Table*, (pp. 90–110, Discharge and Discipline), McGraw-Hill Book Company, Inc., New York, 1945.

MOORE, E. A.: "Making Discipline Enforcement Easy for Supervisors" (The Discipline Control Board at Ryan Aeronautical Co.), *Industrial Relations*, Vol. 4, No. 1, pp. 29–31ff., 1946.

MURPHY, M. J., and R.C. SMYTH: "Discipline: A Case Study in the Development and Application of a Discipline Procedure," *Factory Management and Maintenance*, Vol. 103, No. 7, pp. 97–104, 1945. (Plant Operation Library No. 88.)

SCOTT, WALTER D., R.C. CLOTHIER, S.B. MATHEWSON, and W.R. SPRIEGEL: *Personnel Management*, 3d ed. (pp. 142–143, Discharge), McGraw-Hill Book Company, Inc., New York, 1941.

TEAD, ORDWAY: *Human Nature and Management*, 2d ed. (Chap. XVIII, The New Discipline), McGraw-Hill Book Company, Inc., New York, 1933.

—— and HENRY C. METCALF: *Personnel Administration*, 3d ed. (Chap. XVI, Shop Rules, Grievances, and Discharge), McGraw-Hill Book Company, Inc., New York, 1933.

UNIVERSITY OF MICHIGAN, BUREAU OF INDUSTRIAL RELATIONS: *Personnel Management in War Industries*, (VI, pp. 61–69, The Treatment of Disciplinary Problems), Vol. II, Bulletin No. 15, University of Michigan Press, Ann Arbor, 1944.

WALTERS, J. E.: *Personnel Relations, Their Application in a Democracy*, pp. 259–262, Discharge, The Ronald Press Company, New York, 1945.

YODER, DALE: *Personnel Management and Industrial Relations*, pp. 540–552, Prentice-Hall, Inc., New York, 1942.

CHAPTER 16

Wage Policies and Wage Administration

AMERICAN MANAGEMENT ASSOCIATION: *Putting Job Rating to Work*, Personnel Series No. 49, New York, 1941.

BAKER, HELEN, and JOHN M. TRUE: *The Operation of Job Evaluation Plans*, Princeton University, Industrial Relations Section, Princeton, N. J., 1947.

BALDERSTON, C. CANBY: *Wage Setting Based on Job Analysis and Evaluation*, Industrial Relations Monograph No. 4, Industrial Relations Counselors, Inc., New York, 1940.

BARKIN, SOLOMON: "Wage Determination: Trick or Technique," *Labor and Nation*, Vol. 1, No. 6, pp. 24–26, 48, 1946.

BENGE, EUGENE J., SAMUEL L.H. BURK, and EDWARD N. HAY: *Manual of Job Evaluation*, Harper & Brothers, New York, 1941.

BURK, SAMUEL L.H.: *A Case History in Salary and Wage Administration*, American Management Association, New York, 1939. (Reprinted from *Personnel*, Vol. 15, No. 3, 1939.)

DICKINSON, Z. CLARK: *Collective Wage Determination*, The Ronald Press Company, New York, 1941.

DUNLOP, JOHN T.: "The Economics of Wage-dispute Settlement," *Law and Contemporary Problems*, Vol. 12, No. 2, pp. 281–296, 1947.

————: *Wage Determination under Trade Unions*, The Macmillan Company, New York, 1944.

ELLS, RALPH W.: *Salary and Wage Administration*, McGraw-Hill Book Company, Inc., New York, 1945.

GOMBERG, WILLIAM: *A Labor Union Manual of Job Evaluation*, Roosevelt College, Labor Education Division, Chicago, 1947.

GRAY, ROBERT D.: *Classification of Jobs in Small Companies*, Bulletin No. 5, California Institute of Technology, Industrial Relations Section, Pasadena, Calif., 1944.

HOPWOOD, J.O.: *Salaries, Wages and Labor Relations*, The Ronald Press Company, New York, 1945.

JOHNSON, F.H., R.W. BOISE, JR., and DUDLEY PRATT: *Job Evaluation*, John Wiley & Sons, Inc., New York, 1946.

KNOWLES, ASA S., and ROBERT D. THOMPSON: *Management of Manpower* (Chap. VI, Job Evaluation), The Macmillan Company, New York, 1943.

KRESS, A. L.: "How to Rate Jobs and Men," *Factory Management and Maintenance*, Vol. 97, No. 10, pp. 60–65, 1939. (Discusses the "degree" plan developed for the National Electrical Manufacturers' Association and the National Metal Trades Association.)

LESTER, RICHARD A., and EDWARD A. ROBIE: *Wages under National and Regional Collective Bargaining: Experience in Seven Industries*, Princeton University, Industrial Relations Section, Princeton, N. J., 1946.

LYTLE, CHARLES W.: *Job Evaluation Methods*, The Ronald Press Company, New York, 1946.

NATIONAL INDUSTRIAL CONFERENCE BOARD, INC.: *Job Descriptions*, Studies in Personnel Policy No. 72, New York, 9146.

————: *Job Evaluation*, Studies in Personnel Policy No. 25, New York, 1940.

————: *Principles and Application of Job Evaluation*, Studies in Personnel Policy No. 62, New York, 1944.

————: *Problems in Wage Adjustment*, Studies in Personnel Policy No. 33, New York, 1941.

NATIONAL OFFICE MANAGEMENT ASSOCIATION: *Clerical Job Evaluation*, NOMA Bulletin No. 1, Philadelphia, 1946.

PERCIVAL, ANDREW J., and GLEN B. GROSS: "Job Evaluation—A Case History," *Harvard Business Review*, Vol. 24, No. 4, pp. 466–497, 1946.

PETERSON, FLORENCE: *Survey of Labor Economics* (Chap. 11, Wage Structure), Harper & Brothers, New York, 1947.

RIEGEL, JOHN W.: *Salary Determination*, University of Michigan, Bureau of Industrial Relations, Ann Arbor, 1940.

————: *Wage Determination*, University of Michigan, Bureau of Industrial Relations, Ann Arbor, 1937.

SCOTT, WALTER D., R.C. CLOTHIER, S.B. MATHEWSON, and W.R. SPRIEGEL: *Personnel Management*, 3d ed. (Chap. XI, The Occupational Description; Chap. XX, Job Analysis, Classification, and Rating; Chap. XXV, Wage and Salary Control), McGraw-Hill Book Company, Inc., New York, 1941.

SHARTLE, CARROLL L.: *Occupational Information—Its Development and Use*, Prentice-Hall, Inc., New York, 1946.

SLICHTER, SUMNER H.: *Basic Criteria Used in Wage Negotiations*, Chicago Association of Commerce, Chicago, 1947.

SMYTH, RICHARD C., and MATTHEW J. MURPHY: *Job Evaluation and Employee Rating*, McGraw-Hill Book Company, Inc., New York, 1946.

SUFRIN, SIDNEY C.: "An Economist Looks at Job Evaluation," *Personnel*, Vol. 23, No. 5, pp. 302–309, 1947.

U. S. WAR MANPOWER COMMISSION, BUREAU OF MANPOWER UTILIZATION: *Informational Manual on Industrial Job Evaluation Systems*, U.S. Government Printing Office, Washington, D. C., 1943.

————: *Training and Reference Manual for Job Analysis*, U.S. Government Printing Office, Washington, D. C., 1944.

WALTERS, J. E.: *Personnel Relations, Their Application in a Democracy* (Chap. 4, Wages; Chap. 6, Job Evaluation), The Ronald Press Company, New York, 1945.

YODER, DALE: *Personnel Management and Industrial Relations* (Chap. V, Job Analysis, Description, and Classification; Chap. XIV, Wage Policies), Prentice-Hall, Inc., New York, 1942.

CHAPTER 17

Methods of Wage Payment; Output Standards

METHODS OF WAGE PAYMENT

AMERICAN MANAGEMENT ASSOCIATION: *Incentives for Management and Workers*, Production Series No. 160, New York, 1945.

BALDERSTON, C. CANBY: *Group Incentives*, University of Pennsylvania Press, Philadelphia, 1930.

DICKINSON, Z. CLARK: *Compensating Industrial Effort*, The Ronald Press Company, New York, 1937.

KENNEDY, VAN DUSEN: *Union Policy and Incentive Wage Methods*, Columbia University Press, New York, 1945.

LOUDEN, J. KEITH: *Wage Incentives*, John Wiley & Sons, Inc., New York, 1944.

LYTLE, CHARLES W.: *Wage Incentive Methods: Their Selection, Installation and Operation*, rev. ed., The Ronald Press Company, New York, 1942.

NATIONAL INDUSTRIAL CONFERENCE BOARD, INC.: *Wage Incentive Practices*, Studies in Personnel Policy No. 68, New York, 1945.

NICKERSON, JOHN W.: *Addresses and Papers on Wage Incentive Plans and Labor-Management Relationships*, Prepared by the Management Consultant Division, U.S. War Production Board, Washington, D. C., 1944.

PRINCETON UNIVERSITY, INDUSTRIAL RELATIONS SECTION: *Wage Payment Systems; A Selected List of References*, Princeton, 1944. (Annotated.)

RIEGEL, JOHN W.: *Paving the Way for an Incentive Plan*, An Address Prepared under the Auspices of the Industrial Relations Section, California Institute of Technology, Pasadena, Calif., 1943.

SCOTT, WALTER D., R.C. CLOTHIER, S.B. MATHEWSON, and W.R. SPRIEGEL: *Personnel Management*, 3d ed. (Chap. XXVI, Wage-payment Plans), McGraw-Hill Book Company, Inc., New York, 1941.

SLICHTER, SUMNER H.: *Union Policies and Industrial Management* (Chap. X, Union Attitudes toward Basic Systems of Wage Payment; Chap. XI, Problems and Policies Created by Piecework), Brookings Institution, Washington, D. C., 1941.

UHRBROCK, RICHARD S.: *A Psychologist Looks at Wage-incentive Methods*, Institute of Management Series No. 15, American Management Association, New York, 1935.

UNITED ELECTRICAL, RADIO AND MACHINE WORKERS OF AMERICA: *U.E. Guide to Wage Payment Plans, Time Study and Job Evaluation*, New York, 1943.

U. S. DEPARTMENT OF LABOR, BUREAU OF LABOR STATISTICS: *Incentive-wage Plans and Collective Bargaining*, Bulletin No. 717, U.S. Government Printing Office, Washington, D. C., 1942.

U. S. WAR PRODUCTION BOARD, MANAGEMENT CONSULTANT DIVISION: *A Handbook on Wage Incentive Plans*, U.S. Government Printing Office, Washington, D. C., 1945.

UNIVERSITY OF MICHIGAN, BUREAU OF INDUSTRIAL RELATIONS: *Personnel Management in War Industries* (III, Essentials in Incentive Compensation; IV, Experience with Incentive Plans), Vol. II, Bureau of Industrial Relations Bulletin No. 15, University of Michigan Press, Ann Arbor, 1944.

WATKINS, GORDON S., and PAUL A. DODD: *The Management of Labor Relations* (Chap. XVIII, Wages and Wage Systems; Chap. XIX, Financial Incentives), McGraw-Hill Book Company, Inc., New York, 1938.

YODER, DALE: *Personnel Management and Industrial Relations* (Chap. XIII, Wage Plans), Prentice-Hall, Inc., New York, 1942.

TIME AND MOTION STUDY

BARNES, RALPH M.: *Motion and Time Study*, 2d ed., John Wiley & Sons, Inc., New York, 1940.

CARROLL, PHIL, JR.: *Timestudy for Cost Control*, 2d ed., McGraw-Hill Book Company, Inc., New York, 1943.

GOMBERG, WILLIAM: *A Trade Union Analysis of Time Study*, Science Research Associates, Chicago, 1947.

LOWRY, STEWART M., HAROLD B. MAYNARD, and G. J. STEGEMERTEN: *Time and Motion Study and Formulas for Wage Incentives*, 3d ed., McGraw-Hill Book Company, Inc., New York, 1940.

PRESGRAVE, RALPH: *The Dynamics of Time Study*, 2d ed., McGraw-Hill Book Company, Inc., New York, 1945.

OUTPUT STANDARDS

AMERICAN MANAGEMENT ASSOCIATION: *The Human Aspects of Methods Improvement*, Production Series No. 170, New York, 1947.

GOLDEN, CLINTON S.: "Attitudes toward Methods Improvement," *Mechanical Engineering*, Vol. 66, No. 7, pp. 465–466ff, 1944.

GOMBERG, WILLIAM: "Union Interest in Engineering Techniques," *Harvard Business Review*, Vol. 24, No. 3, pp. 356–365, 1946.

RIEGEL, JOHN W.: *Management, Labor, and Technological Change*, University of Michigan Press, Ann Arbor, 1942.

SELEKMAN, BENJAMIN N.: "Resistance to Shop Changes," *Harvard Business Review*, Vol. 24, No. 1, pp. 119–132, 1945.

SLICHTER, SUMNER H.: *Union Policies and Industrial Management* (Chaps. VII, VIII, and IX, Technological Change), Brookings Institution, Washington, D. C., 1941.

SMITH, ELLIOTT DUNLAP: "The Management of Technological Change," *Personnel*, Vol. 22, No. 6, pp. 376–384, 1946.

————: *Technology and Labor*, Yale University Press, New Haven, 1939.

TEAD, ORDWAY, and HENRY C. METCALF: *Personnel Administration*, 3d ed. rev. (Chap. XVIII, The Joint Control of Production Standards), McGraw-Hill Book Company, Inc., New York, 1933.

UNIVERSITY OF MICHIGAN, BUREAU OF INDUSTRIAL RELATIONS: *Addresses on Industrial Relations*, 1945 (III, Obtaining Employee Acceptance of Production Standards), Bureau of Industrial Relations Bulletin No. 16, University of Michigan Press, Ann Arbor, 1945.

————: *Personnel Management in War Industries* (I, Obtaining Employee Acceptance of Production Standards; II, The Administration of Production Standards in the Murray Corp.) Vol. II, Bureau of Industrial Relations Bulletin No. 15, University of Michigan Press, Ann Arbor, 1944.

PROFIT SHARING

BALDERSTON, C. CANBY: *Profit Sharing for Wage Earners*, Industrial Relations Counselors, Inc., New York, 1937.

EDITORIAL RESEARCH REPORTS: *Sharing Profits in Industry*, by Thomas K. Ford, Vol. 1, 1946, No. 8, Washington, D. C., 1946.

"Experience with Profit Sharing," *Conference Board Management Record*, Vol. 8, No. 2, pp. 33–38, 1946.

RUST, DAVID W.: A Plan to Share Cost Savings with Employees, in *Economic Fundamentals of Collective Bargaining*, pp. 19–25, Personnel Series No. 103, American Management Association, New York, 1946.

STEWART, BRYCE M., and WALTER J. COUPER: *Profit Sharing and Stock Ownership for Wage Earners and Executives*, Industrial Relations Monograph No. 10, Industrial Relations Counselors, Inc., New York, 1945.

U. S. SENATE, SUBCOMMITTEE OF THE COMMITTEE ON FINANCE: *Survey of Experience in Profit Sharing and Possibilities of Incentive Taxation: Report*, 76th Congress, 1st Session, Report No. 610, U.S. Government Printing Office, Washington, D. C., 1939.

WINSLOW, C. MORTON, and K. RAYMOND CLARK: *Profit Sharing and Pension Plans*, 2 vols., Commerce Clearing House, Inc., Chicago, 1946.

ANNUAL WAGE AND GUARANTEED EMPLOYMENT PLANS

AMERICAN MANAGEMENT ASSOCIATION: *Annual Wages and Employment Stabilization Techniques*, Research Report No. 8, New York, 1945.

CHERNICK, JACK, and GEORGE C. HELLICKSON: *Guaranteed Annual Wages*, University of Minnesota Press, Minneapolis, 1945.

DALE, ERNEST: "The Guaranteed Annual Wage," *Personnel*, Vol. 21, No. 3, pp. 146–151, 1944.

FELDMAN, HERMAN: "Annual Wage Plans and Some of Their Practical Problems," *Advanced Management*, Vol. 10, No. 3, pp. 104–112, 1945.

"Guaranteed-wage Plans in Practice," *Conference Board Management Record*, Vol. 8, No. 4, pp. 101–105, 1946.

NATIONAL INDUSTRIAL CONFERENCE BOARD, INC.: *Annual Wage and Employment Guarantee Plans*, Studies in Personnel Policy No. 76, New York, 1946.

SCHMIDT, EMERSON P.: "Annual Wage and Income-security Plans," *The Journal of Business* (University of Chicago), Vol. 14, No. 2, pp. 127–149, 1941.

SNIDER, JOSEPH L.: *The Guarantee of Work and Wages*, Harvard University, Graduate School of Business Administration, Division of Research, Boston, 1947.

———: "Management's Approach to the Annual Wage," *Harvard Business Review*, Vol. 24, No. 3, pp. 326–338, 1946.

U. S. DEPARTMENT OF LABOR, BUREAU OF LABOR STATISTICS: *Guaranteed Employment and Annual-wage Provisions in Union Agreements*, Bulletin No. 828, U.S. Government Printing Office, Washington, D. C., 1945.

U. S. NATIONAL WAR LABOR BOARD, WAGE STABILIZATION DIVISION: *Guaranteed Employment and Annual Wage Plans*, by Alice L. Nielsen, Research and Statistics Report No. 25, Washington, D. C., 1944.

U. S. OFFICE OF WAR MOBILIZATION AND RECONVERSION, OFFICE OF TEMPORARY CONTROLS: *Guaranteed Wages*, Report to the President by the Advisory Board, Murray W. Latimer, Research Director, Jan. 31, 1947. U.S. Government Printing Office, Washington, D. C., 1947.

WITTE, EDWIN E.: "Steadying the Worker's Income," *Harvard Business Review*, Vol. 24, No. 3, pp. 306–325, 1946.

CHAPTER 18

Hours of Work and Shifts

AUSTRALIA, DEPARTMENT OF LABOUR AND NATIONAL SERVICE, INDUSTRIAL WELFARE DIVISION: *Planning Hours of Work*, Bulletin No. 4, Melbourne, 1945.

CAHILL, MARION C.: *Shorter Hours*, Columbia University Press, New York, 1932.

GREAT BRITAIN, INDUSTRIAL HEALTH RESEARCH BOARD: *Hours of Work, Lost Time and Labour Wastage*, Emergency Report No. 2, His Majesty's Stationery Office, London, 1942.

———: *A Study of Variations in Output*, Emergency Report No. 5, His Majesty's Stationery Office, London, 1944.

"Hours of Work in Manufacturing, 1914–43," *Monthly Labor Review*, Vol. 58, No. 4, pp. 838–855, 1944.

METROPOLITAN LIFE INSURANCE COMPANY, POLICYHOLDERS SERVICE BUREAU: *Vacations for Industrial Workers*, New York, 1947.

————: *Vacations for Office Workers*, New York, 1947.

MINTZ, BEATRICE: "Problems of Shift Rotation," *Industrial Bulletin* (New York State Department of Labor), Vol. 21, No. 12, pp. 423–427, 1942.

NATIONAL INDUSTRIAL CONFERENCE BOARD, INC.: *Multiple-shift Operation*, Studies in Personnel Policy No. 3, New York, 1937.

————: *Vacation and Holiday Practices*, Studies in Personnel Policy No. 75, New York, 1946.

NEW YORK STATE DEPARTMENT OF LABOR, DIVISION OF INDUSTRIAL RELATIONS, WOMEN IN INDUSTRY AND MINIMUM WAGE: *Health and Efficiency of Workers as Affected by Long Hours and Night Work: Experience of World War II*, New York, 1946.

————: *Long Hours and Night Work: Experiences and Views of Women Workers, New York State*, New York, 1946.

NEW YORK STATE DEPARTMENT OF LABOR, DIVISION OF WOMEN IN INDUSTRY AND MINIMUM WAGE: *Hours of Work in Relation to Health and Efficiency*, Albany, 1941.

PETERSON, FLORENCE: *Survey of Labor Economics* (Chap. 15, Hours of Work; Chap. 16, Government Regulation of Hours), Harper & Brothers, New York, 1947.

PIGORS, PAUL, and FAITH PIGORS: *Human Aspects of Multiple Shift Operations*, Publications in Social Science, Series 2, No. 13, Massachusetts Institute of Technology, Department of Economics and Social Science, Cambridge, Mass., 1944.

PRINCETON UNIVERSITY, INDUSTRIAL RELATIONS SECTION: *Optimum Hours of Work in War Production*, Princeton, N. J., 1942.

————: *Re-organization of Hour Schedules*, Industrial Relations Digests III, Princeton, N. J., 1941.

————: *Shift Schedules for Continuous Operation*, Industrial Relations Digests XV, Princeton, N. J., 1943.

"Problems in Operating Shifts," *Conference Board Management Record*, Vol. 6, No. 3, pp. 59–63, 1944.

STANFORD UNIVERSITY, DIVISION OF INDUSTRIAL RELATIONS: *Shift Schedules in Continuous-Process Industries*, Study No. 9, Stanford University, Calif., 1942.

TEAD, ORDWAY, and HENRY C. METCALF: *Personnel Administration*, 3d ed. rev. (Chap. VII, Hours and Working Periods), McGraw-Hill Book Company, Inc., New York, 1933.

U. S. DEPARTMENT OF LABOR, BUREAU OF LABOR STATISTICS: *Paid Vacations in American Industry, 1943 and 1944*, Bulletin No. 811, U.S. Government Printing Office, Washington, D.C., 1945.

————: *Pay Differentials for Night Work under Union Contracts*, Bulletin No. 748, U.S. Government Office, Washington, D.C., 1943.

————: *Studies of the Effects of Long Working Hours*, by Max D. Kossoris (Parts 1 and 2), Bulletins Nos. 791 and 791-A, U.S. Government Printing Office, Washington, D.C., 1944.

U. S. DEPARTMENT OF LABOR, WOMEN'S BUREAU: *Women's Wartime Hours of Work*, Bulletin No. 208, U.S. Government Printing Office, Washington, D.C., 1947.

UNIVERSITY OF MICHIGAN, BUREAU OF INDUSTRIAL RELATIONS: *Personnel Management in War Industries* (XII, What Work Schedules are Best?), Vol. II, Bureau of Industrial Relations Bulletin No. 15, University of Michigan Press, Ann Arbor, 1944.

WATKINS, GORDON S., and PAUL A. DODD: *The Management of Labor Relations* (Chap. XXVI, Hours of Labor in Relation to Health and Output), McGraw-Hill Book Company, Inc., New York, 1938.

YODER, DALE: *Personnel Management and Industrial Relations* (Chap. XI, Working Hours), Prentice-Hall, Inc., New York, 1942.

CHAPTER 19

Services for Employees

COOPER, JOSEPH D.: "Criteria for the Organization of Employee Service Activities," *Personnel Administration*, Vol. 6, No. 1, pp. 15–17, 1943.

DARTNELL CORPORATION: *Educational Programs for Employees*, Chicago.

DIEHL, LEONARD J., and FLOYD R. EASTWOOD: *Industrial Recreation; Its Development and Present Status*, Purdue University, Lafayette, Ind., 1940.

DUGGINS, G. HERBERT, and FLOYD R. EASTWOOD: *Planning Industrial Recreation*, Purdue University, Lafayette, Ind., 1941. (Digest in *Personnel*, Vol. 19, No. 1, pp. 398–407, 1942.)

INDUSTRIAL RELATIONS COUNSELORS, INC.: *Company-financed Sickness and Disability Benefit Plans*, Industrial Relations Memos No. 78, New York, 1945.

LAIRD. LEE: "Employee Benefit Programs," in *Papers Presented at the Second Annual Stanford Industrial Relations Conference*, 1939, pp. 52–60, Stanford University, Graduate School of Business, Division of Industrial Relations, Stanford University, Calif., 1939.

METROPOLITAN LIFE INSURANCE COMPANY, POLICYHOLDERS SERVICE BUREAU: *Lunchrooms for Employees*, New York, no date.

NATIONAL INDUSTRIAL CONFERENCE BOARD, INC.: *Company Group Insurance Plans*, Studies in Personnel Policy No. 70, New York, 1945.

———: *Health Insurance Plans: A—Mutual Benefit Associations*, Studies in Personnel Policy No. 9, New York, 1938.

———: *Health Insurance Plans: B—Group Health Insurance Plans*, Studies in Personnel Policy No. 10, New York, 1939.

———: *Health Insurance Plans: C—Company Non-contributory Disability Benefit Plans*, Studies in Personnel Policy No. 11, New York, 1939.

———: *Music in Industry*, Studies in Personnel Policy No. 78, New York, 1947.

———: *Trends in Company Pension Plans*, Studies in Personnel Policy No. 61, New York, 1944.

———: *What Employers Are Doing for Employees*, Studies No. 221, New York, 1936.

NATIONAL RECREATION ASSOCIATION: *Recreation for Industrial Workers*, New York, 1945.

PRINCETON UNIVERSITY, INDUSTRIAL RELATIONS SECTION: *Company Sickness Benefit Plans for Wage Earners*, by Eleanor Davis, Princeton, N. J., 1936.

———: *Educational Refunds in Industry*, by Eleanor Davis, Princeton, N. J., 1935.

———: *The Use of Credit Unions in Company Programs for Employee Savings and Investment*, Princeton, N. J., 1935.

SCOTT, WALTER D., R.C. CLOTHIER, S.B. MATHEWSON, and W.R. SPRIEGEL: *Personnel Management*, 3d ed. (Chap. XVII, Financial Aids to Employees), McGraw-Hill Book Company, Inc., New York, 1941.

U. S. WAR DEPARTMENT: *Planning Employee Services*, Civilian Personnel Pamphlet No. 7, Washington, D.C., 1944.

WALTERS, J.E.: *Personnel Relations, Their Application in a Democracy* (Chap. 14, Employee Service Work), The Ronald Press Company, New York, 1945.

WATKINS, GORDON S., and PAUL A. DODD: *The Management of Labor Relations* (Chap. XXX, Miscellaneous Personnel Services), McGraw-Hill Book Company, Inc., New York, 1938.

YODER, DALE: *Personnel Management and Industrial Relations* (Chap. XXIII, Personnel Services), Prentice-Hall, Inc., New York, 1942.

CHAPTER 20

Employee Health and Safety

AMERICAN COLLEGE OF SURGEONS: *Medical Service in Industry and Workmen's Compensation Laws*, rev. ed., Chicago, 1946.

AMERICAN STANDARDS ASSOCIATION: *American Standard Method of Compiling Industrial Injury Rates*, New York, 1945.

BLAKE, ROLAND P., editor: *Industrial Safety*, Prentice-Hall, Inc., New York, 1944.

CHAMBER OF COMMERCE OF THE UNITED STATES, HEALTH ADVISORY COUNCIL: *Medical Services for Workers in Smaller Plants*, Washington, D.C., 1944.

COLLIER, HOWARD E.: *Outlines of Industrial Medical Practice*, The Williams & Wilkins Company, Baltimore, 1941.

GAFAFER, WILLIAM M., editor: *Manual of Industrial Hygiene and Medical Service in War Industries* (prepared by the Division of Industrial Hygiene, National Institute of Health, U. S. Public Health Service), W. B. Saunders Company, Philadelphia, 1943.

HEINRICH, H. W.: *Industrial Accident Prevention*, 2d ed., McGraw-Hill Book Company, Inc., 1941.

JUDSON, HARRY H., and JAMES M. BROWN: *Occupational Accident Prevention*, John Wiley & Sons, Inc., New York, 1944.

LIPPERT, FREDERICK G.: *Accident Prevention Administration*, McGraw-Hill Book Company, Inc., New York, 1947.

METROPOLITAN LIFE INSURANCE COMPANY, POLICYHOLDERS SERVICE BUREAU: *Safeguarding the Woman Employee*, New York, no date.

METROPOLITAN LIFE INSURANCE COMPANY, WELFARE DIVISION: *Developing Safe Employees*, New York, no date.

NATIONAL ASSOCIATION OF MANUFACTURERS: *Health on the Production Front*, New York, 1944.

———: *Industrial Health Practices*, New York, 1941.

NATIONAL INDUSTRIAL CONFERENCE BOARD, INC.: *Medical and Health Programs in Industry*, Studies in Personnel Policy No. 17, New York, 1939.

NATIONAL RESEARCH COUNCIL, COMMITTEE ON WORK IN INDUSTRY: *Fatigue of Workers: Its Relation to Industrial Production*, Reinhold Publishing Corporation, New York, 1941.

NATIONAL SAFETY COUNCIL: *Industrial Health and Safety; A Bibliography*, 1945 ed., Chicago, 1945.

———: *Industrial Safety Manual*, Chicago, 1944.

———: *Accident Facts* (annual publication); *National Safety News* (monthly periodical); *Safe Practices Pamphlets*.

NEW YORK STATE DEPARTMENT OF LABOR, DIVISION OF INDUSTRIAL HYGIENE: *Essentials of Health Maintenance in Industrial Plants*, Albany, 1942.

PRINCETON UNIVERSITY, INDUSTRIAL RELATIONS SECTION: *Medical Services in Industry: A Selected Annotated Bibliography*, Princeton, N. J., 1942.

SCHAEFER, VERNON G.: *Safety Supervision*, McGraw-Hill Book Company, Inc., New York, 1942.

TIFFIN, JOSEPH: *Industrial Psychology*, (Chap. 11, Accidents and Safety), Prentice-Hall, Inc., New York, 1942.

U. S. DEPARTMENT OF LABOR, BUREAU OF LABOR STATISTICS: *Accident Record Manual for Industrial Plants*, Bulletin No. 772, U.S. Government Printing Office, Washington, D.C., 1944.

U. S. DEPARTMENT OF LABOR, DIVISION OF LABOR STANDARDS: *Joint Safety Committees at Work: A Report of Union Participation*, Bulletin No. 61, U.S. Government Printing Office, Washington, D.C., 1944.

————: *Occupation Hazards and Diagnostic Signs*, Bulletin No. 41, U. S. Government Printing Office, Washington, D.C., 1942. (Also other bulletins and special bulletins of the Division of Labor Standards.)

WALTERS, J. E.: *Personnel Relations, Their Application in a Democracy* (Chap. 11, Health Activities; Chap. 13, Safety), The Ronald Press Company, New York, 1945.

WATKINS, GORDON S., and PAUL A. DODD: *The Management of Labor Relations* (Chap. XXIV, Safeguarding the Worker's Health; Chap. XXV, Industrial Accidents and Their Prevention), McGraw-Hill Book Company, Inc., New York, 1938.

YODER, DALE: *Personnel Management and Industrial Relations* (Chap. XVI, The Health of Employees), Prentice-Hall, Inc., New York, 1942.

CHAPTER 21

Employee Participation in Production Problems

EMPLOYEE SUGGESTION SYSTEMS

AMERICAN MANAGEMENT ASSOCIATION: *Getting and Using Employees' Ideas*, Production Series No. 165, New York, 1946.

"Employee Suggestions," *Factory Management and Maintenance*, Vol. 100, No. 5, pp. 73–84, 1942, Plant Operation Library No. 51.

METROPOLITAN LIFE INSURANCE COMPANY, POLICYHOLDERS SERVICE BUREAU: *Suggestion Systems*, New York, no date.

NATIONAL ASSOCIATION OF SUGGESTION SYSTEMS: *Suggestion Systems, A Brief Survey of Modern Theory and Practice*, Chicago, 1944.

U. S. BUREAU OF FOREIGN AND DOMESTIC COMMERCE: *An Employee Suggestion System for the Small Plant or Store*, Economic (Small Business) Series No. 45, U.S. Government Printing Office, Washington, D.C., 1946.

LABOR-MANAGEMENT COMMITTEES

AMERICAN MANAGEMENT ASSOCIATION: *Development and Operation of Joint Management-labor Committees*, Production Series No. 136, New York, 1942.

CHALMERS, W. ELLISON: "Joint Production Committees in United States War Plants," *International Labour Review*, Vol. 47, No. 1, pp. 22–45, 1943.

INTERNATIONAL LABOUR OFFICE: *British Joint Production Machinery*, Studies and Reports, Series A (Industrial Relations), No. 43, Montreal, 1944.

QUINN, THEODORE K.: *The Original Manual for Labor and Management Committees*, T. K. Quinn Company, Inc., New York, 1945.

U. S. WAR PRODUCTION BOARD, WAR PRODUCTION DRIVE HEADQUARTERS: *Basic Guide for Labor-management Committees; Ways of Operating a Labor-management Production Committee*, Washington, D.C., 1945.

————: *Production Guide for Labor-management Committees; Ways of Handling Production Problems*, Washington, D.C., 1944.

WALPOLE, GEORGE S.: *Management and Men; A Study of the Theory and Practice of Joint Consultation at All Levels*, Jonathan Cape, Ltd., London, 1945.

"Wartime Methods of Labour-management Consultation in the United States and Great Britain," *International Labour Review*, Vol. 52, No. 4, pp. 309–334, 1945.

UNION-MANAGEMENT COOPERATION

CANADA, INDUSTRIAL PRODUCTION COOPERATION BOARD: *Teamwork in Action. The Story of Joint Consultation at the Howard Smith Paper Mills, Cornwall, Ontario*, Ottawa, 1946.

COOKE, MORRIS L., and PHILIP MURRAY: *Organized Labor and Production*, rev. ed., Harper & Brothers, New York, 1946.

"From Conflict to Cooperation; A Study in Union-management Relations," Statements by Herbert J. Buchsbaum, Samuel Laderman, and Sidney Garfield; Introduction and Analysis by Andrew H. Whiteford, William F. Whyte, and Burleigh B. Gardner, *Applied Anthropology*, Vol. 5, No. 4, 1946.

GARMAN, PHILLIPS L.: "How Organized Labor can Cooperate with Management," in *Conciliation and Cooperation in Collective Bargaining*, pp. 3–13, Personnel Series No. 44, American Management Association, New York, 1940.

GOLDEN, CLINTON S.: "The Role of Labor in Modern Industrial Society," *Advanced Management*, Vol. 12, No. 1, pp. 35–38, 1947.

————: and HAROLD J. RUTTENBERG: *The Dynamics of Industrial Democracy*, Harper & Brothers, New York, 1942.

HARBISON, FREDERICK H.: "Some Reflections on a Theory of Labor-management Relations," *The Journal of Political Economy*, Vol. 54, No. 1, pp. 1–16, 1946.

HOCHMAN, JULIUS: *Industry Planning through Collective Bargaining; A Program for Modernizing the New York Dress Industry*, International Ladies Garment Workers Union, New York, 1941.

McGREGOR, DOUGLAS, and IRVING KNICKERBOCKER: *Union-management Cooperation: A Psychological Analysis*, Publications in Social Science, Series 2, No. 9, Massachusetts Institute of Technology, Department of Economics and Social Science, Cambridge, Mass., 1942. (Reprinted from *Personnel*, Vol. 19, No. 3, 1942.)

NYMAN, RICHARD CARTER, and ELLIOTT D. SMITH: *Union-management Cooperation in the "Stretch-out,"* Yale University Press, New Haven, 1934.

PRINCETON UNIVERSITY, INDUSTRIAL RELATIONS SECTION: *Union-management Cooperation with Special Reference to the War Production Drive*, A Selected Annotated Bibliography, Princeton, N. J., 1942.

SLICHTER, SUMNER H.: *Union Policies and Industrial Management* (Chaps. XIV–XIX), Brookings Institution, Washington, D. C., 1941.

STEEL WORKERS ORGANIZING COMMITTEE: *Production Problems*, Publication No. 2, Pittsburgh, no date.

"Union Management Cooperation," *Monthly Labor Review*, Vol. 52, No. 6, pp. 1351–1359, 1941.

"Union-management Cooperation in Full-fashioned Hosiery Industry," Vol. 53, No. 5, pp. 1180–1185, 1941.

WALTERS, J. E.: *Personnel Relations, Their Application in a Democracy* (Chap. 22, Labor-management Cooperation), The Ronald Press Company, New York, 1945.

Index of Names

541

Subject Index[1]

A

Ability, as factor in layoff, 395c.
as factor in promotion, 383c.
"Ability to pay" as factor in wage negotiation, 218
Absence, an index of organizational stability, 86–88
Absence rate, formula for, 87n.
Absences, comparative study of, 86–88
Absenteeism, 86n.
Accident, definition of, 283–284
Accident analysis, 276n., 283–287, 289–290, 465c., 474c.
Accident frequency rate, formula for, 90n.
Accident prevention, 89–90, 464c.
Accident process, 284–285
Accident-proneness, 94
Accident rates, formula for computing, 80
Accident severity rate, formula for, 90n.
Accidents, causes of 89–94, 286
costs of, 286–287
and health, 92–93
an index of stability, 452c.
nature and frequency of, as index of organizational stability, 87–92
and supervision, 93–94
Afternoon shift, description of, 253
American College of Surgeons, principles for health service, 278–279
Annual wage plans, 243–244
Application blank, proper design of, 129–130
Apprentice training, 163
Aptitude tests in employee selection, 132
Arbitration, part of grievance procedure, 111, 113–114

Attitudes of employees toward authority, 112n.
on bonus payments, 243
on employment policy, 338c.
on transfer, 326c.
on wage incentives, 233–235
on work sharing, 352c.
Authority, workers' attitude toward, 112n.

B

Baltimore and Ohio Railroad, plan of union-management cooperation, 302–303
Base rate of pay, 237
Baseball team, company, 266–267
Basic variables in personnel administration, 39–41
Bedaux system of wage payment, 232n.
"Black-Out" week end, 252
Boards, discipline, 207n.
fact-finding, 219
"Bogie Posters," usefulness of, 480
Bonus payments, employee attitude toward, 243
Branch plant, personnel administrator in, 19
British industry, hours and efficiency in, 246n., 248n.
Bulletin boards, 203

C

Case method, description of, 323–324
Collective bargaining as public policy, 27
Cooperation as basis of organization, 7
Committee shop, 111
Committees, departmental scrap, 482

[1] Numerals marked with c. indicate the first page of a case illustrating the point in question.